Lecture Notes in Computer Science 13325

More information about this series at https://link.springer.com/bookseries/558

Norbert A. Streitz · Shin'ichi Konomi (Eds.)

Distributed, Ambient and Pervasive Interactions

Smart Environments, Ecosystems, and Cities

10th International Conference, DAPI 2022
Held as Part of the 24th HCI International Conference, HCII 2022
Virtual Event, June 26 – July 1, 2022
Proceedings, Part I

 Springer

Editors
Norbert A. Streitz
Smart Future Initiative
Frankfurt am Main, Germany

Shin'ichi Konomi
Kyushu University
Fukuoka, Japan

ISSN 0302-9743   ISSN 1611-3349 (electronic)
Lecture Notes in Computer Science
ISBN 978-3-031-05462-4   ISBN 978-3-031-05463-1 (eBook)
https://doi.org/10.1007/978-3-031-05463-1

This Springer imprint is published by the registered company Springer Nature Switzerland AG
The registered company address is: Gewerbestrasse 11, 6330 Cham, Switzerland

Foreword

Human-computer interaction (HCI) is acquiring an ever-increasing scientific and industrial importance, as well as having more impact on people's everyday life, as an ever-growing number of human activities are progressively moving from the physical to the digital world. This process, which has been ongoing for some time now, has been dramatically accelerated by the COVID-19 pandemic. The HCI International (HCII) conference series, held yearly, aims to respond to the compelling need to advance the exchange of knowledge and research and development efforts on the human aspects of design and use of computing systems.

The 24th International Conference on Human-Computer Interaction, HCI International 2022 (HCII 2022), was planned to be held at the Gothia Towers Hotel and Swedish Exhibition & Congress Centre, Göteborg, Sweden, during June 26 to July 1, 2022. Due to the COVID-19 pandemic and with everyone's health and safety in mind, HCII 2022 was organized and run as a virtual conference. It incorporated the 21 thematic areas and affiliated conferences listed on the following page.

A total of 5583 individuals from academia, research institutes, industry, and governmental agencies from 88 countries submitted contributions, and 1276 papers and 275 posters were included in the proceedings to appear just before the start of the conference. The contributions thoroughly cover the entire field of human-computer interaction, addressing major advances in knowledge and effective use of computers in a variety of application areas. These papers provide academics, researchers, engineers, scientists, practitioners, and students with state-of-the-art information on the most recent advances in HCI. The volumes constituting the set of proceedings to appear before the start of the conference are listed in the following pages.

The HCI International (HCII) conference also offers the option of 'Late Breaking Work' which applies both for papers and posters, and the corresponding volume(s) of the proceedings will appear after the conference. Full papers will be included in the 'HCII 2022 - Late Breaking Papers' volumes of the proceedings to be published in the Springer LNCS series, while 'Poster Extended Abstracts' will be included as short research papers in the 'HCII 2022 - Late Breaking Posters' volumes to be published in the Springer CCIS series.

I would like to thank the Program Board Chairs and the members of the Program Boards of all thematic areas and affiliated conferences for their contribution and support towards the highest scientific quality and overall success of the HCI International 2022 conference; they have helped in so many ways, including session organization, paper reviewing (single-blind review process, with a minimum of two reviews per submission) and, more generally, acting as goodwill ambassadors for the HCII conference.

This conference would not have been possible without the continuous and unwavering support and advice of Gavriel Salvendy, founder, General Chair Emeritus, and Scientific Advisor. For his outstanding efforts, I would like to express my appreciation to Abbas Moallem, Communications Chair and Editor of HCI International News.

June 2022   Constantine Stephanidis

HCI International 2022 Thematic Areas and Affiliated Conferences

Thematic Areas

- HCI: Human-Computer Interaction
- HIMI: Human Interface and the Management of Information

Affiliated Conferences

- EPCE: 19th International Conference on Engineering Psychology and Cognitive Ergonomics
- AC: 16th International Conference on Augmented Cognition
- UAHCI: 16th International Conference on Universal Access in Human-Computer Interaction
- CCD: 14th International Conference on Cross-Cultural Design
- SCSM: 14th International Conference on Social Computing and Social Media
- VAMR: 14th International Conference on Virtual, Augmented and Mixed Reality
- DHM: 13th International Conference on Digital Human Modeling and Applications in Health, Safety, Ergonomics and Risk Management
- DUXU: 11th International Conference on Design, User Experience and Usability
- C&C: 10th International Conference on Culture and Computing
- DAPI: 10th International Conference on Distributed, Ambient and Pervasive Interactions
- HCIBGO: 9th International Conference on HCI in Business, Government and Organizations
- LCT: 9th International Conference on Learning and Collaboration Technologies
- ITAP: 8th International Conference on Human Aspects of IT for the Aged Population
- AIS: 4th International Conference on Adaptive Instructional Systems
- HCI-CPT: 4th International Conference on HCI for Cybersecurity, Privacy and Trust
- HCI-Games: 4th International Conference on HCI in Games
- MobiTAS: 4th International Conference on HCI in Mobility, Transport and Automotive Systems
- AI-HCI: 3rd International Conference on Artificial Intelligence in HCI
- MOBILE: 3rd International Conference on Design, Operation and Evaluation of Mobile Communications

List of Conference Proceedings Volumes Appearing Before the Conference

1. LNCS 13302, Human-Computer Interaction: Theoretical Approaches and Design Methods (Part I), edited by Masaaki Kurosu
2. LNCS 13303, Human-Computer Interaction: Technological Innovation (Part II), edited by Masaaki Kurosu
3. LNCS 13304, Human-Computer Interaction: User Experience and Behavior (Part III), edited by Masaaki Kurosu
4. LNCS 13305, Human Interface and the Management of Information: Visual and Information Design (Part I), edited by Sakae Yamamoto and Hirohiko Mori
5. LNCS 13306, Human Interface and the Management of Information: Applications in Complex Technological Environments (Part II), edited by Sakae Yamamoto and Hirohiko Mori
6. LNAI 13307, Engineering Psychology and Cognitive Ergonomics, edited by Don Harris and Wen-Chin Li
7. LNCS 13308, Universal Access in Human-Computer Interaction: Novel Design Approaches and Technologies (Part I), edited by Margherita Antona and Constantine Stephanidis
8. LNCS 13309, Universal Access in Human-Computer Interaction: User and Context Diversity (Part II), edited by Margherita Antona and Constantine Stephanidis
9. LNAI 13310, Augmented Cognition, edited by Dylan D. Schmorrow and Cali M. Fidopiastis
10. LNCS 13311, Cross-Cultural Design: Interaction Design Across Cultures (Part I), edited by Pei-Luen Patrick Rau
11. LNCS 13312, Cross-Cultural Design: Applications in Learning, Arts, Cultural Heritage, Creative Industries, and Virtual Reality (Part II), edited by Pei-Luen Patrick Rau
12. LNCS 13313, Cross-Cultural Design: Applications in Business, Communication, Health, Well-being, and Inclusiveness (Part III), edited by Pei-Luen Patrick Rau
13. LNCS 13314, Cross-Cultural Design: Product and Service Design, Mobility and Automotive Design, Cities, Urban Areas, and Intelligent Environments Design (Part IV), edited by Pei-Luen Patrick Rau
14. LNCS 13315, Social Computing and Social Media: Design, User Experience and Impact (Part I), edited by Gabriele Meiselwitz
15. LNCS 13316, Social Computing and Social Media: Applications in Education and Commerce (Part II), edited by Gabriele Meiselwitz
16. LNCS 13317, Virtual, Augmented and Mixed Reality: Design and Development (Part I), edited by Jessie Y. C. Chen and Gino Fragomeni
17. LNCS 13318, Virtual, Augmented and Mixed Reality: Applications in Education, Aviation and Industry (Part II), edited by Jessie Y. C. Chen and Gino Fragomeni

39. CCIS 1582, HCI International 2022 Posters - Part III, edited by Constantine Stephanidis, Margherita Antona and Stavroula Ntoa
40. CCIS 1583, HCI International 2022 Posters - Part IV, edited by Constantine Stephanidis, Margherita Antona and Stavroula Ntoa

http://2022.hci.international/proceedings

Preface

The 10th International Conference on Distributed, Ambient and Pervasive Interactions (DAPI 2022), an affiliated conference of the HCI International Conference, provided a forum for interaction and exchanges among researchers, academics, and practitioners in the field of HCI for DAPI environments. The DAPI conference addressed approaches and objectives of information, interaction and user experience design for DAPI-Environments as well as their enabling technologies, methods and platforms, and relevant application areas.

The DAPI 2022 conference developed on topics and treatment of issues already discussed in previous years. Two tendencies were observed in this year's proceedings. On the one hand, there are papers addressing basic research questions and technology issues in the areas of new modalities, augmented and virtual reality, immersive environments, pattern recognition, blockchains, solar-powered beacons, smart furniture, etc. On the other hand, there was an increase in more applied papers that cover comprehensive platforms and smart ecosystems addressing the challenges of cyber-physical systems, human-machine networks, public spaces, smart cities, smart islands, theme parks, and even wildlife in the Himalayas. The application areas also include education, learning, culture, art, music, and interactive installations, as well as security and privacy, and the currently prominent topic of the COVID-19 pandemic.

Two volumes of the HCII2022 proceedings are dedicated to this year's edition of the DAPI Conference, entitled Distributed, Ambient and Pervasive Interactions: Smart Environments, Ecosystems, and Cities (Part I), and Distributed, Ambient and Pervasive Interactions: Smart Living, Learning, Well-being and Health, Art and Creativity (Part II). The first volume focuses on topics related to user experience and interaction design for smart ecosystems, smart cities, smart islands and intelligent urban living, smart artifacts in smart environments, as well as opportunities and challenges for the near future smart environments. The second volume focuses on topics related to smart living in pervasive IoT ecosystems; distributed, ambient, and pervasive education and learning; distributed, ambient, and pervasive well-being and healthcare; as well as smart creativity and art.

Papers of these volumes are included for publication after a minimum of two single–blind reviews from the members of the DAPI Program Board or, in some cases, from members of the Program Boards of other affiliated conferences. We would like to thank all of them for their invaluable contribution, support, and efforts.

June 2022

Norbert A. Streitz
Shin'ichi Konomi

10th International Conference on Distributed, Ambient and Pervasive Interactions (DAPI 2022)

Program Board Chairs: **Norbert A. Streitz**, Smart Future Initiative, Germany, and **Shin'ichi Konomi**, Kyushu University, Japan

- Pedro Antunes, University of Lisbon, Portugal
- Paul Davidsson, Malmö University, Sweden
- Boris De Ruyter, Philips Research Europe, The Netherlands
- Morten Fjeld, Chalmers University of Technology, Sweden
- Nuno Guimarães, Instituto Universitário de Lisboa - ISCTE, Portugal
- Jun Hu, Eindhoven University of Technology, The Netherlands
- Oskar Juhlin, Stockholm University, Sweden
- Eiman Kanjo, Nottingham Trent University, UK
- Nicos Komninos, Aristotle University of Thessaloniki, Greece
- Irene Mavrommati, Hellenic Open University, Greece
- H. Patricia McKenna, AmbientEase/UrbanitiesLab Initiative, Canada
- Tatsuo Nakajima, Waseda University, Japan
- Guochao (Alex) Peng, Sun Yat-Sen University, China
- Carsten Röcker, TH OWL, Germany
- Tomoyo Sasao, University of Tokyo, Japan
- Konrad Tollmar, KTH and EA, Sweden
- Reiner Wichert, National Research Center for Applied Cybersecurity ATHENE, Germany
- Chui Yin Wong, Multimedia University, Banting, Selangor, Malaysia
- Woontack Woo, KAIST, South Korea
- Takuro Yonezawa, Nagoya University, Japan
- Chuang-Wen You, National Tsing Hua University, Taiwan

The full list with the Program Board Chairs and the members of the Program Boards of all thematic areas and affiliated conferences is available online at

http://www.hci.international/board-members-2022.php

HCI International 2023

The 25th International Conference on Human-Computer Interaction, HCI International 2023, will be held jointly with the affiliated conferences at the AC Bella Sky Hotel and Bella Center, Copenhagen, Denmark, 23–28 July 2023. It will cover a broad spectrum of themes related to human-computer interaction, including theoretical issues, methods, tools, processes, and case studies in HCI design, as well as novel interaction techniques, interfaces, and applications. The proceedings will be published by Springer. More information will be available on the conference website: http://2023.hci.international/.

General Chair
Constantine Stephanidis
University of Crete and ICS-FORTH
Heraklion, Crete, Greece
Email: general_chair@hcii2023.org

http://2023.hci.international/

Contents – Part I

Smart Artifacts in Smart Environments

Opportunities and Challenges for the Near Future Smart Environments

Contents – Part II

Distributed, Ambient, and Pervasive Well-Being and Healthcare

Smart Creativity and Art

User Experience and Interaction Design for Smart Ecosystems

Social Product Design:

An Approach to Improving Behavior Relationship for Chinese Older Adults in Community Space

Lei Bai[(⊠)]

Nanjing University of the Arts, Nanjing 210013, China
272870153@qq.com

Abstract. At present, China is in the stage of rapid aging, and the innovation of China's pension model must face the great pressure of social isolation of the elderly. The Shanghai model has many shortcomings in practice, and the lack of industry innovation methods urges us to go back to the root of the problem to explore the way of innovation. The Spatio-temporal difference of aging is the main reason for the barriers in the pension model, which also provides the social impetus to promote the innovation of pension model. Combined the Nanjing case study and social technology methods, We propose Social Product Design Approach to improving behavior relationship for Chinese Older Adults in Community Space.

Keywords: Product design · Social integration · Older adult · Community space

1 The Current Situation of China's Aging Population

Nowadays the aging of population has become a worldwide trend. As a developing country with the largest population in the world, China's aging degree has been increasing since 1999 when it entered the aging society. According to the latest data of the National Bureau of Statistics, as of the end of 2018, the population over 60 years old in China has reached 250 million, among which the population over 65 years old is about 167 million, accounting for 11.9% of the total population [1], making it the first country in the world with a population over 200 million. Compared with developed countries, the aging process in China is far beyond the level of economic and social development, with the characteristics of a large base, large differences, rapid development and getting old before getting rich [2]. At present, China is in a rapid aging stage. According to WHO's prediction, it will usher in a stable and severe aging stage in the mid-21st century. By then, the population over 60 years old in China will account for 35% of the total population, making China one of the most aging countries in the world. From the perspective of the elderly population structure, "disabled and semi-disabled, old age, empty nest" three groups account for a large proportion. The results of the fourth Sample survey on the living conditions of the elderly in China's urban and rural areas show that 40.63 million elderly people in China are disabled or semi-disabled, accounting for about one-fifth of the elderly population. The elderly will reach 29 million by 2020, and the elderly living alone and empty-nest will increase to about 118 million [1], which shows that the innovation of China's pension model must face the great pressure of social isolation of the elderly.

N. A. Streitz and S. Konomi (Eds.): HCII 2022, LNCS 13325, pp. 3–12, 2022.
https://doi.org/10.1007/978-3-031-05463-1_1

2 "9073" Model

Shanghai has the oldest registered population in China, accounting for more than 30% of its registered population by 2015. Therefore, Shanghai is also the first city to explore the adjustment of the pension system to adapt to the aging population, and its landmark policy is the 11th Five-Year Plan for the Development of Civil Affairs in Shanghai issued on January 24, 2007 (which was already issued in 2005). According to the plan, "90% of the elderly with household registration in the city are cared by their families, 7% are provided with home-based care services in communities, and 3% are provided with institutional care services". The pension system was named "9073" (see Table 1). The "9073" model proposed by Shanghai has a profound impact on China's pension pattern. Some provinces and cities then directly apply the "9073" model, or derive a new version based on the model structure.

Although the "9073" mode has become the basis of institutional design, there are still many deficiencies from the experience of Shanghai. Professor Yang Cuiying from Shanghai University of Finance and Economics summed it up as "two maladaptations and one defect": The first is that 90% of the elderly are "maladjusted" to the positioning of family pension services. According to the sampling data of 1% population in 2015, only 57.48% of the elderly live with adult family members. It can be seen that 90% of family-style pension accounts for too high a proportion, which cannot meet the needs of the elderly for institutional pension. In addition, the proportion of nursing beds in institutional endowment beds is too low. The demand for long-term care services far exceeds the current supply. Second, the family pension and community pension completely separate "not adapt". Family pension cannot share the services provided by community pension institutions, the elderly cannot enjoy professional services without leaving the familiar environment. Third, there is no clear boundary of government responsibility in 7% and 3%, so it is difficult for market institutions to enter, and the supply is small and the government has a heavy burden.

In 2014, Shanghai issued the Implementation Opinions on Accelerating the Development of Old-age Service Industry and Promoting the Construction of Social Old-age Service System. Based on the original "9073" pattern, Shanghai proposed a "five-pronged" social old-age service system, deepening reform in five aspects, including supply, security, policy support, demand assessment and industry supervision. Especially launched "family of the elderly care" fusion pension services (both can provide short-term nursing services, and to provide daytime care services, can provide professional service and support for the pension that occupy the home), through "90" "7" "3" three plates, promote original service keep at the same time, the old people without leaving the familiar community environment also can enjoy professional pension services, It is convenient for family members to visit them daily. But such aggressive reforms still face huge barriers to development. There are some problems in "family of the elderly care", such as lack of model innovation, weak industrial support and slow development. According to our interview results, the key is the lack of innovation methods in the industry, which urges us to go back to the root of the problem to explore the way of innovation.

Table 1. Mode for elderly

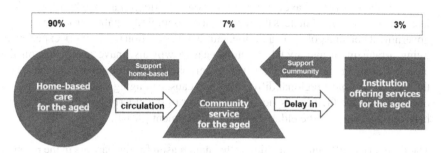

3 Spatio-temporal Differences and Mechanisms of Regional Population Aging

The positive and negative effects of aging in different environments (rural to urban) and different scales (family to global) include the following research contents [9, 10]: (1) Spatial distribution and causes of aging, (2) Study on residential space isolation of the elderly (3) Research on mobility of the elderly. (4) Research on housing choice of the elderly.

1. Spatial distribution and causes of aging. There are great differences in aging at different regional scales. American studies have found that 75% of the elderly live in urban areas, and 1/2 of them are clustered in central urban areas [4]. The aging phenomenon in Japan is concentrated in the rural areas where a large number of young people emigrate, while the aging degree in urban areas is low. McCarthy divided the aging process into three types: accumulation caused by the emigration of young people and the residue of the old, recomposition caused by the emigration of the old and the emigration of the young, and congregation caused by the simultaneous emigration of the old and the young [5].
2. Study on residential space isolation of the elderly. By comparing the social spatial differentiation between urban and suburban areas, it is found that the elderly tend to live in the suburbs and stay away from the urban areas that have undergone residential transformation (gentrification) [6]. However, this phenomenon shows great differences in China's vast region. For example, some elder are willing to follow their children to join the city life.
3. Research on mobility of the elderly. As the income, health and mobility of older persons change, quantitative identification of the factors that influence the choice of place of residence is crucial for maintaining physical health, disease repair and improving the quality of life of older persons. Coughlin points out that mobility also determines how older people care in place, and that the ability to move freely around the community has both practical and strong emotional meaning that is essential for older people to feel socially integrated [7].
4. Research on housing choice of the elderly. Based on the theory of life course and retirement migration, the author constructs a model of the elderly's future housing

expectation. It is found that the socioeconomic status and social inequality of the elderly in their early life have a lasting impact on the differentiation of housing in their later years, and then influences the formation of community spatial structure through government housing policy. In addition, family reproduction mode, work experience, living arrangement and social structure change will also have an impact on the elderly's housing choice [8]. Domestic geographers' research on aging focuses on the following topics: regional differences and causes of aging, spatial configuration of elderly service facilities, space-time behavior of the elderly, and the relationship between the health of the elderly and the environment [9, 10].

The time-space differences of aging is the main reason for the barriers in the pension model, which also provides the social impetus to promote the innovation of pension model.

4   Case of Nanjing

As an area with significant difference in population aging between urban and rural areas, the Yangtze River Delta is related to inter-regional and rural-urban population migration caused by the establishment of national and regional urban agglomerations. These areas show a significant spatial pattern of rural population aging higher than urban population. The inner core area of the Yangtze River Delta, as the inflow population concentration area, has a lower level of aging than the surrounding suburban counties, and is mostly in the early or late stage of growth. Population migration is the key factor of the regional difference between urban and rural population aging, and the migration rate shapes the spatial pattern of rural population aging higher than urban population in the Yangtze River Delta.

The case of this study is located in Nanjing city of Yangtze River Delta. There are 1.63 million old people over 60 years old and 1.0758 million old people over 65 years old in Nanjing, which has reached the deep aging. By the end of 2019, the population aged 60–69 accounted for 54.57%, 70–79 for 30.58%, and 80 for 14.85% of the population aged 60 and above in The city. According to the "Report on the Aging Population Information and the Development of aging Undertakings in Nanjing in 2019" [11], Gulou District, Jiangning District and Qinhuai District accounted for 16.74%, 14.50% and 12.80% of the population aged 60 or above in Nanjing in 2019. The least elderly population is in Pukou District, Yuhuatai District and Jianye District, accounting for 3.91%, 4.94% and 4.96% of the elderly population aged 60 and above in the whole city, respectively. There is a great difference in the number of elderly population in all regions. In 2019, the three regions with the highest degree of aging are Qinhuai District, Gulou District and Lishui District, with the proportion of elderly population aged 60 and above reaching 24.09%, 22.97% and 22.57%, respectively. The three regions with the lowest degree of aging are Jianye District, Jiangbei New District and Qixia District. The proportion of elderly population aged 60 and above was 12.72%, 12.96% and 14.21%, respectively. The degree of aging in different districts also showed great differences. In terms of regional distribution, Gulou District, Lishui District and Qinhuai District have the highest number of empty nesters, with 48362, 21472 and 16406, respectively. Pukou District, Jiangbei

New District and Yuhuatai District have the lowest number of empty nesters, with 934, 1140 and 2404, respectively. Lishui District, Gulou District and Xuanwu District have the highest proportion of empty-nesters in the population aged 60 and over, accounting for 21.29%, 17.70% and 10.56%, respectively. Jiangbei New District, Jiangning District and Pukou District have the lowest proportion of empty-nesters in the population aged 60 and over. The proportion of empty nesters in the population aged 60 and above was 0.14%, 0.28% and 0.29%. Jiangning district, Lishui District and Gulou District have 6117, 5208 and 5032 old people living alone, respectively. Pukou District, Jiangbei New District and Qixia District have 478, 875 and 937 old people living alone, respectively. In terms of the proportion of the elderly living alone, lishui District, Gaochun District and Jiangning District have the highest proportion of the elderly living alone in the population aged 60 and over, which are 5.16%, 3.01% and 2.58%, respectively. Pukou District, Jiangbei New District and Qixia District have the lowest proportion of the elderly living alone in the population aged 60 and over. The proportion of the elderly living alone in the population aged 60 and above was 0.75%, 0.80% and 0.91%, respectively.

The above data show that Gulou District in the central city and Lishui District in the suburbs of Nanjing have become the areas with the highest aging level as two completely different types. They respectively correspond to McCarthy's accumulation caused by the migration of young people and the residue of the old, and the congregation caused by the simultaneous migration of the old and the young. Zheng-He Park in this case study is typical in that it is not only located in the earlier developed area of Hexi New Urban district of Nanjing, but also comes from Gulou District with a high degree of aging. The aging situation of Gulou District shows the great pressure of social isolation for the elderly. In the interview with 20 elderly people over 60 years old, the lack and unreasonable functions in transports aspects (including personal and public) are these top three problems reflected in: mismatching with the target place, security problems and price factors. The problems of immovable public space facilities are reflected in the lack and mismatch of shared leisure facilities, unreasonable walking paths, and the lack of barrier-free design. Meanwhile, combining with the shadowing survey of 10 elderly people, the structure of the needs of the elderly in the communities surrounding Zheng-He Park shows that their social activities are limited. Our survey of social mobility limitations included the following satisfaction items: public transport accessibility, personal transport accessibility, shared space services, care and safety facilities. In the survey of 7 parks in Hexi District of Nanjing, we found that even including Nanhu, an old city with a high degree of aging, its community space still has a great deficiency in the survey of limited social activities. According to the interviews with the three main managers of the above parks, it is difficult to make comprehensive planning and transformation through the social management system when the community space is built. The more realistic way is to achieve community embeddedness through the design innovation of community space products.

5   Social Technology: A Concept to Guide the Aging Design Approach

In the past two years, the global economy, politics and society are facing huge adjustments due to the impact of COVID-19 epidemic. The enormous pressure on the health sector in various countries also brings the impetus for adjustment and improvement. The trend of population aging has not changed at all, and the accelerated adjustment of global industrial structure has also accelerated the growth of digital technology industry, which makes people believe that the convergence of aging and digitization has become a matter of course. The new generation prefers to grow old at home rather than stay in CCRC collectively. Technological innovation has brought this possibility.

Arthur Kleinman (Harvard University) team proposed in the social technology app-roach that the aging of this century is a challenge to the system, and only the systematic solution can be solved through careful analysis and integration [12]. The social science and technology they put forward refers to the comprehensive selection and integrated development in the two main aspects of social operation and cultural environment. In the cooperation of multi-disciplinary teams, the source of the problem is found in the research, and solutions based on individuals, families and society are formulated to face a series of problems caused by the disability of the elderly, and help families and orga-nizations that provide care for the elderly who cannot live independently to reduce the burden. This series of problems may include: cognitive disorder, depression, restricted movement, dementia, social isolation, etc. The program of social science and technol-ogy, especially according to the two conditional variables of social system and culture, involves the combination of technology and social system designed for the provision of medical services. The social technology tend to improve the quality of nursing for the elderly, combined technology with complex social system. For example, the new design thinking in product design, that is, how to combine design and technological innovation with social ethics with cultural diversity. Although the details of social technology theory need to be explored and developed, they have brought specific direction and vision to this activity. As social technology proposed the following six specific considerations: (1) Fostering Multidisciplinary Collaboration, (2) Including Ethical and Humanistic Stan-dards in Evaluation of Innovation, (3) Improving Social Systems, (4) Promoting Social Justice Through Policy Research and Innovation, (5) Fostering Social Integration, (6) Seeking nationwide Benefit Through Best Practices. The concept of social technology must be an important idea to guide the aging design approach.

6   Design Case

In our research, we developed a design scheme of escort robot (see Figs. 1 and 2) to solve the specific problems of the aging community in Nanjing. We extracted the simulation scene of Zhenghe Park and established a persona based on the specific semi-disabled elderly in this scene. We also extracted similar family samples and community pension data samples. Based on these samples, we finally focused on the problem of limited social action of the elderly in the region, which comes from the lack of mobile tool products. At the same time, our research found that there is a lack of suitable products from the market. The results of further design research lie in two points: (1) The use and service of products are oriented to leasing. (2) The products based on this positioning have wider applicability. We have developed the systematic value of the product in the design, that is, it meets the auxiliary functions of elderly users from bed to park, organically combines community service institutions and urban public space, and maximizes the role of infrastructure in solving the social isolation of semi-disabled elderly people.

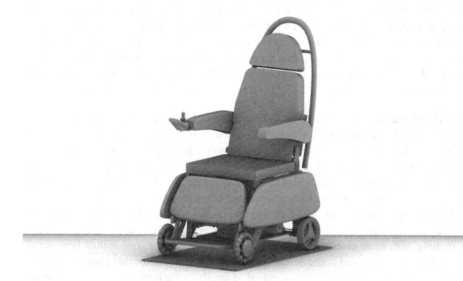

Fig. 1. Sitting position of the escort robot

Fig. 2. Lying position of the escort robot

7 Social Product Design Approach

Based on our specific research and the Social Technology approach, we proposed Social Product Design approach to improving behavior relationship in community space. Our points would include six considerations which could define social product design.

Interdisciplinary Design. First of all, we advocate immersive research methods. Interdisciplinary experts go deep into the life scenes of the elderly to understand their real needs, and consider the local culture and social comprehensive current conditions to guide technology-based design innovation. The proposal here refers not only to the interactive dialogue among designers, engineers and scientists, but also to the way of interaction and cooperation among their organizations. That means new design management or design contract emerging.

Ethical and Humanistic Standards in Evaluation of Design. The evaluation standard of design has always been constantly updated. In the history of design, the renewal of design evaluation standard is even self negation. We believe that no matter how many design evaluation criteria there are, the standard of social product design is at least not business oriented, because that will potentially affect the standard of ethical and human. Of course, the standard will include commercial considerations.

For nursing problems, the standard of good product design should be the feedback of the elderly and families, the feedback of nursing service providers, whether they are compatible with local cultural traditions and social conditions, rather than how many new technologies are used in the design and the maximum added value generated by the design. The ethical and humanistic standard of family is the basis of design evaluation, and then extended to individuals and organizations on this basis, which is also determined by the decisive position of family pension in China's pension system in the future. In addition, the participatory design method will also be promoted and used in aging design, which not only helps the production process of products and services, but also helps us to create and improve social product design applications. This evaluation standard is a conscious commitment, that is, to ensure that the cultural values of the specific environment and social requirements are combined in all solutions. Designers' emotional and moral participation will be reflected in the design of products and services, and become the driving force of innovation, rather than the usual commercial driving force.

Design for Social Service Systems. Social product design is an integrated system design, which is participated and benefited by several levels of stakeholders related to the pension system. China's pension planning is mainly based on family pension, and then forms a system of community pension and institutional pension. The design system should also be carried out around this framework. Professional product and service design supporting home care, product and service design of community day care and exercise, long-term care facilities in nursing institutions, and design process participation of large social policy institutions to ensure nursing Sustainability (such as insurance policy and housing policy institutions) are all part of system design.

We will work closely with all those who provide or manage care for the elderly to improve service design, conduct feasibility testing, and optimize the use of support resources across physical and social distances. In particular, although social product design is a non-commercial oriented design method, we advocate actively strengthening cooperation with commercial resources, especially seeking technical and financial support from the commercial sector. In some cases, social product design may be aimed at developing new social infrastructure and strengthening and integrating often fragmented care service systems (e.g., community rehabilitation rental equipment) with innovative solutions. It also includes the training of personnel using such products and services to promote and accelerate the dissemination and diffusion of innovation in the whole society and industry.

Promoting Social Equilibrium Through Systematic Pre-design. Based on the large base of low-income and difficult elderly in China, it is very important to design solutions to ensure that ordinary elderly people in marginal communities with less resources are the beneficiaries of the solutions. Lower priced technologies will be the focus of selection and redesign to make such products and services affordable. At the same time, we will explore close cooperation with policy researchers and policymakers to promote systematic pre-design, explore social welfare product and service innovation, and pro-vide solutions for social product design for disadvantaged groups.

Fostering Social Integration Through Design. We especially hope that the introduction of new technologies can promote mutual understanding and cohesion of social 10 groups. For example, the engineering technology used in our design case will help to solve the problem of restricted movement of semi disabled elderly people, increase their activity ability in outdoor space and reduce their social isolation. This may also mean that digital technology-based design will enhance the social integration level of the elderly not only in the physical community space but also in the virtual media space, so that they can continue to communicate, learn and maintain their physical and mental health.

Design should increase opportunities to create a true intergenerational social integration. The design based on AI technology and new media image technology can narrow the intergenerational gap between the elderly and the younger generation and delay the social aging and decline of the elderly. Here, the elderly-centered social products design will help to reduce the rigid impression and negative reflection of the elderly among young people.

Seeking Nationwide Benefit Through the Best Local Design. These design solutions based on the huge sample base of China's social endowment problems could be promoted and applied to a wider range of fields, Regions and countries. These solutions meet the challenges of population aging and related nursing challenges by designing mindset and methods that combine technology, social sciences and sensitive local cultural values. By identifying and studying the best practices of social product design implementation in the local environment, we expect to evaluate and promote the experience systematically.

8   Thoughts

We believe that social product design is a design method proposed as the urgency and complexity of China's pension problem, and many of its details need to be explored, evaluated and improved in practice. It needs to seek the opinions and cooperation of experts in different fields also needs to be applied in China's vast region. We recognize that some concepts contained in the social product design method may be similar to those already used in the design community (such as service design or design thinking), but as mentioned conditions in the article, these are explicit to constitute the essential differences in concepts. We regard social product design as a systematic concept, and its framework comes from our research on aging society, exploring the great potential of technology and design in improving nursing needs. More importantly, we will continue to explore the possibility of social product design methods in the face of other social problems, and continue to evaluate, improve and iterate. The goal of design is to help technology become an organic part of complex and dynamic social system, which is the consistent social function of design. Design innovation must be linked to people's current concerns and cultural systems in real social life in order to create human well-being.

References

1. Di, G., Hongjie, Z.: The model of combining medical care with old-age care in the context of population aging, Med. Res. Educ. **37**(2), 55–62 (2020)
2. Ling, Z.: Research on long-term care insurance under medical care model. Job Ind. Health. **33**(6), 842–845 (2017)
3. Riming, N.: Shanghai's "9073" pension model. Tong zhou gon jin (04) (2018)
4. Golant, S.M.: The Suburbanization of the American Elderly Migration and Population Redistribution-a Comparative Study. Belhaven Press, London (1992)
5. Mccarthy, K.F.: The Elderly Populations Changing Spatial Distribution: Patterns of Change Since 1960. Rand Corporation, Santa Monica (1983)
6. Smith, G.C.: Change in elderly residential segregation in Canadian metropolitan areas, 1981–91. Can. J. Aging **17**(1), 59–82 (1998)
7. Coughlin, J.: Transportation and Older Persons: Perceptions and Preferences: A Report on focus Groups. AARP Public Policy Institute (2001) http://assets.aarp.org/rgcenter/il/2001_05_transport.pdf. Accessed 13 Mar 2013
8. Izuhara, M., Heywood, F.: A life-time of inequality: a structural analysis of housing careers and issues facing older private tenants. Ageing Soc. **23**(2), 207–224 (2003)
9. Ribang, L., Wuyi, W., Jian 'an, T., et al.: The development stage, trend and region difference of aging population in China. Geograph. Res. **18**(2), 113–121 (1999)
10. Peng, D., Wulin, W.: On the transformation of the difference between urban and rural population aging degree. Popul. Res. **34**(2), 3–10 (2010)
11. "Report on the Aging Population Information and the Development of aging Undertakings in Nanjing in 2019". Nanjing Municipal Health Kang Commission (2020)
12. Kleinman, A., et al.: Social technology: an interdisciplinary approach to improving care for older adults perspective, Front. Public Health **9,** 729149 (2021). https://doi.org/10.3389/fpubh.2021.729149

A Study on Projection-Based Public Displays that Attract People with Peripheral Vision

Chihiro Hantani, Airi Tsuji$^{(\boxtimes)}$, and Kaori Fujinami

Department of Computer and Information Sciences, Tokyo University of Agriculture and Technology, 2-24-16 Nakacho, Koganei, Tokyo 184-8588, Japan
`atsuji@go.tuat.ac.jp, fujinami@cc.tuat.ac.jp`

Abstract. In this paper, we propose a presentation position determination method to improve the noticeability of information presentation in floor and wall projection public displays. Two types of information presentation methods: fixed position presentation and moving presentation, and four parameters: distance to the person, distance from the gazing point, difference in position, and direction of movement from other moving information, were considered and evaluated in this study. The experimental results showed that the method using the distance to the person was the most effective in both presentation methods.

Keywords: Public displays · Position determination method

1 Introduction

Recently, there has been an increase in the installation of displays in public spaces. Public displays are used in public spaces such as transportation facilities like stations and airports, and commercial facilities such as shopping malls. As an example of an advertising display, a large display was installed in a commercial facility to promote sales by transmitting information about the facility, with images introducing each store, and event information [1]. A similar example is a transportation system in which a display was installed at a bus stop to show bus operation information, route maps, and tourist information [2]. Although the mainstream means of information dissemination in the past were through static content such as signs and posters, there has been an increase in the use of dynamic content such as videos and slide shows on digital displays. Public displays have the advantage of easily changing content compared to paper media.

However, public displays still have a problem in that users often ignore uninteresting content such as advertisements [15]. Most passersby do not pay attention to public displays placed on walls near the passageway [13]. Moreover, stationary people such as those in waiting rooms or rest areas in shopping malls are more likely to concentrate on their tasks, such as using a smartphone or reading, and are less likely to recognize the content of the display. If a display method

N. A. Streitz and S. Konomi (Eds.): HCII 2022, LNCS 13325, pp. 13–27, 2022.
https://doi.org/10.1007/978-3-031-05463-1_2

with high attraction effect is clarified, more effective advertisement display will be possible.

The purpose of this study is to attract attention to information by changing the display position, assuming a situation where multiple different information is displayed on a public display simultaneously. Two types of information presentation methods were proposed: fixed position presentation, in which the information suddenly appears in one place (Fig. 1(a)), and moving presentation, in which the information moves on the screen (Fig. 1(b)). Since public displays are used by multiple people, it is necessary to attract attention concurrently. It is possible to attract the attention of multiple people to a single piece of information by changing the display position. The position and direction of a person's gaze around the display are fluid, and the appropriate parameters are likely to change accordingly. Therefore, a method that presents information in the most appropriate position or path depends on the user's situation. In the case of a fixed position presentation, the position where new information appears is determined. Conversely, a series of positions to the destination is found incrementally in the moving presentation. Thus, in either case, the problem is to determine a position that maximizes the *noticeability* of the information. For example, in the case of a sitting person using a smartphone or reading a book, the person is looking down; therefore, the presentation of information on the floor is considered to be suitable.

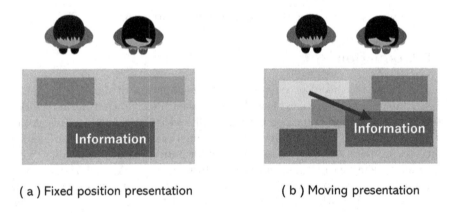

(a) Fixed position presentation   (b) Moving presentation

Fig. 1. Information presentation methods.

In this paper, we propose position determination methods for fixed and moving presentations that consist of three and four parameters. The remainder of this paper is organized as follows: Sect. 2 examines related work; Sect. 3 presents the display position determination methods; Sect. 4 describes the experiment to investigate the impact of each parameter and the combination of all parameters in the most suitable position determination; Sect. 5 discusses the results; and Sect. 6 concludes the paper.

2   Related Work

Public displays come in a variety of shapes and methods according to their intended use. The widespread use of displays with LED lighting, which consumes less electricity and generates less heat, has made information presentation in public spaces more dynamic, while projectors have made it possible to present information in a more interactive and location-independent manner. Anthony et al. investigated and clarified the differences in user behavior between horizontal floor-mounted displays and vertical wall-mounted displays [3]. An evaluation of the interactivity of the displays was also conducted [6]. Since most public displays are designed to present information to several people simultaneously, studies have also been conducted with multiple users [7,16,17].

In a motion-related study on noticeability that investigated the movement of icons in peripheral vision [4], it was found that motion-based methods attracted more attention. Howard et al. [12] investigated the relationship between changes in the direction of object movement and attention and found that response accuracy decreased when objects not being tracked by the subject made unexpected movements such as bouncing. Horowitz et al. [11] thought that moving objects characteristically would help users to recognize objects. They compared three types of motion: ballistic motion, which moves in a straight line; random walk motion, which moves in a random direction; and compound motion, which randomly fluctuates around a ballistic trajectory. The visual search task suggested that changes in the direction of motion affected the task. In a study that investigated the position of the display in addition to the motion, Klauck et al. [14] investigated the effect of the design of the notification on the display on attention and disturbance to the task. The results of this experiment showed that dynamic characteristics such as blinking and moving, were associated with higher levels of attention and disturbance to work. In addition, the degree of attention and disturbance were both higher when the notification was displayed close to the gazing position.

An example of an eye-catching public display is Chueng et al.'s study [5], which aimed to attract people by adding motion to the content and interaction with users. Ghare et al. [9] investigated the impact of visual elements on user attention in public displays. The results of their experiment showed that randomly-initiated animation attracts more attention than distance-based animation. A delay in the animation start timing was cited as a reason for distance being less likely to attract attention.

As described previously, research has been conducted to improve noticeability through movement and display position, and to develop eye-catching displays based on these findings and knowledge. In this study, we assume a rich public display that simultaneously targets both horizontal and vertical planes as a public display that presents information more effectively and examines information presentation methods that simultaneously attract multiple people based on previous research.

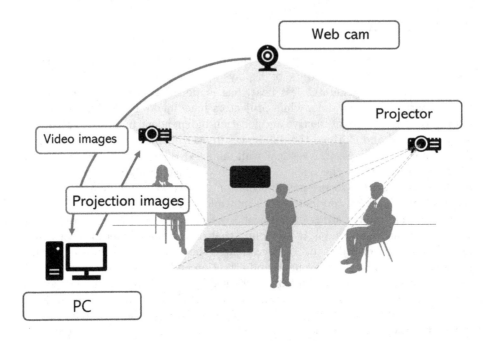

Fig. 2. Information presentation methods.

3   Display Position Determination Methods

3.1   Experimental System Configuration

In this study, we present information that incorporates the gaze direction and dynamic display based on the person's position and head orientation, grounded on the knowledge of related work. We propose two types of information presentation methods with high noticeability: fixed and moving presentations. The wall or floor public displays and the experimental system targeted in this study are intended for multiple users in different states (standing or sitting). Figure 2 shows an example of the system environment, including the display device and users. The display targets both standing and sitting users simultaneously. This implies a difference in the user's standing/sitting position and may clarify the hypothesis of whether the user can look at the wall or the floor depending on their standing/sitting position (standing users prefer to look at the wall while sitting users prefer to see information presented on the floor). Thus, two projectors were installed to display the information on these two surfaces. To present the information within the subject's field of view, a visual marker on the subject's head was used to detect the direction of the face and a web camera was installed on the ceiling to detect the visual marker. The intersection point between the face direction and each plane was assumed to be the gazing point in this study.

3.2   Proposed Method

We performed a preliminary questionnaire survey and introduced four parameters to determine the presentation position: 1) distance to the person (dp); 2) distance from the gazing point (dv); 3) positional difference from other moving information (do); and 4) difference in moving direction from other moving information $(\Delta\theta)$, which are shown Fig. 3.

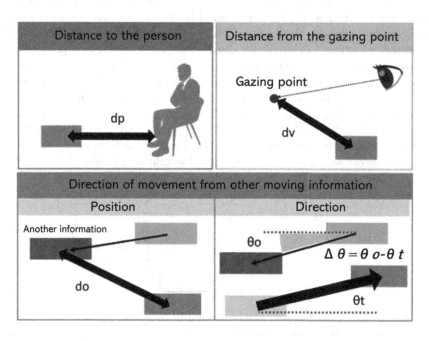

Fig. 3. Parameters of information presentation methods

To increase the noticeability of information, the information should be in the person's field of vision. Thus, the closer the display is to a person, the better it is. However, some subjects in the preliminary experiment said that they might feel that their personal space is being intruded on and feel uncomfortable if the distance is too close. Thus, the evaluation value in terms of the distance to the person is set to zero when the distance between the display position and the person (dp) is closer than the personal distance of 1.2 m [10]. In addition, because it is presumed that the probability of the object being within the visual field range is higher when it is closer to the gazing point, the position closer to the gazing point is given a higher rating. Therefore, we set the distance to the gazing point as dv. Bartram et al. [4] showed that objects in motion attract more attention than static objects. In the case of a fixed position presentation, the information should be displayed further from other moving objects because such a static object might not be noticeable. After all, attention is drawn to the moving object. Furthermore, Duncan et al. [8] showed that the larger the difference between the target and other disturbing elements (the information), the easier it is to find the target (the newly-projected information). Thus, the larger difference in position (do) and the direction of movement $(\Delta\theta = \theta o - \theta t)$ might make it easier to find the target information. The noticeability measure is calculated for each candidate position by changing the parameters defined previously, and the position with the highest value was selected as the projection position. The objective function for the noticeability measure of the fixed position representation (W_f) is represented by Eq. (1), which consists of three terms calculated by dp, dv, and do. The first and second terms indicate the normalized "closeness" from the candidate position to the user's position and the user's gazing point. The terms were averaged over all persons in the public display area (Np). The third term represents the average distance between the path of the other no-moving information and the candidate position. Here, Nr is the number of passing points plus the point to move next. The constants dp_{max}, dv_{max}, and do_{max} were used to normalize the terms and were all set to 3.0 m as the largest distance in the projection area. Finally, the three terms are added using the weights $w_{i \in 1,2,3}$, so that the sum of weights is 1.0 (Eq. (2)).

$$W_f = \omega_1 \frac{1}{N_p} \sum_{i=1}^{N_p} \left(1 - \frac{dp_i}{dp_{max}} \right) + \omega_2 \frac{1}{N_p} \sum_{i=1}^{N_p} \left(1 - \frac{dv_i}{dv_{max}} \right)$$
$$+ \omega_3 \frac{1}{N_o} \sum_{i=1}^{N_o} \frac{\frac{1}{N_r} \sum_{j=1}^{N_r} do_{ij}}{do_{max}} \tag{1}$$

$$\omega_1 + \omega_2 + \omega_3 = 1.0 \tag{2}$$

In the moving presentation, the noticeability measure W_m is represented by Eq. (3) by adding the average normalized difference of the moving direction $(\Delta\theta)$ at each passing point as the fourth term in Eq. (1). The four terms were also added to the weights (Eq. (4)).

$$W_m = \omega_1 \frac{1}{N_p} \sum_{i=1}^{N_p} \left(1 - \frac{dp_i}{dp_{max}} \right) + \omega_2 \frac{1}{N_p} \sum_{i=1}^{N_p} \left(1 - \frac{dv_i}{dv_{max}} \right)$$
$$+ \omega_3 \frac{1}{N_o} \sum_{i=1}^{N_o} \frac{\frac{1}{N_r} \sum_{j=1}^{N_r} do_{ij}}{do_{max}} + \omega_4 \frac{1}{N_o} \sum_{i=1}^{N_o} \frac{\frac{1}{N_r} \sum_{j=1}^{N_r} \Delta\theta_{ij}}{180} \tag{3}$$

$$\omega_1 + \omega_2 + \omega_3 + \omega_4 = 1.0 \tag{4}$$

4   Evaluation

The effectiveness of the proposed parameter determination methods was evaluated based on the rate of detection of the presented character rate and the time required to find the characters (Fig. 4) using an experimental system.

The system can project information on both the floor and the wall to respond to various states of the person, such as standing and sitting, as mentioned previously. A schematic of the experiment is presented in Fig. 5. The visual fiducial marker (Fig. 6) to obtain the person's position and facial orientation was used to calculate the noticeability in this research.

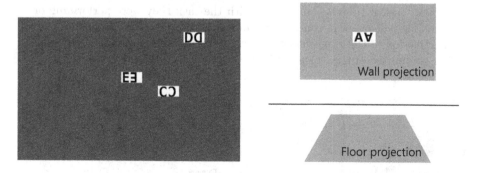

Fig. 4. Characters using an experimental system

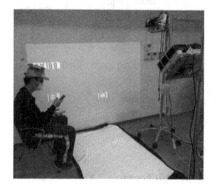

Fig. 5. Experimental scene   **Fig. 6.** Visual fiducial marker

Eleven students in their 20s participated in the experiment. To examine the impact of each evaluation item, various weights were used to determine the display position using equal weights (Eqs. (2) and (4)): The characters were displayed at random positions and paths as a control group. The evaluation was performed with subjects in both standing and sitting positions. Figure 7 shows the positions of the subjects and display in each condition. To simulate the situation where multiple people use the system simultaneously when the subject was sitting, the dummy marker information was used on the assumption that the person was in the standing position and when the subject was standing, we set it as the person in the sitting position. As the dummy marker coordinates, the average of the marker coordinates obtained by the experimenter in the sitting and standing conditions was used to determine the appropriate values. The subjects were asked to perform a task in which they could concentrate best using their smartphones as a dual-task. The subjects were instructed in advance to switch to another task if they became bored with the task they were performing or if they noticed a decrease in concentration. A questionnaire was administered after the completion of the experiment. The experiment was approved by the ethical review committee of the Tokyo University of Agriculture and Technology.

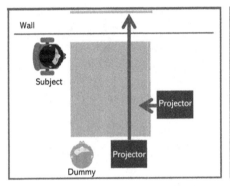 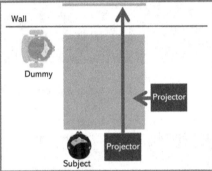

(a) Sitting condition   (b) Standing condition

Fig. 7. Parameters of information presentation methods

5   Result

5.1   Detection Rate and Time Required for Detection

Figure 8 shows graphs of the detection rate in the fixed position and moving presentation. The detection rate was higher when the display position was determined using the distance from the person, as shown in Fig. 8. Therefore, noticeability may be improved when the position of a person is used in both methods. However, the detection rate was lower when the distance from the gazing point was used.

Figure 9 shows the difference in the detection rate and time required for detection for each presentation method. The detection rate was found to be higher in the case of moving presentation, and the time required for detection was shorter in the case of fixed position presentation.

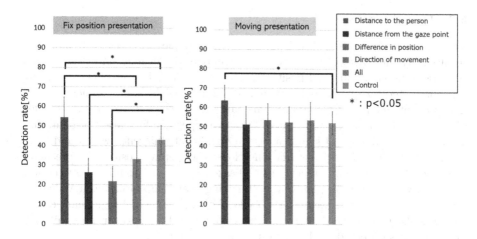

Fig. 8. Average detection rates per method of calculating noticeability measure.

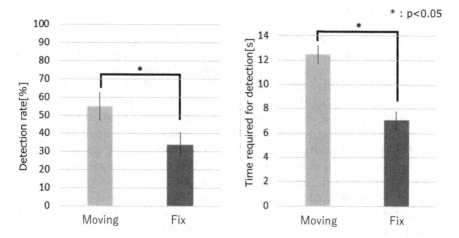

Fig. 9. Average detection rates and time required for detection in the two presentation methods.

Table 1. Average rates of questionnaire in the two presentation methods

Questionnaire	Answer
1) Eyes for a moving presentation {5:attracted/1:not attracted}	4.4
2) Eyes on the fixed position presentation {5:attracted/1:not attracted}	3.7
3) Moving presentation is {5:annoying/1:not annoying}	3.0
4) Fixed position presentation is {5:annoying/1:not annoying}	2.3
5) The position that was {5:nearer/1:farther} to me is attracted	4.0
6) When sitting the projected floor surface is {5:easy to see/1:hard to see}	4.5
7) When sitting, the wall projection is {5:easy to see/1:hard to see}	2.1
8) When standing, the floor projection is {5:easy to see/1:hard to see}	3.8
9) When standing, the wall projection is {5:easy to see/1:hard to see}	2.9

5.2   Questionnaire

The questionnaire consisted of 5-point Likert-scale questions. Table 1 shows the results of the average of the subjects. To compare the evaluation of the attractiveness of moving and fixed position presentation, a Wilcoxon signed-rank test was conducted for questions between 1 and 2 at a 5% level of significance, and a significant difference was found. The same rank test was also conducted for Questions 3 and 4 for the annoyance of the two types of information presentation methods at a 5% level of significance; no significant difference was found. The results of Question 5 indicate that the closer the display position is, the more attentive the subjects are. Questions 6–9 asked about the visibility between the floor and wall projection planes in each sitting/standing state, and a Wilcoxon signed-rank test was conducted at a 5% level of significance. A significant difference was observed in the sitting state (between Q6 and 7), however, no significant difference was observed in the standing state (Q8 and 9).

5.3   Weight Evaluation

To examine the weighting, we interviewed the subjects about the display positions and movement directions. The results of the interviews and display positions determined by changing the ratio of weights for each item were compared. A system that can display information at specified display positions and routes was created to determine the most eye-catching display positions and routes. For the display position, the subjects were asked in which area they thought the display was the most eye-catching. The experimenter manipulated the display at the specified position, and if there was a correction from the subject, the display position was changed accordingly. When there was no problem, the position was determined. As for the movement path, the subject was first asked in which direction it would attract the most attention when it was displayed on the center of the floor. The final direction of movement was determined by showing the movement and asking again in which direction it would attract the eye. The fixed-position presentation used three evaluation items. For all combinations in which the sum of the weights for all evaluation items is 1.0, the evaluation values are calculated with a tick size of 0.1, and the display position and movement path are determined. Therefore, the display positions of 66 combinations were determined. For the moving presentation, because four items are used, the position of the destination is also determined in 286 combinations.

The difference in the distance between the determined position from weighting and the position selected by each subject is calculated, and the top 10 patterns for the sitting states are shown in Table 2. The table is arranged in descending order by the average of all the subjects. Table 3 shows the results for the standing state for the fixed presentation, and Tables 4 and 5 show the results for the moving presentation.

6   Discussion

As shown in Fig. 8, the detection rates of the moving and fixed position presentation were higher when the display position was determined using the distance to the person compared to the control group. Because the detection rate was higher than that of the control group, which was displayed randomly, the proposed parameter determination method was considered effective.

However, in the fixed position presentation, the detection rates were lower than that of the control group when the distance from the gazing point was used, and when the difference in position from other moving information was used. In addition, the detection rates were lower when all items of the movement presentation were used compared to when the distance from the person was used. This may be because of the inclusion of evaluation items with low noticeability, such as the distance from the gazing point; thus, it is necessary to set only evaluation items that are effective in improving noticeability.

The average detection rate was higher for the moving presentation than for the fixed position. In addition, the time required for detection was shorter for the fixed position presentation than for the moving presentation. It is possible to be detected by moving even if it cannot be detected at the start of the display in the moving presentation. However, it will take longer to find them because the visibility of the character will be reduced by movement. Based on these results, it is necessary to use different information presentation methods for different purposes, such as using a moving presentation for reliable information transmission and using a fixed position presentation for quick information transmission.

The average distance between the position where the subject selected and determined using weighting was tend to short under the condition giving the heaviest weight to ω_1 in the all ωs, in the case of the fixed position presentation

Table 2. Distance between the display position and the subject's answer for each weights in the fixed presentation (sitting)

Weights in objective function for W_f (Eq. (1))			Difference from interview [cm]
ω_1	ω_2	ω_3	
0.4	0.5	0.1	60.3
0.3	0.5	0.2	61.3
0.8	0.2	0.0	63.0
0.7	0.3	0.0	63.0
0.6	0.4	0.0	63.0
0.5	0.5	0.0	63.0
0.5	0.4	0.1	63.0
0.9	0.1	0.0	63.0
0.1	0.5	0.0	64.6
0.2	0.5	0.3	65.5

Table 3. Distance between the display position and the subject's answer for each weights in the fixed presentation (standing)

Weights in objective function for W_f (Eq. (1))			Difference from interview [cm]
ω_1	ω_2	ω_3	
0.4	0.3	0.3	49.2
0.7	0.2	0.1	50.2
0.6	0.2	0.2	50.2
1.0	0.0	0.0	50.2
0.5	0.3	0.2	50.2
0.8	0.1	0.1	50.2
0.9	0.0	0.1	56.9
0.5	0.2	0.3	58.1
0.7	0.1	0.2	58.1
0.8	0.0	0.2	58.1

Table 4. Distance between the display position and the subject's answer for each weights in the moving presentation (sitting)

Weights in objective function for W_m (Eq. (3))				Difference from interview [cm]
ω_1	ω_2	ω_3	ω_4	
0.1	0.0	0.4	0.5	19.9
0.1	0.2	0.2	0.5	19.9
0.1	0.4	0.0	0.5	19.9
0.1	0.3	0.1	0.5	19.9
0.2	0.0	0.0	0.8	19.9
0.1	0.5	0.0	0.4	19.9
0.1	0.1	0.3	0.5	19.9
0.1	0.0	0.5	0.4	20.7
0.1	0.4	0.1	0.4	20.7
0.1	0.2	0.3	0.4	20.7

(5 cases of Table 2, and all cases of Table 3). This is consistent with the results of the detection rate, which was higher in the distance-to-person condition.

In the sitting condition of the moving presentation shown in Table 4, the difference in distance from the subject's answer was tend to smaller when the heaviest weight is given to ω_4 in the all ωs than others (7 cases of the top 10). On the other hand, in the standing condition, the average distance was almost (9 cases in the top 10) shorter when the heaviest weight was given to ω_3 than others in Table 5. This is because, in the moving presentation, many of the candidate locations are close to the subject. To avoid displaying the information in the

Table 5. Distance between the display position and the subject's answer for each weights in the moving presentation (standing)

Weights in objective function for W_m (Eq. (3))				Difference from interview [cm]
ω_1	ω_2	ω_3	ω_4	
0.0	0.0	1.0	0.0	20.3
0.0	0.4	0.6	0.0	20.5
0.0	0.1	0.9	0.0	20.5
0.0	0.2	0.8	0.0	20.7
0.0	0.3	0.7	0.0	20.9
0.0	0.0	0.9	0.1	22.6
0.0	0.1	0.8	0.1	22.9
0.0	0.2	0.7	0.1	23.2
0.3	0.7	0.0	0.0	26.4
0.1	0.2	0.7	0.0	26.6

subject's personal space, we set the evaluation value of the distance to a person to zero when the distance is closer than 1.2 m in this evaluation. Therefore, the evaluation value of the distance to the person becomes zero when the distance to the person is closer than 1.2 m for any weight, and these positions were seldom selected.

The results of the questionnaire showed that there was a significant difference in noticeability between moving and fixed position presentations, and no significant difference in annoyance of both presentation method. The test results showed that the floor presentation was more visible in the sitting condition. In the sitting condition, the head position was closer to the floor surface, therefore the participants felt it was easier to see. However, the subject in sitting was positioned too close to the wall, and his/her line of sight was close to the wall, which may have made it difficult to see.

7 Conclusion

In this paper, we proposed parameters of presentation position determination method to improve the noticeability of information presentation in floor and wall projection public displays. The experiment showed that the method using distance to the person was the most effective. In addition, the difference in the detection rate and the time required for detection indicates that it is necessary to use fixed position presentation and moving presentation differently depending on the purpose. In the future, we aim to further study the weighting method and adapt the system to various environments.

References

1. Large multi-signage | Clopdpoint. https://www.cloudpoint.co.jp/case/case-181207/. Accessed 1 Feb 2022. (in Japanese)
2. Intelligent bus stop outdoor LCD digital signage | fengshi, https://cnnlcd.com/intelligent-bus-station-lcd-digital-signage-used-in-songyang/. Accessed 1 Feb 2022
3. Anthony, L., Stofer, K.A., Luc, A., Wobbrock, J.O.: Gestures by children and adults on touch tables and touch walls in a public science center. In: Proceedings of the 15th International Conference on Interaction Design and Children. IDC 2016, pp. 344–355. Association for Computing Machinery. https://doi.org/10.1145/2930674.2930682
4. Bartram, L., Ware, C., Calvert, T.: Moticons: detection, distraction and task. Int. J. Hum. Comput. Stud. **58**(5), 515–545. https://doi.org/10.1016/S1071-5819(03)00021-1, https://linkinghub.elsevier.com/retrieve/pii/S1071581903000211
5. Cheung, V., Scott, S.D.: Studying attraction power in proxemics-based visual concepts for large public interactive displays. In: Proceedings of the 2015 International Conference on Interactive Tabletops & Surfaces - ITS 2015, pp. 93–102. ACM Press. https://doi.org/10.1145/2817721.2817749, http://dl.acm.org/citation.cfm?doid=2817721.2817749
6. Camba, D.J., Feng, J., Kwon, E.: Interactive experiences in public spaces: A novel floor display system based on luminous modular units. https://doi.org/10.24251/HICSS.2018.040, http://scholarspace.manoa.hawaii.edu/handle/10125/49927, accepted: 2017-12-28T00:34:46Z
7. Dostal, J., Hinrichs, U., Kristensson, P.O., Quigley, A.: SpiderEyes: designing attention- and proximity-aware collaborative interfaces for wall-sized displays. In: Proceedings of the 19th international conference on Intelligent User Interfaces, pp. 143–152. ACM. https://doi.org/10.1145/2557500.2557541, https://dl.acm.org/doi/10.1145/2557500.2557541
8. Duncan, J., Humphreys, G.W.: Visual search and stimulus similarity. Psychol. Rev. **96**(3), 433 (1989)
9. Ghare, M., Pafla, M., Wong, C., Wallace, J.R., Scott, S.D.: Increasing passersby engagement with public large interactive displays: a study of proxemics and conation. In: Proceedings of the 2018 ACM International Conference on Interactive Surfaces and Spaces, pp. 19–32. ACM. https://doi.org/10.1145/3279778.3279789, https://dl.acm.org/doi/10.1145/3279778.3279789
10. Hall, E.T.: The Hidden Dimension, vol. 609. Doubleday, Garden City (1966)
11. Horowitz, T.S., Wolfe, J.M., DiMase, J.S., Klieger, S.B.: Visual search for type of motion is based on simple motion primitives. Perception **36**(11), 1624–1634. https://doi.org/10.1068/p5683, http://journals.sagepub.com/doi/10.1068/p5683
12. Howard, C.J., Holcombe, A.O.: Unexpected changes in direction of motion attract attention. Attent. Percept. Psychophy. **72**(8), 2087–2095. https://doi.org/10.3758/BF03196685, http://link.springer.com/10.3758/BF03196685
13. Huang, E.M., Koster, A., Borchers, J.: Overcoming assumptions and uncovering practices: when does the public really look at public displays? In: Indulska, J., Patterson, D.J., Rodden, T., Ott, M. (eds.) Pervasive 2008. LNCS, vol. 5013, pp. 228–243. Springer, Heidelberg (2008). https://doi.org/10.1007/978-3-540-79576-6_14

14. Klauck, M., Sugano, Y., Bulling, A.: Noticeable or distractive?: A design space for gaze-contingent user interface notifications. In: Proceedings of the 2017 CHI Conference Extended Abstracts on Human Factors in Computing Systems, pp. 1779–1786. ACM. https://doi.org/10.1145/3027063.3053085, https://dl.acm.org/doi/10.1145/3027063.3053085

15. Müller, J., et al.: Display blindness: the effect of expectations on attention towards digital signage. In: Tokuda, H., Beigl, M., Friday, A., Brush, A.J.B., Tobe, Y. (eds.) Pervasive 2009. LNCS, vol. 5538, pp. 1–8. Springer, Heidelberg (2009). https://doi.org/10.1007/978-3-642-01516-8_1

16. Nutsi, A., Koch, M.: Readability in multi-user large-screen scenarios. In: Proceedings of the 9th Nordic Conference on Human-Computer Interaction, pp. 1–4. ACM. https://doi.org/10.1145/2971485.2971491, https://dl.acm.org/doi/10.1145/2971485.2971491

17. Tafreshi, A.E.S., Marbach, K., Troster, G.: Proximity based adaptation of content to groups of viewers of public displays. Int. J. Ubiquitous Comput. 9(1), 01–09. https://doi.org/10.5121/iju.2018.9201, http://aircconline.com/iju/V9N2/9218iju01.pdf

The Landscape of Digital Platforms for Bottom-Up Collaboration, Creativity, and Innovation Creation

Aikaterini Katmada[1]([⊠]), Nicos Komninos[2], and Christina Kakderi[1]

[1] School of Spatial Planning and Development, Aristotle University of Thessaloniki, Thessaloniki, Greece
{akatmada,kakderi}@plandevel.auth.gr
[2] URENIO Research, Aristotle University of Thessaloniki, Thessaloniki, Greece
komninos@urenio.org

Abstract. The widespread use of digital networks, technologies, and platforms, that allow humans, physical objects, and machines to interact with each other, has significantly affected the structure, components, and knowledge processes of innovation systems that have been transformed into cyber-physical innovation environments. Such environments operate at various scales and spaces, involve a wider set of actors, and demonstrate collective intelligence, exhibiting, thus, higher efficiency and impact than traditional innovation systems. Therefore, it is justified that there is an increasing research interest for understanding digital crowdsourcing platforms and online communities as a channel of collaborative innovation. Despite the attention such systems receive from different disciplines, there is still limited empirical evidence on their structure and coordination, as well as the mechanics that lead to sustained user participation and the generation of inventive and creative ideas, especially in urban planning and civic participation. This paper aims to conduct an overview of key platform attributes and common human-computer interaction patterns, based on an examination of the pertinent literature, as well as an indicative sample of notable platforms which allow large networks of individuals or communities to access, explore, and exchange knowledge and ideas.

Keywords: Digital platforms · Human-computer interaction · Crowdsourcing · Planning & urban design · Citizen engagement

1 Introduction

Over the last decade, we have witnessed the emergence of new digital tools and technologies that transform modern societies, bringing together people, organizations, and resources, creating cyber-physical interactive ecosystems characterized by novel ways of innovation and value creation. A core component of these tools are platforms; digital participative infrastructures accompanied by new governance conditions that create network effects and externalities by consummating matches and facilitating the exchange of goods, services, ideas, and data [1].

N. A. Streitz and S. Konomi (Eds.): HCII 2022, LNCS 13325, pp. 28–42, 2022.
https://doi.org/10.1007/978-3-031-05463-1_3

Platforms disrupt industries, economies and have a detrimental effect on society. Due to their intrinsic characteristics that leverage technology to trigger social creativity [2], they are increasingly linked to grand societal challenges such as those of sustainability and climate change, as well as to complex and persistent urban problems that are characterized by multiple conflicting forces, such as those of congestion, pollution and economic degradation [3].

Digital innovation and platform-based solutions in the urban environment fuel new processes for creativity and innovation creation, form new governance conditions, but also pose implications that city authorities must address. Given their broad/universal character and the interconnected processes that they trigger, it is suggested here that their full potential and dynamics have not been thoroughly analyzed. Empirical studies from different disciplines (economics, ICT) focus on different dimensions of the platforms, such as their structure (technical architecture and specifications), value proposition (new product development and entrepreneurship), and network effects. What these studies rarely consider is the dynamic effects that these attributes have at the spatial level, especially through the interaction of digitalization-enabled factors with any non-digital elements in an urban context.

This paper aims to contribute towards filling this gap by clustering digital platforms with regards to several characteristics that reflect their way of operation, governance, and outcomes. More specifically, we review the literature of digital platforms and collect attributes that seem to affect their impact and prospect of innovation creation, such as ownership, openness, and application domain. We use these attributes to examine twenty (20) different digital crowdsourcing platforms and reach insights on the elements that differentiate digital platforms compared to analog means of collective intelligence.

2   Digital Crowdsourcing Platforms: Definition and Key Attributes

Digital platforms constitute a new organizational form; based on digital technology, they mediate the relationships between producers or workers and consumers. Common types of digital platforms include transaction platforms, such as Amazon and Airbnb, and technology platforms, such as the app stores of Google and Apple [4]. The rise of digital platforms is rapidly changing the landscape of many industries, such as transportation, software development, and hospitality [5], leading to increasing research interest. Prior research has offered various definitions for digital platforms, i.e., definitions based on a technical view that addresses the technical elements and processes that interact to form a digital platform, as well as definitions based on a non-technical view that present platforms as commercial or two-sided networks that enable interactions between interdependent groups of users [5]. Similarly, in [1] the authors define a platform as a business based on enabling value-creating interactions between external producers and consumers. The platform provides an open, participative infrastructure for these interactions and sets governance conditions for them, to consummate matches among users and facilitate the exchange of goods, services, or social currency [1].

Recently, there has also been an ongoing interest in crowdsourcing platforms. In his defining work, Howe [6] suggested that crowdsourcing is *"the act of a company or institution taking a function once performed by employees and outsourcing it to an undefined network of people in the form of an open call"*. According to a comprehensive study that compiled and examined several different definitions of crowdsourcing [7], crowdsourcing *constitutes a distributed online process that requires the participation of the crowd for the accomplishment of specific tasks.* Thanks to the recent advances in information technologies and the emergence of collaborative Web 2.0 digital platforms, organizations or companies can now benefit from the "wisdom of the crowd", which is typically heterogeneous, comprising volunteers, enthusiasts, amateurs, as well as experts and companies [8]. Furthermore, crowdsourcing is also considered a mechanism that can be used to organize and facilitate worldwide volunteer efforts, or "collective intelligence" [9].

Crowdsourcing has already been applied in many areas, from business projects to non-profit initiatives, and there are many examples of successful crowdsourcing platforms, such as Amazon Mechanical Turk (a crowdsourcing website where businesses can find remotely located "crowdworkers" to perform micro tasks), Wikipedia (a free, multilingual online encyclopedia created and maintained by a community of volunteers), and InnoCentive (an open innovation platform which allows organizations to post their unsolved problems to InnoCentive's "solver" network).

Furthermore, it has also been suggested that crowdsourcing is an appropriate method for motivating and facilitating citizen participation in urban projects [10]. Indeed, many scholars have advocated for more participatory processes where civic technologies are publicly owned and led by citizen initiatives [11]. Participatory innovation is thought to provide a viable alternative to more traditional official-led planning, as it is believed that the increasing number of open data sets could facilitate citizens in becoming active participants and urban innovators, instead of mere civic technology users [12]. Accordingly, there is also an ongoing research interest on the design and use of crowdsourcing platforms as participative ecosystems for *e-governance*, see, e.g. [13–15]; *urban planning*, see, e.g. [16–19]; *transit planning*, e.g., [20, 21]; as well as *air quality and environmental awareness*, e.g., [22, 23], among others.

So far, several crowdsourcing platforms that facilitate citizens have been created around the world in finding information, collaborating, and voicing their perspectives on important urban issues. Some noteworthy examples comprise: (a) Better Reykjavik, an online civic participation and open innovation platform; (b) Spacehive, a UK-based crowdfunding platform for citizen-led neighborhood improvement projects; (c) Ushahidi, a Kenyan-based platform allowing people to submit, collect and map crowdsourced information for crisis response, environmental justice, election monitoring, etc.; (d) Carticipe, or Debatomap for non-French speakers, a participatory mapping tool designed to promote citizen debates and consultation on a city or urban territory; (e) Colouring London, a knowledge-exchange platform providing open data on London buildings to help make the city more sustainable, and (f) Decide Madrid, a platform aiming to engage the public in decision-making and to ensure transparency of government proceedings. These platforms vary greatly in aims, characteristics, and organizational structures; for example, they can be instigated by researchers or governing bodies, or they can be bottom-up community-led ones, where citizens are directly involved in the organization of the project and the development or improvement of the platform.

Due to their broad spectrum and sociotechnical implications, it is difficult to truly understand the attributes of digital platforms, especially since research on the subject is fragmented into many different domains. Efforts have been made to create taxonomies and analyze their specific characteristics. [24] and [25] both use the method of taxonomy mentioned in [26] to group digital platforms' instances and conceptualizations, facilitating thus the identification of archetypes. The first study is focused on dimensions and characteristics and suggests that digital platforms exhibit characteristics on at least four dimensions—namely, infrastructure, core, ecosystem, and service dimensions. The second one analyzes digital platforms from a business model perspective and derives four archetypes with distinct design configurations, i.e., business innovation platforms, consumer innovation platforms, business exchange platforms, and consumer exchange platforms. Other efforts to create a classification system focus on digital platforms' core building blocks such as platform architecture, platform orchestrator and ownership, value-creating mechanisms, coordination mechanisms, as well as market control [27–29]. Based on an extended review of this literature we have identified attributes that seem to define the nature of digital platforms and affect their overall impact, not only in terms of innovation outcome within the specific context in which they are being used but also with regards to their prospect for facilitating innovation in wider contexts. These attributes and characteristics include the type of crowdsourcing, the platform's ownership, openness, and affordance and are analytically explained below.

2.1 Typology of Crowdsourcing Platforms

Concerning crowdsourcing platforms, an overview of relevant studies revealed various proposed typologies. First, a more generic categorization would be based on the mode of interaction between contributors, so platforms could be characterized as either competitive or collaborative. In the first category, contributors provide competing products/services or take part in contests for rewards. In the second category, open access to information is promoted among contributors [5]. There are also other categorizations based on various dimensions, e.g., the objective of the platform and the type of need it addresses. In [8], the authors propose an integrated typology composing five main types of crowdsourcing: (a) *Crowdcasting* – contests where participants are presented with a problem and the best solution is rewarded; (b) *Crowdcollaboration* – crowdsourcing initiatives in which the initiator remains on the sidelines in order to allow participants to interact on their own. It can be divided into *Crowdstorming* (online brainstorming sessions, in which the crowd can vote for preferred ideas) and *Crowdsupport* (where the customers themselves solve the problems of other customers); (c) *Crowdcontent* – in this category of crowdsourcing tasks, the crowd creates or finds content on the Internet or inside multimedia documents, but not in a competitive way; (d) *Crowdfunding* – the crowd can fund various initiatives, in exchange for a reward; and (e) *Crowdopinion* – participants contribute by sharing their opinions about a particular issue or product through votes, comments, shares, etc.

Common subtypes of crowdsourcing have also been used effectively in the commercial world. These include e.g. microwork (online platforms that allow users to do small tasks that cannot be automated but also do not require any special training or expertise, for low amounts of money, e.g. Toloka, Amazon Mechanical Turk); macrowork (online platforms that in which tasks require specialized skills and typically take longer, e.g. Upwork, Fiverr); creative crowdsourcing (online platforms where clients can solicit a wide variety of creative work, such as graphic or apparel design, at lower cost, e.g. 99designs, DesignCrowd); crowdvoting (a subtype of crowdopinion where a platform gathers users' opinions on a certain topic by upvoting/downvoting, e.g. Reddit), and others. Even though this is not an exhaustive list, the above-mentioned types and subtypes of crowdsourcing cover the present major ways in which people use the wisdom of the crowds to perform tasks.

2.2 Capabilities of Platform Leaders or Suppliers

Capabilities may refer to the distribution of benefits and the nature of the motivation to participate [9] or the platform ecosystem orchestration [30]. Regarding supplier capabilities, these can be characterized based on the simplicity of the outsourced task. Simple tasks are of relatively low complexity, can easily be performed without formal training, and can be easily evaluated; moderate tasks require a moderate level of complexity and difficulty, and, finally, sophisticated tasks are complex and require highly skilled suppliers [9]. The distribution of benefits refers to who has benefited from the crowdsourcing activity. Based on that, crowdsourcing can be labeled individualistic (activities that provide personal or company benefits), community (activities that are designed to benefit a community of some kind), and mixed (both individualistic and community) [9]. Finally, crowdsourcing can also be characterized by users' incentives for participation. Some common incentives include learning and motives related to personal achievement, (ii) altruism, (iii) enjoyment and intellectual motives, i.e., curiosity, (iv) social motives, (v) self-marketing, and (vi) financial motives [31].

Lastly, crowdsourcing can be characterized as implicit or explicit, based on the way users contribute data to the platform. More specifically, crowdsourcing platforms can be distinguished between platforms where data is provided directly by users (explicit crowdsourcing), and platforms where data is indirectly provided by users' sensors, e.g., geolocation info from mobile devices (implicit crowdsourcing or "crowdsensing") [31]. Usually, the goal of these applications is to monitor indicators such as radiation levels or air quality and to raise awareness on local issues.

2.3 Platform Ownership

Platform ownership is not just about the legal entity that owns the digital platform; it is also related to content ownership, the relationships among partners, and the distribution of power in the ecosystem, which can be centralized or decentralized. Rules of ownership and governance mechanisms are usually stated in the Terms of Service, although in most cases it is not very well-suited for governing the relationship between user and platform [32]. In [27] three categories of platform ownership are defined: (a) centralized platforms, controlled by a single owner (usually a company or an organization), who defines, establishes, and maintains the governance mechanisms of the platform (e.g. Google, Apple); (b) owned by consortia, a group of actors or a community of independent developers, where there is a distribution of power over multiple stakeholders (e.g. Cloud Foundry); and (c) decentralized platforms, governed by peer-to-peer communities that allow individuals to make changes in the design and functionality of the platform (e.g. blockchain platforms).

2.4 Platform Openness

Openness, an important factor for knowledge sharing and innovation creation, refers to the degree to which other firms or individuals can freely use, modify, and develop the platform technologies, terms of use, and outcomes [33]. It is directly linked to platform ownership and affordance and can be examined through different dimensions. Several aspects of openness are identified in the relevant bibliography, such as (i) architectural openness, (ii) standards compliance, (iii) open intellectual property regime, (iv) absence of lock-in mechanisms, (v) free and open market, and (vi) open governance [34].

2.5 Platform Affordance

It is a relational property comprising (a) decoupling, that reduces the importance of asset specificity in regulating power and dependency relationships within manufacturing value chains, (b) disintermediation, the ability to support direct interactions between service providers and users, thereby enabling them to bypass intermediaries, and (c) generativity, i.e. facilitate unprompted innovative inputs from large, uncoordinated audiences, the outcome of several architectural features that jointly reduce transaction costs in interactions conducted through the internet and infuse an extent of unpredictability and fluidity into innovation outcomes) [35].

The literature on platform attributes and characteristics is going on with studies focusing on a) resource richness, i.e. the types of inputs or contributions b) the platform's structure, either as an innovation platform that facilitates collaboration between customer groups or as an exchange platform that promotes transactions between them, c) the network's attributes, such as network structure and intensity, since the platform can be considered as an intermediary interface that facilitates interactions between entities (nodes) comprising both individual participants and collectives [36].

3 Methodology

We collected and analyzed 20 international crowdsourcing platforms based on specific attributes that have need described in the section before. Compared to previous empirical studies we analyze platforms of different types (crowdcontent, crowdfunding, crowdopinion, crowdcasting) as they are listed below.

Crowdcontent platforms

- Ushahidi (http://www.ushahidi.com/): Crowdsourcing tools for democratizing information, increasing transparency, and lowering the barriers for individuals to share their stories. Users can submit their reports by text message, e-mail, online posts, etc. Ushahidi tools have been used for crisis response, election monitoring, advocacy, and human rights.

- Neighborland (https://neighborland.com/): Neighborland is a proprietary public engagement platform designed for government agencies, developers, and civic organizations. It allows stakeholders to publish their feedback (ideas, votes, comments) on maps and scenario renderings, interact with others on the discussion forum, and take part in surveys. Resident ideas, insights, and solutions are mapped to specific locations and categorized by topic. It can also be characterized as a crowdopinion/crowdvoting and crowdcollaboration platform.
- Actipedia (https://actipedia.org/): An open-access, user-generated database of creative activism, that can also be characterized as a crowdopinion/crowdvoting platform. Users can share projects they found on the Web or participated in themselves, improve the platform's user-generated content, keep track of projects they like, and upvote their favorite projects.
- ColouringLondon (https://colouringlondon.org/): A free knowledge exchange platform designed to provide over fifty types of open data on London buildings, to help make the city more sustainable. Users can contribute their knowledge on London's building, check the platform's data, and submit links to databases of relevance.
- OpenStreetMap (https://www.openstreetmap.org/): A collaborative project to create a free editable geographic database of the world. Contributors use aerial imagery, GPS devices, and low-tech field maps to verify that the platform's maps are accurate.
- WikiHouse (https://www.wikihouse.cc/): An open-source project aiming to democratize the creation of low-cost, low-energy homes. Contributors include a distributed network of small, local fabricators and assemblers, as well as architects, designers, engineers, entrepreneurs, etc.
- Block by Block (https://www.blockbyblock.org/): A project providing the tools and platform to involve community members –especially underrepresented, such as kids, elders, disabled residents, and refugees– by integrating the computer game Minecraft into public space planning. Given the fact that Minecraft is easy to learn and to play by people of all ages and backgrounds, it is used to enable neighborhood residents to model their surroundings, visualize possibilities, and express ideas.

Crowdfunding platforms

- Spacehive (https://www.spacehive.com/): UK-based crowdfunding platform for projects aimed at improving local civic and community spaces. Individuals, local groups, and businesses can start a project on the platform and raise funds from the crowd or partners of the platform.
- DigVentures (https://digventures.com/): Platform for crowdfunded and community archaeology and heritage projects. Users can support and take part in various crowdfunded projects.
- IOBY (https://ioby.org/): US-based civic crowdfunding platform that connects local leaders with support and funding from their communities to make neighborhoods more sustainable, healthier, and greener.

Crowdopinion/crowdvoting platforms

- Crowdscope (https://www.crowdoscope.com/): Survey and discussion tool for gathering quantitative and qualitative data and generating real-time collective intelligence.
- Polis (https://pol.is/home): Open-source real-time system for gathering, analyzing, and understanding large groups of people's opinions, enabled by advanced statistics and machine learning. Used by governments, academics, independent media, and citizens.
- Terrifica (http://climatemapping.terrifica.eu/): A crowdmapping platform built to collect people's experiences and opinions regarding climate change in their local environment. Users are invited to put marks on an interactive map and explain why they decided to mark this place.
- MindMixer (https://www.mindmixer.com): Online community engagement platform that connects municipal decision-makers and elected officials with their constituents in a cost-effective manner. Participants can submit their ideas or support other ideas. They can also vote in instant polls or take part in surveys.
- DecideMadrid (https://decide.madrid.es/): Open-source platform which can be used to engage the public in decision-making and ensure transparency of government proceedings. Participants can propose and support ideas for new legislation, and provide opinions about/vote on council proceedings, among others.
- Decidim (https://decidim.org/): Free open-Source digital platform providing spaces for participatory democracy for cities and organizations enriched with tools such as proposal creation, voting, surveys, comments, etc.
- Better Reykjavik (https://betrireykjavik.is/domain/1/communities): The City of Reykjavik's online engagement platform is used for the crowdsourcing of solutions to urban challenges. Better Reykjavik uses Your Priorities (open-source software to organize and crowdsource ideas). Participants can submit ideas and vote on proposals submitted by other users.

Crowdcasting and Open Innovation platforms

- Innocentive (https://www.innocentive.com/): Open innovation and crowdsourcing platform. Solvers can visit the platform's challenge center and find open challenges to tackle. If their submission is selected they may receive a monetary reward.
- OpenIdeo (https://www.openideo.com/): An open innovation platform where people collaboratively tackle global issues. The purpose of the platform is to virtually drive the creative process to solve challenges, by facilitating people of different expertise and backgrounds to collaborate, innovate, and win various prizes.
- IdeaScale (https://ideascale.com): Innovation management platform allowing organizations to crowdsource the opinions of public and private communities regarding various challenges. Users can create a profile on IdeaScale and submit ideas as members of a community. They can also comment and vote on other ideas.

We analyze the platforms comparatively based on three characteristics: the domain they are used, the type of the platform, the contributors' incentives, the platform ownership as well as their openness. First, with regards to platform typology, we use the following types: (i) crowdcollaboration, mainly crowdstorming, (ii) crowdcreation, (iii) crowdopinion and crowdvoting, and (iv) crowdfunding, although we have noticed that some platforms can incorporate attributes from several crowdsourcing types at the same time. We then categorize platforms according to ownership status. We also focus on three different dimensions of openness: a) the platform's technological openness, i.e. the openness of the digital platform architecture and the boundary resources (APIs) that affects the ability of external entities to build on and complement one another's contributions, b) access openness, i.e. the platform's rules for entrance and exit along with the ability of different types of actors to participate, and c) outcome openness, i.e. the openness of data and the ability to use the platform outcomes for purposes outside the scope of the platform. These dimensions show that openness is not just about the platforms' artifacts but also refers to the transparency and inclusiveness of its governance [34].

4   Research Findings

The findings are based on the analysis of the sample of 20 crowdsourcing platforms based on five attributes: their domain of application, their type, the incentives of platform contributors, the platform's ownership, and openness. More specifically, most of the platforms analyzed aim at community engagement and civic participation, while a limited number of others focus on volunteered geographic information, crisis mapping, knowledge exchange, participatory democracy, and election monitoring. Participation is considered a key feature in the innovation process, as it strengthens and seizes network effects, and enhances the ability of people to collaborate and create bottom-up innovative solutions to complex problems.

With regards to their type, 45% of the sample platforms were crowdopinion platforms, 35% crowdcontent platforms, and a smaller percentage was crowdfunding, collaborative project creation, crowdmapping, and crowdcasting platforms. Most of the reviewed platforms facilitate collaboration among participants, while only a few platforms (i.e., crowdcasting/open innovation platforms) urge the participants to compete –as individuals or members of a team– in order to submit the best solution and gain a reward. Reflecting on the context of grand challenges and of complex urban problems, crowd-opinion moves one step further from collecting resources and captures the collective wisdom of the crowd facilitating, complementing, and increasing thus the capacities and effectiveness of urban authorities, leading to better-informed decision-making processes and empowered governmental entities and citizens.

With regards to ownership, most platforms are owned by non-profit organizations, and only a small percentage of them are owned by a private company. The non-profit nature of ownership does not affect the technological openness of the platform, since a large percentage of them is using proprietary software. Finally, almost all platforms give open access to users (either individuals or organizations) with the requirement to create an account although the openness to different types of contributions may vary depending on the platform. For example, in almost all platforms anyone can register and contribute content to the platform, but there may be limitations or specific rules for editing inputs from other users, participating in conversations, voting, etc. (Table 1).

Table 1. Crowdsourcing platforms and their attributes

	Domain	Contributors' motives	Platform ownership	Technological openness	Access openness	Outcome openness
Crowdcontent						
Ushahidi	Human rights & Crisis mapping Election monitoring	- Altruism - Learning - Personal achievement - Intellectual motives	Non-profit company	Open-source technology Paid plans for custom enterprise platform	Anyone can participate through various channels, e.g., SMS, e-mail, Twitter	Supports import and export of user-contributed data
Neighborland	Public engagement	- Altruism - Learning - Personal achievement - Intellectual and social motives	Private for-profit company	Proprietary software	Citizens, governments, and civic organizations	Material and platform code cannot be modified, used, or distributed without permission
Actipedia	Creative activism	- Altruism - Learning - Personal achievement - Intellectual motives	Non-profit company	Proprietary software	Anyone can participate by creating a free account	Collect and share users' submissions outside of the platform
Colouring London	Citizen social science & knowledge exchange platform Volunteered Geographic Information	- Altruism - Learning - Personal achievement - Intellectual motives	Non-profit company	Open-source software	Anyone can participate by creating a free account	All data and code are free to download, use and share under our open license terms
OpenStreetMap	Volunteered Geographic Information	- Altruism - Learning - Personal achievement - Intellectual motives	Non-profit organization	Not open source	Anyone can edit the maps	Open data: users are free to copy, distribute, transmit and adapt OSM data if they credit the platform and its contributors
Wikihouse	Open-source architecture	- Altruism - Learning - Personal achievement - Intellectual and social motives	Non-profit company	Open-source project	Anyone can contribute, improve or even create a new product based on the WikiHouse building system	Users can download Creative Commons-licensed files, customize them and use them in construction

(continued)

Table 1. (*continued*)

	Domain	Contributors' motives	Platform ownership	Technological openness	Access openness	Outcome openness
Block by Block	Community engagement Urban planning	- Altruism - Learning - Personal achievement - Intellectual and social motives	Non-profit foundation	Workshops using Minecraft (proprietary software)	Local community members can participate and contribute	The Block by Block Methodology is free to download

Crowdfunding

	Domain	Contributors' motives	Platform ownership	Technological openness	Access openness	Outcome openness
Spacehive	Community engagement Civic projects	- Altruism - Learning - Personal achievement - Intellectual and social motives	Private company	Proprietary platform. It also provides specialized software to foundations that it partners with to fund projects	Anyone can submit a project after registering. Organizations can become fund owners	The content of the platform may be accessed only for non-commercial use and cannot be distributed or modified
DigVentures	Community engagement in archeology and heritage projects Civic participation	- Altruism - Learning - Personal achievement - Enjoyment - Intellectual and social motives	Private company	Proprietary platform. They also offer consultation services	Anyone can use the platform to back a project and take part in community projects	The material or the platform cannot be modified. Users cannot contribute or edit content
IOBY	Civic participation Community engagement	- Altruism - Learning - Personal achievement - Intellectual and social motives	Non-profit company	Proprietary platform	Users can submit ideas as individuals or organizations or back projects	Users retain ownership of their works but cannot modify or use other users' projects

Crowdopinion/Crowdvoting

	Domain	Contributors' motives	Platform ownership	Technological openness	Access openness	Outcome openness
Crowdscope	Collective intelligence	- Personal achievement - Social and professional motives	Private company	Proprietary platform	Users participate in surveys and discussions	Users retain ownership of their content
Polis	Collective intelligence Civic participation	- Altruism - Learning - Personal achievement - Intellectual and social motives	Non-profit organization	Open source	Organizations can invite citizens to take part in conversations	Users can store, transfer, display and distribute content from the platform

(*continued*)

Table 1. (*continued*)

	Domain	Contributors' motives	Platform ownership	Technological openness	Access openness	Outcome openness
Terrifica	Community engagement	- Altruism - Learning - Personal achievement - Intellectual and social motives	Non-profit organization EU-funded project	Proprietary software	Anyone can register and contribute. Users from six pilot region	No data policy in place. Users can contribute but not export data
MindMixer	Community engagement	- Altruism - Learning - Personal achievement - Intellectual and social motives	Private company	Proprietary platform	Municipal decision makers and elected officials can connect with citizens	Users can view/download content solely for personal and non-commercial purposes
DecideMadrid	Community engagement Participatory democracy	- Altruism - Learning - Personal achievement - Intellectual and social motives	Non-profit organization	Open-source software	Anyone can participate, vote and collaborate	Data is open to be freely used, reused and redistributed
Decidim	Community engagement Participatory democracy	- Altruism - Learning - Personal achievement - Intellectual and social motives	Non-profit organization	Open-source platform	Any group of people can use it. However, it is addressed primarily to users based in Barcelona	The data available through the platform will be published and licensed under Open Data Commons Open Database License
Better Reykjavik	Community engagement Participatory democracy	- Altruism - Learning - Personal achievement - Intellectual and social motives	Non-profit organization	Open-source software provided by Citizens.is	Anyone can participate, even anonymously	Supports easy access and export of data for administrators. Ideas can be shared on social media
Crowdcasting/Open innovation						
Innocentive	Open innovation	- Altruism - Learning - Personal achievement - Intellectual - Social and financial motives	Private for-profit company	Proprietary platform	Open participation after signing a specific agreement	The solvers own their proposed solutions. They can transfer the intellectual property rights to seekers

(*continued*)

Table 1. (*continued*)

	Domain	Contributors' motives	Platform ownership	Technological openness	Access openness	Outcome openness
OpenIdeo	Open innovation	- Altruism - Learning - Personal achievement - Intellectual - Social and financial motives	Private for-profit company	Proprietary platform	Open participation from anyone in most cases	All ideas publicly contributed to OpenIDEO become shareable, remix-able and reusable by anyone
IdeaScale	Open innovation management	Rewards (and subsequently user motives) are dependent on the company or organization that uses IdeaScale's platform	Private for-profit company	Proprietary platform	Freemium model and paid subscriptions	Users retain ownership of the intellectual property rights of the content they submit. They cannot reproduce or modify derivative works of the platform's content

5 Discussion and Further Research

The open collaborative approach of innovation has resulted in fundamental changes in problem-solving capabilities as (a) it enhances wider participation in the innovation process, and (b) it enables network effects to take place while also reducing transaction costs. Digital platforms and web-based tools for open collaborative innovation provide a virtual environment for knowledge transfer and integration and can be leveraged for the design and implementation of bottom-up innovative solutions to complex problems, creating new sources of value. The digital, collaborative platform provides an open, participative infrastructure of interactions and sets governance conditions for them while the Internet allows wider aggregation and integration of different members in an innovation community [37]. We approached the different aspects of digitalization and openness of the innovation process through the analysis of different attributes of platforms that vary significantly with regards to their domain and type. We find that most platforms present similar features of ownership and openness which might be characteristics innate to digital technologies that set motion to the mechanisms for engagement, sharing, collaboration, and co-creation.

References

1. Parker, G.G., Van Alstyne, M.W., Choudary, S.P.: Platform Revolution: How Networked Markets are Transforming the Economy and How to Make Them Work for You. WW Norton & Company (2016)

2. Anttiroiko, A.-V., Valkama, P., Bailey, S.J.: Smart cities in the new service economy: building platforms for smart services. AI Soc. **29**(3), 323–334 (2013). https://doi.org/10.1007/s00146-013-0464-0

3. Komninos, N., Kakderi, C. (eds.): Smart Cities in the Post-algorithmic Era: Integrating Technologies, Platforms and Governance. Edward Elgar Publishing, Cheltenham (2019)

4. van der Aalst, W., Hinz, O., Weinhardt, C.: Big digital platforms. Bus. Inf. Syst. Eng. **61**(6), 645–648 (2019)

5. Asadullah, A., Faik, I., Kankanhalli, A.: Digital platforms: a review and future directions. In PACIS, p. 248 (2018)

6. Howe, J.: Crowdsourcing: a definition (2006). http://crowdsourcing.typepad.com/cs/2006/06/crowdsourcing_a.html. Accessed 5 Feb 2022

7. Estellés-Arolas, E., González-Ladrón-de-Guevara, F.: Towards an integrated crowdsourcing definition. J. Inf. Sci. **38**(2), 189–200 (2012)

8. Estellés-Arolas, E., Navarro-Giner, R., González-Ladrón-de-Guevara, F.: Crowdsourcing fundamentals: definition and typology. In: Garrigos-Simon, F., Gil-Pechuán, I., Estelles-Miguel, S. (eds.) Advances in Crowdsourcing. Springer, Cham (2015). https://doi.org/10.1007/978-3-319-18341-1_3

9. Rouse, A.C.: A preliminary taxonomy of crowdsourcing. In: ACIS 2010 Proceedings (2010)

10. Brabham, D.C.: Crowdsourcing the public participation process for planning projects. Plan. Theory **8**(3), 242–262 (2009)

11. Saunders, T., Baeck, P.: Rethinking Smart Cities from the Ground up. Nesta, London (2015)

12. Wolff, A., Gooch, D., Cavero, J., Rashid, U., Kortuem, G.: Removing barriers for citizen participation to urban innovation. In: de Lange, M., de Waal, M. (eds.) The hackable city, pp. 153–168. Springer, Singapore (2019). https://doi.org/10.1007/978-981-13-2694-3_8

13. Warner, J.: Next steps in e-government crowdsourcing. In: Proceedings of the 12th Annual International Digital Government Research Conference: Digital Government Innovation in Challenging Times, pp. 177–181 (2011)

14. Motta, G., You, L., Sacco, D., Ma, T.: City feed: a crowdsourcing system for city governance. In: 2014 IEEE 8th International Symposium on Service Oriented System Engineering, pp. 439–445. IEEE (2014)

15. Certoma, C., Corsini, F., Rizzi, F.: Crowdsourcing urban sustainability. Data, people and technologies in participatory governance. Futures **74**, 93–106 (2015)

16. Lu, H., et al.: Evaluating urban design ideas from citizens from crowdsourcing and participatory design. In: Proceedings of the 23rd International Conference of the Association for Computer-Aided Architectural Design Research in Asia (CAADRIA) 2018, vol. 2, pp. 297–306 (2018)

17. Segedinac, G., Reba, D.: Crowdsourcing in participatory planning: online platforms as participative ecosystems. Facta Univ. Ser. Architect. Civil Eng. **17**, 81–91 (2019)

18. Liao, P., et al.: Applying crowdsourcing techniques in urban planning: a bibliometric analysis of research and practice prospects. Cities **94**, 33–43 (2019)

19. Chaves, R., et al.: Understanding crowd work in online crowdsourcing platforms for urban planning: systematic review. In: 2019 IEEE 23rd International Conference on Computer Supported Cooperative Work in Design (CSCWD). IEEE (2019)

20. Brabham, D.C.: Motivations for participation in a crowdsourcing application to improve public engagement in transit planning. J. Appl. Commun. Res. **40**(3), 307–328 (2012)

21. Hara, K., et al.: Improving public transit accessibility for blind riders by crowdsourcing bus stop landmark locations with google street view: an extended analysis. ACM Trans. Access. Comput. (TACCESS) **6**(2), 1–23 (2015)

22. Overeem, A., et al.: Crowdsourcing urban air temperatures from smartphone battery temperatures. Geophys. Res. Lett. **40**(15), 4081–4085 (2013)

23. Kanhere, S.S.: Participatory sensing: crowdsourcing data from mobile smartphones in urban spaces. In: Hota, C., Srimani, P.K. (eds.) ICDCIT 2013. LNCS, vol. 7753, pp. 19–26. Springer, Heidelberg (2013). https://doi.org/10.1007/978-3-642-36071-8_2

24. Blaschke, M., Haki, K., Aier, S., Winter, R.: Taxonomy of digital platforms: a platform architecture perspective. In: Internationale Tagung Wirtschaftsinformatik (WI2019) (2019)

25. Staub, N., Haki, K., Aier, S., Winter, R.: taxonomy of digital platforms: a business model perspective. In: Hawaii International Conference on System Sciences (HICSS 54) (2019)

26. Nickerson, R.C., Varshney, U., Muntermann, J.: A method for taxonomy development and its application in information systems. Eur. J. Inf. Syst. 22(3), 336–359 (2013)

27. Hein, A., et al.: Digital platform ecosystems. Electron. Mark. 30(1), 87–98 (2019). https://doi.org/10.1007/s12525-019-00377-4

28. Maffie, M.D.: Are we 'sharing' or 'gig-ing'? A classification system for online platforms. Ind. Relat. J. 51(6), 536–555 (2020)

29. Gawer, A.: Bridging differing perspectives on technological platforms: toward an integrative framework. Res. Policy 43(7), 1239–1249 (2014)

30. Helfat, C.E., Raubitschek, R.S.: Dynamic and integrative capabilities for profiting from innovation in digital platform-based ecosystems. Res. Policy 47(8), 1391–1399 (2018)

31. Katmada, A., Satsiou, A., Kompatsiaris, I.: Incentive mechanisms for crowdsourcing platforms. In: Bagnoli, F., Satsiou, A., Stavrakakis, I., Nesi, P., Pacini, G., Welp, Y. (eds.) INSCI 2016. LNCS, vol. 9934, pp. 3–18. Springer, Cham (2016). https://doi.org/10.1007/978-3-319-45982-0_1

32. Zhou, M., Leenders, M.A., Cong, L.M.: Ownership in the virtual world and the implications for long-term user innovation success. Technovation 78, 56–65 (2018)

33. Choi, G., Nam, C., Kim, S.: The impacts of technology platform openness on application developers' intention to continuously use a platform: from an ecosystem perspective. Telecommun. Policy 43(2), 140–153 (2019)

34. Teixeira, J.: On the openness of digital platforms/ecosystems. In: Proceedings of the 11th International Symposium on Open Collaboration, pp. 1–4 (2015)

35. Autio, E., Nambisan, S., Thomas, L.D., Wright, M.: Digital affordances, spatial affordances, and the genesis of entrepreneurial ecosystems. Strateg. Entrep. J. 12(1), 72–95 (2018)

36. McIntyre, D.P., Srinivasan, A., Chintakananda, A.: The persistence of platforms: the role of network, platform, and complementor attributes. Long Range Plan. 54(5), 101987 (2021)

37. Battistella, C., Nonino, F.: Open innovation web-based platforms: the impact of different forms of motivation on collaboration. Innovation 14(4), 557–575 (2012)

Exploring the Implementation of Web, Mobile, and VR Technology for Cultural Heritage Presentation

Junyang Li[1] , Guochao Peng[1(✉)] , and Ning Zhang[2]

[1] School of Information Management, Sun Yat-sen University, Guangzhou 510006, China
penggch@mail.sysu.edu.cn
[2] Research Center for Digital Publishing and Digital Humanities, Beijing Normal University, Zhuhai 511449, China

Abstract. As an important base for collecting cultural heritage resources, cultural and museum institutions in smart cities play an increasingly important role in public education. VR technology has received extensive attention because of its immersion, interaction, and imagination advantages. This paper explores the current Implementation and problems of digital cultural heritage in the world and proposes the optimization scheme of VR Museum design and development. VR museum can provide multi-modal information provision in five aspects: exhibition hall, collection display, interpretation, collection interaction, and guide, which involves human sight, hearing, and tactile sense. From the perspective of user experience, this paper analyzes the problems of the current digital cultural and museum websites, app and VR applications in terms of software features, hardware features, and digital content, designed and constructed a VR Museum application to show a potential future development path of VR cultural heritage applications,

Keywords: Virtual reality · Cultural heritage · Interface and interaction design · Information resources

1 Introduction

Cultural heritage in a smart city is enabling technologies connecting cultural institutions, visitors, and cultural artefacts [1]. Museums, libraries, archives, cultural institutions, tourism institutions, and other cultural institutions are committed to opening digital curation data for users to easily use information technology to access knowledge. As an important institution for the preservation and presentation of cultural heritage in the smart city, Museums provide digital cultural heritage information resources access services. Virtual reality is a technology that can simulate the real environment in computers and other electronic devices and bring users an approximate real experience from the senses of sight, hearing, tactile, and so on [2]. VR cultural heritage application combines VR technology with cultural heritage information resources to enrich the provision of cultural heritage information on multi-modal information which can help visitors to

© The Author(s), under exclusive license to Springer Nature Switzerland AG 2022
N. A. Streitz and S. Konomi (Eds.): HCII 2022, LNCS 13325, pp. 43–58, 2022.
https://doi.org/10.1007/978-3-031-05463-1_4

understand the museum collections, instead of only present objects [3]. VR technology provides different types of cultural heritage presentation, including text, audio, pictures, video, 3D model, and virtual environment. It offers multi-functions of communication and dissemination of information and knowledge between users and cultural heritage collections. Therefore, how to use VR technology to put forward the presentation and dissemination mode of cultural heritage information is a problem to be solved in the process of VR museums. This study explores the current situation and existing problems of digital cultural heritage resources and proposes an integrative VR museum information system in smart cities. The objectives of this paper are:

1. What are the key features to be used in digital cultural heritage applications.
2. Investigate the implementations of the current web, mobile, and VR museum.
3. To propose a VR museum model to improve users' experience in digital cultural heritage.

2 Literature Review

Various types of digital technologies have been used to improve visitors' experience in museums [4]. For example, web technology, mobile technology, and VR technology. Digital cultural heritage can be accessed on websites, smart devices, and VR devices, each platform presents cultural heritage information resources in different technology and using different features.

2.1 Web Technology

The website takes the Internet as the media and uses information technology to digitize cultural heritage resources, convert them into text, picture, audio, video, and other types of data that can be stored in the computer, and spread them through web pages. Website is an important channel to spread cultural heritage information. Users usually obtain digital cultural heritage information from museum websites, but the features of each museum website are different. Users mainly use the website to browse and query cultural artefacts information, as well as obtain relevant information such as activities and current exhibitions held by cultural institutions [5]. Various technologies can be used to build cultural heritage websites to meet the information needs of different users. The online digital exhibition hall is built by taking high-definition photos of the exhibition hall by using high-definition camera technology and making 360° panoramic pictures for users to watch from multiple angles. For example, the Palace Museum website provides "panoramic Palace Museum" and "V Palace Museum" features to take panoramic photos of multiple palaces in the Palace Museum. Users can click the corresponding button on the computer screen to jump to visit the palace, to achieve the effect of a panoramic tour. The web plug-in can be utilized to display 3D models of collections on the web page. WebGL technology achieves the function of web page 3D scene rendering, which provides technical support for the construction of a 3D virtual museum on the web page. Some websites integrate a variety of display technologies to display collections. For example, Europeana is a website established by the European Union containing

European cultural resources such as digital libraries, archives, and museums. It covers digital information resources such as text, pictures, audio, video, panoramic images, and 3D models, providing users with a comprehensive experience in querying cultural heritage information on the web page.

2.2 Mobile Technology with Smart Devices

The cultural heritage smartphone app uses human-computer interaction technology to integrate mobile devices with digital resources. In the review of early research on digital cultural heritage, mostly to explore how to guide users to visit museums and improve users' visit experience. Semper proposed to use the mobile positioning function of portable electronic devices to provide navigation services for users in museums [6]. In recent years, smartphone apps integrate augmented reality (AR) technology which combines the real world and the virtual world. virtual objects can be shown in the real environment and displayed through smart devices. Vlahakis proposed a system for cultural heritage reconstruction, education, and research-based on augmented reality technology. Users can see the reconstructed temple on the ruins of the Hera Temple site through smartphones, tablets, and other electronic devices [7]. Spallone introduced the 3D reconstructive modeling technology in AR and VR systems for the digital reconstruction of cultural heritage [8]. The real scene is combined with the virtual 3D model so that users can view the reconstructed building through smart devices. In the museum, smart devices can be used to sense and scan the corresponding labels of the exhibits to identify the information of the exhibits. It also provides location functions with a convenient experience for users to browse independently. QR code recognition technology, represented by QR code, can scan QR code through the camera, read corresponding information, display it on screen, and convey it to users. Smartphones usually have many built-in sensors, such as WiFi, Bluetooth, infrared, RFID, etc., which help users to identify cultural artefacts and to locate their position in museums.

2.3 VR Technology

Since the invention of the first head-mounted display system for immersive simulation applications [9], more and more institutions and enterprises have participated in the research and production of VR equipment. VR devices are commonly divided into three types: PC VR, mobile VR, and all-in-one VR. PC VR connects the helmet with the computer host. After running through the computer host, the computer screen is transmitted to the helmet display. PC VR has strong performance and good display effect, as well as space binding and high cost. Mobile VR is to put mobile devices such as smartphones into a headset box, and the application runs using the mobile phone and is displayed on the mobile phone screen. The advantages of mobile VR are easy to carry and low cost; The disadvantage is poor performance and poor display effect. The all-in-one VR has an independent processor and display device, which can run the application independently and display it on the helmet display screen. All-in-one VR has strong independence and better spatial freedom, but with high cost, poor display effect, and great influence by the battery power supply. The three popular VR devices in the world are HTC VIVE,

Oculus, and PS VR. All these devices are PC VR which is supported by a powerful computer host.

3 Human-Computer Interaction in Cultural Heritage Applications

Dale's core of experience theory divides learning experience into concrete and abstract [10], which corresponds to different information channels of human hearing, sight, and body senses. These information channels are responsible for processing voice information, image information, and spatial environment information respectively. Human-computer interaction in a VR environment allows humans to communicate with the computer system through the application interface by using multi-modal interaction such as sight, hearing, and gesture [11].

3.1 Modules of the Digital Cultural Heritage Applications

According to the VR Cultural Heritage Application of website, mobile app, and PC, based on the multi-modal interaction theory, this paper divides the exhibition hall, collection display, interpretation, collection interaction, and navigation mode from the three channels of sight, hearing, and tactile sensation. Lin conducts interviews with some experts who are from museums or educational institutions; and indicates that appearance, accessibility, interactivity, and ease of use are features to encourage learning activity on e-learning websites [12]. This paper divides digital museums into 5 modules which are Exhibition Hall, Collection Display, Interpretation, interaction, and Guide.

Module 1. Exhibition Hall
There are two popular implementation techniques to create an exhibition hall. One is to use 360° panoramic camera technology to take panoramic pictures of the exhibition hall, and the other is to make a virtual environment of the exhibition hall. A particular feature for mobile apps is enable AR to users to explore collections with museum apps. The PC VR application default contains a virtual environment. Therefore, this paper investigates whether it provides free-roam in a virtual environment with background music and sound effects to improve users' immersion experience.

Module 2. Collection Display
Picture and 3D models can visually display digital collections in cultural heritage applications, combining with the interpretation of artefacts.

Module 3. Interpretation
The content of digital cultural heritage is mainly output through text, audio, and video media. PC VR can carry out interpretation using narrative story scenes which restores characters, time, and place of the story in the virtual environment.

Module 4. Collection Interaction
The three types of applications can technically achieve the features of moving, rotating, and scaling. On websites and mobile apps, users can interact with the touch screen

by clicking or touching the area on the screen for interacting with digital collections [13]. In addition to screen interaction, PC VR interacts with a virtual environment and object through a stereo monitor and glass, together with a pair of controllers.

Module 5. Guide

It helps beginners quickly familiar with device operations. The user needs to understand how to use a VR headset and start playing. Therefore, it is necessary to apply the operation instructions and the map of the place to ensure that the user will not feel lost in the environment.

3.2   Features in the Digital Cultural Heritage Applications

There is several features are implemented in virtual museums. Panoramic virtual tour simulates exhibition rooms which allow visitors to look around [14].

Table 1. Illustration of features for digital cultural heritage sites and applications

Features	Illustration
Panorama	Photos are taken in the full scene range of 90° to 360°
Free-roam	Allowing users to walk in the virtual environment & interact with objects
3D environment	A virtual environment that is created by 3D modeling
Environment effect	Effect in a virtual environment such as sound, light, weather, etc
Scene	A virtual environment presents the time, place, characters of a story
Picture	Image of cultural heritage artefacts
3D model	Simulating a three-dimensional object in the virtual environment
Augment Reality (AR)	Allowing users to observe virtual objects in the real world
Text	Using words to describe a cultural heritage artefact
Audio	Providing recorded vocal commentary of the collections
Video	Providing collections information by videos
Movement	Capable to move the position of an object
Rotation	Capable to rotate the angle of an object
Scale	Capable to scale the size of an object
Eye tracking	Using eye-track technology to interact with objects and interfaces
Pickable	Capable of picking up an object
Navigation	Navigating users use application functions
Map	Showing overview area of the museum & the current position of the user

Huang illustrates 3D modeling, scene building, and roaming are three key features in VR digital museums [15]. Boiano indicates that the main content for mobile museums is text, image, audio, video, and map [16]. Table 1 shows the features are explored in this paper.

Table 2 shows the features in museums based on different technologies. The panorama is not necessary for VR technology, instead, the user can experience a virtual environment, and its effect and scene. Moreover, it is not possible to have an immersive free-roam experience on a website and mobile phone because users can only observe a virtual environment on devices rather than inside it. Picture and 3D models are supported in all three technologies, but AR is implemented in mobile technology only. Three types of museums provide all features in interpretation modules. 3D models should be able to be moved, rotated, and scaled. VR devices integrate with the eye-tracking feature. In mobile and VR museums, objects allow users to pick them. The Navigation and map are friendly to help users visit a virtual museum.

Table 2. Comparison of indicators of three types of digital cultural heritage technologies

Module	Features	Website	Mobile	VR
	Panorama	✓	✓	
Exhibition Hall	Free-roam			✓
	3D Environment	✓	✓	✓
	Environment Effect			✓
	Scene			✓
Collection Display	Picture	✓	✓	✓
	3D Model	✓	✓	✓
	AR		✓	
Interpreta- tion	Text	✓	✓	✓
	Audio	✓	✓	✓
	Video	✓	✓	✓
Collection Interaction	Movement	✓	✓	✓
	Rotation	✓	✓	✓
	Scale	✓	✓	✓
	Eye Tracking			✓
	Pickable		✓	✓
Guide	Navigation	✓	✓	✓
	Map	✓	✓	✓

4   Case Studies and Analysis

In the case selection, this study focuses on the category of History & cultural heritage and filters out museums in categories such as nature, science, and technology. The museum websites that do not provide collection online access services were also excluded.

4.1 Website Cases

This paper selected 21 provincial museum websites from the report on the ranking of the Chinese museums in 2019 released by Intelligence Research Group, as well as selected 6 museums among the top 10 most visited museums announced in 2019–2020 released by Statista.

In the website case study, users can move through the click of the arrow button in the panoramic tour of web pages; but it is difficult to control the exact stop position and the user easily lost direction. To guide users' movement in the panoramic tour, some museums use the minimap to show the user's current location in the exhibition hall and support clicking on the small map to directly jump to the clicked location. For example, in the digital exhibition "Tianxia Longquan" exhibition hall of Zhejiang Provincial Museum, the text prompts of "forward" and "backward" are added to the position arrow mark; In the panoramic exhibition hall "Queen of yin and Shang Dynasty", Changsha Museum indicates the tour order with numbers on the position arrow button, as well as informs the user of "areas visited" and "areas not visited".

Changsha Museum, The British Museum, and New York Metropolitan Museum of Art provide a different experience in web tours. Changsha Museum has developed the virtual tour function by using Unity WebGL. It can perform 3D rendering and smoothly display 3D environments and models in the browser. Panoramic exhibition hall jumps by clicking the preset position. The virtual exhibition hall uses the keys W, S, A, and D to move forward, backward, left, and right respectively. Users can move freely and accurately to the exhibits they want to see. The British Museum uses Google's Street View to allow users to enter the museum directly from Google Maps for the virtual tour. Unlike the panoramic tour, users click the ground within the visual range and move freely to the corresponding position without being fixed at the preset position. The Metropolitan Museum of Art in New York produced and released many panoramic tour videos, which are shot in 360° with a 3D camera. Users can adjust the visual angle of the video while watching the video. However, this technology does not allow users to walk freely in the video scene.

4.2 Mobile Apps Cases

This paper selects 18 high-ranking apps related to historical and cultural heritage from various app stores for research. Cases are selected from the Apple App Store of IOS OS, and Google Play, Huawei, and Xiaomi App Stores of Android OS by searching the keywords "History and cultural", "cultural heritage", or "Museum".

The number of digital cultural heritage resources of the mobile app is less than that of the website, especially in the display of 3D models and video resources. In addition, there is less development of interactive functions of mobile app exhibits. Most of them only provide picture scaling and do not develop more interactive functions. The panoramic digital exhibition hall is not popular on mobile apps. A few of those who have carried out panoramic views are simply converted and transferred from the website. Some museum apps have utilized AR scanning which can identify cultural artefacts, such as the Hunan Museum app and the Suzhou Museum app. But the app needs to detect the user's position in the museum when running the AR, so it cannot be used by users who are not in the museum. The display methods of APP digital resources in foreign museums are not diverse. They are still dominated by traditional text and pictures, and there are few resources such as audio, video, and 3D models. However, in terms of user navigation, it can provide a complete exhibition hall map and exhibit location information.

4.3 PC VR Cases

This paper selects PC VR among VR device types, and the research objects are selected from the two VR application platforms with the most PC VR users in the world: Steam and Viveport. This study searches "cultural heritage" or "Museum" as keywords in the platform, and selects 9 VR applications.

The free-roam experience in the virtual environment is very different from the panoramic tour. For example, The Louvre of France, in cooperation with the HTC VIVE team, launched a VR application called "Mona Lisa: beyond the glass at the Louvre", which uses 3D modeling to allow users to see the "real person" Ms. Mona Lisa sitting in front of the user in the VR environment. In the VR environment, users can observe cultural artefacts closely, not through the transparent window, but in front of them. The application represented by "the VR Museum of fine art" is one of the earliest VR cultural heritage applications on the Steam platform, which displays some of the world's famous cultural heritage, such as Terracotta Warriors, Mona Lisa portrait, David sculpture, etc. Users can browse freely in it. Each exhibit is equipped with text descriptions, and some exhibits are also equipped with environmental simulation and sound effects. The "Rome reborn" application has developed a feature that users can shuttle between the past and present times of the Roman city.

5 Findings

Table 3 describes the relative frequency in feature usage among three types of technologies. These data show the number of times a value of feature occurs in the set of the total number of cases. It divides each frequency of features by the total number of each case.

Table 3. The ratio of frequency in feature utilization of the three technologies

Module	Features	Website	Mobile	VR
Exhibition hall	Panorama	0.8571	0.25	\
	Free-roam	\	\	0.8889
	3D environment	0.0952	0.0625	1
	Environment effect	\	\	0.4444
	Scene	\	\	0.1111
Collection display	Picture	0.9524	0.875	0.8889
	3D model	0.2857	0.1875	0.7778
	AR	\	0.1875	\

(*continued*)

Table 3. (*continued*)

Module	Features	Website	Mobile	VR
Interpretation	Text	1	1	1
	Audio	0.4286	0.6875	0.5556
	Video	0.381	0.3125	0.1111
Collection interaction	Movement	0.5238	0.1875	0.1111
	Rotation	0.3333	0.25	0
	Scale	0.7143	0.75	0
	Eye tracking	\	\	0.2222
	Pickable	\	0.0625	0.5556
Guide	Navigation	0.2857	0.0625	0.6667
	Map	0.6667	0.625	0.1111

The result of the case study shows that most museum websites created panoramic tours for users, however, mobile has fewer implementations in terms of this feature. Regardless of users can get inside the virtual environment, not all VR applications allow them to have free walking in the virtual environment. A VR museum is fully constructed in a 3D environment, which is rare to observe in web and mobile museums. But not too many story scenes have been created in the VR museum. Picture and image are commonly used in digital museums, the utilization rate of the 3D model of VR museum is much higher than that of the other two technologies. AR feature only to be found in the mobile museum, and a small number of museums use it. Text is the basic interpretation feature that all digital museums provide. Each technology type of digital museum has more audio interpretation than video interpretation elements. The scaling feature is the most frequently used feature in web and mobile technology. However, in VR applications none of the museums carries out the rotation and scale feature on 3D cultural heritage objects. Due to the advantage of the equipment, VR offers an eye-tracking feature to interact with objects. More than half of Mobile museums and VR museums allow users to pick up objects so that they can have a close observation of them. Most VR museums provide navigation to teach users how to use the application, but a few give the map of the virtual environment. On contrary, most web museums and mobile museums offer maps of the real or virtual museum to users.

As Fig. 1 shows, features such as pictures, text, and audio have a similar utilization rate. VR technology uses more 3D models and navigation features than web technology. But the web technology has a higher rate of the video, movement, rotation, and scale usage.

In Fig. 2, picture, text, and audio are widely used in mobile museums and VR museums. Due to VR museums having more utilization of 3D models than mobile museums, the pickable feature usage rate is higher as well. Similar to web museums, mobile museums use more video, movement, rotation, and scale features. VR museum is constructed by a full of 3D models in terms of environment, rooms, and artefacts.

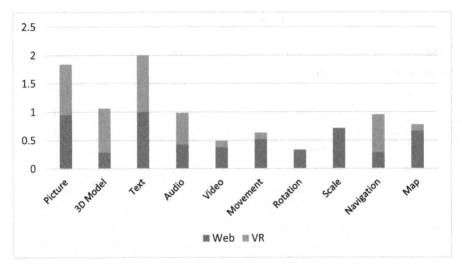

Fig. 1. Comparison of the ratio of feature utilization in web and VR technology

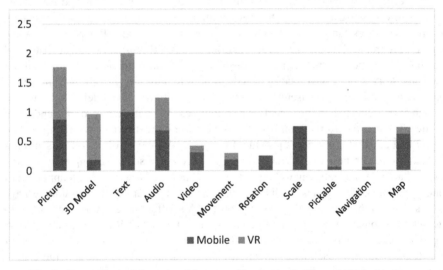

Fig. 2. Comparison of the ratio of feature utilization in mobile and VR technology

Astonishingly, there is no VR museum develop functions on 3D objects such as rotation and scale.

6   Problems in the VR Environment

6.1   Software Layer

Most VR exhibition halls provide free-roam adventure, but in terms of display and interpretation feature of virtual exhibits is not deeply developed. It is common to use simple pointing and clicking functions, and lack interaction between users and exhibits. Some applications carry out the functions of taking and rotating objects, but they cannot meet the expectations of users to obtain sufficient exhibit information in VR cultural heritage [17]. VR applications are still quite weak in improving the overall body perception, mainly manifested in less interactive functions and low user participation in the virtual scene.

6.2 Hardware Layer

An issue in VR cultural heritage is that most people have no experience in using VR equipment and have not received relevant training. Therefore, they will feel complex and difficult while presenting in the virtual world [18]. PC VR is limited by the site space, so it is difficult to move freely in a large area. VR interaction forms are mainly divided into two types: virtual hands and virtual pointing. The interaction process affects the user experience from interaction efficiency and interaction accuracy [19]. In the display effect of VR helmet, resolution and refresh rate are the main factors affecting users' observation of the virtual environment.

6.3 Digital Content

The reasons for the scarcity of 3D models of collections in digital resources are in terms of resolution, accuracy, and high cost [20]. The 3D models and virtual environments are not easy to create. It requires high technical difficulty and the high cost of it are the main factors affecting VR cultural heritage application development.

7   VR Museum Construction

According to the analysis of the implementation of the feature in the current VR museum, after defining the problems of VR environment for information presentation. This paper proposes a model of a VR museum that contains features necessary to present for users.

7.1 VR Museum Interaction Model

Figure 2 shows the construction of an interface model of VR cultural heritage application, which is divided into three components: User's Senses, VR Devices, and VR Application Interface. Multi-modal interaction in VR human-computer interaction can reduce user cognitive load, make user operation more flexible and improve operation recognition rate [21].

Figure 3 is a human-computer interaction model of a VR museum, Users' cognition and perception to the interface of application through multimodal integration input and output to VR devices. The devices input operations of the user and interact with the application interface. After the process in the software system, the interface output result of processes to VR devices. So that VR devices could respond to users with the pictures, sounds, vibrations, etc.

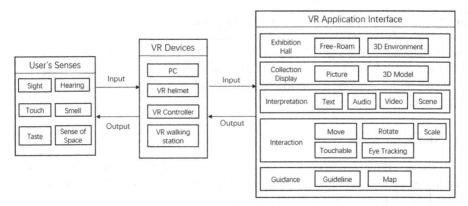

Fig. 3. VR cultural heritage application human-computer interaction model

7.2 Creation of VR Museum

VR museum presents virtual objects and a virtual environment for users to visit. A number of issues regarding the construction of a VR museum may affect users' experience in the VR museum. such as 3D model generation, virtual museum exhibition hall construction, and virtual environment creation.

3D Model Generation

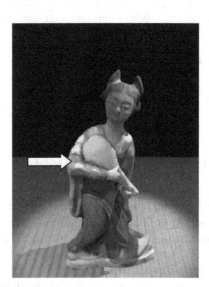

Fig. 4. Transform a real object into a 3D model

In the virtual environment, objects are presented in a form of a 3D model. The museum collections need to be transformed into 3D models so that they could be placed and interacted with. This study uses a 3D scanner to scan objects and generate 3D models.

Figure 4 shows a real object transformed into a 3D model and being placed on a virtual table.

Virtual Museum Exhibition Hall Construction

Fig. 5. The virtual exhibition hall in the VR museum

The virtual exhibition hall in the VR museum is the place to put scanned objects. The design of the exhibition hall follows the reality museum, but the exhibit and display cases are removed from the VR museum. Users are freely touching, rotating, and scaling the exhibits. As Fig. 5 shows, all the artefacts are put on pedestals, so that users to "grab" them using VR controllers/gloves.

Virtual Environment Creation

Fig. 6. The virtual environment of a VR scene

A VR scene is used to interpret a story of exhibits. Users who want to understand a story will surely be teleported to a virtual environment related to the story. The virtual environment is created according to the time, place, and characters of the story. Figure 6 shows a virtual environment that is built in the style of ancient China. It is matched the character's historical background of the previously generated 3D model.

8 Future Opportunities in VR Cultural Heritage

8.1 Creating Virtual Cultural Heritage Resources

Cultural heritage artefacts provide plenty of information. In addition to the background story information, it also presents its appearance characteristics such as shape, color, and material. VR application requires a larger number of digital objects than other digital types of application. VR technology has well compatible with the existing digital resource formats, so it is easy to transfer the existing pictures, audio, and video to the VR environment.

8.2 Adding More Interaction Functions

VR cultural heritage application calls users' multi-modal perception to interact with the system to help users understand information. In the process of using web pages and mobile apps, sight and hearing senses play an important role in information acquisition. Increasingly, in the VR environment, the enhancement of body perception can improve the user's sense of presence and enhance the understanding of the situation [22]. VR cultural heritage should not be satisfied with the simple control function of objects. To make users are connected to the characters and issues in the story.

8.3 Telling Stories of Collections Using Virtual Scenes

It is a commonly used narrative interpretation in the dissemination of cultural heritage, which provides users with a personalized storytelling experience and helps users learn and understand cultural heritage information [23, 24]. Using VR technology can create story-related virtual scenes with the virtual environment, characters, and objects. To stimulate the story scene and make it easier for users to empathize with the characters in the story [25].

9 Conclusion

VR museum is a potential form of presentation of museum collections information. The transfer of digital information resources from websites and app applications to VR will be a trend of the virtual reality of cultural heritage. This paper explores the interactive features of three types of VR cultural heritage application interfaces: Web page, mobile terminal, and PC VR, and summarizes the problems that may be faced in the display and dissemination of VR cultural heritage information resources. The study proposed a VR museum model and structures that can be used as a reference for the design and development of VR cultural heritage applications. It has certain limitations that websites and applications are selected from public reports and rankings. Therefore, a system evaluation approach is necessary to be implemented in the future.

References

1. Board, A., Bowen, J.: Smart cities and cultural heritage-a review of developments and future opportunities. In: EVA. BCS (2017)
2. Steuer, J.: Defining virtual reality: dimensions determining telepresence. J. Commun. **42**(4), 73–93 (1992)
3. Schweibenz, W.: The "virtual museum": new perspectives for museums to present objects and information using the internet as a knowledge base and communication system. In: Knowledge Management und Kommunikationssysteme, Workflow Management, Multimedia, Knowledge Transfer - Proceedings des 6. Internationalen Symposiums für Informationswissenschaft (ISI 1998), vol. 34, pp. 185–200 (1998)
4. Mohd Noor Shah, N.F., Ghazali, M.: A systematic review on digital technology for enhancing user experience in museums. In: Abdullah, N., Wan Adnan, W.A., Foth, M. (eds.) i-USEr 2018. CCIS, vol. 886, pp. 35–46. Springer, Singapore (2018). https://doi.org/10.1007/978-981-13-1628-9_4
5. Marty, P.F.: Museum websites and museum visitors: digital museum resources and their use. Mus. Manag. Curatorship **23**(1), 81–99 (2008)
6. Semper, R., Spasojevic, M.: The Electronic Guidebook: Using Portable Devices and a Wireless Web-Based Network to Extend the Museum Experience (2002)
7. Vlahakis, V., et al.: Archeoguide: an augmented reality guide for archaeological sites. IEEE Comput. Graph. Appl. **22**(5), 52–60 (2002)
8. Spallone, R., Lamberti, F., Trivel, M.G., Ronco, F., Tamantini, S.: 3D reconstruction and presentation of cultural heritage: AR and VR experiences at the Museo d'arte orientale di torino. Int. Arch. Photogram. Remote Sens. Spatial Inf. Sci. **46**, 697–704 (2021)
9. Sutherland, I.E.: A head-mounted three dimensional display. In: Proceedings of the Fall Joint Computer Conference, Part I, 9–11 December 1968, pp. 757–764 (1968)
10. Dale, E.: The cone of experience. Audio-Vis. Methods Teach. **1**, 37–51 (1946)
11. Jaimes, A., Sebe, N.: Multimodal human–computer interaction: a survey. Comput. Vis. Image Underst. **108**(1–2), 116–134 (2007)
12. Lin, A.C., Gregor, S.D.: Designing websites for learning and enjoyment: a study of museum experiences. Int. Rev. Res. Open Distrib. Learn. **7**(3), 1–21 (2006)
13. Petridis, P., et al.: Exploring and interacting with virtual museums. In: Proceedings of the Computer Applications and Quantitative Methods in Archaeology (CAA) (2005)
14. Tjahjawulan, I., Sabana, S.: Panoramic virtual museum: representation or simulation. Int. J. Innov. Manag. Technol. **6**(1), 40 (2015)
15. Huang, L., Lv, N.: Design and implementation of digital museum system based on AR-VR hybrid technology. In: 2021 4th International Conference on Information Systems and Computer Aided Education, pp. 2675–2679 (2021)
16. MacDonald, G.F., Alsford, S.: The museum as information utility. Mus. Manag. Curatorship **10**(3), 305–311 (1991)
17. Boiano, S., Bowen, J.P., Gaia, G.: Usability, design and content issues of mobile apps for cultural heritage promotion: The Malta culture guide experience. arXiv preprint arXiv:1207.3422 (2012)
18. Carrozzino, M., Bergamasco, M.: Beyond virtual museums: experiencing immersive virtual reality in real museums. J. Cult. Herit. **11**(4), 452–458 (2010)
19. Roessler, A., Grantz, V.: Performance evaluation of input devices in virtual environments. In: Designing Effective and Usable Multimedia Systems, pp. 205–212. Springer, Boston (1998). https://doi.org/10.1007/978-0-387-35370-8
20. Gomes, L., Bellon, O.R.P., Silva, L.: 3D reconstruction methods for digital preservation of cultural heritage: a survey. Pattern Recogn. Lett. **50**, 3–14 (2014)

21. Wang, X., Ong, S.K., Nee, A.Y.C.: Multi-modal augmented-reality assembly guidance based on bare-hand interface. Adv. Eng. Inform. **30**(3), 406–421 (2016)
22. Coelho, C., Tichon, J.G., Hine, T.J., Wallis, G.M., Riva, G.: Media presence and inner presence: the sense of presence in virtual reality technologies. In: From Communication to Presence: Cognition, Emotions and Culture Towards the Ultimate Communicative Experience, pp. 25–45. IOS Press, Amsterdam (2006)
23. Palombini, A.: Storytelling and telling history. Towards a grammar of narratives for cultural heritage dissemination in the digital era. J. Cult. Herit. **24**, 134–139 (2017)
24. Vayanou, M., Karvounis, M., Katifori, A., Kyriakidi, M., Roussou, M., Ioannidis, Y.E.: The CHESS project: adaptive personalized storytelling experiences in museums. In: UMAP Workshops (2014)
25. Shin, D.: Empathy and embodied experience in virtual environment: to what extent can virtual reality stimulate empathy and embodied experience? Comput. Hum. Behav. **78**, 64–73 (2018)

An Applied Research of Persuasion Theory in the Design of Weight Management Applications

Hongyu Liu$^{(\boxtimes)}$ and Junsong Hu

School of Digital Media and Design, Guangdong Neusoft University, Shishan University Town, Nanhai, Foshan, Guangdong, China
905410578@qq.com

Abstract. Weight management is a critical way to maintain a healthy posture. At present, doing exercise, eating functional food and taking medicines are popular ways of weight management, which is mainly conducted spontaneously or under the supervision of others. However, with high cost and poor persistence, these two forms also fail to take psychological factors into full consideration, showing great limitations in general. Therefore, the research philosophy of this study lies in "behavioral supervision and psychological guidance". This study introduced persuasion theory to discuss the application of persuasion theory in weight management applications (apps). In addition, this study put forward an application model of persuasion theory in weight management apps, and verified the satisfaction degree of weight management apps based on this model. The purposes of this study are to: 1) Promote the multi-directional flexible development of weight management apps' design at both academic and practical levels; 2) Establish a more usable design model for the design of weight management apps through the research and exploration of this study, so as to improve the effect of weight management and provide reference for the weight management practice.

Keywords: Persuasive Theory · Persuasive design · FBM behavioral motivation model · Weight management · Persuasive design strategies

1 Introduction

1.1 Background Information

Weight problem has become a major health problem in the world. For one thing, obesity is one of the main inducing factors leading to high blood pressure, diabetes, cardiovascular disease and other chronic diseases; for another, attending activities for pursuing physical beauty such as weight reducing and fitness has been a fashion already. Nevertheless, with wrong perceptions of their somatotype and poor correct knowledge of healthy weight management, many people's understanding concerning healthy weight management is one-sided [1]. For pursuing the fashion of physical beauty, many people often blindly reduce weight through all kinds of methods, which then causes the problem

© The Author(s), under exclusive license to Springer Nature Switzerland AG 2022
N. A. Streitz and S. Konomi (Eds.): HCII 2022, LNCS 13325, pp. 59–71, 2022.
https://doi.org/10.1007/978-3-031-05463-1_5

of underweight [2]. Inappropriate weight management can seriously affect the physical and mental health of users [3], and even well-educated medical school students can't avoid making this mistake [4].

Therefore, since there are a large number of obese people, and the public blindly treats thinness as beauty and lacks knowledge of health, diet and nutrition, it is of great significance to explore and study the method model that can effectively guide the design of weight management apps.

1.2 Motivation and Goal

A great deal of researches have shown that the increase or decrease of body mass index(BMI) may result in the increase of mortality, that is, the U-shaped relationship between BMI and mortality is high at both ends and low in the middle [5, 6]. A research referring to the relationship between mortality and BMI showed that the mortality decreases to its lowest when male BMI is between 23.5 to 24.9 kg/m^2 and female BMI is between 22.0 to 23.4 kg/m^2, while overweight people have a much higher mortality risk than normal-weight people [7].

Persuasion theory is a theory in the field of computer science, mainly featuring with continuous and timeless guiding of human behaviors [8], meanwhile, weight management is a long-term and repeating process [9]. Therefore there is a basis for the match of the two. In the process of weight management, to better stimulate users' motivation, users' behaviors and psychological characteristics should be taken into special consideration, and reminder and supervision mechanism should be adopted as an assistance. Only when both physical and psychological factors are considered, can enhancing users' motivation and ability to manage their weights be best achieved. Therefore, how to attract users' long-term participation and help users manage weight scientifically and effectively has very high research value for design practice. The main research reason of this study is to provide ideas for the development of weight management apps by applying persuasion theory to the design of weight management apps through relevant researches.

Currently, most weight management products only work on a physiological level, and are either ineffective in practice or can't be used consistently due to users' lacking of self-discipline [10]. Therefore, the purposes of this study are to: 1) Introduce persuasion theory into weight management apps; 2) Establish the design strategy model of weight management apps, and study its feasibility and effectiveness from the theoretical level based on in-depth understanding of persuasion theory, behavior and other related concepts, combined with the user model of weight management; 3) Promote people's understanding of weight management, so as to guide people to establish a correct concept of health, cultivate good living habits, and improve life quality.

2   Related Literature

2.1   Persuasion Theory

Regarding to persuasion, there are varied theories and methods targeting different fields. Persuasion was previously seen in public relations or commercial sales [11], also known as persuasive method that usually means to persuade and guide the public to understand and recognize their organizations or buy their products. It is a direct and effective method of establishing public relations by actively affecting the public psychology and can change the will of users in a flexible and unforced way.

2.2 Persuasive Design

Proposed by professor BJ Fogg of Stanford University [12], persuasive design is the design practice and application of persuasion theory, a method of changing people's will through unforced guidance. Persuasive design can also be called "influence design" or "persuasion design", which is a method that uses persuasive technology to change the attitudes or behaviors of users, namely design with intend of persuasion. The focus of interaction design is to improve the communication effectiveness between users and machines, and most of interaction design are process-oriented design. So its designers pay more attention to the operating fluency and experience of users, emphasizing process design. Meanwhile, persuasive design, stressing on what the users plan to do or what they are doing, and how the design might affect them, is results-oriented design [13]. Persuasive design not only concerns the process of man-machine interaction, but also pays more attention to whether the possible effect of the interaction process or procedure on users meets the stated goals [14]. It concentrates on improving users' motivation and ability to complete the target behavior.

According to the expected persuasion effect, we divided users' behavior changing process into three types that are stated in the Table 1.

Table 1. Behavior changing types

Behavior changing types	Description
Type I	Single behavior
Type II	Long-term behavior
Type III	Habitual behavior

Among them, type I represents that the users behavior is motivated under the influence of triggers and begin to change for the first time or several times; type II stands for the change in the users' long-term behavior, meaning that persuasion has been effective; type III represents that users successfully achieve the desired effect of persuasion, and the implementation of the target behavior becomes a habit. Therefore, the purpose of this study is to change the weight management behavior of the target user group into type II or III, that is, long-term behavior or habitual behavior, and ultimately help the user group to understand and develop scientific and healthy weight management behavior.

At the same time, during user behavior changes, users will be affected by different factors at different times, as shown in Fig. 1.

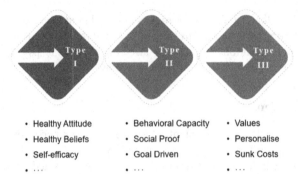

- Healthy Attitude
- Healthy Beliefs
- Self-efficacy
- …

- Behavioral Capacity
- Social Proof
- Goal Driven
- …

- Values
- Personalise
- Sunk Costs
- …

Fig. 1. Influencing factors of weight management in different behavioral stages

In persuasive design, as shown in the Fig. 2, professor Fogg put forward an eight-step method for the application of persuasive technology in design [15], emphasizing the significance of target selection, selection of persuasive methods, as well as testing and iteration.

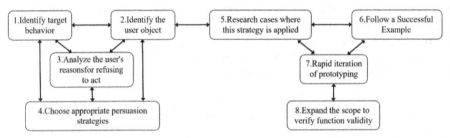

Fig. 2. Eight-step method for the application of persuasive technology in design

2.3 Persuasive Behavior Model

As a tool for analyzing behavior change, the conceptual framework of Fogg Behavior Model (FBM) [16], as shown in the Fig. 3, aims to help designers find the opportunities and obstacles in the design, thus establishing the relationship between the target behavior and the product. The model should be able to answer questions about what kind of design will improve users' implementation ability, and which type of design or technology will give users encouragement and guidance, or enhance users' motivation of persistence [17].

There are four design elements in this model, simply B = MAT, that is, behavior (B) = motivation (M) + ability (A) + triggers (T). The first element is target behavior (B) that means the behavior of users this product targets at. The second is motivation (M) referring to the internal reasons of the users' operation or usage behavior. The third is ability (A) that is considered as the most scarce resource of users. The fourth is triggers (T) because an effective stimulus is needed to trigger the behavior after the motivation and ability are possessed.

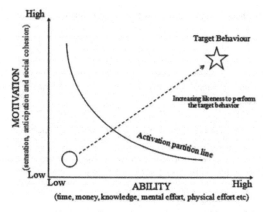

Fig. 3. Behavior model for persuasive design

Different types of users need different motivation models. For example, as for users with poor motivation and ability, considering a single trigger may end up with low efficiency, instead, two or more triggers should be taken into account. In other words, when encountering different types of users, whether the user lacks motivation, ability, or both is the question to be answered. Especially, due to the slight interest of users with poor motivation and ability, priority should be given to stimulate triggers by persuasive strategy that encourages users' motivation to enhance using motivation, and then users' ability can be gradually improved in the subsequent process. Otherwise, directly adopting the strategy to improve users' ability will get half the results.

2.4 Persuasive Strategy

Persuasive strategy refers to the concrete strategy and method to realize persuasive technology [18]. In order to achieve the main goal of changing behavior or attitude, it is necessary to specify the behavior model according to appropriate persuasive strategies and realize it through computer technology. Computer technology can play the roles of tool, medium and social personage in persuasive technology, and different roles require corresponding persuasive strategies. Whalen summarized the persuasive strategies used in website development [19], and Hamid innovatively proposed some new persuasive strategies in the self-management system [20]. Table 2 lists some of these persuasive strategies with brief descriptions. In the actual design and development process, one or more persuasive strategies can be selected, or from which a series of new persuasive strategies can be derived [21].

Table 2. Persuasive strategies with brief descriptions

Persuasion Strategy	Instructions
Streamline	Simplify complex goal behaviors into one or more simple tasks to make them easier to achieve
Personalized	Provide relevant information based on users' needs, interests and personalities
Authority	Providing users with information from experts in the field is easier to achieve when they are in a competitive environment
Competition	Provide necessary reminders at appropriate times
Reward	Rewarding the completion of the target behavior can make the target behavior more stable.
Social identity	Goal behaviors that most people have are more attainable
The instance	Provide successful examples of user target behavior to better persuade users
Simulated causality	The visual relationship between simulation behavior and results can persuade users more vividly
The game	Use games or other means to make the target behavior fun and easy
Free	Offering a service for free or at a low price makes targeted behavior easier to achieve
...	...

3 Research Framework

3.1 Summary of Typical User Models

The user persona is a kind of typical user image that is classified by the designer after collecting and approaching the user information. The image includes various information, such as user background, user life, daytime habits, and product demand. The creation of the user is conducive to guiding the following design and checking out the design orientation.

In light of FBM, users of weight management apps can be divided into four types: self-explorers (with high ability and motivation), self-learners out of interests (with poor ability and strong motivation), persistent actors out of feedback (with strong ability and poor motivation), and negative hider (with poor ability and motivation).

1. Self-explorers: They demonstrate respectably strong ability and motivation in the process of weight management. As they are relatively willing to keep a healthy

weight, they proactively have a healthy diet, do exercises, and get informed of the latest knowledge of physical state and weight management.

2. Self-learners out of interests: They feature relatively strong motivation for weight management and take an interest in learning knowledge of weight management and keeping a healthy weight. However, they lack solid implementation ability for consistent weight management. Therefore, they need external encouragement to insist on consistent weight management.

3. Persistent actor out of feedback: Boasting strong implementation ability, they are characterized by poor motivation for proactive weight management due to their shallow knowledge of weight management, deficiency of weight management demand as well as corresponding feedback. It also explains why they lack interest in weight management.

4. Negative hider: This kind of user is found with poor motivation and implementation ability in weight management. It is often the case that they embark on weight management out of external encouragement but eventually give up for lacking confidence, implementation ability, and other factors.

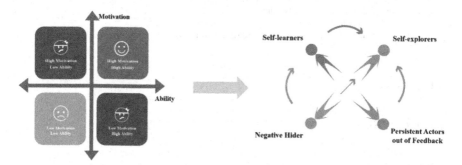

Fig. 4. Classification and conversion of weight management users

As shown in Fig. 4, the four user models represent the typical states of the user groups of weight management apps. The foregoing states are not immutable and can achieve reciprocal transformation under certain conditions. Therefore, users can be persuaded with persuasive strategies combined with the behavior model and thus transformed to another type. In this sense, a negative hider can be transformed to a self-learner out of interest or a persistent actor out of feedback with strengthening monitoring and persuading via the persuasive design. A self-explorer is made, once reinforced is the ability of a self-learner out of interest, and aroused is the interest of a persistent actor out of feedback. Moreover, a daily habit of weight management of the self-explorer can be formed.

3.2 Design Framework of Weight Management Apps

The persuasion theory is theoretically established on the behavior changing model and the persuasive strategy is a method of the theory specifically. Relied on the behavior changing model and combined with the persuasive focus of the service model, corresponding persuasive models should be applied in different design stages of weight management apps according to diverse user types.

As shown in Fig. 5, Based on corresponding concepts of the persuasion theory, persuasive design, FBM, and target user models, established are design models of weight management apps with universalism so that evaluations for the user type and user stage can be done by designers and researchers and corresponding persuasive strategies can be applied.

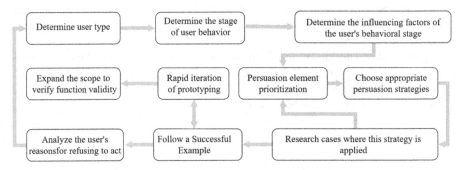

Fig. 5. Design framework of weight management apps

3.3 Case Study

Case Study 1: Keep

Fig. 6. Keep app and interface display diagram

Launched in 2015, Keep, an online fitness app, is targeted at junior bodybuilders initially. The APP interface is shown in Fig. 6. It primarily focuses on meeting the fitness demands of the mass majority and cultivating fitness habits for users. An analysis is made from the perspective of the persuasive design: 1) Keep boasts fitness of odd moment which triggers the user motivation with low time cost, attracts users of type I, and lays the ground for transforming users of type I to users of type II and type III; 2) It offers a reward mechanism for users with "free playground" and "user growth system", providing positive feedback for user behavior and setting a long-term user goal; 3) Various fitness training of Keep is prepared for users to choose according to individual states. The training plans are designed for users with different sports apparatuses and fitness goals of all kinds of states, suitable for a range of fitness scenes. The plan involves daily motion sports of a certain amount for some body parts. With personalized service and a gradual assignment setting, it improves the ability of users; 4) "One-spot fitness solutions" of Keep covering fitness teaching, the guidance of running, cycling, friend-making, diets, and fitness outfits and the like amplify the professional and personalized content and combine online classes with offline guidance. Keep also launches its offline gym, Keepland, as well as smart hardware to provide more advanced fitness services for users. Moreover, it enhances users' motivation and consolidates their ability at ease via streamlining the fitness process and establishing social contacts. While serving users, Keep primarily makes efforts to generate users' motivation with a focus on major behavior types of the targeted, such as attracting users of type I to take advantage of their odd moment. Personalized fitness plans are made after the evaluation of users' certain qualifications. In other words, users' motivation is boosted with authoritative but low-cost strategies and thus users have more confidence in Keep. The users' ability is gradually upgraded too thanks to "one-spot fitness solutions" and "small one-by-one assignments". Keep also raises the user stickiness by making the user behavior meaningful. For instance, it defines what can be qualified as an "achievement", offers rewards for users, and builds social contacts between users. A conclusion can be drawn after a careful analysis that Keep transforms users of type I to type II and type III primarily by means of boosting users' motivation and ability.

Case Study 2: Boohee

Fig. 7. Boohee app and interface display diagram

Started in 2007, Boohee is a weight management app. The APP interface is shown in Fig. 7. In view of the persuasive design, its success should give credit to the following five reasons: 1) The "story" section of Boohee displays considerable successful cases of weight-losing, highlights Boohee's think tank composed of senior dietitians and professional weight-losing consultants, lifts users' expectation with real-life cases, authorities, and simulated cause-effect relation, and boosts users' confidence, enhancing users' motivation for the app eventually; 2) Before using the app, weight management goals for each stage and corresponding diet and workout plans are designed according to users' physical conditions, diet and workout habits. Splitting one big goal into several small goals will help users to maintain their motivation and ability. 3) Reasonable diet suggestions are provided via diet-grading and calorie-evaluating based on users' exercise and diet intake. In this sense, Boohee's strategy is to communicate knowledge to users and develop their ability; 4) The app offers visualized a weekly summary as triggers, allowing users to get informed of their changes directly and be encouraged to stick to their goals and surpass their counterparts via posture comparison, workout and diet records, ranks and relative suggestions; 5) The "community" function invites users to share their moments and see others' as well as comment on and give a like on them. With social interaction among users, their sense of social identity is improved and motivation boosted. During the whole process, the interaction between Boohee and the user mainly revolves around authority supports of experts and personalized plans, encouraging cases with current users' outcomes, quantitative assignment of weight management, visualized posture and body records demonstrated to help users to know themselves, in-time feedback for users' workouts and diets, social-recognition-driven sharing, weekly summary for users' consistency, and knowledge communication of the fitness and diet and the like. It can be noticed that Boohee achieves its design from three dimensions, that is, motivation boosting, ability enhancing, and trigger adding. Based on the three dimensions, different persuasive strategies are utilized to achieve persuasion and fulfill anticipatory goals.

Case Study 3: Nike+ Training Club

Fig. 8. Nike+ Training Club and interface display diagram

Nike+ Training Club, a weight management app owned by Nike. The APP interface is shown in Fig. 8. From the perspective of the persuasive design, the design of the app is analyzed: 1) The app's training contents are given by professional coaches and athletes of Nike, shaping an authoritative image with the brand and professional teams and allowing users to have an expectation for the app. In a word, it applies authority strategy to boost users' motivation; 2) The users' motivation can also be boosted by the building of Nike+ personal profile, introducing of social and teaming systems to establish social contacts, joint participating with friends, and mutual encouragement and competing. The foregoing methods can transform users of type I to type II and type III; 3) According to the user situation, the app boasts personalized training plans containing proper training time and content. With split training assignments, users' ability to achieve training improves and their fear of difficulties fades away; 4) The app records all activities of users during a certain time period and further adjust the training plan intelligently. In this sense, it boosts users' motivation and ability with the authority strategy; 5) When doing exercise, users can import their favorite music to complete weight management assignments with a more positive mindset and obtain better ability. The interaction between Nike+ Training Club and the user represent itself in this way: It reinforces users' confidence in the app with its brand image and professionals, increases user stickiness by compiling personal profiles and establishing social contacts, figures out an initial weight management plan in terms of the user demand and then schemes a scientific personalized weight management plan adhering to frequent workouts and relative information of the user. It is observed that Nike+ Training Club works with the following process: First, it is endorsed by the authorities and brand. Then, it establishes convincing social links and introduces competition and cooperation mechanisms. At the same time, it perfects its weight management solutions in light of the actual habits of users and splits the final goals with trivial training assignments to boost users' motivation. Moreover, it offers in-time feedback and personalized service in the training, for example, music-playing. Prominent in the whole process, the authority factor boosts users' motivation and ability and thus achieves the anticipatory goal.

4   Discussion

The core of persuasive design is that, in the process of design, conditions of whether users have the corresponding motivation and ability and whether there are triggers in apps motivating users are fully considered in each interaction process between users and products or services. At the same time, since the design problems faced vary with the change of behavior changing stages, designers are expected to focus on the characteristics of users in different behavior stages. The analysis results of the above three cases showed that most of the weight management apps lay particular emphasis on the motivation and ability cultivation of users during the design process. However, to a certain extent, the full consideration of triggers is ignored. As well, the user group classification method is relatively simple without a systematic classification, and users are directly divided into elementary, intermediate and advanced users in most cases. What's more, more targeted motivation and ability improvement designs are scare. As a result, there is still a lot of room for improvement.

5   Conclusion

Based on persuasion theory, this paper studied the general persuasive design frame-work model of weight management apps. By analyzing the user classification, stage classification of user behavior and factors affecting user behavior in persuasion theory, this model specified persuasive goals, applied different procedures in different stages of these persuasive goals, and adopted corresponding persuasive strategies to design weight management apps.

Future research will further explore the impact of different persuasive strategies on behavioral and attitudinal changes, and the effectiveness evaluation of persuasion theory on users of weight management apps will be one of the key research points.

References

1. Xiang, N.: The obese population in China is 325 million and 40% of the dieters are normal weight or underweight. J. Communist Party Members Sec. Half. **5**, 24 (2012)
2. Shi, X., Hu, S.: Effect of healthy weight loss intervention on weight loss cognition and behavior of female college students. J. Collect. **90** (2019)
3. Liu, Y., Ye, Y.: Current status analysis of weight loss behavior of overweight college students in a medical college. J. Luzhou Med. Coll. **5**, 563–565 (2010)
4. Hua, J.: Diet management of obesity and weight loss. In: The 6th Yangtze River Delta Science and Technology Forum—Nutrition Sub-forum and the 5th Academic Conference of Jiangsu Nutrition Society. Chinese Nutrition Society; Jiangsu Association for Science and Technology; Jiangsu Provincial Nutrition Society (2009)
5. Liu, F., Cai, H.: Insulin resistance, blood lipid and dietary analysis of normal BMI abdominal obesity patients. J. Chin. Mod. Med. **21**(30), 3782–3786 (2011)
6. Wen, Z., Hou, J.: Comparison and application of moderating effect and mediating effect. J. Acta Psychol. Soc. **02**, 268–274 (2005)
7. Fang, J., Wen, Z.: Analysis of moderating effect based on multiple regression. J. Psychol. Sci. **38**(03), 715–720 (2015)
8. Bian, J.: Design and evaluation method of human-computer interaction with persuasion characteristics. D. Shanghai Jiaotong University (2010)
9. Jiang, J., Jia, X.: The effect of weight management on obesity control in long-term hospitalized patients with schizophrenia. Chin. J. Health Psychol. **22**(6), 809–812 (2014)
10. China Market Research Online: 2017–2023 China Weight Loss Industry Market In-depth Analysis And Investment Prospect Forecast Report. China Market Research Online, Beijing: (2017)
11. Hovland, C.I., Janis, I.L.: Communication and persuasion. Audiov. Commun. Rev. **2**(2) (1954)
12. Fogg, B.J., Iizawa, D.: Online persuasion in Facebook and Mixi: a cross-cultural comparison. In: Oinas-Kukkonen, H., Hasle, P., Harjumaa, M., Segerståhl, K., Øhrstrøm, P. (eds.) PERSUASIVE 2008. LNCS, vol. 5033, pp. 35–46. Springer, Heidelberg (2008). https://doi.org/10.1007/978-3-540-68504-3_4
13. Fogg, B.J.: A behavior model for persuasive design. In: Fourth International Conference, on Persuasive Technology, Xi 'an (2009)
14. Creed, C.: Using computational agents to motivate diet change. In: IJsselsteijn, W.A., de Kort, Y.A.W., Midden, C., Eggen, B., van den Hoven, E. (eds.) PERSUASIVE 2006. LNCS, vol. 3962, pp. 100–103. Springer, Heidelberg (2006). https://doi.org/10.1007/11755494_14
15. Fogg, B.J.: Creating persuasive technologies: an eight-step design process. In: Proceedings of the 4th International Conference on Persuasive Technology, pp. 1–6 (2009)
16. Fogg, B.J.: Persuasive technology: using computers to change what we think and do. Ubiquity **5** (2002)
17. Shih, L.: Persuasive design for products leading to health and sustainability using case-based reasoning. Sustainability **8**(4), 318 (2016)
18. Fogg, B.J.: The behavior grid: 35 ways behavior can change. In: International Conference on Persuasive Technology. ACM (2009)

19. Whalen, J.: Persuasive design: putting it to use. Bull. Am. Soc. Inf. Sci. Technol. **37**(6), 16–21 (2011)
20. Mukhtar, H., Ali, A.: Persuasive healthcare self-management in intelligent environments. In: 2012 Eighth International Conference on Intelligent Environments, pp. 190–197. IEEE (2012)
21. Hurling, R., Catt, M.: Using internet and mobile phone technology to deliver an automated physical activity program: randomized controlled trial. J. Med. Internet Res. **9**(2), e7 (2007)

Interaction Design in Residence Mode of Health and Tourism

Yanlin Liu[1][✉], Ruichao Wang[2], and Tingwei Zhao[3]

[1] University of Jinan, No. 336, West Road of Nan Xinzhuang, Jinan, Shandong, China
liuyanlin269@163.com
[2] Shandong Ruisheng Investment Co., Ltd., Weihai, China
[3] CDI College, 3D Modeling and Animation Design, Montreal, Canada

Abstract. Under the background of the healthy country strategy, new health industries, new business forms and new models have emerged and expanded, and the big health industry has entered a golden period of rapid development. The integrated development of new technologies such as artificial intelligence, interactive design, health maintenance, tourism and elderly care, community e-commerce, cloud computing technology and big data makes human-computer interaction have a wider range of application fields and burst out new vitality. With the support of artificial intelligence technology, the big health industry, because of its strong relevance, a wide range of areas, deep fusion innovation with interaction design, culture, tourism, electricity, medical, big data, etc., makes the comprehensive service mode of interactive design + intelligent tourism + health maintenance + community e-commerce ushered in a new challenge. Relying on big data "design + service + text brigade + maintenance + intelligent terminal", with the support of government service platform, with artificial intelligence, integration of community electricity resources, efforts to build to "human-computer interaction, kang, brigade service and health records management" as the center, intelligent health country service network, more effectively provide more support and services for the society.

Keyword: Health country · Interactive design · Community e-commerce · Health care · Artificial intelligence

1 Introduction

Since the beginning of the new century, due to the continuous growth of the population, health and pension industries, which affect social civilization and progress, have shown unprecedented development opportunities and created unlimited market space. From 2020, the generation born in the 1970s began to gradually enter the age of 60, that is, this generation began to enter the needs of retirement and pension. This makes the people who control the vast majority of the wealth and resources of the society appear blowout into the era of aging, which is bound to promote China's pension industry to the historical era of surging wind and cloud and disputes!

It is expected that in the next 20 years, China's pension industry will enter the golden 20 years of rapid development. The government took the report of the 19th National Congress of the Communist Party of China, which indicates that the design and policy structure of the multi-platform integrated development of China's pension industry has taken shape. Therefore, we firmly believe that in the great process of human history, a number of world-class star enterprises and great IP will emerge, which will bring many classic cases involving the most populous country with the pension industry!

At the same time, with the support of artificial intelligence technology, health pension industry because of its correlation, wide coverage, depth and interaction design, big data, electricity, medical, culture, tourism fusion innovation, efforts to build to "human-computer interaction, kang, brigade service and health records management" as the center, intelligent health country service network, more effectively provide more support and services for the society (Fig. 1).

Fig. 1. Interaction design under Big Data

In today's China health town has become a figure and rapidly developed as a national strategy! The concept of health town here refers to the "health" as the starting point and destination of the town development, health industry as the core, the health, health, pension, leisure, tourism and other diversified operation functions are integrated, forming a characteristic tourism vacation pension industry town on the premise of beautiful ecological environment. According to the Outline of the Healthy China 2030 Plan released by The State Council, the integration of health with elderly care, tourism, the Internet, fitness and leisure, and food should be actively promoted, so as to promote new health industries, new business forms and new models." The health industry will develop into an important pillar industry of the national economy" can be said to inject a shot in the arm for the medical and health industry people, and the country's determination to vigorously develop the medical and health industry is exciting. The Healthy China 2030 Plan directly shows that the scale—of the health industry will reach 16 trillion yuan by 2030. How will the market size of 16 trillion yuan be achieved? How can we mobilize all resources to join the cake of the medical and health industry? One of the very important points is the reform in the medical and health sector (Figs. 2 and 3).

Fig. 2. Health industry

Fig. 3. Big data platform

Yesterday, doctors were registered as units, overnight became regional registration; yesterday, doctors were difficult to open clinics, overnight individual clinics are no longer subject to planning restrictions…

In this regard, it can be seen from a series of intensive reform measures to liberate the productivity in the medical and health field in recent years that the reform will continue and deepen in terms of deregulation and service. It is expected that larger and larger reform measures will be introduced one after another.

2 Planning Ideas

1. Resource advantage: to discover the value of the countryside from the perspective of ecological civilization.

For a long time, looking at the countryside, people are used to use the perspective of industrial civilization and the standard of urbanization. The most common evaluation index is scale efficiency. From this perspective, rural production and consumption seems to have become less "economic" nor a field for people to obtain economic benefits. Think that the countryside can only be attached to the city (Figs. 4 and 5).

Fig. 4. Health town

Fig. 5. Featured pension

However, when we change the evaluation system and look at the countryside from the perspective of ecological civilization, we will find its unique value in modern society. As a matter of fact, rural civilization is based on respect and reverence for nature. It maintains the harmony between ways of production, life, beliefs and customs, and maintains the harmony between man and the environment, and between man and nature.

In this case, how to build a community culture that makes people willing to stay, is very important. In a secluded and beautiful land, if there is a group of friends, friends, family can accompany, have feelings can comfort here, have an ideal to look forward to, the meaning of life will appear rich and complete. In essence, the needs of the current Chinese people are not only material wealth, but also mental health and spiritual wealth are more important.

In 1992,1,575 scientists published a Warning of World Scientists to Humanity, which began with the proposal that "mankind and nature are on a conflicting path", which is precisely related to the excessive demand of the industrial age. This "excessive demand" seriously endangers a generation because of health problems, premature "heroic death", therefore, the development of natural health care, pension industry is imminent, work in the present, benefit for generations. **Those who are relatively rich and can enter the suburbs for holiday health care, not only need excellent hardware facilities and warm heart services, but also the sense of belonging is very important.** A new environment, can let people stay, must be because of the spiritual sustenance, some comfort. The pension market has an annual share of 1.500 billion yuan per year, and the average permanent urban resident spends more than 2,000 yuan per year for health care. These positive factors will ferment rapidly, thus promoting the first-class demand of the big health industry, and getting sustainable development (Fig. 6).

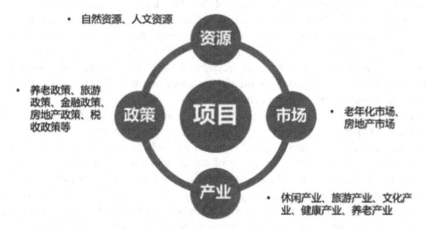

Fig. 6. Compound project development mode

Areas suitable for the creation and development of health care towns should usually have a good ecological environment and climate conditions, which is an important basic condition to achieve a healthy life. In this condition, according to different local resources, health towns with different theme contents can be designed and planned. For example, in the town to "forest", "garden", central meeting room, reading audio-visual, chess and card sports, calligraphy music, dance yoga, tea drinking bar, leisure guests, sunshine private banquet and so on, Create a different, functional space, So that people with different needs can freely choose to participate in various interest activities, Build ecological experience, vacation health, summer health, island health, mineral health, pastoral health and other different theme health formats, Build leisure farm, health resort, health valley, hot spring resort, ecological hotel/home stay and other products, Form a small town industrial system integrating ecology, health preservation, health, tourism and culture.

3   Industrial Characteristics

The industry of health care town should be based on health care, supplemented by cultural tourism. According to the Institute of the Elderly of the Chinese Academy of Social Sciences, the current business opportunities in China's pension market are about 4 trillion yuan, which is expected to increase to 13 trillion yuan by 2030, with huge potential. At the same time, the concept of pension living has changed greatly: 41% of the elderly choose to live with their children. With the change of the concept, this trend will rise, increasing people's yearning for rural + health + health care model life. Life changes like the sun and the moon! In front of the children and grandchildren are also like the old trees in front of the door long bud rotation! In the face of wrinkles on the face before not feel young old. In the face of various diseases, the threat to human beings, the treatment of disease prevention on the important agenda of life. People pay more attention to "health", but can not find a good "health" land.

According to the "China Health Care Big Data Report", women pay much more attention to health preservation than men. Women accounted for 63.2%, men 36.8%, women are nearly twice the needs of men; the health people trend and younger, more and more young people, 18 to 35 group accounted for 80%, this data fully shows that health care is not only the patent of the elderly, more and more young people in their own health problems, and put into action.

With the increasing pressure of work, the competition pressure also increases accordingly. After a period of high load work, people often choose to find a beautiful scenery place, to relieve the body and mind, slow down to smell the healthy air, taste healthy food ingredients, slowly enjoy the peace of the countryside, looking for the feelings of the past. Therefore, the health care into leisure agriculture + health care + pension as the upgraded version of the security. As a result, the proportion of unit teams and individuals resting increases fast every year. Companies with good welfare benefits, at least two to three times a year, and once in general terms. Uncontaminated ingredients is the guarantee of life safety, draw part of the farmland, according to the demand of consumers, young people can farming, the elderly can be interested in crops on the rented land, to give guidance, guide the choice of their hobby which varieties, pay attention to scarce benefit, cause people's planting desire, for the future large-scale development as a demonstration effect. From eating safely to the advanced level of eating healthy, these functional upgraded version of agricultural leisure places can attract the majority of people while vacation, while conditioning the body, to get a full range of physical and mental care (Figs. 7 and 8).

In such a country with a large population, the government has always continued to attach great importance to the agriculture, rural areas and farmers issues, and has always given them the top priority in all its work. In the face of major changes in

Fig. 7. Health care services   **Fig. 8.** Health data

the domestic development environment and the new situation and new requirements of China's economy entering the new normal, the CPC Central Committee has further placed stable agriculture and rural economic development at a higher position, and made a series of major decisions and arrangements, which has provided an important historical opportunity for accelerating agricultural modernization and the construction of a new socialist countryside (Fig. 9).

Fig. 9. Beautiful countryside

4 Clear Function

People have been deeply aware that with the concept of ecological civilization to understand, the countryside is like a dusty treasure house, but also like a carefully carved handicraft. With a heart of awe to treat it, experience it, you will find the irreplaceable value (Fig. 10).

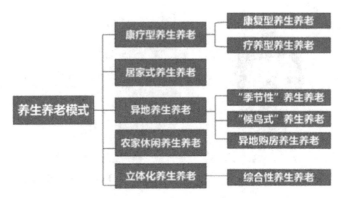

Fig. 10. Health preservation, pension model

According to the driver factors, it is divided into five major health care and pension modes like that.

Which methods are operational and are also popular?

(1) **leisure agriculture + pastoral + health factors**
Draw part of the farmland, according to the demand of consumers, young people can plow, the elderly can be in the rented land grow their interested in crops, at the same time using pension people for planting experienced experts to give guidance, cause people's planting desire, from the heart solve a lot of retired pension personnel have nothing to do, make its "full blood resurrection".

(2) **will provide good agricultural technical services**
Modern people are not arable land, not to mention planting technology, we must have a special person to provide, and patient technical guidance, make friends with them, increase trust and expand influence, establish a good reputation.

(3) **sets up a membership picking mechanism to improve land value**
Due to the limitation of land area, it is impossible for all customers to be equipped with the corresponding vegetable fields, and those who do not rent the supporting land, or are unwilling to farm, can handle picking members. Pay a certain annual fee every year, which can be quantitatively picked in the vegetable field of the farm. Picking vegetables to meet the needs of the elderly, can also be given to their children, killing two birds with one stone.

(4) **is suitable for health function and diversified picking**
In the picking area design, to humanized layout, picking trails, high and narrow have design, suitable for the needs of different ages, unified planting, unified management, green and healthy vegetables, planting competition activities, taste the joy of harvest and a series of activity innovation, in order to achieve labor is not monotonous, feel the joy of labor and enrichment.

(5) **enriches the community culture and makes the farming culture a driving force**
According to each season, with seasonal varieties set cultural creativity as the proposition, can be planting, can be sketch master, can be tea picking expert, with the theme of season, dance winners, and give spiritual and material encouragement, here into a modern pastoral, pastoral, hope the field.

(6) **health catering is the standard match**

Young people have work pressure, the degradation of the organism, minor problems, big problems, health diet effect is big, to the heart suggests plays a product effect, can be classified, to different physique, different ages, in the special human custom not only meet the needs of the guests, also create higher economic benefits.

In the development of health garden, we should combine people's physical and mental needs, in addition to do a good job in health catering, but also to provide people's favorite leisure health services, bring different experience.

In such a life, also feelings, also healthy, also happy rural + health pension + health mode of land, three or five years after 80% of the people will rush to the pastoral + health pension + health mode of life, enjoy her, fall in love with her, cannot leave her a way of life.

Cultural tourism + Kangyang town is different from the previous town, and its functions are more targeted.

5   Construction Standards and Development Types

The average annual PM2.5 value of Kangyang + Cultural Tourism Town is less than or equal to 50.

The standard concentration of negative oxygen ions in this area is greater than or equal to 5000 units per cubic centimeter (according to the World Health Organization, the standard concentration of negative oxygen ions in fresh air is not less than 1000–1500 units per cubic centimeter).

Village and town environment is beautiful, clean and tidy.

Nearby within 100 km of high-speed rail, airport, high-speed, convenient transportation.

The activity range is more than 3 km^2.

It is an environmental basis for developing the medical industry.

1. **Relying on, cultural and health preservation**

According to different regional characteristics depth mining project unique religion, folk, history and culture, combined with market demand and modern way of life, combining planning and design and innovation means, build yangxin spiritual level of cultural tourism industry, make the tourists experience different cultural characteristics at the same time, can cultivate one's morality, return to the heart, edify sentiment. For example, under the current environment of vigorously advocating sinology, relying on sinology resources, to build a cultural resort, relying on traditional Chinese culture, and to build a sinology experience base.

2. **Relying on it, longevity resources**

Relying on the longevity culture, vigorously develop the longevity economy, and form a health care pension system with food therapy, forest health, climate health, health catering, leisure and entertainment, health vacation and other functions with health products as the auxiliary.

3. **Relying on it, traditional Chinese medicine medicinal diet**

4. **Relying on it, ecological health preservation**

   Based on the original ecological environment, with health care and leisure tourism as the core of development, we focus on the construction of health care, leisure tourism, ecological planting and other health industries, which are generally distributed in ecological leisure tourist attractions or areas with good natural ecological environment. Is relying on the project to good climate and ecological environment, build ecological experience, vacation health, spa, forest health, mountain summer health, island cold health, lake health, mineral health, rural health, health formats, build leisure farm, health resort, health valley, hot spring resort, ecological hotel/home stay facility products, form ecological health health town industry system.

5. **Relying on the comprehensive pension type**

   Have certain environmental resources, at the same time has a certain economic strength of the elderly, the medical, climate, ecology, rehabilitation, leisure and other elements into the pension industry, developing rehabilitation, living pension, leisure vacation "migratory birds" pension, elderly sports, elderly education, elderly cultural activities, build pension living, pension, pension service as a pension base of comprehensive development projects, for the elderly pension living, medical care, leisure vacation as the main function of pension town. Drive the common development of nursing, catering, medicine, supplies for the elderly, finance, tourism, education and other industries.

6. **Relying on, vacation industry**

   Residential health care is a kind of health care mode formed with the concept of health care and vacation real estate development as the leading role. This kind of health living community provides people with not only living space, but also a healthy lifestyle. In addition to the characteristics of architectural ecology, good environment, food health and other characteristics, it also provides a full range of health care and health facilities and services, and provides people with meditation space and environment, to achieve the purpose of self-cultivation in a quiet atmosphere.

7. **Relying on, sports culture**

Fig. 11. Green ecology   **Fig. 12.** Cultural tourism town

With the theme of building "naked heart" sports, the town plans "one belt, two wings and many districts" to build a town with sports characteristics. We will organically combine sports, health, culture and tourism, and explore sports, outdoor leisure and cycling culture to promote the integrated development of production, life and ecology (Figs. 11 and 12).

8. **Relying on medicine**

Kang nursing products are mainly in traditional Chinese medicine, western medicine, nutrition, psychology and other theoretical knowledge as guidance, combined with the human physiological behavior characteristics of drug rehabilitation, drug treatment as the main means, with certain leisure activities of rehabilitation health tourism products, including health inspection products, it is one of the important contents in the development of medical tourism development (Figs. 13 and 14).

Fig. 13. Medical service   **Fig. 14.** Cultural tourism health care

6 How to Plan

1. **Reconstruction of ecology**

The planning, design and development of any place should go through three stages: the original ecological stage, the ecological destruction stage, and the ecological reconstruction stage. For example, the most typical British London, 100 years ago was the world recognized as the "fog capital", now as long as there is no rain is the blue sky. After 30 years of renovating the environment and spending two hours walking on the streets of Tokyo, you will feel very good enough to see no garbage. Therefore, seeking development should not only look at the present, look at the long term, take ecological reconstruction as the direction, and lead the industry to the high-end. Whether doing tourism, agriculture or science and technology, the idea should be the same. In the future, there is great hope for enterprises to do industries related to ecology.

As planners and designers should follow the concept of green development, retain green mountains and clear waters, carry out overall protection and comprehensive management of mountains, rivers, fields, forests and lakes, and practice the design way of seeing mountains, seeing water and remembering homesickness. We will effectively address problems such as clean agriculture and a prominent agricultural environment.

We will establish diversified rural industrial land supply methods, and support the development of landscape agriculture, agricultural experience, sightseeing and picking, research and education, leisure fishing, boutique home stay, and shared farms.

Innovate industrial forms. We will make good use of idle rural housing and homestead, and develop boutique homestay, shared farms, health and elderly care, and farmhouse entertainment. Effectively develop the "four wasteland", develop leisure agriculture (animal husbandry, fishing) garden, forest families, healthy oxygen bar, ecological experience, characteristic animal and plant viewing and other formats.

(1) **planning is the leading, rural change park**

Promote the pastoral transformation into a park, organize the pastoral landscape according to the principle of garden art, highlight different characteristics and styles, provide visitors for leisure and appreciation, and transform the unique ecological value, cultural value and social value of the countryside into economic value. The first thirty years will focus on "eating, accommodation and transportation"; the second thirty years will focus on "swimming, raising and entertainment". The extensive economic development of the past three decades is a stage of satiety." Eating" refers to the diet. In the first 30 years, one Wahaha can make Zong Qinghou the richest man in China, and selling drinks and food can have a great development. In more than a decade, more than half of the richest people in China are engaged in real estate. In the future, Chinese real estate enterprises may have a considerable part of their assets discounted, or even lose their money, so it is impossible to build houses or sell houses. "Line" refers to the car. In recent years, our country's car sales have been the first in the world for several years. As a result, traffic jams everywhere, resulting in bad urban environment. Now with the development of high-speed railway, there may be many rich but environmental protection people will choose high-speed rail travel, environmental protection travel (Fig. 15).

Fig. 15. Garden park

(2) **industry is the foundation, products into commodities**

Under the background of the dual strategies of "healthy China" and "rural revitalization", the Kangyang Cultural Tourism Town and rural revitalization project, as a new business form, will eventually usher in a golden period of development. But how to adapt to the development trend of The Times and enjoy the favorable national policies? How to grasp the tuyere, strong layout? (Fig. 16).

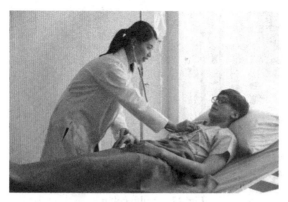

Fig. 16. Community Services in the health industry

In view of the problems faced by the health care, cultural and tourism industry and rural revitalization projects, Yifang City specially selects the most representative cases of different types, Invite relevant political, industry, academic and research authorities in the industry and a number of famous experts in the field of health care, cultural tourism and rural revitalization and representative health care, cultural tourism and rural revitalization project operators, Focusing on the core issues such as the top-level design, profit model, planning, industrial introduction, operation and finance of the health and tourism industry and the creation process of rural revitalization projects, Discuss the road of health care, cultural tourism and rural revitalization and development together, Jointly promote the sustainable and healthy development of health care and cultural tourism industry and the implementation of the rural revitalization strategy!

(3) **culture is the soul, turning the farm houses into the guest rooms**
The pension industry is a huge rigid need for the public. Especially in the education industry, why did meng's mother move three times? There is an old Chinese saying, called "dyed in god is green, dyed in yellow is yellow", there is a sentence in "Confucius Language": "Living with good people, if into the room of lanzhi, long and do not smell its fragrance, with it. With the wicked, such as into the abalone four, long time and do not smell its smell, also with it." This is a focus that we need to educate our children for a long time to come, and there is a great market prospect (Fig. 17).

(4) **ecology is an advantage, and the environment is more livable**
Unified planning, sorting out value, and establishing a sticky and sentimental community culture must be based on market research combined with local culture and natural environment advantages, and explore the main selling points of health, health, pension, living and residence. Travel is not to say that the ticket charge is over, now China's tourism is still "tied with grass, while hungry cattle",

In a secluded and beautiful land, if there is a group of friends, friends, family can accompany, have feelings can comfort here, have an ideal to look forward to, the meaning of life will appear rich and complete. In essence, the needs of the current Chinese people are not only material wealth, but also mental health

Fig. 17. Health culture

and spiritual wealth are more important. Therefore, from this point of view, the first-class health care project is not a real estate, let alone a hospital, but a sentimental, beautiful scenery, high-quality life vacation community (Figs. 18 and 19).

Fig. 18. Original ecological landscape   **Fig. 19.** Landscape planning according to local conditions

2. **Adjust measures to local conditions**
   First of all, according to their own characteristics, determine the town development type of development. If there are no characteristic resources, relevant features and functions can be implanted. For the towns without obvious characteristic resources, we should enter the health town and implant them through the carrying function of tourism. This type is generally only suitable for longevity culture type, ecological health preservation type, medical care combination type or pension town type development.

   Ecological health requires the town to have a good environmental foundation, the later stage to improve and maintain the ecological environment of the town, at the same time to cultivate and guide the health care industry to enter, develop health industry, carry out ecological health development.

3. **Diversified development**
   Secondly, the planning should strengthen the health theme and carry out diversified development. Health care town must strengthen the theme of health and health

care, and carry out diversified development. With health industries such as health care, leisure and pension vacation as the core, the multi-functional development of leisure agriculture, medical services, leisure and entertainment, health vacation is etc. (Figs. 20 and 21).

Fig. 20. Data collection platform

Fig. 21. Data application instances

4. **Integrated operation**

Finally, in terms of operation and management, based on the characteristics of the town, dominated by market-oriented development, determine the development subject, development mode, investment attraction and operation mode of the project, form a systematic operation and management process, promote the efficient development of the healthy industry chain, and realize the growth of economic benefits of the town.

7 Design and Application of the Interactive Platform

Wisdom, big data, artificial intelligence and other fine management tools will be the necessary capabilities of elderly care service enterprises.

1. **Development of interactive platform (V-Care smart care platform) to achieve fine management**

In order to standardize and refine its services, Vanke has developed the V-Care smart care platform. At present, Fangshan · Suiyuan uses V-Care system 3.0. The system has customized care plans for each elderly person according to the nursing level, and standardizes 64 nursing actions of caregivers. Through fingerprint punching and data upload, daily services can be recorded in every time period (Figs. 22 and 23).

In addition, after V-Care is fully applied in Fangshan Suiyuan, the entertainment system will also be incorporated into the data management system. Through the form of elderly clocking and butler statistics, regional heat map and club activity heat map are provided, so as to find which space and activity design need to be optimized, which are clearly presented in the form of data.

Up to now, Beijing Vanke Pension has sorted out 165 service items in 8 categories of service modules, covering product hardware services, health management, nursing, rehabilitation, medical treatment, colorful life, nutrition and catering, characteristic housekeeping, etc. (Figs. 24 and 25).

Fig. 22. Interactive design platform development

Fig. 23. Interactive Platform application design

Fig. 24. Health management

Fig. 25. Featured service

2. **Different spatial function designs correspond to the requirements of different product lines**

   In the Yiyuan Guangxi project, for the surrounding medical treatment, living facilities on the higher requirements. Yiyuan Guangxi is located in the core of Beijing's North Third Ring Road, rich in medical resources, is a rare central apartment in Beijing. The scarce location and high-quality environment make it a Taoyuan retirement residence in the bustling downtown.

   In terms of space design, more attention is paid to bringing home-like experience for the elderly. Multi-storey theme garden, sunshine corridor, family meeting room and other diversified functional Spaces, and the indoor living environment is warm and elegant.

3. **Fangshan · Suiyuan—introduced the concept of "full life cycle housing"**

   Vanke invited well-known Japanese designer TsuXiaosheng (once designed Vanke Liangzhu Beautiful Zhou Church) to design Fangshan · Suiyuan and introduce the concept of whole life cycle residence.

   Fangshan · Suiyuan has a total construction area of about 40,000 m², with an overall planning of 7 buildings with 475 rooms and nearly 800 beds. It is mainly aimed at all-age elderly who live independently and need different degrees of care services.

After three years of studying the social activity scenes suitable for the elderly in the garden, the designer designed five functional landscape Spaces of "music, forest, court, welcome, health" for the garden, covering a total area of 16,000 m².

When the elderly are in good physical condition, they can participate in more than 20 functional Spaces such as "forest", "garden" and central meeting room to participate in various interest activities. At the same time, the surrounding Yonghui Supermarket, Carrefour supermarket, Changyang Shopping Center, and the Capital Outlets can also meet the needs of leisure shopping (Figs. 26 and 27).

Fig. 26. Application of smart care platform   **Fig. 27.** Application of smart care platform

When the self-care ability of the elderly gradually declines, they can move to the nursing building to continue living, and the surrounding medical resources are rich. In addition to the 24-h medical team of Guangxi, the five-kilometer emergency channel in the community can go directly to many hospitals.

8 Research Summary

1. Most of the domestic health and care projects deviate from the market in the main urban area. Whether the sales and operation customers are only for local regional customers, or for a wider range of markets and customers, and what class of customers are locked is the basis for the planning and positioning of the whole project.

2. Unified planning, sorting out value, and establishing a sticky and sentimental community culture must be based on market research combined with local culture and natural environment advantages, and explore the main selling points of health, health, pension, living and residence. On the other hand, those who are relatively rich and can enter the suburbs for holiday health care, not only need excellent hardware facilities and warm heart services, but also a sense of belonging is very important. In this case, how to build a community culture that makes people willing to stay, is very important. In essence, the needs of the current Chinese people are not only material wealth, but also mental health and spiritual wealth are more important. Therefore, from this point of view, the first-class health care project is not a real estate, let alone a hospital, but a sentimental, beautiful scenery, high-quality life vacation community.

3. Attach great importance to the service system and confirm the basic health care function structure and service system. The basic functions of a health care project

include living function, learning and communication function, leisure and entertainment function, medical care function, health care function, etc. The functions of different themes will be distinguished and emphasized. In general, the above four categories of products and services are the basic content of the project. In addition, different types of hotels or home stay clusters are also important supporting facilities for such projects to come to recuperate for vacation.

4. Different from the urban pension projects, in fact, the biggest selling point is the good space environment quality and comfortable environmental atmosphere. Therefore, shaping a park-oriented health environment is the development concept that developers should uphold. The first-class health vacation project should be not only reflected in the functional buildings and space, but more importantly in the high-quality, garden-like environmental attraction. Only by planning and designing projects from the perspective of landscape urbanism can we create a unique and comfortable vacation space to attract customers.

5. Effective allocation of cash flow, build the best financial model with the control of real estate financial policy, health vacation comprehensive projects with investment scale, public part of the long investment cycle leads to the characteristics of relatively high cost of capital, therefore, this is in the early development, rigorous measuring cash flow and investment time, and the late operating costs. Under normal circumstances, health and project development investment are carried out in stages. In this process, it is necessary to accurately calculate the investment intensity of different types of public construction construction, landscape facilities and real estate and hotel properties, so as to achieve the balance of benign cash flow in stages and in stages.

6. The core key of building a professional operation team, designing a gradually integrated operation strategy, and constantly improving the long-term operation capacity of health care projects is the operation. Operational ability is an important key point to measure the success of the project. Especially in the early stage of project development, in the face of generally low occupancy health projects with low resident population, how to attract consumers, ensure popularity, have the ability of long-term healthy operation is the top priority.

From the case summary, in general, the cost of paying a professional and multi-functional health care team in the early stage is relatively high, and most developers will choose the strategy of taking sales first. This is the main problem in the Chinese market. After development projects were used to making quick money, they were unwilling to win reputation and customer trust with operation. As a result, a large number of health projects in China opened hot in the early stage. However, due to the lack of operation ability, the reputation declined and sales fell into the mire. So there will be an unfinished project.

In order to solve the difficulties of such projects, the most important thing is to prepare the corresponding operation of supporting resources in advance. The early operating expense investment must be highly valued in the early use forecast of cash flow, and the appropriate proportion of funds is withheld in the sales profit for operation. At this time, how to design the operation system, how to develop and operate the public construction products by stages is very important.

References

1. Liuyuhao: Indoor Scene Reconstruction Technology Based on Depth Information. Yanshan University, Qinhuangdao (2016)
2. Luomingxuan: Talking about the Technology and Application of Motion Capture, 15 March 2013. http://blog.sina.com.cn/s/blog_6be92b950101bqtt.html
3. Jiangyajie: Human Body Gesture Recognition and Robot Control Based on Kinect. Shenzhen University, Shenzhen (2017)
4. Zhanqinchuan: Analysis of the application and development status of virtual reality technology. Ind. Technol. Forum **7**, 75–76 (2014)

On Research and Exploration of New Media Interaction Design in Display Design

Le Liu[(⊠)]

Shandong University Art & Design, Jinan, China
549084617@qq.com

Abstract. As the information age has come, more and more new things have entered and changed our lives, among which exhibition design has gradually developed into a systematic discipline. Exhibition design is not only classified as a science, but also a culture. With the continuous integration of various cultures, the exhibition industry is also developing rapidly. The themes of the exhibition have become more and more diversified as well as the dramatically increased scale, furthermore, the pattern of the exhibition becomes more and more eye-catching. However, the informatization has gradually changed people's life style, and the traditional display design idea needs further improvement because of its inadaptability with the development of the times.

With the rapid development of new media art, exhibition design has become a dynamic space with a intensive interaction instead of a rigid interface of just a product display. During the 2010 Shanghai World Expo, the design of the pavilions of various countries has already combined interactive art with the exhibition design, which has achieved very good results, and has been praised by visitors from all countries. At present, interaction design has become one of the representative technologies and multimedia technology is constantly improving the way of communication between people, improving the way of information dissemination, and improving the efficiency of people-to-people, people-to-information exchange. The development of interactive technology has been closely accompanied by the development of high-tech. The development of these technologies provides the core for the development of interactive technology, which enables the comprehensive dissemination of exhibition information, and simultaneously provides the audience with a multi-channel "Comprehensive Feeling." But this development is not one-direction, because the development of exhibition technology also promotes the development of various network technology during the development of exhibition technology.

Keywords: Exhibition design · New Media

1 Introduction of Interactive Media

The development and application of computer technology has promoted the development of technology based on new media, and in this new era, the expression forms of new media technology are becoming richer and more complex. Especially in recent years, new media, multimedia, interaction media and other related words has frequently appeared in our daily life. In a broad sense, media is a relatively extensive concept.

Media refers to those works or products based on computer or digital devices, involving a series of electronic fields such as film, game, animation, digital disks and so on. Interactive media, however, refers to connecting to process during which information and data received from external sensors could be transformed, through a certain transformation technology, into machine language that can be recognized by computer, and then transmit signals through corresponding programs, so as to realize the interaction of different media.

While performing exhibition design, as the name suggests, interaction design is the interaction between the audience and the exhibits, so that the audience can communicate directly with the exhibits. Therefore, interaction design is a bridge connecting the audience and the exhibition. This kind of design is often supported by science and technology. When performing the exhibition design, we should also add a theme to the exhibition and take the audience's personal emotional needs into consideration, so as to realize the effective communication of multi-sensory, multi-level and three-dimensional information for exhibition.

In recent years, with the continuous development of high-tech industry, multimedia technology has been applied more frequently. It includes the application of multimedia technology in interaction design and exhibition design. Interaction design can not only provide more ideas for exhibition design, but also simultaneously promote the conceptual realization of exhibition design. For the exhibition design, interaction design combines the audience with the exhibits, so that the audience can communicate with the exhibits more directly. For example, interactive design helps the gradual transformation of the exhibition mode of exhibition design from static to dynamic. The traditional exhibition mode is related to real scenes, while interactive design gradually turns it to virtual scenes. This transformation could present a more dazzling effect for the exhibition, and at the same time improve the sensory experience for the audience. During this process, the product, audience and environment are closely interconnected, highlighting the audience's main position, which could present the audience with a more real and empathetic experience.

2   Application Status of Exhibition Technology

The emergence of new media interactive technology enriches the form of exhibition and provides space for the content exhibition. It appears to be that new media technology breaks through the traditional form of exhibition and creates infinite effect for the space of exhibition material supported by new media technology. Exhibition refers to promotion activities related to commercial activities, which is closely related to art and business. Therefore, the management of commercial exhibition is also the fundamental requirement to promote the healthy development of every enterprise. The use of new media technology shortens the distance between exhibitors and audiences and effectively improves the efficiency of exhibition. With the development of society, people are also pursuing the cultural enjoyment while becoming more and more wealthy. Cultural and artistic workers could gather together to create a relatively concentrated exhibition area.

Commercial exhibition activities promote the development of commerce to a certain extent.

3 Principles for Interactive Technology in Exhibition

The Shanghai World Expo held in 2010 is a grand world-class cultural and economic event. The designers all over the world give full play to their talents and cooperate with each other to realize the full potential of the new media technology within the exhibition space. For the World Expo, the designers widely applied new media technology and adhered to the following design principles:

Everything is based on the exhibits. Presenting the exhibits is the ultimate goal of interactive new media. The most important thing is not the exhibition process, but the perfect understanding and arrangement of the concept of exhibition products before exhibition design process, therefore, the design and implementation of interactive media must comply with the exhibition concept. For example, for science and technology commodities, the main exhibition contents should include technical concepts, applied technologies, technological methods and other substantive aspects. Therefore, during the designing process, interactive new media technology should be clearly applied and effectively integrated, so as to truly exhibit the characteristics and performance of commodities to the greatest extent.

We need to clarify the goal for the exhibition. The ultimate purpose of the exhibition is to benefit the enterprise participants. Therefore, the use of technology must be taken into consideration to integrate with interactive new media technology, so as to realize the seamless connection between the technology and the exhibits. We should highlight the content expression, and pay attention to the coherence and concentration of content information. The common problem in the exhibition is that the inappropriate arrangements cause the dispersion of exhibition information, and the lack of obvious indication sign leads to the audience's confusion of the type of the exhibition.

4 Application of Interactive Technology in Exhibition

The use of audio technology. The use of audio technology is not the main direction of research for previous exhibition, but with the new media interaction technology, it becomes an important topic in the research of exhibition design.

Generally speaking, the use of audio design refers to the design of sound in movies or TV programs, so as to effectively integrate sound and other factors in the exhibition process and improve the effect of exhibition. In space design, we should use porous materials instead of hard materials, because of the sound sputtering phenomenon. Porous materials can absorb surrounding noise and echoes and improve the sound effect.

The use of film and television technology. LED lights are used for exterior design. The external characteristics of the exhibits are the first factor to attract the audience. A well-designed exterior exhibition can leave people with visual impact and deep impression. The use of different pictures for different products would integrate art into the exhibits, so that the audience can understand the characteristics of the exhibits while appreciating the beauty of the art.

5   Advantages of Interactive New Media Technology

New media interaction technology is based on digital media which involves an effective combination of modern science, technology and art. During the exhibition process, the final expression is enhanced through pictures, texts, sound and video. The introduction of new media technology improves the information storage, and has removed the space limitation in previous exhibitions. Before the exhibition, designers can perform simulation on the computer in advance, which improves the possibility of a successful exhibition. Under these circumstances, people have really entered the digital age. Interactive new media technology is an extension and update of the traditional model. The progress of science and technology not only facilitates people's life, but also meets people's diverse needs.

6   Disadvantages of Interactive New Media Technology

The effective combination of new media technology and exhibition increases the replicability of exhibition and makes it more and more flexible in the process of information communication. There are fewer and fewer restrictions. It can vividly show the characteristics of the exhibits, shorten the distance between the audience and the exhibits, immerse the audience in the exhibition to improve its effectiveness. However, the complex information increases the difficulty for the audience to absorb effective information. Whether the audience can find beneficial information is related not only to the designer but also to the audience itself. Before the exhibition, the audience must understand their purpose, stay awake and find the information they need like a needle in the haystack. Because the interactive new media is based on the computer, on the connection between the external sensors and signal data interface through circuits, and on the transmission the information through a series of translation inside the computer, highly qualified designers and operators are required for the process, and special maintenance personnel must be needed to deal with any problems.

7   The Design of Exhibition Interactive System Based on Internet of Things (IOT) Technology

7.1   Introduction of Key Technologies

7.1.1   Application of Traditional Indoor Positioning Technology in Exhibition

The traditional indoor positioning technology, represented by infrared detection technology, has been widely used in the exhibition. When a visitor walks close to an exhibit, the light will automatically light up, and when the visitor picks up an exhibit and changes the content on the screen, it is obvious that these exhibition items may use the traditional indoor positioning technology. The application of indoor positioning technology in exhibition can present the flexibility and diversity of the exhibits, and can fulfill some display effects that cannot be achieved by traditional technology, so as to make interactive exhibition reach a new height. However, due to the limitations of traditional indoor positioning technology, it can not be widely used in exhibitions, and it plays a role of auxiliary exhibition technology for some specific exhibitions.

7.1.2 Application of New-Generation Indoor Positioning System in Exhibition

With the development of indoor communication technology, its indoor positioning function has made great progress and its application form in exhibition has also undergone great changes. Most of the new-generation indoor positioning technologies need the binding between visitors and terminals. Therefore, it is necessary to distribute intelligent terminals to visitors before they visit. The style of the terminal can be diversified according to different technical requirements, and it should match the theme of the exhibition.

Application of new-generation indoor positioning system in exhibition

1) In the form of intelligent terminal. When visitors enter the exhibition area, intelligent terminals with positioning tags are distributed to visitors, so that the exhibition system can perceive the position of visitors from time to time and push information to visitors through the intelligent terminal. The cost of this identification terminal is usually relatively high, which is not suitable for mass-distribution despite of its powerful function and feasibility for visitors. Technologies like Bluetooth can make better use of this form of identification.

2) In the form of souvenirs or combination with tickets.

   This form is suitable for ordinary visitors because the cost is usually low, and the terminal can be designed as a disposable product. RFID and other technologies are usually adopted for this terminal form. While distributing the terminal to the visitors, the personal information of the visitors will also be collected, and the collected information can be used in the later exhibition items. The forms of information collection are divided into active collection and passive collection. Active collection requires visitors to actively input relevant personal information. More comprehensive information about the visitors will be collected through this method, so as to fulfill a more effective positioning function. Static collection can collect relevant information of visitors, such as height, weight and so on.

   Despite of the small amount of information collected, a stronger sense of surprise to the audience is intensified when the collected information is utilized in subsequent exhibitions, because of its invisibility during the process of information collection. Different forms of information collection shall be adopted for different display themes. The collected information will be bound with the terminal identification system, so that it can be mapped to the corresponding visitor. In this way, the exhibition hall identification system can realize real-time capture of the visitor's location and confirm the identity of visitors according to the terminal, so as to push customized display information according to the different characteristics of various visitors,

3) Through the utilization of the visitors' mobile phones and other electronic devices which functions, such as position and Bluetooth, should be switched on by the visitors themselves, this method can effectively reduce the cost, but raise the requirements for visitors.

2 Functions

Due to its own limitations, the traditional indoor positioning technology can only function as an auxiliary technology for certain exhibits, while the function of the new-generation indoor positioning system breaks through the limitations of the original technology. Its function can be implemented not only in the area of one exhibition, but can be expanded to the whole venue, thanks to its own functional characteristics. Compared with the traditional positioning technology, it has two obvious functional advantages

1) One advantage is its wider coverage area and better accurate-positioning. Therefore, the new-generation indoor positioning system can be applied in the whole range of the venue, rather than one individual exhibition, so that designers can revise the display content based on the whole-area-coverage positioning function from a new perspective.
2) The new-generation indoor positioning system provides terminals for each visitor, so as to provide customized services based on the fact that each visitor's personal information is bound to the attached terminal. This facilitates the system not only to locate the visitors, but also to track their real-time browsing route. The system is aware of the location, identification and even the exact action of the visitors.

7.1.3 Performance Analysis of Some Positioning Technologies for Exhibition Application

1) Infrared indoor positioning technology. Infrared indoor positioning technology is a relatively traditional positioning technology. The basic principle of infrared indoor positioning technology is that portable IR-ray emission tag emits infrared rays, and optical sensors receives infrared rays to position the tag. Despite of the relatively high accuracy of infrared indoor positioning technology, its poor penetration through obstacles causes the fact that the emission and reception of infrared is affected by the indoor environment. Therefore, the infrared indoor positioning technology has a relatively poor effect. When the tags are blocked by objects such as clothes or buildings, infrared positioning function cannot work normally. In addition, infrared positioning technology is also under the influence of ambient light, which will reduce its accuracy. Nevertheless, the infrared positioning technology is relatively mature and can function perfectly when applied to a single exhibition, which is why it is applied to traditional display projects which require positioning system service.
2) Ultrasonic positioning technology
   The basic principle of ultrasonic positioning technology is to use the reflection characteristics of ultrasonic to carry out ranging and accurate positioning through triangulation. Although the accuracy of ultrasonic positioning technology is high, like infrared positioning technology, it can neither penetrate obstacles to realize accurate positioning. Furthermore, the relative high cost prevents its application to normal exhibitions.

3) Wi-Fi Technology

Wireless LAN technology, based on its own network node position, can realize indoor positioning function with high accuracy. When it is applied to the exhibition, the requirements for the terminals used by users is relatively high, which is not convenient for the development of disposable terminals for each visitor. On the other hand, it can provide more diversified functions for VIP visitors,

4) ZigBee Technology

The basic principle of ZigBee technology is to use a large number of nanosensors to coordinate and perform its positioning function. The cost of this technology to realize the positioning function is relatively low, but it can not be used in large-scale exhibitions due to its poor positioning accuracy.

5) UWB Technology

UWB technology is a medium and short distance communication technology, which can perfectly help to construct an indoor positioning system. However, its high cost restricts its wide application in exhibitions.

6) Bluetooth Technology

Bluetooth technology is a short-distance transmission technology, and positioning function can be realized by measuring its signal strength. Its biggest advantage is that the device is small and easy to be integra ted into computers and mobile phones. However, its high cost prevents its usage for disposal terminals for exhibition. For some exhibitions, the exhibition cost can be reduced by utilizing visitors' own devices with Bluetooth function to fulfill the positioning functions.

7) RFID Technology

The basic principle of RFID technology is that the tag sends a signal of a certain frequency, and the receiver sends the information to the central information processing system, so as to fulfill the corresponding positioning function. A complete RFID system consists of three parts: receiver, electronic tag and its application software system. Compared with other indoor positioning technologies, RFID technology is characterized with its small size and low cost, which is more suitable for large-scale application in exhibitions by distributing to users in various forms to realize the function of disposal use. However, it also has its own shortcomings. It does not have communication functions, which makes it impossible to provide a more optimized interactive experience for some users or push complex information to visitors more effectively.

Each positioning technology has its own advantages and disadvantages. For example, RFID is suitable for ordinary visitors, while Wi-Fi technology is more suitable for VIP visitors. Traditional positioning technologies such as IR can be designed for specific exhibition items, while Bluetooth technology can be effectively used for exhibition where visitors have smart phones. Comprehensive application of various positioning technologies, according to different exhibition themes and requirements, can well achieve the exhibition's purpose and make the science exhibition more lively and interesting, by immersing visitors in the exhibition.

7.2 Example of Interactive System Based on the Technology of Internet of Things (IOT)

Here we take the exhibition design of Wuxi IOT Center – Sensing China Windows as an example to carry out a further introduction about the design and application of interactive system based on IOT technology in science exhibition.

The exhibition's theme is to display IOT technology through the comprehensive utilization of the new-generation indoor positioning system, so that visitors can experience the future life brought by IOT technology in an immersive way. The exhibition construction is designed according to a future imaginary city, which simulates the real experience in the scene of the city, including restaurants, parks, hospitals, etc. After entering the exhibition hall, visitors can walk freely through different exhibition items by taking multi-path route. During this period, visitors can experience the specific contents of exhibition items respectively, as if they were in a real future city.

The terminal of the indoor positioning system based on RFID technology is distributed to visitors in the form of "city" map, and simultaneously collect the personal information of visitors (such as height, weight and so on) in the form of static data collection. The collected data is bound with the corresponding terminal to realize real-time location of visitors when they walk through the exhibition area. At the same time, intelligent positioning terminals are distributed to visitors to record visitors' real-time browsing routes as visitors make their way through the exhibition area. Together with the visitors' personal information collected when receiving the terminal, a customized experience can be provided to visitors when browsing through the exhibition are. This method is not only consistent with the theme of the exhibition, but also gives visitors a strong sense of immersion.

The functional change of the application of the new-generation indoor positioning system in the exhibition brings visitors a different feeling compared with the past. The new-generation sensor positioning system, based on one-to-one sensor terminals, can not only perceive the location of visitors, but also record personal information of visitors. This enables different customized feedback to be pushed to different visitors while experiencing different exhibition projects. For example, the sensor system will record the height and weight of visitors and present them with customized information. Take the above exhibition area as an example. When visitors enter the "store", while experiencing the simulated future urban life, the sensor network in the "store" will get the positioning information sent by the sensor terminal carried by visitors, so as to know that visitors enter the "store" exhibition area. While locating visitors, the exhibition system will identify the personal information of visitors carrying corresponding terminals according to the ID of different terminals. Therefore, the "store" exhibition area can automatically present visitors with clothes suitable for their height and weight. This exhibition mode highly simulates the future life based on the IOT technology. The visitors are presented with a real-life experience, and "passively" experience the core design concept in the exhibition area, which is based on the function of the new-generation indoor positioning system to record visitors' personal information.

The improvement of the new-generation sensor positioning technology enables it not only to record personal information of different visitors, but also to be applied to all display items throughout the whole exhibition area. This means that the sensor positioning technology is no longer only an auxiliary exhibition technology of a single exhibit, but can be used as the basic exhibition technology for the whole exhibition area. Because the sensor positioning technology can record the route of visitors, the connection between different exhibition items can be effectively utilized in the design of the exhibition area. Taking the above exhibition as an example, the free and multi-path experience means various choices for visitor's route. Based on the sensor positioning technology, the system records the relation between the visitor's route and the exhibition items means the whole exhibition area can be organically combined into one integral whole, which shows visitors a real-existed "future city", not just independent exhibits with urban settings. The designer presents the relationship between different exhibits based on real-life environment. Taking a certain route of the visitors as an example, the visitor first enters the "future hospital" exhibition item to experience future medical service which relevant results will be recorded in the corresponding terminal of the visitor, then the visitor marches to the "future restaurant" exhibition item, which is also recorded by the sensor positioning technology. When the visitor enters the restaurant to experience this exhibition item, the exhibition system will give relevant tips to the visitor according to his information collected through his previous experience in exhibition item "future hospital". The tips include 'one of your test is above normal level, please avoid such food' and so on. The visitor's experience information in the "future restaurant" will also be recorded on his corresponding sensor positioning terminal. When he comes out from the "future restaurant" to the park, the sensor positioning terminal will always send feedback information about the visitor's browsing order in each exhibition to the system. Based on this information that he has just come out of the "future restaurant", the park exhibition system will prompt relevant contents according to the information brought by the sensor positioning terminal carried by visitors. Exhibition, such as: "If you have just finished your meal, please be careful not to take vigorous exercise". If the visitor enters other exhibitions after coming out of the restaurant, they will not be prompted with such information. According to the following table, the system will actively push customized information according to the user's different route choices. Visitors will receive different information according to which they will carry out relevant activities, so as to complete the interaction and achieve the purpose of exhibition.

For VIP users, the intelligent terminal they carry not only has the above functions, but also has a more specific information push function. For example, intelligent terminals will present different information according to which exhibition area the visitors enter. Its screen will be switched to "menu" in the restaurant and "medical record" in the hospital.

Thus, the active-push-mode interactive system, based on IOT technology, dynamically integrates the whole exhibition venue by recording the personal information of visitors and using the real relationship between exhibition items, effectively presents visitors with the immersive experience process and achieves the purpose of exhibition perfectly.

8   Research on New Media Interaction Design in Exhibition Design

8.1   The Combination of Senses

Traditional display design is often single-channeled, which can not give the audience an all-round sensory experience. Interaction design is a multichannel design. During the interaction between human and computer, multi-channel refers to the use of two or more sensory systems of the human body to capture the user's intention. This way improves the reliability and naturalness of human-computer interaction. Interactive design utilizes virtual system to output the information of the exhibits from different channels so that customers can not only observe more carefully, but also experience the exhibits in an all-round way through senses of hearing, touching and so on.

At present, interaction design has become one of the landmark technologies of the current era. Multimedia technology is constantly improving the way of communication between people, improving the way of information dissemination, and improving the efficiency of human-human and human-computer communication. However, the development of interactive technology is inseparable from the development of high-tech technology. The development of these technologies provides the core for the development of interactive technology, enables the exhibited information to spread comprehensively, and also provides the audience with multi-channel "three-dimensional feeling". However, this is not a one-way development. There is a mutual promotion to each other between the development of exhibition technology and computer-internet technology.

8.2   Combination of Virtual Environment and Reality

Interaction technology also achieves the combination of reality and virtuality. The traditional exhibition design is often limited to real life scenes and needs the support of sufficient materials. Virtual technology is the opposite. It can be seen from the above that the exhibition technology relies on the development of new media technology, and this virtual design often does not need a lot of materials. Moreover, due to the availability of technology, the exhibition can reappear for many times, which also reduces the consumption of resources to a certain extent. With the development of interactive technology, the combination of virtual and reality has become one of the main exhibition modes of exhibition design. The combination of virtual and reality can stimulate the audience's sensory system and add a lot of interest to the exhibition design.

8.3   Combination of Single Dimension and Multi Dimension

Due to its characteristics, interaction design is destined to be a combination of single dimension and multi dimension. The development of human-computer interaction interface is a process of continuous superposition of dimensions. This feature of interaction design will be illustrated based on the development of dimension.

The first stage, one-dimensional. The exhibition relies on the texts, which shows only the arranged letters and characters, and lacks of obvious spatial coordinates. The second stage, two-dimensional. At this stage, exhibition can be displayed on the screen in graphics with colors. Data can also be used for input. The development of two-dimensional form enriches the content that can be displayed in one-dimensional stage, but the exhibits still has certain limitations because the information provided can only be determined by x-axis and y-axis.

8.4 Promoting the Exchange of Information Between the Audience and the Exhibition

For the design of new media exhibition, the initiative of the audience has also developed. Because of the continuous development of the above technologies, the exhibition is more fun, which arouses people's interest in the exhibition. The audience has gradually changed their attitude from passive viewing to active viewing. This initiative is reflected in the following two aspects.

Finally, the current interaction design has developed to the three-dimensional stage. This stage mainly depends on the development of computer-based three-dimensional graphics. Audience can visit the exhibits from multiple angles. They can see the characteristics of the exhibits from the side and from the rear. It seems to bring the audience the most interesting and real experience with direct feelings.

First of all, China's GDP is growing rapidly and the mass consumption level is also improving, and the number of exhibitions is increasing. At the same time, it also involves all aspects of life, such as history, economy, science and so on. In order to make the exhibition more relevant to the theme, the social division of labor has gradually become more distincitve. People need to cooperate with each other to complete a exhibition. Therefore, people's demand for information is also growing. Due to the demand for information, people began to gradually realize the importance of information dissemination and exchange, and take action for it. Such actions often result in conscious and active participation in exhibitions.

Secondly, science and technology is the primary productivity. With the continuous development of various science and technology, interactive technology is also changing with each passing day. The development of this technology is shown in the exhibition with people's active participate in the exhibition, which not only enhances the speed of information dissemination, but also deepens the audience's impression of the development of interactive technology. At the same time, this kind of actively selected information is more conducive to the audience's digestion, absorption and feedback, so as to make the whole exhibition more natural, efficient and interactive.

In the past, the exhibition mode was relatively simple, and the most vivid one was the market. The seller (curator) will exhibit their goods and lock them in a certain space, while the buyer (audience) will visit to obtain the desired products. However, this mode of communication has great disadvantages, and the choice of the exhibits is only determined by the curator. In the later stage, with the development of exhibition design, especially with the development of new media technology in recent years, more buyers (viewers) have greater demand and begin to actively participate in the exhibition, so recent exhibitions pay more attention to audience's requirements. For example, many current exhibition designs have begun to involve "customer participation", changing the traditional one-way communication into multi-party exhibition and multi-party communication. During the exhibition, the public has the opportunity to participate in the whole exhibition or a certain program. For example, some museums carried out public education activities with schools or other groups to attract the masses and effectively mobilize the public's desire and behavior of participation. At this stage, exhibition design is far beyond a simple "sales relationship".

In the early exhibition design, the mode of communication was also relatively simple. People often looked at some pictures, calligraphy and painting, texts and other information with their eyes. The senses of hearing, touching and tasting did not participate in the process. This single sensory experience is static with poor interaction and participation of the audience, which means the efficiency of information dissemination is gradually getting worse. With the development of information technology, this single sensory exhibition design has been gradually eliminated. The audience prefer direct and on-the-spot personal feelings, so there comes enriched exhibition methods. Relying on the development of multimedia technology, people can hear or even touch the "sound" of the exhibits. This multi-sensory combination makes the audience feel more involved and more willing to participate, which improves the efficiency and the speed of information dissemination.

8.5 Integration of the Green Design Concept

As mentioned above, interactive technology can achieve the combination of reality and virtuality. The traditional exhibition design is often limited to real life scenes and needs the support of sufficient materials. Virtual technology, is on the contrary, often has low requirements for the exhibition environment and does not need the support of large number of materials. Moreover, the results and technologies applied in the exhibition can reappear for many times, and reduces the consumption of resources to a certain extent, which is also a representation of green design in exhibition design.

In foreign countries, information technology and new media have an early start and its development in the field of interaction design is also prior to that in China. Although the development of interactive technology in China is growing vigorously, it is still slightly insufficient compared with foreign countries. Firstly, there are few professional discussions in the field of interaction design of new media exhibition design in China, resulting in the lack of solid theoretical foundation. Moreover, teachers need to improve them according to their own reality because the foreign research results can only be used for theoretical reference. Secondly, compared with the excellent foreign technology in the field of multimedia and its diversified effect, China is slightly left behind. However, with the advent of economic globalization, in recent years, China have gradually enhanced the exchange in various fields. Many national museums have gone abroad to hold exhibitions for many times, and world-class exhibitions have frequently been held in our country. This mutual exchange is quite beneficial to the development of interactive technology in China. However, at present, most of the exhibitions in China are still static and lack of exhibition products with multi-sensory combination. These aspects need to be improved in the later stage.

9   Conclusion

There will be various problems in the emergence of any new thing. There are deficiencies and shortcomings in the application of exhibition, such as stability and technical limitations. In the process of exhibition, designers should constantly improve their ability and understand the relevant knowledge of computer, aesthetics, design and other related aspects because the information technology involves new media technology and many other aspects of knowledge, which levels up the requirement for talents. In order to hold a successfully exhibition, senior designers and operators are also needed, which has brought certain challenges to the whole process. Efforts are still needed to solve this problem, which can finally make the digital exhibition more mature and perfect. The development of interaction design was delayed and has a short period. It cannot compete with the same industry around the world. But practice makes true knowledge. At present, the number of exhibitions in China is continuously rising, and artists will have enough time and practice opportunities. Therefore, at present, the development of new media exhibition design in China has been gradually enhanced, which provides a good beginning for the later development. Artistic Works are artificially created by people and closely related to people's way of thinking. Works inspired by their own ideas are artistic creation. The above concept has gradually penetrated into the exhibition, which in turn illustrated the new media art's impact on the exhibition.

References

1. Danilov, V.J.: Science and Technology Centres. MIT Press, Cambridge (1982)
2. Boer, T.: Global user research methods. In: Handbook of Global Research, pp. 145–201 (2010)
3. Flórez Ochoa, R.: Hacia una pedagogía del Conocimiento. McGraw-Hill, Bogotá-Colombia (2000)
4. Dewey, J.: El Arte Como Experiencia. Paidós, Barcelona (2008)
5. Mc Lean, K.: Planning for People in Museum Exhibitions. Association of Science-Technology Centers, Washington (1993)
6. Michel, R.E.: Design Research Now. Birkhäuser Verlag AG, Berlin (2007)
7. Ross, P.R.: Designing behavior in interaction: using aesthetic experience as a mechanism for design. Issue Des. **4**, 3–13 (2010)
8. Saffer, D.: Designing for Interaction: Creating Innovative Applications and Devices. New Riders Publishing, New York (2009)

Smart Cities, Smart Islands, and Intelligent Urban Living

From 'Smart-only' Island Towards Lighthouse of Research and Innovation

Norbert A. Streitz[1][✉] ⓘ, Christine Riedmann-Streitz[2], and Lúcio Quintal[3]

[1] Smart Future Initiative, Frankfurt am Main, Germany
norbert.streitz@smart-future.net
[2] MarkenFactory, Frankfurt am Main, Germany
christine.riedmann-streitz@markenfactory.com
[3] ARDITI, Funchal, Madeira, Portugal
lucio.quintal@arditi.pt

Abstract. This paper presents a systematic approach on how to transform islands into Lighthouses of Research and Innovation (R&I) by moving beyond 'smart-only' islands towards humane, self-aware, and cooperative hybrid islands. It requires the following prerequisites: First, to adopt an Open Innovation 4.0 approach based on the Quintuple Helix Model. Second, to critically reflect on 'smart-only' developments as characterized by the 'Smart Everything Paradigm' and focus on different design trade-offs when designing future smart environments. Third, to be aware of the lessons learned from moving beyond 'smart-only' cities towards humane, self-aware, and cooperative hybrid cities, where 'self-awareness' provides a new definition of 'smartness'. Fourth, to identify the special issues of islands and so called 'Outermost Regions' (ORs) addressed in the EU-funded FORWARD project which provided our application context. Based on these prerequisites, we applied the lessons learned from 'smart-only' cities to 'smart-only' islands, including a semantic extension of the notion of 'hybrid' for islands. A transformation and change approach based on participatory design and associated methods provided the foundation for the Island Design Café held on the island of Madeira in October 2021 with active participation of a group of researchers, stakeholders from local businesses and institutions, and people of Madeira. The goal of the Island Design Café was to develop ideas, strategies, and a road map for transforming Madeira into a 'place to be' as a Lighthouse of Research and Innovation (R&I). The results of this extensive group effort are reported supplemented by conclusions and perspectives for follow-up activities.

Keywords: Citizen-Centered Design · Human-Centered Design · Participatory Design · Design Trade-offs · Human Control · Automation · Artificial Intelligence · Internet of Things · Smart-Everything Paradigm · Privacy · Trust · Human-Technology Symbiosis · Humane City · Hybrid City · Self-aware City · Cooperative City · Smart City · Smart Island · Hybrid Island · Outermost Region · Madeira · Living Lab · Sustainability · SDG · Open Innovation · R&I · Quintuple Helix Model · Participatory Innovation Model · Empowerment-Coherence Concept · Levels of Participation · Big Talk · Transformation · Change · Smart People · Smart Living · Smart Environment · Smart Infrastructure · Smart Economy · Smart Government

© The Author(s), under exclusive license to Springer Nature Switzerland AG 2022
N. A. Streitz and S. Konomi (Eds.): HCII 2022, LNCS 13325, pp. 105–126, 2022.
https://doi.org/10.1007/978-3-031-05463-1_8

1 Introduction and Overview

Islands have always played a special role in history being the subject of dreams, of hopes and expectations. They provided a destination, a goal to reach and finally secure places and safe harbors for those sailing for a long time with no land in sight. While these might be reminiscences of a maritime past, these properties are still valid and become a new meaning in the context of developments we observe sailing under the new flag 'smart island'.

They are part of a general trend that everything must be 'smart': phones, TVs, cars, buildings, cities, and now also islands. Streitz [21] calls this trend the 'Smart-Everything Paradigm' (SEP). It is a mainly technology-driven development where smart objects and services provide the main constituents of our current and future working and living environments. They are based on an Internet of Things (IoT) infrastructure in combination with dedicated software, increasingly relying on Artificial Intelligence (AI) and Machine Learning (ML) which has severe and problematic implications. In parallel, we observe an increasing degree of importunate automation and privacy infringements. Humans are being removed from being the 'operator' and thus in control of their interactions and decisions in their hybrid (virtual and physical) environments. So called 'smart cities' are telling examples of these developments. Thus, we must ask – and answer – the question: *What kind of cities and islands do we want to live in?*

Answering this question requires to address issues of transformation aiming at an improvement of the current status. To achieve the transformation goals in a sustainable fashion and to gain broad acceptance it is necessary to apply proven methods and criteria. Every transformation implies change processes and therefore a corresponding change methodology, e.g., participatory design, is needed.

We investigate these questions and answers in the context of the EU-funded FOR-WARD project [6]. It addresses the specific challenges of the so called 'Outermost Regions' (ORs) of Europe and aims to foster Research Excellence & Innovation Capacity in ORs. The analysis of the status quo provided the 'why' for the transformation needs. Our particular focus is the island of Madeira as an example of a European OR.

A currently common answer to advance transformations is the proposal of ubiquitous and comprehensive digitalization. It results in many cases in a primarily technology-driven development which does not reflect severe implications for humans, society, and environment. Analyzing transformations of cities to 'smart' cities in the framework of the 'Smart-Everything Paradigm' (SEP) [21] reveals the associated problems.

To avoid these problems for the transformation of islands, we apply the lessons learned from 'smart' cities by adapting and elaborating the criteria and features for cities now for outermost regions and islands. *Our guiding thesis for the transformation is to move beyond 'smart-only' cities, regions, and islands towards humane, self-aware, and cooperative hybrid cities, regions, and islands* [23, 26]. We propose to pursue a transformation path determined by converging change processes and participatory design approaches. We also believe that the transformation should be future oriented and not past oriented, while at the same time recognizing and fostering existing strengths that are valid in the future. Creating innovations plays a central role for the transformation, because the goal of becoming a humane, self-aware, and cooperative hybrid island requires not only rethinking and redefining, but rather research and innovation for developing and spreading new functions, services, and properties. For the special case of Madeira as part of the FORWARD project, we proclaimed the goal that *Madeira should become a Lighthouse of Research and Innovation (R&I)*.

This way, Madeira can shape its future under its own steam and with increasing independence and autonomy. The advantage is that beyond the typical R&D stakeholders the civil society and other stakeholders play an important role in the transformation process. To ensure, that the transformation process does not slip into the pitfalls of many smart city processes, we developed a special participatory design as well as a participatory innovation model. Participation, properly understood and implemented, bridges the gap between stakeholder needs and government requirements as well as between different expectations and needs. Moreover, it unlocks hidden strengths and boosters creative and innovative ideas and solutions.

The empirical work based on this framework consisted of an Island Design Café held in Funchal, Madeira, in October 2021 with active participation of a group of researchers, stakeholders from local businesses and institutions, and citizens of Madeira (all experts in their specific areas). The goal of the Island Design Café was to develop ideas, strategies, and a road map for transforming Madeira into a '*place to be*' as a Lighthouse of Research and Innovation (R&I).

2 Islands and Outer Most Regions (ORs)

Islands are not only separated territories of land surrounded by water (and not big enough to be a continent), but they also carry a backpack of associations as mentioned in the introduction. Europe has 147 island territories (659 islands) with an estimated population of 17 million. Half of those islands extend for no more than 50 km^2. While we focus here on a special collection of islands, the European Outermost Regions (ORs) (see Figure 1), and, in particular, on the island of Madeira, many results and insights are valid for islands in general.

Fig. 1. Geographical distribution of the nine European ORs

The nine European Outermost Regions (ORs) of Europe include the Azores (PT), Madeira (PT), Canaries (ES), Guadeloupe (FR), French Guiana (FR), Martinique (FR),

Saint Martin (FR), La Reunion (FR) and Mayotte (FR), and only French Guiana is not an archipelago. ORs are exposed to problems mainly linked to: their remoteness from continental Europe; small size (with concentration of activities in some sectors); limited natural resources; dependent on goods and services supplied from the exterior; higher levels of underemployment and difficult topography.

Despite their low economic and demographic weight in the EU as a whole (5 vs 448 million inhabitants), the ORs also offer advantages to Europe. Its geographical location and its natural environment add another dimension to the European Union: a vast maritime zone and a valuable geostrategic position; privileged places for the implementation of scientific research activities and high technology; a great potential to develop renewable energies and an exceptional natural framework for a safe and environmentally friendly tourism, among others. Located at geostrategic positions across different hemispheres, oceans, and continents (see Figure 1), ORs constitute perfect test beds and living labs for the implementation, monitoring and evaluation of impacts and solutions to current major societal challenges posed to mankind and life on earth in general, namely those associated to Climate Change, Energy Transition and Biodiversity.

3   FORWARD: Fostering Research and Excellence in ORs

The FORWARD H2020 project [6], involving 24 quadruple helix partners from all the nine ORs, aims to boost Research Excellence and Innovation Capacity in ORs. FORWARD is organized in three logical phases: 1) Defining a vision: from a regional diagnosis, passing by a comparative analysis between ORs and co-creation of common joint strategies. 2) Building capacities: through thematic working groups, training, networking, and consortium building activities. 3) Strengthening connections: between research and policymaking and ensuring sustainability and impacts of the project results in the long term. Three main objectives and corresponding approaches have been proposed (see Table 1).

Table 1. Objectives and Approach of the FORWARD Project

FORWARD Objectives	Approach to achieve the Objectives
Improve ORs excellence in research and their innovation potential	By a diagnosis of ORs R&I ecosystems and designing of a joint strategy
Improve their participation in EU research and innovation funded projects	Through a capacity building action plan and co-creation and implementation of common thematic action plans
Link research activities with territorial development	Favoring mutual training and networking with the connecting of research and policymaking

The FORWARD project main activities and results are listed below.

- **Diagnosis of ORs R&I ecosystems** aiming at: 1) Establish a state of play of each OR participation to FP7 & H2020. 2) Explore the main explanatory: lack of connection to major networks, regional innovation system structure and performance, regional organizations characteristics, individual profiles and motives. 3) Construct a collective regional diagnostic and action plan, through the involvement of the local community. 4) Produce comparative analysis of results.
- **OR R&I cooperation: co-creation and implementation of Thematic Action Plans**, aiming at: 1) Identification of R&I themes relevant to ORs. 2) Building inter regional Thematic Working Groups (8 TWGs created). 3) Implementation of the thematic action plans.
- **Capacity building: development & strengthening**, aiming at designing and implementing a Capacity Building Plan in ORs that supports and builds competences in the R&I ecosystem on EU programs, international outreach & ORs regional officers and network.
- **Networking Activities,** aiming at: 1) Organization and participation of networking and brokerage events. 2) Organization of short-term mobilities for researchers.
- **Connecting research and policy making, recommendations, tools, and events** aiming at: 1) Facilitating the dialogue between the research community and policy makers. 2) Contributing to further development and implementation of Smart Specialization Strategies (S3/RIS3). 3) Contributing to more tailored EU policies for ORs and fine-tuned programming of regional policies.

The FORWARD project partners are designing a dedicated *"OR-izon Network"* to continue the work done by the consortium and their regional R&I ecosystems, ensuring the sustainability of the FORWARD legacy after the formal end of the project (planned for June 2022).

4   Open Innovation and the Quintuple Helix Model

The intended transformation of Madeira should adopt an Open Innovation 4.0 approach. Like with software versions, people are labeling different development generations as Open Innovation 2.0, 3.0, 4.0. This indicates a change of mindsets by including a wider range of players and drivers relevant for innovation strategies and processes. They are often connected to the extension of the Triple and Quadruple Helix towards the Quintuple Helix Model[1] (see Figure 2). The inclusion of the natural, resp. the socio-ecological environment implies to consider issues of sustainability. As an example of considering Open Innovation 4.0 as an enhancer of sustainable innovation ecosystems, we quote from Costas and Matias [3]: "Creating an innovative ecosystem has a multilayer effect: It contributes to regional digitalization, technological start-up emergence, open innovation promotion, and new policy enhancement retro-feeding the system. Public policy must create open innovation environments accordingly with the quintuple helix harmonizing the ecosystem to internalize emerging spillovers."

---

[1] https://en.wikipedia.org/wiki/Quadruple_and_quintuple_innovation_helix_framework.

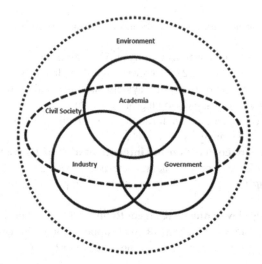

Fig. 2. The five helices of the Quintuple Helix (Source: Wikipedia)

The comprehensive Quintuple Helix approach involves institutional and government bodies, academic and research spheres, industry and business sectors, the civil society with its citizens as well as the natural ecological environment in the innovation process. This new generation of open innovation should lead to stronger economic impact and improved user experience.

Innovation economists believe - based on early ideas by Schumpeter [17] - that what primarily drives economic growth in today's knowledge-based economy is not capital accumulation as neoclassical economics asserts, but innovative capacity spurred by appropriate knowledge and technological externalities. Economic growth in innovation economics is the end-product of:

- knowledge (tacit or implicit vs. codified or explicit)
- regimes and policies allowing for entrepreneurship and innovation
    (=>R&D expenditures, permits and licenses)
- technological spillovers and external effects between collaborative organizations
- systems of innovation that facilitate creative and innovative environments
    (=>clusters, agglomerations, and metropolitan areas).

Since we believe that Silicon Valley or other metropolitan areas are not the only ones providing the necessary framework conditions for creating innovations, we ask the disruptive question: *How about transforming an Island into a Lighthouse of Research and Innovation (R&I) representing a 'place to be' by facilitating a creative environment providing the key factors?*

Before we develop the specific answers to this question, especially for the island of Madeira, we present a framework - the 'Smart Everything Paradigm' - that allows us to position and critically reflect the developments towards smart cities and smart islands, thus extending the problem solution space for the issues raised.

5   The Smart-Everything Paradigm and Design Trade-offs

Innovations and technological progress developed over the last centuries and decades are very much appreciated by most of us because they provide valuable functionality in our everyday life, ease hard physical work, and provide comfort at numerous levels. The flip side of the coin is that our society - at a local and global level - is exposed to many dependencies we usually do not consciously reflect and move into the background, e.g., disposability of proper resources, secure availability of electricity (danger of blackouts) and reliable functioning of traditional software and infrastructure platforms. Soon, we will also be dependent on ubiquitous and pervasive infrastructures providing 'smart' services in many areas of our daily life. We see the beginnings in smart homes, smart cars, and smart cities. Everything must be *'smart'*. It is a self-reinforcing trend resulting from the combination of different developments in IoT, AI, ML, and their combinations. It includes a shift towards substantial partial or even full automation of activities and services which before used to be controlled by human operators. There will be increasing control by AI-based algorithms, which are often non-transparent and not traceable. This is reason enough to reflect on the underlying rationale and challenges associated with what Streitz [21] calls the 'Smart-Everything Paradigm (SEP)'.

Here, we focus on selected core challenges. A major challenge is caused by the technology-driven approaches and results of AI methods or rather ML (much of what is marketed as AI is 'only' machine learning). Streitz [21] identified three problem sets of AI and ML and described examples for each set: a) Inability and error-prone behavior, b) Rigidity, and c) Missing transparency, traceability, and accountability. These problems are not only outside views as demonstrated by a quote of an AI/ML researcher reported by Knight [10]: "We can build these models, but we don't know how they work." There is an increasing awareness that AI/ML 'black boxes' must be critically examined [1]. They are not only rejected by everyday citizens, but also by regulators, authorities, and companies, because they do not meet regulatory, compliance and risk management requirements [5]. The White House report "Preparing for the Future of Artificial Intelligence" [29] called for establishing practices and protocols to build understanding and trust in the mechanisms of algorithms.

One learning is that claims and high expectations about AI/ML are fueled by venture capitalists and stakeholders with vested interests although progress is limited. But the main problem is not failures and limited progress. It is the overall technocentric approach trying to reduce or even eliminate the human from the equation as the alleged reason for errors.

Fortunately, there is light at the horizon, e.g., activities on explainable AI and human-centered AI [9, 18] and awareness of ethical aspects, e.g., IEEE Global Initiative on 'Ethics of Autonomous and Intelligent Systems (A/IS)'. It provides recommendations for Ethically Aligned Design [7] which connect to our design trade-offs (see section 5.1). A discussion of the IEEE recommendations is provided in [24]. In April 2021, the European Commission published a regulatory framework proposal on AI[2], part of the Coordinated Plan on AI. They aim at guaranteeing the safety and fundamental rights of people and businesses. Thus, critical, but constructive views proliferate.

---

[2] https://digital-strategy.ec.europa.eu/en/policies/regulatory-framework-ai.

5.1   Design Trade-offs Based on Human-Technology Symbiosis

The counter proposal to the technocentric version of the 'Smart-Everything Paradigm (SEP)' is based on a different view of the relationship between humans and technology. In Stephanidis et al. [19], 'Human-Technology Symbiosis' was identified as the major approach for our understanding of how to design future 'smart' environments. It is based on the Greek word 'symbiosis' for 'to live together' and defines how humans will live and work harmoniously, cooperatively, and respectfully together with technology. This human-centered perspective is closely related to the Ambient Intelligence approach [20, 24, 25] developed in contrast to a technocentric artificial intelligence view. It goes beyond a traditional user-centered design of human-computer interaction and addresses more comprehensive issues of human-environment interaction [20, 22].

There is usually not a unique solution when designing human-technology systems. Designers evaluate different options meeting the objectives and desired properties and consider the constraints. The mechanisms to deal with the limiting factors are 'design trade-offs'. We refer here to two major design trade-offs described before in [21].

• Design Trade-off: Human Control and Empowerment vs. Automated Systems

This design trade-off addresses the observed shift towards more or even full automation in human-technology systems. Humans are increasingly removed from being the operator, supervisor or at least being in charge, thus losing control and the option of being empowered. Services and devices as well as the interactions with humans are controlled by algorithms. In most cases, they are created by an external institution with no option to interfere. They are opaque and not accountable although in many cases error prone. The design goal is to accomplish a balance between keeping the human in the loop and in control vs. automated system behavior as, e.g., in fully automated vehicles at SAE Level 5 [16] and autonomous robots or drones. Thus, one is confronted with a design trade-off between 'human control and empowerment vs. system automation' [21]. One could also say that "people should be empowered to own the loop" and not be at the mercy of an automated system with no means of intervention. In his book on 'Smart Cities and Connected Intelligence', Komninos [11] relates directly to this view and states: "Connectivity and integration of different types of intelligence – human, collective, organizational, AI – offer capabilities and ways for addressing the grand challenges of the 21st century".

• Design-Trade-off: Usable Privacy vs. Importunate Smartness

This design trade-off addresses the conflict of assuring privacy vs. providing smartness by collecting and exploiting personal data. Most people agree at an abstract level that privacy is an important aspect of their life. Looking at their digital activities in social communities, e-commerce, and use of location-based services, shows that privacy is often compromised. The observation that many, especially younger users do not care too much about it is also called the 'privacy paradox' [2]. Our interpretation is that users are not provided with transparent, easy, flexible access to control their privacy settings.

Obviously, a smart system can be 'smarter' offering a personalized service if it has more data and knowledge about the person and the environment compared with a system with no or insufficient data. There is a tricky trade-off between providing smartness (by collecting and processing data for personalization) and maintaining privacy. On the other hand, people have the right to control which data are collected and exploited. Thus, the challenge is to find the right balance. Streitz [21] proposed that the respective person determines and controls the extent of this balance. Users should have a transparent view of their options: how much privacy are they willing to compromise for which benefits they get in return. As a basis, system designers must be aware of and implement the requirements of the European General Data Protection Regulations [4] (adopted already in 2016), which took effect on May 25, 2018. All companies doing business in Europe with European citizens must adhere to them – independent of the location of their registered headquarters. More aspects of this design trade-off are discussed in [21]. Among others, the ubiquitous appearance of 'urban spies' (e.g., smart cars with sensors not being shut off when parking, smart streetlights using radar for observing the streets) creates new challenges for dealing with privacy in real world urban environments [23].

- **Combination of Design Trade-offs**

In a realistic setting, design trade-offs do not exist independent of each other. The overall design should account for combinations of the different aspects expressed in the requirements of the trade-offs discussed above. One could summarize this approach as "smart spaces make people smarter" [21]. This is achieved by providing information and facilitating the situation so that informed decisions can be made, and mature actions can be taken by responsible people. At the same time, the extent and quality of the necessary data collection and aggregation is under the control of the individual deciding dynamically on the pros (added value benefits) and cons (privacy infringements). The overall insight is to realize true human-technology symbiosis. Promising examples can be found in human-centered automation resulting in 'human-robot collaboration' via 'collaborative robots' or 'cobots' assisting humans and augmenting their capabilities.

6   Moving from 'Smart-only' Cities to Humane, Self-aware, and Cooperative Hybrid Cities

In the next step, we apply our insights on how to deal with the 'Smart-Everything Paradigm' in the domain of 'smart cities', a research and application area that needs new perspectives as expressed also by Komninos [11] and McKenna [12]. The answer to our guiding question *What kind of cities do we want to live in?* is based on moving from 'smart-only' cities towards *humane, self-aware, and cooperative hybrid cities*. Since the foundation is a recap of previous work [21–23], we keep it short here and provide only the essentials needed for the transfer to the main issue of this paper, i.e., transforming 'smart-only' islands. The main aspects of our vision of future cities are:

- **Smart Cities as self-aware Cities.** We redefined the smartness of a city by how much the city knows about itself and how it communicates the collected data and their aggregations to its citizens and to the city administration. This approach relates to the open data model and motivates citizens to contribute relevant city data themselves and in return have access to data collected by the city administration creating a win-win situation.

- **Citizens in the Loop.** Keeping citizens in the loop facilitating co-provision, co-creation and co-exploitation is the foundation of a citizen-centered design approach. It enables citizens to develop a better and more comprehensive perspective of the city when they engage and participate in urban issues and decisions.
- **Privacy as a Basic Right of Citizens.** Contributing and being part of the processes for creating a comprehensive perspective of the many facets that make up a city and describing the state of a self-aware city in a dynamic fashion must be in accordance with a transparent privacy governance. The requirements of the EU-GDPR [4] are a good reference and obligatory for all services and activities in European cities.

  So far, privacy infringements are mainly discussed in the virtual world of social media, e-commerce, etc. But the main privacy challenges will be in current and future urban environments with ubiquitous sensors, location-based services, etc. constituting hybrid environments. The concept of 'ambient privacy' provides a new approach of addressing them. For more details see [23].
- **Future Cities are Hybrid Cities.** The distinctive treatment of virtual worlds and real worlds was useful and valuable as long as they were reflected in different worlds of people's experiences. With increasing coexistence, overlap and finally smooth transitions between them, one can no longer treat them separately. Real urban environments tend to contain more and more smart artefacts augmented by sensors and actuators, constituting 'digital shadows' and corresponding entities in the virtual world that can be accessed and controlled remotely. In addition, they are connected and can influence each other. Due to the problems of the 'disappearing computer' approach [20, 22], citizens are usually not aware of the sensors embedded in the environment causing a severe privacy problem (see above). Thus, it is necessary to develop and disseminate 'hybrid affordances' [23] and context-dependent notifications [15], providing transparency and informing about potential interaction options in the hybrid urban environment.
- **Citizen ⇔ Cooperative City Contract (CCCC).** Viewing citizens, city administration and additional service providers as 'mutual cooperation partners' was the basis for proposing the '*Citizen ⇔ Cooperative City Contract (CCCC)*' [21, 23]. It requires to develop a shared vision and a common purpose. Based on the common purpose one must develop trust and respect of all parties involved despite vested interests and certain conflicts. They form the basis for creating new citizen-centered city operations as well as business models for delivering urban services. The CCCC defines the rules and regulations for providing the services and guarantees the rights of the citizens in terms of performance, security, and privacy. An approach based on block chains providing so called 'smart contracts' could be the foundation for the implementation of the CCCC.

These characteristics and requirements for moving beyond 'smart-only' cities provide the foundation for rethinking and redefining the current notion of 'smart islands' [26], addressed in the next sections by applying the lessons learned from cities to islands.

7   Rethinking Smart-only Islands

Parallel to the increasing number of activities targeting the special challenges of islands in terms of climate and energy issues, sustainability, clean water, transportation, waste, ICT infrastructure, etc., the term 'smart island' is gaining popularity. Especially in the context of applying digitalization as the prominent means for developing solutions, almost everything is now labeled as 'smart' according to the 'Smart-Everything Paradigm' described in section 5. Accordingly, one can find numerous initiatives and projects associated with the term 'smart island'. Without claiming completeness, we list a few of them for information purposes.

In Europe, there is the Smart Island Initiative[3] with 35 islands from 16 European countries. It formulated a declaration with rather general "action points towards becoming smart, inclusive, and thriving societies" and organized two major events (Smart Islands Forum) in 2016 and 2018. According to the website and its news section, it does not seem to be active currently. According to its history website[4], it builds on several previous activities starting in 1993 with "ISLENET: European Islands Energy and Environment Network" funded by the European Commission, was continued in 2009 with the ISLE-PACT project[5] and the Pact of Islands signed by 64 insular communities in 2011, followed by several specific projects. A national activity in Greece is DAFNI - Network of Sustainable Greek Islands[6] which was founded in 2006 with 56 members from 52 island municipalities. Another currently still active initiative with a particular focus is "Clean Energy for EU Islands"[7]. There are numerous other activities, workshops, conferences, newsletters, etc. in and beyond Europe, e.g., the Conference of Peripheral Maritime Regions (CMPR) bringing together more than 150 regions from 24 states from the European Union and beyond, with its special Islands Commission[8].

7.1   Moving Towards Humane, Self-aware, and Cooperative Hybrid Islands

Guided by the lessons learned from the critical analysis of 'smart-only' cities [21, 23], we can reflect on how to move beyond 'smart-only' islands towards humane, self-aware, and cooperative hybrid islands. A major aspect is to develop (in analogy to the CCCC for cities in Sect. 3) an '*Islanders ⇔ Cooperative Island Contract*' (ICIC). Rethinking 'smart-only' islands implies to facilitate co-provision, co-creation, and co-exploration by keeping islanders in the loop and in control and respecting their rights on privacy. Beyond several analogies to cities, we must account for specific characteristics of islands. This includes to extend the semantics of the property 'hybrid' used before for cities. In '*Hybrid Islands*', the term 'hybrid' is now used to indicate the combination of several separate, sometimes opposite properties. We now define islands as 'hybrid' in the following sense [26]:

---

[3] http://www.smartislandsinitiative.eu.

[4] https://www.smartislandsinitiative.eu/en/history.php.

[5] https://www.islepact.eu/

[6] https://dafninetwork.gr/en/

[7] https://www.euislands.eu/

[8] https://cpmr-islands.org/

- combining and integrating real and virtual environments (like cities)
- combining urban and rural environments on a limited defined territory
- combining earth and water (or land and sea) as two material states.

Designing Hybrid Islands requires to look at the boundaries between the different situations and states and a careful design of the 'hybrid seams' between them facilitating smooth transitions. Due to their limited and defined territory, islands can very well serve as test beds for prototypes and proof-of-concept demonstrators and provide Living Labs. These features can be part of the foundation for initiatives to transform an island into a humane, self-aware, cooperative and hybrid island. But there is more to it as we will show in the following sections when we apply the general ideas of a participatory transformation and change approach to the specific case of transforming the island of Madeira towards a Lighthouse of Research and Innovation (R&I).

8   A Transformation Approach Based on Participatory Design

8.1   Successful Transformation Starts with a Visionary Objective

The overall goal was formulated in the FORWARD project [6]: European outermost regions, in our case Madeira, should improve their Research Excellence and their Innovation potential. Since 'improvement' is a relative and very general goal description, it was of strategic importance to sharpen the target.

One strategic way for improvement is to reduce vulnerabilities as "concentration of activities in some sectors", "smallness of the market" or "dependence on goods and services supplied from the exterior" through research and innovation (the obvious path).

Based on the insight that the strategic mindset determines the result, we redefined the goal. For example, in designing road traffic, it makes a huge difference, if the goal is to reduce road accidents or to have a so called 'vision zero'[9] postulating that deaths or serious injuries must not be accepted. It started in Sweden, spread across Europe, and was also adopted in Canada and several states in the US. Currently, we observe examples of different strategic mindsets on how to cope with Covid-19 ('flatten the curve', 'herd immunity' or 'zero covid'). Different mindsets result in huge differences in terms of acceptance of necessary actions by people and in the overall results.

Thus, we modified the goal from 'improvement' to a declared clear objective that is attractive, ambitious, and achievable and moreover positions Madeira – according to its strengths – within the group of outermost regions. This resulted in the declared objective: To make the island of Madeira the '*place to be*' by becoming a *Lighthouse of Research and Innovation* – as a humane, self-aware, cooperative, hybrid island.

We adopt here the new paradigm of the Open Innovation 4.0 approach. This is due to the fact, that innovation could have a huge impact, but only if it creates added values that matter and results in sustainable improvements.

---

[9] https://visionzero.lu/en/origin/
https://en.wikipedia.org/wiki/Vision_Zero

8.2 Successful Transformation Requires Understanding the Change Process

An island, as well as a city, a region, or an organization forms a community. Transforming a community is always a process of change. Applying a shortcut to success by announcing what should be done (the classical top-down-approach), hinders change more than that it promotes it. Thus, it is of critical importance to consciously decide on the approach and respect the crucial factors of successful change. Still, about 70% of all change projects fail. One acknowledged change model is the "8-step process for leading change" developed by Kotter [13].

Nevertheless, when it comes to the transformation of a city into a smart city many approaches are still 'top-down', which we call the *Transformation Approach* TA 1.0. Here, only few selected people are in charge, decide on a plan, put it into practice and communicate it to the stakeholders. One example of such a TA 1.0 is the often-criticized effort of building the smart city Songdo in South Korea[10]. TA 1.0 is only apparently more efficient and faster. It leads to the accumulation of hurdles, especially in smart city or smart island projects, which prevent the change from being accepted and from bringing the intended benefits to the stakeholders.

While TA 2.0 is more oriented to respect the needs of stakeholders, only the next level, Transformation Approach TA 3.0, follows the concept of an integrated top-down and bottom-up approach combined with an interdisciplinary participatory cooperative process. Here, islanders' needs and wishes, government goals, requirements of business, education, culture, and environment as well as new technologies improving life and work are linked and considered in a holistic view.

8.3 Participatory Design Creating Ownership and Acceptance of Innovation

TA 1.0, TA 2.0, and TA 3.0 are tightly connected with different levels of participation – as is the success of transformation and change. Just like the TA-level, the depth of possible participation determines the quality of the results. In this context, it is necessary to mention that informing people does not mean that they actually participate, which is a common misunderstanding. Therefore, we present a taxonomy of different *Levels of Participation* (LoP) (see Figure 3).

The levels 'LoP 1 = information' and 'LoP 2 = consultation' are one-dimensional instruments: people are informed, or they are asked for their wishes and needs. The effect is mainly a reinforcement of the status quo. Only when people are invited to participate and to be active, there is the chance that hidden strengths and new ideas can emerge leading to innovations, new business models and a lively community.

Creative processes are based on exchange, thinking ahead of other people's ideas, get inspired by ideas and statements of others. Acceptance of the results and ownership (which means being a promoter of the project and being committed to make it successful) emerges only in a real participatory process. Only at higher levels of participation ('LoP 3 = contribute/co-design' and – if possible – 'LoP 4 = co-decision'), valuable wisdom is unlocked, and incredible ideas emerge. Moreover, it is here, where broad acceptance, commitment, engagement, and ownership is created. Successful change requires participatory formats empowering and inviting active contributions and involvement.

---

[10] https://www.archdaily.com/962924/building-a-city-from-scratch-the-story-of-songdo-korea.

Participatory Levels of Formats

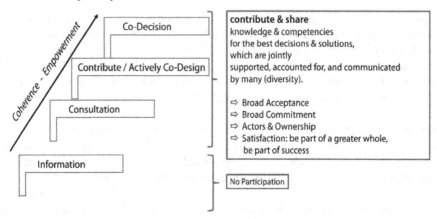

Fig. 3. Taxonomy of different levels of participation (LoP). (Copyright C. Riedmann-Streitz)

Consequently, creating the Madeira Islander Participatory Design followed a special 'mindset for success.' We strongly believe that transformations of cities and islands cannot be subordinated to individual political and economic interests or to what is technologically feasible [14]. Therefore, professional, recognized methods and instruments should be used to make cities/islands livable and prosperous in the long term. The starting point is an attractive vision and a strong identity. The city and the island of the future should be developed in a participatory, cooperative manner to release existing knowledge and skills and to strengthen acceptance, identification, and commitment. Simply because: there is no vibrant community without committed humans.

9   The Madeira Island Design Café

The Madeira Island Design Café was conceived according to TA 3.0. and stakeholder level of participation LoP 3.0, named *'Islander Participatory Design'*. It was designed as a special contribution to the FORWARD project addressing Excellence in Research and Innovation in Madeira. The conversational creative process strengthens a culture of collaborative research and engaging in constructive dialogues around challenging and critical questions. There are *three key objectives* of the Madeira Island Design Café:

1. Strengthening and increasing Madeira's *Excellence in R&I* by

   - identifying key parameters of humane, self-aware, cooperative, hybrid islands, and applying them for the transformation of Madeira,
   - identifying current and future fields of excellence and competitive advantages of Madeira,
   - considering Madeira as a 'living laboratory' for designing islands of the future by focusing on the innovative and creative potential.

2. Strengthening the regional, national, European, and worldwide *Visibility and Recognition* of Madeira.
3. Creating a *road map* for *"Madeira as a Lighthouse of R&I"* – as a plan-to-action and a starting point of future research and follow-ups during implementation phase.

9.1 Key Elements Providing Innovation, Focus, and Orientation

The Madeira Island Design Café was dedicated to enable and empower transformation. Therefore, it was essential to show and practice with the participants a proven way for a successful transformational process avoiding the classical pitfalls and fostering innovative ideas and approaches. *Three key elements* form the basis of the Design Café:

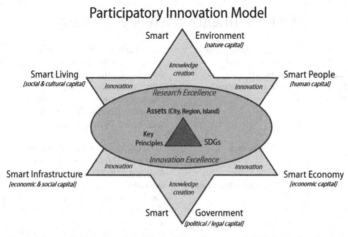

Fig. 4. The Participatory Innovation Model contains the essential 'fields of action' for the development of a 'really smart' (in the new sense as defined before) island/city/region: Smart Environment (energy & environment), Smart People (access to information & education), Smart Economy (industry, trade), Smart Government (information, digitization, guidelines) Smart Infrastructure (IoT, ICT, Security, Data Platforms) Smart Living (Mobility, Health, Society, Culture). (Copyright: Christine Riedmann-Streitz).

The Participatory Innovation Model. The work was structured by the six-dimensional 'Participatory Innovation Model' (PI-M) shown in Figure 4. Its dimensions have an overlap with a taxonomy proposed by Giffinger et al. [8] who had the objective to evaluate and rank cities. Among others, it differs with respect to positioning infrastructure and mobility. Furthermore, PI-M facilitates a structured process for providing access to existing knowledge and information and allowing to exploit valuable synergies

Frames. The work was guided by overarching 'frames.' Shaping the future towards a declared goal must necessarily consider at least three aspects: 1) Communicating a common understanding of the goal. 2) Identifying and respecting identity-forming characteristics (here: of Madeira). 3) Identifying and following indispensable future requirements (here: the 17 UN Sustainable Development Goals – SDGs [28]).

Interdisciplinarity. The invited participants were researchers, stakeholders from local businesses and institutions, and citizens of Madeira – an interdisciplinary group of experts in their fields. All were familiar with the conceptual framework of 'Moving Be-yond Smart-Only Islands' towards 'Humane, Self-aware, Cooperative, Hybrid Islands.

9.2   Methods to Empower and Ease Transformation

Every transformation is a change and changes are always difficult because our brain loves the accustomed and practiced. Therefore, proven methods are needed to empower and ease the transformation.

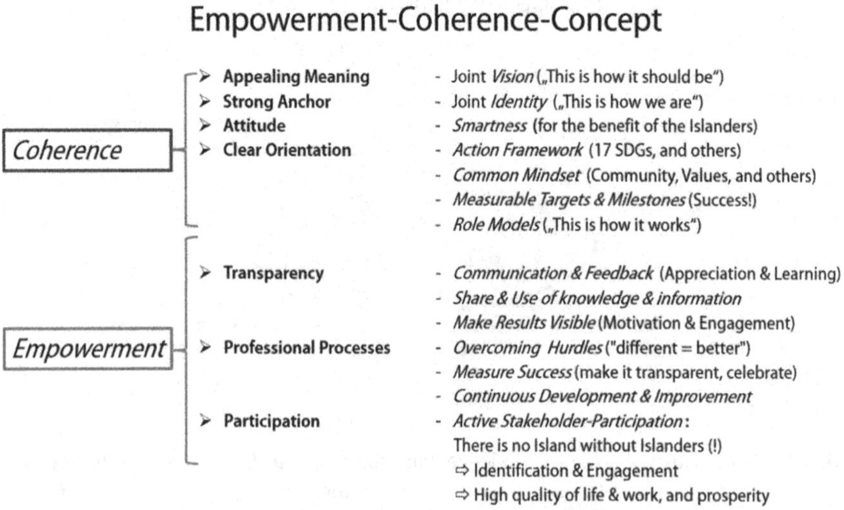

Empowerment-Coherence-Concept

Coherence	➤ Appealing Meaning	- Joint *Vision* („This is how it should be")
	➤ Strong Anchor	- Joint *Identity* („This is how we are")
	➤ Attitude	- *Smartness* (for the benefit of the Islanders)
	➤ Clear Orientation	- *Action Framework* (17 SDGs, and others)
		- *Common Mindset* (Community, Values, and others)
		- *Measurable Targets & Milestones* (Success!)
		- *Role Models* („This is how it works")
Empowerment	➤ Transparency	- *Communication & Feedback* (Appreciation & Learning)
		- *Share & Use of knowledge & information*
		- *Make Results Visible* (Motivation & Engagement)
	➤ Professional Processes	- *Overcoming Hurdles* ("different = better")
		- *Measure Success* (make it transparent, celebrate)
		- *Continuous Development & Improvement*
	➤ Participation	- *Active Stakeholder-Participation*:
		There is no Island without Islanders (!)
		⇨ Identification & Engagement
		⇨ High quality of life & work, and prosperity

Fig. 5. The empowerment-coherence-concept (Copyright: Christine Riedmann-Streitz)

Empowerment-Coherence-Concept. One crucial approach is the 'Empowerment to Change'. Decisive questions during changes are: Why and where to? What gives us the necessary orientation? We derived the Empowerment-Coherence-Concept [14] (Figure 5), from the success drivers in change management. It ensures a value-based consistent process, triggering engagement, ownership, and broad acceptance of the results.

Easing Transformation via Nudging. There is a proven instrument for easing transformations from concept to lived reality. This instrument makes it easy for individuals to jump in and engage. It is called '*nudging*'. According to the *nudge theory* developed by Thaler [27], nudges may help people to exercise better self-control. Nudges bridge the gap between knowing and doing by steering individuals in a particular direction without imposing any regulatory or financial sanctions as well as by making it easy for people to choose the 'better option'.

Nudges help people because behavioral economics has shown that people often choose the easiest route, the default answer, or the first option they are presented with. Thus, nudging means changing the choice architecture (the way in which potential decisions or products are designed and presented). A nudge is any aspect of the choice architecture that alters people's behavior in a predictable way without forbidding any options or significantly changing their economic incentives. Adopting nudges help people to change their behavior. It is of highest importance that the intervention must be easy and cheap to avoid – and that the nudge is grounded in democratic participation, digital fairness and equity, and transparency. Nudges are no mandates. They involve no sanctions, commands, or bans.

9.3 Process and Results

The results of this systematic approach on how to transform islands into Lighthouses of Research and Innovation and not being trapped by a 'smart-only" approach was elaborated in the format of a specific and consistent road map for Madeira to become a Lighthouse of R&I – as a humane, self-aware, and cooperative hybrid island. The road map is a milestone and starting point for the follow-up realization of selected projects. The results are grounded in the leadership approach formulated in the strategic question, discussed by the interdisciplinary group in the participatory format called *Big Talk*.

Smart People *[human capital]*	**Collaboration**	How to promote collaboration between stakeholders, especially between academia and industry?
	Talents	How to leverage local talent and get advantage of it? How to attract talented people to Madeira?
Smart Economy *[economic capital]*	**Diversification** **Talents** **Sustainability**	Economic Diversification (for not being dependent on tourism) Digital Nomads for R&I Smart Tourism
Smart Environment *[nature capital]*	**Sustainability**	Renewable Energy. New Energy Supply. Food Production Systems. Take advantage of the blue economy that surrounds Madeira. Energy & water consumption digitized and available to people in real time.
Smart Infrastructure *[economic & social capital]*	**Innovation /** **Madeira as testbed**	Create a pilot zone in the ocean to test the new ideas & projects.

Excerpt of 40 Big Topics for Madeira elaborated during BIG TALK.

Fig. 6. Excerpt of the results: 40 Big Topics for Madeira

The guiding strategic issue of the *Big Talk* was "What are the big questions that move us to make Madeira the Lighthouse of R&I?" The participants discussed and prioritized their ideas, based on the Participatory Innovation Model (Figure 4). The *Big Talk*, framed by the assets of Madeira, the 17 UN SDGs, and structured by the Participatory Innovation Model, resulted in about 40 Big Topics for Madeira (see Figure 6).

After the *Big Talk*, the experts selected four essential key questions with highest priority to reach the declared goal: 1) In which fields/topics should Madeira become a testbed for a self-aware island to foster successful implementation of new, innovative ideas? 2) Island as a service – What are the services that should be part of the Islander ⇔ Cooperative Island Contract (ICIC)? 3) How could Madeira become a Lighthouse of R&I by exploiting the unique three hybrid dimensions, a) real ⇔ virtual, b) urban ⇔ rural, and c) earth/land ⇔ water/sea? 4) Madeira's maritime environment ocean: How to create a pilot-zone in the ocean to test new ideas and projects?

These four key questions were then discussed with the aim to develop ideas and rough concepts having an impact for Madeira. This was organized in a special participatory setting, where subgroups worked at four tables (with one question each) in a rotating process so that each subgroup addressed all questions but building on the ideas created by the previous subgroup at a table. In this way, all participants contributed to all key questions in an iterative process. A big, focused picture emerged about key drivers and key activities for achieving the overall goal. One of the four tables was dedicated to the ICIC. These participants discussed it from the perspective of 'Island-as-a-service'. Four fields for activities were identified and further elaborated (see Figure 7).

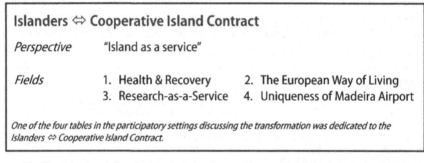

Fig. 7. 'Island as a Service' in the Islanders ⇔ Cooperative Island Contract (ICIC)

The interdisciplinary group of stakeholders decided to focus on four of the six dimensions of the Participatory Innovation Model (Figure 4):

Smart People covers the ideas on exploiting existing resources and knowledge by building collaborative value creation with strong networking of relevant stakeholders. This includes fostering creativity, promoting proximity, and increasing the typical strength of Madeira for attracting more talents in Madeira, but especially from abroad.

Smart Economy was framed by the requirements of the SDGs and focused on economic independence from tourism. If tourism, then it should be transformed to 'smart' in the sense of sustainable tourism. Moreover, entrepreneurship, excellence of research and innovation as well as 'glocal' interconnectedness were discussed in depth.

Smart Environment. This refers to the assets of Madeira and the 'blue economy' surrounding the island. One concept should allow islanders to monitor their energy and water consumption in real time, enabling them to change their behavior to 'the better'.

Smart Infrastructure focused on the third hybrid dimension (land/earth ⇔ sea/water) with the aim of creating a pilot zone in the ocean beneficial for Madeira and the rest of the world. This concept exploits the hybrid character of an island by combining e.g., an experimental pilot zone in the sea with energy issues at sea and land. Moreover, new interdisciplinary business models were created.

After the development of the rough concepts, answering big questions of the transformation of Madeira, consequently, the interdisciplinary group created nudges that should support Madeira to achieve its lighthouse goals and promote islander engagement. Those nudges were applied to the key activities. Well-designed nudges also support the shift from the criticized approach of a 'smart-only' island where islanders are regarded and function as passive data-providing subjects to a participatory approach of a humane, self-aware, cooperative, hybrid island perceiving islanders as active contributors and informed decision makers in the sense of the 'Islanders ⇔ Cooperative Island Contract'. In this way, Islanders are motivated and get involved in the 'management' of Madeira issues and in co-designing of innovations beneficial for all of Madeira.

An extensive report was prepared presenting the ideas, concepts and approaches resulting from the Madeira Island Design Café. It included suggestions for future work based on the road map and beyond. The results and the report were very well received by the Madeira organizers and the participants of the Island Design Café.

10   Conclusions and Outlook

The results and the positive feedback show that the carefully prepared Madeira Island Design Café – based on an innovative conceptual framework and a structured toolbox with fine-tuned participatory design methods – yields excellent results. Participants were very motivated and highly engaged, produced creative ideas and innovative solutions. They expressed how valuable the whole experience was for them, especially in terms of knowledge transfer and new ideas for their own future activities.

Follow-up activities in Madeira. The report opens new perspectives and provides sound chances for relevant follow-up activities. The results indicate that a clear focus for further activities should be on four aspects: 1) *Talents* (attract, develop, retain, involve, collaborate, better use of existing resources). 2) *Autonomy and Independence* of Madeira: focus on human capital and resources, innovation addressing local needs, economic diversification, testbeds for innovation, reconsidering supply and value chains. 3) *Sustainability*: covering energy transition, consumption, smart tourism, and circular economy. 4) The *European Way of Living*: Europe suffers from fragmentation at various levels. Madeira, where islanders and tourists represent a diversity of lifestyles, cultural heritages, and languages, could become a social integration laboratory and a flagship of the European Way of Living, sending a strong signal for a united Europe.

After the Design Café, several activities started in Madeira or are in the application phase for funding in the following areas (in accordance with topics in Figure 6): 1) *Blue Economy*: Related to the proposal of a 'pilot zone to test new ideas', a new research vessel is under construction as well as the installation of a test bed area for oceanic technologies (marine renewable energy, aquaculture, artificial reefs, ocean observation, monitoring marine environment, algae production for CO_2 capture). They are part of Madeira's Operational Program 2021–2027. 2) *Economic Diversification* (beyond tourism): Initiatives promoted by ARDITI, e.g., the Smart Islands Hub (SIH) being part of the national network proposal submitted in February 2022 to the European Digital Innovation Hubs, and the Startup Madeira and the startNOW acceleration program 2022. 3) *Sustainable Agriculture and Food Production*: The proposal 'Boost Agriculture Research in Madeira' was submitted by the University of Madeira to the EC Twinning call in January 2022. It targets assessment and monitoring of agrosystems, improving crops resiliency to new climate constraints and sustainability of food production.

Transfer and scaling to other islands. The results and feedback from the Island Design Café show that rethinking the 'old' notion of 'smart islands' has a great potential for future developments not only in Madeira, but for all Outermost Regions, the many islands in the Mediterranean Sea and along the coastlines of Europe, and finally at a worldwide scale. Characteristics of islands are physical isolation, respectively being surrounded by water, and proximity of people due to short to medium distances of locations and institutions. Rethinking, restructuring, and empowering the so-called 'local network integration' is a central lever for future success. It also is a booster for an island becoming a flagship for selected exceptional competences. Identifying and labeling the assets of an island is important to strengthen the awareness of its assets and uniqueness of a particular island. This is the basis for creating a unique identity and new strong brand, e.g., beyond traditional tourism, and thus creating new options and perspectives.

Acknowledgements. This activity was supported by the EU-funded project FORWARD "Boosting Research Excellence & Innovation Capacity in EU's Outermost Regions". The first two authors like to thank the Madeira partners of FORWARD, especially Rui Caldeira (President of ARDITI), Lucio Quintal (ARDITI), and Élia Vieira (University of Madeira), for their support, including the invitation to and the arrangement of the visit in Madeira.

References

1. AI NOW: Algorithmic Accountability for the Public Sector (2021). https://www.opengovpa rtnership.org/wp-content/uploads/2021/08/executive-summary-algorithmic-accountability. pdf. Accessed 6 February 2022
2. Barth, S., de Jong, M.: The privacy paradox – Investigating discrepancies between expressed privacy concerns and actual online behavior. *Telematics and Informatics* **34**(7), 1038–1058. https://doi.org/10.1016/j.tele.2017.04.013
3. Costa, J., Matias, J.: Open Innovation 4.0 as an enhancer of sustainable innovation ecosystems. Sustainability **12**(19), 8112 (2020). https://doi.org/10.3390/su12198112
4. EU-GDPR. https://www.eugdpr.org/ is currently under construction. An alternative is: https:// gdpr.eu/. Accessed February 2022
5. Financial Stability Board: Artificial intelligence and machine learning in financial services (2017). https://www.fsb.org/2017/11/artificial-intelligence-and-machine-learning-in-financial-service/. Accessed February 2022
6. FORWARD Project: Boosting Research Excellence & Innovation Capacity in EU's Outermost Regions. https://forward-h2020.eu/. Accessed February 2022
7. IEEE (Institute of Electrical and Electronics Engineers): IEEE Ethics in Action in Autonomous and Intelligent Systems. https://ethicsinaction.ieee.org. Accessed February 2022

8. Giffinger, R., Fertner, C., Kramar, H., Kalasek, R., Pichler-Milanovic, N., Meijers, E.: Smart cities - Ranking of European Medium-Sized Cities. Report of the Centre of Regional Science (SRF), Vienna University of Technology. http://www.smart-cities.eu/download/smart_cities_final_report.pdf. Accessed February 2022

9. HCAI: European network of Human-Centered Artificial Intelligence. https://www.humane-ai.eu/. Accessed February 2022

10. Knight, W.: The dark secret at the heart of AI *MIT Technology Review* (2017). https://www.technologyreview.com/2017/04/11/5113/the-dark-secret-at-the-heart-of-ai/. Accessed February 2022

11. Komninos, N.: Smart Cities and Connected Intelligence: Platforms, Ecosystems and Network Effects. 292 p. Routledge, Taylor & Francis (2020). https://www.taylorfrancis.com/books/mono/10.4324/9780367823399/smart-cities-connected-intelligence-nicos-komninos. ISBN: 978-0-367-42305-6

12. McKenna, H.P.: Perspectives on smart cities. In: Seeing Smart Cities Through a Multi-dimensional Lens Perspectives, Relationships, and Patterns for Success, pp. 3–16. Springer, Cham (2021). https://doi.org/10.1007/978-3-030-70821-4_1

13. Kotter, J.P.: Leading Change. Harvard Business School Press. Boston. https://www.kotterinc.com/8-step-process-for-leading-change/. Accessed February 2022

14. Riedmann-Streitz, C.: Achieving broad acceptance - success factors of effective participation. Keynote at "Digital Cities – Digital Regions - Smart development of municipalities" Hessen Ministry for Digitalization (2021). https://markenfactory.com/focus-topics/smarte-staedte-regionen-inseln-und-die-relevanz-der-wirkungsvollen-partizipation/

15. Röcker, C., Bayon, V., Memisoglu, M., Streitz, N.A.: Context-dependent email notification using ambient displays and mobile devices. In: Tarumi, H., Li, Y., Yoshida, T. (eds.). Proceedings of the International IEEE Conference on Active Media Technology (AMT 2005), 19–21 May 2005. pp. 137–138 (2005). https://doi.org/10.1109/AMT.2005.1505288

16. SAE: Taxonomy and definitions for terms related to driving automation systems for on-road motor vehicles. SAE standard J3016. Original in 2014, revised in 2016, 2018 and 2021. https://www.sae.org/standards/content/j3016_202104/. Accessed February 2022

17. Schumpeter, J.A.: Capitalism, Socialism, and Democracy. Harper & Brothers, New York (1942)

18. Shneiderman, B.: Human-Centered AI. Oxford University Press, London (2022)

19. Stephanidis, C., et al.: Seven HCI grand challenges. International Journal Human-Computer Interaction **35**(14), 1229–1269 (2019). https://doi.org/10.1080/10447318.2019.1619259

20. Streitz, N.A.: From human–computer interaction to human–environment interaction: ambient intelligence and the disappearing computer. In: Stephanidis, C., Pieper, M. (eds.) UI4ALL 2006. LNCS, vol. 4397, pp. 3–13. Springer, Heidelberg (2007). https://doi.org/10.1007/978-3-540-71025-7_1

21. Streitz, N.: Beyond 'smart-only' cities: redefining the 'smart-everything' paradigm. Journal of Ambient Intelligence and Humanized Computing **10**(2), 791–812 (2019). https://doi.org/10.1007/s12652-018-0824-1

22. Streitz, N.A.: Empowering citizen-environment interaction vs. importunate computer-dominated interaction: let's reset the priorities! In: Escalona, M.J., Ramirez, A.J., Silva, H.P., Constantine, L., Helfert, M., Holzinger, A. (eds.) Computer-Human Interaction Research and Applications. Communications in Computer and Information Science, vol. 1351, pp. 41–59. Springer, Cham (2021). https://doi.org/10.1007/978-3-030-67108-2_3

23. Streitz, N.A.: From smart-only cities towards humane and cooperative hybrid cities. Technology | Architecture + Design **5**(2). 127–133 (2021). https://doi.org/10.1080/24751448.2021.1967050

24. Streitz, N., Charitos, D., Kaptein, M., Böhlen, M.: Grand challenges for ambient intelligence and implications for design contexts and smart societies. *Journal of Ambient Intelligence and Smart Environments* **11**(1), 87–107 (2019). https://doi.org/10.3233/AIS-180507

25. Streitz, N., Privat, G.: Ambient intelligence. In: Stephanidis, C. (ed.) The Universal Access Handbook, pp. 60.1–60.17. CRC Press Taylor & Francis (2009). ISBN: 978-0-8058-6280-5

26. Streitz, N.A., Riedmann-Streitz, C.: Rethinking 'Smart' Islands towards Humane, Self-Aware, and Cooperative Hybrid Islands. Interactions, pp. 54–60. ACM Press. May–June Issue 2022. https://doi.org/10.1145/3527200

27. Thaler, R., Sunstein, C.: Nudge: Improving Decisions about Health, Wealth, and Happiness. Yale University Press, New Haven (2008). ISBN: 978-0-14-311526-7

28. UN Sustainable Development Goals: https://sdgs.un.org/goals. Accessed 2 January 2022

29. White House: Preparing for the future of artificial intelligence. Prepared by the Executive Office of the President National Science and Technology Council Committee on Technology. https://obamawhitehouse.archives.gov/sites/default/files/whitehouse_files/microsites/ostp/NSTC/preparing_for_the_future_of_ai.pdf. Accessed February 2022

Understanding Intra-regional Flow of Vehicles Using Automatic License Plate Recognition

Kenro Aihara[1,2,3]([⊠]) [iD]

[1] Tokyo Metropolitan University, Tokyo, Japan
kenro.aihara@tmu.ac.jp
[2] National Institute of Informatics, Tokyo, Japan
[3] Joint Support-Center for Data Science Research, Research Organization
of Information and Systems, Tokyo, Japan
https://researchmap.jp/aihara/

Abstract. In order to realize a smart city, it is essential to understand the ever-changing flow of people in the city. Regarding transportation by public transportation, such as trains, bus, and taxis, probe information generated from their operational data of such services are one of the clues, but private cars are operated independently by the citizens and out of such probe data. It is not easy to comprehensively grasp their dynamics because there are also social demands for privacy protection.

In this paper, in order to exceed the limit of covering many mobile objects with probe data alone, a hybrid of fixed-point observation on the environment side and the probe is used to obtain an outline of inbound and outbound to the target area and also transitions of major points in the area. The methodology for grasping dynamics is introduced. Here, cameras are installed at major spots and transportation hubs in the city to identify individual vehicles.

Keywords: ITS · Smart city · Crowdsourcing · Drive recording

1 Introduction

In order to realize a smart city, it is essential to understand the ever-changing flow of people in the city. Regarding transportation by public transportation, such as trains, bus, and taxis, probe information generated from their operational data of such services are one of the clues, but private cars are operated independently by the citizens and out of such probe data. It is not easy to comprehensively grasp their dynamics because there are also social demands for privacy protection.

In this paper, in order to exceed the limit of covering many mobile objects with probe data alone, a hybrid of fixed-point observation on the environment side and the probe is used to obtain an outline of inbound and outbound to the target area and also transitions of major points in the area. The methodology

N. A. Streitz and S. Konomi (Eds.): HCII 2022, LNCS 13325, pp. 127–138, 2022.
https://doi.org/10.1007/978-3-031-05463-1_9

for grasping dynamics is introduced. Here, cameras are installed at major spots and transportation hubs in the city to identify individual vehicles.

From a privacy standpoint, vehicle images are only retained in an edge system equipped with a camera, and individual vehicle feature values are calculated including visual features such as color and vehicle type and the registration area provided by an automatic license plate recognition device. The exact license number recognized is converted into an irreversible signature that cannot identify vehicle individually.

By using this methodology, it becomes possible to grasp the overview of the inbound and outbound of vehicles to the target area, and also to grasp the transition of the same vehicle recognized at multiple points within the area. This paper describes the system and data processing and introduce a case study in a city with a population of about a hundred thousand.

2   Background

2.1   Automatic License Plate Recognition

Automatic License Plate Recognition (ALPR) [3], or automatic number-plate recognition (ANPR), is a technology that uses optical character recognition on images to read vehicle registration plates to create vehicle location data. ALPR is used by police forces around the world for law enforcement purposes, including to check if a vehicle is registered or licensed. It is also used for electronic toll collection and also grasping the movements of traffic.

Automatic license plate recognition can be used to store the images captured by the cameras as well as the text from the license plate. Since recognition accuracy is greatly affected by illuminance, systems commonly use infrared lighting to allow the camera to take the picture even at night.

Privacy issues have caused concerns about ALPR, such as government tracking citizens' movements, misidentification, high error rates, and increased government spending. Critics have described it as a form of mass surveillance.

2.2   Car Probe

In order to realize a smart city, it is essential to understand the ever-changing flow of people in the city. For public transportation, such as trains, bus, and taxis, probe information generated from their operational data of such services are one of the clues.

In the recent IoT era, smartphones and IoT devices capable of wide-area wireless communication have become widespread, and it is not uncommon for them to be incorporated into personal objects carried by individuals. One of the well-known personal IoT devices for a long time is the automobile. They have been called probe cars [4]. Each manufacturer delivers their vehicles equipped with a communication module and implements a mechanism to constantly collect information during driving.

In recent years, there have been an increasing number of cases in which drivers themselves additionally attach devices to automobiles. A typical example is a drive recorder [6]. Users mount the recording appliance on the dashboard or attach it to the windshield to record the behavior of the car during the journey, such as the trajectory (a sequence of locations with time stamps), acceleration, and speed. One of the strongest motivations for using such appliances is that they can provide evidence in relation to an accident if necessary. Therefore, drivers should use an appliance of some sort whenever they drive. Ordinary appliances, such as the Garmin Dash Cam, are commercial products that usually work automatically. The appliance begins recording when the driver starts his/her engine and stores the data it records. From the viewpoint of reducing car insurance premiums, drive recording appliances that records not only data relating to accidents but also the whole driving are on the market. They monitor and record the driver's behavior by assessing speed, braking, acceleration, cornering and the time of day when journeys are made. The data are transmitted to the insurance provider via mobile networks.

Even if it doesn't have as clear a purpose as a drive recorder, there is a need to record driving activities using an appliance. There is also known an effort to collect data for each vehicle using a dongle that connects to the odb2 port that is equipped as standard on each vehicle, reads status data from the onboard computer, and collects it together with its location and acceleration data.

On the other hand, instead of those dedicated appliances, some smartphone applications are proposed. AutoGuard Dash Cam and Safety Sight[1] are smartphone applications for drive recording. Although Safety Sight is provided by an auto insurance company, it only assesses the driver's behavior and provides feedback. It does not transmit data back to the insurance company. It also provides a warning to drivers by estimating the distance to the vehicle ahead, which it calculates by analyzing an image of the scene to detect the shapes and sizes of objects (Fig. 1). It automatically records a 10-second video of the scene in front of the vehicle before and after impact when the app detects the possibility of an impact, such as from sudden braking.

The author and his collaborators have proposed a drive recorder application that collects sensor data for assessing road surface conditions using a crowdsourcing approach [1,2,5].

One of the major problems of collecting probe car data is the social demands for privacy protection. There are large individual differences in resistance to the provision of personal data, even for the public good. Therefore, if the collected probe car data is biased, there remains a problem in using it for grasping social activities.

In this paper, in order to exceed the limit of covering many mobile objects with probe data alone, a hybrid of fixed-point observation on the environment side and the probe is used to obtain an outline of inbound and outbound to the target area and also transitions of major points in the area. The methodology for grasping dynamics is introduced. Here, cameras are installed at major spots and transportation hubs in the city to identify individual vehicles.

---

[1] Distribution of this application ended in 2020.

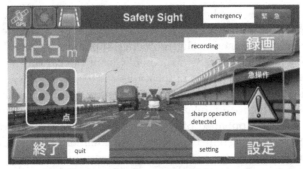

(a) approaching forward vehicle warning

(b) event data recorder

Fig. 1. Safety Sight by Sompo Japan Nipponkoa Insurance Inc.

3   Proposed Methodology

3.1   Overview

Here, the target is a city where the intercity roads that are the routes of inflow and outflow are limited. Since it is premised on measurement at the point of inflow and outflow, the proposed method is not effective for a large city with many inflow and outflow routes or a town with a structure in which the urban area expands continuously.

Figure 2 overviews the proposed methodology. Edge systems are deployed in the town and each of them detects vehicles and its identifications. Such identifications are anonymized and replaced with the corresponding signature before being stored in the cloud. The dashboard (Fig. 5) prepared on the cloud is used by several stakeholders, such as experts of traffic, experts of road maintenance, and managers of the road.

Figure 3 illustrates the proposed methodology for collecting the appearance of vehicles in the town. At first, some checkpoints on the inflow and outflow routes are selected. For these checkpoints, its location that is advantageous for identifying the traveling vehicle should be selected. Specifically, they are places

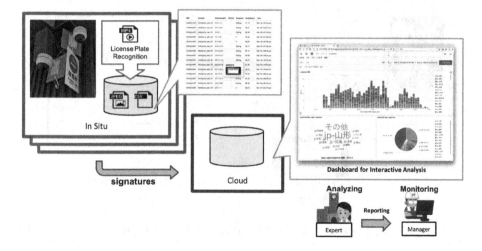

Fig. 2. Overview of collecting data

where the vehicle speed is not very high, the number of lanes is limited, the vehicle can be easily grasped from the front, and the brightness is high. ALPR is used for local identification on the edge side and these conditions are required for better ALPR results.

3.2 Edge Systems

An edge system consists of an IP camera, a computer (the black box in Fig. 4), and a network appliance (the white box with a grey circle on the top) for communicating both in the local network and to the Internet. Once the system detects a vehicle and identifies it, the result is then transmitted to the ALPR service to merge data from all edges. The proposed methodology uses the OpenALPR service[2] by Rekor Systems, Inc. for this part. The service consists of an agent software running on the edge device and a web service for monitoring and analyzing results with dashboard. The agent software watches a video stream from the camera and detects vehicle and extract a minimum bounding rectangle of the license plate. It recognizes characters on the plate. In addition, the software identifies the vehicle manufacturer, model, and color. The web service collects identifications from all agents though the Internet. It holds such results for specified period and then drop them after they expire. The service also can send all results in JSON format to a specified endpoint. It plays a role of a repeater in this methodology.

---

[2] https://www.openalpr.com/.

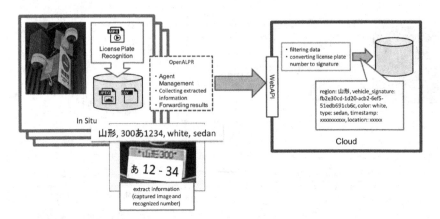

Fig. 3. Recognizing vehicles on-site and collecting data

3.3 Cloud Server

The methodology contains its own cloud storage with the REST API, as the endpoint for accepting results. When receiving a result, it produces a text string as the corresponding signature for the vehicle identifier using plate number, manufacturer, model, and color. It stores such signature instead of plate number itself and drop the plate number. The region is not used as one of seeds of signature because the accuracy of recognition for region is less than other features, such as plate number, color, and model.

3.4 Remarks

Accuracy. This methodology clealy depends on the recognition accuracy of ALPR. The accuracy of the license plate number part is quite high in preferable conditions, but the accuracy of the region is a little lower in Japanese plates. From the perspective of generating signatures, it is important to reduce the dependence on the accuracy of ALPR alone. In other words, it should be avoided that the identity cannot be determined unless the number recognition is perfect. Here, after making the license plate part a signature, it is treated as a multidimensional feature including other attributes, and the identity is handled with similarity measure.

Since the recognition accuracy depends on the illuminance and the angle, the installation conditions of the camera are important.

Privacy Preserving. Irreversible signatures basically protect the privacy of the individual. On the other hand, it is expected to be used for crime prevention purposes, so these will be covered by data stored locally in the edge system for a certain period of time.

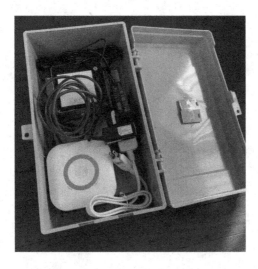

Fig. 4. The edge system

4   A Case Study

In this section, an example of experimental implementation of this methodology in Yonezawa City is introduced.

4.1   Overview of Yonezawa City

Yonezawa City is located at the southernmost tip of Yamagata Prefecture, and is located in the Yonezawa Basin surrounding high mountains. Its population is less than 100,000 and one of typical local cities in Japan. It takes about 2 h from Tokyo by train and 4 h by car. The highest point in the city area is Mt. Nishi-Azuma at an altitude of 2,035 m, and the highest point in the city is 260 m above sea level. The climate is hot and humid in summer, but the cold weather is severe in winter. It is designated as a special heavy snowfall area. In addition to abundant hot springs, you can easily enjoy summer mountain climbing and skiing.

Yonezawa is also famous in samurai period of Japanese history. This city was governed by the Uesugis, one of popular families of load, and especially the 9th feudal lord Harunori Uesugi as known as Yozan who was under tight financial conditions took the initiative in making a great deal of frugality and developed a number of policies to promote breeding. The townscape with its rich nature and history of samurai culture is popular for sightseeing.

Figure 6 illustrates the daily traffic volume of major transportation in Yonezawa, according to the census. The passengers at the main station is about 5,000, even though Shinkansen, the bullet train of Japan, stops here.

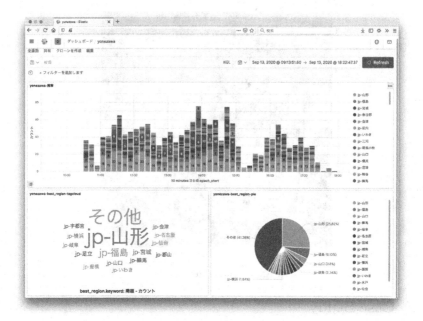

Fig. 5. A example of the dashboard on the cloud

The major route from large cities is the highway E13 and its traffic is about 9,000. The highway passes on the east side of the city and three exits can be used for accessing the city. There is a new roadside station next to the nearest exit and it is functioning as a gateway to the city.

4.2   Settings

Since opening in April 2018, "the roadside station Yonezawa" has been crowded with many visitors. In contrast, the number of tourists in the city center is said to be sluggish. The decrease in the number of tourists is a phenomenon that can be seen in various places, and there are various reasons for the decrease, and it varies from city to city. The problem is that it is not possible to clearly estimate these causes from conventional statistics such as the number of visitors, the number of passengers of train, and traffic volume on road, which is the main reason for policies that rely on beliefs, subjectivity, and intuition. In fact, in Yonezawa, it has been heard that the popular roadside station is vacuuming tourists from the city center where conventional point-of-interests are located. In such situations, it is necessary to grasp the behavior from a micro perspective in real time in order to objectively grasp the situation and manage the city scientifically.

Therefore, here, edge systems including a camera are installed and measured at two roadside stations, which is the gateway, and the parking lot for tourists in the city center where the most popular POIs are located (Fig. 7).

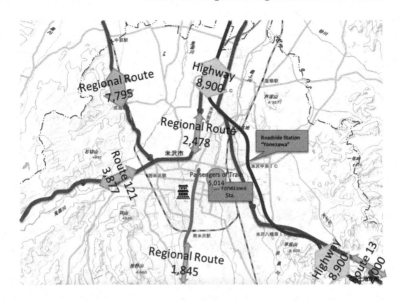

Fig. 6. Field of the case study: daily traffic of Yonezawa City according to Traffic Census

4.3   Preliminary Tests

The preliminary test was conducted in September 2020, which is the autumn holiday season in Japan. The weather was fine throughout the week and a lot of visitors visited this city.

Here, the author focuses on the flow between the roadside station Yonezawa, which is the gateway, and the city center. Figure 8 shows the transitions. The graph on the upper left shows the transition from the roadside station to the city center, and the upper right shows the opposite. The graph shows the number of vehicles with the color darkness which are detected in both sites. The vertical axes show regions of vehicles, and the horizontal axes show hours of the day. The bar graph in Fig. 8 shows the number of vehicles in time series. From 9am to 12pm, 88 out of 730 (12.1%) of vehicle from Fukushima, one of the neighbor regions, stop at the city center via the roadside station. Vehicles from Sendai, the major city in the northeast Japan apart from one and half hour by car, were 38 out of 218 (17.4%). On the other hand, 55 out of 64 Sendai numbers (85.9%) that stopped at the roadside station at around 2pm stopped at the city center before that, and it can be seen that a high percentage of them stopped at the roadside station on their way home.

Figure 9 shows hours of each region that visited the roadside station. The blue line denotes weekdays, and the red line denotes weekend. In the top graph, vehicles in Yamagata including Yonezawa itself come early in the morning on weekdays, compared with other regions and weekends. In contrast, vehicles from Fukushima apart a half hour distance visited more in the evening on weekends.

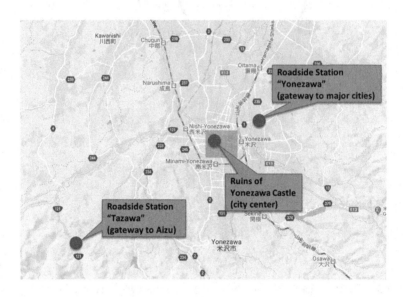

Fig. 7. Locations of cameras

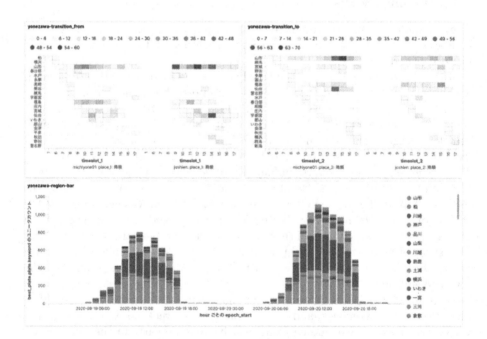

Fig. 8. Transitions between spots

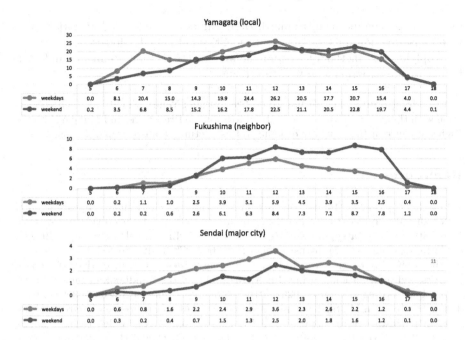

Fig. 9. Visiting hours to "the roadside station Yonezawa"

4.4 Discussion

A major limitation of the methodology is that it becomes less accurate or unusable at night and in bad weather. In fact, actual problems such as unrecognizable situations due to snow accretion on the license plate and occlusion due to snowy mountains piled up on the side of the road were also confirmed in Yonezawa. Of course, it is possible to raise the conditions for license plate recognition, such as installing the camera on an ideal overhead position above the road and irradiating it with stronger infrared rays, but an excessive increase in installation cost is an acceptable solution in this methodology.

One of possible solutions is crowdsourcing of moving objects, that is, drive recorders on the driving vehicles in the city. Images captured by the recorder includes other vehicles around the city. If such images or extracted vehicle features onboard can be collected online, we don't even need to deploy edge systems at fix positions.

5 Conclusions

In this paper, in order to exceed the limit of covering many mobile objects with probe data alone, a hybrid of fixed-point observation on the environment side and the probe is used to obtain an outline of inbound and outbound to the target area and also transitions of major points in the area. The methodology for grasping dynamics is introduced. Here, cameras are installed at major spots and transportation hubs in the city to identify individual vehicles.

Applying this methodology and the system for real environments and verifying through experiments are future issues.

Acknowledgments. The author would like to thank Yonezawa City for their cooperation with this research. He is also grateful to Shimane Prefecture, and Matsue National Highway Office of the Ministry of Land, Infrastructure, Transport and Tourism.

References

1. Aihara, K., Bin, P., Imura, H., Takasu, A., Tanaka, Y.: A smart city application for sharing up-to-date road surface conditions detected from crowdsourced data. In: Streitz, N., Markopoulos, P. (eds.) DAPI 2017. LNCS, vol. 10291, pp. 219–234. Springer, Cham (2017). https://doi.org/10.1007/978-3-319-58697-7_16

2. Aihara, K., Imura, H.: Crowdsourcing for smart cities that realizes the situation of cities and information sharing. In: Augusto, J.C. (ed.) Handbook of Smart Cities, pp. 1–42. Springer, Cham (2020). https://doi.org/10.1007/978-3-030-69698-6_67

3. Du, S., Ibrahim, M., Shehata, M., Badawy, W.: Automatic license plate recognition (ALPR): a state-of-the-art review. IEEE Trans. Circuits Syst. Video Technol. **23**(2), 311–325 (2013). https://doi.org/10.1109/TCSVT.2012.2203741

4. Miwa, T., Morikawa, T.: The model analysis on route choice behavior based on probe-car data. Infrastruct. Plan. Rev. **21**, 553–560 (2004). https://doi.org/10.2208/journalip.21.553

5. Piao, B., Aihara, K.: Detecting the road surface condition by using mobile crowd-sensing with drive recorder. In: IEEE Conference on Intelligent Transportation Systems, Proceedings, ITSC 2018, pp. 1–8, March 2018. https://doi.org/10.1109/ITSC.2017.8317818

6. Toledo, T., Lotan, T.: In-vehicle data recorder for evaluation of driving behavior and safety. Transp. Res. Rec. **1953**(1), 112–119 (2006). https://doi.org/10.1177/0361198106195300113

Designing City Service Ecosystems: The Case of the City of Espoo in the Capital Region of Finland

Ari-Veikko Anttiroiko[(⊠)] [ID] and Kaisu Sahamies [ID]

Tampere University, 33100 Tampere, Finland
{ari-veikko.anttiroiko,kaisu.sahamies}@tuni.fi

Abstract. This article discusses the evolution, scope, and impact of ecosystem thinking in public service management in the city of Espoo, Finland. Discussion starts with a brief introduction to the emergence of ecosystem thinking and the ideas on which the conceptualization of ecosystems in the given local context have been anchored. The second task is to describe, on the basis of the document analysis and two key informant interviews, how the city of Espoo started to build the conceptual tools, models, and strategies associated with ecosystem thinking. We will assess the added value of such an approach in four areas of public management, which deal with service innovation, competence issues, customer relationships, and citizen engagement. Lastly, this article will elaborate briefly three contextual ecosystem-related issues. First, to what extent the ecosystem thinking depends on the critical mass of producers, developers, and other stakeholders in terms of scalability, urbanization economies, and opportunity enhancement? Second, what is the role of digitalization in the development of ecosystem thinking? Third, how is the application of ecosystem thinking in public service management conditioned by its inherent institutional context, such as the democratic and bureaucratic aspects of local self-government? This article highlights the preconditions and forms of the real-life ecosystem thinking in the context of a progressive local government in the Nordic welfare society, and further assesses the promise of ecosystem thinking as a paradigmatic approach to public service management adjusted to the conditions of the global digital age.

Keywords: City · Espoo · Finland · Ecosystem · Public service · Public service ecosystem · Public management · Innovation management

1 Introduction

Profound technological, political, economic, social, and environmental changes are sweeping through communities of all shapes and sizes in different parts of the world. While some of these changes are alarming, as with climate change, coronavirus pandemic, or increased economic polarization, many of them create new opportunities. Among the most important factors on the opportunity side of the equation are technological advancements and a wide range of related socio-technological and organizational trends that are at a fast pace reshaping the current techno-economic paradigm and,

N. A. Streitz and S. Konomi (Eds.): HCII 2022, LNCS 13325, pp. 139–157, 2022.
https://doi.org/10.1007/978-3-031-05463-1_10

along with it, essential aspects of our urban future. Areas that have attracted increasing attention among local developers and urban researchers alike within such a broad framework are platformization and ecosystem thinking, which are crystallizations of the recent changes taking place at the intersection of technological, economic, and social development [1–4].

Radical changes associated with platform logic and ecosystem thinking have a natural connection with the way we conceptualize urban communities [5]. Furthermore, these trends penetrate to the preconditions and forms of local institutions themselves, local government included. In this sense, the novel trends referred to above are gradually reshaping public governance, management, and service provision, or to be more precise, further accelerating the development that begun a few decades ago when the hierarchical mode of public governance was supplemented with markets, partnerships, networks, and various new methods of citizen participation. In the traditional hierarchically organized system, public services are decided by politicians, managed by public managers, provided as an in-house solution, and controlled primarily by political-administrative machinery. In the advanced Western countries, the managerial turn took place in the 1980s and more so in the decade that followed it, most notably along the principles of New Public Management (NPM), according to which political control was loosened, managerialism increased, services contracted out, and citizens seen primarily as service users [6, 7].

A re-evaluation of public administration and management (PAM) theory has been going on for some time [8]. Due to several challenges especially with business-style NPM, the next significant wave in public management was to strengthen political steering, utilize networks, and enhance citizen involvement under the loose umbrella of New Public Governance [9–13]. We focus here on the next phase of public governance and service management, which is emerging as a response to technological advancements, overall development of tech-savvy environments, and related socio-technical changes. Particular manifestations of these changes in the administrative logic are associated with digital platforms and innovation and service ecosystems [14, 15]. Especially the concept of ecosystem is still underdeveloped vis-à-vis its promise derived from the business ecosystem analogy [16]. There is a need for theoretical analyses of the premises of ecosystem thinking and empirical analyses of its early manifestations in local government.

This article aims to provide empirical insights into the pros and cons of the real-life ecosystem thinking in the context of a progressive local government in a welfare society. We focus on the following research questions:

(a) How is *ecosystem thinking* emerging in the local governments in the advanced Western countries?
(b) What is the added value of ecosystem thinking in *public service management*, especially in such areas as innovation management, competence management, customer relationship management, and citizen engagement?
(c) How does *local embeddedness* affect critical mass and further scalability, urbanization economies, and opportunity enhancement of urban service ecosystem?
(d) What is the role of *digitalization* in the operationalization and utilization of ecosystem thinking?

(e) How does ecosystem thinking in public service management relate to its *institutional context*, especially to the democratic and bureaucratic aspects of local self-government?

We will provide empirical evidence for the emergence, forms, and impact of ecosystem thinking in local government through an illustrative case, as it allows an in-depth analysis of nuances of the novel phenomenon under investigation. This article forms a part of a larger on-going research project, which started from platform governance and broadens the view to ecosystem thinking [15, 17–19]. Research strategy and methodological choices are discussed in detail in the next section.

2 Methodology

Our approach can be characterized as exploratory case-based research with strong emphasis of the illustrative role of the case in making sense of the preconditions and introduction of ecosystem thinking in a progressive tech-savvy cities (cf. [20, 21]). The setting of our case selection is similar with Sahamies et al. [17], the pool of potential cases being evidently large. We wanted to shed light on ecosystem thinking through a single case study, which requires that the case is illustrative enough. Beside explicit commitment to ecosystem thinking, this implies the existence of such preconditions as advances in intersectoral collaboration, democratic culture, and sufficient digital infrastructure. In addition, special characteristics of local government, such as openness, inclusiveness, transparency, innovativeness, and the culture of experimentation, can be expected to be essential for the ecosystem thinking to thrive. With such criteria, several notable cities especially in both Anglo-American and European country groups stand out.

When we sharpened the criteria to the early adoption of urban platforms and ecosystem-related service innovations in the public domain, the group of potential cases is narrowed down. We ended up making the case selection among Nordic region for as a context it fulfils practically all the criteria mentioned above. After screening different options through both literature and case descriptions in the Web, a particular program, Six City Strategy or 6Aika in Finnish, attracted our attention as a nationally backed up program co-funded by the EU. It facilitated platform and ecosystem development among six largest cities in Finland. After screening the cities involved – Helsinki, Espoo, Vantaa, Turku, Tampere, and Oulu – the most impressive case in applying ecosystem thinking appeared to be the city of Espoo in terms of its reputation, explicit commitment to platform and ecosystem thinking, relevant project portfolio, and availability of relevant materials (see [22–26]). This selection implies that discussion is tightly tied to a Nordic style democratic local government in the context of a tech-savvy welfare society.

The primary data sources used are selected documents and two semi-structured expert interviews. In order to obtain and analyze documentary evidence of how ecosystem thinking has been introduced, conceptualized, and communicated in the city government, we focused on relevant strategic documents among the set of policy documents, frameworks, and handbooks that (a) are published by the city of Espoo, (b) discuss new ecosystem thinking, and (c) are presented the way that indicates that they manifest

Espoo's approach to or application of ecosystem thinking (see Tools to Support Development at https://www.espoo.fi/fi/espoon-kaupunki/innovatiivinen-espoo/tyokaluja-kehitt amisen-tueksi). On the basis of preliminary thematic selection, eight documents were selected for a closer inspection. Documents are referred to in the text with codes D1 to D8 (see List of analyzed documents of the city of Espoo in Appendix 1).

Document analysis was supplemented by two interviews of the employee of the city of Espoo, chosen on the basis of their role in the introduction of ecosystem thinking in city government. They were Director for City as a Service Development interviewed in December 2021 and Senior Innovation Ecosystem Manager interviewed in February 2022, both having a key role in the Service Development Unit of the city government (see List of expert interviews in Appendix 2). Interviews were essential for making sense of the context for the research questions and understanding the organizational processes through the eyes of senior and project managers who had a hands-on role in introducing ecosystem thinking in the city government. Such exploratory expert interviews are used to gain tacit knowledge in a conceptually fuzzy field (see [27]). At the same time, they provide insights into and content validation of the factual organizational processes in the given real-life case.

3 Public Service Ecosystem

3.1 Emergence of Ecosystems in the Public Management Literature

The two novel concepts that emerged recently the field of PAM as a reflection of changing techno-economic paradigm and related organizational and social ramifications include platforms and ecosystems. The role of platforms in urban development, services, and governance emerged as a fairly coherent research agenda in the mid-2010s [14, 18, 19, 28–35], whereas ecosystem thinking has remained somewhat elusive and vaguely conceptualized [8, 36–38].

In the local affairs, ecosystems have been primarily associated with digital ecosystems [39], semantic city service ecosystems [40], and innovation ecosystems [25, 26], and regarding services, with generic view of service ecosystems [41], smart service ecosystems [42], and innovation in service ecosystems [43, 44]. The concept has been rarely used in the context of public governance, even though there are concepts like 'open governance ecosystem' that conceptualize governance field using ecosystem analogy [45]. In some conceptualizations this discussion developed from services towards broader views of cities as services systems [46] or as a kind of service platform as in the concept of City-as-a-Service [47]. This discussion poses a challenge to our understanding of the nuances and utility of the concept of ecosystem in the given context. In particular, what is the added value of the concept of ecosystem in the public domain, and what this concept refers to in concrete terms, especially regarding public service management.

3.2 Conceptualizing Public Service Ecosystem

Service ecosystem can be defined as a "relatively self-contained, self-adjusting system of resource-integrating actors connected by shared institutional arrangements and mutual value creation through service exchange" [48]. When this is applied to the public domain, essential aspects remain the same, even though public services are conditioned by a few critical factors – including democratic control, legal framework, and public funding – that are ontologically and institutionally relevant aspects of the reality affecting the ontogenesis and operations of every public entity.

The idea of public service ecosystem (PSE) has emerged as novel approach to public service management, which can be seen as a step forward in the evolution of new public governance. PSE reshapes the view of the utilization of networks in providing public services [38, 49]. It has emerged as a unifying framework through which to understand the complexities of public service delivery and value creation within a multi-level setting [36]. In terms of service logic, it implies a move beyond "the transactional and linear approach associated with NPM, towards a relational model where value is shaped by the interplay between all of these dimensions and not least by the wider societal context and the values that underpin it" [37, p. 436]. Such a view provides new opportunities for value creation and enhancement by combining resources and competences in a multi-layered setting, which poses obvious managerial challenges, as indicated in the current discussions about public service ecosystem management [8].

4 Ecosystem Thinking in the City of Espoo

4.1 The City of Espoo in the Capital Region of Finland

Espoo is a city in the capital region of Finland. It is located in the Helsinki Metropolitan Area by the Gulf of Finland. Its neighboring municipalities are Vihti, Nurmijärvi, Vantaa, Helsinki, and Kirkkonummi. In addition, the municipality of Kauniainen is enclaved within it. The population of Espoo was close to 300,000 in June 2021, making it the second largest city in the country.

Espoo's development is tightly connected with the capital region, in which the three largest cities are Helsinki, Espoo, and Vantaa. Helsinki as the capital city is the most well-known and most internationalized city in the region. Espoo due to its polycentric urban structure and quick and fairly recent urbanization has for long been in the shadow of Helsinki, even if the location of the main campus of Aalto University in Otaniemi, the collection of headquarters in Keilaniemi, and cultural and business center in Tapiola have increased its reputation as a city of business and technology. Vantaa is considerably smaller than Helsinki and Espoo and has a stronger multicultural, residential, and edge city atmosphere. Vantaa's strength is the location of Helsinki-Vantaa Airport and the development of Aviapolis, which is a business area branded as an internationally oriented airport city.

In all, Espoo is a part of a dynamic capital region in which cities have their own specializations and profiles. It is a city of business, technology, and innovation, which is functionally connected with other cities of the wider metropolitan area (see e.g. [23, 25]). Cities in the capital region and in the wider metropolitan area have collaborated in many areas of urban development, including the promotion of strategic business and regional innovation system development [50]. Helsinki, Espoo, and Vantaa have also been involved in the collaboration between six largest cities in Finland, known as Six

City Strategy, which had a decisive role in the introduction of ecosystem thinking in Finnish local government (see e.g. [24, 25]).

4.2 The Emergence of Ecosystem Thinking

Espoo's road to ecosystem thinking has its root in the impact of the technical university in Otaniemi and the gradual emergence of regional innovation ecosystem around it. We may see Espoo as the case in which the city is modeled according to the political economy of its resource base or signature institution. Espoo is in essence a city that is inspired by and in a sense even modeled itself on the technical university. The story goes back to the 1950s, when Helsinki University of Technology, the oldest and largest technical university in Finland, started its operations in Espoo. In 2010 it was merged with other educational institutions to become Aalto University. The university with its close connection with business development was a particularly influential model because during these formative post-war decades Espoo had neither a strong urban profile nor other dominating institutions. Such a thinking was merged with the gradually urbanizing Finnish welfare society, in which the role of municipalities as important self-governing and development-oriented local institutions were generally seen prominent.

The spirit of the city of Espoo resembles that of innovative and entrepreneurial technical university and urban innovation milieu, even to the extent that its urban form and multipolar and networked structure resembles that of a campus life. In this, Espoo actually resembles many post-industrial cities and a range of cases in which universities have left their mark on their host cities, such as Cambridge or Oxford in the UK, or Berkeley, Stanford, and Chicago in the United States (cf. [51]) as well as cities that have adopted some of the attitudes and working methods from business incubators, innovation hubs, and technopolises, epitomized by cities like Palo Alto in Silicon Valley, California [52]. This view is further sedimented in how essential role the entrepreneurial university – Aalto University in this case – plays at the heart of place-based innovation ecosystem [25]. The key brand of this system is Espoo Innovation Garden within Keilaniemi-Otaniemi-Tapiola area of Espoo [23], within which Urban Mill is a good example of a hub that facilitates learning and collaboration (https://urbanmill.org/). It is thus no wonder why the city of Espoo has adopted a range of radical approaches to its governance and service development, such as openness to disruption, the culture of experimentation, platformization, and ecosystem thinking.

The other essential aspect of the Espoo story is the innovation-driven Finnish economy, and the role of public sector organizations in promoting it, including the input of progressive local governments. City's openness to new ideas and new business models, productization and contracting out developed in the 1990s and more so in the following decades [Sutinen, P., Personal interview, December 10, 2021]. A milestone in this respect was, however, the beginning of the collaboration between six largest cities in Finland, known as Six City Strategy, abbreviated to 6Aika in Finnish [Sjöholm, K., Personal interview, February 7, 2022]. It began with three large-scale spearhead projects, those of open data and interfaces (2014–2017), open innovation platforms (2015–2018), and open participation and customership (2015–2018), which promoted the development of Finnish smart city model (cf. [22]). These three spearhead projects and a range of related projects gave significant impetus to the adoption of platform and ecosystem thinking in the six cities involved (see https://6aika.fi/). For example, one of the outcomes of the open innovation platforms project was that platform thinking was incorporated into the strategies in all six cities.

This Six City Strategy collaboration had a huge impact on the city of Espoo's involvement in ecosystem thinking in the latter half of the 2010s (e.g. [53]). Among the first important outcomes of this work was a document titled "Ekosysteemien innovaatiojohtamisen viitekehys" (The framework for the innovation management of ecosystems) published in 2018 [D1]. It was drafted as a part of Open participation and customership spearhead project of the Six City Strategy in the Service Development Unit of the city in collaboration with KPMG. An additional element in the policy context was the connection with the EU funding instruments and various EU programs, such as smart specialization strategies (S3) for territorial development [25].

The city of Espoo has a city strategy that is written in the form of a story, which is a collaboratively drafted view of the orientation and strategic actions of the city for 2021–2025 (https://www.espoo.fi/en/city-espoo/espoo-story). While the idea of City-as-a-Service appears in The Espoo Story, it only scratches the surface of the issue. The true work in this respect was done when a range of strategic documents and guidelines were drafted within Six City Strategy in the latter half of the 2010s. They are published on a site titled Tools to Support Development Work ("Työkaluja kehittämisen tueksi" in Finnish) at https://www.espoo.fi/fi/espoon-kaupunki/innovatiivinen-espoo/tyokaluja-kehittamisen-tueksi.

4.3 Ecosystems in Different Areas of Public Management

In this section we will illustrate the managerial view of public service ecosystems by highlighting how the city of Espoo has adopted this framework in a few special aspects of public service management, including the management of service innovations, public service competence, customer relations, and citizen engagement. They can be seen as managerial fields of their own, each having nevertheless overlapping areas with or providing specific view of public service management. In the case of Espoo, *innovation management* is the kind of framing managerial field, which determines the approach to the ecosystem thinking, as it primarily seeks resources and competences outside the administrative apparatus of the city to be utilized in developing services and, more broadly, in urban renewal. Another outward oriented area is *citizen engagement*, usually seen as a governance rather than managerial issue. The organization of the forms of citizen participation includes anyway an obvious managerial dimension. Lastly, *customer relationship management* operates at the core of public service management, while *competence management* is primarily an internally oriented function that builds the capacity of the organization.

It is worth emphasizing that the evolution of ecosystem thinking within the city's administrative and service organization is asynchronous. There is a general tendency in the highest political decision-making bodies towards ecosystem style thinking, but at the practical level a kind of natural inertia manifests itself in the process. For example, while the city strategy states that "[w]e will promote the implementation of the City as a Service multi-provider model" (https://www.espoo.fi/en/city-espoo/espoo-story), the way ecosystem thinking and City-as-a-Service idea is conceptualized within Service

Development Unit is much broader and radical. The Service Development Unit applies a principle that each unit must adopt such new ways of thinking on the basis of their own motivation and learn from their own experiences. This makes the organizational transformation asynchronous. Nevertheless, ecosystem thinking is visible throughout the municipal organization, even though it is most developed in those organizational units that seek resources and competences outside the organization, that deal with urban development, and that are involved in education and learning [Sjöholm, K., Personal interview, February 7, 2022].

Innovation Management.   To start with, defining Espoo's role in innovation management has required that the entire mindset was changed regarding the role of the city government in promoting innovativeness in its organization and within a broader urban community [Sjöholm, K., Personal interview, February 7, 2022]. The most important generic framework for ecosystem thinking in the city of Espoo is documented in The Framework of Innovation Management of Ecosystems, which determines the city government's overall approach to ecosystem thinking [D1]. It emphasizes "the attempts to direct innovative energy towards shared goals for the benefit of all members of the ecosystem". This framework identifies the need to deal with potentially tensional aspects of such a setting, such as having a sufficient degree of conformism in the field of differing objectives of various ecosystem players as a precondition for synergy, coordination, and smooth collaboration [D1, pp. 18–22].

The city government has to define its own role on this scene. This discussion raises the issue of the publicness of local government [54, 55], which requires that the city government defines its role in the service ecosystem. There is a natural duality of the role of local government in innovation ecosystems: the city government is an enabler that contributes to the learning and renewal processes in the local society, while at the same time the units of the local government are learning organizations themselves and operate as members of various innovation ecosystems [D1, pp. 27–29]. As an institution, the city government is involved in the networks of customers and other institutions and participates in co-creation processes in the pursuit of creating innovations that benefit local actors. While doing this, it participates in service activities that are "adjusted to the realities of urban life, platform economy, and service logic" [D1, p. 29]. Espoo aims at becoming active player in the ecosystem not only as a purchaser but also as an enabler, partner, learner or in other roles [Sjöholm, K., Personal interview, February 7, 2022].

The city government – and the public sector as a whole – serves as an enabler in ecosystems, which implies that it has a special role in maintaining local conditions that are conducive to long-term development of ecosystems, including infrastructures, research, education, and public funding. City of Espoo's strategic position as a primus inter pares in the field of public governance is built on its connections with all local actors, including inhabitants, companies, and associations, as well as its connections with the wider society. Related to this role, it represents a democratic society that operates within the rule of law [D1, pp. 27, 30–31].

Competence Management.   Ecosystem thinking has its inherent connection with talent and competence management, which has both internal and external dimensions. Regarding the latter, Espoo has started to organize its talent attraction activities within the city's line organization (see [56]; see also at https://www.espoo.fi/en/working-life/talent-espoo). At the same time, it is an internal issue, revolving around the question of how the competences of the city government should be developed and increased in order to be able to best utilize various service ecosystems [Sjöholm, K., Personal interview, February 7, 2022].

This issue is addressed in the strategic document titled The Handbook of Talent Management [D2]. The relevance of competences can be derived from both resource-based view of an organization and service-dominant logic, as both of them have competence as their core category. Competence is a key resource for any service system, and that resource must be managed if one wishes to acquire best competences to be utilized in its service system and nurture existing competences within city government.

In the case of the city of Espoo 'competence' is a cross-cutting theme that is expected to help in mapping out, planning, and directing development efforts in a holistic and contextual manner. This broadens the perspective beyond administrative duties or skills. The key idea of applying ecosystem thinking is to acknowledge that the city as an organization does not have to meet the future challenges alone if it "includes in its development efforts the competences from outside its organization". This is where ecosystems can be extremely useful, as they serve as a pool of various kinds of businesses, research institutes, and other expert organizations [D2, p. 9]. This relates to an open-minded attitude towards new technologies, innovative work methods, partners, networks, and other ecosystem components, which helps to strive for continuous development and higher goals. As crystallized in the given document, "[t]his development road map is also called organization's stretching towards strategic goals through the competence development" [D2, p. 16].

Customer Relationship Management (CRM). Public service management is not only about innovation and competence management. It is also about managing the service delivery processes and creating value with the customer. How is ecosystem thinking applied in this core area of service provision and especially in managing customer relationships? The city of Espoo has addressed these issues in four documents that deal with the customer-based knowledge management [D3], the production and utilization of customer knowledge [D4], and multi-channel customer service [D5, D6]. Let us focus here on the framing issue of customer-based knowledge management.

The city of Espoo has modeled this area with a focus on two major dimensions. First, it focusses on determining the role of local government in relation to its customers. Local government either organizes required services or serves as an enabler within its jurisdiction. In this context, the latter is more pronounced than the former. Second, the other key dimension is the benefit that the customer reaps from public services. Beside immediate benefits to a customer, many benefits materialize later, and some are indirect as with the creation of public value [D3, p. 11].

The city's approach to customer relationship management focusses on conceptualizing and modeling service processes and enabling full utilization of open data and data analytics. The aim has been to develop tools for collecting and analyzing customer data, which is made available to all stakeholders involved in the development of multi-channel services and setting up new businesses [D4, D5]. In such constellations the utilization of ecosystem thinking requires new attitudes and competences, as the content and value of service will be ultimately determined by the customer. This approach entails joint visioning, holistic understanding of the field and stakeholders' relationality, and creating conditions for smooth interaction. The entire rationale of ecosystem management is derived from the ultimate purpose of co-creating value for customer. In the same vein, service as a system is understood in a dynamic and market-oriented fashion, including value networks and revenue logics, which is vital in the long-term development of service ecosystems [D6].

Citizen Engagement. Added value of ecosystem thinking in co-creation and citizen participation brings democratic control into the picture. This has been addressed especially in two strategic documents of the city of Espoo, those of The Handbook of Co-creation [D7] and The Handbook of Open Participation [D8]. The city's documents focus more on inclusive value-creation than, say, political inclusion or citizens' democratic rights. Within this framework, participation and inclusion are seen from the view-point of managerialism [D7, D8].

The city is seen in this context as a meeting place, open innovation platform, or as an open ecosystem, in which all the local actors can meet on equal terms while pursuing their own interests. This kind of facilitative and enabling activity setting is characterized as City-as-a-Service or city as a Living Lab, which revolves around co-creation. The methods of co-creation are supposed to help all players of the service ecosystem to design better environment and services [D7, p. 5]. This reveals a kind of ecosystem logic that resembles market mechanism: the interaction between ecosystem actors is assumed to lead to either the finding of the solution to the problem or a successful launch of a product or a service [D7].

From a service management point of view, the approach applied by the city of Espoo emphasizes the role of enabling, encouraging, and orchestrating. It is a 'systemic' approach that focusses on the facilitation of peer networks and collaborative opportunity enhancement. It rests on the idea of shared leadership [D7]. The other side of the coin is well designed model for open participation and the facilitation of both physical and digital environments, which brings digital platforms into the picture [D8].

5   Urban, Digital, and Institutional Embeddedness

In the previous chapter ecosystem thinking has been described as an organizational and managerial issue. However, there is a range of contextual aspects to be taken into account when considering the preconditions for successful adoption of ecosystem thinking in public service management. In this section, these matters are discussed under three broadly defined themes, which revolve around urban, digital, and institutional aspects of ecosystem thinking.

5.1   Urbanization, Critical Mass, and Scalability

Urban platforms that facilitate city service ecosystems are locally embedded, which poses a challenge to scaling up innovations and other service-related solutions [19].

Even if the case of Espoo shows certain degree of potential association with scaling, it is too early to assess the success or failure in this respect. In the case of Espoo, instructions for scaling up co-creation solutions have been included in the co-creation handbook [D7, p. 26–28]. The city government does not conceptualize this issue as an integrated city-level ecosystem, but rather as a constellation of multiple ecosystems, each of which have different conditions and requirements for critical mass and scaling up. Such a thinking is called City-as-a-Service (CaaS) or city-at-your-service, which emphasizes the facilitating and enabling role of the city with connections with multiple micro-environments (ecosystems) thus including varying sets of relevant actors [Sutinen, P., Personal interview, December 10, 2021].

The other issue is the utilization of the external scale economies – determined by such factors as economic densities, variations, connections, and distances – in ecosystem thinking. *The localization economies* refer to the benefits derived from the close proximity of industrial, institutional and social players within the given service ecosystem. This may materialize in urban service provision in the form of inter-municipal collaboration and in the involvement of partners and service providers in service provision within the local government jurisdiction. City governments may enhance productivity and innovation through localization economies, though the added value of ecosystem thinking remains somewhat fuzzy in this respect. In any case, the tendencies for seeking location economies by the city of Espoo are manifest in its service ecosystem development. It is noteworthy that there is a tendency to overcome the spatial limitations of ecosystem creation via increased use of digital platforms.

Larger cities have better chances of utilizing service ecosystems, even if the relationship between the size of the city and *urbanization economies* may be non-linear [57, 58]. As concluded by Turok and McGranahan, "the potential of urbanization to promote growth is likely to depend on how conducive the infrastructure and institutional settings are" [59]. In the case of Espoo, such initial conditions are fairly good. In any case, in a simplified sense, it is the larger cities or metropolises that enable urbanization economies to emerge [60].

A few implications for policymakers are worth pinpointing here. The city government's policies play an intervening role, for they mediate demand and supply, which affects urbanization economies. The underlying premise is that a larger city size guarantees a wider and richer set of inputs, which have a potential to lower costs and increase innovativeness. However, as the urban settlements are shaped by dynamic forces and market agents, this logic should be given sufficient role as the conditioning factor that affect ecosystem building. In other words, city government's role in ecosystem building should be based on the utilization of the dynamic relations of the naturally evolving system rather than on an attempt to control it. Regarding jurisdiction size, the former is in line with the public choice principle outlined in Tiebout hypothesis [61], while the latter seeks "internalization of externalities" through the formation of the larger regional or metropolitan governance structures. One of the outcomes of this is that city governments should pay primary attention to the functioning of urban settlements and in 'fertilizing' business and innovation ecosystems rather than being obsessed neither with the population size of the metropolitan area nor their ability to control it [60]. Espoo represents in general a public choice type orientation supported by gradually weakening localism, while at the same time in its context there are strong regionalization tendencies, most radical changes in the recent years being the health, social, and rescue services reform decided by the Finnish Government in 2021. In this sense Espoo's ecosystem thinking is evolving in an institutional setting with some underlying structural tensions.

5.2   The Role of Digitalization

There has been a lot of discussion about the role of digitalization in the public sector reforms. The development of Finnish local e-government started slowly in the 1960s, computerization increased in the 1980s, and the great leap took place in the 1990s due to the Great Internet Explosion. Espoo followed this trend. Since then Espoo has been promoting the digitalization of local public services, which in recent years has been organized within Digiagenda Program of 2015–2021 (https://www.espoo.fi/fi/esp oon-kaupunki/innovatiivinen-espoo/digiagenda). In this area the city aims at increasing productivity and cost-effectiveness, on the one hand, and creating increasingly smooth and high-quality services, on the other. Its development efforts have been based on pilots and experiments along the principles of the culture of experimentation (see [62]). The view of digitalization is strategic in the sense that the city sees digitalization as a leverage in local renewal, which emphasizes the effectiveness and added value of digitalization. In other words, the issue itself is not digitalization *per se*, but the changes in organizational practices and culture. This connects digitalization with competence development, as the latter is essential in achieving the desired results by smart utilization of digital tools, applications, and environments [Sutinen, P., Personal interview, December 10, 2021; Sjöholm, K., Personal interview, February 7, 2022].

In Espoo, there is a high degree of openness towards new ways to doing things. Its innovation management framework emphasizes that the tools of hierarchical network management have become largely obsolete in the global age in which data, knowledge and learning have become essential for the organizational success. Most notably, digitalization will reduce transaction costs dramatically, which will have a revolutionary impact on transactions and the forms of social interaction [D1, pp. 5–6].

One of the consequences of this development is the dramatic change in the premises of the social organization of society, starting from the decreased utility of the economies of scale. Resources do not have to be fully controlled by an individual organization, especially regarding such resources and competences that are largely frictionless and abundantly available in the global resource pool. Digitalization will reduce the need to acquire resources inside the boundaries of the organization and rely on in-house solutions. Such a frictionlessness is likely to favor decentralized business models and smaller size of organizations, which are able to operate successfully in an increasingly dynamic competitive environment [D1, p. 6, 13]. Practical aspects of this development have their expression in various fields of public service management, most notably in customer relationship management [D3] and service co-creation [D7], which in their ideal forms are served by digital platforms that facilitate the processes of creating and nurturing ecosystems [Sjöholm, K., Personal interview, February 7, 2022]. One of the early formations of such development is Make With Espoo innovation platform (https:// makewithespoo.espoo.fi/en).

5.3 Institutional Setting

Local governments are local public institutions with overall responsibility of the well-being of local inhabitants and of promoting local development. The two dimensions of this institutional setting are of vital importance when thinking about the adoption of ecosystem thinking in public service management, those of democratic governance and policy making, on the one hand, and the role of public service and administrative organization, on the other.

In the same way as there have been concerns about democracy during the previous phases of the development of the models and theories of public management and governance, the same holds with ecosystems. The best reference for an analogy is the discussion about the democratization of network governance [63]. The dilemma is that while creating and nurturing ecosystems have positive impact on public service management as they widen resource base and competences and strengthen customer and stakeholder orientation in value co-creation, large part of this kind of action takes place outside the control vested in elected representatives. As such a control would limit the managerial and professional freedoms that are practical preconditions for the materialization of the added value of service ecosystems, there is obvious need to supplement conventional democratic framework with increasingly subtle forms of citizen and stakeholder influence (cf. [8, 37, 49]). In the case of Espoo, political steering affects service development through visions, principles, and broad political objectives. Political leaders of the city neither hinder innovative service development nor attempt to intervene employees' work, which makes the city government essentially a freedom-centered organization with self-directed service units [Sjöholm, K., Personal interview, February 7, 2022].

Within the democratic system, policies are as a rule implemented through coordinated actions in a multi-actor field to address public problems and to create public value. As service ecosystems deal with multi-level issues in the sense that they include usage motivations and situations (micro), organizational arrangements (meso), and value constellations derived ultimately from cross-contextual resource pool (macro), it poses a challenge in terms of how policy interventions affect across such value constellations [64]. These issues have been addressed in Espoo's framework documents and handbooks, which emphasize the need to strike a balance between conformism and various stakeholder-specific objectives [D1, D7].

Lastly, ecosystems thinking reflects the premises of New Public Governance, which has been evolving since the 1990s in the advanced Western countries. This approach is open for flexibility, empowerment, and wider use of community and extra-local resources, which has evolved through stakeholder, network, innovation, and service management, and is arguably developing towards platform and ecosystem management. From the point of view of service management, one of the key issues is how ecosystem thinking matches with the Public Service-Dominant Logic (PSDL) [65]. In this sense there is a far-reaching tension built in this setting. Namely, while service science has contributed to the understanding of the role of service users or customers as co-creators of value and as actors that ultimately determine value of service, the very existence of the public value as a framing value concept is rooted in democratic control executed primarily by the representative system of government. Thus, the issue of the creation of public value, as vague as it has proved to be, becomes an inherent part of the puzzle of the value creation in public service ecosystems, determining how the selected aspects of 'common good' in the context of the given service benefit all sectors of society through categories rooted on subsystems of society (cf. [66]). In fact, moving away from NPM paradigm points to the direction, which naturally increases the complexity of the value perspective on public services [67–69].

6 Conclusion

This article discusses the evolution, manifestations, and impact of ecosystem thinking in the Nordic tech-savvy city, the case being the city of Espoo in the capital region of Finland. Espoo is an innovation, technology, and business oriented city with Aalto university as its signature institution. Its involvement in ecosystem thinking developed primarily within Six City Strategy collaboration with other five large Finnish cities, which evolved during the latter half of the 2010s. Its approach has a genuine urban entrepreneurial and managerial tone. Adoption of ecosystem thinking is asynchronous process in the sense that different units have different preconditions and needs for the utilization of ecosystems in their service development.

Regarding local embeddedness of ecosystem thinking, Espoo has a fairly high degree of institutional thickness, well-developed business community, and sufficient population base. Its proximity to Helsinki and integration into the wider Helsinki Metropolitan Area supports the generation of urbanization economies. It seems that Espoo has in this sense good preconditions for the utilization of ecosystem thinking, even if the population of the city proper is only some 300,000.

The focus in Espoo's ecosystem approach is on "the social" in the sense that the precondition for success with ecosystems lies in openness, shared understanding of the common good, and smooth institutional relations. This implies that digitalization is not the framework through which this agenda is designed. However, digitalization has entered this agenda naturally through platformization, as seen in the establishment of platforms that facilitate locally rooted innovation ecosystems.

Finnish cities have been eager to adopt new management and governance models, and ecosystem thinking makes no exception. It fits well with the long-lasted development towards New Public Governance, which focuses on the utilization of the resources and competences of the local community and also of the wider environment. The need for democratic control over ecosystem development is a matter yet to be addressed much the same way as the issue of network governance. The decreased publicness of public administration may have happened in Espoo as in most other Western cities, yet it is compensated to a degree by a broad involvement of the members of the urban community in local policy making and development processes, through which the seeds have been planted for the emergence of decentralized forms of real-life ecosystem democracy that operates within the broader framework of representative system of government.

Appendix 1. List of Analyzed Documents of the City of Espoo

D1. Ekosysteemien innovaatiojohtamisen viitekehys. [The Framework of the Innovation Management of Ecosystems]. The city of Espoo. Retrieved September

29, 2021, from https://issuu.com/espoonkaupunki/docs/tuotos_editointi_oskivi_ekosysteemi_4cb399f6775265

D2. Kyvykkyyksien johtamisen käsikirja. [The Handbook of Talent Management]. The city of Espoo. Retrieved September 29, 2021, from https://static.espoo.fi/cdn/ ff/nrB37l--KNoSWgjoM4wZXOJCcDrJ7wS2ivHwSD2jXGE/1629461058/pub lic/2021-08/k%C3%A4sikirja_Kyvykkyyksien_johtamisen%20_k%C3%A4siki rja_ei%20saavutettava.pdf

D3. Asiakkuusperustaisen tietojohtamisen viitekehys. [The Framework for Customer-based Knowledge Management]. The city of Espoo. Retrieved September 29, 2021, from https://static.espoo.fi/cdn/ff/LXvbTblesC6kU3S0HebLkbMg rPam6kU8vfe8H5wsFqE/1629273361/public/2021-08/viitekehys_Asiakkuusp erustaisen_tietojohtamisen_viitekehys_ei%20saavutettava.pdf

D4. Asiakkuustiedon tuottamisen ja hyödyntämisen käsikirja. [The Handbook of the Production and Utilization of Customer Knowledge]. The city of Espoo. Retrieved September 29, 2021, from https://static.espoo.fi/cdn/ff/Xj2nMquFK TANMZfRKBHFWXuoUBw9Mun5upUPS7LJtvY/1629460848/public/2021- 08/k%C3%A4sikirja_Asiakkuustiedon_tuottamisen_ja_hy%C3%B6dynt%C3% A4misen_k%C3%A4sikirja_ei%20saavutettava.pdf

D5. Monikanavaisen asiointipalvelun johtaminen. [The Management of Multi- channel Customer Service]. The city of Espoo. Retrieved September 29, 2021, from https://static.espoo.fi/cdn/ff/ON62lK56AyXV63W3EtOY6Pfcm4E GVSVCPwhhV2PwvmI/1629273094/public/2021-08/esite_Monikanavaisen_asi ointipalvelun_johtaminen_ei%20saavutettava.pdf

D6. Monikanavaisen asiointipalvelun käsikirja. [The Handbook of Multi- channel Customer Service]. The city of Espoo. Retrieved September 29, 2021, from https://static.espoo.fi/cdn/ff/sjf5UPXVJoS5YBDe6vUXlfaS1TglkD kXeCVYfcpA5iQ/1629461116/public/2021-08/k%C3%A4sikirja_Monikanav aisen_asiointipalvelun_k%C3%A4sikirja_ei%20saavutettava.pdf

D7. Yhteiskehittämisen käsikirja. [The Handbook of Co-creation]. The city of Espoo. Retrieved September 29, 2021, from https://issuu.com/espoonkaupunki/ docs/yhteiskehittaminen-a4-web-issuu

D8. Avoimen osallisuuden käsikirja. [The Handbook of Open Participation]. The city of Espoo. Retrieved September 29, 2021, from https://static.espoo.fi/cdn/ff/ ZPo-kcoOy5DxUJI7tlV6u4a-d1ox1wsjH8IgJ-_OYjQ/1629460958/public/2021- 08/k%C3%A4sikirja_Avoimen_osallisuuden_k%C3%A4sikirja_ei%20saavute ttava.pdf

Appendix 2. List of Expert Interviews

Sutinen, Päivi, Director for City as a Service Development, City of Espoo, interviewed by Ari-Veikko Anttiroiko and Kaisu Sahamies on December 10, 2021.

Sjöholm, Katja, Senior Innovation Ecosystem Manager and Head of Co-creation and Innovation, City of Espoo, interviewed by Ari-Veikko Anttiroiko on February 7, 2022.

References

1. Komninos, N.: The Age of Intelligent Cities: Smart Environments and Innovation-for-all Strategies. Routledge, London (2015)
2. Kenney, M., Zysman, J.: The rise of the platform economy. Iss. Sci. Technol. Spring **2016**, 61–69 (2016)
3. Brynjolfsson, E., McAfee, A.: The Second Machine Age: Work, Progress, and Prosperity in a Time of Brilliant Technologies. W.W. Norton & Company, New York (2014)
4. Parker, G.G., Van Alstyne, M.W., Choudary, S.P.: Platform Revolution: How Networked Markets Are Transforming the Economy and How to Make Them Work for You. W.W. Norton & Company, New York (2017)
5. Barns, S.: Platform Urbanism: Negotiating Platform Ecosystems in Connected Cities. Palgrave Macmillan, Basingstoke (2020)
6. Hood, C., Peters, G.: The middle aging of new public management: into the age of paradox? J. Public Adm. Res. Theory **14**(3), 267–282 (2004)
7. Funck, E.K., Karlsson, T.S.: Twenty-five years of studying new public management in public administration: accomplishments and limitations. Fin. Account. Manag. **36**, 347–375 (2020)
8. Osborne, S.P., Powell, M., Cui, T., Strokosch, K.: New development: "Appreciate-Engage-Facilitate" - The role of public managers in value creation in public service ecosystems. Public Money Manag. **41**(8), 668–671 (2021)
9. Jones, C., Hesterly, W., Borgatti, S.: A general theory of network governance: exchange conditions and social mechanisms. Acad. Manag. Rev. **22**(4), 911–945 (1997)
10. Osborne, S.: The new public governance? Public Manag. Rev. **8**(3), 377–387 (2006)
11. Osborne, S.: The New Public Governance? Emerging Perspectives on the Theory and Practice of Public Governance. Routledge, London (2010)
12. Rhodes, R.A.W.: Understanding governance: ten years on. Organ. Stud. **28**(8), 1243–1264 (2007)
13. Klijn, E., Koppenjan, J.: Governance Networks in the Public Sector. Routledge, London (2016)
14. Ansell, C., Gash, A.: Collaborative platforms as a governance strategy. J. Public Adm. Res. Theory **28**(1), 16–32 (2018)
15. Haveri, A., Anttiroiko, A.-V.: Urban platforms as a mode of governance. Int. Rev. Adm. Sci. First Published 22 April 2021, 1–18 (2021)
16. Rong, K., Lin, Y., Li, B., Burström, T., Butel, L., Yu, J.: Business ecosystem research agenda: more dynamic, more embedded, and more internationalized. Asian Bus. Manag. **17**, 167–182 (2018)
17. Sahamies, K., Haveri, A., Anttiroiko, A.-V.: Local governance platforms: roles and relations of city governments, citizens, and businesses. Adm. Soc. First Published January 11, 2022 (2022)
18. Anttiroiko, A.-V.: City-as-a-platform: the rise of participatory innovation platforms in Finnish cities. Sustainability **8**(9), 922 (2016)
19. Anttiroiko, A.-V.: Digital urban planning platforms: the interplay of digital and local embeddedness in urban planning. Int. J. E-Plan. Res. **10**(3), 35–49 (2021)
20. Yin, R.K.: Case Study Research—Design and Methods, 3rd edn. Sage, Thousand Oaks (2003)
21. Morgan, M.S.: Exemplification and the use-values of cases and case studies. Stud. Hist. Philos. Sci. Part A **78**, 5–13 (2019)
22. Ylipulli, J., Luusua, A.: Smart cities with a Nordic twist? Public sector digitalization in Finnish data-rich cities. Telemat. Inform. **55**, 101457 (2020)
23. Lappalainen, P., Markkula, M., Kune, H. (eds.): Orchestrating Regional Innovation Ecosystems: Espoo Innovation Garden. Aalto University, Espoo (2015)

24. European Commission: Espoo as a digital launch pad. Digital Entrepreneurship Monitor, European Union (2016). https://www.intelligentcitieschallenge.eu/sites/default/files/2018-06/Case-Study-Deep-Dive-Espoo-v1.pdf, Accessed 12 Nov 2021

25. Rissola, G., Hervás, F., Slavcheva, M., Jonkers, K.: Place-based innovation ecosystems Espoo Innovation Garden and Aalto University (Finland). Joint Research Centre. JRC Science for Policy Report, EUR 28545 EN. Publications Office of the European Union, Luxembourg (2017)

26. Markkula, M., Kune, H.: Making smart regions smarter: smart specialization and the role of universities in regional innovation ecosystems. Technol. Innov. Manag. Rev. 5(10), 7–15 (2015)

27. Bogner, A., Menz, W.: The theory-generating expert interview: epistemological Interest, forms of knowledge, interaction. In: Bogner, A., Littig, B., Menz, W. (eds.) Interviewing Experts, pp. 43–80. Palgrave Macmillan, Basingstoke (2009)

28. O'Reilly, T.: Government as a platform. Innovations: technology, governance, Globalization 6(1), 13–40 (2011)

29. Janssen, M., Estevez, E.: Lean government and platform-based governance—doing more with less. Gov. Inf. Q. 30(1), S1–S8 (2013)

30. Desouza, K., Bhagwatwar, A.: Technology-enabled participatory platforms for civic engagement: the case of U.S. cities. J. Urban Technol. 21(4), 25–50 (2014)

31. Bollier, D.: The City as a Platform: How Digital Networks are Changing Urban Life and Governance. The Aspen Institute, Washington, D.C. (2016)

32. Brown, A., Fishenden, J., Thompson, M., Venters, W.: Appraising the impact and role of platform models and Government as a Platform (GaaP) in UK government public service reform: towards a platform assessment framework (PAF). Gov. Inf. Q. 34(2), 167–182 (2017)

33. Falco, E., Kleinhans, R.: Digital participatory platforms for co-production in urban development: a systematic review. Int. J. E-Plan. Res. 7(3), 52–79 (2018)

34. Janowski, T., Estevez, E., Baguma, R.: Platform governance for sustainable development: reshaping citizen-administration relationships in the digital age. Gov. Inf. Q. 35(4), S1–S16 (2018)

35. Ansell, C., Miura, S.: Can the power of platforms be harnessed for governance? Public Adm. 98(1), 261–276 (2020)

36. Petrescu, M.: From marketing to public value: towards a theory of public service ecosystems. Public Manag. Rev. 21(11), 1733–1752 (2019)

37. Strokosch, K., Osborne, S.: Co-experience, co-production and co-governance: an ecosystem approach to the analysis of value creation. Policy Polit. 48(3), 425–442 (2020)

38. Kinder, T., Stenvall, J., Six, F., Memon, A.: Relational leadership in collaborative governance ecosystems. Public Manag. Rev. 23(11), 1612–1639 (2021)

39. Paulin, A.A.: Informating public governance: towards a basis for a digital ecosystem. Int. J. Public Adm. Digit. Age 4(2), 14–32 (2017)

40. Celino, I., Carenini, A.: Towards a semantic city service ecosystem. In: Omitola, T., Breslin, J.G., Barnaghi, P.M. (eds.), Proceedings of the Fifth Workshop on Semantics for Smarter Cities. CEUR Workshop Proceedings, vol. 1280, pp. 3–8. CEUR-WS.org. (2014)

41. Vargo, S.L., Akaka, M.A., Wieland, H.: Rethinking the process of diffusion in innovation: a service-ecosystems and institutional perspective. J. Bus. Res. 116, 526–534 (2020)

42. Bruneo, D., et al.: An IoT service ecosystem for smart cities: The #SmartME project. Internet Things 5, 12–33 (2019)

43. Aal, K., Di Pietro, L., Edvardsson, B., Renzi, M.F., Guglielmetti Mugion, R.: Innovation in service ecosystems: an empirical study of the integration of values, brands, service systems and experience rooms. J. Serv. Manag. 27(4), 619–651 (2016)

44. Koskela-Huotari, K., Edvardsson, B., Jonasc, J.M., Sörhammard, D., Witell, L.: Innovation in service ecosystems: breaking, making, and maintaining institutionalized rules of resource integration. J. Bus. Res. **69**(8), 2964–2971 (2016)
45. de Magalhães Santos, L.G.: Toward the open government ecosystem: connecting e-participation models and open government to analyze public policies. In: Rodríguez Bolívar, M., Bwalya, K., Reddick, C. (eds.) Governance Models for Creating Public Value in Open Data Initiatives, pp. 85–102. Springer, Cham (2019)
46. Polese, F., Botti, A., Monda, A., Grimaldi, M.: Smart city as a service system: a framework to improve smart service management. J. Serv. Sci. Manag. **12**, 1–16 (2019)
47. Klassen, G., Buske, M.: City as a service and city on-demand – new concepts for intelligent urban development. In: Linnhoff-Popien, C., Schneider, R., Zaddach, M. (eds.) Digital Marketplaces Unleashed, pp. 795–807. Springer, Heidelberg (2018). https://doi.org/10.1007/978-3-662-49275-8_70
48. Vargo, S.L., Lusch, R.F.: Institutions and axioms: an extension and update of service-dominant logic. J. Acad. Mark. Sci. **44**(1), 5–23 (2016)
49. Kinder, T., Six, F., Stenvall, J., Memon, A.: Governance-as-legitimacy: are ecosystems replacing networks? Public Manag. Rev. **24**(1), 8–33 (2022)
50. Anttiroiko, A.-V., Laine, M., Lönnqvist, H.: City as a growth platform: responses of the cities of Helsinki Metropolitan area to global digital economy. Urban Sci. **4**(4), 67 (2020)
51. Haar, S.: The City as Campus: Urbanism and Higher Education in Chicago. University of Minnesota Press, Minneapolis (2011)
52. Castells, M., Hall, P.: Technopoles of the World: The Making of the 21st Century Industrial Complexes. Routledge, London (1996)
53. Tukiainen, T., Sutinen, P.: Cities as open innovation platforms for business ecosystems. In: Lappalainen, P., Markkula, M., Kune, H. (eds.) Orchestrating Regional Innovation Ecosystems: Espoo Innovation Garden, pp. 313–322. Aalto University, Espoo (2015)
54. Haque, M.S.: The diminishing publicness of public service under the current mode of governance. Public Adm. Rev. **61**, 65–82 (2001)
55. Pesch, U.: The publicness of public administration. Adm. Soc. **40**(2), 170–193 (2008)
56. Räty, R.: Espoo eager to make way for global talent. Aalto PRO, November 15, 2018. https://www.aaltopro.fi/en/aalto-leaders-insight/2018/espoo-eager-to-make-way-for-global-talent. Accessed 10 Feb 2022
57. Sarkar, S., Arcaute, E., Hatna, E., Alizadeh, T., Searle, G., Batty, M.: Evidence for localization and urbanization economies in urban scaling. R. Soc. Open Sci. **7**(3), 191638 (2020)
58. Chen, M., Zhang, H., Liu, W., Zhang, W.: The global pattern of urbanization and economic growth: evidence from the last three decades. PLoS ONE **9**(8), e103799 (2014)
59. Turok, I., McGranahan, G.: Urbanization and economic growth: the arguments and evidence for Africa and Asia. Environ. Urban. **25**(2), 465–482 (2013)
60. Gill, I.S., Goh, C.-C.: Scale economies and cities. World Bank Res. Observer **25**(2), 235–262 (2010)
61. Tiebout, C.M.: A pure theory of local expenditures. J. Polit. Econ. **64**, 416–424 (1956)
62. Wistuba, V.: Loppuraportti: Digiagenda-ohjelma 30.6.2021 [Final Report: Digiagenda Program, June 30, 2021]. Espoon kaupunki, Espoo (2021)
63. Sørensen, E., Torfing, J. (eds.): Theories of Democratic Network Governance. Palgrave Macmillan, London (2007). https://doi.org/10.1057/9780230625006
64. Trischler, J., Charles, M.: The application of a service ecosystems lens to public policy analysis and design: exploring the frontiers. J. Public Policy Mark. **38**(1), 19–35 (2019)
65. Osborne, S.P.: From public service-dominant logic to public service logic: are public service organizations capable of co-production and value co-creation? Public Manag. Rev. **20**(2), 225–231 (2018)

66. Bryson, J.M., Crosby, B.C., Bloomberg, L. (eds.): Creating Public Value in Practice: Advancing the Common Good in a Multi-Sector, Shared-Power No-One-Wholly-in-Charge World. Routledge, New York (2015)
67. Sønderskov, M., Rønning, R.: Public service logic: an appropriate recipe for improving serviceness in the public sector? Adm. Sci. **11**(3), article 64 (2021)
68. Eriksson, E.M.: Representative co-production: broadening the scope of the public service logic. Public Manag. Rev. **21**(2), 291–314 (2019)
69. Hodgkinson, I.R., Hannibal, C., Keating, B.W., Chester Buxton, R., Bateman, N.: Toward a public service management: past, present, and future directions. J. Serv. Manag. **28**(5), 998–1023 (2017)

A Broad Platform for Smart City Projects Idea Contribution and Interaction

Julia Lee[✉] and Lawrence Henschen

Northwestern University, Evanston, IL 60208, USA
j-leeh@northwestern.edu, henschen@eecs.northwestern.edu

Abstract. We propose a broad platform for smart city project idea contribution and interaction. The platform/application can be downloaded by citizens to participate in the conceiving, designing, and implementation of a project that will impact their life.

Keywords: Smart city project · Interactive application · Common goal · Guided exploration

1 Introduction

Smart city projects are rapidly rolling out in cities all over the world [3–5]. As the number of projects grows, the richness of the projects also grows. Nowadays, the ideas for smart city projects are not only exchanged through articles and websites, but also through classes [12] and large expos [2].

Some planed smart city projects delineate very impressive environments and lives of citizens of future smart cities, and these are not just pictures or videos of proposed ideas – they are smart city projects in progress [13, 14].

This growing richness can be significantly enhanced by contributions and interactions among a much broader audience in ways that support, extend, critique, etc. the work of the engineers and immediate stakeholders [6, 7]. When ideas go through such a broad interactive process, they can change, grow, and produce much more interesting results. Meetings of engineers, city officials, and immediate stakeholders do not allow for broad participation from the community. Large expos are usually focused on commercial aspects of smart cities and in any case include too broad a community. We propose a system in which the right community of interested people can participate in the discussion of a smart city project. Allowing input from the general population of the city should certainly benefit any smart city project. After all, the general population will be the real/major occupants, users, enjoyers, and sustainable human resources. This work represents a significant extension to our prior work in this area [1].

Our proposed system includes an application that can be downloaded into individuals' smart phones or tablets. To join the interactive community, an individual provides basic personal information such as name, email address, area of profession or experience, etc. The system can verify that the individual is a relevant community member

N. A. Streitz and S. Konomi (Eds.): HCII 2022, LNCS 13325, pp. 158–168, 2022.
https://doi.org/10.1007/978-3-031-05463-1_11

(for example, actually lives in the city for which the project is being developed) and will save the information by creating an account for the individual. After getting registered into the system, the individual can perform different activities: browsing the list of ideas by category, inputting ideas by category [2, 8, 9], making comments on an existing idea, suggesting a new category/topic, etc.

2 Purpose of Proposed Platform/System

Traditionally, for large projects like smart city projects, only the immediate stakeholders and their representatives are involved in the planning and designing stages. This is understandable for the reason of being easier to manage the project and avoiding any chaos introduced by unorganized opinions without focus. The stakeholders contribute to the requirements of the project from their own point of view and/or aspects. Because these people are likely to be part of the occupants of the future smart city, they certainly carry relevant opinions on how the project can be shaped. However, their ideas are more focused from the point of view of their particular area of expertise and from the point of view of their particular requirements. They might be able to carry opinions of others through different means of communication with broader groups of "beneficiaries" of the smart city project. Their focus of interest and strength of professional background might give them the ability of summarize and filter a large amount of information related to the smart city project from broader bases.

However, there are many reasons to involve broader segments of the population and collect some "hidden ingenuities". We all have experiences of good ideas "bursting out" suddenly when broader groups of individuals are motivated and focused. When more people with direct interest are involved, more such ideas will be generated. Further, we know that when more people are involved there is more chance for interaction and ideas from different participants feeding on each other. More ideas and more interaction lead to "sparks" of good and new ideas. This is similar to "aggregation" of hidden ingenuities.

However, if the community of participants is too large, the discussions often stray away from the topics of interest. The system we are proposing is different from general social media; we are not proposing another platform to allow people to "freely" express themselves in any aspect. We are proposing a platform focused on a common goal – to conceive, design, and implement a smart city project that will meet all the requirements from stakeholders and general citizens. The focus on the common goal and the supporting features provided by our system will avoid chaos and help assure progress towards the goals of the smart city project.

3 Key Features

As we mentioned in the previous section, our proposed platform/application has some key features to support the focused goal. In this section we will discuss the key features of our proposed system.

3.1 Motivation

The first important feature of our system is to motive the users. The ways to motive users to be involved and to contribute their ideas can be:

- List some issues of the current city that can be improved.
- List the impact of the current issues to daily life of individuals.
- List the features that can be introduced to the "smart city".
- Show the tentative smart city project plan for this city.
- Show some of the smart city projects around the world that have been implemented.

3.2 Guided Exploration

The platform provides guided exploration and interaction. A user will not be allowed to post material unrelated to the goal. Guided exploration will assure the system resources are used for the purpose of the smart city project. This will also ensure to collect useful ideas and to lead to useful results (Figs. 1 and 2).

After a user logs in to the system, an eye-catching headline, such as "Your city, Your project, Your idea matters!!" motivates the user to be involved. The main menu will include topics such as:

- Information.
- Forums.
- Contribution.

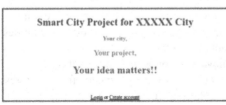

Fig. 1. Login/Register   **Fig. 2.** Select action to perform

The above figures show the home/login/register page and after-login page which asks the user to select an action to continue.

Information. When the user chooses "information", a sub menu will drop down to show the possible categories of information related to the smart city project. The submenu could contain but is not limited to the following:

- Smart city projects – the goals and the technologies. This sub-menu will open up a page that has a brief description of what a "smart city project" is and the issues that a smart city project would try to deal with. It will also summarize the technologies available to support the project [15].

- Smart city project activities around the world. The internal search engine will search the web and display links related to smart city projects around the world. The normal Google search will be used plus some filters built in to this application, for example, based on date, reputation of the website, etc. After clicking one of the links, the information provided by the site will be displayed. It will have links to the relevant web pages to give some details of those projects. The search results will include smart city projects planned around the world. Many of the planned smart city projects around the world have been publicized on the web, and there are some very impressive videos on the internet showing some of the planned/initiated smart city projects [13]. These videos can provide information and motivation to the user in a more concrete/intuitive way.
- Smart city projects of our city. This sub-menu will give some details of the projects planned by the city. It can list the public issues currently existing in the city and the plans of the projects to "attack" those issues. It should also give the current progress and future schedules of the projects.

The following figures illustrate how the "Information" menu can get the users different types of information related to world-wide or home-city smart city projects.

When the user selects the sub-menu "Smart City Projects in the World" a page will list all the links found by the modified search engine as illustrated in Fig. 3. When the user clicks one of the links, say "Cities of the Future | The World in 2050", the user will be able to watch a video describe some of the planned smart city projects around the world (Fig. 4).

On the other hand, if the user selects the sub-menu "Smart City Project in XXXXX City" as in Fig. 5, then a list of city related issues/topics will be displayed as in Fig. 6.

Fig. 3. Smart City projects in the world   **Fig. 4.** Cities of the future | The world in 2050 [14]

Fig. 5. User selects local city issue   **Fig. 6.** Local city issues displayed

Forums. When the user selects the "Forums" menu, a submenu drops down to let the user chose a category to browse and contribute:

- Current focus topic
- Smart city project general
- Existing issues
- Planned goals
- Technologies
- Resources
- Schedule

When the user selects one of the sub-menus, a page displays the on-going discussion about that category. The page shows the list of posted opinions of the individual users with their names and possibly picture icons in addition to the posted texts. The page provides an input area for the user to post his/her opinion on the subject. The input area allows the user to upload pictures and/or files to post with the typed text. What he/she posted will be displayed immediately on the screen with some way to distinguish his/her post from the posts from other users, for example, on two different columns of the screen.

In Fig. 7, Rick Goodman joined a forum discussion about city traffic lights. John Dow raised the issue of city traffic light pole damage. May Smith added some idea on changing the lights into LED lights to save energy. Rich first agreed with the idea of LED lighting. Then he is typing in more ideas to make traffic light poles into "smart poles" that can perform other functions in addition to lighting. The buttons on the right side of the text area allow him to upload related pictures or files.

Contributions. When a user selects the "Contribution" menu, a submenu drops down to let the user chose a category to contribute to:

- View contributions
- Comment
- Make a contribution

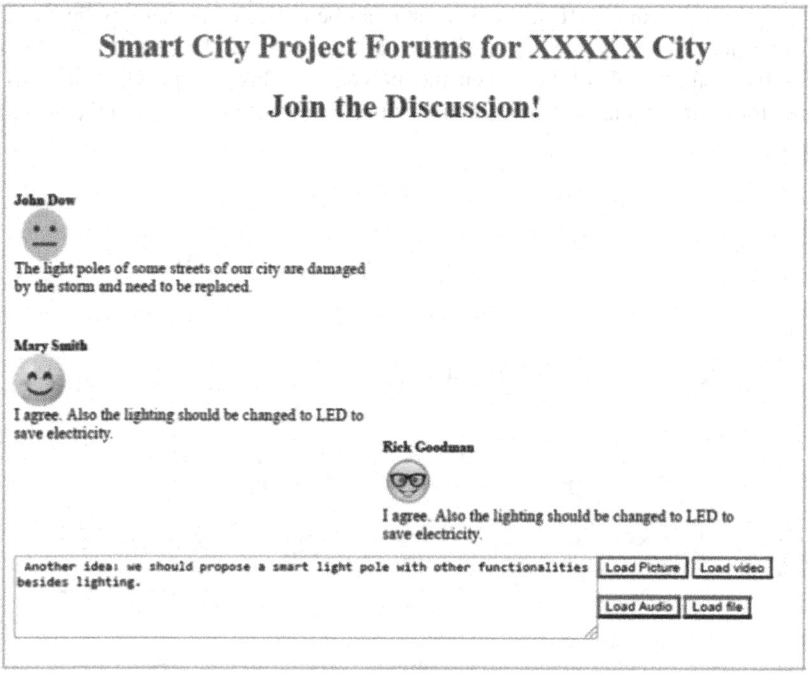

Fig. 7. Joining a forum discussion

Each of the above sub-menus will drop the following sub-categories to choose from:

- Existing issues in the city
- Planned goals
- Technologies
- Resources
- Schedule

One may wonder what is the difference between "Forum" and "Contribution". We distinguish "Contribution" from a discussion in forum by the extensive effort made by the contributors. Extensive effort involves serious study, not just a spontaneous reaction. When submitting a contribution, the user needs to provide evidence, supporting data, and/or references. A user can summarize some forum discussion topics into a contribution post, but to do so the user needs to provide some high-level overview and the focal point(s) of the discussion.

When a contribution idea has been input in a category, the system will ask the user to also provide some preliminary self-evaluation using criteria such as: feasibility, impact to the city, economic impact, environmental impact, policy conformation, references, etc. Similarly, when the contribution is to make comments on an existing idea/issue, the systems will also ask for evaluation using the same kind of criteria.

In Fig. 8, Mary is making a contribution on an existing issue related to parking. She is suggesting to install sensors in the parking space area to indicate whether or not the parking space is occupied. If the sensor data can be collected and an application, say on a smart phone, can display the available parking space in the city, it will certainly improve the quality of life of the citizen and the visitors. This page provides not only the text area for typing in the contribution idea but also the buttons to upload the necessary references.

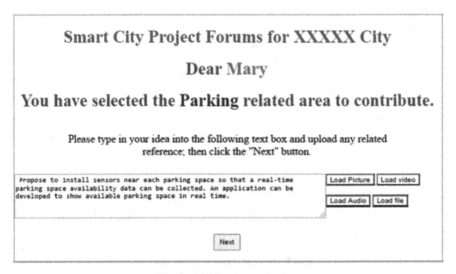

Fig. 8. Making a contribution

After Mary clicks the "Next" button, another page comes up to ask for a self-evaluation of the contributed idea. Figure 9 displays the possible criteria used for evaluation. In this case, Mary puts a 5 in the "Improvement on Citizen Life", which is a reasonable evaluation. She is not sure about the impact on the environment by putting sensors in the parking space area, so she puts a "N/A" for that criterion.

Note that we cannot put all reasonable criteria in the illustration due to space limitation.

If another user tries to comment on a contributed idea, he/she can select the "Comment" drop down menu and appropriate sub-menu to see a list of contributed ideas in that category and pick the one he/she would like to comment on. For example, in Fig. 10 John wants to make a comment on the contribution made by Mary on parking space sensor installation.

He has more concerns about the implementation of the sensor (network) system and the budget required. Obviously both Mary and John have put a lot of thought into this plausible project that can be part of the smart city project for the XXXXX city. This could be a good contribution to the Smart City Project planning team.

Fig. 9. Self-evaluation for a contribution

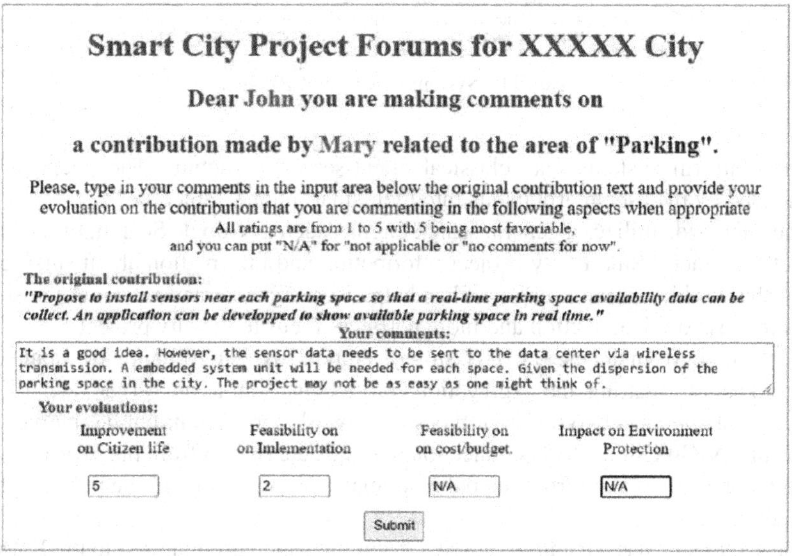

Fig. 10. Commenting a contribution

4   System Structure

The following figure depicts the system structure of our proposed platform/system. We abbreviate the name as BPCI (Broad Platform for Contribution and Interaction) to save space.

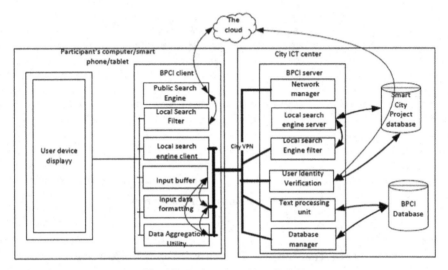

Fig. 11.   System structure of BPCI

The platform system is a "classical client-server" structure. The client side is downloaded by the users/participants into their smart phone, tablet, or PC.

The client side utilizes a general search engine, such as Google Search, to search the internet for general Smart City Project information and information about smart cities around the world. A search engine filter helps to reorganize and reformat the search results for ease of visualization and more pertinent focus to the city project.

All the input from the users will be stored, temporarily, in the client-side input buffer subject to data formatting and aggregation before being sent to the server side.

The client side has two different types of network connection: public internet connection and XXXXX city VPN connection. All the data sent to/from the server side are via VPN connection. Data from the public domains are sent through the public internet connection.

The server side has a local/private search engine which is connected to the XXXXX city smart city database. There is a filter for this search engine. It filters the data to be more focused on the discussions by the BPCI users, and it prevents compromising proprietary information from unintentionally going public.

There is a "User Identity Verification" unit that tries to verify the identity when a user registers to BPCI system. It serves two purposes: to avoid potentially harmful "invasion" to the system by people who are not relevant to the city and to identify potential experts in needed areas who can be invited to the core project team.

A text processing unit extracts useful information from the "Forums" discussion and reformats the data into concise information that can be stored into a longer-term data storage. The raw data of the "Forums" discussion should be periodically moved to some secondary storage or even cleared depending on how much the data-flow would be.

The data from users' contributions, including the reference material and comments made by other users, will be stored in the system database in the city data center. Since contribution inputs have well defined format, a relational database [10] could well serve the purpose. Data-mining software (not shown in Fig. 11) can be used to extract information that can be promptly sent to the project's core system, including the OMS4SC [1], so that highly rated contributions can be adopted as soon as possible to the project development.

5   Summary

We have proposed a broad platform for citizens to participate in their city's smart city projects. Our proposed platform/application has some key features to support the focused goal. The system motivates the users to participate and to contribute by showing the big picture of smart city projects around the world present and in the future. The platform/system provides guided exploration on discussion and contribution, so the user will focus on the issues that are needed by the city and their own life.

The system can be incorporated by the OMS4SC [1] and other possible smart city project platforms to collect useful ideas from a broad base.

References

1. Lee, J.C., Henschen, L.J.: A smart city stakeholder online meeting interface. In: Kurosu, M. (ed.) HCII 2021. LNCS, vol. 12764, pp. 554–565. Springer, Cham (2021). https://doi.org/10.1007/978-3-030-78468-3_38
2. Smart City Expo World Congress: City Possible Summit (2021). https://citypossible.com/events/city-possible-summit-2021/?cmp=2021.q4.glo.glo.others.dir-res.purp.others.city-possible-summit-2021.301102.sep.txt.googles.scr
3. Deloitte. https://www2.deloitte.com/us/en/pages/consulting/solutions/smart-cities-of-the-future.html. Accessed 08 Nov 2021
4. GuidehouseInsights. https://guidehouseinsights.com/news-and-views/more-than-250-smart-city-projects-exist-in-178-cities-worldwide. Accessed 08 Nov 2021
5. The Future of Smart Cities: Barclays. https://www.cib.barclays/our-insights/Rethinking-smart-cities-prioritising-infrastructure.html?cid=paidsearch-textads_google_google_themes_smart_cities_us_research_general_phrase_300433502566&gclid=EAIaIQobChMIi_Gh_JOJ9AIVaW5vBB1g9QSEEAAYAiAAEgIVYfD_BwE&gclsrc=aw.ds
6. Jayasena, N., Mallawarachchi, H., Waidyasekara, A.: Stakeholder Analysis For Smart City Development Project: An Extensive Literature Review. https://www.researchgate.net/publication/331225610_Stakeholder_Analysis_For_Smart_City_Development_Project_An_Extensive_Literature_Review. Accessed 26 May 2020
7. Willems, J., Van den Bergh, J., Viaene, S.: Smart City Projects and Citizen Participation: The case of London, Public Sector Management in a Globalized World. Part of the series NPO-Management, pp. 249–266. https://doi.org/10.1007/978-3-658-16112-5_12

8. Sydney Stone, Key Challenges of Smart Cities & How to Overcome Them. https://ubidots.com/blog/the-key-challenges-for-smart-cities/. Accessed 08 Nov 2021
9. Smart city – Wikipedia. https://en.wikipedia.org/wiki/Smart_city. Accessed 2 Jan 2021
10. Ullman, J.D.: The Relational Model Principles of Database Systems, pp. 145–173. Computer Science Press, Inc., Cambridge (1982)
11. Hoffer, J., Ramesh, V., Topi, H.: Modern Database Management, 13th edn. Pearson Publishing Company, London (2019)
12. MIT School of Architecture and Planning; Smart Mobility: Reimagining the Future of Transportation Tech & Sustainable Cities. Accessed 18 Dec 2021
13. YouTube: Future Smart Cities Planned By 2050. https://www.youtube.com/watch?v=SZZ2N2DcLi4. Accessed 18 Dec 2021
14. YouTube: Cities of the Future | The World in 2050. https://www.youtube.com/watch?v=T6mK-Ukr_ts. Accessed 30 Dec 2021
15. Bartz/Stockmar, CC BY-SA 4.0. https://commons.wikimedia.org/w/index.php?curid=69505744. Accessed 31 Dec 2021

Exploring the Usefulness and Usability of Ambient Theory for Smart Cities

H. Patricia McKenna[(✉)]

AmbientEase, Victoria, BC V8V 4Y9, Canada
mckennaph@gmail.com

Abstract. The purpose of this paper is to explore the usefulness and usability of ambient theory for smart cities. This work is motivated by the need for theory in assisting to provide understanding of, and insight into, the evolving development of smart cities. While ambient theory for smart cities has been advanced, assessed as a theory, and evaluated as a good theory, this paper highlights the importance and nature of usefulness and usability for ambient theory in smart environments. A theoretical perspective is provided based on a review of the research literature for the concepts of theory usefulness and usability. An overview of research works associated with ambient theory and smart environments is then provided along with emergent variables explored. Using an exploratory case study combined with an explanatory correlational design, variables relevant to usefulness and usability are explored in the context of ambient theory for smart cities. Quantitative findings emerging from survey results reveal the nature and possible usefulness of correlations for variables such as *mixed-use spaces* and *urbanizing* (e.g., adapting for urban uses). Among the advantages of exploring the usefulness and usability of ambient theory for smart cities is that guidance on potential variables for researchers and practitioners to consider is provided while involving people meaningfully in thinking about and assessing their everyday urban experiences. The impact of these findings for the application of ambient theory for smart cities could influence directions for smart cities and regions in terms of planning, design, development, evaluation, and creative uses going forward.

Keywords: Smart cities · Theory usability · Theory usefulness · Urban theory · Urbanizing

1 Introduction

In response to the under-theorizing of the smart cities' domain identified by Batty [1] and Roy [2] and the need for theory to address 21st century urban environments articulated by Brenner [3] and Harrison and Abbott Donnelly [4], McKenna [5] advanced the notion of ambient theory for smart cities. The three key propositions of ambient theory for smart cities are awareness in relation to technologies and to people; awareness-based spaces that foster an evolving interplay of one or more elements (e.g., adaptive, dynamic, emergent, interactive, pervasive); and meaningfully involving people in action such as planning, design, development, implementation, evaluation, or creative use(s)

N. A. Streitz and S. Konomi (Eds.): HCII 2022, LNCS 13325, pp. 169–180, 2022.
https://doi.org/10.1007/978-3-031-05463-1_12

of the ambient dimension of technologies, as identified by McKenna [5]. Highlighting the importance of the usefulness of a theory, Higgins [6] explores ways of "making a theory useful" giving rise to the exploration in this paper of this challenge in relation to ambient theory for smart cities. Löwgren [7] describes usability as a central concept in human-computer interaction (HCI) where it is said that a range of perspectives have emerged. Windlinger and Tuzcuoğlu [8] explore usability in relation to workplace environments, noting key efforts pertaining to ergonomics in human-computer interaction (HCI) while seeking to add a user-centric perspective. It is worth noting that the International Standards Organization (ISO) identifies three dimensions of usability – effectiveness, efficiency, and satisfaction – in ISO 9241-11 [9], all of which include in their descriptions the importance of the element of usefulness. As such, the main objectives of this paper are to provide a) a review of the research literature pertaining to theory usefulness and usability; and b) an exploration of ambient theory for smart cities in relation to theory usefulness and usability.

2   Background

From a health education perspective, Van Ryn and Heaney [10] discuss "barriers to the use of theory" using social learning theory (SLT) and the explanatory variables of behavioral capacity, efficacy expectations, and outcome expectations to show "how theory can guide practice" while "exposing common misconceptions of the nature and usefulness of theory." From a business administration perspective, Brunsson [11] discusses the use and usefulness of theory, as in, to "allow for discoveries, theorizing, and new concepts" that are "experience and intuition based." Speaking in terms of a "long and unsettled future" for smart cities, Karvonen, Cugurullo, and Caprotti [12] assert that "we are closer to the beginning of the smart city journey than to its endpoint." As such, the "smart agenda" is said to be "unavoidably bound up" with several elements including that of the "messy processes of translating ambitious visions into real-world applications." In keeping with the potential for guiding and informing practice, Kordts, Gerlach, and Schrader [13] refer to "ambient applications" as "applications that are used within smart environments." In this paper, ambient theory for smart cities and the explanatory variables associated with "meaningfully involving people in action" with implications for "planning, design, development, implementation, evaluation, or creative use(s) of the ambient dimension" are explored in terms of the potential for guiding practice in urban environments.

Definitions for key terms used in this paper are provided in Sect. 2.1 based on real world practice, dictionaries, and the research literature.

2.1   Definitions

Definitions for key terms used in this work in the context of the ambient, as in, aware people and awareness-enabling technologies in support of smart environments include the following:

Smart Cities. According to Kris Carter [14] in the Boston Mayor's Office of New Urban Mechanics, what contributes to the smartness of a city is "the recognition of the strengths community members possess and how to lift them up, how to build partnerships, how to learn together, and how to be accepting of failure as part of that learning process" and technology may be used "to answer questions and move community-enabled plans forward."

Useful. Merriam-Webster [15] defines useful as "capable of being put to use."

Usability. In the context of human-computer interaction (HCI) and software systems, Lin, Choong, and Salvendy [16] refer to the definition of usability by Brian Shackel [17] as "the capability in human functional terms to be used easily and effectively by the specified range of users, given specified training and user support, to fulfil the specified range of tasks, within the specified range of environmental scenarios."

2.2 Paper Overview

What follows is the development of a theoretical perspective for theory usefulness and usability and discussion of emerging variables pertaining to ambient theory for smart cities (ATSC). A conceptual framework showing independent variables influencing potential outcomes for ATSC is then formulated for use in this paper. The methodology underlying the exploration in this paper is described followed by the presentation of findings. A discussion of findings is provided, followed by a conclusion including limitations of this work, future directions for research and practice, and identification of the intended audience.

3 Theoretical Perspective: Usefulness, Usability, and ATSC

Higgins [6] discusses the notion of "making a theory useful" identifying the varying purposes of theory in being, for example, "generative of new ideas and new discoveries." Additionally, Higgins [6] argues that "for a theory to be useful, it needs to be studied thoroughly for what it is and what it is not." Further, Higgins [6] advises that the "test for a theory is whether its logic concludes with an implication, often surprising, that suggests new research that otherwise would not be done" as in, "research that ends in a discovery." Solove [18] describe theories as "not lifeless pristine abstractions but organic and dynamic beings" that "are meant to live, breathe, and grow" and "will, it is hoped, be tested, doubted, criticized, amended, supported, and reinterpreted" and as such "are not meant to be the final word, but a new chapter in an ongoing conversation." Theory is also said by Wise and Shaffer [19] to be important for the identification of variables in terms of "what variables a researcher should attend to" and how to "make them actionable." In the formulation of ambient theory for smart cites, variables have been identified by McKenna [5] pertaining to *creative opportunities* and *technology-driven services*, and *creative opportunities* and *access to public data*, that when correlated yield what Creswell [20] considers to be within the range of "very good" relationships, at Spearman correlation coefficients for ordinal data of .70. Similarly, when *awareness* is correlated with *interactivity*, using the proxies of *heightening urban sensibilities* and *interactive public spaces* respectively, a "very good" correlation of .81 emerges. However, when *privacy* is correlated with *ICTs* (Information and Communication Technologies) a Spearman correlation coefficient of .57 emerges with "limited prediction" potential according to Creswell [20]. Variables have also been explored resulting in typology development by McKenna [21] and taxonomy development by McKenna [22] in the context of smart city explorations.

Regarding usability, Zambonelli, Salim, Loke, De Meuter, and Kanhere [23] remind us of the attributes identified by Krug [24] for the usability of an interface, namely, useful, learnable, memorable, desirable, and delightful. The notion of "interface" is reminiscent perhaps of "smart spaces" as articulated by Streitz et al. [25] where awareness by people, extended by awareness-enabling technologies contributes to environments wherein "the world around us becomes the interface". Designing cities to be humane and cooperative hybrid cities, Streitz [26] advances the notion of usable privacy and data being useful in terms of "useful services to citizens" and "smart car data collection" being "useful for maintenance, or providing navigation support" and citizens being motivated "to contribute data about the city" as such data "can be useful for the city administration" in providing services to people. Thinking in terms of the notion by Streitz [26] of designing cities to be humane and cooperative hybrid spaces could perhaps be combined with the notion by Krug [24] of an interface for the city with usability features.

Based on this review of the research literature, an ambient theory for smart cites framework is formulated in Fig. 1 showing a series of independent variables pertaining to usefulness and usability (e.g., access to public data, connecting, heightening urban sensibilities, innovative opportunities to make use of data, mixed-use spaces, urbanizing), interacting with, and possibly influencing, the dependent variable identified by ATSC (e.g., meaningfully involving people in actions), with implications for outcomes.

Application of Ambient Theory for Smart Cities

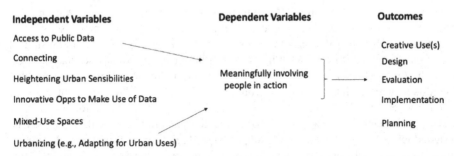

Fig. 1. Ambient theory for smart cities framework: independent variables influencing dependent variables with implications for outcome potentials.

As such, independent variables are explored in this paper in terms of the potential for influencing a particular dependent variable for ambient theory for smart cities with implications for outcomes pertaining to usability and usefulness potentials.

4 Methodology

Methodologically, this paper uses an exploratory case study approach combined with an explanatory correlational design in exploring the usefulness and usability of the application of ambient theory for smart cities. Data collection methods include use of a pre-tested survey instrument with open-ended and closed questions about smart cities and in-depth interviews guided by a pre-tested interview protocol. Using an online space, people were invited to sign up for the study and demographic data were gathered during this process including age range, gender, location, and self-categorization (e.g., educator, student, community member, etc.). Study participants emerged from cities in Canada, the United States, Europe, and the Middle East. Survey respondents were asked to assess various aspects of smart cities, based on their everyday experiences. A selection of aspects assessed by survey respondents constitute the independent variables (Fig. 1) selected for exploration in this paper pertaining to use, usability, and usefulness. In parallel with the study underlying this work, data were also systematically collected through individual and groups discussions across many sectors in a variety of Canadian cities (e.g., Toronto, Vancouver, Greater Victoria) and beyond (e.g., Asia). Overall, an analysis was conducted for n = 79 consisting of 42% females and 58% males for people ranging in age from their 20s to their 70s.

5 Findings

Findings from a range of elements assessed in a survey on smart cities shed light on the usefulness and usability of the application of ambient theory for smart cities. For example, survey respondents were asked to assess the extent to which they associate smart cities with *mixed-use spaces* and the extent to which aware technologies give rise to possibilities such as *urbanizing*, as in, *adapting for urban uses*. As shown in Table 1, on a seven-point Likert-type scale, with 1 = not at all and 7 = absolutely, for *mixed-use spaces*, respondent assessments show 17% at position 5 on the scale, 33% at position 6, and 50% at position 7. For *urbanizing* (e.g., *adapting for urban uses*), respondent assessments show 50% at position 5; 17% at position 6; and 33% at position 7.

Table 1. Correlation between mixed-use spaces and urbanizing.

Element	Assessments	Correlation
Mixed-use spaces	17% (5); 33% (6); 50% (7)	.56
Urbanizing	50% (5); 17% (6); 33% (7)	

Using an explanatory correlational design as described by Creswell [20], a relationship emerges between *mixed-use spaces* and *urbanizing* (e.g., adapting for urban uses) in the form of a Spearman correlation coefficient for ordinal data of .56, through use of the correlation feature of the Real Statistics Resource Pack containing an-add in for Microsoft Excel [27]. Creswell [20] cautions that correlations in the .35 to .65 range "are useful for limited prediction." Exploring further, as shown in Table 2, when asked to assess the extent to which aware technologies give rise to possibilities such as *heightening urban sensibilities,* respondent assessments show 33% at position 5, 17% at position 6 and 50% at position 7. When assessments for *urbanizing* (e.g., adapting for urban uses) are correlated with assessments for *heightening urban sensibilities,* a Spearman correlation coefficient of .43 emerges.

Table 2. Correlation between urbanizing and heightening urban sensibilities.

Element	Assessments	Correlation
Urbanizing	50% (5); 17% (6); 33% (7)	.43
Heightening urban sensibilities	33% (5); 17% (6); 50% (7)	

Continuing the exploration further, as shown in Table 3, for *heightening urban sensibilities,* respondent assessments show 33% at position 5, 17% at position 6 and 50% at position 7. For *connecting,* respondent assessments show 17% at position 5 and 83% at position 7. When assessments for *heightening urban sensibilities* are correlated with assessments for *connecting,* a Spearman correlation coefficient of .56 emerges.

Table 3. Correlation between heightening urban sensibilities and connecting.

Element	Assessments	Correlation
Heightening urban sensibilities	33% (5); 17% (6); 50% (7)	.56
Connecting	17% (5); 83% (7)	

Continuing the exploration further, as shown in Table 4, when asked to assess the extent to which factors such as *access to public data* contribute to the livability of a smart city, respondent assessments show 25% at positions 4, 5, 6, and 7. When asked to assess the extent to which factors such as *innovative opportunities to make use of data* contribute to increased value for data in smart cities, respondent assessments show 50% at positions 6 and 7. When assessments for *access to public data* are correlated with assessments for *innovative opportunities to make use of data,* a Spearman correlation coefficient of .44 emerges.

Table 4. Correlation between access to public data and innovative opportunities.

Element	Assessments	Correlation
Access to public data	25% (4); 25% (5); 25% (6); 25% (7)	.44
Innovative opps – use of data	50% (6); 50% (7)	

In addition to survey-based assessments, guided by the use of ambient theory for smart cities and the proposition of meaningfully involving people in action, other ways of exploring the usefulness and usability of the theory include putting the theory out in the world through international conferences. For example, ATSC was first advanced through a conference paper [5]. A second conference paper assessing ATSC by McKenna [28] was presented virtually through video, in the future technologies space, where among viewers, a response of particular interest was received from a conference participant resulting in an invitation to deliver a talk to a doctoral course on critiquing theory. In response, a video presentation was prepared for the doctoral course on critiquing theory using ambient theory for smart cities as an example of critiquing a contemporary theory developed for real-world environments. As such, ambient theory for smart cities was put to work, demonstrating a type of usability, and hopefully making the theory useful for educational purposes.

A third paper assessing whether and how ambient theory for smart cities fulfills the criteria for a "good" theory was prepared for presentation at a conference in the international intelligent human systems integration space by McKenna [29]. This paper resulted in the author being selected to co-chair a session on "applications and future trends" where the paper was presented virtually via video as the first in a series of paper presentations during the session.

6 Discussion

A discussion of findings for the usefulness and usability of ambient theory for smart cities is presented in this section where Sect. 6.1 focuses on usefulness and Sect. 6.2 focuses on usability.

6.1 Usefulness

A series of independent variables are explored in this paper, based on assessments by people of their everyday experiences of smart cities, as a way of evaluating the usefulness of ambient theory for smart cities. Findings from correlations conducted in Sect. 5 are summarized in Table 5.

While the correlations found among the variables in Table 5 are useful for limited prediction they also are said to be "the typical values used to identify variable membership in the statistical procedure of factor analysis" [20] and as such, present a form of usefulness in the guiding of further research.

Gregor [30] describes several types of theory where studies that focus on explaining and predicting (EP) are said to "usefully contribute to either theory building or theory testing." While some prediction potential is demonstrated in the findings for this paper, albeit limited, this work demonstrates usefulness in theory building for ambient theory for smart cities in terms of the variables identified and activated for use. This work also tests ambient theory for smart cities in terms of the relationship between variables and the potential for variables to influence the proposition of meaningfully involving people in action, providing potentially useful guidance to researchers and practitioners engaged in the design, planning, development, implementation, evaluation, or creative use(s) of smart city initiatives.

Table 5. Ambient theory for smart cities: assessment of variables for usefulness.

Independent variables	Relationships	Usefulness
Mixed-use spaces & urbanizing	.56 Spearman correlation Useful for limited prediction Useful for factor analysis	Yes
Heightening urban sensibilities & urbanizing	.43 Spearman correlation Useful for limited prediction Useful for factor analysis	Yes
Connecting & heightening urban sensibilities	.56 Spearman correlation Useful for limited prediction Useful for factor analysis	Yes
Access to public data & Innovative opps for data use	.44 Spearman correlation Useful for limited prediction Useful for factor analysis	Yes

6.2 Usability

Considering ambient theory for smart cities in the context of interfaces as articulated by Streitz et al. [25] for working with smart cities, it may be important to keep Krug's attributes in mind when thinking about and evaluating the usability of a theory. As such, ATSC is discussed here in relation to the attributes of usability identified by Krug [24] – delightful, desirable, learnable, memorable, and useful.

Delightful. Whether ambient theory for smart cities can be said to be "delightful" remains to be determined (TBD). In the meantime, a conference video presentation of a paper assessing ambient theory for smart cities by McKenna [28] was found to be "very interesting" by a conference participant with expressions of interest in possible collaborations going forward.

Desirable. The many individuals who are downloading and reading the paper on advancing ambient theory for smart cities by McKenna [5] and the paper assessing ATSC by McKenna [28] is perhaps indicative of the "desire" to engage with the theory in some way.

Learnable. Again, the many individuals who are downloading and reading the paper on advancing ambient theory for smart cities by McKenna [5] and the paper assessing ATSC by McKenna [28] are perhaps providing indications that people are wanting to learn about the theory. The extent that the theory is put-to-use going forward will provide insight into the nature of the learnability of the theory which to date remains to be determined (TBD).

Memorable. The sharing of the theory paper in a conference venue where it received the best paper award when the theory was first advanced in the research community by McKenna [5] was certainly memorable for the author of the paper and possibly for those involved in the decision to select the paper for the award, and possibly also for the many individuals who are attentive in some way to the conference paper and to other conference papers presented on ATSC [28, 29].

Useful. Indeed, when the paper assessing the theory was presented in a conference (virtual video presentation) by McKenna [28], interest in the theory emerged in the form of an invitation to the author to speak to a class of doctoral students in a course on critiquing theory, possibly indicative of the usefulness potential of the theory for educational purposes and other potential purposes.

Table 6 provides a summary of usability attributes and their assessments in relation to ambient theory for smart cities.

Table 6. Ambient theory for smart cities: assessment of usability attributes.

Attributes	Ambient theory for smart cities	Usability
Delightful	Interest in conference paper presentation	TBD
Desirable	Interest in the theory (paper views/downloads)	Yes
Learnable	Interest in learning about the theory	Yes/TBD
Memorable	Best paper award	Yes
Useful	Doctoral course on critiquing theories invitation	Yes

Regarding outcomes, to the extent that the role of theory is said by Gieseler, Loschelder, and Friese [31] to "inspire new research, lead to discoveries that make contributions beyond the previously known, and promote theoretical progress", it would seem that ambient theory has begun to inspire developments for smart cities in terms of explorations pertaining to variables in assessing the usefulness and usability of the theory; is shown to be influential for the work of other researchers as the recipient of the Best Paper Award by McKenna [5] at a recent conference; and may have further potentials associated with an invitation to present to a doctoral course on critiquing theories in response to a future technologies conference presentation by McKenna [28]. As such, this paper is significant in that a contemporary, real-world theory in the emergent and evolving domain of smart cities is being, in the words of Higgins [6], "allowed to develop through contact with the world" while undergoing explorations of usefulness and usability and possibly revealing "theory-generated discovery" since "what distinguishes a theory" it is said "are the discoveries that it generates" [6] as in, variables that matter to people in smart environments such as *access to public data, connections, heightening urban sensibilities, innovative opportunities to make use of data,* and *urbanizing* (e.g., *adapting for urban uses*).

7 Conclusion

This paper provides an exploration of the usefulness and usability of ambient theory for smart cities by demonstrating how the theory may be applied on the one hand and by discussing how the theory is being received on the other hand. While findings in this paper show limited prediction capability for variables associated with theory usefulness and usability when correlated – for example, *access to public data* correlated with *innovative opportunities to make use of data* shows a Spearman correlation coefficient for ordinal data of .44 and *mixed-use spaces* correlated with *urbanizing* (e.g., adapting for urban uses) shows a correlation of .56 – relationships are nevertheless shown to be present providing opportunities going forward for further explorations in research and in practice. This paper contributes to the theory testing literature for ambient theory for smart cities while pointing to early signs of progress for the theory in terms of usefulness and usability. As such, this paper is significant in that it highlights emergent developments for ambient theory for smart cities in real world spaces as the theory makes ongoing "contact with the world" [6].

Limitations of this work pertaining, among other things, to the small sample size are mitigated by the potential to extend the inquiry more broadly, providing opportunities for further research going forward, and more particularly, for the potential to achieve stronger prediction capabilities for the variables explored. This work may also be limited by the theoretical perspective provided for theory usefulness and usability, opening opportunities for further review and exploration going forward. And finally, another limitation of this work may be the variables used to explore the usefulness and usability of ambient theory for smart cities, providing opportunities going forward to identify and explore other, possibly more relevant variables. This paper will be of interest to urban researchers concerned with urban theory to guide research and to practitioners concerned with design, planning, development, implementation, evaluation, and creative use(s) in smart city initiatives and meaningfully involving people in action in smart cities and regions, more generally.

References

1. Batty, M.: Big data, smart cities and city planning. Dialog. Hum. Geogr. **3**(3), 274–279 (2013). https://doi.org/10.1177/2043820613513390
2. Roy, A.: The 21st century metropolis: new geographies of theory. Reg. Stud. **43**(6), 819–830 (2009). https://doi.org/10.1080/00343400701809665
3. Brenner, N.: New Urban Spaces: Urban Theory and the Scale Question. Oxford University Press, New York (2019)
4. Harrison, C., Abbott Donnelly, I.: A theory of smart cities. In: Proceedings of the 55th Annual Meeting of the ISSS. International Society for Systems Sciences, pp. 521–535. ISSS, UK (2011)
5. McKenna, H.P.: The importance of theory for understanding smart cities: making a case for ambient theory. In: Streitz, N., Konomi, S. (eds.) HCII 2021. LNCS, vol. 12782. Springer, Cham (2021). https://doi.org/10.1007/978-3-030-77015-0
6. Higgins, E.T.: Making a theory useful: Lessons handed down. Pers. Soc. Psychol. Rev. **8**(2), 138–145 (2004)
7. Löwgren, J.: Perspectives on Usability. IDA Technical Report. Linköping University, Linköping, Sweden (1995)
8. Windlinger, L., Tuzcuoğlu, D.: Usability theory: adding a user-centric perspective to workplace management. In: Danivska, V., Appel-Meulenbroek, R., (eds.) A Handbook of Management Theories and Models for Office Environments and Services. Routledge, Milton Park (2021). https://doi.org/10.1201/9781003128786

9. ISO.: ISO 9241 – Ergonomics of human-system interaction – Part 11: Usability: Definitions and concepts. International Standards Organization, Geneva, Switzerland (2018). https://www.iso.org/obp/ui/#iso:std:iso:9241:-11:ed-2:v1:en. Accessed 8 Jan 2022

10. Van Ryn, M., Heaney, C.A.: What's the use of theory? Health Educ. Q. **19**(3), 315–330 (1992). https://doi.org/10.1177/109019819201900304

11. Brunsson, K.: The use and usefulness of theory. Scand. J. Manag. **37**(2), 101155 (2021). https://doi.org/10.1016/j.scaman.2021.101155

12. Karvonen, A., Cugurullo, F., Caprotti, F.: Conclusions: the long and unsettled future of smart cities. In: Karvonen, A., Cugurullo, F., Caprotti, F., (Eds.) Inside Smart Cities: Place, Politics and Urban Innovation. Routledge, Milton Park (2018)

13. Kordts, B., Gerlach, B., Schrader, A.: Towards self-explaining ambient applications. In: The 14th PErvasive Technologies Related to Assistive Environments Conference (PETRA 2021), June 29-July 2, 2021, Corfu, Greece, 8p. ACM, New York, NY, USA (2021). https://doi.org/10.1145/3453892.3461325

14. McLean, D.: 15 city leaders define a 'smart city'. Smart Cities Dive, 2 November 2021 (2021). https://www.smartcitiesdive.com/news/back-to-basics-what-is-a-smart-city/609225/. Accessed 2 Jan 2022

15. Merriam-Webster. Useful (2022). https://www.merriam-webster.com/dictionary/useful. Accessed 2 Jan 2022

16. Lin, H.X., Choong, Y.-Y., Salvendy, G.: A proposed index of usability: a method for comparing the relative usability of different software systems. Behav. Inf. Technol. **16**(4/5), 267–278 (1997)

17. Shakel, B.: Usability – context, framework, definition, design and evaluation. In: Shackel, B., Richardson, S. (eds.) Human Factors for Informatics Usability. Cambridge University Press, Cambridge (1991)

18. Solove, D.J.: Understanding Privacy. Harvard University Press, Cambridge (2008)

19. Wise, A.F., Shaffer, D.W.: Why theory matters more than ever in the age of big data. J. Learn. Anal. **2**(2), 5–13 (2015). https://doi.org/10.18608/jla.2015.22.2

20. Creswell, J.W.: Educational Research: Planning, Conducting, and Evaluating Quantitative and Qualitative Research, 6th edn. Pearson, Boston (2018)

21. McKenna, H.P.: Seeing Smart Cities through a Multi-Dimensional Lens: Perspectives, Relationships, and Patterns for Success. Springer, Cham (2021). https://doi.org/10.1007/978-3-030-70821-4

22. McKenna, H.P.: Visibilities and Invisibilities in Smart Cities: Emerging Research and Opportunities. IGI Global, Hershey (2021). https://doi.org/10.4018/978-1-7998-3850-0

23. Zambonelli, F., Salim, F., Loke, S.W., De Meuter, W., Kanhere, S.: Algorithmic governance in smart cities: the conundrum and the potential of pervasive computing solutions. IEEE Technol. Soc. Mag. **37**(2), 80–87 (2018). https://doi.org/10.1109/MTS.2018.2826080

24. Krug, S.: Don't Make Me Think: A Common Sense Approach to Web Usability. Pearson, India (2005)

25. Streitz, N., et al.: Smart artefacts as affordances for awareness in distributed teams. In: Streitz, N., Kameas, A., Mavrommati, I. (eds.) The Disappearing Computer. LNCS, vol. 4500, pp. 3–29. Springer, Heidelberg (2007). https://doi.org/10.1007/978-3-540-72727-9_1

26. Streitz, N.A.: From smart-only cities towards humane and cooperative hybrid cities. Technol. Architect. Des. **5**(2), 127–133 (2021). https://doi.org/10.1080/24751448.2021.1967050

27. Zaiontz, C.: Real statistics using excel (2021). www.real-statistics.com

28. McKenna, H.P.: is ambient theory for smart cities even a theory? An affirmative assessment. In: Arai, K. (ed.) FTC 2021. LNNS, vol. 359, pp. 550–558. Springer, Cham (2022). https://doi.org/10.1007/978-3-030-89880-9_41

29. McKenna, H.P.: Ambient theory for smart cities: is it a good theory? In: Ahram, T., Karwowski, W., Di Bucchianico, P., Taiar, R., Casarotto, L., Costa, P. (eds.) Proceedings of the 5th International Conference on Intelligent Human Systems Integration (IHSI 2022): Integrating People and Intelligent Systems, Venice, Italy, 22–24 February 2022, 1410 p. AHFE International, 24 February 2022 - Technology & Engineering. https://doi.org/10.54941/ahfe100931

30. Gregor, S.: The nature of theory in information systems. MIS Q. **30**(3), 611–642 (2006)

31. Gieseler, K., Loschelder, D.D., Friese, M.: What makes for a good theory? How to evaluate a theory using the strength model of self-control as an example. In: Sassenberg, K., Vliek, M.L.W. (eds.) Social Psychology in Action, pp. 3–21. Springer, Cham (2019). https://doi.org/10.1007/978-3-030-13788-5_1

Extended Reality for Smart Built Environments Design: Smart Lighting Design Testbed

Elham Mohammadrezaei and Denis Gračanin$^{(\boxtimes)}$ (iD)

Virginia Tech, Blacksburg, VA 24060, USA
{elliemh,gracanin}@vt.edu

Abstract. Smart Built Environment is an eco-system of 'connected' and 'smart' Internet of Things (IoT) devices that are embedded in a built environment. Smart lighting is an important category of smart IoT devices that has recently attracted research interest, particularly for residential areas. In this paper, we present an extended reality based smart lighting design testbed that can generate design prototypes based on the functionality of the physical environment. The emphasis is on designing a smart lighting system in a controlled residential environment, with some evaluation of well-being and comfort.

Keywords: Smart lighting · Design · Internet of Things · Extended reality

1 Introduction

Smart built environment (SBE) or smart home provides an eco-system of 'connected' and 'smart' Internet of Things (IoT) devices situated in the built environment [12]. The main goal of SBE is to provide and promote user comfort, quality of living, convenience and security to satisfy residents' needs. To help achieve this goal, we build on our previous results [10–12] to provide an SBE design testbed where designers can use the designs prescribed by the testbed as well as to explore original designs.

The Internet has fundamentally altered our way of life, allowing people to engage virtually in a variety of settings ranging from work to social relationships. By facilitating communications with and among smart objects, IoT has the potential to add a new layer to this process, resulting in the idea of "anytime, anywhere, anymedia, everything" communications [4].

New sensor, mobile, and control technologies have a lot of potential for connecting people with their surroundings. Individuals, groups, and the broader community can benefit from smart built environments (e.g., a smart house) that are enhanced with technology, such as increased awareness of information in the user's surroundings, integrated control over factors in one's surrounding and home environments, and increased ability to support sustainable living for both individuals and groups.

N. A. Streitz and S. Konomi (Eds.): HCII 2022, LNCS 13325, pp. 181–192, 2022.
https://doi.org/10.1007/978-3-031-05463-1_13

IoT [4] is a concept that defines the ubiquitous presence of things or devices that utilize a unique addressing system to interact with one another and collaborate with their neighbors to achieve common goals. These physical items have a social existence that IoT might sustain. IoT has a wide range of applications, from automation and manufacturing to assisted living and e-health. The ability to change how systems behave and how users interact with them is provided by designing and deploying IoT into built settings. Design, simulation, planning, monitoring, optimization, and visualization technologies could all help with sustainability [11].

IoT has penetrated the daily operations of numerous industries as a result of recent improvements in communication and mobile computer technology; applications include, but are not limited to, smart agriculture, smart grids, smart buildings, and e-health.

Smart buildings are an important part of smart cities, and they've been the subject of a lot of research in recent years. Despite the fact that a vast variety of infrastructures, platforms, and systems have been developed, implemented, and deployed, several barriers such as upfront technology investment and continuing system maintenance costs have stymied their widespread adoption.

The equipment is often purchased by the owners of these solutions, who are also responsible for its implementation and upkeep. The inherent hazards have become one of the most significant impediments to wide-scale adoption of IoT technology. Furthermore, a great number of past systems have only been installed and tested in a single building or a testbed that only covers a few levels, therefore their availability and scalability in large-scale real buildings are unclear [22].

Smart lighting is a novel concept that has emerged over a decade now and is being used and tested in commercial and industrial built environments. Currently, smart lighting research is predominantly dedicated to energy saving in non-residential environments; the residential environments have not been explored [20]. The focus is mostly on designing and developing a smart lighting system in a controlled environment, with a limited evaluation of well-being and comfort.

In this paper, we focus on designing and developing an Extended Reality (XR) based SBE smart light design testbed that is capable of generating design solutions and alternatives based on the functionality of the space.

2   Related Work

Several smart home systems based on IoT applications have recently been developed with the goal of making human life more convenient and ecologically friendly. Real-world situations, on the other hand, present a number of difficulties. A smart home is built to be energy efficient and provide basic functionality such as lighting and switch settings.

Furthermore, a low-cost network can be created by combining embedded controllers, such as Arduino with Ethernet, ZigBee technology, and an Android device that acts as a home environment controller. The system's drawbacks don't apply to all security solutions, and such a solution isn't new in a smart home [15,24].

There are methods for evaluating IoT-based built environments that employs a large-scale virtual environment (VE) in which a building model is aligned with the physical space [11]. To model user interaction with constructed spaces, this approach takes advantage of affordances and embodied cognition in a vast physical setting.

The model is based on an enclosed space with real-time tracking and spatial audio capabilities. Several users can move around the physical space at the same time and view the simulation results from various perspectives. The corresponding view in the VE is determined in real-time based on a user's physical location and orientation. The user can also monitor and cooperate with other users to change the simulation.

A smart home system employs integrated sensors, actuators, wireless networks, and graphical user interfaces to provide positive, adaptable, secure, and cost-effective results. By incorporating sensors for lighting, temperature, pressure, humidity, motion, fire alarms, and dust/air, among other things, a sensor network may transform an existing home into a smart home [5]. However, this platform faces numerous challenges, one of which is the issue of security and privacy.

Similarly, [14] provides a simple platform based on open-source code, in which the authors present a solution for remote monitoring in a smart home by using ESP8266 micro-controller and MQTT protocol [3]. This minimizes the IoT system's security risk while also increasing its cost.

2.1   Extended Reality for Smart Built Environments Design

The architectural, engineering, and construction (AEC) industry has increasingly recognized XR technology for its ability to provide multisensory three-dimensional (3D) environments that immerse the user in a virtual world, specifically to meet the high demand for visual forms of communication during the work related to designing, engineering, construction, and management of the built environment over the past decades [13].

The first application of XR technology for the built environment can be traced back to the 1990s, when this simulation technology was first brought to the attention of architects, piqued the interest of other disciplines involved in architectural engineering, and led to further exploration of XR technology's possibilities.

Recent advances in computer graphics and virtual reality equipment have resulted in a slew of useful XR applications in pilot testing and industry, including client walkthroughs, review, and building sequence visualization. AEC professionals have increasingly pushed and implemented XR technology to many other disciplines, leveraging on its sophisticated functions such as visualization, in addition to these traditional methods.

It's worth noting that XR might refer to a simulation of specific features of the real world, a symbolic world, or an imaginative world, among other things.

XR technology and associated applications have been progressively investigated and deployed in the AEC industry because to its huge potential.

Nonetheless, such technology has yet to be embraced as a standard tool in the workplace. According to market reports, user experience (i.e., cumbersome gear and technological faults), content offering, and cost are among the challenges preventing XR from becoming popular [2].

As a summary for discussion, challenges and opportunities of XR applications for the built environment, potential research needs, such as 1) user-centered adaptive design, 2) human cognition-driven virtual reality information system, 3) construction training system incorporating human factors, 4) occupant-centered facility management, and 5) industry adoption, are proposed to shed light on future research directions [23].

2.2   Light

In home automation, smart lighting is one of the main components. Integrating it into the Smart House platform is a fundamental part of using the benefits that new technologies give us in everyday life. The use of centralized lighting control contributes to more efficient use of electricity and adds an extra dose of comfort in the home.

Xu et al. proposed a smart construction framework that solution providers can use as a starting point when designing their own solution architecture. Following that, they present a smart lighting system for smart buildings based on the framework. In their system, the standard emergency lights can be augmented to a smart router by simply replacing the old product with a low-cost wireless module [22].

It's worth noting that in recent years, an increasing number of researchers have worked on improving control algorithms. Methods such as statistics, data modeling, and machine learning have been utilized to save energy. A neural network controller, for example, was created and tested. It may regulate the brightness of bulbs in a classroom based on the ambient light and the number of students [8].

Besides saving energy, some studies also considered to improve user experience [6,16,19]. For consumers' convenience and a better experience, some researchers supported integrated lighting control with occupancy sensors, photocells, and a central control module [17]. A few researchers developed mobile applications for better user experience in terms of operability and mobility [7,9,18,21]. Evidence suggests that a well-designed mobile application can enhance user experience while simultaneously ensuring compliance with lighting rules and lowering energy use [7].

Every lighting designer, architect and project manager should have suitable tools to plan their project in the best way possible. Table 1 shows a comparative study of the features of different packages that are suitable for use in lighting design.

Table 1. Comparative analysis of different lighting simulation packages.

Feature	AGI 32	CalcuLux	DIALux	Radiance	MicroLux	LightCalc	Visual 3D	Unity
Interior and exterior study	✓	✓	✓				✓	✓
Analysis and visualization of lighting design				✓				
Designing in 2D and 3D organize					✓			✓
Irregular geometries	✓							✓
Analysis of the appropriate distances between objects						✓	✓	✓
Analysis and comparison of different lighting scenarios	✓		✓				✓	✓
Calculation tools		✓					✓	
QuickTime Virtual reality (QTVR)								✓
Virtual Reality Markup Language (VRML)								✓
Walkthrough animation								✓

3 Problem Description

There are many intelligent lighting control strategies, but they are all based on basic lighting control methods: on-off control and dimming control. Constant illuminance control refers to using luminance management in conjunction with intelligent sunshade to keep the illuminance within a consistent range. When an infrared sensor detects that someone has entered the room, the luminaire will automatically turn on, while an illumination sensor detects the room's illumination and adjusts the luminaire's brightness, keeping the room's illumination close to the default. At the same time, manage the shading blind's rotation angle automatically to minimize direct glare and excessive indoor temperatures. The lighting qualities of lamps produce varied levels of illumination in different areas of a room.

Timing control refers to the use of a timer to switch on and off a luminaire. Timing control can be used in the bedroom, for example. Turn on luminaire automatically at a specific time in the morning to assist people in waking up as quickly as possible; in the evening, turn off luminaire automatically at a given time to encourage people to go to bed as quickly as possible.

A combination of timer and illumination sensor can manage lighting in places like balconies and green plants. The landscape lighting in the region is automatically turned on when the illumination falls below a specified threshold during a certain time period; otherwise, it is turned off. As a result, it's both attractive and functional, as well as energy-efficient and environmentally beneficial.

Intelligent lighting now not only offers light to people but also promotes a healthy lifestyle. Scene control refers to the ability to turn on different luminaires based on different conditions in order to provide the desired lighting atmosphere. People must do a wide range of activities in a relatively short space due to the peculiarities of dwelling. The lighting requirements for various behaviors aren't always the same. People can watch TV, read, chat, and sip tea in the living room, for example. To create a comfortable, energy-efficient lighting atmosphere, scene control can be used to initiate multiple scene illumination schemes.

By studying and forecasting people's behavior, linkage control refers to automatically turning luminaires on and off in a relevant zone. When individuals open the closet, for example, the luminaire in it will automatically turn on for picking clothes, and when they close it, the luminaire will turn off. When individuals sit in front of a dresser, the mirror light will turn on and stay within a predefined illumination range; in the meantime, the luminaire will turn off automatically when they depart. When people get up in the middle of the night, the nightlight in their bedroom will automatically switch on. The luminaires in the respective region will automatically switch on and maintain a reasonably low-light standard when people enter the living room, bathroom, and other rooms, and will automatically turn off when people leave.

To produce an intelligent, pleasant lighting environment, linkage control enhances and strengthens existing management measures. These control strategies are, in reality, accomplished on the basis of on-off and dimming control, and they are not mutually independent. A good intelligent lighting system should develop a technologically reasonable, cheap, practical, healthy, and comfortable intelligent lighting management scheme by considering all control techniques in the context of actual applications.

Intelligent lighting offers the following benefits as compared to traditional lighting. In intelligent lighting, lighting in various environments is precisely and intelligently controlled by various means, and minimum amounts of energy are used to ensure required illumination standards, effectively avoiding the phenomena of "everlasting lamps" and overly strong illumination while also drastically reducing energy consumption. According to statistics, intelligent lighting may save more than 30% of energy.

A decent working or living environment requires a proper lighting environment. Intelligent lighting makes use of advanced electronic and information technology to automatically control the on-off and brightness of lamps in order to increase uniformity of illumination and reduce the stroboscopic effect, resulting in more comfortable and healthy lighting environments for people's work and lives, as well as reducing dizziness and eyestrain.

There is a strong need for a comprehensive framework for the smart lighting design as a part of the SBE design process. As a result, smart capabilities of lighting design are underutilized in terms of improving occupants' overall spatial experience and influencing activity patterns. We looked at existing systems

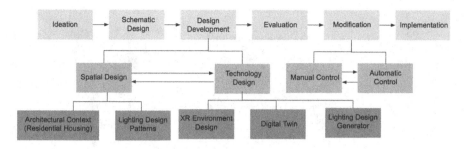

Fig. 1. Design process diagram.

from a variety of domains to help us establish a smart lighting design system for smart home design. Our proposed system stands in the intersection of full manual and full automatic control where the user will be provided with embedded design ideas that are automatically suggested based on the geometry and its functionality and in the next step, the user will be able to manually change the settings and modify them based on their needs, activities and the weather condition and probably many other factors.

4 Proposed Approach

We studied SBE research to understand the architectural concerns for smart home design. We also reviewed smart lighting design for SBE and identified the components and the current research focus to identify the existing smart lighting systems and the role of light in a successful architectural design and how the smartness in lighting design can help increasing the quality of users' experience of their living spaces.

Additionally, we reviewed XR technology and its application to architecture and construction industry and its ability to create multi-sensory and three dimensional environments which provides an opportunity for users to experience and interact with a virtual version of the future building and modify it based on their needs and fix the flaws in pre-construction phase.

To investigate the current state, challenges, and best practices of the smart lighting design process, we studied past researches in lighting design and existing intelligent lighting system and how these systems add smartness to the system. We also studies about current software package which are being used for simulating the lighting systems and had a quick review of the features of each software and what are the pros and cons of each option.

Smart capabilities are often underutilized in terms of improving occupants' overall spatial experience and influencing activity patterns. We explored design methods from a variety of domains to help us designing a smart lighting design generator system.

Our SBE smart lighting design testbed (Fig. 1) includes control, communication and interconnection capabilities and enables designers to have full control over light characteristics and how occupant control those lights (interaction

Fig. 2. Ideation diagram.

modalities). The proposed testbed targets a sweet spot between having a full manual and full automatic control over the lighting design and modifications which means at the very first step, given the input, it automatically generates and proposes the prototypes and later in the development process, it allows for manual changes and modifications by users.

Using cross-platform tools, we provide a visual representation of lighting design prototypes, as well as management and monitoring capabilities, manual control and modification in parallel with having automatic control on generating prototypes based on the geometry and also functionality of the input context.

The testbed is capable of understanding what the functionality of the space is and propose design prototypes based on the guidelines and use design patterns to provide an initial design without user intervention.

The testbed includes a collection of lighting design patterns and outlines of different room types which are developed according to the U.S. Interior and Exterior Lighting Systems and Controls Guideline [1] and are embedded in the system. For example, a design pattern for a bedroom in residential housing provides a solution that includes a ceiling mounted luminaire which provides ceiling surface brightness as well as two table light sources that provide task lighting.

5   Case Study

For our case study we focus on a simple bedroom outline from a residential unit since it's one of the most important sections in a house and has direct influence on the residents' well-being and preservation of their comfort. We design the system to generate lighting design prototypes and let the users get involved with the environment and have interaction with the system and evaluate it and give us

Fig. 3. Comparative analysis of different lighting scenarios: **Left:** ceiling lamp and **Right:** wall mounted lamps on two sides of bed and/or TV.

Fig. 4. Comparative analysis of different lighting scenarios: **Left:** ceiling lamp and **Right:** wall mounted lamp on top of bed and/or TV.

feedback. A sample bedroom outline has been designed and used as the context of this study and the proposed system has been implemented in Unity. Figure 2 is a diagram that shows how the system first scans the room and figures out the outline and identifies the geometry and objects inside the room and in the next step it proposes situating the lighting fixtures inside that geometry and based on the function we have already assigned to the room. Five different lighting design scenarios (Figs. 3, 4, and 5) have been proposed by system.

One of the corresponding rendering alternative is shown in Fig. 6.

6   Discussion

Our SBE smart lighting design testbed includes control, communication and interconnection capabilities and enables designers to have full control over light characteristics and how occupant control those lights (interaction modalities).

The initial design solution could be modified by a designer using the SBE testbed. The designer can explore how a smart lighting system in an SBE responds to occupants' behavioural habits and how a smart lighting system can have impacts on the occupants, how it can change the habits and also what are the effects on the occupants from a psychological perspective.

The described SBE smart lighting design testbed represents just one of the aspects of the SBE design. Therefore, our future work will include expanding the testbed to include the support for other SBE functions and services.

Fig. 5. Comparative analysis of different lighting scenarios: ceiling lamp.

Fig. 6. Real time lighting design rendering of Fig. 3 left.

Also, this system can be expanded to be implemented for other architectural contexts and environment rather than residential buildings and we also can develop the system and provide the outdoor and area lighting simulator too which can also generate design ideas for those spaces and so will be applicable to a broader range of buildings and functionalities.

References

1. Unified facilities criteria (UFC): Interior and exterior lighting systems and controls. Change 4 UFC 3–530-01, U.S. Department of Defense. Accessed 1 Nov 2019
2. Augmented and virtual reality survey report: Industry insights into the future of immersive technology, vol. 4, Perkins Coie. Accessed Mar 2020
3. Arlitt, M., Marwah, M., Bellala, G., Shah, A., Healey, J., Vandiver, B.: MQTT version 3.1.1 plus errata 01. Standard, OASIS. Accessed 10 Dec 2015

4. Atzori, L., Iera, A., Morabito, G.: The internet of things: a survey. Comput. Netw. **54**(15), 2787–2805 (2010)
5. Bhatt, A., Patoliya, J.: Cost effective digitization of home appliances for home automation with low-power WiFi devices. In Proceedings of the 2nd International Conference on Advances in Electrical, Electronics, Information, Communication and Bio-Informatics (AEEICB), pp. 643–648. IEEE (2016)
6. Byun, J., Hong, I., Lee, B., Park, S.: Intelligent household led lighting system considering energy efficiency and user satisfaction. IEEE Trans. Cons. Electron. **59**(1), 70–76 (2013)
7. Castillo-Martinez, A., et al.: Evaluation and improvement of lighting efficiency in working spaces. Sustainability **10**(4), 1110 (2018)
8. Chen, Y., Sun, Q.: Artificial intelligent control for indoor lighting basing on person number in classroom. In: Proceedings of the 9th Asian Control Conference (ASCC), pp. 1–4. IEEE (2013)
9. Choi, K., Suk, H.-J.: Dynamic lighting system for the learning environment: performance of elementary students. Optics Exp. **24**(10), A907–A916 (2016)
10. Dasgupta, A., Handosa, M., Manuel, M., Gračanin, D.: A user-centric design framework for smart built environments. In: Streitz, N., Konomi, S. (eds.) HCII 2019. LNCS, vol. 11587, pp. 124–143. Springer, Cham (2019). https://doi.org/10.1007/978-3-030-21935-2_11
11. Gračanin, D., Matković, K., Wheeler, J.: An approach to modeling Internet of Things based smart built environments. In: Yilmaz, L., Chan, W.K.V., Moon, I., Roeder, T.M.K., Macal, C., Rosetti, M. (eds.) Proceedings of the 2015 Winter Simulation Conference (WSC), 6–9 December 2015, pp. 3208–3209 (2015)
12. Handosa, M., Dasgupta, A., Manuel, M., Gračanin, D.: Rethinking user interaction with smart environments—a comparative study of four interaction modalities. In: Streitz, N., Konomi, S. (eds.) HCII 2020. LNCS, vol. 12203, pp. 39–57. Springer, Cham (2020). https://doi.org/10.1007/978-3-030-50344-4_4
13. Kim, M., Wang, X., Love, P., Li, H., Kang, S.-C.: Virtual reality for the built environment: a critical review of recent advances. J. Inf. Technol. Constr. **18**(2013), 279–305 (2013)
14. Kodali, R.K., Soratkal, S.R.: MQTT based home automation system using esp8266. In: Proceedings of the 2016 IEEE Region 10 Humanitarian Technology Conference (R10-HTC), pp. 1–5 (2016)
15. Lee, H., Ahn, C.R., Choi, N., Kim, T., Lee, H.: The effects of housing environments on the performance of activity-recognition systems using Wi-Fi channel state information: an exploratory study. Sensors **19**(5), 983 (2019)
16. May, Z.B., Yaseen, Y.A.A.B.M.: Smart energy saving classroom system using programmable logic controller. In: Advanced Materials Research, vol. 660 of Advanced Materials Research, pp. 158–162. Trans Tech Publications Ltd. (2013)
17. Middleton-White, S., et al.: Integrated lighting system and method. US Patent 8,436,542. Accessed 7 May 2013
18. Moon, S.-M., Kwon, S.-Y., Lim, J.-H.: Implementation of smartphone-based color temperature and wavelength control led lighting system. Cluster Comput. **19**(2), 949–966 (2016)
19. Parise, G., Martirano, L., Cecchini, G.: Design and energetic analysis of an advanced control upgrading existing lighting systems. IEEE Trans. Ind. Appl. **50**(2), 1338–1347 (2013)
20. Soheilian, M., Fischl, G., Aries, M.: Smart lighting application for energy saving and user well-being in the residential environment. Sustainability **13**(11), 6198 (2021)

21. Suresh, S., Anusha, H.N.S., Rajath, T., Soundarya, P., Vudatha, S.V.P.: Automatic lighting and control system for classroom. In: Proceedings of the 2016 International Conference on ICT in Business Industry & Government (ICTBIG), pp. 1–6. IEEE (2016)
22. Xu, W., et al.: The design, implementation, and deployment of a smart lighting system for smart buildings. IEEE Internet Things J. 6(4), 7266–7281 (2019)
23. Zhang, Y., Liu, H., Kang, S.-C., Al-Hussein, M.: Virtual reality applications for the built environment: research trends and opportunities. Autom. Constr. 118, 103311 (2020)
24. Su, Z.: Design of smart home system based on zigbee. In: Proceedings of the 2016 International Conference on Robots & Intelligent System (ICRIS), pp. 167–170. IEEE (2016)

Integrating Uni-messe and FIWARE for Low-Code Development of Complex Context-Aware Applications

Takuya Nakata[1]([✉])(iD), Tasuku Watanabe[1], Sinan Chen[1](iD),
and Masahide Nakamura[1,2]

[1] Graduate School of System Informatics Kobe University,
1-1 Rokkodai, Nada, Kobe 657-8501, Japan
{tnakata,tasuku,chensinan}@ws.cs.kobe-u.ac.jp
[2] Riken Center for Advanced Intelligence Project, 1-4-1 Nihonbashi,
Chuo-ku, Tokyo 103-0027, Japan
masa-n@cs.kobe-u.ac.jp

Abstract. A smart system with context-aware technology can dynamically coordinate heterogeneous distributed services according to various contexts in the physical world and cyberspace. Two technologies, context management and rule-based system, are important elements in developing context-aware applications, and these implementation technologies can reduce the manpower required for service development. *FIWARE*, an open-source context management platform, and *Uni-messe*, a rule-based event routing hub, are examples of previous research. This study explores an integrated architecture that connects Uni-messe and FIWARE. We first propose the overall structure of the integrated architecture. The coordination and behavior of the five modules that constitute the architecture are discussed. Finally, a demonstration service based on the proposed architecture is constructed and implemented, and the work processes required for development are discussed. By linking Uni-messe and FIWARE, the development of context-aware applications can be carried out efficiently.

Keywords: Smart system · Context awareness · Rule-based system · FIWARE · Data covnert

1 Introduction

With the development of *information and communication technology (ICT)*, digital devices such as smartphones and smart speakers have entered people's lives, enabling them to obtain services that enrich their lives through various applications. In recent years, there has been a remarkable development of *smart systems* that create value-added services (i.e., *smart services*) by linking things and objects in the physical world with computational resources in cyberspace through networks [17]. Smart systems have various fields of application. Examples include the *smart home* [10,19], where home appliances are operated via the Internet of Things (IoT), and the *smart city* [15, 24], where urban operating systems are constructed to improve the efficiency of city operations.

Context is an important concept that supports these smart systems, which represents the situation of an entity such as a person or a thing. For example, the context of a room is expressed by address and room temperature and other attributes. *Context awareness* is a technology that aims to read and aware the context with sensors and services, and provide appropriate services according to the situation [7, 13, 18]. *Rule-based system* is a typical technology to realize context awareness [27, 28]. Rule-based systems are inference-based Artificial Intelligence (AI) systems that operate according to Event Condition Action (ECA) rules [16], evaluating events based on the rules and decide whether to take actions. In previous research, our group has developed a routing hub service, *Unified Rule-based Message Delivery Service (Uni-messe)* [22], to reduce the implementation cost of context-aware services by neutrally servicing the rule-based system. For context management platforms, *FIWARE* is open source and publicly available [9, 23]. FIWARE makes it possible to construct various services such as visualization and log management of contexts, by managing the database of contexts with the core module *FIWARE Orion* and connecting other sub-modules.

In this study, we investigate an integrated architecture linking Uni-messe and FIWARE with the aim of lowering the development cost of complex context-aware applications by combining the advanced context processing of FIWARE with the rule-based system of Uni-messe.

The proposed integrated architecture consists of the following five modules:

- **(Module 1)** Northbound Adapter
- **(Module 2)** FIWARE
- **(Module 3)** Data Converter
- **(Module 4)** Uni-messe
- **(Module 5)** Southbound Adapter

The (Module 1) Northbound Adapter is the module responsible for sending contexts from the application to FIWARE, and the (Module 5) Southbound Adapter is the module responsible for sending events from Uni-messe to the application. The (Module 3) Data Converter is a module that converts the Next Generation Service Interfaces (NGSI) data format handled by FIWARE into the 6W1H data format handled by Uni-messe.

In this study, we also implemented a demo service that mocks the (Module 3) Data Converter in order to investigate the improvement of development efficiency by the integrated architecture. By examining the development process of this demo service, we analyzed the work required for developers to develop services using the integrated architecture. The analysis revealed that the only modules that need to be developed by the developer, excluding the applications to be linked, are the (Module 1) Northbound Adapter and (Module 5) Southbound Adapter, which are easy to develop, and the (Module 3) Data Converter, which absorbs the differences in data formats. Moreover, although FIWARE and Uni-messe need to be configured, they can be easily configured using the Web User

Interface (Web UI) and Application Programming Interface (API). From the results of the analysis, it is clear that the development and configuration of the modules for the integrated architecture can be done with less man-hours.

2 Preliminary

2.1 Smart Service

A smart system realizes value-added services by linking information in the physical world and computational resources in cyberspace through a network. In recent years, research and development of *smart services* running on smart systems has been active, and our laboratory has been working on various services, such as a monitoring service for the elderly using LINE application [21] and a speaker for preventing forgetfulness [5]. Smart services are being deployed in a variety of fields, with applications ranging from smart home, smart city, smart healthcare, and smart agriculture.

A common feature of these smart systems is that they dynamically coordinate heterogeneous distributed services to read and aware the context of a room or a person using sensors and services, and provide appropriate services (*context-aware services*) according to the situation. Context-aware services acquire a variety of context data, such as indoor environmental sensing data acquired using Sensorbox [25], traffic data, health data, and store inventory data. These data applications enable the provision of practical services closely related to the lives and health of individuals [8,12] and efficient urban-scale systems that utilize big data [26]. The research on composite context aware using these various data is becoming active. Moreover, many commercial services using context-aware technology, such as IFTTT [2,20] and Nature Remo [4], have been commercialized and are becoming popular among the general public.

Rule-based system is a typical technology to realize context-aware services, which is an inference-based AI system that operates based on ECA rules. It evaluates Events generated by services and sensors using Conditions, and executes Actions based on the evaluation results. The other technology for handling contexts is *context management*, which enables analysis such as tracking and visualization of the temporal changes of the accumulated context by managing the context in the database. *FIWARE*, an open source software, is a typical context management service.

2.2 Previous Research: Uni-messe [22]

Our previous work, Unified Rule-based Message Delivery Service (*Uni-messe*), is a technology for constructing services that incorporate rule-based systems. Uni-messe is a neutralized service for rule-based systems. The architecture of Uni-messe is shown in Fig. 1. It is a hub service that receives events generated by applications via the Publish/Subscribe messaging infrastructure (Pub/Sub) [29], evaluates them using pre-registered conditional expressions, and routes them.

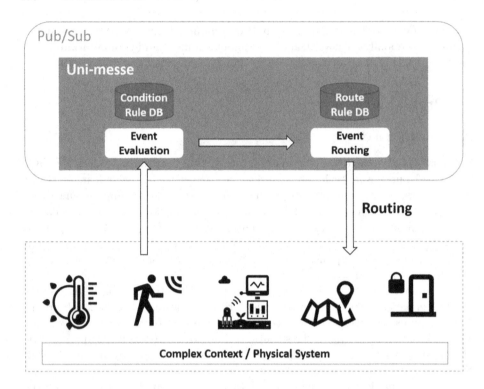

Fig. 1. Uni-messe architecture.

Each application receives the routed events, interprets the event contents, and sends them to the routed events are received by each application, and various smart services can be provided by interpreting the event contents.

The data format of events in Uni-messe is *6W1H attributes (Who, Whom, When, What, Why, Where, How)*. Two types of rules, Condition rules and Route rules, are registered and used in Uni-messe. The Condition rule holds an evaluation formula for 6W1H conditions. The content of the evaluation expression is a string comparison, a cron expression, and a string of Java conditional expression. The Route rule holds the destination information of the event and the additional information attached at the time of transmission. Each Route rule is associated with the Condition rule and registered in Uni-messe. Since Uni-messe has a Web UI to manage these rules, users of Uni-messe can register and delete rules without writing source code.

By using Uni-messe, it is no longer necessary to implement a rule-based system, and it is now easy to create services that maintain loose-coupling between applications with a high degree of integration.

2.3 Technical Challenge

One of the challenges of Uni-messe is that it does not have the capability to manage the context. Uni-messe is a service that handles the events that occur when the context changes, not the context itself. Hence, Uni-messe is not good at processes that refer to the state of smart services, such as getting whether the TV is on or not, or using room temperature data at the current time. It is also difficult to detect how the actual context has changed as the application interprets the event and executes the service. As an example, consider an automatic window-opening service. This service receives events from other services that trigger the opening of a window. Uni-messe does not obtain the context of whether the window is open or closed as a precondition for processing. It also does not acquire the status of whether the window is actually opened or not after processing.

2.4 FIWARE [1]

FIWARE is a data management infrastructure that focuses on CRUD management of contexts. The data format of the contexts managed by FIWARE is NGSI, supporting NGSI-v2 and NGSI-LD. By using the NGSI data format, contexts can be represented hierarchically in terms of Type and Value. FIWARE provides a variety of sub-modules, facilitating the provision of various context-centric services such as linkage to IoT devices, log management, authentication and visualization.

FIWARE Orion is the core module of FIWARE that stores contexts in a database and provides an API to CRUD the contexts. Moreover, FIWARE Orion provides a subscription function. This is a function that can pass (i.e., POST) part or all of the context to a pre-registered URL when the context in the database is changed by the CRUD process. Since many of the sub-modules provided by FIWARE are designed to work with FIWARE Orion, they are essential modules for an architecture using FIWARE.

IoT Agent is a module that mediates between the protocols of IoT devices and FIWARE Orion. It can receive communications using JSON, Lightweight M2M, UltraLight2.0, LoRaWAN, etc. used by IoT devices and convert them into the NGSI format handled by FIWARE Orion. IoT Agent can mediate two-way communication, and the communication from the IoT devices to FIWARE is defined as northbound traffic, and the communication from FIWARE to the IoT devices is defined as southbound traffic. An example of a configuration using FIWARE Orion and an IoT Agent is shown in Fig. 2.

FIWARE is expected to play an active role as a foundation for urban OS [6], and many local governments are paying attention to it for Digital Transformation (DX). However, the development and operation of FIWARE requires specialized knowledge.

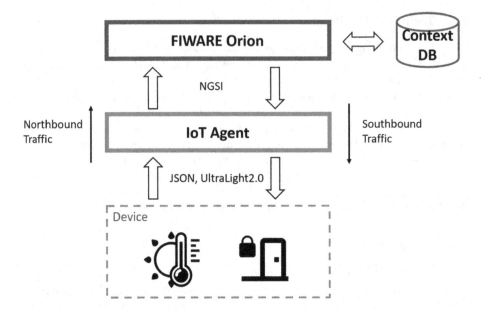

Fig. 2. Example architecture using FIWARE orion and IoT agent.

3   Proposal Method

3.1   Purpose and Key Idea

The purpose of this research is to reduce the development cost of context-aware applications that perform complex processing by utilizing context. As a key idea of the research to achieve the purpose, we integrate Uni-messe and FIWARE. A unique feature of the collaborative architecture is that Uni-messe not only facilitates the construction of context-aware applications, but also enables the easy deployment of applied services by using the context managed by FIWARE. The technical challenges to be solved are that the way to integrate Uni-messe and FIWARE is not obvious and that the data formats handled by Uni-messe and FIWARE are different.

The approach of this study is as follows:

– **(A1)** Study on the Integration Architecture of Uni-messe and FIWARE
– **(A2)** Consideration of Modules for Collaboration and Integration
– **(A3)** Examining Development Efficiency with Mock Services

3.2   Integration Architecture of Uni-messe and FIWARE

The integration architecture of Uni-messe and FIWARE is shown in Fig. 3.

– **(Module 1)** Northbound Adapter
– **(Module 2)** FIWARE

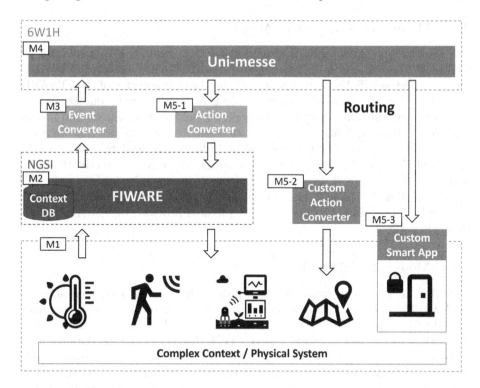

Fig. 3. Integration architecture of Uni-messe and FIWARE.

– **(Module 3)** Data Converter
– **(Module 4)** Uni-messe
– **(Module 5)** Southbound Adapter

Contexts composed by services and sensors are sent to (Module 2) FIWARE by (Module 1) Northbound Adapters. Changes in the context on FIWARE are passed to the (Module 3) Data Converter, which converts the context format from NGSI to 6W1H. The Data Converter passes the formatted context to the (Module 4) Uni-messe, which evaluates and routes it according to the Condition and Route rules registered in advance. Finally, since there are three routes from Uni-messe, and each route requires different modules, there are three types of (Module 5) Southbound Adapters:

– **(Module 5-1)** Action Converter
– **(Module 5-2)** Custom Action Converter
– **(Module 5-3)** Custom Smart App

Through these modules, events are sent to the new service, which interprets the events and provides various functions.

3.3 (Module 1) Northbound Adapter

The Northbound Adapter is the application that sends the context data to FIWARE. There are two ways to send the data to FIWARE, directly to FIWARE Orion or via the IoT Agent, which depends on the configuration of the FIWARE used. The processing flow of the application is as follows. First, contextual data such as environmental data (e.g., temperature, human perception) and health data (e.g., stress, weight) are acquired through sensors and external services. Next, the acquired data is formatted into NGSI format. If the data is sent directly to FIWARE Orion, the NGSI format data needs to be created directly. However, if the IoT Agent is used, the data formatting process can be performed by the IoT Agent. Finally, the FIWARE API is used to register and update the context data in FIWARE. The API used in this process is provided by FIWARE Orion or the IoT Agent.

3.4 (Module 2) FIWARE

FIWARE is a context management infrastructure, as we have described in Sect. 2.4. The only essential module in this architecture of FIWARE submodules is FIWARE Orion. The IoT Agent is used as needed, paying attention to the characteristics of the service to be used. FIWARE receives context data through APIs and FIWARE can receive context data through APIs, and can communicate context changes to any URL through a subscription function. Moreover, by linking with submodules other than FIWARE Orion, it will be possible to develop a variety of services utilizing the context, such as linking with IoT devices, log management, authentication, and visualization.

3.5 (Module 3) Northbound Adapter

The Data Converter is an intermediary service that converts NGSI format data of contexts managed by FIWARE into 6W1H format data suitable for Uni-messe condition evaluation. It receives NGSI format data from FIWARE via a subscription function, converts the data using an appropriate algorithm, and then sends the converted 6W1H data to Uni-messe via a Pub/Sub topic.

3.6 (Module 4) Uni-messe

Uni-messe is a hub service for conditional evaluation and routing of events, as we have described in Sect. 2.2. In this architecture, events are received from Data Converters via Pub/Sub, evaluated and routed, and then sent to Pub/Sub topics based on Route rules.

3.7 (Module 5) Southbound Adapter

The Southbound Adapter is an application that receives events from the Uni-messe and passes them on to a service. A subscription to a Pub/Sub topic is used to receive events from Uni-messe. Southbound Adapters can be classified into three types according to the route they take to return events to the service.

The (Module 5-1) Action Converter is used as a route to run the service through FIWARE. Since the Uni-messe service is intended for routing events, it is usually difficult to specify how the context is changed by triggering an event. However, if the changed context can be identified, it would be desirable to register the changed context in FIWARE before the service process changes the real physical world context. In such cases, the Action Converter will be needed as a module that is responsible for uniquely converting events from the Uni-messe to the post-change context. The execution of services via FIWARE can use the southbound traffic of the IoT Agent as described in Sect. 2.4.

The (Module 5-2) Custom Action Converter is used in the route to run services without FIWARE. In other words, the Custom Action Converter is a module that converts Uni-messe events into commands to run the service. The service that receives commands from the Custom Action Converter needs to prepare an API.

The (Module 5-3) Custom Smart App is used in the same way as the Custom Action Converter, but without FIWARE. The difference is that the smart application itself has the function to interpret the Uni-messe events. If the application is large size, it can have the event interpretation function, so it can process events without the need to create a new Custom Action Converter. However, there are many cases in which small-scale applications are desirable from the perspective of power consumption, so the choice of which module to use depends on the design.

4   Implementation

4.1   System Architecture

In this study, we briefly implemented a part of the proposed architecture as a demonstration. The implemented system architecture is shown in Fig. 4. The Northbound Adapter measures the temperature, humidity, etc. of the room using a Sensorbox equipped with various sensors and passes the data directly to FIWARE Orion. FIWARE passes the data when the room context is changed. The Data Converter is a mock service that describes only the program to convert the room data into 6W1H. The Uni-messe adds a string of the speech content according to the Condition satisfied by the Route rule. The Southbound Adapter is a Custom Action Converter that does not go through FIWARE (Module 5-2) and commands the speaker service to speak the string.

4.2   Technical Details of Implementation

In this section, we describe the technical details of Module 1, Module 3, and Module 5 in the demo architecture. The Northbound Adapter uses Python scripts to retrieve room data from the Sensorbox API. It formats the data into NGSI

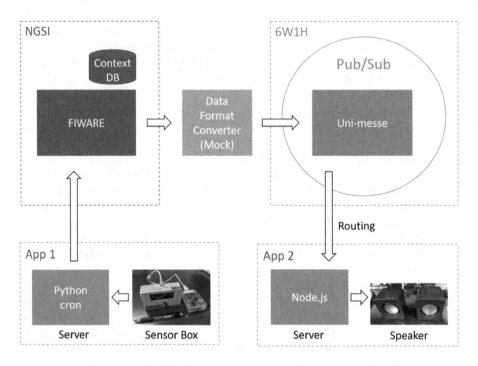

Fig. 4. System architecture of demonstration service.

Listing 1.1. NGSI-v2 format.

```
{
    "id": "urn:ngsi-ld:Room:001",
    "type": "Room",
    "address": {
        "type": "Text",
        "value": "1-1 Rokkodai, Nada, Kobe",
        "metadata": {}
    },
    "name": {
        "type": "Text",
        "value": "S101",
        "metadata": {}
    },
    "temperature":{
        "type": "Number",
        "value": 22.67
    },
}
```

Listing 1.2. 6W1H format.

```
{
    "when": "20211201T12:00:00",
    "where": "S101, 1-1 Rokkodai, Nada, Kobe",
    "what": {
        "temperature": 22.67
    },
    "why": ["fiware"]
}
```

format and sends the context data via the FIWARE Orion API. This sequence of operations in Python is executed every minute using a cron daemon. The Data Converter receives the data from FIWARE Orion as a POST request on the Node.js server. It then executes the data conversion program for the room context only, and converts the NGSI format into 6W1H format. Finally, the data is sent (published) to the topic used by the Pub/Sub Uni-messe. An example of the data before and after conversion is shown in Listing 1.1 and 1.2.

The Southbound Adapter receives events from the Uni-messe via Pub/Sub on the Node.js server (i.e., subscription). It then commands the speaker service to speak the string via the API.

5   Consideration

5.1   Potential for Combined Context-Aware

By devising a Data Converter, composite context aware can be realized in the whole architecture. Specifically, the Data Converter can be designed not only to convert a single context into an event, but also to combine multiple contexts into a single event. In this way, the evaluation of a composite event in Uni-messe is in effect the simultaneous evaluation of multiple contexts. As an idea for a general-purpose Data Converter, a method that describes conversion rules that link NGSI attributes to 6W1H attributes and automatically converts them according to the conversion rules can be considered. Specifically, we can manually create a conversion rule that describes the connection for each attribute, such as Who attribute for the name of Person:001, Who attribute for the name of Person:002, and Where attribute for the name of Restaurant:001. This method eliminates the need to implement Data Converters for each data format, and it is thought that composite context-aware can be realized by only registering conversion rules without knowledge of programming. As future work, it is necessary to implement a general-purpose Data Converter based on these ideas, and to evaluate the realized composite context aware.

5.2   Potential for Development by Non-experts

By using the integrated architecture of Uni-messe and FIWARE proposed in this study, service developers can use both the context management using FIWARE and the rule-based context awareness using Uni-messe. Some services and items must be configured by the developer in order to use the integrated architecture. First, it is necessary to set up the adapters for Module 1 and Module 5. However, with the exception of Module 5-1, the implementation is relatively easy since it is a simple service that only receives data and makes requests using the API. Next, we need to register a routine rule to Uni-messe and a Pub/Sub topic to receive events. Routing rules can be intuitively designed in 6W1H format and can be easily registered using the Web UI. The API also facilitates the registration of Pub/Sub topics. Finally, the Data Converter needs to be configured. In the case study, we implemented a mock service that converts only specific data formats. However, we believe that no-code data conversion will be possible with some ingenuity, such as rule registration in a general-purpose Data Converter as discussed in the previous section. From the above discussion, we believe that the development of complex context-aware applications can be made easier by using the integrated architecture.

6   Related Research

FIWARE Perseo [3,14] is a rule-based component of FIWARE that makes it possible to perform mail linking and HTTP requests by evaluating contexts managed by FIWARE Orion using conditional expressions. Since conditional expressions need to be written using the Event Processing Language (EPL) and there is no easy-to-use UI, it is difficult for non-experts to set up conditional expressions. Moreover, FIWARE Perseo does not use Pub/Sub, and therefore, unlike Uni-messe, the services are tightly coupled.

7   Conclusion

In this study, we have newly investigated an integrated architecture of Uni-messe, a rule-based routing hub without context management functions, and FIWARE, a context management infrastructure. Through the analysis, we have discovered the possibility of implementing a context-aware service that can make extensive use of contexts with a small development cost. In this research, (Module 5-1) Action Converter and (Module 5-3) Custom Smart App have not been implemented and need to be further verified. Furthermore, the quantitative evaluation of the development cost reduction by the integrated architecture has not been conducted. For quantitative evaluation of the architecture, it is possible to evaluates the APIs of Uni-messe, FIWARE, and Data Converters that need to be used during development based on the SQuaRE quality characteristics [11].

As future research, we plan to (Step 1) study and construct the general-purpose 6W1H format Data Converter, (Step 2) study and construct an Action

Converter that converts Uni-messe events into contexts, and (Step 3) quantitatively evaluate the development cost of context-aware services using the integrated architecture.

Acknowledgements. This research was partially supported by JSPS KAKENHI Grant Numbers JP19H01138, JP18H03242, JP18H03342, JP19H04154, JP19K02973, JP20K11059, JP20H04014, JP20H05706 and Tateishi Science and Technology Foundation (C) (No. 2207004).

References

1. Fiware - open apis for open minds. https://www.fiware.org/. Accessed 14 Dec 2021
2. IFTTT. https://ifttt.com/. Accessed 14 Dec 2021
3. Introduction - Perseo context-aware complex event processing. https://fiware-perseo-fe.readthedocs.io/en/latest/. Accessed 29 Dec 2021
4. Nature Remo. https://nature.global/nature-remo/. Accessed 14 Dec 2021
5. Akashi, T., Nakamura, M., Yasuda, K., Saiki, S.: Proposal for a personalized adaptive speaker service to support the elderly at home. In: 22nd IEEE-ACIS International Conference on Software Engineering, Artificial Intelligence, Networking and Parallel Distributed Computing (SNPD2021), November 2021
6. Araujo, V., Mitra, K., Saguna, S., Åhlund, C.: Performance evaluation of FIWARE: a cloud-based IoT platform for smart cities. J. Parallel Distrib. Comput. **132**, 250–261 (2019). https://doi.org/10.1016/j.jpdc.2018.12.010
7. Chen, S., Saiki, S., Nakamura, M.: Integrating multiple models using image-as-documents approach for recognizing fine-grained home contexts. Sensors **20**(3), 666 (2020)
8. Chen, S., Saiki, S., Nakamura, M.: Toward flexible and efficient home context sensing: capability evaluation and verification of image-based cognitive APIs. Sensors **20**(5), 1442 (2020)
9. Corista, P., Ferreira, D., Gião, J.a., Sarraipa, J.a., Gonçalves, R.J.: An IoT agriculture system using FIWARE. In: 2018 IEEE International Conference on Engineering, Technology and Innovation (ICE/ITMC), pp. 1–6 (2018). https://doi.org/10.1109/ICE.2018.8436381
10. Dong, B., Shi, Q., Yang, Y., Wen, F., Zhang, Z., Lee, C.: Technology evolution from self-powered sensors to AIoT enabled smart homes. Nano Energy **79**, 105414 (2021)
11. Esaki, K., Azuma, M., Komiyama, T.: Introduction of quality requirement and evaluation based on ISO/IEC SQuaRE series of standard. In: Yuan, Y., Wu, X., Lu, Y. (eds.) ISCTCS 2012. CCIS, vol. 320, pp. 94–101. Springer, Heidelberg (2013). https://doi.org/10.1007/978-3-642-35795-4_12
12. Esposito, M., et al.: A smart mobile, self-configuring, context-aware architecture for personal health monitoring. Eng. App. Artif. Intell. **67**, 136–156, 105414 (2018). https://doi.org/10.1016/j.engappai.2017.09.019
13. Ferraz, Jr, N., Silva, A.A., Guelfi, A.E., Kofuji, S.T.: Performance evaluation of publish-subscribe systems in IoT using energy-efficient and context-aware secure messages, June 2021. https://doi.org/10.21203/rs.3.rs-387836/v1
14. Gonçalves, R., J. M. Soares, J., M. F. Lima, R.: An IoT-based framework for smart water supply systems management. Fut. Internet **12**(7), 114 (2020). https://doi.org/10.3390/fi12070114, https://www.mdpi.com/1999-5903/12/7/114

15. Gopikumar, S., et al.: A method of landfill leachate management using internet of things for sustainable smart city development. Sustain. Cities Soc. **66**, 102521 (2021)
16. de Ipiña, D.L., Katsiri, E.: An ECA rule-matching service for simpler development of reactive applications. In: Published as a supplement to the Proceedings of Middleware (2001)
17. Ishaq, M., Afzal, M.H., Tahir, S., Ullah, K.: A compact study of recent trends of challenges and opportunities in integrating internet of things (IoT) and cloud computing. In: 2021 International Conference on Computing, Electronic and Electrical Engineering (ICE Cube), pp. 1–4. IEEE (2021)
18. Jara, A.J., Bocchi, Y., Fernandez, D., Molina, G., Gomez, A.: An analysis of context-aware data models for smart cities: towards FIWARE and ETSI CIM emerging data model. Int. Arch. Photogr. Remote Sens. Spatial Inf. Sci. **XLII-4/W3**, 43–50 (2017). https://doi.org/10.5194/isprs-archives-XLII-4-W3-43-2017, https://www.int-arch-photogramm-remote-sens-spatial-inf-sci.net/XLII-4-W3/43/2017/
19. Lu, C.H.: Context-aware service provisioning via agentized and reconfigurable multimodel cooperation for real-life IoT-enabled smart home systems. IEEE Trans. Syst. Man Cybern. Syst. **50**(8), 2914–2925 (2020). https://doi.org/10.1109/TSMC.2018.2831711
20. Mi, X., Qian, F., Zhang, Y., Wang, X.: An empirical characterization of IFTTT: ecosystem, usage, and performance. In: Proceedings of the 2017 Internet Measurement Conference, pp. 398–404. IMC 2017, Association for Computing Machinery, New York, NY, USA (2017). https://doi.org/10.1145/3131365.3131369
21. Miura, C., Saiki, S., Nakamura, M., Yasuda, K.: Implementing and evaluating feedback feature of mind monitoring service for elderly people at home. In: The 22nd International Conference on Information Integration and Web-based Applications and Services (iiWAS2020), pp. 390–395, November 2020
22. Nakata, T., Chen, S., Nakamura, M.: Developing event routing service to support context-aware service integration. In: 22nd IEEE-ACIS International Conference on Software Engineering, Artificial Intelligence, Networking and Parallel Distributed Computing, SNPD 2021, November 2021
23. Rampérez, V., Soriano, J., Lizcano, D., Lara, J.A.: An innovative approach to improve elasticity and performance of message brokers for green smart cities. In: Proceedings of the Fourth International Conference on Engineering and MIS 2018. ICEMIS 2018, Association for Computing Machinery, New York, NY, USA (2018). https://doi.org/10.1145/3234698.3234732
24. Reddy, K.H.K., Luhach, A.K., Pradhan, B., Dash, J.K., Roy, D.S.: A genetic algorithm for energy efficient fog layer resource management in context-aware smart cities. Sustain. Cities Soc. **63**, 102428 (2020). https://doi.org/10.1016/j.scs.2020.102428
25. Sakakibara, S., Saiki, S., Nakamura, M., Matsumoto, S.: Implementing autonomous environmental sensing in smart city with IoT-based sensor box and cloud services. Inf. Eng. Express (IEE) **4**(1), 1–10 (2018)
26. Schürholz, D., Kubler, S., Zaslavsky, A.: Artificial intelligence-enabled context-aware air quality prediction for smart cities. J. Clean. Prod. **271**, 121941 (2020). https://doi.org/10.1016/j.jclepro.2020.121941
27. Takatsuka, H., Saiki, S., Matsumoto, S., Nakamura, M.: Design and implementation of rule-based framework for context-aware services with web services. In: Proceedings of the 16th International Conference on Information Integration and Web-based Applications and Services, pp. 233–242 (2014)

28. Takatsuka, H., Saiki, S., Matsumoto, S., Nakamura, M.: A rule-based framework for managing context-aware services based on heterogeneous and distributed web services. In: 15th IEEE/ACIS International Conference on Software Engineering, Artificial Intelligence, Networking and Parallel/Distributed Computing (SNPD), pp. 1–6. IEEE (2014)

29. Zhao, Y., Li, Y., Mu, Q., Yang, B., Yu, Y.: Secure pub-sub: blockchain-based fair payment with reputation for reliable cyber physical systems. IEEE Access **6**, 12295–12303 (2018)

The Use of AI to Develop Smart Infrastructure in Indonesia

Cindy Fabrizia Suling[1][(✉)], Achmad Nurmandi[1], Isnaini Muallidin[1],
Eko Priyo Purnomo[1,2], and Danang Kurniawan[1]

[1] Department of Government Affairs and Administration, Jusuf Kalla School of Government,
Universitas Muhammadiyah Yogyakarta, Yogyakarta, Indonesia
Cindy.fabrizia.psc21@mail.umy.ac.id, {nurmandi_achmad,
eko}@umy.ac.id
[2] E-Governance and Sustainability Institute, Yogyakarta 55183, Indonesia

Abstract. This study aims to see how the government sector implements Artificial Intelligence (AI) to develop smart infrastructure in Indonesia. Artificial Intelligence is now widely used by various sectors, including the government sector. Applying the AI concept in government will greatly help the government because it can greatly support the running of a smart city, which will later realize one of the dimensions of the smart city itself, called smart society. This study used descriptive qualitative research methods. There are three main characteristics of this method: (1) exploring the existing problem; in this case, is the problem of parking lots in Jakarta (2) identifying potential problems; potential problems that arise this time regarding the security of user data from the Jakparkir application (3) identifying potential solutions. Once the problem and its causative factors have been identified, an overarching theory will be developed to solve the current problem. This study used secondary data collected from various sources, including articles, journals, and official government websites, such as transportation services for the Special Capital Region of Jakarta.

Keywords: AI · Smart city · Smart infrastructure

1 Introduction

This study examined how the government sector employs Artificial Intelligence (AI) in-service activities to foster the development of a smart society capable of with Society 5.0 in Indonesia. Society 5.0, which was launched in 2019, is a concept being explored by the Japanese. This concept emphasizes the application of current science to human needs. This notion seeks to strengthen further the role of people, meaning that each human person must be capable of thinking critically and creatively when confronted with a challenge and in conjunction with artificial technology [1]. Each year, technology advances introduce new technologies that are anticipated to improve human lives. The rapid advancement of technology directly affects humans, altering how they communicate and receive information from cyberspace. These innovations have changed how individuals communicate and how they interact with the government [2]. Artificial

Intelligence is one technological advancement that has made a significant contribution to human life. It is a computer-based program designed to perform jobs that humans often perform [3]. Artificial intelligence can accelerate government-organized public services [4]. Artificial intelligence implementation is a service transformation encompassing e-services, community monitoring, and innovation [5]. Artificial intelligence ensures that data and information are integrated and high-quality as a document processor in government management [6].

AI development in Indonesia focuses on four areas: ethics and policy, talent development, infrastructure and data, and industrial research innovation. Such extent to which government policies will facilitate open data and cross-border data flow while ensuring data security and personal data protection, promoting transparency and accountability, promoting economic democratization, and mitigating the unintended consequences of AI use [7]. AI is an important element in the ideal concept of a smart city [8]. This concept is part of artificial intelligence (AI) and the Internet of Things (IoT) in daily governance to increase efficiency, improve public services, and improve the welfare of citizens [9]. The object of this smart city is none other than the government, society, and city infrastructure [10]. AI and IoT play a critical role in realizing the smart city concept since both technologies can transmit and track data across a network with minimal human intervention. They can automatically perform various functions [11]. The focus of smart cities is centered on new infrastructures, such as the internet and mobile communication networks [12]. Its intelligent urban services include police early warning, real-time querying of public transportation information, intelligent traffic signals, intelligent parking, and telemedicine, all of which improve residents' quality of life while promoting urban spatial optimization.

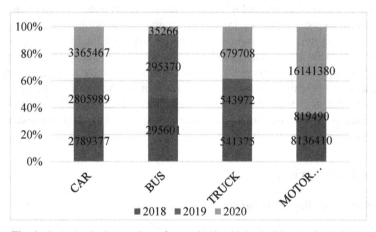

Fig. 1. Increase in the number of motorized vehicles in Jakarta (2018-2020)

One example of applying the AI concept in the government sector in Indonesia is the Jakparkir application. Increased population and vehicle ownership in metropolitan areas will affect the growth and development of human activities, particularly in places with a high level of commercial activity [13]. Naturally, such conditions should necessitate a suitable parking place. However, parking places are typically few in the city center [14]. The primary issue with parking is the scarcity of available spaces compared to vehicles requiring parking [15]. Parking issues not only contribute to congestion, but many losses are incurred as a result of parking violations. The large number of parking spaces that are not used for the benefit of the community has resulted in illegal parking due to the lack of parking space from the government, such as parking in areas that should not be used for parking [16]. A policy innovation parking lot is required to reduce the presence of illegal parking by withdrawals that do not adhere to applicable regulations. Jakparkir is a mobile application that allows to reserve street parking in DKI Jakarta. Motorized vehicle users can use this app to make parking reservations ahead of time, examine parking location information, and make non-cash payments. The application's GPS feature allows users to locate the reserved parking location [17]. This application is linked to the DKI Jakarta Provincial Transportation Service's Motor Vehicle Test Technical Implementation Unit (UPT KIR), the DKI Jakarta Provincial Environment Service, and the DKI Jakarta Provincial Revenue Agency (Bapenda) [18]. Figure 1 shows the increasing number of motorized vehicles in Jakarta during 2018–2020. Every year this number has increased. Indirectly, this also affects the growth of taxes originating from the parking sector. With the prospect of such a significant increase, e-parking is a positive step because it can assist the government in data collection related to income from the parking sector, data collection related to parking lots, and providing information about parking to the general public.

Smart infrastructure is the backbone of a smart city, driven by a wireless sensor network. The intelligent energy subsystem, the intelligent information, and the intelligent communication subsystem work together to deliver desirable outcomes such as improved adaptability, longevity, and efficiency of services provided to consumers and businesses [19]. Using ICT and other technologies to implement smart infrastructures can assess a city's readiness to provide better services and equipment to its citizens. By cooperating with the private sector, the government can apply Artificial Intelligence to the public service process in their country. The e-parking service is the latest innovative solution to solve parking management problems and challenges for local governments. This study wants to see how the government sector implements Artificial Intelligence (AI) to develop smart infrastructure in Indonesia using Artificial Intelligence. This study used qualitative research methods with a descriptive approach, and the data sources used were from previous research.

2 Literature Review

2.1 Artificial Intelligence in Smart City to Develop Smart Infrastructure

John McCarthy is credited with coining the term "Artificial Intelligence" in a 1956 proposal for a Dartmouth summer conference [20]. Approximately over 70 alternative definitions have been presented. While the term "artificial," which in this context primarily refers to "machines" or "computers," is straightforward to define and experts cannot agree on the term "intelligence". According to one definition, intelligence in AI refers to an artificial organism that can "act appropriately and predictably" in a given context [21]. Artificial intelligence is a technological advancement that occurs due to a paradigm shift in a system in which machines are extremely reliable for human life [22]. Artificial intelligence refers to a computer system capable of performing tasks normally performed by humans [23]. This technology can make decisions based on the analysis and data stored in the system [24]. Artificial intelligence processes include learning, reasoning, and self-correction. This process is analogous to how humans analyze situations before making a decision [25]. Artificial intelligence can conduct analyses and forecasts in various areas related to smart cities. This process can yield valuable insights for smart infrastructure, making city planning more manageable and enabling smart mobility [26].

One popular "smart" concept that has captured the public imagination in the previous decade is "smart city" [27]. It is also one of the most important and politically significant, guiding and molding the work of urban planners, architects, infrastructure operators and real-estate developers, transit officials, mayors, and entire industries [28]. The smart city program intends to improve the quality of the city's transformation into a 'smart' city by strengthening technology infrastructure, particularly ICT in the region, developing software applications, and collaborating with the private sector [29]. However, the evolution of the smart city concept has seen tremendous advancements throughout time, both in terms of publication and application [30]. A smart city can develop new forms of involvement that combine new technology and new types of social contact to renew and reinvent the fabric of human interactions and discourse opportunities [31]. Since its inception, this concept has become one of the innovations highly emphasized by the government because the smart city concept is a modernization step that connects technology to a broader sector [32]. A smart city is seen as a thriving urban plan that employs technology to improve urban space quality of life, environmental quality, and citizen service delivery [33]. Smart living, smart governance, smart citizens (people), smart mobility, smart economy, and smart infrastructure are already established components of smart cities [34].

Government regulations, resource readiness, and infrastructure are critical to the successful implementation of smart cities [35]. Internet of Things (IoT), Big Data, Cyber-Physical Systems, and Cloud Computing are also required to run smart city applications and infrastructure systems to support social and economic systems [36]. By utilizing ICT technology to integrate all elements in these aspects, the smart city concept attempts to connect physical, social, and economic infrastructure to create a more efficient and livable city [37]. The notion of smart infrastructure has emerged, where enabling technologies like linked sensors and big data analytics are coupled with physical infrastructure to accomplish real-time monitoring, efficient decision-making, and improved service delivery [19]. Smart infrastructure may cut maintenance costs, reduce damage and interruption costs, and improve service quality and value (on-demand use and flexible tariffs) [38].

3   Research Method

This study used descriptive qualitative research methods. There are three main characteristics of this method: (1) exploring the existing problem; in this case, is the problem of parking lots in Jakarta (2) identifying potential problems; potential problems that arise this time regarding the security of user data from the Jakparkir application (3) identifying potential solutions. Once the problem and its causative factors have been identified, an overarching theory will be developed to solve the current problem. This study used secondary data collected from various sources, including articles, journals, and official government websites, such as transportation services for the Special Capital Region of Jakarta.

4 Finding and Discussion

Smart City is a city with a secure network and infrastructure. Smart cities can also make residents' lives easier and more comfortable. However, Smart City provides smart solutions for businesses. An example of a Smart City uses smart data, smart mobility, smart energy, smart transportation, smart IoT devices, smart healthcare, governance and smart citizen services [26]. Smart cities produce services and infrastructures. It could be used to assess the smart city's intensity: the more citizens use smart services, the higher the output [39].

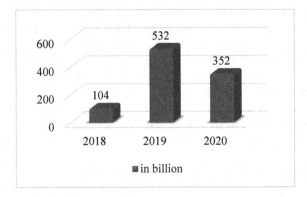

Fig. 2. Jakarta's local tax revenue derived from the parking sector

Every car or motorcycle driver, particularly in large cities such as Jakarta, requires parking. Still, the availability of parking spaces in this city is unbalanced in comparison to the number of private vehicle users, resulting in a variety of issues such as the number of vehicles exceeding the parking capacity, meaning that if the parking capacity is too large in comparison to the number of cars, many cars will be unable to be accommodated. These concerns can exacerbate existing ones, such as increased road congestion, lengthy waits restricting public highways, unlawful parking, and traffic accidents [40]. Parking issues are a never-ending source of contention. Every year, the growing number of inhabitants in Jakarta impacts the increasing number of automobiles, causing a parking problem. With this particular situation, the Jakarta government took the initiative to introduce new parking services in Jakarta. This service was made possible by implementing an application known as Jakparkir, which was integrated with some essential parties throughout the process. Jakarta's local tax revenue derived from the parking sector is depicted in Fig. 2 from 2018 to 2020. Parking can contribute significantly to regional income, as evidenced by a fairly substantial increase in the number of parking spaces available from 2018 to 2019. Another decline in 2020 is attributed to the COVID-19 pandemic, which forces people to spend more time in their respective homes [41]. The DKI Jakarta Provincial Government is digitizing parking management to increase regional income. This system is integrated with a payment system, which will make it easier to monitor and manage parking operations in the future. Since every transaction report is recorded and monitored in real-time, revenue receipts become more accurate and transparent as a result of this application.

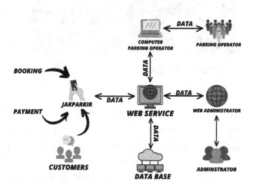

Fig. 3. The app work system

This parking technology applies to 479 locations, including 79 off-street parking spaces and 400 on-street parking spaces. Users can search for parking slot availability information using the Jakpakir application, place an order in advance, receive directions to the parking spot, pay with electronic money or QRIS, and prolong the parking time using the Jakpakir application. They can download the application on Google Play Store and complete the registration process. To register for the Jakparkir application, prospective users enter their mobile number and email address; they will receive an OTP code and begin using the application. One mobile number can only be used for one account. To book a parking space in the Jakparkir application, they must click the Parking Order icon and select a parking location from the map or type it into the Search Bar, select Book Ticket and enter the desired parking length. Then, they will proceed with the payment process. If the user cancels the parking reservation before 15 min or does not show up within 15 min, the reservation will be canceled, and their cash will be reimbursed automatically. Jakparkir operates between 07.00 am until 11.00 pm.

Although this service is application-based, users can park without using their application because each parking point has a Jukir (Juru Parkir) who will record the vehicle's registration number and parking location via the Jukir mobile application, allowing users to pay parking rates via the QRIS application. Upon leaving the parking area in line with the applicable tariff connected to the electronic money application or mobile banking. Between JakOne, LinkAja, Ovo, Dana, and GoPay, a QRIS application or e-Wallet has worked with Jakparkir. Jakparkir has also partnered with over 30 banks to facilitate the QRIS payment mechanism. The parking rate at Jakparkir is 5,000/h for vehicles and 2,000/h for motorcycles, in compliance with the DKI Jakarta province government's requirements. This application can determine the duration of the KIR test, emission test, and vehicle tax. Vehicles that have not paid the emission test tax or the KIR test will be assessed a high fee following DKI Jakarta governor regulation no. 31 of 2017 on parking service rates.

Fig. 4. The jakparkir app on playstore

When it comes to Smart Cities, digital technologies are critical since they are a crucial facilitator in increasing their attractiveness and sustainability and their impact on the social, economic, and environmental environments. When it comes to sustainable transportation, the efficient management of parking lots is a critical factor to consider. Parking space is typically scarce in major cities, resulting in traffic congestion, air pollution, and driver dissatisfaction among the general public. Indeed, it has been estimated that locating a vacant parking space could take upwards of 20–30 min on average in some areas [42]. The elimination of the parking problem in Jakarta necessitates the collaboration of all parties involved. Since the private sector and government organizations frequently fail to prepare a large parking lot, many residents are forced to park carelessly on the side of the road, causing the problem to occur. The advancement of technology can provide a foolproof solution for Jakarta, which experiences high levels of movement daily. By involving all stakeholders capable of presenting a surefire innovation to reduce the problems in the city, the Jakarta city government has taken a surefire step toward achieving its goals. Artificial Intelligence (AI) is being implemented in smart cities, a surefire step toward achieving its goals. According to data from Google Play, this application has been downloaded a significant number of times and has received a wide range of good reviews, as illustrated in Fig. 4. The Jakparkir application is capable of alleviating Jakarta's parking problems. In addition, this application serves as evidence that the Jakarta government is serious about creating a suitable city for its citizens and is making every effort to bring the concept of smart infrastructure to fruition.

5   Conclusion

Artificial intelligence is unquestionably beneficial to the public sector because it enables the realization of a concept that encourages the availability of various public facilities that are so beneficial. Thus, the government can fully present the idea of smart infrastructure, one of the dimensions of smart cities. The Jakarta government's commitment to city development continues to be demonstrated through the presentation of numerous innovations that are relevant to the city's residents. The Jakparkir application addresses one of the major issues facing this metropolitan city, namely parking. The community benefits and does not have to worry about parking fees through this application, as they are under applicable regulations. Additionally, this application assists the government in coordinating with one another in monitoring the movement of motor vehicles, which are abundant in Jakarta.

References

1. Pereira, A.G., Lima, T.M., Charruasantos, F.: Industry 4.0 and society 5.0: opportunities and threats. Int. J. Recent Technol. Eng. **8**(5), 3305–3308 (2020). https://doi.org/10.35940/ijrte. d8764.018520
2. Mohammed, Z.K.A., Ahmed, E.S.A.: Internet of things applications, challenges and related future technologies Zeinab. World Sci. News **67**(2), 126–148 (2017)
3. Kasiwi, A.N., Nurmandi, A., Mutiarin, D., Azka, M.F.: Artificial data management in reaching conditional cash transfer of Program Keluarga Harapan (PKH) utilizing simple addictive weighting. IOP Conf. Ser. Earth Environ. Sci. **717**(1), 12013 (2021). https://doi.org/10.1088/ 1755-1315/717/1/012013
4. Grove, H., Clouse, M., Schaffner, L., Xu, T.: Monitoring ai progress for corporate governance. J. Gov. Regul. **9**(1), 8–17 (2020). https://doi.org/10.22495/jgrv9i1art1
5. Kerr, A., Barry, M., Kelleher, J.D.: Expectations of artificial intelligence and the performativity of ethics: Implications for communication governance. Big Data Soc. **7**(1), 1–2 (2020). https:// doi.org/10.1177/2053951720915939
6. Pi, Y.: Machine learning in governments: benefits, challenges and future directions. eJ. eDemoc. OpenGov. **13**(1), 203–219 (2021). https://doi.org/10.29379/jedem.v13i1.625
7. Admin: Kecerdasan Artifisial Bantu Ungkit Perekonomian Nasional di Masa Depan. Kementerian Komunikasi dan Informatika Republik Indonesia
8. Yun, Y., Lee, M.: Smart city 4.0 from the perspective of open innovation. J. Open Innov. Technol. Mark. Complex. **5**(4), 92 (2019). https://doi.org/10.3390/joitmc5040092
9. Subandi, Y., Qodir, Z., Jubba, H., Nurmandi, A.: Artificial intelligence in election party of broker clientelism Joxzin (Jogjakarta Islamic Never Die). IOP Conf. Ser. Earth Environ. Sci. **717**(1), 012040 (2021). https://doi.org/10.1088/1755-1315/717/1/012040
10. Dewanti, M., Purnomo, E.P., Salsabila, L.: Analisa efektifitas bank sampah sebagai alternatif pengelolaan sampah dalam mencapai smart city di kabupaten kulon progo. Publisia J. Ilmu Adm. Publik. **5**(1), 21–29 (2020). https://doi.org/10.26905/pjiap.v5i1.3828
11. Lv, Z, Qiao, L., Kumar Singh, A., Wang, Q.: AI-empowered IoT security for smart cities. ACM Trans. Internet Technol. **21**(4), 1–21 (2021). https://doi.org/10.1145/3406115
12. Samih, H.: Smart cities and internet of things. J. Inf. Technol. Case Appl. Res. **21**(1), 3–12 (2019). https://doi.org/10.1080/15228053.2019.1587572
13. Kazazi Darani, S., Akbari Eslami, A., Jabbari, M., Asefi, H.: Parking lot site selection using a fuzzy AHP-TOPSIS framework in Tuyserkan, Iran. J. Urban Plan. Dev. **144**(3), 04018022 (2018). https://doi.org/10.1061/(asce)up.1943-5444.0000456
14. Ridwan, A., et al.: Evaluation of the strength of coconut shell aggregate concrete block for parking area. IOP Conf. Ser. Earth Environ. Sci. **277**(1), 012002 (2019). https://doi.org/10. 1088/1755-1315/277/1/012002
15. Ajeng, C., Gim, T.H.T.: Analyzing on-street parking duration and demand in a Metropolitan city of a developing country: a case study of Yogyakarta city, Indonesia. Sustain. **10**(3), 591 (2018). https://doi.org/10.3390/su10030591
16. Maulana, M.F., Adhy, S., Bahtiar, N., Waspada, I.: Development of a smart parking system based on internet of things using object-oriented analysis and design method. J. Phys. Conf. Ser. **1524**(1), 012111 (2020). https://doi.org/10.1088/1742-6596/1524/1/012111

17. Prasetya, E.: Pemprov DKI Uji Coba Aplikasi JakParkir, Bisa Cek Lokasi dan Pesan Parkir. Merdeka (2021)
18. Amalia, Y.: Lewat Jakparkir, Tempat Parkir Bisa Dipesan Lebih Dahulu. Liputan6 (2021)
19. Ogie, R.I., Perez, P., Dignum, V.: Smart infrastructure: an emerging frontier for multidisciplinary research. Proc. Inst. Civ. Eng. Smart Infrastruct. Constr. **170**(1), 8–16 (2017). https://doi.org/10.1680/jsmic.16.00002
20. Press, G.: A very short history of artificial intelligence (AI). Forbes. **30**, 6 (2016)
21. Truby, J., Brown, R., Dahdal, A.: Banking on AI: mandating a proactive approach to AI regulation in the financial sector. Law Financ. Mark. Rev. **14**(2), 110–120 (2020). https://doi.org/10.1080/17521440.2020.1760454
22. Hovy, E., Navigli, R., Ponzetto, S.P.: Collaboratively built semi-structured content and artificial intelligence: the story so far. Artif. Intell. **194**, 2–27 (2013). https://doi.org/10.1016/j.artint.2012.10.002
23. Lewis, D., Moorkens, J.: A rights-based approach to trustworthy AI in social media. Soc. Media Soc. **6**(3), 14 (2020). https://doi.org/10.1177/2056305120954672
24. Larsson, S., Heintz, F.: Transparency in artificial intelligence. Internet Policy Rev. **9**(2), 1–16 (2020). https://doi.org/10.14763/2020.2.1469
25. Morrar, R., Arman, H., Mousa, S.: The fourth industrial revolution (Industry 4.0): a social innovation perspective. Technol. Innov. Manag. Rev. **7**(11), 12 (2017). https://doi.org/10.22215/TIMREVIEW/1396
26. "Here are 6 Important Technologies to Build a Smart City. Hardayaperkasa (2019)
27. Allam, Z., Newman, P.: Redefining the smart city: culture, metabolism and governance. Smart Cities **1**(1), 4–25 (2018). https://doi.org/10.3390/smartcities1010002
28. Meijer, A., Bolívar, M.P.R.: Governing the smart city: a review of the literature on smart urban governance. Int. Rev. Adm. Sci. **82**(2), 392–408 (2016). https://doi.org/10.1177/0020852314564308
29. Budiarti, N., Putra, Y.P., Nurmandi, A.: Digital signature implementation as a new smart governance model. Society **8**(2), 628–639 (2020). https://doi.org/10.33019/society.v8i2.222
30. Susanti, R., Soetomo, S, Buchori, I., Brotosunaryo, P.M.: Smart growth, smart city and density: in search of the appropriate indicator for residential density in Indonesia. Proc. Soc. Behav. Sci. **227**, 194–201 (2016). https://doi.org/10.1016/j.sbspro.2016.06.062
31. Kirimtat, A., Krejcar, O., Kertesz, A., Tasgetiren, M.F.: Future trends and current state of smart city concepts: a survey. IEEE Access **8**, 86448–86467 (2020). https://doi.org/10.1109/ACCESS.2020.2992441
32. Tanwar, S., Tyagi, S., Kumar, S.: The role of internet of things and smart grid for the development of a smart city. In: Hu, Y.-C., Tiwari, S., Mishra, K.K., Trivedi, M.C. (eds.) Intelligent Communication and Computational Technologies. LNNS, vol. 19, pp. 23–33. Springer, Singapore (2018). https://doi.org/10.1007/978-981-10-5523-2_3
33. Torre, T., Braccini, A.M., Spinelli, R. (eds.): Empowering Organizations. LNISO, vol. 11. Springer, Cham (2016). https://doi.org/10.1007/978-3-319-23784-8
34. Silva, B.N., Khan, M., Han, K.: Towards sustainable smart cities: a review of trends, architectures, components, and open challenges in smart cities. Sustain. Cities Soc. **38**(January), 697–713 (2018). https://doi.org/10.1016/j.scs.2018.01.053
35. Dameri, R.P.: Smart City Implementation: Creating Economic and Public Value in Innovative Urban Systems (2017)
36. Rathore, M.M., Paul, A., Ahmad, A., Jeon, G.: IoT-based big data: from smart city towards next generation super city planning. Int. J. Semant. Web Inf. Syst. **13**(1), 28–47 (2017). https://doi.org/10.4018/IJSWIS.2017010103
37. Ma, S., Zhang, H., Xing, X.: Scalability for smart infrastructure system in smart grid: a survey. Wirel. Pers. Commun. **99**(1), 161–184 (2017). https://doi.org/10.1007/s11277-017-5045-y

38. Chen, Y., Shen, L., Zhang, Y., Li, H., Ren, Y.: Sustainability based perspective on the utilization efficiency of urban infrastructure — a China study. Habitat Int. **93**(174), 102050 (2019). https://doi.org/10.1016/j.habitatint.2019.102050

39. Rahman, M.A., Rashid, M.M., Shamim Hossain, M., Hassanain, E, Alhamid, M.F., Guizani, M.: Blockchain and IoT-based cognitive edge framework for sharing economy services in a smart city. IEEE Access **7**, 18611–18621 (2019). https://doi.org/10.1109/ACCESS.2019.289 6065

40. Sandra, C.F.K.: Kebijakan Strategi Parkir (Studi Kasus : Ibu Kota Metropolitan Jakarta). September, pp. 103–108 (2020)

41. Data Penerimaan Pajak Daerah. Bapenda Jakarta (2021)

42. Herawati, Y.: Potret Jakarta, Setengah Jam Mencari Tempat Parkir. Viva (2019). https://www.viva.co.id/otomotif/1123438-potret-jakarta-setengah-jam-mencari-tempat-parkir

Universality and Interoperability Across Smart City Ecosystems

Ioannis Tsampoulatidis[1,2(✉)], Nicos Komninos[1], Evangelos Syrmos[3], and Dimitrios Bechtsis[3]

[1] URENIO Research, Faculty of Engineering, Aristotle University of Thessaloniki, Thessaloniki, Greece

[2] Infalia PC, Thessaloniki, Greece
itsam@infalia.com

[3] Department of Industrial Engineering and Management, School of Engineering, International Hellenic University, Thessaloniki (IHU), Greece

Abstract. Contemporary smart cities involve a very high number of software applications and hardware devices that connect to the physical and social space of cities and form complex global ecosystems in different knowledge and activity domains (transportation, logistics, healthcare, local communities, industry, governance, social care and many more). In this context, smart cities can be considered multi-layered complex systems, systems of systems, that provide ubiquitous access to services, applications, platforms, and infrastructures. Although the inherent heterogeneity of Internet-of-Things (IoT) devices and their platforms, is one of the challenges smart city ecosystems face, several implementations promote digital transformation methodologies that attempt to bridge the different domains. Multiple IoT and software platforms, ranging from open source to proprietary solutions, implement different architectures and communication protocols for exchanging data streams. The diversity of these platforms though disrupts the creation of smart city ecosystems and prohibits the establishment of holistic and universal access models.

Keywords: Universality · Universal access · Datastream integration · Smart city ecosystem

1 Introduction

To foster and facilitate the development of new applications, flexible smart systems and complex architectures are proposed. Specifically, these systems are able to connect different domains from different smart city ecosystems together, avoiding single vertical implementations that limit the scalability of solutions and infrastructure.

Available solutions and systems that are developing in vertical markets at various domains, offer little interoperability and sharing of resources and there is a knowledge gap about developing cross-sector smart city systems. To handle these challenges, Komninos et al. [1] proposed the concept of 'Connected Intelligence Spaces' that enables

N. A. Streitz and S. Konomi (Eds.): HCII 2022, LNCS 13325, pp. 218–230, 2022.
https://doi.org/10.1007/978-3-031-05463-1_16

synergies between human, machine, and collective intelligence and assess a universal architecture of high impact smart city projects. These spaces for interconnecting distributed smart city ecosystems can be utilised for information sharing.

Existing decentralised smart city ecosystems can be connected via information sharing pipelines as a horizontal layer that contributes to decreased load, but also offers extensive flexibility by promoting a unified architecture. Adjustments are mandatory for overcoming the underlying fragmentation of smart city ecosystems and for contributing to a more universal architecture scalability. This can promote the decision-making process and conclude to universal access frameworks and architectures that are customised to the citizens' needs.

Discussions for evaluating the performance of heterogeneous architectures and communication protocols are triggered by the research community, to develop a universal smart infrastructure and a universal architecture of city intelligence categorised in four parts (agglomeration, orchestration, empowerment, and instrumentation according to N. Komninos [2]) that appears within smart cities and enables interoperability across smart city ecosystems.

Numerous challenges though, need to be tackled via the collaboration of all involved stakeholders and real-world implementations are needed to assess the theoretical frameworks and architectures in this nascent area.

2 Approaching Smart City Ecosystems from Legacy to New Initiatives

With the advancement of smart city technologies, 27 billion IoT devices are expected by 2025 [3]. This network of interconnected physical devices and software applications constantly produces and exchanges data over the Internet, and creates clusters and networks. Smart cities do not have a single definition, but they are considered as an abstract multi-layered structure that utilises information and communication technologies, data and analytics to operate efficiently, improve the quality of governance and citizen well-being. From a wider scope, a smart city ecosystem includes people, organisations, businesses, policies and laws cooperating to provide solutions in a domain of activity, such as governance, economy, mobility, healthcare, public safety, environmental sustainability, and others [4].

One of the first initiatives that have been proposed for implementing a smart city ecosystem, suggests that every application, service, and IoT device should comply with specific connectivity criteria and communication protocols. This approach is mainly based on standards, principles and strict software architectures and limits the implementation freedom of developers while restricting the types of devices. Compatibility issues arise and the information distribution channels are restricted. Hence, legacy applications are difficult to maintain as they follow deprecated standards and eventually should be abandoned. New initiatives that tackle the problem of legacy ecosystems should be substituted by new holistic approaches that have no limitations and follow open connectivity standards. Universality will not only reduce the overall cost across software tools and hardware devices (human labour, maintenance and hardware cost) but will also gradually transform legacy applications to open standards solutions that digitally transform the old ecosystem.

The purpose of any newly established ecosystem is to provide a path for the next generation of applications. All stakeholders involved in this ecosystem will be able to operate via open data streams. Due to its highly open design, start-ups, SMEs, and big tech companies can equally develop applications to be connected to the ecosystem despite their dynamics. Application interoperability across smart city ecosystems is another major goal of this initiative. Different types of services are seamlessly interconnected and provide communication solutions at the social, political, and environmental domains. Stakeholders can use data from a variety of different sources focusing on the provided services and not on backend developments which will be orchestrated horizontally.

Contemporary smart city ecosystems need to define open architectures and open standards to support interoperability and interconnection of applications by producing and using data in the form of data streams. The adaptation of new standards ensures interoperability across all services and applications. Moreover, accessibility standards need to be integrated at every level of services, organisations, federations, from design to implementation, to promote inclusion. End-users can benefit from the adoption of the new approach by having access to numerous applications and services customised to their needs and accessibility requirements. Organisations and federations on the other hand can collect and combine data from different sources to make predictions, analysis, and apply machine learning methodologies or any other post-processing of data. The utilisation of cross-platform data will immensely support optimisation techniques that could be applied to well-established domains (public transportation, energy, or water consumption) and affect our daily routines.

3 Data and Surveys

3.1 Architectures Towards Systems Integration

The technological growth of the last decade in terms of available open-source and proprietary solutions for managing large scale software ecosystems, in conjunction with their constantly reduced costs, has led to a blooming transition from monolithic architectures into modular, scalable, and auto-deployable containerised environments. Additionally, there is a continuously increasing trend of moving from on-premises and legacy systems to multi and hybrid cloud-based ecosystems. This migration is applied not only to enterprises and private companies but to local authorities and the public sector. According to Danielsen et al. [5] the transition is due to proven cloud computing benefits that include among others, cost reduction, security, flexibility and scalability, mobility and availability, and infrastructure. The tendency for hybrid cloud computing is highlighted in Gartner's 2021 overview of the top trend hype cycle for digital government [6]. The same report also identifies a clear focus on solution design to meet the agility demands of governmental organisations through the inclusion of Digital Government Technology Platforms (DGTPs), event stream processing, full life cycle Application Programming Interface (API) management, microservices, and packaged business components.

Undeniably, the IoT concept plays a major role in the context of smart cities and several surveys have been conducted to highlight the importance of open cross-compatible IoT platforms and their underlying architectures. Mineraud et al. [7], identified the technical gaps and differences during the integration and development phase among open-source and proprietary IoT platforms and concluded that although open-source platforms can be expanded more rapidly to cope with the emergence of new technologies, proprietary solutions also tend to adapt on new requirements even at a slower pace. Due to the wide diversity of sensors and their supported systems, there is no global architecture to cover all needs. Still, some universally accepted architectural characteristics should be applied to every proposed solution, such as scalability, high availability, and flexibility. The most commonly accepted architecture for IoT projects consists of three layers, namely; the perception (e.g., how data are produced from sensors and IT systems), the network (e.g., how data are transferred), and the application (e.g., how data are displayed to end-users). MongoDB's technical article [8] considers the three-layer architecture and proposes a five-layer architecture that stacks to perception, transportation, processing, application, and business layers. Another approach to define an IoT architecture according to several studies is a four-stage workflow consisting of sensors and actuators, Internet gateways and Data Acquisition Systems (DAS), Edge IT, and data-centre and cloud, while some others include a fifth stage which involves user interaction, control, and feedback.

At a lower level, the most widely used IoT standards to support interoperable data exchange between devices and the cloud, are the MQTT, an OASIS standard messaging protocol that offers bi-directional secure communication, and the CoAP, a service layer protocol mainly for use in resource-constrained devices. For larger universal implementations supporting a wider variety of backend applications and services, a common approach is to apply the oneM2M standards that most importantly support a syntactic and semantic interoperability solution via a set of ontologies and XML schemas for connecting cross-silo IoT systems. Thus, it is of high importance that a semantic vocabulary is used across systems to minimise the integration complexity.

Besides the IoT context, a smart city ecosystem is composed of thousands of heterogeneous larger IT systems, each one having its business logic and handling its data. A well-established method to interconnect these systems is each one to acknowledge every other system's API (tightly coupled). The use of APIs is the most widely used methodology of integration; gateway-service implementation is mostly used in systems without access to source code, and proxy-service implementations based on extended SDK are used at device-level platforms that are frequently inaccessible. Although using APIs, to connect contrasted systems is broadly used, it demands bilaterally agreements between providers and deep knowledge of their available methods (e.g., REST with the use of open API standards). It also requires constant monitoring for possible API's schema updates, newly introduced parameters, endpoints revisions, and other issues. To overcome these obstacles, an architecture based on the MQTT approach at a much larger scale, is suggested. Every system keeps its existing operations and logic but in addition, it produces a payload of data that streams under one or more topics (aka categories) without necessarily knowing a priori which systems or other smart city ecosystems are going to receive them (loosely coupled). Vice versa, systems willing to receive data from others, just need to know the topic names. To support such architecture, a cluster of messaging brokers, easily scalable, must be included in the ecosystem. The use of data streams over Kafka is a proven solution offering distributed coordination and can support such a large-scale implementation, allowing new kinds of real-time function-alities. Such an approach is adopted by the "Improve My City" application [9] which produces and streams data in kafka topics, which are then consumed by a dashboard. A controlled parking system in Thessaloniki [10] uses kafka streams to fetch data from differerent sources and creates interactive visualisations. Moreover, for newly incoming IT systems into the smart city ecosystem, it is suggested to avoid monolithic designs and use modern cloud computing as-a-service approach such as infrastructure-as-a-service (IaaS), platform-as-a-service (PaaS), and software-as-a-service (SaaS) and also to adopt the microservices architecture for their applications, orchestrated by solutions such as Kubernetes, Mesos, Docker Swarm, OpenShift, and others.

3.2 Platforms and Services

The enforcement of specific communication protocols and connectivity criteria in smart city ecosystems limit the use of IoT devices and software modules and restrict the easy development of niche, reusable and scalable software applications and services. Holistic approaches better engage the ecosystem's layers and pave the way for universality and interoperability across them. Multi-layered smart city platforms are robust solutions that tackle the heterogeneous nature of IoT devices and seemingly connect them to the smart city backbone. In the early years, smart city platforms mainly included protocols and methodologies for on-demand data aggregation. More sophisticated platforms focus on the distributed nature of the smart cities and make extensive use of APIs for interoper-ating with hardware and software devices. As a next step, push protocols are used for data retrieval and communication. Data streams and topics are broadcasting data from multiple sources while distributed cloud platforms are collecting them. This enables the implementation of hardware and software agnostic methodologies, and the development of a plethora of services.

A common solution is the implementation of platforms that support numerous APIs and provide a set of libraries for establishing connections to IoT devices and third-party software tools. FIWARE is a widely used platform that offers such APIs for developing web applications and many contemporary solutions are using FIWARE as a building block. Pereira et al. [11] reviewed several smart city platforms regarding their func-tional requirements, indicatively; data management, application runtime, sensor man-agement, data processing, external data sources, services, tools, city models, distributed sensing, resource discovery, resource, and events management. The authors' research output SGeoL is a multi-layered smart city platform for handling heterogeneous data. Trilles et al. [12], presented the SmartUJI platform that aggregates university-related data sources and offers them to the public using RESTful APIs and web services. Smar-tUJI provides the content, the service, and the application layers. Similar is the case of Webinos and CityPulse that enable the development of applications through APIs as well.

Massana et al. [13] proposed a multi-layered framework to monitor activities in the smart city ecosystem. The services layer handles data streams while the applica-tion layer provides the dashboards that interoperate with the end-users. The platform Sense Our Environment (SEnviro) follows an inherent IoT and Web of Things (WoT) approach using low-cost, open-hardware and open-software, energetically autonomous and interoperable solutions. At the application layer, a set of web applications are provided. The European Commission also supported the SmartSantander project as a part of the Future Internet Research and Experimentation initiative, for monitoring the environment's pollution, the parking positions, and irrigation systems. PortoLivingLab has been developed in Porto and has a multi-source sensing infrastructure for data aggregation and management applications.

Middleware solutions are also taken into consideration for tackling heterogeneity both in hardware and software components. The EPIC (European Platform for Intelligent Cities) project proposed a middleware tool for tacking interoperability, extensibility, and reconfigurability in smart cities. Sofia2 is a middleware that enables interoperability between multiple systems and devices, offering a semantic platform that makes real-world information available to smart, mainly IoT-oriented applications. Similarly, Civitas could be used for application development and could tackle the heterogeneity of the smart cities using abstract interfaces.

Cloud-based platforms are connecting IoT devices to the smart city ecosystem. SIGMA and Kaa are cloud-based solutions for storing, handling, processing and presenting IoT data. The SureCity platform is using Azure Cloud services and provides dashboards for smart app development (Pardo-García et al. [14]). Snap4City platform is a cloud IoT solution that focuses on microservices (Badii et al. [15]).

Service-dominant platforms are also proposed to focus on key contributors in a smart city and describe that value be co-created in the establishment of a platform (Yu et al. [16]). Carriots is a Platform as a Service (PaaS) solution designated for IoT and can be used to connect the information-providing infrastructure to a smart city. InterSCity is an open-source platform that could be also used for the development of microservices.

Agent-based distributed platforms are tackling scalability issues and support the implementation of nodes for establishing a robust network infrastructure and handling the IoT devices. The design and development of distributed smart city IoT platforms for handling large volumes of data is presented while an approach for reusing functionalities of legacy applications is examined. The IoT landscape includes many manufacturers, protocols and communication technologies and current platforms have difficulties transparently supporting them while having scalability issues. An Apache Kafka based platform could tackle scalability and reusability issues using a database, a data streaming, and an application layer (Chamoso et al. [17]).

3.3 Cross-ecosystem IoT Infrastructure

As smart cities continue to grow, the migration of citizens to urban areas has imposed various challenges. Most of the established IoT ecosystems are combining multiple information flows into one single platform and do not fully support integration with third-party applications. This approach results in IoT ecosystems known as silos. To solve this inherent problem that involves multiple proprietary and open IoT platforms, the EU's ambition is the establishment of Open IoT ecosystems. The US government supports multinational corporations such as Google, Amazon, Facebook and Apple to develop state of the art IoT ecosystems (Miguel et al. [18]). On the other hand, the EU is also funding SMEs for the development of innovative ecosystems that contribute to the growth of a more sustainable smart city ecosystem (Kubler et al. [19]).

The establishment of widely used open IoT platforms imposes challenges from an integration perspective and usually concludes with the development of APIs and web sockets for linking third-party applications. To exchange information with multiple platforms, to support the vertical silos and to create a unified ecosystem that guarantees interoperability across all services, standards are adopted. Ubiquitous connectivity and disruptive innovations in several sectors (e.g., transportation, energy, manufacturing, healthcare, cities, etc.), demand the creation of open IoT ecosystems as sustainable connectivity and information gathering solutions. The design of state-of-the-art platforms should support ad hoc and loosely coupled data flows among hardware devices, software components, data sources, and users.

Cross Platform Interoperability. Extensive research has been conducted in published papers and funded projects to support cross-platform interoperability. Standards and abstract interfaces enable the connection of IoT devices and software applications to a multi-layered ecosystem that aggregates data streams from various sources. Chaturvedi and Kolbe [20] proposed the use of OGC (Open Geospatial Consortium) standards to address cross-platform interoperability issues. They conducted their study at Queen's Elizabeth Olympic Park in London and highlighted the advantages of integrating geospatial standards for collecting information from heterogeneous data sources in a semantic architecture approach. Similarly, Bröring et al. [21] state that cross-platform interoperability is critical for avoiding vertical silos. To validate their statements, the BiG-IoT project developed an open-source ecosystem for interoperable communication across multiple IoT platforms based on discovery methodologies, marketplaces for data gathering and monetization schemes.

Although standards for communicating between multiple IoT platforms have been proposed, their adoption rate is significantly low. This is due to the fact that companies use commercial proprietary products which are difficult to be adapted to open ecosystem initiatives and solutions. Standards such as O-MI (Open Messaging Interface) and O-DF (Open Data Format) have been tested on projects such as bIoTope funded by the H2020 Research and Innovation Programme (Javed et al. [22]). In order to assess the potential of the standards, extensive trials were performed in three European cities. The VITAL platform has been proposed as a solution for connecting and integrating diverse data sources using semantic data models (Kazmi et al. [23]). There is evidence that standards can promote cross-platform interoperability.

Open IoT Ecosystems. The concept of open IoT ecosystems has been proposed recently. Open stands for the ability to support open standards for interoperating with third-party platforms, applications and services. Citizens and companies benefit from the utilisation of data pools that aggregate heterogeneous data sources in the smart city ecosystem (Ahlgren et al. [24]). Robert et al. [25] stated that a scalable open IoT ecosystem should be broken down into multiple layers and each layer should have specific communication and access rights. More importantly, to integrate heterogeneous data sources and avoid the creation of IoT silos, methodologies for discovering, connecting and integrating IoT devices from external platforms must be adopted as means of standardising a communication layer.

Automated discovery and connection methodologies have been tested on a scalable IoT testbed (Javed et al. [26]). The authors implemented O-MI and O-DF standards as the messaging format across the connected devices. The hierarchy was structured based on XML which eliminates unnecessary conflicts from connected IoT devices during integration in a unified schema. Although open standardisation is promising for avoiding IoT platform isolation, software limitations should be addressed for shifting to a more scalable and sustainable approach.

3.4 Data Interoperability and Data Transfer Across Ecosystems

Smart cities follow the system-of-systems architecture of cities and an important challenge in developing smart city solutions across (sub)systems relates to data. In particular, the compilation of data from different sources, the orchestration of data, the use of datasets across city (sub)systems, the re-use of same datasets to support different functionalities, and the use of dataset from one system to develop solutions for another system (Liu et al. [27]; Bischof et al. [28]; Gupta et al. [29]). To discuss these challenges of data interoperability across smart city ecosystems, we refer to three cases and experiments.

The IBM design for an open data system in Thessaloniki was a free consultation offered by the company to the city. Thessaloniki, Greece, was selected through a competitive process as one of 16 cities to be awarded a "Smarter Cities Challenge" grant in 2015–2016. A team of six IBM experts worked in the city for three weeks in collaboration with many stakeholders from universities, the government, and the business community. They delivered recommendations on how to organise an open data system that encourages transparency, benchmarking, performance measurement, and data-sharing between public departments, businesses, universities, non-governmental organisations, and citizens (IBM [30]). The findings of this assignment highlighted the fragmented and scattered data among multiple recording systems and departments, incomplete data collection, data storage in different formats, data that is not shareable or readily consumable, inaccurate data because of undefined and non-standardised collection and storage, and unclear data ownership. The IBM assignment concluded with five strategic recommendations to the city administration and stakeholders to develop a collaborative city dashboard.

- Reorganise IT-related departments to enable open data policies and practices, designate a leader for open data, policy and process and streamline services to create efficiency in open data efforts.
- Establish an open data strategy and consistent understanding across City departments and stakeholders, managing the coordination between stakeholders
- Foster an environment that supports collaboration in dashboard development with ideas from technology, academia and business that enable diverse groups to work together
- Establish a publishing process and maturity model that put open data into practice, increasing the City's ability to govern and publish data and transparency of City activities
- Address resource constraints through investments, strategic partnerships, and change management.

Gaia-X is a more complex system, a federated data infrastructure establishing an ecosystem in which data is made available, collated and shared in a trustworthy environment [31]. GAIA-X is not a monolithic organisation or platform but a cloud ecosystem. In the ecosystem, data are not stored centrally but at the source and are shared via semantic interoperability. A key concept to achieve this type of collaboration is the concept of "Data Space". The term refers to the relationship between trusted partners that apply the same standards and rules for data storage and sharing. Data spaces are created by participants that decide to share data. They can be data providers, users, or intermediary organisations. Each organisation can participate in many data spaces and therefore data spaces are nested and overlapping. To ensure data sovereignty and trust, Gaia-X has developed a reference architecture model, which defines the open data infrastructure and how Gaia-X facilitates interconnection, interoperability, and integration of data spaces (Gaia-X [32]). Existing examples include Gaia-X data spaces in the domains of SMEs and industry 4.0, health, education, energy, mobility, finance, in which many organisations collaborate in data sharing. For instance, in the case of smart homes, Gaia-X is building a platform for organising, orchestrating, and optimising data from smart meters on gas, water and electricity consumption. Gaia-X is a European initiative towards a "sovereign cloud" that would end the dependence of the European economy on large US and Chinese hyperscalers (AWS, Microsoft Azure, Google Cloud, Alibaba, IBM). However, there are concerns about whether Gaia-X will achieve this ambitious objective and develop a sustainable business model taking into account the real needs of the market (Autolitano and Pawlowska [33]).

An advanced case of data sharing in Europe is the Open Research Data Pilot. It was launched by the European Commission in the framework of Horizon 2020 as a pilot for open access to research data and improving the re-use of research data across all thematic areas of H2020. The pilot adopts the FAIR data principles (Findable, Accessible, Interoperable, and Reusable) assisting humans and machines in their discovery of, access to, integration and analysis of data associated algorithms and workflows. Findable data relate to metadata, which is registered or indexed in a searchable resource, specify the data identifier as a globally unique and eternally persistent identifier. Accessible data are retrievable by their identifier using a standardised communications protocol, which is open, free, and universally implementable, and allows for an authentication and authorisation procedure. Interoperable data are those using a formal, accessible, shared, and broadly applicable language for knowledge representation. Finally, reusable data have a plurality of accurate and relevant attributes, are released with a clear and accessible data usage license, and meet domain-relevant community standards (Wilkinson et al. [34]). In this direction, a literature review of academic articles published between 2016 and 2019 on the use of FAIR Guiding Principles is presented by van Reisen et al. [35].

The three cases, we summary presented, shows that data reuse and interoperability across smart city ecosystems rely on three pillars. First, on agreements for collaboration between data providers and users belonging to different ecosystems or sectors of activity, establishing partnerships, data sharing strategies, and data spaces for collaboration. Second, on adopting open ("as open as possible, as closed as necessary") and FAIR principles of data organisation and semantic annotation enabling data sharing and re-use.

Third, by appropriate Human-Computer-Interaction, using semantic technologies and identifiers, formal languages for data representation, and rich and searchable metadata.

4   Discussion

Smart cities involve diverse software applications and hardware devices that constitute complex architectures in multiple knowledge domains and according to N. Komninos [36], along with big data and social media analytics and civic technologies, these architectures and their supported technologies allow the creation of smart ecosystems in which connected intelligence emerges. The establishment of a universal access schema across the smart city ecosystem necessitates the adoption of open standards on the communication and integration layer while providing a trustworthy infrastructure for data acquisition and management. Although technologies for connecting diverse IoT ecosystems have been proposed and utilised, third-party applications are still striving to identify and adopt efficient standards that minimise the total development time for building connectors and middleware software tools.

To support the connectivity of ecosystems, data streams and data spaces are continuously under study and new hardware and software solutions are proposed. It is critical to have a consensus on the conceptual design and planning scheme and explicitly propose next generation universal access services. This study analyses four echelons for promoting universal access to smart city data providers: (i) architecture; (ii) platform and services; (iii) IoT infrastructure; and (iv) data interoperability and transfer. At the architecture level, there is a trend for adopting multi-layered cloud-based systems that support both microservices and classic infrastructure, platform and software-as-a-service solutions. This is also the case for platforms and services as distributed multi-layered cloud platforms are proposed for supporting both developers and end-users with services. The IoT infrastructure is focused on providing hardware and software integration middleware tools for avoiding the creation of IoT silos and unify heterogeneous devices and services in a scalable, hardware and software agnostic communication layer. Finally, data interoperability and data transfer rely on the adoption of (i) common strategies at the data provider level; (ii) open and FAIR principles; and (iii) effective and efficient Human-Computer-Interaction interfaces.

Eventually, the collaboration of all the aforementioned technologies that compose a smart city, such as; software platforms, system architectures, IoT, but also, social media, data science, and lately blockchain (as used in the context of intelligent cities [37]), are actually constituting the algorithmic logic under which they operate. In the book "Smart Cities in the Post-algorithmic Era", the editors [38] conclude that the algorithmic logic should be combined with creativity, innovation and collective and collaborative intelligence in order to be efficient and effective.

Smart city stakeholders should elaborate on the reorganisation of IT processes and establish consistent open data strategies. Heterogeneous data streams should be handled by a multi-layered ecosystem that provides focused services to the citizens with the use of state-of-the-art flexible dashboards. As a last step, there is a continuous need for investments that could be fostered by strategic partnerships between the public and the private domain.

5 Conclusions

The HCI community is examining universality and interoperability in order to provide global protocols, standards and methodologies. This schema expands the usage levels of heterogeneous devices and data sources and supports the decision making process. The cross-ecosystem area of IoT technologies is expected to transform the well-established IoT platforms into a unified ecosystem minimising the heterogeneity while providing the building blocks for future ecosystems. Specifically, initiatives that address the importance of the ubiquitous connectivity and interoperability of the underlying ecosystems are the first steps to a futureproof interconnected ecosystem. Standardisation across all IoT layers, from the data models to the application connectivity layers are crucial for enabling future technologies to be built upon. This will enable the development of new ecosystems that prohibit the formation the vertical silos. Although, innovative projects are already being funded, we are far from concluding to universality and interoperability standards. Future research and experimentation are mandatory to assess the importance and added benefits of standardisation. Messaging, connectivity standards and data provisioning are the underlying pillars of the aforementioned initiatives, that will shape the future of cross-ecosystems interoperability.

The multi-layered approach is considered as a viable solution for aggregating heterogeneous data sources in the global smart city ecosystem. IoT agnostic solutions are needed in a global landscape that should embrasse a very high number of billions of software applications and hardware devices that connect to the physical and social space of cities and form complex global ecosystems. At the same time, the platforms are evolving and provide distributed cloud services based on multi layered architectures.

Acknowledgments. The research work of two of the authors (D. Bechtsis and E. Syrmos) was supported by the European Regional Development Fund (ERDF) 2014–2020, Central Macedonia Operational Programme, Project 'iWet: Intelligent IoT System for Quantitative and Qualitative Measurements for water distribution networks' MIS 5136429.

References

1. Komninos, N., Kakderi, C., Mora, L., Panori, A., Sefertzi, E.: Towards high impact smart cities: a universal architecture based on connected intelligence spaces. J. Knowl. Econ. **4**, 1–29 (2021). https://doi.org/10.1007/s13132-021-00767-0
2. Komninos, N.: Architectures of intelligence in smart cities: pathways to problem-solving and innovation. ArchiDoct. **6**(1), 11 (2018)
3. IoT Analytics: State of IoT 2021. https://iot-analytics.com/number-connected-iot-devices. Accessed 29 Jan 2022
4. IIoT World: The Smart City Ecosystem Framework – A Model for Planning Smart Cities. https://www.iiot-world.com/smart-cities-buildings-infrastructure/smart-cities/the-smart-city-ecosystem-framework-a-model-for-planning-smart-cities. Accessed 29 Jan 2022
5. Danielsen, F., Flak, L.S., Ronzhyn, A.: Cloud computing in e-government: benefits and challenges. In: ICDS 2019: The Thirteenth International Conference on Digital Society and eGovernments, Athens, Greece (2019)

6. Gartner Inc.: Hype Cycle for Digital Government Technology, 2021, Alia Mendonsa, 21 July 2021, Whitepaper (2021)
7. Mineraud, J., Mazhelis, O., Su, X., Tarkoma, S.: A gap analysis of Internet-of-Things platforms. Comput. Commun. **89–90**, 5–16 (2016). https://doi.org/10.1016/j.comcom.2016.03.015
8. What is IoT Architecture: MongoDB. https://www.mongodb.com/cloud-explained/iot-archit ecture. Accessed 29 Jan 2022
9. Tsampoulatidis, I., Nikolopoulos, S., Kompatsiaris, I., Komninos, N.: Geographic citizen science in citizen-government communication and collaboration: lessons learned from the Improve My City application. In: Geographic Citizen Science Design: No one Left Behind, pp. 186–205. UCL Press (2021)
10. Chalikias, A.P., et al.: Evidence-driven policy-making using heterogeneous data sources—the case of a controlled parking system in Thessaloniki. Data Policy **2**(2020), e15 (2021)
11. Pereira, J., Batista, T., Cavalcante, E., Souza, A., Lopes, F., Cacho, N.: A platform for integrating heterogeneous data and developing smart city applications. Futur. Gener. Comput. Syst. **128**(March), 552–566 (2022). https://doi.org/10.1016/j.future.2021.10.030
12. Trilles, S., Calia, A., Belmonte, Ó., Torres-Sospedra, J., Montoliu, R., Huerta, J.: Deployment of an open sensorized platform in a smart city context. Futur. Gener. Comput. Syst. **76**(November), 221–233 (2017). https://doi.org/10.1016/j.future.2016.11.005
13. Massana, J., Pous, C., Burgas, L., Melendez, J., Colomer, J.: Identifying services for short-term load forecasting using data driven models in a smart city platform. Sustain. Cities Soc. **28**(January), 108–117 (2017). https://doi.org/10.1016/j.scs.2016.09.001
14. Pardo-García, N., Simoes, S.G., Dias, L., Sandgren, A., Suna, D., Krook-Riekkola, A.: Sustainable and resource efficient cities platform – SureCity holistic simulation and optimization for smart cities. J. Clean. Prod. **215**(April), 701–711 (2019). https://doi.org/10.1016/j.jclepro.2019.01.070
15. Badii, C., Bellini, P., Difino, A., Nesi, P., Pantaleo, G., Paolucci, M.: Microservices suite for smart city applications. Sensors (Switzerland) **19**(21), 4798 (2019). https://doi.org/10.3390/s19214798
16. Yu, J., Wen, Y., Jin, J., Zhang, Y.: Towards a service-dominant platform for public value co-creation in a smart city: evidence from two metropolitan cities in China. Technol. Forecast. Soc. Chang. **142**(May), 168–182 (2019). https://doi.org/10.1016/j.techfore.2018.11.017
17. Chamoso, P., González-Briones, A., de La Prieta, F., Venyagamoorthy, G.K., Corchado, J.M.: Smart city as a distributed platform: toward a system for citizen-oriented management. Comput. Commun. **152** (February), 323–32 (2020). https://doi.org/10.1016/j.comcom.2020.01.059
18. Miguel, J.C., Casado, M.A.: GAFAnomy (Google, Amazon, Facebook and Apple): The Big Four and the b-Ecosystem (2016)
19. Kubler, S., et al.: IoT platforms initiative. In: Vermesan, O., Friess, P., (Eds.), "Internet of Things Connecting the Physical, Digital and Virtual Worlds: Digitising the Industry, pp. 265–292 (2016)
20. Chaturvedi, K., Kolbe, T.: Towards establishing cross-platform interoperability for sensors in smart cities. Sensors. **19**(3), 562 (2019). https://doi.org/10.3390/s19030562
21. Broring, A., et al.: Enabling IoT ecosystems through platform interoperability. IEEE Softw. **34**(1), 54–61 (2017). https://doi.org/10.1109/MS.2017.2
22. Javed, A., et al.: BIoTope: building an IoT open innovation ecosystem for smart cities. IEEE Access. **8**, 224318–224342 (2020). https://doi.org/10.1109/access.2020.3041326
23. Kazmi, A., Jan, Z., Zappa, A., Serrano, M.: Overcoming the heterogeneity in the internet of things for smart cities. In: Podnar Žarko, I., Broering, A., Soursos, S., Serrano, M. (eds.) Interoperability and Open-Source Solutions for the Internet of Things. LNCS, vol. 10218, pp. 20–35. Springer, Cham (2017). https://doi.org/10.1007/978-3-319-56877-5_2

24. Bengt, A., et al.: Internet of things for smart cities: interoperability and open data. IEEE Internet Comput. **20**(6), 52–56 (2016). https://doi.org/10.1109/mic.2016.124
25. Robert, J., et al.: Open IoT ecosystem for enhanced interoperability in smart cities—example of Métropole de Lyon. Sensors. **17**(12), 2849 (2017). https://doi.org/10.3390/s17122849
26. Javed, A., Malhi, A., Kinnunen, T., Framling, K.: Scalable IoT platform for heterogeneous devices in smart environments. IEEE Access **8**, 211973–211985 (2020). https://doi.org/10.1109/access.2020.3039368
27. Liu, X., Heller, A., Nielsen, P.S.: CITIESData: a smart city data management framework. Knowl. Inf. Syst. **53**(3), 699–722 (2017). https://doi.org/10.1007/s10115-017-1051-3
28. Bischof, S., Karapantelakis, A., Nechifor, C.S., Sheth, A.P., Mileo, A., Barnaghi, P.: Semantic modelling of smart city data (2014)
29. Gupta, A., Panagiotopoulos, P., Bowen, F.: An orchestration approach to smart city data ecosystems. Technol. Forecast. Soc. Chang. **153**, 119929 (2020)
30. IBM: Thessalonki, Greece. Smarter Cities Challenge report. IBM Corporate Citizenship & Corporate Affairs (2017)
31. Gaia-X: https://www.gaia-x.eu. Accessed 29 Jan 2022
32. Gaia-X: Gaia-X architecture document. Gaia-X European Association for Data and Cloud AISBL (2021)
33. Autolitano, S., Pawlowska, A.: Europe's quest for digital sovereignty: GAIA-X as a case study. IAI Papers. **21**, 14 (2021)
34. Wilkinson, M.D., et al.: The FAIR guiding principles for scientific data management and stewardship. Sci. Data **3**(1), 1–9 (2016)
35. van Reisen, M., Stokmans, M., Basajja, M., Ong'ayo, A.O., Kirkpatrick, C., Mons, B.: Towards the tipping point for FAIR implementation. Data Intell. **2**(1–2), 264–275 (2020)
36. Komninos, N.: Smart Cities and Connected Intelligence: Platforms, Ecosystems and Network Effect Regions and Cities Series. Routledge, Milton Park (2021)
37. Tsampoulatidis, I., Bechtsis, D., Kompatsiaris, I.: Moving from e-Gov to we-Gov and beyond: a blockchain framework for the digital transformation of cities. In: Smart Cities in the Post-algorithmic Era: Integrating Technologies, Platforms and Governance, pp. 176–200. Edward Elgar (2019)
38. Komninos, N., Panori, A., Kakderi, C.: Smart cities beyond algorithmic logic: digital platforms, user engagement and data science. In: Smart Cities in the Post-algorithmic Era: Integrating Technologies, Platforms and Governance, pp. 1–15. Edward Elgar (2019)

An Evaluation System of One-Stop Smart City App Performance Based on ANP

Bingqian Zhang, Siyuan Wu, and Guochao Peng[(✉)]

School of Information Management, Sun Yat-Sen University, Guangzhou 510006, Guangdong, China
penggch@mail.sysu.edu.cn

Abstract. Exploring the performance evaluation index system of one-stop smart city app is helpful to promote the design, improvement and development of one-stop city app under the digital society. It is also beneficial for exploring new ways of city operation and building a new model of city governance. Based on the theoretical lens of the improved D&M model, this study proposed an evaluation system with 7 primary indicators which consist of function, design, information quality, service quality, system quality, privacy specification and city influence and 32 secondary indicators by means of literature analysis and expert interviews. It then adopts experts survey and ANP algorithm to determine the indicator weights. From the comparative analysis, it is found that functional indicators and service quality are key to the performance evaluation of one-stop smart city app, and countermeasures and suggestions for improving such app are proposed in terms of core competencies, operation promotion and privacy norms.

Keywords: One-stop smart city app · Performance evaluation · ANP · D&M model

1 Introduction

In many cases, it is difficult for citizens to participate in the design or implementation of smart city through ICT, one of the reasons is that information technology (IT) is deployed internally in public organizations, hardware such as sensors do not interact with citizens and citizens only passively use these facilities [1]. Smart city apps, as part of city governance revolutionary change, are expected to address this problem. This kind of apps links citizens with the city's IoT network and city service providers, aggregating the online and offline public resources of a city through seamless networks, to enhance the monitoring and management capabilities of cities through tasks collaboration and data sharing among systems [2].

The diversified public needs have led to the continuous integration of multiple channels of city services, forming a city smart service network characterized by a one-stop app [3]. The one-stop smart city app can make full use of city Internet of Things to sense and monitor key city data in real-time. In particular, the data will be transmitted to the cloud, and then be aggregated, processed and analyzed with the other data provided by public service departments in different fields, such as city management, government services, transportation, community, energy, and medical care. Thus, citizens can enjoy various convenient services in the city ecosystem by using their smartphones [4]. On the one hand, smart city apps provide city services to citizens at the front end. On the other hand, different types of data collected by sensors can be shared and analyzed by smart service providers to further promote city planning and create other practical values [5]. As explicated above, one-stop smart city apps link the three stakeholders of citizens, city IoT and service providers. And these apps also play an important role in improving communication and information sharing between citizens and the government, as well as promoting the use efficiency of infrastructure and social services [6].

Some scholars have pointed out that in China, many smart city apps are not effective after implementation. Zhang et al. have conducted a survey of 333 smart city apps in China and found that the user satisfaction response is not high, and the average user score is only 2.994. The key reason is that these smart city apps have quality problems, including program design, user needs, technology, information, services, and systems. These problems make it difficult to realize its value, resulting in a lot of waste of human and material resources [5]. It can be seen that the one-stop smart city needs continuous optimization and upgrading to better meet the needs and requirements of users.

To sum up, for the service performance and service capabilities of one-stop smart city apps in the context of smart cities, there are currently many studies focusing on the evaluation system of global smart cities. The evaluation indicators include smart infrastructure, smart infrastructure, governance, people, economy, environment, etc. [7, 8]. There are also some studies focusing on the evaluation of ICT facilities in smart cities, city Internet of Things and high-performance sensors in different scenarios [9, 10, 11]. However, there is no systematic evaluation index for smart city apps, a new type of city governance tool. Identifying and analyzing the key influencing factors of one-stop smart city app user evaluation can provide reference and basis for one-stop smart city app service capability evaluation, service optimization and innovation, and has important research value. Specifically, this paper explores the following questions:

- What are the indicators included in the performance evaluation index system of one-stop smart city apps?
- Which are the key influencing factors?
- What are the beneficial implications?

To answer these questions, this study adopts the improved D&M model and combines the existing literature, user interviews and the actual characteristics of one-stop smart city apps to construct a performance-influencing factor system for one-stop smart city apps. The Analytical Network Process (ANP) is used to calculate and analyze the expert scoring results, determine the weight of indicators, identify the key influencing factors of the performance of the one-stop smart city app, and put forward optimization suggestions accordingly.

2 Literature Review

Smart governance is a strategic issue of increasing global concern in recent years. Smart city applications are an important way for citizens to directly enjoy convenient services in smart cities [12]. That is to say, the government relies on network systems (such as the Internet of Things and the Internet) to achieve a seamless connection between management and services, providing people with more humane service choices, more thorough demand analysis, and more convenient intelligent responses [13].

A city app is an open and complex information system based on network and city information resources, and is the city's digital virtual space, information service market and information resource allocation center. It builds a mobile city ecosystem that integrates city links, scene links and people links, realizes real-time online and efficient coordination of various entities, businesses, business opportunities and other elements, and improves the efficiency of resource utilization, innovation vitality and business coordination capabilities of the entire city. It is not only the primary project of city digital transformation, but also an important platform for each individual's localized online services, which will bring great benefits to the city itself, organizations and individuals [4, 14]. The application of smart city is based on the integrated cloud data platform, and its fields include smart transportation, smart medical care, smart elderly care and smart life [15]. Compared with other types of applications, it relies on government platforms and channels, and is an important convenient means of government public services, allowing citizens to participate in city smart governance in various ways, including participating in public services, publishing public service opinions and suggestions, using public devices based on IoT and other smart technologies to access open government data, in an attempt to improve citizens' perception of public values [16].

After a further review of the literature, we found that current research on smart city applications mainly focuses on the following three aspects: (1) digital platform construction, technology implementation, sensors and algorithms; (2) Problems and obstacles in the process of program promotion of smart city applications in social and local political contexts; (3) the analysis of the user's adoption and related influencing factors based on the theory of information system.

2.1 Related Work on Smart City App Technology

Research on smart city app technology is mostly about sensor improvement, system design, and how to improve the data set management and measurement accuracy of city data collection. In the aspect of sensor improvement, previous studies focused on improving the built-in sensors in wearable devices to track and collect the user's vital signs such as temperature, heart rate, blood oxygen, and blood pressure in real time [17]. In this way, health care professionals can innovate the traditional health care mode, promote self-health management by means of wisdom, and alleviate the pension problem caused by the aging population to a certain extent [18]. In terms of system design, the smart tracking system embedded in the smart city app can help health authorities and government to track and trace citizens' actions at the most subtle level, so as to respond and control the spread of the epidemic [19]. As for algorithms, researchers improve those of smart transportation systems to analyze the location data in the IoT,

RFID and big data platforms and strengthen traffic monitoring and intelligent scheduling, which can effectively alleviate city congestion, reduce the probability of accidents, and provide real-time travel information for citizens [20]. Further to database management, smart city app is a combination of transportation, health care, public management and education, and integrates different sensor infrastructure and other information data sources. Researchers improve the democratization of the development of mobile city applications based on open data by optimizing the database components [21], to better achieve business collaboration and data sharing, enhance the ability of city operation and management, and provide integrated services for citizens.

It can be identified from related studies that smart city apps are effective in coping with various major city diseases (e.g. traffic congestion, shortage of medical resources, population aging, energy shortage, etc.), improving people's quality of life, promoting local economic development, and enhancing the core competitiveness of both cities and countries [22]. Numerous technical facets have laid the foundation for the realization and efficient operation of a one-stop smart city app. Several studies have also looked at evaluation systems for smart city projects and technological hardware. For example, based on the Kano model, the quality of smart city projects is evaluated from the aspects of importance and satisfaction [23]. And some studies have evaluated the adoption rate and maturity of IoT facilities and sensors from a technical point of view. Application scenarios include smart irrigation and smart parking systems [24, 25].

In addition, for various smart apps and smart products emerging in smart cities, the evaluation system generally evaluates from the dimensions of technology, design, usability, efficiency, and economy. Some studies also consider environmental factors (e.g. work condition and influence) and social factors (e.g. community feelings, safety and health, etc.). These researches are mostly concentrated in the field of smart transportation and smart education [26, 27, 28]. In terms of public governance, it pays attention to the evaluation of smart government, and some researchers believe that institutional, organization, and strategy factors are crucial in smart government initiatives [29]. However, most studies focus on the impact of advanced ICT technologies on smart cities, but do not evaluate one-stop smart apps. Compared with other types of smart apps, a one-stop smart city app integrates more service modules and databases, realizes the all-around interconnection of the city, shoulders the role of the city's gateway and strives to achieve transparency in governance. Therefore, an evaluation system for single-type smart city apps cannot comprehensively evaluate one-stop smart city apps, especially in terms of city collaboration. To sum up, a more complete evaluation system is needed to systematically evaluate it.

3 Evaluation Index System of One-Stop Smart City Apps

3.1 Theoretical Basis

Based on Mason's information influence theory (Information Influence Theory) [30], DeLone and McLean proposed an information system success model (Information System Success Model, ISSM), also known as D&M model [31]. It is a classic model in the field of information system (Information System, IS), which has been proved to be effective in IS research in many fields and situations [32]. In this model, System

Quality is the measurement of information system technology; Information Quality is the measurement of information system output-information. In the subsequent revision of the model, DeLone introduced the service quality variable. Service quality refers to the evaluation of all service support provided by the information system [33]. That is, the improved D&M model proposes that users' satisfaction with IS is affected by three variables: system quality, information quality and service quality of IS. Taking this as a theoretical basis, this paper identifies the one-stop smart city app system quality, service quality and information quality as the basic primary indicators.

Since the one-stop smart city app has the attributes of actual effect and hedonic value, the research adds two primary indicators, i.e., the functional level and the design level, from the perspective of APP characters [34]. The functional level focuses on whether users can use the one-stop smart city app to complete tasks successfully, efficiently and with ease, while excellent design can increase the user's pleasure and hedonic experience when using it. In addition, since the one-stop smart city app needs to obtain attributes such as user identity information, primary indicators of privacy norms are added. Combined with the characteristics of the city information resource service center and the important platform of localized online services, the city influence is added as a primary indicator. Combined with the existing literature in the IS field and the actual situation of the one-stop smart city app, the secondary indicators corresponding to each primary index are initially proposed, and then a complete one-stop smart city APP performance evaluation index system is constructed.

The one-stop smart city app evaluation covers a wide range of content, the evaluation indicators are complex and diverse, and there are many methods for selecting indicators. In view of the one-stop smart city app as a new type of city governance tool and its own particularity, in order to further ensure the reliability of the extracted factors, combined with the functions and characteristics of the one-stop smart city app, the researchers aimed at city users and smart cities. City app product managers and smart city app researchers conducted in-depth interviews to further supplement and revise their performance evaluation indicator system.

3.2 Contents of Evaluation Indicators

Starting from the reality of one-stop smart city apps, we comprehensively consider the previous evaluation indicators of mobile government apps or e-government services [28, 29], as well as some influencing factors for related smart city apps [35]. Through literature review, we can find that these standards and indicator systems are incomplete, focusing only on government services, ignoring other functional modules of the one-stop smart city app and the collaboration between different service systems in the city. To this end, we combine the research of the above experts and perform systematic analysis and reasonable integration of the evaluation indicators that affect the smart city app to establish a hierarchical evaluation index from the function of the app to the city impact according to the affiliation between the indicators. The evaluation index system of the station-type smart city app is divided into two layers: the first layer is the function layer that includes seven primary indicators, i.e., system quality, design aesthetic, privacy standard, service quality, information quality, and city influence. The second layer is the specific subdivision of the primary indicators, with a total of 32 items.

Table 1. One-stop smart city performance evaluation indicators.

Primary indicators	Secondary indicators	Connotation of indicators
C_1 functions	C_{11} account linking	Whether the app provides other app account linking functions, and whether other methods can be used to log in after binding the mobile phone
	C_{12} personalized function	Whether to support users' autonomous operations such as recommending, collecting and subscribing to the content and columns they are interested in
	C_{13} retrieve function	Whether to provide search function, and support keyword fuzzy search and combination search
	C_{14} interaction and feedback	Whether to provide various interactive methods to enable users to consult and feedback with the app, such as online messages, etc.
	C_{15} functional classification	Whether the app column classification is scientific and reasonable, it should include information, life, services, and user homepages
	C_{16} intelligent user service	Whether it can actively push and provide citizen services to users according to their preferences
C_2 design	C_{21} column layout	Whether the various functions and column layout of the app are beautiful and reasonable, and there is no large area of blank space
	C_{22} webpage navigation	Whether the navigation of each column page of the app is clear and reasonable
	C_{23} page color	Whether the color matching of the app interface design is beautiful and comfortable
	C_{24} logo icon	Whether the logo design of the app has city characteristics and can attract users' attention
C_3 information quality	C_{31} information authority	Whether the source of the information provided on the app platform is authoritative
	C_{32} information richness	Whether the information provided by the app is systematic, complete, and comprehensive
	C_{33} information availability	Whether the information is displayed intuitively and is relatively easy to obtain
	C_{34} information timeliness	Whether the information on the app platform is updated in a timely and frequent manner, and whether the information is invalid
	C_{35} accuracy of information	Whether the information published by the app is true, and whether the content of the information is consistent with the facts, etc.

(continued)

Table 1. (*continued*)

Primary indicators	Secondary indicators	Connotation of indicators
C4 system quality	C_{41} system fluency	Whether the app runs quickly in response to user instructions, and there is no lag, display delay, etc.
	C_{42} system stability	Whether the app is running stably, and there are no technical failures such as errors, interruptions, and flashbacks
	C_{43} system ease of use	Whether the functions and services of the app are easy to use, and the operation settings are reasonable, etc.
	C_{44} system security	Whether the app has user information and privacy security risks
	C_{45} system integration	Whether the app can effectively integrate the functions belonging to different service departments
C5 service quality	C51 service convenience	Whether the service content published by the app is convenient and the process is simple
	C_{54} service personalization	Whether the app can actively push and provide services to users according to their preferences, and allow users to customize services according to their own needs
	C_{52} service coverage	Whether the coverage of the service content published by the app is rich and suitable for the needs of different users
	C_{53} service humanization	Whether the app and its service personnel can truly understand users, think about users, and consider different user characteristics
C6 privacy specification	C_{61} privacy agreement	Whether the app provides users with the privacy protection agreement
	C_{62} user agreement	Whether the app provides users with the user agreement, and the content of the agreement meets the policy requirements
	C_{63} information collection and push permissions	Whether the app dynamically applies for the permissions required when the user uses the corresponding business function
	C_{64} agreement option	Whether the content of the user agreement and privacy agreement on the app registration/login page asks the user to agree

(*continued*)

Table 1. (*continued*)

Primary indicators	Secondary indicators	Connotation of indicators
C7 city influence	C71 city promotion	Whether the app provides an introduction to the basic situation of the region, such as geographical location, human climate, historical allusions, customs, etc.
	C72 city collaboration	Whether the app provides city collaboration services, such as publishing city tasks, around the characteristics of the digital city portal
	C73 local online community	Whether the app provides city community services, such as friend circle recommendation, and personal opinion sharing
	C74 share and spread	Whether the app supports users to share app services and has multiple channels and easy operation

4 Calculation of Index Weights Based on ANP

4.1 Determining Index Weights

Analytical Network Process (ANP) is the further improvement and optimization of Analytical Hierarchy Process (AHP), and ANP is a more scientific and effective decision-making method of complex structure which also developed on the basis of AHP [35]. This method has been applied in the research of identifying index systems in various fields for many times, and it is scientific and widely applicable [36]. The one-stop smart city APP index system has a relationship of interplay and feedback, that is, the indicators are not independent of each other. Therefore, it is more reasonable and effective to choose the ANP as the method to determine the weight of the one-stop smart city app performance evaluation indicators. According to Table 1, a one-stop smart city app performance evaluation network diagram is constructed, as shown in Fig. 1.

The calculation core of the ANP method is based on the supermatrix of the feedback system. Each primary indicator and the secondary indicators in the system may be affected by other indicators, and the whole system is also dominated by certain attributes. The study adopts the method of indirect dominance comparison, combined with smart city app researchers and industry experts to judge the importance of each indicator according to the 1–9 scale, then constructs a judgment matrix, and uses Super Decision software to complete ANP calculations. The discriminant matrix is constructed in turn, and the eigenvector sorting weight is obtained after normalizing the judgment result to construct the initial supermatrix and weighted supermatrix. At the same time, in order to make the correlation between the elements more reflected, the secondary performance evaluation indicators must be more fully weighted, so that the weighted supermatrix tends to be stable, and normalized, and finally the limit supermatrix is obtained, then the vector of each column is the weight vector of the one-stop smart city app performance evaluation index. The weight results of each index are shown in Table 2.

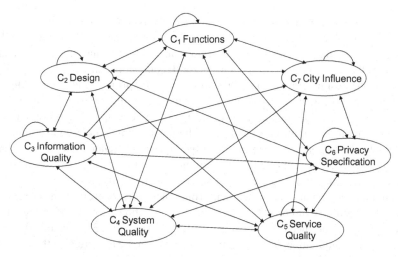

Fig. 1. ANP model of one-stop smart city app performance evaluation

Table 2. One-stop smart city performance evaluation indicators.

Primary indicators	Global weight	Secondary indicators	Local weight	Global weight	Primary indicators	Global weight	Secondary indicators	Local weight	Global weight
C_1 functions	0.258	C_{11}	0.174	0.045	C_4 system quality	0.183	C_{41}	0.053	0.010
		C_{12}	0.172	0.044			C_{42}	0.066	0.012
		C_{13}	0.355	0.092			C_{43}	0.506	0.092
		C_{14}	0.044	0.011			C_{44}	0.289	0.053
		C_{15}	0.145	0.037			C_{45}	0.086	0.016
		C_{16}	0.110	0.029	C_5 service quality	0.225	C_{51}	0.302	0.068
C_2 design	0.044	C_{21}	0.363	0.016			C_{52}	0.122	0.027
		C_{22}	0.341	0.015			C_{53}	0.388	0.088
		C_{23}	0.243	0.011			C_{54}	0.188	0.042
		C_{24}	0.054	0.002	C6 privacy specification	0.090	C_{61}	0.141	0.013
C_3 information quality	0.143	C_{31}	0.344	0.049			C_{62}	0.088	0.008
		C_{32}	0.062	0.009			C_{63}	0.712	0.064
		C_{33}	0.076	0.011			C_{64}	0.059	0.005
		C_{34}	0.107	0.015	C_7 city influence	0.056	C_{71}	0.075	0.004
		C_{35}	0.411	0.059			C_{72}	0.200	0.011
							C_{73}	0.571	0.032
							C_{74}	0.154	0.009

According to the comparative analysis of the indicator weights, it can be seen that among the primary indicators, the importance of C_1 Functions is significantly higher than that of other indicators. This shows that as a utilitarian information system, the first consideration in the construction of a one-stop smart city app is to meet the daily needs of citizens and solve city problems. Therefore, the completeness of functions and the availability of functions are of the highest importance. This evaluation result is a direct reflection of the functions and needs of users for the one-stop smart city app [4]. Correspondingly, the design factor ranks last among the seven primary indicators. Although the system's navigation introduction and clear column classification may have an impact on ease of use, due to the maturity of the design of various apps, the aforementioned parts are similar to different types of apps, so the impact of this problem is not obvious.

Secondly, the importance of information quality, service quality and system quality is basically the same, and service quality is slightly higher than the other two indicators. On the one hand, the unique government service functions of one-stop smart city app are the main features that distinguish them from other apps. Therefore, the coverage of services is particularly important. If the service of the app covers a wide range, it can better cover the various needs involved in the life of citizens [14, 37]. On the other hand, the convenience and humanization of various services in the app are also the important basis for measuring the performance of smart city apps. These two indicators not only reflect the service efficiency of the app but also show the people-oriented service [3]. In addition, system quality determines the service supply. Since the one-stop smart city app is for the public, it needs to be considered in terms of ease of use to serve different user groups more comprehensively (e.g., the elderly) [38]. Moreover, the quality of information is less concerned than the former two, the reason may be that some users prefer to obtain information in social media or news apps [39]. Compared with social media such as Weibo, smart city apps can release some government information in a more reliable, authoritative, and timely manner, so the authority and accuracy of information have a greater impact on one-stop smart city apps.

Besides, privacy security and user authorization have also attracted more attention. Because smart city app needs to authenticate users and bind ID cards when they register or use services, some payment services also need to bind the payment tools such as bank cards or Alipay. Therefore, they are also considered to have a significant impact on privacy and payment security. Service providers can provide users with user agreements and privacy protection agreements that meet policy requirements through pop-up windows, text links and attachments in a concise and easily accessible form, and comply with the relevant provisions of the cybersecurity law in the collection, storage, and use of personal information, which can better guarantee the user's security experience when using it [40].

As a manifestation of city service and governance, the local influence of smart city app also determines its service ability and success in society [41]. The core of promoting the utilization of city apps is to stimulate the initiative of users to participate, so that users can actively and voluntarily use the app. City collaboration and local social services are expected to have a positive impact on this area [42]. In other words, these two factors can link the relationship between people and organizations, and even between cities. We must admit that this will improve the utilization efficiency of various city resources and the tightness of personnel cooperation. Finally, as one of the city's business cards, the smart city app provides city introduction services, gives full play to the characteristics of the digital city portal, and gives a vivid and detailed introduction to the local basic geographical conditions, customs, and historical background, showing the local culture. Therefore, the aspects of city publicity and sharing should also be fully considered during the operation of the app.

5 Conclusions and Policy Recommendations

Using scientific methods to evaluate the one-stop smart city app is of great significance for improving the design, development, promotion and application of these apps, so as to better help implementations of smart cities and smart governance. Based on the lens of information success theory (D & M), this paper constructs a one-stop smart city app performance evaluation index system to measure the performance and development of these apps from seven aspects: the app function, design level, service quality, system quality and information quality, as well as privacy norms and city influence. The research results show that in the construction of one-stop smart city apps, attention should be paid to the functional level, as well as strengthening service capabilities and city influence, and focus more on the formulation and permission settings of privacy and user agreements.

Based on the above analysis, the following suggestions are put forward to promote the construction and development of one-stop smart city app:

First, improve core competence. It can be seen that the functional level and service quality are the two core indicators of one-stop smart city app performance evaluation. The strong functional system and wide coverage services are the core competitiveness of this app different from other apps. However, the current one-stop smart city app generally has the problem of strong information supply and weak service supply, and it is difficult to reflect its own advantages and characteristics, especially compared with other apps such as social media. Therefore, service providers and policy makers may emphasize the function construction and service quality of the apps, which satisfy the needs of users, integrate multiple resources, and provide services in multiple forms and channels. The service providers thus need to focus on users' daily high-frequency service such as errands, inquiries, bill payment, appointments, complaints and communications, to meet residents' diversified needs. At the same time, construction mode of the one-stop smart city apps is expected to rationally plan to avoid blind investment, repeated construction and waste of resources. Engineers need to optimize the platform architecture and set aside standard interfaces to facilitate the improvement of other service functions during the operational process.

Second, create a city digital portal. One-stop smart city app should be combined with social context to enhance social influence as well as city collaboration. Effective and timely inter-city collaboration services and cross-city collaboration services will enhance the social influence of the app in the local community, such as providing epidemic tracking, patient trajectories, and epidemic prevention policies in the context of epidemic prevention and control. One-stop smart city app should also strengthen support in city community services, raise the awareness of the operation of city communities and improve the community activity, make local city communities form good interaction with e-commerce and new media, and develop more high-quality and characteristic city activities. In addition, one-stop smart city apps should also combine local characteristics, develop strategies to ensure special functions and column contents, provide personalized, active, accurate and intelligent services for local users, and build a digital window of the city.

Third, strengthen the privacy specification settings. The use of many functions of the smart city app requires real-name authentication of user identity information, and some personalized function services and preference recommendation mechanisms also require access to user usage footprint information. Therefore, a large amount of sensitive user privacy information is stored in the app's database. In order to enhance the professionalism of app design, development and maintenance, many cities have introduced third-party development companies to develop the app instead of relying only on the government's internal technical team, which has the risk of user data leakage. As stated above, the app should formulate a complete user agreement and privacy agreement to ensure the users' right to know and give their full privacy information protection authority to avoid compulsory access to the user agreement and privacy agreement consent. This means that on the one hand, the authorities of the app should strengthen the data protection to prevent the loss of user property and missing data information caused by the system run-down, or the intrusion into the system to steal user information. On the other hand, the government needs to be stricter in specifying user data management requirements when signing contracts with third parties to prevent development teams from leaking user data and guaranteeing user information security.

This study also has several limitations, such as the establishment of the index system in the process of considering the opinions of experts and users, but did not conduct interviews for app service providers. In the next step, app providers' interviews can be added to strengthen the completeness and accuracy of evaluation indicators. Besides, a case study can be conducted for some specific one-stop smart city apps from different cities to verify and revise the evaluation index system.

Acknowledgement. This research was supported by two grants respectively funded by the Natural Science Foundation of Guangdong (No.: 2018A030313706), the National Natural Science Foundation of China (No.: 71974215) and the International Program for Ph.D. Candidates, Sun Yat-Sen University.

References

1. Zheng, Y., Schachter, H.L.: Explaining citizens' e-participation use: the role of perceived advantages. Public Organ. Rev. **17**(3), 409–428 (2016). https://doi.org/10.1007/s11115-016-0346-2
2. Wang, G., Chen, Q., Xu, Z., Leng, X.: Can the use of government apps shape citizen compliance? The mediating role of different perceptions of government. Comput. Hum. Behav. **108**, 106335 (2020)
3. Zhang, B., Peng, G., Xing, F., Liang, X., Gao, Q.: One-stop smart urban apps and determinants of their continuance usage: an empirical investigation based on CSCM. J. Glob. Inf. Manag. **29**(6), 1–21 (2021)
4. Zhang, B., Peng, G., Xing, F., Chen, S.: Mobile applications in China's smart cities: state-of-the-art and lessons learned. J. Glob. Inf. Manag. **29**(6), 1–18 (2021)

5. Peng, G.C.A., Nunes, M.B., Zheng, L.: Impacts of low citizen awareness and usage in smart city services: the case of London's smart parking system. Inf. Syst. eBus. Manag. **15**(4), 845–876 (2016). https://doi.org/10.1007/s10257-016-0333-8
6. Johnson, P.A., Robinson, P.J., Philpot, S.: Type, tweet, tap, and pass: how smart city technology is creating a transactional citizen. Gov. Inf. Q. **37**(1), 101414 (2020)
7. Qi, J., Ba, Y.:. Smart city construction evaluation system study based on the specialists method and analytic hierarchy process method. In: 2016 International Conference on Smart City and Systems Engineering (ICSCSE), pp. 149–152. IEEE, November 2016
8. Li, C., Dai, Z., Liu, X., Sun, W.: Evaluation system: evaluation of smart city shareable framework and its applications in China. Sustainability **12**(7), 2957 (2020)
9. Luque-Vega, L.F., Carlos-Mancilla, M.A., Payán-Quiñónez, V.G., Lopez-Neri, E.: Smart cities oriented project planning and evaluation methodology driven by citizen perception—IoT smart mobility case. Sustainability **12**(17), 7088 (2020)
10. Abba, S., Wadumi Namkusong, J., Lee, J.A., Liz Crespo, M.: Design and performance evaluation of a low-cost autonomous sensor interface for a smart iot-based irrigation monitoring and control system. Sensors **19**(17), 3643 (2019)
11. Perković, T., Šolić, P., Zargariasl, H., Čoko, D., Rodrigues, J.J.: Smart parking sensors: state of the art and performance evaluation. J. Clean. Prod. **262**, 121181 (2020)
12. Sharma, S.K., Al-Badi, A.H., Rana, N.P., Al-Azizi, L.: Mobile applications in government services (mG-App) from user's perspectives: a predictive modelling approach. Gov. Inf. Q. **35**(4), 557–568 (2018)
13. Tangi, L., Benedetti, M., Gastaldi, L., Noci, G., Russo, C.: Mandatory provisioning of digital public services as a feasible service delivery strategy: evidence from Italian local governments. Gov. Inf. Q. **38**(1), 101543 (2021)
14. Yeh, H.: The effects of successful ICT-based smart city services: from citizens' perspectives. Gov. Inf. Q. **34**(3), 556–565 (2017)
15. Talari, S., Shafie-khah, M., Siano, P., Loia, V., Tommasetti, A., Catalão, J.P.S.: A review of smart cities based on the Internet of Things concept. Energies **10**(4), 421 (2017)
16. Pereira, G.V., Macadar, M.A., Luciano, E.M., Testa, M.G.: Delivering public value through open government data initiatives in a Smart City context. Inf. Syst. Front. **19**(2), 213–229 (2016). https://doi.org/10.1007/s10796-016-9673-7
17. Marsico, M.D., Mecca, A., Barra, S.: Walking in a smart city: investigating the gait stabilization effect for biometric recognition via wearable sensors. Comput. Electr. Eng. **80**, 106501 (2019)
18. Papi, E., Osei-Kuffour, D., Chen, Y.M.A., McGregor, A.H.: Use of wearable technology for performance assessment: a validation study. Med. Eng. Phys. **37**(7), 698–704 (2015)
19. Rahman, M.T., Khan, R.T., Khandaker, M.R.A., Sellathurai, M., Salan, M.S.A.: An automated contact tracing approach for controlling COVID-19 spread based on geolocation data from mobile cellular networks. IEEE Access **8**, 213554–213565 (2020)
20. Nurnawati, E.K., Ermawati, E.: Design of integrated database on mobile information system: a study of Yogyakarta smart city app. IOP Conf. Ser. Mater. Sci. Eng. **306**(1), 012036 (2018)
21. Murshed, S.M., Al-Hyari, A.M., Wendel, J., Ansart, L.: Design and implementation of a 4D web application for analytical visualization of smart city applications. ISPRS Int. J. Geo Inf. **7**(7), 276 (2018)
22. Lin, Y.: A comparison of selected Western and Chinese smart governance: the application of ICT in governmental management, participation and collaboration. Telecommun. Policy **42**(10), 800–809 (2018)
23. Abba, S., Wadumi Namkusong, J., Lee, J.A., Liz Crespo, M.: Design and performance evaluation of a low-cost autonomous sensor interface for a smart iot-based irrigation monitoring and control system. Sensors **19**(17), 3643 (2019)

24. Yan, J., Liu, J., Tseng, F.M.: An evaluation system based on the self-organizing system framework of smart cities: a case study of smart transportation systems in China. Technol. Forecast. Soc. Chang. **153**, 119371 (2020)
25. Lee, J.S., Kim, S.W.: Validation of a tool evaluating educational apps for smart education. J. Educ. Comput. Res. **52**(3), 435–450 (2015)
26. Niculescu, A.I., Wadhwa, B., Quek, E.: Smart city technologies: design and evaluation of an intelligent driving assistant for smart parking. Int. J. Sci. Eng. Technol. **6**(6), 1096–1102 (2016)
27. Song, W., Niu, Z., Zheng, P.: Design concept evaluation of smart product-service systems considering sustainability: an integrated method. Comput. Indust. Eng. **159**, 107485 (2021)
28. Al-Obthani, F., Ameen, A.: Towards customized smart government quality model. Int. J. Softw. Eng. App. **9**(2), 41–50 (2018)
29. Albreiki, S., Ameen, A., Bhaumik, A.: Impact of internal government efficiency and service delivery infrastructure on the smart government effectiveness in UAE. Int. J. Emerg. Technol. **10**(1), 1–8 (2019)
30. Mason, R.O.: Measuring information output: a communication systems approach. Inf. Manag. **1**(4), 219–234 (1978)
31. DeLone, W.H., McLean, E.R.: Information systems success: the quest for the dependent variable. Inf. Syst. Res. **3**(1), 60–95 (1992)
32. Petter, S., DeLone, W., McLean, E.R.: Information systems success: the quest for the independent variables. J. Manag. Inf. Syst. **29**(4), 7–62 (2013)
33. DeLone, W.H., McLean, E.R.: The DeLone and McLean model of information systems success: a ten-year update. J. Manag. Inf. Syst. **19**(4), 9–30 (2003)
34. García-Gómez, J.M., de La Torre-Díez, I., Vicente, J., Robles, M., López-Coronado, M., Rodrigues, J.J.: Analysis of mobile health applications for a broad spectrum of consumers: a user experience approach. Health Inform. J. **20**(1), 74–84 (2014)
35. Saaty, T.L.: Fundamentals of the analytic network process—multiple networks with benefits, costs, opportunities and risks. J. Syst. Sci. Syst. Eng. **13**(3), 348–379 (2004)
36. Wu, C.R., Lin, C.T., Tsai, P.H.: Analysing alternatives in financial services for wealth management banks: the analytic network process and the balanced scorecard approach. IMA J. Manag. Math. **20**(3), 303–321 (2009)
37. Ameen, A., Alfalasi, K., Gazem, N.A., Isaac, O.: Impact of system quality, information quality, and service quality on actual usage of smart government. In: 2019 First International Conference of Intelligent Computing and Engineering (ICOICE), pp. 1–6. IEEE, December 2019
38. Salim, T.A., Barachi, M.E., Onyia, O.P., Mathew, S.S.: Effects of smart city service channel- and user-characteristics on user satisfaction and continuance intention. Inf. Technol. People **34**(1), 147–177 (2020)
39. Veeramootoo, N., Nunkoo, R., Dwivedi, Y.K.: What determines success of an e-government service? Validation of an integrative model of e-filing continuance usage. Gov. Inf. Q. **35**(2), 161–174 (2018)
40. Ismagilova, E., Hughes, L., Rana, N.P., Dwivedi, Y.K.: Security, privacy and risks within smart cities: literature review and development of a smart city interaction framework. Inf. Syst. Front. **2020**, 1–22 (2020). https://doi.org/10.1007/s10796-020-10044-1
41. Gupta, P., Chauhan, S., Jaiswal, M.P.: Classification of smart city research-a descriptive literature review and future research agenda. Inf. Syst. Front. **21**(3), 661–685 (2019)
42. Zhang, B., Liu, C., Kong, Y., Wang, Y., Peng, G.: Users adaptation and infusion of smart city app. In: Streitz, N., Konomi, S. (eds.) HCII 2021. LNCS, vol. 12782, pp. 68–81. Springer, Cham (2021). https://doi.org/10.1007/978-3-030-77015-0_6

Smart Artifacts in Smart Environments

Caregivers' Perceived Usefulness of an IoT-Based Smart Bed

Davide Bacchin[1](✉) , Gabriella F. A. Pernice[1], Marcello Sardena[3],
Marino Malvestio[3], and Luciano Gamberini[2]

[1] Department of General Psychology, University of Padova, via Venezia 8, 31121 Padova, Italy
davide.bacchin.2@phd.unipd.it,
gabriellafrancescaamalia.pernice@unipd.it
[2] Human Inspired Technology (HIT) Research Centre, University of Padova, via Luigi Luzzatti 4, 35121 Padova, Italy
luciano.gamberini@unipd.it
[3] Malvestio S.p.a., via Marconi 12D, 35010 Villanova di Camposampiero, PD, Italy
{sardena.marcello,marino}@malvestio.com

Abstract. Health facilities worldwide have been struggling for years with the low number of care personnel compared to the demand for assistance, even before the recent pandemic emergency. This problem has made the caregivers a category characterized by a high-workload job, with consequent risks of stress and burnout. In these cases, technology can often help people mitigate these issues, but only if it is accepted and perceived as useful by users. This study investigates caregivers' perceived usefulness, a key factor of the Technology Acceptance, of an innovative IoT patient monitoring system, called smart-bed, able to provide valuable information about patients without being in contact with them. The study carries out a series of focus groups with employees from hospitals, elderly retirement homes and home-care assistance. Through a thematic analysis of the discussion topics that emerged, the reasons to perceive the IoT system useful are investigated and analyzed, together with caregivers desired functions and the possible limitations that these technologies could have if inserted in this context. In addition to providing an overview of these elements for this particular system, the results bring some reflections relevant to IoT in healthcare environments, therefore contributing to the design of future technologies that will take into account the wishes and needs of users.

Keywords: Healthcare · IoT · Smart bed · Focus group · Perceived usefulness

1 Introduction

The healthcare environment is facing a challenging historical period due to the COVID-19 pandemic, which has been affecting health systems around the world for two years in various waves. This recent problem was added to a series of pre-existing problems, starting from the simultaneous lack of care personnel and increased demand due to demographic changes [1]. Therefore, the working conditions of health care personnel are increasingly characterized by risks, precarious working conditions, long and irregular shifts, and emotional pressures [2]. Indeed, these and other factors contribute to creating a stressful environment which causes, according to a 2018 study [3], 40–43% of burnout and 22–29% of intention to leave the profession cases.

1.1 Internet of Things (IoT)

Therefore, problems of this magnitude have prompted researchers worldwide to develop possible solutions, often in the form of technological innovations designed to lighten or simplify the work of caregivers [4] or to try to improve patient stay [5].

Among the types of technologies used for this purpose, it is undoubtedly important the one that refers to the concept of the Internet of Things (IoT), i.e. a network of mutually connected devices, capable of exchanging information and interacting with each other [6]. These systems are able, in general, to reduce management costs, simplify and support the organization and activities of an infrastructure [7, 8] and have been used in numerous fields of application, from traffic to manufacturing and supply chain management [9–11]. The numerous possible uses for these technologies have allowed their introduction in numerous fields of application, such as the Internet of Medical Things (IoMT) [12], telemedicine [13], e-health [14] and patient monitoring [15]. The IoT potential and flexibility are also intuitive from the market forecasts, which estimate a total value of $ 3.9 and $ 11.1 trillion per year up to 2025 [16]. Despite this considerable prospect, nowadays, the IoT still struggles to establish itself as a frequent investment by companies that deal with Information Technology (IT) [17]. More specifically, in the medical environment, they have been used for the most various reasons, such as hospital management [18], the fight against the COVID-19 pandemic [19], remote monitoring of patients and telemedicine [20, 21], and for the material management in the hospital [22].

1.2 IoT in Hospitals

The next step in this series of essential innovations is to imagine a hospital or an elderly caring environment where an IoT system can support operators. For example, Chiuchisan and colleagues [23] proposed a patient monitoring system capable of monitoring patients at risk in an Intensive Care Unit (ICU), thanks to the integration of signals coming from technologies already in use in the hospital. This system used a Microsoft XBOX KinectTM to detect patient movement and a sensing board to monitor environmental parameters such as temperature and humidity. Other works, such as those described by Dhariwal and Mehta [24] and Catarinucci and colleagues [25], proposed different system architectures to make a hospital smart. Many of these systems operate thanks to a series of sensors positioned inside the room. Instead, other studies aim to centralize all data collection on a single object, easily accessible to operators and in contact with the patient, such as the hospital bed. For example, some studies monitor the patient's pressure on the bed to inform the operator of any dangers regarding ulcers and pressure sores [26–28]. In other cases, however, monitoring concerns the physiological signals related to the patient, as in the studies by Sivanantham [29] and Hart and colleagues [30], which develop systems for monitoring cardiac and respiratory signals. Finally, some studies have also focused on the nursing home environment, developing technologies capable of detecting the presence or absence of the patient in bed and their incontinence [31]. However, few works consider all these characteristics in a single IoT system to date. An example in the literature is the work of Nakajima and Sakaguchi [32], while there are some commercial solutions by the hospital-beds leading companies, such as Hillrom with its Centrella Smart + bed [33] and the stryker iBed Wireless [34].

1.3 Perceived Usefullness in Technology Acceptance

To date, however, a topic that still requires in-depth analysis is how operators would react to the introduction of these systems into their work environment and, in particular, their opinions regarding the social and behavioural implications [17, 35]. In literature, the intention to adopt new technology is called Technology Acceptance (TA), and it is often described by the Technology Acceptance Model [TAM; 36] or, more recently, by the Unified Theory of Acceptance and Use of Technology [UTAUT and UTATU 2; 37, 38]. Over time, the TAM has become the dominant model for investigating the TA of users regarding numerous technological systems [39] in various fields of application [40–42], including healthcare [43, 44].

One of the model's critical variables is Perceived usefulness (PU), the dimension for which the users think that using a particular system, they can obtain useful results, solve a problem, improve their performance and overcome their possible limitations [35]. Therefore, this TAM dimension has been studied to determine its importance concerning IoT technologies for healthcare and non-healthcare personnel. For example, generally speaking, the study by Tsourela and colleagues [45], carried out with an online questionnaire on a sample of 812 subjects, showed how PU is one of the factors that most influence users to have a positive attitude, and therefore a higher behavioural intention, towards IoT products. Focusing on the medical environment, a recent study [46] highlighted, through a questionnaire with 348 nursing students, how PU is the most strongly correlated factor to the intention to accept a technology within one's work environment. Another work by Martinez-Caro and colleagues [47] has instead shown how the PU of IoT-based systems is a key factor in the formation of a positive environment and high perceived satisfaction in patients.

A further study analyzed 181 subjects via an online questionnaire [48]. The study showed that for people over 20 years of age, defined by them as IOT immigrants, facilitating conditions play an important role in adopting IoT technologies. Since these facilitating conditions are connected to perceived usefulness [49], it can be assumed that they too play an important role in the TA of the IoT in healthcare.

1.4 Objective of the Study

These are some examples of how research has tried to address this issue. All the studies listed in the previous paragraph examined PU with online questionnaires administered to nursing students or people outside the healthcare environment. The present study wanted to approach the problem differently, using a qualitative method, the Focus Group, carried out with hospital staff which, in our opinion, is the category of user who will be most involved with the system in the future. Therefore, the goal was to analyze PU through these discussion groups to draw conclusions about the fundamental elements for the acceptance of IoT technologies in different environments, from hospitals to care.

2   Materials and Methods

2.1   IoT-Based Smart Bed

The system proposed in this study and described to the participants makes the hospital bed a patient data centre. For example, it can obtain the bed position in the structure, allowing operators to be directed to the source of the alarms. The bed weighting system also allows having information regarding the patient's presence and his/her eventual exit or fall. In addition, an algorithm that works on the weight data can predict the patient's exit, thus speeding up the intervention of the nurses. As for the patient's physiological signals, a non-invasive tool can detect heartbeat and respiratory rate signals. Finally, the bed can inform the system about its status, providing data like minimum height, the side rails status, or the backrest positioned at 30°. All these data are accessible from any browser, where the healthcare staff can consult the status of the bed and the associated patient and set the monitoring rules that trigger the alarms. These alarms are then sent to the web application and can also be viewed on common smartphones anywhere in the hospital. Finally, the bed has two touch interfaces mounted on the side rails, allowing to manage the single bed and modify and view the alarms.

2.2   Focus Group

This study exploits the Focus Group technique [50], which consists of forming a selected group of participants to discuss some problems proposed by the researchers. In addition to the participants were present two researchers. The first was the moderator, who presented the questions, managed any problems between the participants, controlled the time of their interventions and maintained the discussion on the desired topics. The second was the observer, instructed to pay attention to the participants' non-verbal language to assist the discussion moderation. The data analysis was carried out with thematic analysis [51].The interviews were transcribed starting from the audio recordings. Afterwards, the researchers have read independently all the transcriptions, and defined and then discussed the emerged themes in which subdivided participants' answers. Accordingly, the three main themes were: Perceived Usefulness (e.g. usefulness to use the system during the night shifts, time saving and improving assistance), Desires (the most desired smart-bed functions e.g. alerts, physiological signals, fall prevention) and Limitations (critics and limits of the smart-bed system e.g. fear of the alarm fatigue, reliability of the system, privacy issue). All the participants' answers were then inserted into these categories, and the number of answers' frequencies across the different focus groups was counted.

2.3   Participants

The experiment involved six groups of subjects, composed of nurses, social health operator (SHO) and physiotherapists belonging to different realities: 2 groups of nurses employed in the hospital, one of which from the University of Padua Hospital (FG1) and one from a mixed group of nurses from various hospitals expert researchers in patient positioning (FG2), 1 group of nurses, SHO and physiotherapists of an elderly retirement home (FG3), 1 group of SHO employed in a facility for people with disabilities (FG4), 1 group of SHO employed in hospital (FG5), 1 group of nurses employed in domiciliary home care (FG6). In total, the study participants were 29 (F $= 19$, $M_{age} = 39$, $SD_{age} =$ 9).

2.4 Experimental Procedure

After welcoming the participants in a large environment, they were seated in a circle to create a place for open discussion where everyone was treated as equals and could freely express their ideas (see Fig. 1A and 1B). They compile an informed consent and a demographic questionnaire. Then some indications of the correct behaviours were given for a peaceful discussion, together with an invitation to profit the refreshment prepared for the participants. Then, a quick phase of acquaintance was carried out with a round of names, followed by some easy and immediate questions useful to break the ice among the participants and introduce them to the study subject. Next, the moderator explained the concept of IoT to the participants and described the concepts and functioning of the "smart-bed" system (see Fig. 2) before asking the research question about their perception of usefulness for the systems.

Fig. 1. A (Left). Focus Group with nurses employed in the hospital of the University of Padua; B (Right). Focus group conducted with a mixed group of nurses, SHO and physiotherapists of a retirement home (Opere Pie, Onigo)

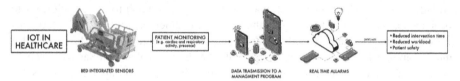

Fig. 2. English translation of the smart bed system brief explanation presented to participants

3 Results

The results were subdivided into themes according to the participant's answers that emerged during the discussions. The participants' answers were inserted into the three main categories and the number of answers' frequencies, across the different focus groups, was counted.

3.1 Perceived Usefulness

The results showed that in 100% of the focus groups, in all 6, the participants declared that they found the system useful for their work. In all environments, therefore, the system is perceived as a potential help (P03-FG3: "I believe that all the listed features are useful).

In particular, the importance of the system during the nocturnal phase of health care has also emerged in 100% of cases. For example, the SHO of FG4 declared that they consider an IoT system to be an aid and a reason for serenity in the case of night shifts (P02-FG4: "I don't mind receiving alarms, it would make me safer, especially at night. I would like to know what happens"), for the identification of the many problems they face (P02-FG4:" We have big problems with people getting up, side rails being lowered etc. Then we have many problems that the system could see, people getting up, epileptics..."). These kinds of answers are common to the participants of other groups (hospital nurses, the elderly retirement home group, and the domiciliary nurses).

This result underlined the usefulness of the system during the night shift, but its use was perceived positively also during the day. As was highlighted by the hospital nurses (FG1), the system would work greatly also during the day, especially for the management of hectic or particularly busy working moments where the attention of the operators is less present (P04-FG1: "Even during the day that would be fine, maybe you are walking around with the doctor or something else and the ward is uncovered and not immediately noticeable").

As for the hospital environment, both SHO and nurses (2 FG out of 6) stated that the system could greatly simplify their work, lightening the load (P03-FG2: "The listed characteristics can certainly make the workload, that so often exceeds due to a deficient workforce, more manageable").

Among the reasons that prompted the participants to define the system as useful, the spared time emerged in 2 of the FG conducted. In the case of FG2, this issue has been extensively discussed, leading to the conclusion that the system can be a valuable aid both to optimize times and improve assistance (P02-FG2: "Maybe you have these tools, they do not diagnose but direct attention, they make work more manageable and easier and help to focus on the assistance that must be directed") and to assign priorities to problems, providing help to speed up the response in emergencies (P02-FG5: "At least you know if they are calling you about more dangerous things"). This last issue also emerged among the SHO of the Padua hospital. They highlight that a similar system could save precious time for patients in emergency cases (P03-FG5: "All precious seconds and minutes to save the life").

Another important aspect for the participants (3 FG out of 6) is the advantage of the real-time monitoring of the patients (P01-FG4:" In the case of the measurement of vital parameters it would be great, because even when you are there, and you have to communicate to the nurses… you can give them an indication by staying in front of the screen").

In 4 of the 6 FG, participants also discussed about how using the data recorded by the smart bed. In summary, some participants expressed their interest in analyzing this data to improve their working environment. In one case, for the participant these data could objectively evidencing the lack of personnel to the management of the structures (P02-FG2: "Tracking data would also allow you to collect information, to understand for example that if there are many falls, then it means that one more person is needed"). In the other cases, however, they want to view the stored data to verify the effectiveness of a procedure (P05-FG3: "I can check if two hours between one posture and the next are adequate"), to view the history (P03- FG5: "Useful… to have the data as soon as you need it. Even the one previously recorded maybe") or to check the effective progress of the anti-pressure injury therapies (P02-FG6: "A motion sensor would be good to understand our absence as much as the patients moved. Even for informational purposes only").

Safety was among the most cited aspects (3 FG out of 6) for the patient and the operator's work. The SHO find useful receiving alarms from the system (P02-FG4: "I do not mind receiving the alarms would make me safer") and the fact that the system would improve the safety of the environment and the patient (P02-FG5:" For the safety of the environment "; P03-FG5:" For the safety of the patient").

Furthermore, during the focus groups, the participants discussed about what is the working environment in which it is more beneficial to insert the bed system (5 FG out of 6). In the case of nurses in the Hospital of Padua (FG1), belonging to a work environment with frequent use of telemetry, they found only some signals advantageous, those not monitored by hospital's tools (P04-FG1: "Ours is a particular environment. We have the telemetry and there are constant alarms. However, breathing could be interesting for those few who are not monitored"). For the second FG with nurses (FG2), the slower rotation of patients in nursing homes (RSA) would make them perfect for using the system as they are less overburdened by bureaucratic obligations (P01-FG2: "In my opinion, it would be more useful in retirement homes where people stay there for many days"). On the contrary, however, this fast rotation in the hospital would make this environment perfect for this system, as it is more challenging to keep track of the peculiarities of each patient (P02-FG5: "They know them, we have only 20 days, so here it would be much more useful"). The opinion of nurses in retirement homes is according to this last opinion. The participants of FG3 have, in fact, declared that most of the guests are manageable with the instruments available, but that the smart-bed would be very useful for those most at risk (P04-FG3: "in subjects not constantly monitored such as those subject to ALS it would be useful".

In FG6, on the other hand, the home nurses underlined that a similar system would be difficult to implement for them because they don't work in a fixed place, but at their patients' home, (P03-FG6: "I cannot intervene in this way from my home. The functions are excellent, but it changes little for us"). Despite this, they have repeatedly pointed out the system's usefulness both for the hospital and for the care environment (P01-FG3: "In the hospital environment it would be an important innovation. Colleagues can tell me that in this bed there is a patient who tends to have tachycardia, I set the alarm and go"). They hypothesized that it could still be useful in their environment but if managed by the informal caregivers, such as a family member (P01-FG6: "Perhaps remotely, for the sons of the patients it could be very useful to monitor and control"). This particularly significant issue finds a possible solution in one of the FGs. In fact, in FG1, the discussion brought to light the need to design a modular system, therefore adaptable to the specific situations of each environment in which it could be inserted (P01-FG1: "It should be adapted because each department has its needs").

One aspect, which emerged only in one of the FGs, appears particularly interesting. In fact, in FG1, one of the participants pointed out how the system could be useful in the case of isolated patients, where the contact between patient and operator should be reduced for the safety of both (P03-FG1: "For me, it would be very useful especially for those who get up from the bed, to put me on pre-alarm or in those in isolation because we can't go out and in all the time, something would be needed to help us").

The results are summarized numerically in Table 1 and graphically in Fig. 3.

Table 1. Appearing frequencies of discussion topic that emerged for the Perceived Usefulness

Discussion argument	Frequence
Perceived usefulness	100%
Usefulness during night shifts	100%
Simplify work	33%
Time saving	33%
Real-time monitoring	50%
Data usage	67%
Safety	50%
Working environment	83%
Isolated patients' monitoring	*17%*

3.2 Desires

During the FGs, the caregivers highlighted the smart-bed system's more important and interesting functions.

The first was the creation of alerts, which emerged in 2 FG out of 6, those with hospital nurses. In particular, the nurses of FG1 expressed the need to have the alarms displayed on a monitor (P04-FG1: "Maybe it could be connected to a computer, to a monitor") or, for reasons of suitability and visibility, on a mobile device such as a telephone (P03-FG1: "We often go away from the PC, so if the alert comes out there I would have difficulty seeing it, while with the ward telephone I would always have it with me"). They also expressed the need to connect the system to the alerts already present in the hospital, increasing their visibility with a colour code (P05-FG1: "It could also be linked to the alerts already existing in the hospital. It should be something that

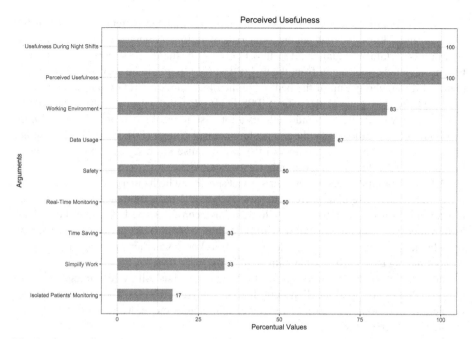

Fig. 3. Graphical summary of appearing frequencies of discussion topic that emerged for the Perceived Usefulness.

flashes, a colour that catches your eye"). The same problem of visibility, and therefore of the need for mobile devices, emerged in FG2 (P02-FG2: "It would be interesting if all this information were mobile, not fixed, perhaps a kind of pad, a tablet that allows me to see from any room where there are problems. Otherwise, one has to work in front of the monitor"). The possibility of having the data easily accessible even from the bed has emerged (P01-FG2: "Unless from each bed it could be possible to control the system as if you were always with it") together with the possibility to visualize data from every point of the ward (P02-FG2: "Even two three five monitors, because at night when you are few in number nobody could control a single monitor"). Furthermore, in FG1, the need for an indication of the place where the emergency is taking place emerged (P03-FG2: "It tells you the room where the problem is").

The patient's vital signs control was a high-discussed point (6 FG out of 6). The nurses of FG1, familiar with telemetry, declared that they might need a sensor of a parameter that they do not usually control, for example breathing (P04-FG1: "However, breathing could be interesting for those few who are not telemetry"). Those of FG2 feel the necessity of a sensor for heart and respiratory rate (P01-FG2: "Respiratory heart rate, that yes"), those of FG3, FG5 and FG6 of heart rate (P03-FG5: "If the patient goes under cardiac arrest at least you see it";), while those of FG4 mentioned the control of the temperature and, in general, of various vital parameters (P05-FG4: "The temperature is also useful").

Another theme is the control of risks for the patient. In 2 out of 6 FG participants discussed about weight/pressure sensors to prevent falls (P01-FG2: "The first cause of adverse events are falling. So, an alert that tells me that the patient has lowered the side rail and I know it, that patient is at risk of falling. Something that catches my attention is certainly fundamental"). In 4 FG out of 6, the discussion regard warnings for uncontrolled patients exit from the bed (P03-FG1: "It would be very useful above all to detect those who get up of the bed"). On the other hand, in 2 FG out of 6, there was the need to be able to weigh the patient (P05-FG4: "Because we have bedridden patients who must be weighed … it would help us a lot, also to establish diuresis"). Finally, in 3 FG out of 6, they discussed about a posture control system (P01-FG3: "It can also be useful if there were pressure points in the mat because knowing them you can adjust how to act on the decubitus. Even only torso or legs").

A further parameter desired by users is wet sensing, which emerged in 2 FG out of 6. It was indicated as useful to prevent injuries (P01-FG2: "Indication of humidity because it is an indicator for operators to say, look, it has been for some hours that the patient lies on the wet. That is essential") or in order not to disturb the patient unnecessarily (P02-FG4: "A humidity sensor could be useful to know whether to change the patient without having to disturb or wake him at all").

In 2 FG out of 6, emerged the need to create a nurse call system integrated into the bed (P04-FG3: "Also a call system that goes beyond the classic bell. Let's see the problem of bedrooms or bedridden patients who cannot move. Maybe touch bells, on the side, or voice command").

Finally, other wishes that emerged individually in only one of the FGs are the integration of the system with the IT medical record (P03-FG2: "It would be useful to have an IT medical record of the patient also for this, which connects to the existing one to make so that I do not have to do the same operation twice"), the creation of checklists for therapies and patient checks (P03-FG2: "It would also be nice to be able to integrate a sort of checklist with the therapies done or missing on that patient"), the creation of different types of users with different degree of access for the flexible setting of the monitoring rules (P04-FG2: "For me, there must also be a manager who decides the settings to be applied for each patient"), and the flexibility of choice for setting times alarms (P02-FG3: "For me, alarms should be able to be set by us, perhaps in time bands").

The results are summarized numerically in Table 2 and graphically in Fig. 4.

Table 2. Appearing frequency of discussion topic that emerged for the Desires.

Discussion argument	Frequence
Alerts	33%
Physiological signals	100%
Fall prevention	33%
Patient outside the bed	67%
Postural monitoring	50%
Bed wet	33%

(continued)

Table 2. (*continued*)

Discussion argument	Frequence
Integrated nurse call	33%
Integration with hospital medical records	17%
Procedures checklist	17%
Users differentiation	17%
Flexible time settings	17%

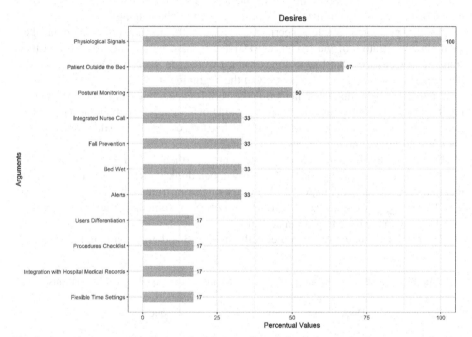

Fig. 4. Graphical summary of appearing frequencies of discussion topic that emerged for the Desires.

3.3 Limitations

The methodology used also revealed some criticalities and limitations of the system.

First of all, in 4 out of 6 FG participants were worried by the presence of alarms other than hospital ones, a possible source of alarm fatigue (P06-FG1: "There are positive and negative aspects, you already have many things to do, if you have to keep up with so many alarms you have a hard time").

There is also a risk, which emerged in 2 FG out of 6, on the acceptance of the system due to the trustworthiness of the data (P06-FG1: "Let's say the bed gets jammed, can I definitely rely on it? It can happen... I don't know if I would totally trust") and on the reliability of the system and therefore on the need for timely technical support (P02-FG1:

"I use the PC very little but it always jams. So currently, you hear swearing because the pc is turned off. You need good support").

It is also interesting to highlight a problem detected in one of the FGs, in which the discretion of mobile devices for receiving alarms was discussed because it could impact on the professionalism of the operators (P02-FG1: "However, currently, when doctors use the telephone in hand the patients say they are not working. It would take something smaller, a clock where you have alarm bells. So yes, but with discretion and without letting the patient doubt").

The need to not overload the already overburdened bureaucratic commitments has also emerged as a possible limitation of the system (P01-FG2: "In the hospital where you also have many papers to fill out for an acceptance if you also have to be there to do the bed and patient settings that gets into it becomes challenging").

Another possible obstacle concerns the feeling of the operators of being controlled by the administrators of the structures (P01-FG3: "Yes, but if I do my 8 h and then someone goes to see what I have done or not, I would feel judged. When they first put the cameras in it was a period of anxiety at the beginning").

Another problem that has emerged is the permissions to view data. One of the FGs points out that the family and the patients should not have access to their data (P03-FG6: "In my opinion the user is not able to manage this data, especially in a domestic context, therefore he should not have access").

Finally, some problems related to incidents and their legal resolution have been highlighted in one of the FG (P03-FG2: "If we then think about the various complaints that many are addressed to us, we could avenge on this instrument by saying that we had it and that maybe we ignored an alarm for any reason, something happened and then with the system we have to give an account").

The results are summarized numerically in Table 3 and graphically in Fig. 5.

Table 3. Appearing frequency of discussion topic that emerged for the Limitations.

Discussion argument	Frequence
Alarm fatigue	67%
Reliability	33%
Display devices discretion	17%
Bureaucracy	17%
Feel of being under control	17%
Data accessibility for patients and families	17%
Legal issues	17%

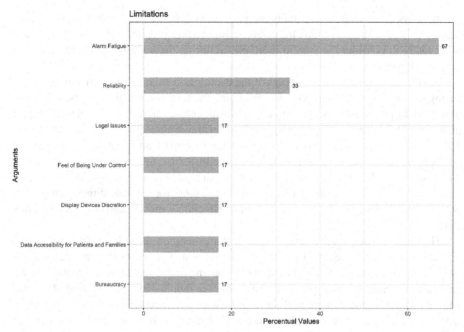

Fig. 5. Graphical summary of appearing frequencies of discussion topic that emerged for the Limitations.

4 Discussion

This study aims to explore the perception of the smart-bed IoT systems' usefulness in the medical environment with the end-users, such as nurses, SHO and physiotherapists, working in different healthcare realities.

The first important result is a general positive feeling of usefulness on all the groups involved. This data allows to state that users understand the potential of these technologies and the possible support they could offer them, which is a fundamental indication that caregivers of all categories involved could accept the use of highly technological systems in their work environment. In particular, the perception of usefulness seems to be related mainly to the nocturnal phase of their work. This distinction between night and day and the statements collected about the perceived usefulness suggests that the concept behind the design of the smart bed, an aid capable of lightening the operator's workload, was understood by the participants. Indeed, night shifts are working hours where the healthcare structures see reduced personnel compared to the diurnal phase. Therefore, in the absence of personnel and the consequent workload and responsibility increment, the results shows that technology is seen as an aid to overcome these problems. However, emphasizing the night-time usefulness of the system by the caregivers is not the same as saying that the result is that the system is harmful during the day. During this last situation, the control system was not opposed but simply less mentioned by participants. The explanation for the minor interest could be founded on one limitation of the system: the number of alarms received. During the day, when the activities are more hectic and numerous, many alarms could cause the phenomenon called alarm fatigue [52, 53]. Therefore, this may have influenced respondents' opinions, who were more likely to consider the system more useful during the night shift, where there is a reduced fatigue alarm occurrence.

Some arguments raised in support of the usefulness of the IoT system were those of saving time and simplifying work. For the latter, the reason is fundable in the workload reduction. Regarding the former, it is interesting to note that alerts and related information management are a way of organizing work, prioritizing some alarms more than others. This would make it possible to deal with severe cases firstly and then move on to minor emergencies, with the consequence of using the little time available by rushing first to the aid of those who need it most. Moreover, the care quality could increment, as the time saved thanks to the use of the system would allow a more focused and direct relationship with patients, consequently increasing their satisfaction with care and clinical outcomes [54].

The issue of the data collected by the system was then faced from different points of view. Participants indicated the collection and visualization of data in real-time as particularly positive, due to the possibility of viewing and monitoring each patient at the desired times. Smartphones, smartwatches, tablets or monitors directly integrated into the bed, in addition to the computer of the guardhouse, were cited as possible visualization devices. This result, therefore, shows the participants' desire to continuously monitor patients to increase safety for the assisted and the operators themselves. In one of the FGs, the necessity of increasing safety for cases of isolated patients and to reduce contacts while maintaining a high level of attention also emerged. Safety represent an important theme because, as mentioned in the literature, continuous monitoring brings, even outside critical areas, benefits in terms of clinical outcomes, length of stay in hospital and cost efficiency especially overcoming barriers such as false alarms [55]. Therefore, the result obtained shows that for half of the operators involved, the IoT-based smart bed data is perceived as a positive factor for adopting this technology in their working environments.

The data collected by the smart bed were also cited for the enormous analytical potential they represent. The participants, for example, expressed the desire to collect them to have objective numbers that support them in asking for an increase in the number of personnel from the administrations. Therefore, this result is particularly interesting, as the shortage of operators is a primary concern in hospitals [56, 57]. Finally, the data collected could also represent an aid to verify the correct carrying out of the procedures by non-professional caregivers (domiciliary nurses brought this statement) and to verify their effectiveness.

Moreover, a topic particularly discussed in these FGs was the ideal environment in which to insert an IoT system with these characteristics. The procedure, carried out with different categories of users, has shown that the common opinion is that the hospital is the most appropriate target, especially if the department involved does not have monitoring instruments. The hospital is a more dynamic environment, with a particularly fast patient turnover and a high number of employees who alternate in administering care. These features make a technological monitoring system a valid aid in managing patients, as it allows to keep track of the less known patients. In addition, given the significant differences between the departments of a hospital, it is interesting the suggestion of one of the groups that highlighted the need to create a modular system, therefore adaptable to different needs. Therefore, choosing the most appropriate formula, allowing for customization and cost reduction for the facility, would represent an important element in the intention to adopt the system and so in acceptance. In support of the greater usefulness in hospitals, in the FG for retirement home nurses, the participants highlighted how in most cases, knowing the patients very well, they are manageable with current resources. However, constant monitoring would be welcome for a few patients, the most unpredictable or non-self-sufficient ones. In opposition, the lower frequency of the documents to be filled in for retirement homes would make them a good target since they would not suffer much of the time it takes to insert patients into the bed system, which instead for the hospital has represented a possible limitation. Finally, the domiciliar caregivers find the system not suitable for their work but discuss about providing it, after a simplification of the systems' language, to family members or informal caregivers to monitor their patients in a more sensitive and timely manner. In summary, the system has advantages for its use in all the environments involved (hospital, nursing homes for the elderly, home care), but it seems more suitable for hospitals.

Summarizing the users' desires, the results show the need to create alerts about the patient's vital parameters, especially the heart and respiratory rate, including temperature. Furthermore, the caregivers were particularly interested in avoiding possible risks for the patient, such as falls, getting out of bed unsupervised, immobility, and liquid spills. All these data would allow a complete overview of the patients and, consequently, increase their safety. Furthermore, the caregivers highlight the need to integrate into the bed the facility medical records, a checklist of specific procedures for the patient, and a function for the voice nurse call with easy-to-use interfaces for every type of patients involved.

The system limits highlighted were many, starting from false alarms. For example, the home care caregivers indicate them as a major issue for the acceptance of the IoT bed in their work. Connected to this important problem is the reliability of the data, which could greatly affect the operators' effective use of the system, given the importance of the information's quality in the model of acceptance of technologies also in the medical field [58]. After these two major problems, a series of minor limitations have been highlighted, allowing some reflections. First, the need to not damage operators' professionalism by using mobile devices that patients would consider suitable for recreational use, such as smartphones. Indeed, the patients could perceive a lower care quality or attention, negatively impacting the perceived caregiver's work. In addition, the feeling of control that the caregivers could experience is another important limit. Initially conceived to protect nurses from lawsuits, save and track data is seen as a potential control tool for the administration, like a video camera. A possible suggestion deriving from the FGs could be to guarantee access to the entire database only in legal disputes. This solution seemed to generate greater serenity in the interviewees. Finally, the operators were concerned that the system could be used against them legally when, for various reasons, a caregiver is forced to ignore an alarm to pay attention to something else. If this action were to have any consequences, the recording of the data and the presence of the alarm would make them the target of the legal action.

5 Conclusion

In summary, this exploratory study on a very varied sample of personal care professionals led to an excellent result in terms of the perceived usefulness of IoT systems, indicating how they can be inserted in the modern hospital working context, considering the importance of PU in the model of acceptance of technologies, also for health [41]. Furthermore, the study provides an overview of the key elements to meet users' needs, as well as the possible limits that should be overcome to increase the possibility that similar systems can be adopted in the various settings of patient care. Ultimately, this work offers important insights for the design and planning of IoT systems devoted to patient monitoring and the reduction of operators' workload.

Acknowledgement. The study was supported by a grant from SMACT scpa competence centre [N. H82C20001350001, I.O.BED project] to the Human Inspired Technology Research Centre (HIT). We also thank Dr Ilaria De Barbieri and Dr Mario Degan for the support of the University Hospital or Padua for the research of the study participants.

Bibliography

1. Krick, T., Huter, K., Domhof, D., et al.: Digital technology and nursing care: a scoping review on acceptance, effectiveness and efficiency studies of informal and formal care technologies. BMC Health Serv. Res. **19** (2019). https://doi.org/10.1186/s12913-019-4238-3
2. Büssing, A., Falkenberg, Z., Schoppe, C., et al.: Work stress associated cool down reactions among nurses and hospital physicians and their relation to burnout symptoms. BMC Health Serv. Res. **17** (2017). https://doi.org/10.1186/s12913-017-2445-3
3. Hämmig, O.: Explaining burnout and the intention to leave the profession among health professionals - a cross-sectional study in a hospital setting in Switzerland. BMC Health Serv. Res. **18** (2018). https://doi.org/10.1186/s12913-018-3556-1
4. Zhou, J., Wiggermann, N.: The effects of hospital bed features on physical stresses on caregivers when repositioning patients in bed. Appl. Ergon. **90** (2021). https://doi.org/10.1016/j.apergo.2020.103259
5. Gunningberg, L., Carli, C.: Reduced pressure for fewer pressure ulcers: can real-time feedback of interface pressure optimise repositioning in bed? Int. Wound J. **13**, 774–779 (2016). https://doi.org/10.1111/iwj.12374
6. Kashani, M.H., Madanipour, M., Nikravan, M., et al.: A systematic review of IoT in healthcare: applications, techniques, and trends. J. Network Comput. Appl. **192** (2021). https://doi.org/10.1016/j.jnca.2021.103164
7. Ullah, F., Habib, M.A., Farhan, M., et al.: Semantic interoperability for big-data in heterogeneous IoT infrastructure for healthcare. Sustain. Cities Soc. **34**, 90–96 (2017). https://doi.org/10.1016/j.scs.2017.06.010
8. Najafizadeh, A., Salajegheh, A., Rahmani, A.M., Sahafi, A.: Privacy-preserving for the internet of things in multi-objective task scheduling in cloud-fog computing using goal programming approach. Peer-to-Peer Network. Appl. **14**(6), 3865–3890 (2021). https://doi.org/10.1007/s12083-021-01222-2
9. Papert, M., Pflaum, A.: Development of an ecosystem model for the realization of Internet of Things (IoT) services in supply chain management. Electron. Mark. **27**(2), 175–189 (2017). https://doi.org/10.1007/s12525-017-0251-8

10. Haass, R., Dittmer, P., Veigt, M., Lütjen, M.: Reducing food losses and carbon emission by using autonomous control - a simulation study of the intelligent container. Int. J. Product. Econ. **164**, 400–408 (2015). https://doi.org/10.1016/j.ijpe.2014.12.013

11. Jiang, H., Shen, F., Chen, S., et al.: A secure and scalable storage system for aggregate data in IoT. Fut. Gener. Comput. Syst. **49**, 133–141 (2015). https://doi.org/10.1016/j.future.2014. 11.009

12. Al Shorman, O., Al Shorman, B., Al-Khassaweneh, M., Alkahtani, F.: A review of internet of medical things (IoMT) - based remote health monitoring through wearable sensors: a case study for diabetic patients. Indonesian J. Electric. Eng. Comput. Sci. **20**, 414–422 (2020). https://doi.org/10.11591/ijeecs.v20.i1.pp414-422

13. Garai, Á., Péntek, I., Adamkó, A.: Revolutionizing healthcare with IoT and cognitive, cloud-based telemedicine. Acta Polytechnica Hungarica **16**, 163–181 (2019). https://doi.org/10. 12700/APH.16.2.2019.2.10

14. Scarpato, N., Pieroni, A., Di Nunzio, L., Fallucchi, F.: E-health-IoT universe: a review. Int. J. Adv. Sci. Eng. Inform. Technol. **7**, 2328–2336 (2017). https://doi.org/10.18517/ijaseit.7.6. 4467

15. Rahaman, A., Islam, M.M., Islam, M.R., et al.: Developing IoT based smart health monitoring systems: a review. Revue d'Intelligence Artificielle **33**, 435–440 (2019). https://doi.org/10. 18280/ria.330605

16. Manyika, J., Chui, M., Bisson, P., et al.: The Internet of Things: mapping the value beyond the hype. McKinsey Global Inst. **144** (2015)

17. Carcary, M., Maccani, G., Doherty, E., Conway, G.: Exploring the determinants of IoT adoption: findings from a systematic literature review. In: Zdravkovic, J., Grabis, J., Nurcan, S., Stirna, J. (eds.) BIR 2018. LNBIP, vol. 330, pp. 113–125. Springer, Cham (2018). https://doi. org/10.1007/978-3-319-99951-7_8

18. Thangaraj, M., Ponmalar, P.P., Anuradha, S.: Internet of Things (IOT) enabled smart autonomous hospital management system - a real world health care use case with the technology drivers. In: 2015 IEEE International Conference on Computational Intelligence and Computing Research ICCIC 2015 (2015). https://doi.org/10.1109/ICCIC.2015.7435678

19. Singh, R.P., Javaid, M., Haleem, A., Suman, R.: Internet of Things (IoT) applications to fight against COVID-19 pandemic. Diabetes Metab. Synd. Clin. Res. Rev. **14**, 521–524 (2020). https://doi.org/10.1016/j.dsx.2020.04.041

20. Ghosh, A.M., Halder, D., Hossain, S.A.: Remote health monitoring system through IoT. In: 2016 5th International Conference on Informatics, Electronics and Vision (ICIEV), pp. 921–926, May 2016. http://doi.org/10.1109/ICIEV.2016.7760135

21. Albahri, A.S., Alwan, J.K., Taha, Z.K., et al.: IoT-based telemedicine for disease prevention and health promotion: State-of-the-Art. J. Network Comput. Appl. **173** (2021). https://doi. org/10.1016/j.jnca.2020.102873

22. Sodhro, A.H., Pirbhulal, S., Sangaiah, A.K.: Convergence of IoT and product lifecycle management in medical health care. Future Gener. Comput. Syst. **86**, 380–391 (2018). https://doi. org/10.1016/j.future.2018.03.052

23. Chiuchisan, I., Costin, H.N., Geman, O.: Adopting the internet of things technologies in health care systems. In: EPE 2014 - Proceedings of the 2014 International Conference and Exposition on Electrical and Power Engineering, pp. 532–535 (2014). https://doi.org/10.1109/ ICEPE.2014.6969965

24. Dhariwal, K., Mehta, A.: Architecture and plan of Smart hospital based on Internet of Things (IOT). Int. Res. J. Eng. Technol. **4**, 1976–1980 (2017)

25. Catarinucci, L., De Donno, D., Mainetti, L., et al.: An IoT-aware architecture for smart healthcare systems. IEEE Internet of Things J. **2**, 515–526 (2015). https://doi.org/10.1109/ JIOT.2015.2417684

26. Yousefi, R., Ostadabbas, S., Faezipour, M., et al.: A smart bed platform for monitoring and Ulcer prevention. In: Proceedings - 2011 4th International Conference on Biomedical Engineering and Informatics, BMEI 2011, vol. 3, pp. 1362–1366 (2011). https://doi.org/10.1109/BMEI.2011.6098589

27. Brush, Z., Bowling, A., Tadros, M., Russell, M.: Design and control of a smart bed for pressure ulcer prevention. In: 2013 IEEE/ASME International Conference on Advanced Intelligent Mechatronics: Mechatronics for Human Wellbeing, AIM 2013, pp. 1033–1038 (2013). https://doi.org/10.1109/AIM.2013.6584230

28. Hong, Y.S.: Smart Care Beds for Elderly Patients with Impaired Mobility. Wireless Communications and Mobile Computing 2018 (2018). https://doi.org/10.1155/2018/1780904

29. Sivanantham, A.: Measurement of heartbeat, respiration and movements detection using Smart Bed. In: 2015 IEEE Recent Advances in Intelligent Computational Systems, RAICS 2015, pp. 105–109 (2016). https://doi.org/10.1109/RAICS.2015.7488397

30. Hart, A., Tallevi, K., Wickland, D., et al.: A contact-free respiration monitor for smart bed and ambulatory monitoring applications. In: 2010 Annual International Conference of the IEEE Engineering in Medicine and Biology Society, EMBC 2010, pp. 927–930 (2010). https://doi.org/10.1109/IEMBS.2010.5627525

31. Fischer, M., Renzler, M., Ussmueller, T.: Development of a smart bed insert for detection of incontinence and occupation in elder care. IEEE Access 7, 118498–118508 (2019). https://doi.org/10.1109/ACCESS.2019.2931041

32. Nakajima, R., Sakaguchi, K.: Service vision design for Smart Bed System^{TM} of paramount bed. Fujitsu Sci. Tech. J. 54, 9–14 (2018)

33. Centrella Smart+ Hospital Bed I Hillrom. https://www.hillrom.com/en/products/centrella-smart-bed/. Accessed 21 Jan 2022

34. iBed Wireless I Stryker. https://www.stryker.com/us/en/acute-care/products/ibed-wireless.html. Accessed 21 Jan 2022

35. Economides, A.A.: User perceptions of Internet of Things (IoT) systems. In: Obaidat, M.S. (ed.) ICETE 2016. CCIS, vol. 764, pp. 3–20. Springer, Cham (2017). https://doi.org/10.1007/978-3-319-67876-4_1

36. Davis, F.D.: Perceived usefulness, perceived ease of use, and user acceptance of information technology. MIS Quar. Manage. Inf. Syst. 13, 319–339 (1989). https://doi.org/10.2307/249008

37. Ammenwerth, E.: Technology acceptance models in health informatics: TAM and UTAUT. Stud. Health Technol. Inform. 263, 64–71 (2019). https://doi.org/10.3233/SHTI190111

38. Venkatesh, V., Sykes, T.A., Zhang, X.: Just what the doctor ordered": A revised UTAUT for EMR system adoption and use by doctors. In: Proceedings of the Annual Hawaii International Conference on System Sciences https://doi.org/10.1109/HICSS.2011.1

39. Legris, P., Ingham, J., Collerette, P.: Why do people use information technology? a critical review of the technology acceptance model. Inform. Manage. 40, 191–204 (2003). https://doi.org/10.1016/S0378-7206(01)00143-4

40. Granić, A., Marangunić, N.: Technology acceptance model in educational context: a systematic literature review. Br. J. Educ. Technol. 50, 2572–2593 (2019). https://doi.org/10.1111/bjet.12864

41. Tubaishat, A.: Perceived usefulness and perceived ease of use of electronic health records among nurses: application of technology acceptance model. Inform. Health Social Care 43, 379–389 (2018). https://doi.org/10.1080/17538157.2017.1363761

42. Salloum, S.A., Alhamad, A.Q.M., Al-Emran, M., Monem, A.A., Shaalan, K.: Exploring students' acceptance of e-learning through the development of a comprehensive technology acceptance model. IEEE Access 7, 128445–128462 (2019). https://doi.org/10.1109/ACCESS.2019.2939467

43. Rahimi, B., Nadri, H., Afshar, H.L., Timpka, T.: A systematic review of the technology acceptance model in health informatics. Appl. Clin. Inform. **9**, 604–634 (2018). https://doi.org/10.1055/S-0038-1668091

44. Holden, R.J., Karsh, B.T.: The technology acceptance model: its past and its future in health care. J. Biomed. Inform. **43**(1), 159–172 (2010). https://doi.org/10.1016/j.jbi.2009.07.002

45. Tsourela, M., Nerantzaki, D.M.: An internet of things (IoT) acceptance model. assessing consumer's behavior toward IoT products and applications. Fut. Internet **12**, 1–23 (2020). https://doi.org/10.3390/fi12110191

46. Kang, J.-Y., Kong, Y.-W., Kim, E.-B., et al.: Relationships among Nursing Students' recognition, perceived usefulness, and intention to accept IoT. koreascience.or.kr **7**, 1–5 (2021). https://doi.org/10.13106/kjfhc.2021.vol7.no7.1

47. Martínez-Caro, E., Cegarra-Navarro, J.G., García-Pérez, A., Fait, M.: Healthcare service evolution towards the Internet of Things: an end-user perspective. Technol. Forecast. Soc. Change **136**, 268–276 (2018). https://doi.org/10.1016/j.techfore.2018.03.025

48. Ben Arfi, W., Ben Nasr, I., Khvatova, T., Ben Zaied, Y.: Understanding acceptance of eHealthcare by IoT natives and IoT immigrants: an integrated model of UTAUT, perceived risk, and financial cost. Technol. Forecast. Soc. Change **163** (2021). https://doi.org/10.1016/j.techfore.2020.120437

49. Bhattacherjee, A., Hikmet, N.: Reconceptualizing organizational support and its effect on information technology usage: evidence from the health care sector. J. Comput. Inform. Syst. **48**, 69–76 (2008). https://doi.org/10.1080/08874417.2008.11646036

50. Kinalski, D.D.F., de Paula, C.C., de Padoin, M.S.M., et al.: Focus group on qualitative research: experience report. Revista brasileira de enfermagem **70**, 424–429 (2017). https://doi.org/10.1590/0034-7167-2016-0091

51. Maguire, M.: Education BD-AIJ of H, 2017 undefined doing a thematic analysis: a practical, step-by-step guide for learning and teaching scholars. AISHE-J. All Ireland J. Teach. Learn. High. Educ. **9**, 3351 (2017)

52. Deb, S., Claudio, D.: Alarm fatigue and its influence on staff performance. IIE Trans. Healthcare Syst. Eng. **5**, 183–196 (2015). https://doi.org/10.1080/19488300.2015.1062065

53. Johnson, K.R., Hagadorn, J.I., Sink, D.W.: Alarm safety and alarm fatigue. Clin. Perinatol. **44**, 713–728 (2017). https://doi.org/10.1016/j.clp.2017.05.005

54. Ng, J.H.Y., Luk, B.H.K.: Patient satisfaction: concept analysis in the healthcare context. Patient Educ. Couns. **102**, 790–796 (2019). https://doi.org/10.1016/j.pec.2018.11.013

55. Downey, C.L., Chapman, S., Randell, R., et al.: The impact of continuous versus intermittent vital signs monitoring in hospitals: a systematic review and narrative synthesis. Int. J. Nurs. Stud. **84**, 19–27 (2018). https://doi.org/10.1016/j.ijnurstu.2018.04.013

56. Metcalf, A.Y., Wang, Y., Habermann, M.: Hospital unit understaffing and missed treatments: primary evidence. Manage. Dec. **56**, 2273–2286 (2018). https://doi.org/10.1108/MD-09-2017-0908

57. Tourigny, L., Baba, V.V., Monserrat, S.I., Lituchy, T.R.: Burnout and absence among hospital nurses: an empirical study of the role of context in Argentina. Eur. J. Int. Manage. **13**, 198–223 (2019). https://doi.org/10.1504/EJIM.2019.098147

58. Chismar, W.G., Wiley-Patton, S.: Does the extended technology acceptance model apply to physicians. In: Proceedings of the36th Annual Hawaii International Conference on System Sciences HICSS 2003 (2003). https://doi.org/10.1109/HICSS.2003.1174354

Human Pose-Based Activity Recognition Approaches on Smart-Home Devices

Tianjia He[✉]

Graduate School of ISEE, Kyushu University, Fukuoka, Japan
`he.tianjia.371@s.kyushu-u.ac.jp`

Abstract. With the gradual improvement of the intelligent degree of smart-home devices, its popularity is also multiplying. These devices dramatically improve the richness of available data, including a large number of indoor family life visual data. At the same time, it also has higher requirements on effectively using these data and further improving the intelligence of smart-home devices. In this paper, we mainly verify the performance of frameworks and feasibility of deploying the human activity recognition models when the computing power of edge computing devices is limited. It includes typical deep learning methods, CNN and GCN-based recognition methods, and a single activity judgment recognition method based on CTW. We also analyze the help of different data preprocessing steps in improving time efficiency and accuracy. In addition, a human activity dataset is built based on the actual home fitness equipment. The experimental results verify the feasibility and effectiveness of deploying the activity recognition model on IoT devices with limited computing capability.

Keywords: Pose estimation · Human activity recognition · Smart home

1 Introduction

Research on human activity recognition has received increasing attention. Especially in recent years, with the development and popularization of IoT devices, the sources of human activity data have become more abundant and accessible. In addition to wearable sensors or acoustic devices, smartphones and smart-home devices produce a large number of pictures and video data related to daily human activities. Surveillance systems, intelligent security systems, smart-home systems, and various human-computer interaction devices produced a significant amount of data quickly, providing more realistic scenes for the study of human activity recognition. Meanwhile, Human activity recognition research on these data can be applied to these surveillance systems, smart-home systems, and other human-computer interfaces. Analyzing and utilizing the visual data from, such as electronic lock surveillance, a house monitoring system, or Smart Fitness Equipment can effectively improve the performance of the devices.

© The Author(s), under exclusive license to Springer Nature Switzerland AG 2022
N. A. Streitz and S. Konomi (Eds.): HCII 2022, LNCS 13325, pp. 266–277, 2022.
https://doi.org/10.1007/978-3-031-05463-1_19

Applying activity recognition to these smart home devices can effectively improve the intelligence of devices. Other functions can also be added on this basis to provide users with more convenient services. In recent years, various popular activity recognition methods or activity recognition methods basically adopt the framework of deep learning, including network structures such as CNN and GCN [6,18], and have achieved good recognition results. However, in practical application scenarios, whether using single-frame images or video sequences, we will encounter some problems and challenges. Although deep learning can directly provide good end-to-end optimization, it also needs a large amount of pre-training data to help the whole framework learn feature extraction and pattern recognition. At the same time, both CNN and GCN have specific requirements for the performance of hardware equipment.

The CNN-based activity recognition framework directly uses the original unprocessed images [6]. The extraction of human features is implicitly included in the network structure, and its efficiency and accuracy are difficult to measure directly. Recent studies show that the 2D human pose estimation method based on heatmap can effectively extract the key points of a human skeleton [13]. The human pose estimation method can skilfully compress the high-resolution 2D image into low-dimensional data containing only multiple key points of human bodies. Taking these key points as the input of the activity recognition model can effectively reduce the complexity of the network structure. The experiments in this paper are verificated on the key points of 2D or 3D human skeletons. The results show that the performance of subsequent recognition algorithms can be improved by extracting human features from 2D images through human pose estimation.

In this paper, we will mainly discuss various activity recognition methods on devices with limited computing power. According to the specific application requirements of intelligent devices, the performance of two different recognition frameworks on the following two tasks is verified. The traditional activity recognition task is to recognize the in the uncertain scene through the well-trained model, and a single activity distinction task is employed to judge whether the actual activity is the target activity. Our contributions can be summarized as (1) We propose several combination methods of human data preprocessing technics and recognition frameworks for human activity recognition, (2) We built an indoor activities dataset PSC from more than 200 h training video of 14 users on several home intelligent fitness devices, (3) Our experiments verify the performance of the proposed methods on PSC dataset, and We tested the feasibility of the proposed method on different platforms with limited computing power.

2   Related Work

It is challenging to analyze and recognize human activities effectively from the data with huge volume and multi-dimensionality. Extracting human skeleton information into landmarks can reduce the data dimension [5]. The early body sensing device Kinect uses TOF-based depth cameras to obtain human pose information [12]. These pose data can be used to analyze the user's body movements while feeding back to the corresponding commands on the computer. Pose data from the depth camera is streamlined, containing only the coordinates of key points of the human body and removing other noise or environmental effects. However, obtaining the depth camera data is too expensive compared to 2D live streaming generated by a regular camera. While processing human action information on 2D video data, traditional vision algorithms do not explicitly extract human action features but directly process all pixel information, making the computational consumption extremely large. With the development of computer vision in recent years, the RCNN based human pose estimation method has been used to obtain human pose data on pictures and videos to get the same structure to pose information as depth cameras [7]. Because the complexity of 3D human pose estimation is much higher than 2D, this paper only discusses 2D human bone data and 2D human bone data transformed from 3D information after simple preprocessing. The mainstream 2D pose estimation algorithms include Openpose [5,13], Postenet [7] and Mediapipe [9]. Among them, the processing speed and performance of Mediapipe are higher than other two. Meanwhile, Mediapipe also supports deployment on mobile devices.

The mainstream deep learning methods in human activity recognition are based on CNN [6] and ST-GCN recognition with human skeleton information [18]. There is no obvious difference in recognition accuracy in simple tasks between the two, but the processing speed of ST-GCN is better than CNN with the same dataset. Compared with the traditional method of analyzing joint coordinate feature vectors, ST-GCN can effectively utilize the spatial relationship between joints to effectively identify human activity in complex situations. ST-GCN regards each key point of human joints as a graph node and uses GCN to identify it [18]. It is believed that applying ST-GCN to some platforms with low computing power is reasonable. Moreover, experiments show that properly simplifying the number of key points in human pose estimation and effective preprocessing can maintain high accuracy while improving speed further. Both of them are suitable for general human activity/action recognition. In our investigation of intelligent devices at this stage, the demand for designated human activity recognition is also huge. This is mainly reflected in some devices that need simple human-computer interaction. The requirements of these tasks are generally to judge whether the specified action flow is a ground truth target activity. Such tasks are also required to quantify the similarity with the target actions. Some related single-frame motion similarity comparison algorithms have been ubiquitous [17]. However, the works will encounter some problems in practical tasks. One of the key points is that the single-frame comparison similarity method is troublesome to apply to continuous frames directly. When different people do the same actions at different speeds, comparing all frames one by one can not solve the problem of clearly comparing the similarity between the two actions. [19] proposed a CTW algorithm combining CCA and DTW to unify sequences with different Spatio-temporal patterns. Our results show CTW is appropriate for handling such tasks.

3 Estimating Human Pose

3.1 2D Human Pose Estimation

2D human pose estimation for the single person needs to build the ground truth for the eventual regression. There are two primary methods. One is the construction method based on image coordinates [16]. The network constructed by this method generally takes the key point coordinates of human joints as the training target of the network so that the specific key point coordinate information can be obtained directly. Another idea using heatmap will directly consider every pixel in the image. According to the pixel coordinates of the image, a whole probability map is constructed to represent the recognition results [5,7,9]. Each pixel in the image will have a quota representing the probability of belonging to a key point category. The model can take the pixel with the highest probability in the category as the actual key point of the category. Alternatively, it calculates the probability of all possible points in the category and takes the average to obtain the average coordinates as the position of that key point. Some early papers show that the network structure based on heatmap performs better than coordinate in both training and recognition. The regression goal of the coordinate network is the distance of each key point in the graph relative to the ground truth. Thus, a long-distance will slow down the training speed, and the regression error will be larger than expected. In contrast, the training speed of the heatmap network will be much faster.

Human pose estimation methods like Mediapipe or Openpose are all multi-person recognition methods. They all adopted the bottom-up method and extended the recognition task to multi-person recognition based on a single-person recognition algorithm. The identification process is generally divided into two parts:

1. Generate the key point heatmap through the trained CNN network and get the relative correlation between the key points.
2. Generate key points according to the probability map obtained by the heatmap, and then classify each group of key points according to the individuals in the map.

The generated human joint key points can be represented by a connected graph $G = (V, E)$. The nodes in set V represent the joint key points $[v_1, v_2, \cdots, v_n]$, while the edges in set E represent the corresponding limbs $[e_1, e_2, \cdots, e_n]$, such as arms and thighs.

Yolo-Based Estimation. Although the model like Openpose and Posenet also contains the similar object detection layers in the network structure, in more complex scenes, human pose estimation may still be affected by environmental noise. Some scholars have proposed that independent object detection method can be used to preliminarily segment the human ROI region, and then carry out the subsequent steps of human pose estimation [1]. We also verify this idea in experiments. The results show that independent object detection steps, such as YOLO, can indeed improve the accuracy of human pose estimation. As shown in Fig. 1.

Fig. 1. The performance of Yolo-based human pose estimation and native human pose estimation in a real scene.

3.2 Procrustes Superimposition

The superior task of single-activity recognition based on human pose estimation is pose matching. Before considering direct end-to-end optimization, practical data preprocessing can reduce the complexity of the model and improve accuracy. To compare two single poses, we should consider the problem of the human coordinate system and consider the rotation and scaling of poses of people with different shapes. Taking this as the first step of pose data processing can facilitate us to analyze and adjust the final performance of recognition. Therefore, to compare the similarity of two poses, the framework should overlap them under the same measurement condition to the greatest extent.

Procrustes superimposition can effectively translate, rotate, and scale two objects [14]. It minimizes the difference in position and size between objects by measuring the Procrustes distance. Make different objects overlap as much as possible without changing the object's shape. This method can avoid the comparison error caused by body and absolute coordinate differences.

Procrustes superimposition takes k points in n-dimensional space as the key points of the target object. This method is suitable for 2D and 3D human pose data. Here the 2D data is mainly discussed because 3D human pose data requires much more computation than 2D, which is hard to deploy on edge computing devices. Even the built-in chips of some consumer depth cameras can directly output 3D pose data. Naturally, the key points of human joints $[J_1, ..., J_K]$ obtained from human pose estimation can be directly used as the landmark points in Procrustes superposition.

From k points in 2D image coordinates $[(j_{x1}, j_{y1}), (j_{x2}, j_{y2}), ..., (j_{xk}, j_{yk})]$, The centroid is denoted as Eq. (1).

$$\bar{J}_x = \frac{\sum_{i=1}^{k} J_{xi}}{k}, \bar{J}_y = \frac{\sum_{i=1}^{k} J_{yi}}{k} \tag{1}$$

By coincident the centroids of different objects with the origin, different objects can be translated to the target position.

Then making the root mean square distance of the inverted translation element as 1 can scale different objects to the same latitude. RMSD is denoted as

$$s = \sqrt{\frac{\sum_{i=1}^{k} [(J_{xi} - \bar{J}_x)^2 + (J_{yi} - \bar{J}_y)^2]}{k}} \tag{2}$$

This removes the rotation component. Then, with the standard object as the reference direction, rotate the target object around the origin at different angles θ to minimize the sum of the squared distance between the corresponding points.

$$\theta = \tan^{-1} \left(\frac{\sum_{i=1}^{k} (J_{ui} J_{yi} - J_{vi} J_{xi})}{\sum_{i=1}^{k} (J_{ui} J_{yi} - J_{vi} J_{xi})} \right) \tag{3}$$

where $[(j_{u1}, j_{v1}), (j_{u2}, j_{v2}), ..., (j_{uk}, j_{vk})]$ are the coordinates of the landmark points from the standard pose.

The processed data can be directly used in the subsequent GCN based model, or the pose matching method based on Procrustes distance and other distance measurement algorithms.

3.3   3D-2D Pose Data Processing

As discussed earlier, many domestic devices can directly provide 3D pose data, such as Microsoft's Kinect and Realsense series depth cameras [11]. Realsense has tried to embed its devices to smart TVs as typical domestic motion sensing devices. However, the analysis of 3D pose data needs enough computation and more training data. Moreover, the related research shows that the activity recognition algorithm based on 3D pose data has no obvious advantage over 2D pose data in performance. Therefore, in our experiment, we tried some ways to convert 3D data into 2D data for analysis.

Because most motion data acquisition only uses a few specific shooting viewpoints in our dataset construction. The lack of training samples will affect the final optimization effect for the deep learning model that needs enough learning objects. The 3D pose data captured from different directions can be projected on the 2D plane with the standard shooting direction as the viewpoint, then the 2D pose data under the unified viewing angle can be obtained. Although some spatial data may be lost in this way, we can use a 2D model for final recognition, which can significantly reduce the recognition model's complexity and computational power consumption.

To project 3D-space points onto a 2D plane, the viewpoint and the projected plane must be determined first. We use the three key points of the neck, left hip, and right hip to construct a plane similar to the human torso. The viewpoint vector is the Normal Vector of that plane. By projecting the human pose key points in 3D space onto this plane, we can obtain the approximate human frontal 2D pose data. The deep learning methods can directly convert 3D-2D data mutually and have good results [15]. However, additional models will also increase the computational cost. Meanwhile, it also needs enough training sets to support the 3D-2D conversion method based on deep learning. More work may be required for application scenarios that need to be highly portable and replicable.

4   Human Activity Recognition

4.1   Graph Convolutional Network (GCN)

Traditional CNN has been widely used in image recognition, including object detection and human pose estimation tasks. GCN has a network structure similar to CNN but specially designed for the graph. The key idea of GCN is to extract the two-dimensional or three-dimensional spatial features of the topological graphs [4]. As mentioned before, the key points and links of human joints after human pose estimation can be regarded as connected graphs. It is very natural to use GCN as the recognition model. Some related works, such as ST-GCN, have achieved good results in human activity recognition and gesture recognition tasks [8,18]. ST-GCN can learn spatial and temporary patterns from data naturally. Compared with the traditional methods that need to define rules and judgment criteria manually, ST-GCN is more intelligent, especially for the tasks of general activity recognition. St-GCN can effectively learn and model dynamic skeletons. Its multi-layer network structure and specially designed convolution kernel can process a continuous pose skeleton sequence. In the general human activity recognition task, its ability to learn continuous Spatio-temporal features is more effective than just considering hand-crafted parts and traversal rules [2,10]. However, at the same time, the method based on deep learning will overfit or underfit when it lacks enough practical training set. This situation will result in lousy performance.

The edge set designed in ST-GCN includes the above E set $\{v_{ti}v_{tj} \mid (i,j) \in H\}$ in $G = (V, E)$. Where H includes the joint pairs that naturally connected considering the human body structure and t is the time stamp of that frame. There is another edge set $E_f = \{v_{ti}v_{(t+1)j}\}$ refers to the same edge between two joints but with different time stamps. E_f actually contains the varying information of the same connection in a time series which provides the possibility for GCN to extract the dynamic Spatio-temporal features from time series of pose data.

As mentioned above, the human activity dataset we built for some specific intelligent devices can not fully meet the training requirements of ST-GCN. In the experiment, we mainly verify the impact of utilizing Procrustes Superimposition, Unified coordinate system, and preprocessing method of 3D-2D data conversion on the GCN-based recognition method. In the case that the model cannot effectively learn Spatio-temporal feature extraction due to the defects of the training set, combined with hand-crafted rules can make up for the model's defects to a certain extent and improve the recognition performance of GCN.

4.2 Canonical Time Warping (CTW)

Unlike the general human activity recognition task, which hopes to select the target activity with the greatest probability from multiple candidate activities, many application scenarios also hope to judge the similarity between the target actions and the actual actions in a quantitative way accurately. In such tasks, the goal is generally to judge whether the actual activity perfectly meets the action requirements of the target activity. Such as whether the action in motion meets the regulations and standards. This kind of demand is very common in some indoor fitness equipment or interactive teaching devices. The recognition model based on a deep learning algorithm has good generalization ability, but it can not give accurate and interpretable results in tasks requiring computing action accuracy and similarity. For this task, manually making rules and traversing key points and vectors are still needed. DTW is a typical time series alignment method [3]. However, in the processing of pose data, different from ordinary 2D data, the alignment of spatial series is also necessary. CTW combines CCA spatial feature extraction and DTW time series alignment to handle Spatio-temporal sequences [19]. It can simultaneously analyze spatial and temporal features to align two action sequences with different Spatio-temporal attributes. Using Procrustes Superimposition combined with CTW, we can construct an interpretable Action Comparison framework. Combining different position matching rules, such as Procrustes distance, can effectively and accurately quantify the similarity between the target and actual activity.

5   Experiment

In this section, we tested the actual performance of different combinations of preprocessing methods and recognition methods in the above framework with the same dataset. In order to test the performance on low-power edge devices, our experiments were tested on two platforms with different architectures. The first is the standard consumer-grade industrial computer with Intel Core I3 6100U, the maximum dominant frequency is 2.3 GHZ, and the operating system is Linux. The second is the Rockchip RK3399 with a multi-core cortex-a series processor of mainstream mobile products, and the operating system is Android. This is since both Mediapipe and Realsense cameras support Android compatible applications. Here, we mainly consider the time consumption and accuracy of different methods to verify the possibility of deploying them on edge computing devices. All experiments were not accelerated by GPUs, and the main chipset completed all calculations. For the test camera, we chose the Realsense series depth camera. Its RGB camera and depth camera can facilitate us to obtain 2D and 3D data at the same time and the data they need for mutual conversion.

5.1 Dataset

We construct a standard activity dataset PSC, mainly consisting of indoor sports activities. The native resolution of the image is 2K, and in training and testing, we resize all the data to 340 * 256. The input of the traditional CNN is the native images, while the GCN and CTW based methods are 18 human key points and corresponding connections processed by Mediapipe. We delete some key points of face and hand to reduce the number of input nodes further. The dataset contains 32 different types of activities, but the shooting angle and background are relatively fixed. For miniaturized commercial applications, this dataset is relatively common. The impact of defective datasets on the deep learning framework is also one of the points we verify. For the data generated by Mediapipe, we also adopt data augmentation to prevent the insufficient number of training samples in some categories. It is not easy to augment the data of the original image. However, the information contained in the key points after the human pose estimation is apparent, so we can use some hand-crafted methods to expand the training set reasonably. In addition to the perspective data in the training set, the test set also includes some image data from different shooting perspectives for testing.

5.2 Experimental Design and Results

Here we mainly measure the speed and accuracy of different frameworks on the test set. Where calculation of the time consumption is the total time to process a time series divided by the total number of frames. We first tested the deployment of CNN method on two platforms. It should be noted that the training process is carried out on another high-performance machine. We deploy the model on the test platforms after training. As shown in Table 1, the CNN model is not ideal in terms of accuracy and speed. We believe that this is not entirely the defect of the method itself, but the method based on CNN has relatively high requirements for the training set. It's not just a matter of shooting perspective. Unlike the HPE method, which can extract human bone data directly, CNN needs enough training sets to learn the feature extraction process. Simplified datasets are not enough to optimize the model to a satisfactory grade. At the same time, the amount of data processed by CNN is much higher than that of GCN, which makes CNN have no advantage in time consumption.

Table 1. Comparison results of deep learning based approaches on PSC dataset

Platform		TC/F	Accuracy
LX	**CNN**	103 ms	30.2%
AA	**CNN**	140 ms	30.2%
LX	**MDP+ST-GCN**	70 ms	83.9%
LX	**MDP+PS+ST-GCN**	73 ms	85.4%
LX	**PS+3-2D+ST-GCN**	90 ms	90.6%

ST-GCN performed much better. Here, although ST-GCN also faces the problem of defective datasets, as we mentioned earlier, pose data can be easily augmented according to hand-crafted rules. Considering the possible node displacement and vector angle changes in the actual situation, we formulate the augmentation rules and increase the same amount of data by ten times for training. Although it can not solve the problem of various shooting points, ST-GCN still performs very well. The accuracy of ST-GCN is more than 80%, but almost all of that is human pose samples from a fixed shooting perspective. The training set lacks enough different shooting angles, making the model unable to recognize human data from different shooting perspectives generically. The 2D model is tough to deal with in the absence of multi-perspective learning data. In applying MDP+PS+ST-GCN, we found that the PS preprocessing method can further improve the accuracy of ST-GCN. Although the network structure of ST-GCN has the ability to extract and unify spatial features adaptively, it is obvious that PS preprocessing method can still help the learning and inference process of ST-GCN. The last is the method of 2D-3D transformation. The model we use here is still the same 2D ST-GCN model as before. In the test set, we use the 3D human pose data captured and extracted by a Realsense depth camera simultaneously and from the same shooting points. These 3D spatial data correspond to the 2D spatial data in the test set one by one. We use the 3D-2D data processing method to project the 3D spatial human body data onto the 2D plane according to the human body plane to unify the viewing angle relative to the human body. These data have greatly improved the method of PS+ST-GCN. This process standardizes the unlearned data in the test set into the perspective learned by the model from the training set to identify the unlearned data correctly. As we discussed earlier, although we can directly use the 3D ST-GCN, the model complexity and processing speed will be further increased. 3D-2D conversion can enable devices that provide 3D information to use 2D recognition models with low consumption.

The results of the recognition method based on CTW are shown in Table 2. CTW is different from GCN in recognition tasks, so accuracy calculation cannot

Table 2. Comparison results of CTW based approaches on PSC dataset

Platform		TC/F	Accuracy	Threshold
LX	**MDP+CTW**	32 ms	77.3%	65%
AA	**MDP+CTW**	70 ms	77.2%	65%
LX	**MDP+PS+CTW**	36 ms	85.3%	65%
AA	**MDP+PS+CTW**	75 ms	85.3%	65%
LX	**PS+3-2D+CTW**	36 ms	95.5%	75%
AA	**PS+3-2D+CTW**	96 ms	95.5%	75%

be directly compared with GCN. Here, we calculate whether the activity with similarity above a certain threshold is the target activity to judge the recognition accuracy. The composition of the test set is the same as that of GCN, and the target activity is the standard action in the data set. The MDP+CTW can achieve 77% accuracy when the threshold is 65%. Combined with PS preprocessing, its accuracy has been significantly improved. It can be seen that PS data processing also has a positive promotion on the CCA step in CTW. The 3D-2D converted data is better recognized, and the recognition rate is 95% at the 75% similarity threshold. Under the same test platform, all the above combinations have lower time consumption than GCN. CTW is obviously more suitable for the task of dealing with this kind of application requirements.

6   Conclusion

Most edge computing devices are challenging to meet real-time HCR system requirements. If the model inference time is much larger than the frame rate, the single frame pictures waiting for recognition will continue to accumulate, resulting in the infinite lag of recognition results. Therefore, the real-time recognition system based on the deep learning model generally will continue to extract the current frame from the video stream after each inference and then carry out subsequent processing. The results show that if the inference speed is too slow, the keyframes in the video will be discarded, resulting in an unsatisfactory recognition effect. Several frameworks we verified prove the feasibility to apply them in real time system. Moreover, the simplified steps can be convenient for real applications. However, this design also sacrifices some of the generalization ability of general activity recognition. In the follow-up work, we will continue to work on HPE and GCN, and focus on the research of general human activity recognition tasks.

References

1. Artacho, B., Savakis, A.: UniPose: unified human pose estimation in single images and videos. In: Proceedings of the IEEE/CVF Conference on Computer Vision and Pattern Recognition pp. 7035–7044 (2020)

2. Baradel, F., Wolf, C., Mille, J.: Pose-conditioned spatio-temporal attention for human action recognition. arXiv preprint arXiv:1703.10106 (2017)
3. Berndt, D.J., Clifford, J.: Using dynamic time warping to find patterns in time series. In: KDD Workshop, pp. 359–370 (1994)
4. Bruna, J., Zaremba, W., Szlam, A., LeCun, Y.: Spectral networks and locally connected networks on graphs. arXiv preprint arXiv:1312.6203 (2013)
5. Cao, Z., Simon, T., Wei, S.E., Sheikh, Y.: Realtime multi-person 2D pose estimation using part affinity fields. In: Proceedings of the IEEE Conference on Computer Vision and Pattern Recognition, pp. 7291–7299 (2017)
6. Ji, S., Xu, W., Yang, M., Yu, K.: 3D convolutional neural networks for human action recognition. IEEE Trans. Pattern Anal. Mach. Intell. **35**(1), 221–231 (2013)
7. Kendall, A., Grimes, M., Cipolla, R.: PoseNet: a convolutional network for real-time 6-DOF camera relocalization. In: Proceedings of the IEEE International Conference on Computer Vision, pp. 2938–2946 (2015)
8. Li, Y., He, Z., Ye, X., He, Z., Han, K.: Spatial temporal graph convolutional networks for skeleton-based dynamic hand gesture recognition. EURASIP J. Image Video Process. **2019**(1), 1–7 (2019). https://doi.org/10.1186/s13640-019-0476-x
9. Lugaresi, C., et al.: Mediapipe: A framework for building perception pipelines. arXiv preprint arXiv:1906.08172 (2019)
10. Luvizon, D.C., Picard, D., Tabia, H.: 2D/3D pose estimation and action recognition using multitask deep learning. In: Proceedings of the IEEE Conference on Computer Vision and Pattern Recognition, pp. 5137–5146 (2018)
11. Lysenkov, I., Eruhimov, V., Bradski, G.: Recognition and pose estimation of rigid transparent objects with a kinect sensor. Robotics **273**(273–280), 2 (2013)
12. Obdržálek, Å., et al.: Accuracy and robustness of kinect pose estimation in the context of coaching of elderly population. In: 2012 Annual International Conference of the IEEE Engineering in Medicine and Biology Society, pp. 1188–1193 (2012)
13. Osokin, D.: Real-time 2D multi-person pose estimation on CPU: Lightweight open-pose. arXiv preprint arXiv:1811.12004 (2018)
14. Peres-Neto, P.R., Jackson, D.A.: How well do multivariate data sets match? the advantages of a procrustean superimposition approach over the mantel test. Oecologia **129**(2), 169–178 (2001). https://doi.org/10.1007/s004420100720
15. Sun, J.J., Zhao, J., Chen, L.-C., Schroff, F., Adam, H., Liu, T.: View-invariant probabilistic embedding for human pose. In: Vedaldi, A., Bischof, H., Brox, T., Frahm, J.-M. (eds.) ECCV 2020, Part V. LNCS, vol. 12350, pp. 53–70. Springer, Cham (2020). https://doi.org/10.1007/978-3-030-58558-7_4
16. Toshev, A., Szegedy, C.: DeepPose: Human pose estimation via deep neural networks. In: Proceedings of the IEEE Conference on Computer Vision and Pattern Recognition, pp. 1653–1660 (2014)
17. Vrigkas, M., Nikou, C., Kakadiaris, I.A.: A review of human activity recognition methods. Front. Robot. AI **2**, 28 (2015)
18. Yan, S., Xiong, Y., Lin, D.: Spatial temporal graph convolutional networks for skeleton-based action recognition. In: Thirty-second AAAI Conference on Artificial Intelligence, pp. 1–9 (2018)
19. Zhou, F., Torre, F.: Canonical time warping for alignment of human behavior. In: Bengio, Y., Schuurmans, D., Lafferty, J., Williams, C., Culotta, A. (eds.) Advances in Neural Information Processing Systems, vol. 22, pp. 2286–2294. Curran Associates, Inc. (2009)

Collective Stress Visualization Enabled by Smart Cushions for Office Chairs

Matthijs Hoekstra[1], Pei-lin Lu[2], Tan Lyu[3], Biyong Zhang[1,4(✉)], and Jun Hu[1]

[1] Department of Industrial Design, Eindhoven University of Technology, Eindhoven,
The Netherlands
[2] Department of Neurology, Neuroscience Center, Sir Run Run Shaw Hospital,
School of Medicine, Zhejiang University, Zhejiang Hangzhou, China
[3] Department of Electrocardiography, Sir Run Run Shaw Hospital, School of Medicine,
Zhejiang University, Zhejiang Hangzhou, China
[4] BOBO Technology, Hangzhou, Zhejiang, China
`biyong.zhang@ish-lab.org`

Abstract. This paper explores the possibility of combining sensory data of multiple individuals into a collective visualization. Using a smart cushion for office chairs that collects several stress-related parameters, namely: heart rate, respiratory rate, and heart-rate variability, individuals' data can be aggregated into a collective stress visualization. Three different visualizations are designed which abstractly, grouped and aggregated, and metaphorically visualize the collective stress. Additionally, two more visualizations are explored for the 'new way of working' during the COVID-19 epidemic, where people work remotely and from the office. Through expert and user interviews, these visualizations are evaluated. Additionally, there is researched on whether measured heart-rate variability can predict perceived stress levels. The results found an inversed correlation than hypothesized.

Keywords: Collective stress · Stress visualization · Smart cushion ·
Ballistocardiograph sensor

1 Introduction

At more and more places, data of individuals is collected. While this data can provide value for these individuals personally, we might combine these individuals' data and create value for the collective. In, for example, offices, daily interactions take place, and well-being is an important topic. Wellbeings' data of individuals combined and aggregated into a collective visualization might add value for collective reflection.

This paper explores how to visualize collective stress by using smart cushions for office chairs. Collective stress in the office is defined as occupational, workgroup level stress which is caused by either a shared stressor (e.g., an approaching deadline) or by other people (e.g., the facial expression of a colleague) [1]. We explore how one can use multiple individuals' collected well-being data to design collective stress visualizations.

N. A. Streitz and S. Konomi (Eds.): HCII 2022, LNCS 13325, pp. 278–290, 2022.
https://doi.org/10.1007/978-3-031-05463-1_20

User research and expert evaluation are done into the associations and experiences with collective visualizations. Additionally, we researched if perceived stress can be predicted through heart rate variability data.

2 Related Work

The current office environment has seen a rapid change in the last decade. Office buildings, the companies who occupy them, and their workforce have always been a discussion ground [2–4]. Nevertheless, the satisfaction and well-being of the workforce have always been considered, as a negative change can have a considerable impact on the workforce and therefore influence its productivity [4].

An example of technologies that provide insights into processes and well-being is the integration of sensors and Internet of Things-enabled devices in the office [5]. Integrating these devices generates data of every individual in the building and can be valuable if visualized the correct way [6]. These visualizations can give insights on several levels of the office, ranging from insights on a more individual level to combining these single employee's data into collective visualizations.

Several visualizations systems are designed primarily to improve well-being on the work floor, which provide both the individual employee with systems where they can track and reflect on their well-being, to systems that provide teams and departments with means to track and reflect on the collective health status.

Different efforts have been made in creating design proposals that should help individuals track their well-being. Snyder and others tried to create a system that visualizes a person's arousal level [7]. Others tried to create bio-feedback systems which visualize stress [8, 9]. Other researchers focus on making systems that collect individual data and transforms the datasets into collective visualizations to create a reflective process for the complete work floor [10–12].

3 Smart Cushion Design

The study was performed using the smart cushion for office chairs with the model number LS-AEA from BOBO Technology (Fig. 1). A piece of PVDF (Polyvinylidene Fluoride) film is integrated into the smart cushion to capture the BCG signals from the users.

The smart cushion includes a Wi-Fi Module to transmit the collected BCG signals to the BOBO Technology's cloud server. BOBO Technology's cloud server provides data analysis services to calculate users' vitals based on BCG signals received. Typically for the smart cushion (Model LS-AEA), the output includes heart rate, respiratory rate, and heart rate variability. The heart rate variability index is usually treated as a valued indication of stress. Additionally, BOBO Technology's cloud server provides an OpenAPI, in which the data can be easily accessed through the OpenAPI. The outputs are stored in an InfluxDB database for further analysis within this study.

Fig. 1. *Left* - smart cushion on an office chair. *Right* - user working on the smart cushion (grey)

4   Data Visualization

Three levels of visualizations were identified on which any technology could add value. Firstly, on an individual level, the tech can generate insights into a person's well-being or productivity levels. Secondly, on a collective level, one visualization shows multiple individuals' merged data (for example, working together in one room or department). Thirdly, combining the data of multiple collectives can generate insights into the entire office or company.

Visualizing on a collective level provides several design opportunities. Data can be visualized in several ways as data generated is from several individuals, and thus can be displayed by either leaving the individual data intact and still visualizing individuals as a collective or by aggregating the data and combining the data into a 'more' collective visualization. Additionally, data can be displayed either more abstractly and factually using colors and size or designed through metaphors.

Furthermore, the COVID-19 epidemic presented a unique opportunity to design for changing office cultures and environments. As collective are not always in one place, the office floor, but also range to home offices, design opportunities arise to design collective visualizations that extend from the office floor into the home office or vice versa.

The above design suggestions are further explored through expert evaluation and user evaluation. Several collective health visualization designs are evaluated in two sessions with one expert on collective visualization and two young professionals.

4.1   Collective Visualizations

Mosaic Visualization (Abstract) (Fig. 2)

Fig. 2. Every block indicates one person their stress-related levels measured over one hour. Visualizations display thus a week's worth of data.

Expert Evaluation. The time dimension of the mosaic visualization is the most valuable of this visualization. Users can see an extended range of days. Thus, it is possible to reflect upon their stress levels on a short-term and long-term basis due to color usage and the number of people listed. Due to the greyness, it looks like a 'misty' landscape. The greyness adds a layer of negativeness to the already negative message of too much stress.

Bar Visualization (Aggregated And Grouped) (Fig. 3)

Fig. 3. Data is mapped per day, where five working days are visualized in this picture. In this visualization, it is apparent that there have been higher stress levels for multiple days as the red bar has the most significant size on the third day. After this day, people are slowly starting to recover from the stress, consequently increasing the size of the green bar. (Color figure online)

Expert Evaluation. There is a low learning effort due to color usage. Green means relaxed, and red means worse. Besides, the colors are also less 'stress-full' compared to the grey shades. It is essential to inform people about the meaning of the visualization. What does it mean if they are in, for example, the green or orange zone? Individuals cannot see data about themselves; thus, it might be more valuable for managers, as the visualization shows aggregated data and the collective's overall state.

Cityscape Visualization (Metaphor) (Fig. 4)

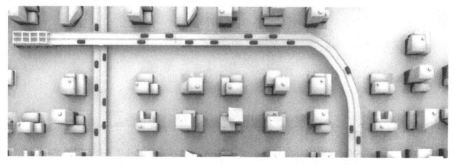

Fig. 4. The number of cars is linked to the amount of traffic. The visualization visualizes traffic jams as a metaphor for stress. The more cars are getting on the road, the more people are stressed.

Expert Evaluation. It is ambient; it will perform in the office environment as a canvas. The visualization will not grab too much attention and make a stressful situation even more stressful. Individual users might have difficulty understanding their stress levels, as their information is not visible.

Overall Evaluation. There are several takeaways from the experts' evaluation: data visualizations must have a versatile time range, which helps users reflect both short-term and long-term. Colors have immense importance; they can negatively influence the user and help understand the data more quickly. Additionally, more aggregated data can be helpful to understand the collective.

4.2 "The New Way of Working" – Visualizations

Two visualizations are proposed, which should help employees and managers reflect on their stress status. These visualizations build upon the already identified takeaways.

Additionally, in these visualizations, the aspects of the COVID-19 epidemic are considered. Several researchers and companies indicate that office and work life will permanently change, and people will be working more remotely [13]. While all employees indicate that they will enjoy their work at home, they risk becoming disconnected from the company and their colleagues.

In both visualizations, the main element visible is the stress visualization itself. It is an abstract representation that tries to summarize one's arousal level. Every horizontal row represents a single employee or user, and every vertical row a single day. The color indicates one's performance level based on the Yerkes-Dodson Law [14], which describes the relationship between arousal levels and performance levels (Fig. 5). In the designed collective visualization, the color is based on this principle. Due to this color differentiation, it is immediately clear if the pressure is too high. Thus, employees directly reflect upon these strains. In addition, four weeks of data are visible so that trends will be visible in the data.

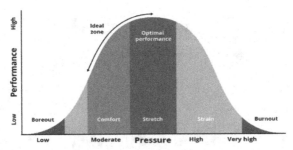

Fig. 5. Yerkes-Dodson law (Cohen [14]) – describes the relationship between pressure and performance

Collective Visualization. In addition to the main performance visualization, the interface allows employees to indicate their emotions. These emotions are ordered based on whether they were sent at home or the office space. The extra addition makes the visualization a twitch more personal, as employees sitting at home and vice versa can view how their colleagues are feeling (Fig. 6).

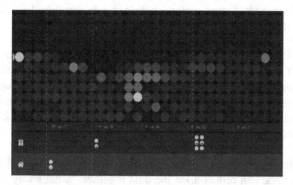

Fig. 6. Collective health visualization is accessible through a central screen and an online webpage. The upper part of the visualization shows individuals horizontally, where every dot represents one day, and the color indicates the performance level. On the bottom part of the visualization, individuals emotions are shown to add a deeper level of emotional data to the visualization.

"Online Video Call" – Collective Visualization. The video call visualization is the leading visualization displayed in the call window of any online meeting. It gives employees the means to reflect on the collective stress at any point of the meeting (Fig. 7).

Fig. 7. Collective visualization visible within an online meeting (e.g., in Microsoft Teams). The visualization shows individuals horizontally, where every dot represents one day, and the color indicates the performance level.

User Evaluation. A validation session is held to review the designed interfaces and evaluate possible users' opinions. Two young professionals were asked to review the interfaces in an open discussion session. A set of topics and questions were set up to prepare the discussions beforehand. The topics discussed were their first thoughts on the system after detailed description, in what kind of setting could the interface be val-uable, and at what point in time could this be helpful? During the session, notes were taken, and the conversation was transcribed after the session. The session was analyzed through thematic analysis, a widely used method within the design world to find themes and patterns within interviews [15]. The following themes are identified:

Identifying Individuals (Acceptance). One of the first though of both interviewees was that the chance of identifying an individual was high. One participant said it never could be anonymous, and chances are to determine who belongs to which row. Another said that if there is one red dot in the system, it is not desirable to know who that is. Additionally, both said that if 50% of the team were red, it would be impossible to solve the situation, and colleagues should take responsibility themselves.

Office Culture (Acceptance). One of the interviewees mentions that office culture needs to be ideal before one can reflect upon the data together. "what's way more important here is the culture of what organization you are working in," [...] "in the ideal world. You do not have an ass of a manager. You can just have an open conversation with him or fellow team members."

Personal Reflection. Both participants mention it might be more helpful as a personal tool: "on a personal level, I can really see this works. If I could see my own data in a personal system, I think that can really help as input for myself."

Tool for Evaluation. One participant mentioned that the tool would be ideal for evaluation after a project. If one can identify stressful periods, you can reflect upon that period with your team and improve future situations.

Aggregation of Data. Both participants said that the tool could be helpful if it aggregates the data into an average score for the entire team. "I guess it could be useful to get a rating of how the full team is doing."

Overall Evaluation. Both participants had positive opinions about the central screen visualization. The visualization within a video call was evaluated as useless, as it would only be a distraction during a meeting. Nevertheless, there are several areas where the tool could be more helpful. One could look at the potential of visualizing data on a more personal level or create a tool that supports managers and employees at the end of the project to reflect upon the stress levels during the project.

5 Effect of Perceived Stress on Measured Heart Rate Variability

Research is conducted to study a relationship between perceived stress and the measured heart rate variability. A generalized rule for predicting a user's perceived stress would mean more insightful data visualizations.

The heart rate variability (HRV) data objectively indicate some bodies' well-being [16]. Even though several research pieces concluded that one could indicate one's perceived stress with HRV measures, it is unknown whether there is a relationship between perceived stress and the measured heart rate variability in this sensor's case. At the start of the research, there is an expected relation between the HRV and perceived stress. When ones perceived stress increases, the HRV drops.

5.1 Method

Design. The study used a repeated-measures experimental design to investigate the relationship between perceived stress level and measured heart rate variability. The measurement ran for every participant for two weeks, thus ten workdays. Perceived stress levels were measured via a self-reported stress scale [17]. The questionnaire was accessible through an online-platform accessible through both desktop and mobile. Heart rate variability was measured through the sensor-equipped cushions. An opportunity sample was recruited (N = 16) from the Eindhoven University of Technology and Hang-zhou Bobo. The recruited participants were only required to do full-time work from their (home) office.

Materials. The study used a self-reported question stress scale (Bartenwerfer[17]). Participants rated how they perceived their current stress level on the scale. The questionnaire was accessible through an online platform available on both desktop and mobile. On submitting, the inputted measure (slider fully up, perceived stress = 1.0, slider fully down, perceived stress = 0.0 – linear scale for all positions in between) is sent to a secure database with a timestamp. The heart rate variability is collected automatically by the sensor-equipped cushion and sent to the same secure database with the corre-sponding timestamp of submitting.

Procedure. Every participant received a sensor-equipped cushion at the start of the project, connected to their preferred Wi-Fi network. Participants were advised to work according to their schedule, not influencing any results. After every working block (morning block (8:00–13:00, afternoon block (14:00–18:00), and evening block (19:00–23:00)1), the participants were asked to reflect upon that block of working (plus-minus 3–4 h of work) and indicate their perceived stress level during that working session.

During the research, all participants were monitored. In a custom-designed webpage, the count of every critical measure in the study was calculated daily. If a participant's cushion failed (most often empty battery), they would receive a message to check their cushion. If the participant worked in a particular block but did not submit their per-ceived stress, one received a reminder through their specified platform.

To create a dataset to analyze the relationship between the measured heart rate variability and the perceived stress, all the submitted survey data (N = 220) was pulled from the database, and the mean HRV data was calculated for all data points in a three-hour block before the submitted perceived stress. Obvious errors in the measurements are dropped (HRV error measurement, submission submitted in the morning, etc.). As a result, a total of 180 submissions and measured HRV levels are present in the dataset (N = 180).

During the research, all participants were monitored. In a custom-designed webpage, the count of every critical measure in the study was calculated daily. If a participant's cushion failed (most often empty battery), they would receive a message to check their cushion. If the participant worked in a particular block but did not submit their perceived stress, one received a reminder through their specified platform.

To create a dataset to analyze the relationship between the measured heart rate variability and the perceived stress, all the submitted survey data (N = 220) was pulled from the database, and the mean HRV data was calculated for all data points in a three-hour block before the submitted perceived stress. Obvious errors in the measurements are dropped (HRV error measurement, submission submitted in the morning, etc.). As a result, a total of 180 submissions and measured HRV levels are present in the dataset (N = 180).

5.2 Statistical Analysis

Linear regression was run to understand submitted perceived stress on measured heart rate variability. A scatterplot of perceived stress and heart rate variability was plotted to assess linearity. Visual inspection of the plots indicated a slight linear relationship between the variables. Residuals were independent, as assessed by a Durbin-Watson statistic of 1.589. There was heteroscedasticity evaluated by visual inspection of a plot of standardized residuals versus standardized predicted values. The data was square transformed to remove heteroscedasticity. After visual inspection, homoscedasticity and Residuals were normally distributed as assessed by visual inspection of a normal probability plot. One outlier was detected with a Casewise diagnostics test. It was decided not to remove the datapoint as it seemed like a genuine datapoint (Fig. 8).

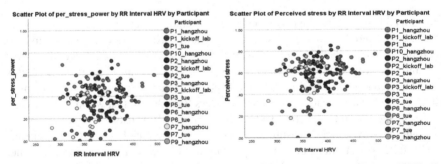

Fig. 8. *left* - Non-transformed perceived stress plotted against the measured mean HRV of a 3-h window. Heteroscedasticity is visually identified. *right* - (perceived stress)^2 plotted against the measured mean HRV of a 3-h window—slight linear relationship between variables present. Homoscedacity visually identified.

The measured HRV statistically significantly predicted the perceived stress, $F(1, 177) = 11.07$, $p < .002$, accounting for 5.89% of the variation in perceived stress with adjusted $R2 = 5,45\%$. An extra point on the scale of HRV leads to a 0.001020 increase in perceived stress. Predictions were made to determine perceived stress levels for people with their measured HRV (Fig. 9); please refer to Table 1 for results. The equation to predict the perceived stress with the measured HRV is:

$$\sqrt{(\text{perceived stress})} = -0.02302 + 0.001020 * \text{measured hrv} \qquad (1)$$

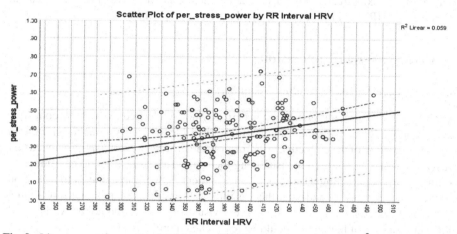

Fig. 9. Linear regression scatterplot. Measured HRV against (perceived stress)^2. 95% Confidence interval plotted, with upper and lower bound.

Table 1. Predictions of (perceived_stress)^2 - calculation of perceived stress - with confidence interval of perceived stress

HRV	(Perceived stress)^2	Perceived stress	Lower bound	Upper bound
350	0.33	0.58	0.55	0.60
375	0.36	0.60	0.58	0.62
400	0.39	0.62	0.60	0.64
425	0.41	0.64	0.61	0.67
450	0.44	0.66	0.62	0.70
475	0.46	0.68	0.63	0.72

5.3 Discussion

The study hypothesized that there is a relation between HRV and perceived stress. When the measured HRV increases, the perceived stress lowers. While the linear regression statistically predicted the perceived stress, the prediction equation contradicts the research's set experimental hypothesis as the relationship is inversed. These findings do not correspond with well-known facts about the HRV. If one HRV decreases, their perceived stress should decrease [16, 18–20]. There has not been any research that validates or explains such an outcome.

Therefore, there is concluded that there is a probable cause for the above result. The participant group is probably too small, and there might have been a confounding variable, resulting in anomalous results. In the future, the research can be rerun to investigate whether the small sample group (N = 16) is the problem. Otherwise, there can be concluded that measured HRV is too personal to find a generalized rule. Thus, it is advised to look at trends in the users' data to detect any negative or positive trend in the measured HRV and inform users based on the trend prediction.

6   Discussion and Conclusion

6.1   Collective Versus Individual Visualization

As already mentioned, it seems that it is currently not yet desired to show the collective ones' data (while anonymized, it might still be possible to identify somebody). Both in the user validation of the collective visualization and the interview, it was mentioned that trust and culture are essential in visualizing such data. Therefore, it might be a direction to further explore creating a more open environment between individuals to reflect on their collective stress. In addition, there is indicated in other research that researching hierarchy is essential when designing stress visualizations for the collective [1], and thus, implications of hierarchy should be researched more in-depth.

Additionally, the consequences of COVID-19 on collective visualizations are explored, but other directions can be explored beyond an online call or webpage. As social contact might be more scarce as more and more people are working at home, it might mean that collective visualizations should adapt and support in creating meaningful reflective moments on the collective stress.

6.2   Measured HRV Versus Real-Life Perceived Stress

As already indicated, a correlation was found between the perceived stress and the measured HRV. This correlation was inversed and not according to the hypothesis set at the start of the research.

As the measured HRV is one of the most valuable parts of the sensor, one could extend upon the research done in this project and see whether there are any other methods to give employees an indication of their fatigue levels. Firstly, as already indicated, one can look at the data trends. If data trends down, one can suggest that an employee might feel more fatigued. Secondly, one can extend the research already done. Several methods exist to adjust or create stress status by, for example, a first-person shooter game [21] or a memory card game [22]. Therefore, we can change participants' stress levels, forcing participants' HRV to go down. One could research whether data can be grouped by certain induced stress levels. If so, a generalized rule can be created.

Acknowledgment. We would like to thank all the participants of this study and Monroe Xue for her expert evaluation of the collective stress visualizations. This work was supported by the [Zhejiang Provincial Natural Science Foundation of China] under Grant [#LY20H090001].

References

1. Xue, M.: AffectiveViz: designing collective stress related visualization (2021)
2. Brennan, A., Chugh, J.S., Kline, T.: Traditional versus open office design: a longitudinal field study. Environ. Behav. **34**(3), 279–299 (2002). https://doi.org/10.1177/001391650203 4003001
3. Leder, S., Newsham, G.R., Veitch, J.A., Mancini, S., Charles, K.E.: Effects of office environment on employee satisfaction: a new analysis. Build. Res. Inf. **44**(1), 34–50 (2016). https://doi.org/10.1080/09613218.2014.1003176
4. Papagiannidis, S., Marikyan, D.: Smart offices: a productivity and well-being perspective. Int. J. Inf. Manag.**51**(October) 0–1 (2020). https://doi.org/10.1016/j.ijinfomgt.2019.10.012
5. Yu, B., Zhang, B., An, A., Xu, L., Xue, M., Hu, J.: An unobtrusive stress recognition system for the smart office. In: Proceedings of the Annual International Conference of the IEEE Engineering in Medicine and Biology Society, EMBS, pp. 1326–1329 (2019). https://doi.org/10.1109/EMBC.2019.8856597
6. Ali, S.M., Gupta, N., Nayak, G.K., Lenka, R.K.: Big data visualization: tools and challenges. In: Proceedings of the 2016 2nd International Conference on Contemporary Computing and Informatics, IC3I 2016, pp. 656–660 (2016). https://doi.org/10.1109/IC3I.2016.7918044
7. Snyder, J., et al.: MoodLight: exploring personal and social implications of ambient display of biosensor data. In: CSCW 2015 - Proceedings of the 2015 ACM International Conference on Computer-Supported Cooperative Work and Social Computing, pp. 143–153 (2015). https://doi.org/10.1145/2675133.2675191
8. Feijs, L., Langereis, G., van Boxtel, G.: Designing for heart rate and breathing movements. In: Proceedings of the 6th International Workshop on DeSForM 2010, pp. 57–67 (2010)
9. Ren, X., Yu, B., Lu, Y., Zhang, B., Hu, J., Brombacher, A.: LightSit: an unobtrusive health-promoting system for relaxation and fitness microbreaks at work. Sensors (Switzerland) **19**(9) (2019). https://doi.org/10.3390/s19092162
10. Li, I.: Designing personal informatics applications and tools that facilitate monitoring of behaviors. Uist (2009). http://www.ianli.org/publications/2009-ianli-uist-designing-personal-informatics.pdf
11. Xue, M., Liang, R.-H., Hu, J., Feijs, L.: ClockViz: designing public visualization for coping with collective stress in teamwork. In: Proceedings of the Conference on Design and Semantics of Form and Movement - Sense and Sensitivity, DeSForM 2017 (2017). https://doi.org/10.5772/intechopen.71220
12. Xue, M., Liang, R.H., Yu, B., Funk, M., Hu, J., Feijs, L.: Affective wall: designing collective stress-related physiological data visualization for reflection. IEEE Access **7**, 131289–131303 (2019). https://doi.org/10.1109/ACCESS.2019.2940866
13. Boland, B., de Smet, A., Palter, R., Sanghvi, A.: The pandemic has forced the adoption of new ways of working. Organizations must reimagine their work and the role of offices in creating safe, productive, and enjoyable jobs and lives for employees (2020)
14. Cohen, R.A.: Yerkes–Dodson Law. In: Encyclopedia of Clinical Neuropsychology, pp. 2737–2738. Springer, New York (2011). https://doi.org/10.1007/978-0-387-79948-3_1340
15. Braun, V., Clarke, V.: Using thematic analysis in psychology. Qual. Res. Psychol. **3**(2), 77–101 (2006). https://doi.org/10.1191/1478088706qp063oa

16. Campos, M.: Heart Rate Variability: A New Way to Track Well-Being - Harvard Health Blog - Harvard Health Publishing (2017). https://www.health.harvard.edu/blog/heart-rate-variability-new-way-track-well-2017112212789. Accessed 2 Jan 2021)

17. Bartenwerfer, H.: Einige praktische konsequenzen der aktivierungstheorie. Zeitschrift für experimentelle und angewandte Psychologie **16**, 195–222 (1969)

18. Harvard Medical School: How's Your Heart Rate And Why It Matters? Hardvard Health Publishing (2020). https://www.health.harvard.edu/heart-health/hows-your-heart-rate-and-why-it-matters. Accessed 16 May 2020

19. McDuff, D., Gontarek, S., Picard, R.: Remote measurement of cognitive stress via heart rate variability. In: 2014 36th Annual International Conference of the IEEE Engineering in Medicine and Biology Society, EMBC 2014, pp. 2957–2960, November 2014. https://doi.org/10.1109/EMBC.2014.6944243

20. Taelman, J., Vandeput, S., Spaepen, A., van Huffel, S.: Influence of mental stress on heart rate and heart rate variability. IFMBE Proc. **22**, 1366–1369 (2008). https://doi.org/10.1007/978-3-540-89208-3_324

21. Bouchard, S., Bernier, F., Boivin, É., Morin, B., Robillard, G.: Using biofeedback while immersed in a stressful videogame increases the effectiveness of stress management skills in soldiers. PLoS ONE **7**(4), e36169 (2012). https://doi.org/10.1371/journal.pone.0036169

22. Admon, R., et al.: Imbalanced neural responsivity to risk and reward indicates stress vulnerability in humans. Cereb. Cortex **23**(1), 28–35 (2013). https://doi.org/10.1093/cercor/bhr369

Smartphone Localization with Solar-Powered BLE Beacons in Warehouse

Kazuma Kano[1]([⊠])[iD], Takuto Yoshida[2], Nozomi Hayashida[2], Yusuke Asai[2],
Hitoshi Matsuyama[2], Shin Katayama[2], Kenta Urano[2], Takuro Yonezawa[2],
and Nobuo Kawaguchi[2]

[1] School of Engineering, Nagoya University,
Furo-cho, Chikusa-ku, Nagoya, Aichi, Japan
kazuma@ucl.nuee.nagoya-u.ac.jp
[2] Graduate School of Engineering, Nagoya University,
Furo-cho, Chikusa-ku, Nagoya, Aichi, Japan
{takuto,linda,asayu,hitoshi,shinsan}@ucl.nuee.nagoya-u.ac.jp,
{urano,takuro,kawaguti}@nagoya-u.jp

Abstract. Workloads in logistics warehouses have been increasing to meet growing demand, and a labor shortage has become a problem. Utilizing information of laborer locations leads to an increase in productivity. We propose an integrated positioning method using solar-powered Bluetooth Low Energy (BLE) beacons. They are easy to install and maintenance-free since they can work without power sources. However, their advertisement interval depends on illuminance and is unstable. Moreover, there are many obstructions in warehouses, such as shelves and products, which cause signal attenuation, interference, and packet losses. We apply particle filters, map matching, and speed prediction with a neural network model to improve robustness and accuracy. We installed 94 beacons in a logistics warehouse. We evaluated the accuracy and found that our method is more accurate than a baseline method.

Keywords: BLE · Indoor positioning · Logistics · Photovoltaics

1 Introduction

In recent years, workloads in logistics warehouses have been increasing due to growing demand for electronic commerce, and additionally, laborers there have been aging. Consequently, a labor shortage in warehouses has become a significant problem. Collaborative work with robots and further improved efficiency are required to solve this problem. Creating digital twins of warehouses is an effective means to implement them. It will enable robots and laborers to keep track of each other consistently, which helps prevent accidents and improve efficiency [4]. It will also allow to simulate workflow and review it quickly. Thus, we tackle estimation of laborer locations in logistics warehouses, essential components of

N. A. Streitz and S. Konomi (Eds.): HCII 2022, LNCS 13325, pp. 291–310, 2022.
https://doi.org/10.1007/978-3-031-05463-1_21

the digital twins. We believe the insights gained through this research can be helpful in other indoor environments such as factories and shopping centers.

Positioning with Global Navigation Satellite System (GNSS) is inaccurate in indoor warehouses. Although vision-based methods such as image recognition and Light Detection and Ranging (LiDAR) can work, they require installing many sensors and power supplies to cover the whole warehouse filled with shields such as shelves. On the other hand, Pedestrian Dead Reckoning (PDR) is a positioning method requiring no infrastructure; however, its errors accumulate over time. It needs to correct accumulated errors by combining other absolute positioning methods to continue positioning for a long duration. In addition, it is difficult for most conventional PDR methods to recognize the practical motions of various laborers in warehouses, such as squatting and climbing a ladder. Then, we focused on trilateration with Bluetooth Low Energy (BLE) beacons and PDR with neural network models.

BLE is superior in power consumption and cost to other wireless technologies such as Wi-Fi and Ultra Wide Band (UWB). We use solar-powered BLE beacons. They are easy to install and maintenance-free since they can work without power sources or batteries. However, their advertisement interval depends on illuminance. We examined the relation between illuminance and their advertisement interval and found it unstable. It is necessary to ensure adequate illuminance. It is also necessary to estimate subject trajectory considering time sequence because not all beacons advertise within a specific interval. Trilateration-based methods are easy to operate because they do not require constant maintenance of radio distribution maps, unlike fingerprinting. At the same time, it has a problem that is likely to be affected by signal attenuation. We also examined signal attenuation in warehouse environments.

From the results of these examinations, we discussed appropriate beacon positions and installed 94 beacons in the warehouse. We propose an integrated positioning method using solar-powered BLE beacons. Figure 1 is concept image of our method. We apply a particle-filter algorithm to improve robustness against reception uncertainty and signal noises. We integrate map-matching to consider the layout of shelves in warehouses. We also integrate speed prediction with a neural network model to simulate subject speed. We evaluated positioning accuracy with data collected in the warehouse and found our method can estimate position more accurately than a baseline method. In summary, our contribution consists of the following points:

- Examined the relation between illuminance and advertisement interval of solar-powered BLE beacons.
- Examined signal attenuation in a warehouse.
- Propose a new integrated indoor positioning method using solar-powered BLE beacons.
- Installed beacons in the warehouse, evaluated accuracy with collected data, and found our method is more accurate than a baseline method.

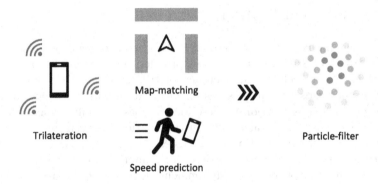

Fig. 1. Concept image of our method.

2   Related Work

Indoor localization with BLE has been well studied [1,6,13]. Most positioning methods with BLE can be categorized into fingerprinting or trilateration-based methods. Positioning by fingerprinting tends to be more accurate, but it requires radio distribution maps to estimate locations. It is extremely time-consuming to maintain radio distribution maps of the whole warehouse where the placement of products frequently changes. Zhao et al. estimated forklift locations in warehouses by fingerprinting or simple trilateration with BLE beacons according to the accuracy required in each warehouse [17]. However, they did not discuss improving the accuracy of trilateration much. Some previous research used particle-filter to improve the robustness of trilateration [16]. Urano et al. used it to estimate trajectories of visitors in an exhibition hall using BLE tags and tandem scanners [12]. Their approach may be effective also in warehouses because these environments share a common characteristic of attenuating. There is no research applying particle-filter to localization with solar-powered BLE beacons to our best knowledge.

PDR is a relative positioning method that is feasible with only smartphones. It is frequently combined with signal-based positioning methods to improve accuracy synergically [8,11]. Ban et al. integrated magnetic field and Wi-Fi fingerprinting and PDR [2]. Dinh et al. integrated fingerprinting with BLE beacons and PDR [3]. However, most conventional PDR methods stand on impractical premises, such as that subjects always walk forward with constant strides. It is difficult for them to track laborers' practical motions in warehouses. Then, we focused on the data-driven approaches to improve robustness against such complex motions and long-duration positioning. Herath et al. predicted subject position and direction with neural network models based on ResNet, LSTM, and TCN [5]. Kawaguchi et al. predicted subject speed with DualCNN-LSTM [7,14,15]. Modularized models can be incorporated into particle-filter.

3   Problem Identification

Advertisement interval of solar-powered BLE beacons depends on illuminance. Many obstructions such as shelves and products in warehouses cause signal attenuation, which declines the accuracy of trilateration. We conducted preliminary experiments to clarify issues on localization with solar-powered BLE beacons in warehouses. Section 4.1 describes the basic specifications of beacons and summarizes experimental results on the relation between illuminance and packet reception interval. Section 4.2 discusses appropriate positions of beacons to ensure adequate illuminance. Section 4.3 summarizes examination results of signal attenuation in warehouse environments and shows the arrangement of beacons in this paper.

3.1   Specification and Performance of Beacons

Figure 2 shows a solar-powered BLE beacon (PulsarGum TM-010 made by Fujitsu) we adopted. Its size is 72 × 19 × 3 [mm] and its weight is about 3 [g]. It conforms to Bluetooth 4.2 and iBeacon. Its transmission strength is fixed to 1 [mW] in this paper; on the other hand, its advertisement interval depends on illuminance.

Fig. 2. Solar-powered BLE beacon (PulsarGum TM-010 made by Fujitsu).

Fig. 3. Beacon set on the upper side of a shelf.

We scanned its advertisement packets for 1 [min] at each illuminance of 300, 400, 500, 550, 600, 650, 700, 750, 800, 900, and 1000 [lx] to examine the relation between illuminance and its advertisement interval. We conducted the scan in a darkroom using variable-brightness LED lighting to suppress the influence of ambient light. Table 1 shows the mode, median, and mean of packet reception interval and the nominal advertisement interval at each illuminance. The nominal advertisement interval at lower than 550 [lx] is not announced. Figure 4 indicates the relation between illuminance and packet reception interval. Intervals were found in about 0.5 [s] increments and were not stable. Most packets were received at about 0.5 [s] intervals with an average of 0.77–0.94 [s] intervals when illuminance was 500 [lx] or higher. Several packets were received at 2.0–4.5

[s] intervals in bad cases. Packet losses are unlikely to have caused most of the outliers because they shall occur equally. Intervals were widely distributed when illuminance was lower than 500 [lx]. From these results, we placed beacons where illuminance was 500 [lx] or higher as much as possible at installation.

Table 1. Mode, median, and mean of packet reception interval and nominal advertisement interval at each illuminance.

Illuminance [lx]	Mode [s]	Median [s]	Mean [s]	Nominal [s]
300	2.35	2.26	2.35	NaN
400	0.50	1.00	1.50	NaN
500	0.51	0.51	0.88	NaN
550	0.50	0.51	0.81	1.0
600	0.50	0.51	0.82	1.0
650	0.50	0.51	0.77	1.0
700	0.51	0.76	0.94	1.0
750	0.50	0.51	0.93	1.0
800	0.50	0.51	0.93	1.0
900	0.50	0.51	0.91	0.5
1000	0.50	0.51	0.82	0.5

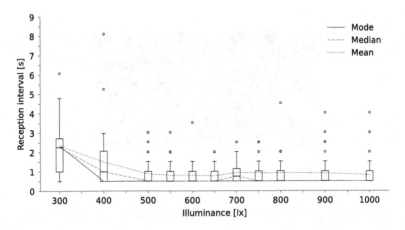

Fig. 4. Relation between illuminance and packet reception interval in 300–1000 [lx].

3.2 Installation of Beacons

Solar-powered BLE beacons do not need power sources and are easy to set with double-sided tapes. However, their positions have the following constraints since they generate their power from light.

– Close to lighting, with their solar panels directed at it.
– Hard for dust to accumulate.
– Unlikely to be covered by products.

The distance from lighting must be short, and their solar panels must face lighting direction to ensure adequate illuminance. Additionally, the location should be hard to accumulate dust and unlikely to be covered by frequently changing products to prevent light from being blocked. Considering these points, we set them on the upper side of shelves and pillars where height is about 3 [m], as shown in Fig. 3. We selected positions of beacons measuring illuminance every time, mostly 500–800 [lx].

3.3   Examination of Signal Attenuation

We iterated the following procedure in an area where the beacons had been installed to examine how signals attenuate in warehouse environments.

1. Set a smartphone for scanning packets at a position 0.8 [m] high in the middle of an aisle using a tripod, as shown in Fig. 5.
2. Scan packets for 30 [s].

We fixed the smartphone with a tripod to prevent the human body from shielding signals. The height was set to 0.8 [m] to simulate subjects wearing the smartphone on their waist. We iterated this procedure for 69 manually selected points shown in Fig. 6.

Fig. 5. Smartphone fixed with a tripod.

Now, we divided relative positions of the scanning points to a reference beacon into 9 groups listed in Fig. 2 according to their aisles seen from it and horizontal distances from it. We took statistics about the proportion of scanning points that received packets from reference beacons more than 30 times (i.e., the average reception interval is shorter than 1 [s]) for 24 beacons, also shown in Fig. 6. Packets were received at intervals of 1 [s] or shorter on most points where 6.5 [m] or nearer in the same aisle (A, B) or 3.5 [m] or nearer in the next aisle (D). On the other hand, packets were frequently lost in 2 aisles away (G, H, I), seemingly due to signal attenuation.

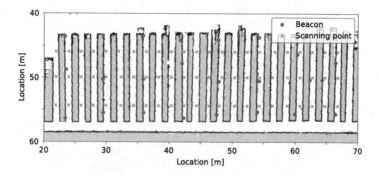

Fig. 6. Location of beacons and scanning points.

Table 2. Statistics about proportion of scanning points where the average reception interval is shorter than 1 [s] in grouped relative positions.

Group symbol	Aisle	Horizontal distance [m]	Proportion of points [%]
A	Same	0.5–1.5	91.7 (22/24)
B	Same	2.5–6.5	96.9 (31/32)
C	Same	6.5–11.0	50.0 (8/16)
D	Next	1.5–3.5	87.0 (40/46)
E	Next	3.5–7.0	51.6 (32/62)
F	Next	7.0–11.5	3.3 (1/30)
G	2 aisles away	3.5–5.0	21.4 (9/42)
H	2 aisles away	5.0–8.0	10.7 (6/56)
I	2 aisles away	8.0–12.0	0.0 (0/28)

The arrangement of beacons in areas expected to receive packets from 1 or more beacons at intervals of 1 [s] or shorter stably should satisfy the following requirements:

- Placed in every 3 or fewer aisles.
- Placed $6.5 \times 2 = 13$ [m] or less apart.

It is desirable to place beacons further denser because the information from at least 3 beacons is necessary to estimate position by trilateration. Figure 7 shows the arrangement of beacons in this paper. We installed 94 beacons. Since spaces between lighting and their brightness are uneven, spaces between beacons are also uneven.

We confirmed the following issues by preliminary experiments in Sects. 3.1 and 3.3. We propose a method to address these issues in Sect. 4.

- The advertisement interval of solar-powered BLE beacons is unstable.
- Signals attenuate, and packet losses frequently occur in warehouse environments.

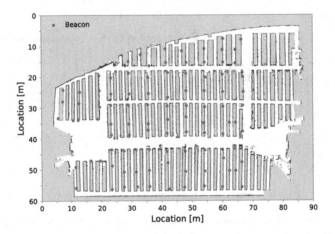

Fig. 7. Arrangement of beacons.

4   Methodology

Trilateration-based methods estimate subject locations by the relation between distance and Received Signal Strength Indicator (RSSI). However, this relation changes depending on the time and place due to signal interference and attenuation. Moreover, we can not always expect packets because the advertisement interval of solar-powered BLE beacons is unstable, and packet losses frequently occur. We propose a new indoor positioning method integrating particle-filter, map-matching, and speed prediction. Section 4.1 gives an overview of our method. Section 4.2 explains our implementation of particle-filter. Section 4.3 explains how to create an aisles network and incorporate map-matching. Section 4.4 introduces the neural network model for speed prediction and explains how to incorporate it.

4.1   Overview

We apply the particle-filter algorithm to improve robustness against reception uncertainty, signal attenuation, and interference. We incorporate map-matching into calculating particles' likelihoods to consider the layout of aisles and obstructions. We also incorporate speed prediction with a neural network model to simulate subject speed instead of a random walk. Figure 8 shows data flow in our method. This method needs the following inputs:

- List of maximum RSSI $(r^{0,t}, r^{1,t}, \ldots)$ received in a window $t - W \sim t$ [s].
- Coordinates of beacons.
- Aisles network.
- Acceleration and angular velocity in a window $t - W \sim t$ [s] resampled at 100 [Hz].

Particle-filter uses a list of RSSI and coordinates of beacons at likelihoods calculation. Aisles network is also necessary for likelihoods calculation after applying map-matching. Acceleration and angular velocity are used in speed prediction.

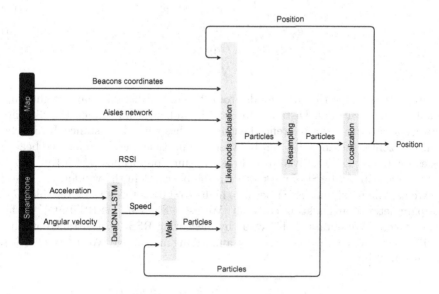

Fig. 8. Data flow in our method.

4.2 Particle-Filter

Particle-filter can improve robustness by stochastic and time-sequential estimation. Urano et al. used it to estimate trajectories of visitors in an exhibition hall using BLE tags and tandem scanners [12]. We extend their implementation. Subject location is estimated by following steps in our method.

1. Specify the initial location and direction of particles.
2. Move the particles.
3. Calculate the likelihood of each particle.
4. Resample the particles.
5. Estimate subject location according to likelihoods.
6. Repeat steps from 2 onward.

Step 1 specifies the initial location and direction of particles as subject location and direction. The number of particles N_p is 128 in this paper. The computational complexity of particle-filter follows order $O(N_p)$.

Step 2 moves the particles randomly. Equation 1, 2, and 3 give the location (x_p^t, y_p^t) [m] and direction θ_p^t [°] of a particle p after a random walk at time t [s]. S_{max} [m] is a parameter of maximum particle stride. α and β follow the uniform distribution and normal distribution, respectively. Particles are likely to move in around the last time direction.

$$x_p^t = x_p^{t-1} + \alpha \, S_{max} \, \cos\theta_p^{t-1} \tag{1}$$

$$y_p^t = y_p^{t-1} + \alpha \, S_{max} \, \sin\theta_p^{t-1} \tag{2}$$

$$\theta_p^t = (\theta_p^{t-1} + 20 \, \beta) \bmod 360 \tag{3}$$

$$\alpha \sim U(0,1)$$

$$\beta \sim N(0,1)$$

Step 3 calculates the likelihoods from 2 weights: distance gap weights and signal strength weights. Distance gap weight indicates how much the distance between a particle and a reference beacon matches with the distance–RSSI relation. Horizontal distance $d_{est}^{b,t}$ [m] between the particle p and a reference beacon b is estimated by Eq. 4 derived from Friis transmission formula. $r^{b,t}$ [dBm] represents the maximum RSSI of packets from the beacon b in the window $t - W \sim t$ [s]. We use the maximum RSSI because high-RSSI data tends to be reliable. C_{att} is a parameter of attenuation constant. We use -80 [dBm] as RSSI at 1 [m] far from beacons. We obtained this value by measuring RSSI at a distance of 1 [m] with a smartphone in a trouser pocket and taking an average. We set the vertical distance to 2 [m].

$$d_{est}^{b,t} = \begin{cases} \sqrt{(10^{-\frac{r^{b,t}+80}{10\,C_{att}}})^2 - 2^2} & \text{if } r^{b,t} \le -10 \log 2 \, C_{att} - 80 \\ 0 & \text{if } r^{b,t} > -10 \log 2 \, C_{att} - 80 \end{cases} \tag{4}$$

Equation 5 calculates the actual distance $d_{true}^{b,t}$ [m] between the particle p and the beacon b whose location is (x_b, y_b).

$$d_{true}^{b,t} = \sqrt{(x_b - x_p^t)^2 + (y_b - y_p^t)^2} \tag{5}$$

The distance gap weight $w_{gap}^{b,t}$ is given by a probability density function P. This function follows the normal distribution whose standard deviation is σ_{gap} [m]. The closer the estimated distance and the actual one are, the more this weight increases.

$$w_{gap}^{b,t} = P(d_{true}^{b,t} - d_{est}^{b,t}) \tag{6}$$

$$P \sim N(0, \sigma_{gap})$$

Signal strength weight indicates how large the RSSI of packets from a reference beacon is. Equation 7 gives the signal strength weight $w_{str}^{b,t}$. This weight is smaller when RSSI is less and takes 0 if it is -100 [dBm] or less.

$$w_{str}^{b,t} = \frac{100 + \max(r^{b,t}, -100)}{10} \tag{7}$$

The total weight $w_{total}^{b,t}$ is given by the product of these two weights if received any packets whose RSSI is more than -100 [dBm] from the beacon b in the window $t - W \sim t$ [s]. On the other hand, the weight $w_{total}^{b,t}$ is given by the function P if not received. The nearer the particle and the beacon, despite not receiving, the more this weight decreases. Parameter $C_{neg} \geq 0$ indicates how much to emphasize receiving no packet.

$$w_{total}^{b,t} = \begin{cases} w_{gap}^{b,t} \, w_{str}^{b,t} & \text{if received} \\ -C_{neg} \, P(d_{true}^{b,t}) & \text{if not received} \end{cases} \tag{8}$$

The likelihood l_p^t of the particle p is given by summing the total weights for all beacons.

$$l_p^t = \sum_b w_{total}^{b,t} \tag{9}$$

Step 4 resamples positive-likelihood particles by picking equidistant points on the Cumulative Distribution Function (CDF) of their likelihoods. The total numbers of particles before and after the resampling are the same. If there is no positive-likelihood particle (i.e., received no packet whose RSSI is over -100 [dBm] in the window $t - W \sim t$ [s]), reinitialize all particles randomly. We reinitialize them on aisles in a 30×30 [m] square centered on the subject position estimated last time.

Step 5 estimates subject location in either of the following 2 strategies.

1. The weighted mean location of the particles' likelihoods.
2. The location of the likeliest particle.

The subject location (x_s^t, y_s^t) is given by Eq. 10 and 11 in strategy 1.

$$x_s^t = \frac{\sum_p l_p^t \, x_p^t}{\sum_p l_p^t} \tag{10}$$

$$y_s^t = \frac{\sum_p l_p^t \, y_p^t}{\sum_p l_p^t} \tag{11}$$

On the other hand, it is given by Eq. 12 and 13 in strategy 2.

$$x_s^t = \{x_p^t \mid l_p^t = \max(l_0^t, l_1^t, \ldots)\} \tag{12}$$

$$y_s^t = \{y_p^t \mid l_p^t = \max(l_0^t, l_1^t, \ldots)\} \tag{13}$$

Step 6 updates time t [s] and repeat steps from 2 onward. The stride of the sliding window is 1 [s] (i.e., the estimation frequency is 1 [Hz]) in this paper.

4.3 Map-Matching

There are many shelves in warehouses. Distances between aisles are about 2 [m] in our environment. We apply the map-matching algorithm to consider the layout of shelves and obstructions. At first, we create an aisles network by the following steps.

1. Set nodes on a map.
2. Draw a line segment between every pairs of nodes. Link the nodes if the length of the segment is 6 [m] or shorter and there is no obstacle on the segment. Set the link's cost as the length of the segment.
3. Link nodes if the summation of the cost is 6 [m] or lower. Set the link's cost as the minimum summation of the cost.

Step 1 sets nodes on a map. Setting many nodes may improve precision but increases computational complexity. Step 2 links pairs of adjacent nodes with a distance of 6 [m] or shorter. We check whether there are any obstacles on the line segment between the nodes referring to pixel values on the map image. The link's cost is the direct distance between the nodes. Step 3 recursively searches pairs of nodes that can reach for 6 [m] or lower cost and links them. The link's cost is the minimum summation of the cost if the nodes can be connected by multiple paths. Then, we create a lookup table of the links in advance to reduce computational complexity at execution of the positioning. The maximum cost of links should be higher than the interval of nodes. We set the maximum cost of links to 6 [m]. Particles move more freely when the maximum cost is higher. Figure 9 shows nodes and links created in this paper.

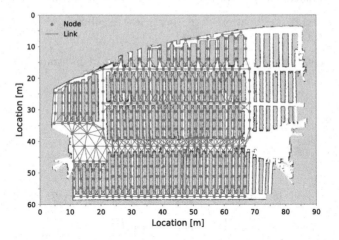

Fig. 9. Aisles network.

We introduce map matching weight to incorporate map-matching into likelihoods calculation at step 3 in particle-filter. The map matching weight indicates how much accessible the particle location is from the subject location estimated last time. Equation 14 gives the map matching weight w^t_{match} of the particle p at time t. f_n is a function to return a node nearest to a given coordinate. f_l is a function to return a list of nodes linked with a given node. This weight is halved if the nearest node of the particle and the nearest node of the last-estimated subject location are not linked. We do not cut off this weight even if the nearest nodes are not linked so that the particle is less likely to be stuck in the wrong location where the likelihood takes local maximum.

$$w^t_{match} = \begin{cases} 1 & \text{if } f_n(x^t_p, y^t_p) \text{ in } f_l(f_n(x^{t-1}_s, y^{t-1}_s)) \\ 0.5 & \text{if } f_n(x^t_p, y^t_p) \text{ not in } f_l(f_n(x^{t-1}_s, y^{t-1}_s)) \end{cases} \tag{14}$$

The likelihood l^t_p of the particle p after applying map-matching is given by multiplying the map matching weight w^t_{match}.

$$l^t_p = w^t_{match} \sum_b w^{b,t}_{total} \tag{15}$$

4.4 Speed Prediction

Most conventional PDR can be categorized into the strap-down algorithm and the step-and-heading approach. It is difficult for them to track the practical motions of various laborers for a long duration. Kawaguchi et al. predicted subject speed using the DualCNN-LSTM model [7,14,15]. We divert their model to our method. See their paper for model details. We predict subject speed with model trained in advance and use it instead of the random walk at step 2 in particle-filter. Equation 16 and 17 gives the location (x^t_p, y^t_p) [m] of the particle p at time t [s] after applying speed prediction. v^t [m/s] is predicted speed. γ follows the normal distribution whose standard deviation is σ_s [m].

$$x^t_p = x^{t-1}_p + (v^t + \gamma) \, \cos \theta^{t-1}_p \tag{16}$$
$$y^t_p = y^{t-1}_p + (v^t + \gamma) \, \sin \theta^{t-1}_p \tag{17}$$
$$\gamma \sim N(0, \sigma_s)$$

5 Evaluation

We performed a simple baseline and our method with log data collected in the warehouse and evaluated accuracy. Section 5.1 describes how we collected log data. Section 5.2 explains the metrics we used for evaluation. Section 5.3 introduces a baseline method and summarizes evaluation results of it. Section 5.4 shows optimized parameters and summarizes evaluation results of our method.

5.1 Data Collection

We collected logs including the following elements:

- RSSI.
- Sensor data of accelerometer and gyroscope.
- Ground truth of subject location.

We used smartphones (TONE e21 made by TONE, Android 10) to collect logs of RSSI and inertial sensor data. Although Micro Electro Mechanical Systems (MEMS) sensors in smartphones have errors, it is reasonable to use them because they can be integrated with other functions such as handy terminals in the future [10]. We logged data walking around the floor with smartphones in trousers pockets. Then, we plotted the ground truth of subject trajectory from videos recorded by another smartphone's camera. We used data of over 10 [min] and 800 [m] for evaluation.

5.2   Metrics

We used the following metrics to evaluate accuracy.

– Circular Error 95 (CE95)
– Circular Error 90 (CE90)
– Circular Error Probable (CEP)

CEP is widely accepted metrics in positioning research. CE95 and CE90 are sometimes used to evaluate error distribution in more detail [9]. These metrics are calculated by the CDF of error between estimated locations and ground truth. CE95, CE90, and CEP correspond to errors when the CDF takes 0.95, 0.9, and 0.5, respectively. For example, CEP indicates the radius of a circle centered on ground truth, including estimated subject positions with a probability of 50 [%] (i.e. the median error).

5.3   Result of Baseline Method

The baseline method estimates subject position as the the beacon's location that RSSI of packets from is highest in a window. The estimation frequency is 1 [Hz]. We interpolated estimated trajectories linearly while no packet with RSSI over -100 [dBm] was received in the window. Table 3 shows a optimized parameter in the baseline method. We compared accuracy changing window size W for 2, 3, 4, 5, and 6 [s]. It was highest when window size W is 2 [s]. Table 5 shows CE95, CE90, and CEP at that time. Figure 10 shows error CDF.

Table 3. Optimized parameter in baseline method.

Parameter	Candidates	Optimum
Window size [s] W	2, 3, 4, 5, 6	2

5.4   Result of Proposed Method

Then, we evaluated the accuracy of our method. The number of particles N_p is 128. The estimation frequency is 1 [Hz], the same as the baseline method. We interpolated estimated trajectories linearly while no packet with RSSI over -100 [dBm] was received in the window as well.

At first, we evaluated plain particle-filter to know the effect of map-matching and speed prediction. Table 4 shows parameters in our method with that the accuracy tended to be higher. We provide multiple optimums for some parameters because accuracy fluctuates due to stochastic estimation and changes depending on the combination of the parameters. We run positioning 5 times with the parameters $(C_{att}, \sigma_{gap}, S_{max}, C_{neg}, W) = (5, 3, 2, 0, 2)$ and the strategy estimating subject position as the weighted mean location of the particles' likelihoods. Table 5 shows the mean of CE95, CE90, and CEP at that time. Figure 10 shows the mean error CDF.

Next, we evaluated our methods after applying map-matching and speed prediction. We run positioning 5 times for each case as well. The maximum cost of links in map-matching is 6 [m]. Stride standard deviation S_{sd} is 0.4 [m]. Other parameters are the same as plain particle-filter. Table 5 shows the mean of CE95, CE90, and CEP at that time. We underlined the highest score for each metrics. Our methods had higher scores than the baseline method in all metrics. Map-matching improved CE95 and CEP. Speed prediction improved CE95 and CE90. Figure 10 shows the mean error CDF. Figure 11 shows sequential error of positioning with the baseline method and our method applied both map-matching and speed prediction. The shaded range, which occupies 18.4 [%] of total time, indicates that received no packet with RSSI over -100 [dBm]. Figure 12 shows the estimated trajectory of the same trial as Fig. 11 and ground truth. Figure 13 shows speed and movement length predicted by DualCNN-LSTM. The mean of predicted speed was 1.09 [m/s] while ground truth was 1.28 [m/s].

Table 4. Optimized parameters in proposed method.

Parameter	Candidates	Optimums
Attenuation constant C_{att}	2, 3, 4, 5, 6	5, 6
Distance gap standard deviation σ_{gap} [m]	1, 2, 3, 4, 5	3, 4
Maximum particle stride S_{max} [m]	1, 1.5, 2, 2.5, 3	1.5, 2
Negative weight coefficient C_{neg}	0, 0.02, 0.04, 0.06, 0.08, 0.1	0
Position estimation strategy	Weighted mean, likeliest particle	Weighted mean
Window size W [s]	2, 3, 4, 5, 6	2
Particle stride standard deviation σ_s [m]	0, 0.2, 0.4, 0.6, 0.8, 1	0.4

Table 5. CE95, CE90, and CEP of baseline method, plain particle-filter, map-matching-applied, speed-prediction-applied, and both-applied.

Method	CE95 [m]	CE90 [m]	CEP [m]
Baseline	7.52	6.24	3.07
Plain	6.71	5.57	2.80
Map-matching-applied	6.68	5.71	<u>2.71</u>
Speed-prediction-applied	<u>6.62</u>	<u>5.46</u>	2.81
Both-applied	6.65	5.59	2.79

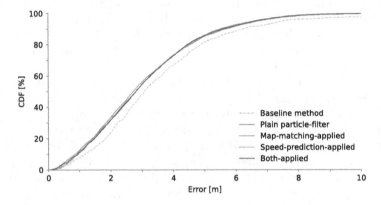

Fig. 10. Error CDF of baseline method and mean error CDF of plain particle-filter, map-matching-applied, speed-prediction-applied, and both-applied.

6 Discussion

We discuss optimized parameters in Sect. 6.1, compare the baseline method and our method in Sect. 6.2, and discuss effect of applying map-matching and speed prediction to particle-filter in Sect. 6.3 based on the result of Chap. 5. We also discuss future perspectives.

6.1 Optimized Parameters

The attenuation constant is 2 in the ideal environment and over 2 in the attenuating environment. In this paper, the accuracy was higher when attenuation constant C_{att} was set to 5 or 6. This result confirms that logistics warehouses are attenuating environments. However, the actual attenuation constant should differ depending on whether the location is Line-of-Sight (LOS) or No-Line-of-Sight (NLOS). We can see the estimated locations concentrated in the same aisle as beacons from Fig. 12. It seems that the parameter attenuation constant C_{att} was too optimized for this method and larger than the actual. It is necessary to correct the distance–RSSI relation according to whether LOS or NLOS for further accuracy improvement.

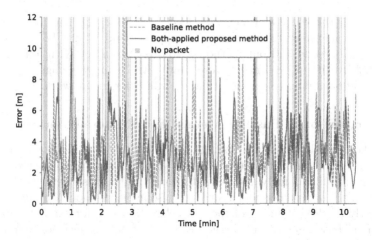

Fig. 11. Sequential errors of baseline method and proposed method applied both map-matching and speed prediction.

The accuracy was highest when negative weight coefficient C_{neg} was 0. Accordingly, we can see that the accuracy improves by not caring about receiving no packet from a beacon even if it is near from estimated subject location. It is natural considering that the advertisement interval is unstable and packets are often lost due to signal attenuation.

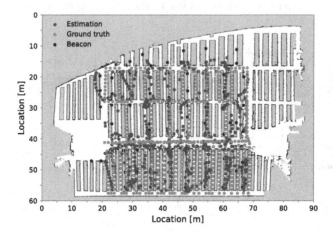

Fig. 12. Trajectory estimated with proposed method applied both map-matching and speed prediction and ground truth.

The baseline and our methods use maximum RSSI in a window to estimate subject position. They can refer to only recent packets when the window is short. At the same time, the shorter the window size is the more likely that no packet is received in the window, which may lead to accuracy decline. In this paper, the positioning accuracy was highest when the window size W was shortest in both the baseline and our methods. However, accuracy with long windows might improve if subjects move more slowly. We plan to change window size dynamically according to predicted subject speed for future work.

6.2 Comparison of Baseline Method and Proposed Method

Our methods had higher scores than the baseline method in all metrics. As shown in Fig. 11, error in our method tended not to fluctuate sharply compared with the baseline method, seemingly due to its stochastic and time-sequential estimation. However, there were some sudden increases also in our method. We can find them particularly at the beginning of the no-packet duration, for example, around 1 and 7 [min]. It seems that our method could not track subject position at those times because they had no information except RSSI of old packets. Weighting RSSI information by how recent it is might prevent getting stuck in the wrong location. We also plan to predict not only speed but also direction and integrate them with particle-filter to reinforce information.

6.3 Effect of Map-Matching and Speed Prediction

Map-matching improved CE95 and CEP. We conclude that map-matching can prevent obvious outliers and faithfully track subject trajectories on a local scale. On the other hand, CE90 declined after applying map-matching, probably because it interfered with returning to the correct position on the contrary.

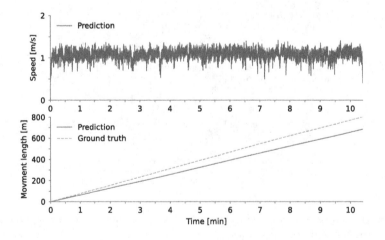

Fig. 13. Speed and movement length predicted with DualCNN-LSTM model.

Speed prediction improved CE95 and CE90; however, CEP declined slightly instead. This experiment was not advantageous for speed prediction because subjects walked consistently. We think about testing our method with data including stays at specific points to simulate laborers' picking.

Accuracy of positioning with our method after applying both map-matching and speed prediction was approximately middle of map-matching-applied and speed-prediction-applied.

7 Conclusion

In this paper, we examined the relation between illuminance and advertisement interval of solar-powered BLE beacons and found it unstable. We discussed appropriate positions of beacons to ensure adequate illuminance. We also examined signal attenuation in warehouse environments and saw packet losses frequently occur beyond shelves. Then, we proposed a new indoor positioning method integrating particle-filter, map-matching, and speed prediction with DualCNN-LSTM. We evaluated accuracy with data collected in the warehouse and found our method had higher scores in all 3 metrics than a baseline method. We also defined some remaining issues and discussed future perspectives.

Acknowledgement. This work is partially supported by JST CREST, NICT, and TRUSCO Nakayama Corporation.

References

1. Ayyalasomayajula, R., Vasisht, D., Bharadia, D.: BLoc: CSI-based accurate localization for BLE tags. In: Proceedings of the 14th International Conference on Emerging Networking EXperiments and Technologies, CoNEXT 2018, pp. 126–138. Association for Computing Machinery, New York (2018). https://doi.org/10.1145/3281411.3281428

2. Ban, R., Kaji, K., Hiroi, K., Kawaguchi, N.: Indoor positioning method integrating pedestrian dead reckoning with magnetic field and WiFi fingerprints. In: 2015 Eighth International Conference on Mobile Computing and Ubiquitous Networking (ICMU), pp. 167–172, January 2015. https://doi.org/10.1109/ICMU.2015.7061061

3. Dinh, T.M.T., Duong, N.S., Sandrasegaran, K.: Smartphone-based indoor positioning using BLE iBeacon and reliable lightweight fingerprint map. IEEE Sens. J. **20**(17), 10283–10294 (2020). https://doi.org/10.1109/JSEN.2020.2989411

4. Halawa, F., Dauod, H., Lee, I.G., Li, Y., Yoon, S.W., Chung, S.H.: Introduction of a real time location system to enhance the warehouse safety and operational efficiency. Int. J. Prod. Econ. **224**, 107541 (2020). https://doi.org/10.1016/j.ijpe.2019.107541. https://www.sciencedirect.com/science/article/pii/S0925527319303676

5. Herath, S., Yan, H., Furukawa, Y.: RoNIN: robust neural inertial navigation in the wild: benchmark, evaluations, amp; new methods. In: 2020 IEEE International Conference on Robotics and Automation (ICRA), pp. 3146–3152, May 2020. https://doi.org/10.1109/ICRA40945.2020.9196860

6. Ji, M., Kim, J., Jeon, J., Cho, Y.: Analysis of positioning accuracy corresponding to the number of BLE beacons in indoor positioning system. In: 2015 17th International Conference on Advanced Communication Technology (ICACT), pp. 92–95, July 2015. https://doi.org/10.1109/ICACT.2015.7224764

7. Kawaguchi, N., Nozaki, J., Yoshida, T., Hiroi, K., Yonezawa, T., Kaji, K.: End-to-end walking speed estimation method for smartphone PDR using DualCNN-LSTM. In: IPIN (Short Papers/Work-in-Progress Papers), pp. 463–470 (2019)
8. Liu, J., Chen, R., Pei, L., Guinness, R., Kuusniemi, H.: A hybrid smartphone indoor positioning solution for mobile LBS. Sensors **12**(12), 17208–17233 (2012). https://doi.org/10.3390/s121217208. https://www.mdpi.com/1424-8220/12/12/17208
9. Moayeri, N., Li, C., Shi, L.: PerfLoc (part 2): performance evaluation of the smartphone indoor localization apps. In: 2018 International Conference on Indoor Positioning and Indoor Navigation (IPIN), pp. 1–8, September 2018. https://doi.org/10.1109/IPIN.2018.8533860
10. Octaviani, P., Ce, W.: Inventory placement mapping using bluetooth low energy beacon technology for warehouses. In: 2020 International Conference on Information Management and Technology (ICIMTech), pp. 354–359, August 2020. https://doi.org/10.1109/ICIMTech50083.2020.9211206
11. Röbesaat, J., Zhang, P., Abdelaal, M., Theel, O.: An improved BLE indoor localization with kalman-based fusion: an experimental study. Sensors **17**(5) (2017). https://doi.org/10.3390/s17050951, https://www.mdpi.com/1424-8220/17/5/951
12. Urano, K., Kaji, K., Hiroi, K., Kawaguchi, N.: A location estimation method using mobile BLE tags with tandem scanners. In: Proceedings of the 2017 ACM International Joint Conference on Pervasive and Ubiquitous Computing and Proceedings of the 2017 ACM International Symposium on Wearable Computers, UbiComp 2017, pp. 577–586. Association for Computing Machinery, New York (2017). https://doi.org/10.1145/3123024.3124405
13. Xiao, C., Yang, D., Chen, Z., Tan, G.: 3-D BLE indoor localization based on denoising autoencoder. IEEE Access **5**, 12751–12760 (2017). https://doi.org/10.1109/ACCESS.2017.2720164
14. Yoshida, T., et al.: Sampling rate dependency in pedestrian walking speed estimation using DualCNN-LSTM. In: Adjunct Proceedings of the 2019 ACM International Joint Conference on Pervasive and Ubiquitous Computing and Proceedings of the 2019 ACM International Symposium on Wearable Computers, UbiComp/ISWC 2019 Adjunct, pp. 862–868. Association for Computing Machinery, New York (2019). https://doi.org/10.1145/3341162.3343765
15. Yoshida, T., Nozaki, J., Urano, K., Hiroi, K., Yonezawa, T., Kawaguchi, N.: Gait dependency of smartphone walking speed estimation using deep learning (poster). In: Proceedings of the 17th Annual International Conference on Mobile Systems, Applications, and Services, MobiSys 2019, pp. 641–642. Association for Computing Machinery, New York (2019). https://doi.org/10.1145/3307334.3328667
16. Zafari, F., Papapanagiotou, I.: Enhancing iBeacon based micro-location with particle filtering. In: 2015 IEEE Global Communications Conference (GLOBECOM), pp. 1–7, December 2015. https://doi.org/10.1109/GLOCOM.2015.7417504
17. Zhao, Z., Fang, J., Huang, G.Q., Zhang, M.: iBeacon enabled indoor positioning for warehouse management. In: 2016 4th International Symposium on Computational and Business Intelligence (ISCBI), pp. 21–26, September 2016. https://doi.org/10.1109/ISCBI.2016.7743254

Emotional Design Strategy of Smart Furniture for Small Households Based on User Experience

Jinglong Li and Han Han[✉]

Shenzhen University, Shenzhen, China
han.han@szu.edu.cn

Abstract. With the rapid development of artificial intelligence (AI) and Internet of Things (IoT) technologies, the designs for small household smart furniture are appearing as an emerging need, but most of which are focusing on the mechanical and functional issues while less attention is paid to the emotional experiences of users. The purpose of this paper is to explore the emotional design strategies of smart furniture in small-sized residential spaces in order to improve the practical value of the design and enhance the user experience of smart furniture for small household. In this paper, qualitative research is the main research strategy, and literature review, field research method, and case study method are used to review and analyze the small household smart furniture, and three types of small household smart furniture corresponding to the theoretical hierarchical framework of emotional design are derived, and according to the above theoretical hierarchical framework of emotional design, corresponding design strategies are given to the three levels of emotional design of small residential smart furniture.

Keywords: Small households · Smart furniture · Emotional design · User experience

1 Introduction

1.1 Research Background

In recent years, due to the rising intensity of the urban housing resources in big cities, small-sized residential space has become a common choice for people with economic consideration. With the rapid development of artificial intelligence (AI) and Internet of Things (IoT) technologies, the designs for small-sized household smart furniture are appearing as an emerging need, but most of which are focusing on the mechanical and functional issues while less attention is paid to the emotional experiences of users [1, 2]. This calls out an urgent need in exploring the possible emotional design strategies for the smart furniture in small-sized residential spaces, so as to enhance the practical value of the design and endure pleasant residential living experience.

1.2   Literature Review

Smart Furniture. Smart furniture refers to the integration of modern intelligent technology (mechanical intelligence, electronic intelligence, IoT intelligence and other technologies) into the design of furniture products based on conventional furniture, so that furniture products have automatic and intelligent characteristics [3, 4]. With the development of smart furniture, furniture in the home space has become more than just as furniture itself, more like a part of the smart home products. Furniture as an important part of the home environment, the traditional business manufacturing model and product features have gradually failed to meet the needs of the times, the development of smart furniture has become an inevitable trend [5]. Strategy Analytics data indicates that the number of connected devices worldwide reached 22 billion by the end of 2018, with 38.6 billion devices expected to be connected by 2025 and 50 billion by 2030 (see Fig. 1). The enterprise IoT accounts for the largest share of these devices, and the smart home is the fastest growing segment. This shows that smart furniture can make people's home life more convenient and comfortable in modern life and has become the main development trend of the furniture product industry in the future.

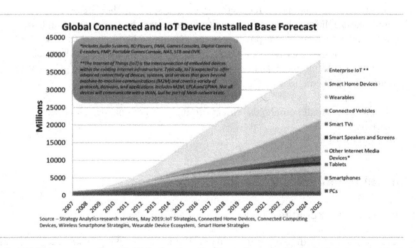

Fig. 1. Global connected and IoT device installed base forecast (Source: Strategy Analytics)

Small-Sized Residential Space. In recent years, small-sized residential spaces have become more and more popular among the public, which is closely related to various factors such as accelerated urbanization worldwide, shortage of land resources, high housing prices and changing lifestyles [6]. At present, there is no clear and standardized concept and definition of small-sized residential space, and different countries, regions and cities have not formed a unified standard in defining small-sized residential space due to the influence of historical, economic and cultural factors [7]. Generally speaking, small-sized residential space in most areas are houses with small space, compact layout, perfect facilities and complete functions, which can meet various living needs of the residents at the same time, usually houses of 40 to 70 square meters, i.e. one- or two-room houses. With the economic development and urbanization construction, a great number of small-sized residential spaces appear in the market to meet the housing needs of the urban population. Social research data shows that the population living in small-sized residential space is mainly urban youth, concentrated in the middle-income group, most of them have received good education, such people have limited economic ability for the time being, and mainly use small-sized residential space as housing in the transitional stage, and small-sized residential space can meet the basic functional needs. In addition, the complete supporting facilities and convenient transportation are very suitable for the rhythm of young people's life. At the same time, they have different needs and thoughts about the design and functional requirements of living space [8].

Emotional Design and User Experience. In his book "Emotional Design", American psychologist Donald Norman explores the relationship between human emotions and product design, and analyzes how to integrate human emotions into design. Donald Norman's theory of emotional design includes visceral level, behavioral level, and reflective level. Similarly, the source of user experience is also divided into these three levels [9]. Visceral level refers to the physical properties of the product, including product shape, material, structure, color, etc. on the five senses of vision, hearing, smell, taste and touch to bring the initial physiological feelings. The information people receive at this level does not need to be processed consciously, and the user experience is generated entirely by subconscious instincts [10]. Behavioral level, as the name implies, is to design the operation mode and usage context of the product according to the user's behavioral habits. Emotional design of products from the behavioral level focuses on the user's ability to quickly and easily master skills and techniques, and to obtain a pleasant experience or even a sense of accomplishment in the process of operation. This level where people's user experience arises from the user's interaction behavior when using the product [11]. The reflective level is a deeper emotion that arises within the consumer as a result of the first two levels and is a complex emotion that intertwines the product with the consumer's personal awareness and understanding, personal experience, and cultural background. In the product emotional design, the reflective level can be reflected in the symbolic meaning of the product shape, which can be the product brand effect, or the local characteristics and cultural meaning contained in the product. The reflective level of experience, i.e. experiential experience, is a psychological activity that occurs after the user compares it with previous experiences and will still have an impact on the user subsequently [12].

Regarding user experience, it focuses on the effect of practical application, that is, whether the product is good or not, and whether it is convenient to use is the criterion to measure the user experience of the product. The international standard (ISO 9241-210) defines its concept: user experience is a purely subjective feeling established by the user when using the product. Based on the current research, people consider user experience more at the level of digital interaction, while the interaction between furniture and people is multi-dimensional, especially with the intelligence of furniture, its user experience also needs our attention, in the small space, the relationship between furniture and people is closer, its user experience is more urgent to be studied [13].

2 Research Objectives

The purpose of this paper is to explore the emotional design strategies of smart furniture in small-sized residential spaces in order to improve the practical value of the design and enhance the user experience of smart furniture in small-sized residential spaces.

3 Research Methods

To achieve this research objective, this study uses qualitative research as the main research strategy and conducts case study with both theoretical and empirical support. Theoretically, the literature on the smart home industry and urban small household furniture design provides the research dimensions in case sampling and analysis. On the basis of theoretical research, the author divides small-sized residential space smart furniture into three basic categories: mechanical intelligent furniture, electronic intelligent furniture, and AIoT intelligent furniture, depending on the type of technology of smart furniture and its human-computer relationship.

4 Small Household Smart Furniture Analysis

4.1 Mechanical Intelligent Furniture

The first type of furniture is mechanical intelligent furniture, which is based on the technology of mechanical manufacturing and control. This type of furniture implants designed mechanical devices into the furniture body, and the user manually controls the furniture to make the mechanical devices move in a certain way (moving, folding, rotating, etc.) to achieve specific functions of mechanical intelligent furniture, such as multifunctional closet (see Fig. 2) by controlling the rotation of mechanical devices, so that ordinary closet has the function of a bed and a desk, while retaining the original storage function of the closet; Folding sofa (see Fig. 3) through the control of mechanical devices folding and moving, so that ordinary sofa can be used as a bed, but also has the function of storage. Through the analysis of these two common mechanical intelligent furnitures, we can easily find that this type of furniture is mainly the use of mechanical devices cleverly designed to change the shape of ordinary furniture, or the integration of a variety of furniture functions to a mechanical intelligent furniture, so as to achieve the role of space saving, more to meet the use of small homes.

This type of furniture, like regular furniture, has a shape and mechanism that is in direct contact with people, and the furniture itself establishes a direct relationship with people, and the user experience is generated entirely by subconscious instincts when using the furniture directly. and the human-machine relationship constructed by the direct contact between the human body and the tangible interface of the product structure. In line with the visceral level of emotional design theory, the design strategy of this type of smart furniture should therefore focus on whether the furniture itself can bring a good experience to the user, including beautiful shape, comfortable material, achievable technology and reliable structure. For example, furniture with comfortable materials often brings a good user experience. However, with the development of society and the advancement of technology, it is difficult for mechanical intelligent furniture to meet the needs of users [14].

4.2 Electronic Intelligent Furniture

The second type (electronic furniture) refers to the products mainly relying on the technology of electronic hardware. On the basis of ordinary furniture and mechanical intelligent furniture, it implants mechatronic accessories or electronic accessories into the furniture. Users can realize the functions of smart furniture through electronic control (wired or wireless), such as remote control of the storage bed (see Fig. 4), which can be controlled by remote control of the storage and opening of the bed; Electronic nightstand (see Fig. 5), the user through a simple touch action to achieve automatic opening or closing of the nightstand drawers, as well as to achieve electronic intelligent furniture additional functions such as fingerprint unlocking, sensor night light, wireless charging, Bluetooth speakers, automatic disinfection, etc. Through the analysis of these two common electronic intelligent furnitures, we can easily find that this type of furniture is mainly used to indirectly control the use of furniture using electronic control technology, while incorporating many electronic products, so that the furniture is more powerful, in the smaller space, compact layout of small-sized residential space to make furniture function more convenient and efficient.

Fig. 2. Multifunctional closet

Fig. 3. Folding sofa

With the popularity of electronic products, electronic intelligent furniture is also becoming more and more popular, touch panel control of furniture simplifies the complexity of the operation, people establish contact with the furniture through the touch panel, the user experience to a large extent with the touch panel has a great relationship [15]. In this case, the human-machine interaction is strongly supported by the electronic panels/controller. This type of furniture is associated with effectiveness and pleasure of use, and it conforms to the behavioral hierarchy of emotional design theory. Therefore this type of smart furniture design strategy should focus on the functionality, ease of understanding, usability and physical feel of the control interface, including safety of use, ease of operation, and reasonable functional design. For example, a reasonable touch panel design often gives a good user experience.

Fig. 4. Storage bed

Fig. 5. Electronic nightstand

4.3 AIoT Intelligent Furniture

The third type (AIoT furniture) is currently the most integrative furniture, which refers to the products mainly relying on AI and IoT technologies. It incorporates advanced intelligent systems or intelligent components (such as embedded systems, sensors, etc.) into the design of furniture. Users interact with the furniture through the mobile terminals (such as cell phones, tablets, etc.) and wireless networks by voice/touch actions to manipulate the multi-dimensional functions carried by the furniture. This not only provides the users smarter ways to manipulate the furniture's mechanical and electronic functions, but also extend the furniture's role as a device connecting with other devices relating to the user's lifestyle by functions like information acquisition, analysis and management, and even automatically provide optimal service for the user, etc. It is worth mentioning that the design of AIoT intelligent furniture incorporates the technology of many smart home products and becomes part of the smart home ecosystem, which develops in the new direction of networking, informatization, realizing the communication and feedback between furniture and furniture, furniture and environment, furniture and people. Therefore, smart home products can also be taken into account when analyzing such furniture. For example, Huawei's "1 + 8 + N" all-scene smart life strategy (see Fig. 6). Huawei builds eight core smart products (tablet, PC, wearable, smart screen, AI speaker, headset, AR/VR, and car) around its own phones outward. Meanwhile, with the support of Harmony OS, Huawei is empowering more pan-IoT terminal devices through the HUAWEI HiLink open platform to expand the IoT ecosystem outward. Through HUAWEI HiLink, Huawei can connect all the hardware and applications to achieve the ultimate experience of one-touch control of devices, voice interaction, and scene linkage. Smart furniture and devices equipped with the Harmony OS rely on Huawei's home router to achieve one-touch connectivity between them, allowing furniture to become part of the smart home ecosystem and achieve informatization and networking. The research fever for smart home at home and abroad has also started to climb rapidly, and the focus of research has begun to shift from smart home products to smart home environment system design and implementation [16]. From this, it is not difficult to find that the design of AIoT intelligent furniture is more dependent on the system with smart home environment, as opposed to a single product, consumers are now also more inclined to an intelligent product system. For example, the smart home furnishings created by the SuperHome (see Fig. 7), It is different from the traditional home function of a single silo experience, it achieves a multi-scene linkage of home products, injecting artificial intelligence, Internet of Things technology into sofas, beds, tables and chairs, and all furniture items to achieve whole-house furniture and home appliances interconnection, creating a new experience for consumers in the Internet home. The design of AIoT intelligent furniture rather than the need for a particular piece of furniture, we prefer an intelligent scene system to achieve the linkage of furniture and environment.

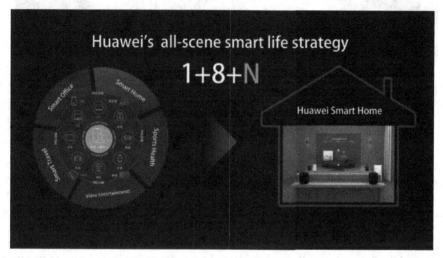

Fig. 6. Huawei's "1 + 8 + N" all-scene smart life strategy (Source: Huawei Developer Conference)

This type of furniture through big data and artificial intelligence technology long-term analysis of user information, more understanding of the user's emotions, furniture and people to establish contact with more diverse ways, and even active service users, can provide more added value and extended services for users, The human-computer relationship achieves a state of interconnection and interoperability that can meet the multi-level needs of people and conform to the user's level of reflection. The reflective level is inclusive of and beyond the first two levels, so AIoT intelligent furniture, in addition to considering the emotional design strategies of the first two types of furniture, should focus on the emotional ties established when furniture serves people, including the satisfaction of users' personalized services and cultural needs. For example, smart furniture self-checking fault contact after-sales, according to the user's body data automatically adjust, detect the user's health status, for the user to develop a scientific travel and diet program can provide users with a full range of life services and comfortable home experience of smart furniture can bring a good user experience.

Fig. 7. SuperHome's smart home furnishings (Source: SuperHome's official website)

5 Emotional Design Strategies for Smart Furniture in Small Households

Based on the above analysis of the technical conditions of the three basic small-sized residential space smart furniture and their human-computer interaction relationships, and by combining Donald Norman's emotional design theory, human emotional needs are incorporated into the user experience design. By correlating the user experience of furniture with the emotional needs of the product, it can be found that as the low-level emotional needs of consumers are satisfied, they will move to the high-level emotional level, and the design of small-sized residential space smart furniture is also in line with this theorem. Mechanical intelligent furniture and electronic intelligent furniture to meet the user visceral level and behavioral level, the design of AIoT intelligent furniture on the need to consider more reflective level, resulting in three small-sized residential space smart furniture corresponding to the theoretical framework of emotional design hierarchy (see Fig. 8).

According to the above theoretical hierarchical framework of emotional design, the corresponding design strategies are given to the three levels of emotional design of intelligent furniture for small households (see Fig. 9). Smart furniture design needs to consider the above requirements of emotional design strategy in addition to the need to fully consider the space and layout of small households, including the precise and appropriate allocation of residential area, compactness of each functional area, and reasonable and perfect spatial relationships. With the development of smart furniture, its form and function can often overturn the previous conventional furniture, under the scientific and reasonable space planning and design, while the ingenious combination with small-sized residential space design, as far as possible in a variety of small-sized residential space living form and limited space to do everything, functional, to enhance the user experience.

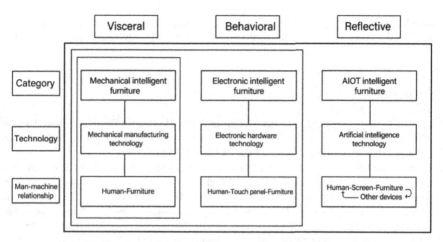

Fig. 8. Categorization structure of the intelligent furniture

Viscera	Beautiful shape (e.g: Simple lines, soft hues, etc.)
	Comfortable materials (e.g: Safe, odorless, lightweight, etc.)
	Reliable structure (e.g: Durable, functional, etc.)
	Achievable Technology (e.g: structural technology and Surface treatment etc.)
Behavioural	Safety of use (e.g: Mechanical Safety, Electrical safety, etc.)
	Easy operation (e.g: Simple interface, clear function buttons, etc.)
	Reasonable functional design (e.g: Avoid useless function stacking, etc)
Reflective	Personalized Service (e.g: Personalized usage solutions, proactive intelligence, etc.)
	Cultural Needs (e.g: Ethnic styles, cultural differences, etc.)

Fig. 9. Emotional design strategy

6 Research Significance

This paper classifies the intelligent furniture products, summarizes the ways and methods of furniture intelligence. The result of the analysis reveals an emotional design strategy considering the technical conditions of different types of small-sized household smart furniture and their human-machine interaction relationships. This strategy provides a structured guideline to explore more integrative design solutions so as to improve users' emotional experience facing multi-disciplinary technological development in the ever-changing future.

Acknowledgment. The author Jinlong Li and corresponding author Han Han would like to express Sincere appreciation to all the participants who contribute advise and data to this study.

References

1. Yu, J.: Research on the Emotional Design of Small Household Furniture. Central Plains College of Technology (2015). https://kns-cnki-net.ezproxy.lib.szu.edu.cn/KCMS/detail/detail.aspx?dbname=CMFD201601&filename=1016043364.nh
2. Gao, L.: Research on the Design Strategy of Small and Micro Living Space Under the Perspective of Innovation. Dalian University of Technology (2019). https://kns-cnki-net.ezproxy.lib.szu.edu.cn/KCMS/detail/detail.aspx?dbname=CMFD201601&filename=1016043364.nh
3. Zhang, X., Wu, W., Zhan, X.: Control technology and design method of intelligent furniture. Furniture **40**(01), 52–57 (2019). https://doi.org/10.16610/j.cnki.jiaju.2019.01.010
4. Duan, H.: Research on Intelligent Furniture. Nanjing Forestry University (2006). https://kns-cnki-net.ezproxy.lib.szu.edu.cn/KCMS/detail/detail.aspx?dbname=CDFD9908&filename=2006110118.nh
5. Bai, X.: Research on the Design of Modern Intelligent Furniture Products. Hebei University of Science and Technology (2015). https://kns-cnki-net.ezproxy.lib.szu.edu.cn/KCMS/detail/detail.aspx?dbname=CMFD201601&filename=1015313766.nh
6. Wang, Z.: Small Should be Beautiful. Tianjin University (2010). https://kns-cnki-net.ezproxy.lib.szu.edu.cn/KCMS/detail/detail.aspx?dbname=CDFD1214&filename=1012007322.nh
7. Li, P., Xu, Z., Wang, Y., Shen, R.: Exploring the consumer demand and space optimization design strategy of small house. Hunan Packag. **36**(05), 122–125 (2021). https://doi.org/10.19686/j.cnki.issn1671-4997.2021.05.034
8. Qu, J.: Research on Adaptive Design of Small House Type for Youth Groups in First-Tier Cities. Guangdong University of Technology (2020). https://doi.org/10.27029/d.cnki.ggdgu.2020.000195
9. Norman, D.A.: Emotional Design: Why We Love (or Hate) Everyday Things. Basic Civitas Books, New York (2004)
10. Wang, W.: Research on the Design of Intelligent Furniture Based on User Experience. Zhejiang University of Technology (2017). https://kns-cnki-net.ezproxy.lib.szu.edu.cn/KCMS/detail/detail.aspx?dbname=CMFD201801&filename=1017083488.nh
11. Chen, Y.: Intelligent Furniture Design and Research Based on User Experience. South China University of Technology (2016). https://kns-cnki-net.ezproxy.lib.szu.edu.cn/KCMS/detail/detail.aspx?dbname=CMFD201701&filename=1017806814.nh
12. Jiang, S.: Research on the design of home fitness application based on user experience. Art Des. **2**(10), 93–95 (2021). https://doi.org/10.16824/j.cnki.issn10082832.2021.10.022
13. Xu, W., Fei, W.: Elements and trends of intelligent furniture design. Design **34**(24), 114–116 (2021)
14. Xiong, X., Li, R., Bai, H.: Current situation and development trend of intelligent furniture industry in China. J. Forest. Eng. **6**(01), 21–28 (2021).https://doi.org/10.13360/j.issn.2096-1359.202003002
15. Pan, M.: Research on the Design of Children's Intelligent Furniture Based on Emotional Interaction. Qingdao University of Technology (2019). https://doi.org/10.27263/d.cnki.gqudc.2019.000215
16. Ruan, X., Cai, C.: Implementation of an example of intelligent lighting application based on ZigBee protocol. J. Chifeng College **27**(08), 38–40 (2011). https://doi.org/10.13398/j.cnki.issn1673-260x.2011.08.004

How People Get Peak Experience When They Using TV?

Kun Wang[✉], Bilan Huang, and Hanxu Bu

Samsung Electronics R&D Centre, Yuhuatai District, Nanjing, Jiangsu, China
{kun777.wang,bilan.huang,hanxu.bu}@samsung.com

Abstract. Peak experience, as an important theoretical tool, is also widely used in experience design. Current research on peak experiences directly applies this theoretical paradigm to emphasize the importance and design optimization of users' experience of critical moments, but rarely related research on the emotional experience of TV use of critical moments. Therefore, research on emotional factors for smart TV peak experiences is necessary.

This paper proposes a performance study based on typical TV user, summarizing the method for guiding design direction to obtain the corresponding peak experience. First, through case analysis and user research, combined with questionnaire surveys to obtain the peak experience description of using TV; Second, through the study, the triggering factors of the TV peak experience are summarized. Finally, based on in-depth interviews, the corresponding relationship between triggering factors and emotional description is obtained, forming a systematic TV peak experience optimization system and tool to help designers better apply in practice.

This study provides a method of obtaining a user experience described in connection with psychology, combined with the sharing concept, obtain the thinking method of contact emotion and design, for the experience design, especially the user-oriented product experience design has highlighted value, and expands the influence of peak-end rule in the design area.

Keywords: Peak experience · Experience design · TV

1 Background

In the era of experienced economic, the additional experience of products and services brought by users have deep affection for preference of using. The concept of peak experience took birth during the humanistic movement in the 1950s, Maslow (1964) was the first one who introduced the concept of peak experience [1]. And then, many researchers explored the definition about "What is Peak Experience?" Besides this, there are also some theory study for further applying, such as Peak-End Rule provided by Daniel Kahneman [5], MOT, etc. all this study enriched the value of this theory. The applying cases in different fields also be valuable, of course. However, there still have some space need to fulfill, the Peak Experience theory used into consumer electronics

© The Author(s), under exclusive license to Springer Nature Switzerland AG 2022
N. A. Streitz and S. Konomi (Eds.): HCII 2022, LNCS 13325, pp. 321–339, 2022.
https://doi.org/10.1007/978-3-031-05463-1_23

is not good enough, we find only 90 result about "Peak Experience & Smart TV", but the result about "Peak Experience (Theory)" is 1,462, "Smart TV/TV" is 78,419 from CNKI, the biggest database of paper research in China. We can see the gap between them.

In summary, although there are many researches on peak experience and peak-end rule, the academic is rarely studied in the TV experience design. Therefore, this article is intended to be based on the framework and methodology of the related theory based on peak experience. In the field of experience design, the evaluation system of the user's peak experience characteristics is summarized through user research. Research peak experience in the excitation state of product use scenarios, and verifies the value of peak experience evaluation system on experience design. Specifically, this research's goal is to learn about how TV design raise people's peak experience and how to evaluate and design for this purpose in the future? This paper wants to answer the following questions:

1   If the users have Peak Experience when they're using TV?
2   What factors will trigger the Peak Experience? In other words, what and why some TV activity or moments make users generate Peak Experience?
3   How to design for TV to trigger users' Peak Experience?

2   Related Work

Maslow initial research through 80 sample interviews, and through the interviews, summarize the impact of some unique moments in life, this is the theoretical basis of the peak experience. Maslow defined peak experiences as "the most joyous, happiest, most blissful moments" in life [1]. Laski (1962) defined transcendent ecstasy as "joyful, transitory, unexpected, rare, valued, and extraordinary to the point of often seeming as if derived from a preternatural source" [2]; In 1983, Gayle Privette demonstrated the intrinsic link between Peak Experience, Peak Performance, and Flow: A Comparative Analysis of Positive Human Experiences in its study "Peak Experience, Peak Performance, And Flow: A Comparative Analysis of Positive Human Experiences". Meet the character emotion needs is an important indicator of peak experience [3]. After that, the Heath Brothers always summarized the moment of the four peak experience in their work "Behavioral Design": Elevation moments; Insight moments; Pride moments; Connection moments. And combined with specific examples, the peak experience can be used to create four peak experience through behavioral design to create different peak experience [4]. The feelings of different peak moments in the peak experience are different. The research pages of various scholars pointed out to create a peak experience by creating emotional resonance in different moments.

The satisfaction of emotional demand based on peak experience is to achieve the satisfaction of the character's service and activities is a significant theoretical study of peak experience in the design area. The Peak-End Rule of the famous Nobel Prize winner, the psychologist Daniel Kahneman, expounds the peak point of the experience in the user's experience period (whether forward or negative) and the end point of the experience, determines the impression of users on the entire product, service experience [5]. This rule is based on psychological subconscious application, in a continuous activity, the most impressed is the feeling of peak and the end of the end, so this part of the feeling also determines the overall impression of the current activity. In others combined with the Moments of Truth theory of Zhan Karlson, former President of Nordic Airlines [6], it can be considered "peak" and "end" herein is actually the "MOT" in the user experience process. Designed for this critical moment can assist in the design team better implementation of service/product experience improvement.

At present, most study of the peak experience has focused on the methods of theoretical mining and user emotional description, and the practice of designing the service and behavior of the peak-end rule, mainly includes three types of research directions: Firstly, a peak experience is targeted in different fields and aspects, summarizing a certain moment as a peak moment, includes emotional and characteristics that bring satisfaction to users. For example, Irina Cojuharenco, Dmitry Ryvkin is proposed in the article "Peak-End Rule Versus Average Utility: How Utility Aggregation Affects Evaluations of Experiences", each instant utility during the experience is worth considering, because the peak moment has the nature of "inclusive", it represents the impact of the experience related to the assessment, including the residual impact of the previous event (for example, satisfying, adapting, fatigue) and related effects [7]. Man Yee Ho, Sylvia Xiaohua Chen, Edward Hoffman in their study "Unpacking Cultural Variations in Peak-Experiences: Cross-Cultural Comparisons of Early Childhood Recollection Between Hong Kong and Brazil" pointed out that memory of individual peak experience is often related to the characteristics of the cultural environment in which it is in its early days [8]. In addition, how to trigger and manufacture peak experience is a very important issue in this field. Such as Matthew G. McDonald, Stephen Wearing & Jess Ponting in their research "The Nature of Peak Experience in Wilderness" by exploring the high peak experience of triggering the experience in the wilderness environment is the performance of the environment and beauty in the wilderness, Beyond the inner lookout of the user, and produce different demands with artificial society, so you can produce a peak experience [9]. Finally, the application of Peak-End Rule is relatively broad, not only service design, including tourism, education, and market management, and achieve a certain effect. For example, the researcher of the Central South University of Business School, Wen-jie Bi, Ying-hui Sun, in its research papers "Reference price complies with the multi-product Dynamic Pricing Model" of Peak-End Rule, designed a dynamic pricing model for multi-products. And indicate that manufacturers can reduce consumers' reference prices by reducing the price of core products, thereby attracting more customers [10]. These different aspects have expanded the connotation of Peak-End Rule and also explore the likelihood that the law has value in a broader field.

Maslow (1964, 1970) identified B-values with 14 items, but the exact number is not important because ultimately all become one, or at least all are highly correlated.

Gayle Privette and Charles M. Bundrick (1987) based on the study of Maslow [3, 5, 14], 8 factors 42 items are proposed to make experience measurement to get six concepts, such as peak experience, peak performance, flow, etc. After the comparison research on these concepts, it found that the unique qualities of peak experience are significance, fulfillment, and spirituality.

3   Methodology

This article plan to invite typical users participate two round of interview, aims to get the specific connection among design factors, emotion characters and TV experience.

3.1   Participants

Participants of this survey are users using TV and have peak experience.

Firstly, a total of 45 participants answered the TV-Related Peak Experience online questionnaire, and 43 were valid.

Then, from the 43 valid participants, 15 representative participants were selected to conduct focus group interviews, thereby deeper to explore their peak experience.

3.2   Instruments

First round online questionnaire:
The questionnaire contains three aspects:

I.   Personal information, such as gender, age, education, etc.;
II. TV usage information, such as TV brands, TV function, etc.;
III. TV-related peak experience related questions, including an open question, which requires the participants to recall the peak experience at the moment of using TV. And a peak experience measurement scale, it consists of 42 statements [18], and each statement provides five options, from most disagree to most agree. Participants need to choose the most suitable one from the five options.

Second Round Focus Group Interview. Participants will be asked to have more discussions about related TV peak experiences under specific five themes which represent peak experience trigger direction, and describe the relationship between experience, trigger, and peak experience characteristics.

3.3   Analysis Method

Quantitative Data. Use the statistical tool to describe the quantitative data in the questionnaire and use cross-analysis to analyze the relationship between different data.

Qualitative Data. Use qualitative content analysis to analyze the participants' Comments (Hsieh & Shannon, 2005, pp.1279–1281) [17]. The purpose of the analysis is to summarize some Themes to extensively represent the peak experience of participants using TV.

Researchers read participants' comments to understand their overall experiences; Then read each answer one by one to highlight accurate words, phrases or ideas, these words, phrases or ideas capture the meaningful information units in the participants' experience. Then, these meaningful information is then coded, and the encoding is classified according to different topics, and the core topic is finally formed.

The research steps can refer to Fig. 1.

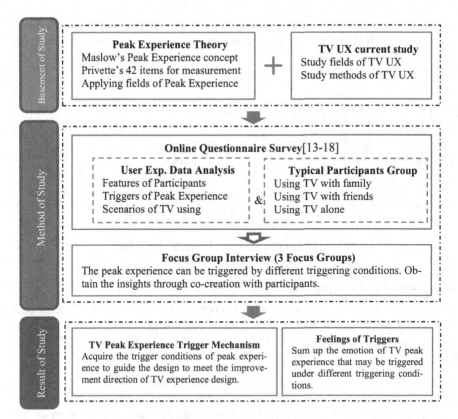

Fig. 1. Research flow

4 Results

This research received a total of 45 online questionnaires, of which 43 were valid.

The age and gender of the participants: mainly aged 20–45, the ratio of male to female is close to 1:1. See Fig. 2.

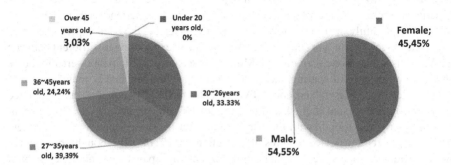

Fig. 2. Participants age and gender

TV usage frequency and brands: ¾ participants used TV frequently, and ¼ participants used TV less often. Most participants used more than one brand of smart TV (Fig. 3):

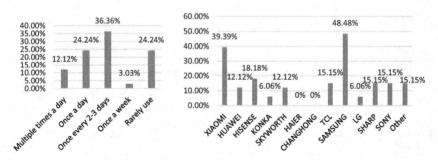

Fig. 3. Participants TV usage frequency and brands

4.1 Features of TV-Triggered Peak Experience

By analyzing questionnaire participants' descriptions of their own TV-triggered peak experiences, researchers summarized the features of TV-triggered peak experience mentioned by the participants from three topics: Devices, Human, Environment. The results refer to Table 1.

Devices. This topic describes the TV services, functions and hardware features involved in the TV-triggered peak experience scenario. Regarding TV services and functions, participants mainly mentioned three items: watching contents (67%), screen casting (35%), voice interaction and split screen (7%). Watching contents refers to watch TV shows, movies and other entertainment contents; Screen casting is mainly used for casting study contents and game on mobile devices to TV; Split screen is used for multiple game players to display their game screens respectively. Regarding hardware, the advantages that are quite different from those of mobile devices are repeatedly mentioned. For example, about 26% of participants mentioned that TV's large screen, high picture quality and excellent sound effects can give them Peak Experience.

Human. This topic describes the human behaviors involved in the TV-triggered peak experience scenario. 51% of participants had the peak experience when they were together with family or friends, and 37% of participants had the peak experience when they were alone. The human behaviors and related peak experience are different between the Multi-user and Alone scenarios. In Multi-user scenario, participants were more care about the experience of sharing and communicating with their family members rather than TV features. They talked about TV contents, made physical contacts, interacted with TV contents, casual chatted, and eaten food. TV is more regarded as a bridge connecting family and friends with the participants. But in Alone scenario, 68% of them more emphasized the device features of TV-self, and 21% of them thought that TV can strengthen their alone state. In other words, when participants were alone, their peak experience was mainly caused by the nature of the device itself, and this device nature in turn further enhanced their sense of alone.

Table 1. TV peak experience characteristics summary table

Topics	Features of peak experience	Rate of participants	Description of features
Device	Watch content (29)	67%	Use TV to watch contents such as TV show, movie
	Intelligent service (18)	42%	Intelligent functions such as voice interaction, screen casting
	Hardware advantage (11)	26%	Excellent characteristics of TV hardware
Human	With your family/friends (22)	51%	Watch and play on TV with family and friends in the same space
	Alone (16)	37%	Use TV alone
	Eating while watching TV (3)	7%	Eating some snacks and fruits while watching TV
	Chatting while watching TV (13)	30%	Chatting with other people while watching TV
	Interact with content (8)	19%	Interact with TV content, such as take screenshot, operating mobile phone according to TV show requirements
	Interact with other people (2)	5%	Body communication based on TV content
Environment	Party (18)	42%	Friends party, family party, parent-kid time
	Special occasions (12)	28%	Use TV at a special, meaningful or commemorative occasion, such as competition, festival
	Atmosphere matching TV (1)	2%	Change the environmental state such as lights, sound, to adapt TV contents
	Comfortable environment (2)	5%	Adjust the environment to be comfortable for the user, such as reclining on the sofa, cover with a blanket

Environment. This topic describes the environment's time and spatial features involved in the peak experience. Regarding time features, 2 types of moments were mentioned: party, special occasion. T he party refers to friend party, family party, and parent-child time, they felt that it was the companion of family and friends on these occasions that made the TV experience memorable and beautiful. The special occasion refers to competition and festival, when there w ere big live competitions such as World Cup, Olympics, or when it was in festival like China New Year, the TV will broadcast the related TV programs, and the participants would like to stay together to watch these programs, which is a good activity for the participants to celebration and stay together. Regarding spatial features, some of the participants would like to set up their home environment to watch TV in a more immersive and comfortable state. For example, changed the environmental state such as lights, sound to adapt TV contents, reclined on the sofa or covered with a blanket to make themselves comfortable.

4.2 Trigger Conditions of TV Peak Experience

After analyzing the characteristics of the TV peak experience, the researchers wanted to understand which factors contributed to the TV peak experience. The researchers classified and analyzed participants with similar or identical peak experience characteristics to obtain triggering conditions for a specific peak experience (Fig. 4).

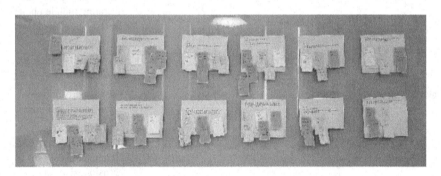

Fig. 4. Participants' peak experience research and workshop

Not all features of peak experience can be triggers. For example, Watch Content, which is a basic function of TV, doesn't lead to a peak experience by itself. But during the Watch Content activity, the peak experience can be triggered by other factors. Finally, the trigger conditions for the TV peak experience are as follows. See Table 2.

Intelligent Service (Hypernormal). Current smart TV has a variety of smart services to help users get better experience. After analyzing the feedback of 18 participants who mentioned intelligent service, researchers found that the peak experience brought by the screen casting function was as high as 83%, and the relevant users have a high evaluation of smart services in the peak experience, for example:

Table 2. TV peak experience trigger condition table

Topics	Features of peak experience	Trigger condition	Trigger description
Device	Intelligent service (18)	Hypernormal	It refers to the TV service that changes users' traditional habits and cognition
		Hypernormal	It refers to the TV service that can help users to achieve their expectation conveniently
	Hardware advantage (11)	Hypernormal	It refers to the characteristics of TV hardware that enhance the watching experience
Human	With your family/friends (22)	Interactive	It refers to having connection and interaction with loved ones and friends via TV
		Common	It refers to having common ground with others through TV services
	Eating while watching TV (3)/Chatting while watching TV (13)	Common Interactive	It refers to other TV related activities performed while using the TV
	Interact with content (8)/Interact with other people (2)	Interactive	It refers to interaction with TV content and other people
Environment	Party (18)	Common	It refers to the common activities that promoted by TV services and functions
	Special occasions (12)	Meaningful	It refers to the occasions that have special meaning to someone
	Atmosphere matching TV (1)/Comfortable environment (2)	Matching	It refers to the changes in TV services that cause the environment to response accordingly

Person 19: "My TV is the old model of TCL brand. After a system update, I suddenly found it support screen casting of Android OS device."

Person 24: "I used XIAOMI TV, it has voice search function, when the elderly and my kids learned to use voice search, it surprised me and unforgettable."

This new experience and service that "break the traditional cognition" will increase the possibility of peak experience; "Convenience" brought by specific functions for specific needs can also trigger the peak experience of users.

Therefore, breakthrough factors are the conditions that trigger user peak experiences, such as breaking the functionality and services of inertial cognition, and providing or strengthening convenience functions and services for specific needs.

Hardware Advantage (Hypernormal). Among the 11 participants who mentioned the TV hardware, 91% of them emphasized the characteristics of the TV inherent characteristics and the TV advantages compared with the mobile device. For example, the TV screen size is larger, the TV picture and sound quality is better.

Person 3: "I'm a HD video user. Every time I watch a good movie on my big TV, coupled with the speakers at home, the visual and auditory impact brings me satisfaction."

Person 26: "I am connecting the screen at home, then open Motion Sensing Game, the picture quality is clearer, the big screen does not have a sense of dizziness, and the game screen is better than the game console and computer screen."

The needs of users have a direct relationship with the hardware advantages of TV, and the difference between TV and mobile screen devices is also the main motivation for users to choose TV.

Therefore, peak experience can directly be triggered by the good hardware characteristics of TV. When watch TV, the application and enhancement of these advantages is also a change in normal state experience, which is also considered to be a triggering factor in the high peak experience. Such as: enhance the color effect of TV display, provide large-size TV screen, etc.

With Family/Friends (Common). In the home scenario, the TV is a kind of public device that plays an important role in intimate social intersection. 67% of participants thought that accompanying by family or friends while watching or playing TV can bring their peak experience, and this "together" scene will satisfy their rich emotional needs. For example,

Person 17: "The most memorable, the happiest event is that, every year, you can watch the Spring Festival Gala and chat with your family. The TV content may not be important, but it makes sense to communicate with family and friends."

Person 38: "I Worked out of town. Occasionally when I go home from vacation, I find that my family and I are chasing the same drama. I can communicate more with my elders through the content of the plot, and I can watch some comedy movies together during family dinners, and the atmosphere is more joyful."

In this intimate social relationship, the TV plays as a bridge to connect people from different regions and eras. Therefore, through TV, more common points can be built, which can be considered as the trigger of TV peak experience.

Eating/Chatting While Watching TV (Interactive). 16 participants said they would like to eat and chat while watching TV. 30% of participants expressed their hopes that can have more ways or opportunities to communicate with people when using TV, and remote communication through the network is also a major demand for users. There are three participants strongly indicated that they will not stop eating snacks when watching the content and thought that it was a good accompanying option:

Person 1: "My most memorable experience was when I got together with my besties. We ordered a lot of takeaways, such as milk tea, fried chicken. We watched the TV Show, we eat and chat, everyone was very happy."

Person 7: "We put fruit, potato chips, melon seeds on the table, lie on the sofa with a small blanket over us ... we are immersed in the movie's picture."

As the participants stated, watching TV content itself is not the factors that trigger their peak experience. TV was more of a background here, and the overall experience brought by the behavior of "eating" and "chatting" shapes the peak experience. The relaxing and interactive activities when alone or with family/friends is the key to making users feel satisfied and memorable. Therefore, providing a combination of content as a core allows users to inspire more common interest or interactive behavior, making the TV experience more abundant.

Interaction with Content/Others (Interactive). 10 participants mentioned that the interactive experience when using TV is very unforgettable, and this interactivity enhances the expectation of the TV scene. For example:

Person 21: "I watched the Spring Festival Gala with my family and followed the TV rhythm to interact with WeChat, such as sending a red envelope, snatching a red envelope ......"

Person 28: "When I watched Kong Fu Panda with my kids, I asked questions and let them find answers in the movie. This greatly increased their interest. After finding the answer, we were all excited, this interaction is interesting. And we continued discussion after movie, and played the role-playing games."

TV content is also not what motivates the peak experience, it is interactivity that drives the peak experience. However, unlike the previous scenario, the content here is specific, and all interactions that generate peak experience must rely on this content, thus creating a content-based interaction scene, which is attractive and arouse peak experience. Therefore, interactive channels or guidance can become a triggering factor in peak experience.

Party (Common). 18 participants mentioned the multi-person party, and they interested in the service for multi-person scenes, such as game:

Person 43: "I played Switch games with my family or friends on TV. Five or six per-sons, each of us allocates a role and displayed on the TV. This is a very happy experience."

It can be seen that providing multi-user services is an important trigger factor in the peak experience in multiplayer scenes.

Special Occasions (Meaningful). In the questionnaire, many users mentioned that the time point of TV usage is an important factor in the peak experience. For example, the Spring Festival, the Mid-Autumn Festival, the World Cup, Olympic Games, and it is easier to enable users to reach emotions. Therefore, TV services matching with emotion points greatly improves the user experience. The following user mentioned:

Person 17: "My happiest is that I can watch the Spring Festival Gala with the family when I have been in the New Year, and I can chat with them."

Person 21: "I watched the Spring Festival Gala with my family."

As the participants stated, during the festival of family or friend reunion such as the Chinese Spring Festival, TV can provide festive atmosphere to bring a peak experience to the user. Therefore, services to significant occasions can be seen as one of the triggered factors of the user's peak experience.

Sense of Ambience/Comfortable (Matching). 3 participants mentioned that the experience of using TV is not only from the TV itself, but the environmental conditions and atmosphere during TV use is an important composition for TV services to become a peak experience, for example:

Person 9: "When I watch a horror movie, I will close all the lights. I won't be disturbed, the environment is quiet and weird. I feel better than the experience of being disturbed in the cinema."

Therefore, when design for the peak experience of TV, it is not only necessary to pay attention to the service and function, but also need to consider the environmental conditions for the experience. Therefore, it can be considered that the matching of environment and TV is also a triggering factor to build user peak experience.

4.3 Design Method Based on Relationship Between Trigger and Feeling

In this part, researchers classified participants as 3 different groups according to 3 typical scenes of TV using, the results of the peak experience scale in their questionnaires were analyzed separately, and a set of general feeling statements about the peak experience of TV using was obtained from the results of each groups; After that, researches selected 15 participants to form 3 focus groups, and explored relationship between triggers and feelings of the peak experience. Finally, the researchers proposed design methods about how to trigger the peak experience of TV use based on the relationship.

General Feelings of Peak Experience: In terms of the user's peak experience of using TV, researchers extracted users' intuitive description of the peak feelings through questionnaire research or user interviews, which forms a preliminary understanding of this part of the user emotions. Then the researchers cross-contrast the emotional characteristics of the TV user using Privette's peak experience scale [18], thereby giving an intensity ranking of emotional description.

According to the results of the questionnaire, the researchers used a weighted ranking method to rank the different inner feelings statements on the basis of the answers to the scale, and selected the top 20% of the statements according to Pareto's law as the most common description of feelings in the TV peak experience. Researchers choose from the 43 valid questionnaires collected, and classify users according to the user's age, living conditions, the frequency and purpose of TV, etc. Get the following three typical user research feature groups.

Group 1: Using the TV with families; A total of 24 have been investigated participants, which mentioned the experience of using TV with their families.

Group 2: Using the TV with friends; A total of 9 have been investigated participants, which mentioned the experience of using TV with their friends.

Group 3: Using the TV alone; A total of 19 have been investigated participants, which mentioned the experience of using TV alone.

Then, researchers integrated the data of the three group participants, and after the weighting sorting, described the peak experience of 20% (9) before the psychological scale of each group according to Pareto Principle. The union of the between-group statements was chosen as the generalized TV peak experience perception description. See Table 3.

Table 3. Peak experience emotional description in the group

TV use peak experience emotional description[18]	Show out in group #		
	Group 1	Group 2	Group 3
1) I experience joy and fulfillment.	✓	✓	✓
2) I felt a need to continue until completions.	✓		✓
3) The event was fun.	✓	✓	✓
4) I was absorbed in what I was doing.	✓	✓	✓
5) The event involved action or behavior.	✓	✓	✓
6) The experience involved unity ... environment.	✓	✓	✓
7) Rules, motivation, and goals ... situation.			✓
8) The event was perceptual, rather than behavioral.			✓
9) Actions or thoughts just came out spontaneously.	✓	✓	✓
10) I was interactive.	✓	✓	
11) I had prior related involvement.		✓	
12) I enjoyed another person or persons during the event.		✓	
13) The experience was its own reward.	✓		

Relationship Between Trigger with Feeling: According to this direction, researchers extract the focus interviews of typical participants from the above group, study the relationship between trigger conditions and peak experience emotional characterization (Fig. 5).

Fig. 5. Tools and records in the focus group interview

Depending on the participant characteristics in each group, researchers select more detailed and clear participants in this group, and consider characteristics such as gender and age. Each group extracted 5 participants with representative, forming a family group, a friend group, and an alone group for focus group discussion.

The main content of focus interview is divided into three parts: First, researchers hope to explore more in-depth exploration based on the experience of the peak experience mentioned in the questionnaire before the participant, by interrogating the behavior of the participant's peak experience, participating in members, the cause of time, environment, unforgettable reasons, and TV playing roles, to guide each group of participants to establish the characteristics of this group of interviews, clearly interviewing the needs of grouping. For example, participants of the family group need more attention to the scene of using the TV with relatives.

After that, guide the participant under each group feature, according to the five feature topics established by the triggered condition before summarizing, the depth experience description, the memories of some details, the following is the corresponding topic:

1. Hypernormal: In the process of using the experience of the TV, participants have experienced changes in regular behavior.

2. Common: Similar or identical experience or tendency.

3. Interactive: In the use of TV, there is an interactive feedback with the device, content or others.

4. Meaningful: Refers to the scene of a special time node.

5. Matching: Environmental conditions for content.

Finally, participants were asked to choose statements (see Table 3) under each theme that matched their inner scene, and obtain the contact between trigger conditions and feelings statements.

Table 4. Overall emotional description (Total = 75 = 3 Group * 5 Triggers * 5 participants)

Emotional description	Count
I experience joy and fulfillment	**43**
I was absorbed in what I was doing	21
The event was fun	27
I felt a need to continue until completions	19
The event involved action or behavior	16
Rules, motivation, and goals were built into the situation	16
Actions or thoughts just came out spontaneously	**33**
The experience involved unity or fusion of self with the environment	17
The event was perceptual, rather than behavioral	14
I was interactive	28
I had prior related involvement	25
I enjoyed another person or persons during the event	27
The experience was its own reward	17

According to the above discussion, researchers obtain the emotional description below the various topics. By calculating statistics, the three groups of emotional descriptions are sorted. See above Table 4.

In general, nearly half or more participants in the three groups believe that "I experience joy and fulfillment" and "Actions or thoughts just came out spontaneously" are indispensable in the peak experience of TV. And different participant groups and different triggers do not affect the performance of these two feeling features, so it can be considered that these two feelings are the basic performance of the TV peak experience. Therefore, these two types of feeling needs are necessary manifestations of peak experience, not the special characteristics need to be concerned.

In addition, from different trigger conditions, participants reflect certain differences in the tendency of emotional performance, so researchers further analyze the remaining results beside two basic feelings.

First, considering that the three groups of scenes can be clustered from the perspective of participant attributes, the participant attributes of the family group and the friend group are more similar than those of the alone group. In addition, there are emotional descriptions that tend to be multi-person in the emotional feedback. Therefore, in order to ensure the universality of the conclusion and exclude the influence of the number base of the participant group in the multi-person scene, researchers first average the frequency data of the multi-person group. For example, under the topic "Hypernormal", 3 people in the family group chose feeling 1, and 4 people in the friend group chose feeling 1. Therefore, in the multiplayer group, the frequency of this triggering factor triggering feeling 1 is 3.5 = (3 + 4)/2, and so on.

After excluding the influence of indifferent emotions and the number of people in the multi-person group, researchers calculated the average value of the frequency of emotional representations between the groups, and obtained the following results. See Table 5.

Table 5. Emotional performance difference chart

Emotional description/Trigger conditions	Tri.1	Tri.2	Tri.3	Tri.4	Tri.5
I was absorbed in what I was doing	2	0.25	1.25	2.25	0.75
The event was fun	**2.75**	2.25	1.25	1.25	1.25
I felt a need to continue until completions	1.5	0.5	1.25	2.25	0.75
The event involved action or behavior	0.75	1.5	0.75	0.5	2
Rules, motivation, and goals were built into the situation	1	0.75	1	1.25	0.75
The experience involved unity or fusion of self with the environment	1	0.5	0.5	1	**2.5**
The event was perceptual, rather than behavioral	1	1	0.5	0.5	1.75
I was interactive	2.25	2	**2.5**	1.5	0.5
I had prior related involvement	1.75	1.5	2	2	1.25
I enjoyed another person or persons during the event	1	2	2	**2.5**	0.75
The experience was its own reward	2	1.25	1.25	1	0

As can be seen from the above table, there are certain differences in the peak experience emotions shown by different trigger conditions. This paper is aim to study the conclusion of universality, therefore, only the results of the research sample whose frequency is greater than the median value of (sample base 5) are selected to confirm the general emotional representation results represented by each trigger condition, and finally the following conclusions are obtained. See Table 6.

Table 6. The relationship of trigger condition and feeling

Tri. conditions	Feeling statement of peak experience
<Basic>	I experience joy and fulfillment Actions or thoughts just came out spontaneously
Hypernormal	The event was fun
Common	<N/A>
Interactive	I was interactive
Meaningful	I enjoyed another person or persons during the event
Matching	The experience involved unity or fusion of self with the environment

Peak-Experience Emotional Design Method: Researchers think that when different triggering conditions are reached through certain means, the corresponding emotional feelings of the participant can be triggered, so as to obtain the corresponding peak TV usage experience.

Combined the Triggers feature description can get the direction that design can be realized, so designers can help users get specific feelings to reach peak experience during using TV. This below is the design principle for TV peak experience:

- ✓ Hypernormal: Create different form from the conventional experience
- ✓ Interactive: Build bridges among users with others/TV equipment/content to ensure two-way information flow
- ✓ Meaningful: Gives a special accessory meaning to the point of time when the TV is used
- ✓ Matching: Arrange Environmental conditions according content category.

5 Conclusion

This study investigates the peak experiences of users in the process of using TV through questionnaires and focus groups, and describes its characteristics and related triggering factors, and finally proposes corresponding design directions. The specific conclusions are summarized as follows:

Firstly, through an online questionnaire study of 43 people, it was found that during the use of TV, users all had experiences that met the definition of peak experience, but most users formed detailed memories of the experience unconsciously.

Secondly, in the Device/Human/Environment fields, the peak experience scenes or behaviors of TV generally have one or more of the following characteristics:

a) Hypernormal: *In the process of using the experience of the TV, participants have experienced changes in regular behavior.*
b) Common: *Having Similar or identical experience or tendency compared with others.*
c) Interactive: *In the use of TV, there is an interactive feedback with the device, content or others.*
d) Meaningful: *Refers to the scene of a special time node.*
e) Matching: *Environmental conditions according to TV contents.*

Finally, realizing different characteristics of scenes and behaviors by means of design, and triggering corresponding emotional tendencies can help users obtain peak experience in the process of using TV to the greatest extent possible. The design directions under specific trigger conditions are described could be as follows (Table 7):

Table 7. Design for trigger peak experience of TV use

Design direction	Trigger	Peak Feeling
Create different form from the conventional experience	Hypernormal	The event was fun
Build bridges among users with others/TV equipment/content to ensure two-way information flow	Interactive	I was interactive
Gives a special accessory meaning to the point of time when the TV is used	Meaningful	I enjoyed another person or persons during the event
Arrange Environmental conditions according content category	Matching	The experience involved unity or fusion of self with the environment

6 Limitation and Discussion

First, this research is only a small scale of participant study, its purpose is to try to apply the peak experience theory to the field of TV design, and to dig out new design ideas that can be used for reference. The conclusion is instructive, but not yet available Universality. It pays more attention to participants who have had a certain TV experience in the participant community, and may not be able to give accurate guidance on the design of new participants. In the future, it is necessary to supplement more extensive participant data and synthesize information from multiple sources to obtain more universal conclusions.

Some insights in the conclusion, although the same findings were found in previous TV research, such as the importance of high-quality hardware factors for TV experience, this research is more about mining TV experience under the theoretical and practical framework of peak experience, including the characteristics of these experiences and the corresponding emotional states.

Finally, the thesis also provides research ideas in psychological description for Experience design, and expands the interdisciplinary approach of experience research.

References

1. Maslow, A.H.: Lessons from the peak-experiences. J. Humanist. Psychol. **2**(1), 9–18 (1962)
2. Majić, T., Schmidt, T.T., Gallinat, J.: Peak experiences and the afterglow phenomenon: when and how do therapeutic effects of hallucinogens depend on psychedelic experiences? J. Psychopharmacol. **29**(3), 241–253 (2015)
3. Privette, G.: Peak experience, peak performance, and flow: a comparative analysis of positive human experiences. J. Pers. Soc. Psychol. **45**(6), 1361 (1983)
4. Consolvo, S., McDonald, D.W., Landay, J.A.: Theory-driven design strategies for technologies that support behavior change in everyday life. In: Proceedings of the SIGCHI Conference on Human Factors in Computing Systems, pp. 405–414, April 2009
5. Kahneman, D.: Evaluation by moments: Past and future. Choices, values, and frames, pp. 693–708 (2000)

6. 朱慧彬. 决定成功的 "关键时刻". 发现, (6), 11–11 (2008)
7. Cojuharenco, I., Ryvkin, D.: Peak–end rule versus average utility: how utility aggregation affects evaluations of experiences. J. Math. Psychol. **52**(5), 326–335 (2008)
8. Ho, M.Y., Chen, S.X., Hoffman, E.: Unpacking cultural variations in peak-experiences: cross-cultural comparisons of early childhood recollection between Hong Kong and Brazil. J. Happiness Stud. **13**(2), 247–260 (2012). https://doi.org/10.1007/s10902-011-9261-y
9. McDonald, M.G., Wearing, S., Ponting, J.: The nature of peak experience in wilderness. Humanistic Psychol. **37**(4), 370–385 (2009)
10. 毕文杰, 孙颖慧, 田柳青.: 参考价格符合峰终定律的多产品动态定价模型. 系统工程学报, **30**(4), 476–484 (2015)
11. Nitu, P., Coelho, J., Madiraju, P.: improvising personalized travel recommendation system with recency effects. Big Data Min. Anal. (03), 139–154 (2021). CNKI:SUN:BDMA.0.2021-03-001
12. 李成 & 鲍懿喜.: 峰终定律在用户体验研究中的应用. 艺术与设计(理论) (06), 179–181 (2011). https://doi.org/10.16824/j.cnki.issn10082832.2011.06.067
13. Mathes, E.W.: Peak experience tendencies: Scale development and theory testing. J. Humanist. Psychol. **22**(3), 92–108 (1982)
14. Maslow, A.H.: Music education and peak experience. Music. Educ. J. **54**(6), 72–171 (1968)
15. Lipscombe, N.: The relevance of the peak experience to continued skydiving participation: A qualitative approach to assessing motivations (1999)
16. DeMares, R.: Human peak experience triggered by encounters with cetaceans. Anthrozoös **13**(2), 89–103 (2000)
17. Hui, S.K., Meyvis, T., Assael, H.: Analyzing moment-to-moment data using a Bayesian functional linear model: application to TV show pilot testing. Mark. Sci. **33**(2), 222–240 (2014)
18. Privette, G., Sherry, D.: Reliability and readability of questionnaire: peak performance and peak experience. Psychol. Rep. **58**(2), 491–494 (1986)
19. Chorianopoulos, K., Lekakos, G.: Introduction to social TV: enhancing the shared experience with interactive TV. Int. J. Hum. Comput. Interact. **24**(2), 113–120 (2008)
20. Vinayagamoorthy, V., Glancy, M., Ziegler, C., Schäffer, R.: Personalising the TV experience using augmented reality: an exploratory study on delivering synchronised sign language interpretation. In: Proceedings of the 2019 CHI Conference on Human Factors in Computing Systems, pp. 1–12, May 2019
21. Mu, M., Knowles, W., Sani, Y., Mauthe, A., Race, N.: Improving interactive TV experience using second screen mobile applications. In 2015 IEEE International Symposium on Multimedia (ISM), pp. 373–376. IEEE, December 2015

Improving User-Centered Interface for Smart Mirror as a Product-Service System Design

Joosun Yum⬤, Juhyun Lee⬤, Po Yan Lai⬤, and Ji-Hyun Lee⁽✉⁾⬤

GSCT, KAIST, 291 Daehak-Ro, Yuseong-Gu, Daejeon, Korea
jihyunlee@kaist.ac.kr

Abstract. As real-time data collection and processing technologies advanced, the demands for customized beauty services have been rapidly increasing. However, existing SBM services are limited to providing results-driven services, such as virtual makeup try-on, than customized services for each makeup process. They are insufficient to address the appearance differences and shortcomings of individual users. Therefore, this study aims to develop a new Product-Service System Design (PSSD) of SBM based on the individual needs and makeup routines of users. Employing the Double Diamond approach, we started off with a case study of SBMs and an in-depth interview with an industry expert to understand the positioning and limitations of existing SBMs used by beauty brands. For suggesting a user-centered interface for customized service, we conducted a survey and an interview with a makeup artist to identify individual users' needs and makeup routines. This paper presents the user persona, the service blueprint, and the wireframe of our PSSD solution of SBM. Our design integrates real-time face-type recognition and rule-based analysis to systemize personalized process-oriented makeup recommendation services. Our system will improve the user experience by providing proper user-centered interfaces and supporting its innate reasoning features.

Keywords: Interface design · User experience design · Blueprint prototyping · Product Service System Design

1 Introduction

The desire to pursue beauty in modern society is manifested in various ways such as fashion, hairstyle, makeup. For the expression of beauty, cosmetics have become an indispensable feature of the modern lifestyle of individuals. According to Allied Market Research, the global cosmetics market size was valued at $380.2 billion in 2019 and is projected to reach $463.5 billion by 2027 [1]. At present, along with women, there is a rise in the use of cosmetics among men in their daily routine, which complements the growth of the global cosmetics market demand. Applying makeup enables people to either emphasize or hide certain features to express the image they want to portray. With the proliferation of AI technologies combined with IoT, an enormous opportunity for personalized beauty services is generated. Along with this background, the emergence of

N. A. Streitz and S. Konomi (Eds.): HCII 2022, LNCS 13325, pp. 340–360, 2022.
https://doi.org/10.1007/978-3-031-05463-1_24

the concept of the smart mirror system has become increasingly widespread. It displays information such as weather conditions, time, calendar, a notification from SNS from the internet [2]. The use of smart mirrors is gradually expanding in various fields.

However, this paper observed three downsides of the current practice. First of all, many kinds of smart mirrors are gradually starting to appear on the market, but users' customed needs are not reflected yet. Existing smart mirror systems in the beauty industry do not reflect individual differences in appearance and needs for each user. It is important to recognize the needs of consumers by interacting with them naturally. So, research is needed to find out what users want through smart mirrors by doing surveys and expert interviews. The second limitation, there is a lack of research on how smart mirrors exchange data with other smart devices and provide personalized services in the IoT environment. Many related studies focus on the platform or framework for the smart home environment. Derrick and his colleagues developed 'SmartReflect' which is a software platform for developing smart mirror applications [3]. Athira and the team proposed a smart mirror which is an interactive system that helps to know schedule notifications [4]. Thus, research on making makeup recommendation services tailored to personal habits or tastes is needed through data collected from other smart devices in the IoT environment. The third limitation is that the recent studies showed the matching algorithms between the users and the make-up images based on AI technologies, but they could not show the make-up process like virtual makeup. Thus, research is needed to show not only the virtual makeup results but also the reason for the recommendation and the makeup process. To overcome these problems, our research aim is to aid people's makeup application by providing personal recommendations as well as creating pleasurable user experiences through designing a Smart Beauty Mirror (SBM).

In this study, we propose a smart mirror method that reflects the user needs of smart PSS. This article adopted a series of service design methods to find the solutions for the new smart PSS, the SBM. As service design includes multiple design-thinking methods which aim at co-design with multiple stakeholders, we report the four design phases (Discovery, Define, Develop and Deliver) of the service design of the SBM. After that, we conducted research to identify the individual needs of users and provide customized makeup recommendation services. The SBM users can not only select the purpose of makeup but also the process of makeup. From this research, our expected contribution is that it can satisfy the extremely contextualized and unique needs and preferences of the customers.

2 Theoretical Background

2.1 Incorporation of AI in Product Service System

The service sector can be divided into two categories, which are material services and immaterial services. Material services, such as the ones provided in beauty salons, are services that require human interaction whereas immaterial services often involve products or technology devices. These days, many enterprises are switching from retailing physical products to providing service-integrated solutions with technological development and consumer sophistication [5]. This market shift of servitization enables enterprises to provide a new value proposition for customers by providing personalized value-added and supporting customer experience during the entire product life cycle [6]. This innovation of service design is known as the Product Service System (PSS), which is a marketing strategy to create customer values that concern the product life-cycle [7]. Adopting PSS shifts the product-centered design paradigm into a service-oriented one. Analogous to this trend, the maturation of the IoT and the rapid advancement of AI allows smart devices to utilize PSS design to provide smart services by understanding customers' needs and responding to them in new approaches. This servitization allows products to become a tool to generate service innovation and the ownership and usage, such as renting and pay-per-use, expects change accordingly [8].

Previous work on the definition of 'Smartness' defined a smart object as something that possesses "wise and interactive management of service systems' assets, goals" [9]. The technology advancement in AI has added learning and adjustment skills to smart products. Thanks to Information Technology, service systems have become smart-service systems [10] to offer personalized experiences. Taken together, the definition of smart Product-Service Systems is the integration of smart products and E-services into single solutions delivered to the market to satisfy the needs of individual consumers [11] Smart PSS is useful for enhancing customer experiences because it is sensible, communicable, and programmable. Thus, Smart PSS allows consumer empowerment, individualization of services, provides both individual and shared experiences, and continuous expansion. The information-based approach is the key to value creation by identifying users' behavioral patterns and providing appropriate services to fulfill needs in Smart PSS. The most noticeable benefit of Smart PSS is providing personalized customer experiences by understanding and adjusting to individual customer values [12]. The current issues of Smart PSS are mass-customization and personalization; however, it is difficult to recognize the needs of customers from their unclear requirements [13]. Therefore, it is important to explore how to utilize data generated by various stakeholders through AI techniques. To sum up, AI in Smart PSS is important to use as a way to strengthen large-scale customization and personalization aspects by identifying various consumer needs. These features of smart PSS imply that it is important to deeply understand individual customers through AI. In particular, AI using image processing began to be utilized exponentially in the field of cosmetics [14].

2.2 Digitization of Beauty Lifestyles

Generations born in the early 1980s and early 2000s are avid consumers of emerging technologies and will continue to use new technologies throughout their lives. The Millenials are already connecting to others via electronic media and messaging and spend more time communicating digitally than face to face. Beauty service consumption is rapidly changing due to the digital transformation of society. The most well-known activity for self-care and enhancing appearance is using cosmetic products to wear make-up. According to the definition from the Oxford dictionary, the word 'Beauty' means "a combination of qualities such as shape, color, or form which is pleasing to the aesthetic senses, especially the sight". As the beauty market grows, various terms are used for new products or trends (e.g., K-beauty to represent Korean cosmetics, MLBB (My Lips But Better), MFBB (My Face But Better), etc.). Considering the user's acceptability for the product and defining the scope of suggestion of new smart PSS, we need to use the appropriate term and consistent expression in the paper. The terms 'Cosmetics' and 'Make-up' are often used interchangeably to convey similar meanings. The Oxford dictionary definition of cosmetics is "substances or products that you put on your face or body to make it more attractive". Also, it is a collective term that includes products designed to be applied to the face, hair, and body. The Food and Drug Administration (FDA), which regulates cosmetics in the U.S., defines cosmetics as "intended to be applied to the human body for cleansing, beautifying, promoting attractiveness, or altering the appearance without affecting the body's structure or functions" [15]. When the industry classifies the products for the market analysis, 'Make-up' usually belongs to the category of 'Cosmetics' [16].

Applying makeup has a long history because it enhances facial contrast which increases both attractiveness and perception of health [16]. Cosmetic products or makeup-related services used to be considered as young women's dominant industry. However, the last two decades showed the market increase in male self-presentation practices. As more women are investing in their appearance, males are making lifestyle choices to enhance their attractiveness by investing in clothing, accessories, or cosmetics. With the widespread use of the Internet along with the human innate appreciation of beauty and health, the beauty-related lifestyle activities and beauty industry distribution are changing. For instance, non-celebrity people share videos of various beauty activities online through YouTube or other social media. Through these channels, people follow non-makeup artists' tutorials or exchange opinions through online platforms. This trend indicates the changes in the beauty industry and emphasizes the need to explore new opportunities that comport with technology embedded lifestyles of people. Applying makeup not only modifies one's appearance but also promotes positive emotions by forming a desirable self-image of an individual. Despite the positive consequences of using cosmetic products, the process of applying makeup can be difficult since all people's facial features and preferences differ. Furthermore, selecting the right type of makeup product is challenging, because there are too many makeup brands and products to choose from.

2.3 Personalization of User Needs and Experience

In the cosmetic and beauty fields, the customers have various and changing needs. The users can have physiological needs that would depend on their physical attributes. For example, a person with dry skin would prefer to use a rich moisturizer. If the user is aware of their skin attributes, the recommendation of cosmetic product usage could be easily reached with, for instance, a preliminary questionnaire to set up the smart mirror.

But refining recommendation is more complex because the usage of makeup also depends on users' likes, geographical trends, and buying preferences. For instance, a recent study on the purchasing behavior of Chinese male adolescents using makeup has shown that these young people are of interest in Korean makeup products and trends [17]. Other studies have showcased the difference in purchase behavior for cosmetics between countries, such as between America and France [18], or between Korea, Japan, and China [19]. Getting recommendations right demands to have awareness of the user's context, but it may still not be enough to propose the correct content for the users. One solution could be the integration of a feedback circuit into the system to adjust the recommendations, which would question the user about the relevance of the information displayed. There are other sources of data collection for personalization for a smart mirror. Smart mirrors can be equipped with sensors such as microphones or a webcam. In the industry, these sensors are used to allow having multiple accounts for the usage of the smart mirror at home. The direct consequence is that the device can adapt the interactions and suggestions according to the corresponding user. The collection of data on the usage of the smart mirror is a second means for enhancing the user interface and the type of content displayed. For example, the smart device could collect the most frequent interactions and requests from the user to adapt its content.

3   Develop Product Service System Design

3.1   The Double Diamond Model

This article adopted a series of service design methods to find service design solutions for the Smart Beauty Mirror as Product Service System Design. As Service design includes multiple design-thinking methods which aim at co-design with multiple stakeholders [20], we have undergone four main design processes (Discover, Define, Develop and Deliver) (Fig. 1).

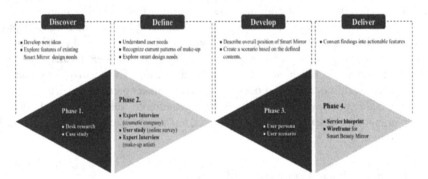

Fig. 1. Four design phases of service design of smart mirror

In phase 1, the initial stage of 'Discover' begins with the case study and desk research. A case study of smart mirrors in the market was conducted to explore the new smart service design. This method is descriptive or explanatory to describe the state of the art of phenomena developing new ideas or testing theories. We have adopted this method since this method has the advantage of providing holistic details of the design deliverable, which is beneficial for service design methodologies. In phase 2, the 'Define' stage includes a user study and two expert interviews. First, we did an expert interview with the president of a cosmetic company. The expert interview with the CEO who is familiar with the cosmetic industry was conducted to explore hidden design needs. Second, an online survey was conducted to understand the users' needs for the smart mirror. Based on the findings, an expert interview with a make-up artist was conducted to understand the current patterns and feasibility of the service. In phase 3, the 'Develop' phase is for creating a scenario based on the defined contents. Based on the findings from the two design phases, a persona that represents the core user need was developed. In phase 4, the 'Deliver' process includes making a service blueprint and wireframe for SBM to convert findings into actionable features.

3.2 Case Study of Existing Smart Beauty Mirrors

The Cosmetic Market has proposed various formats of smart beauty systems. Our research team analyzes 9 companies to provide the smart mirror for cosmetics (Table 1). We categorized the analysis through the platform, interface, and support functions. These mirrors are using cameras to track the face of users and provide the make-up results of selected styles. They could be divided into two purposes; to enhance the user experience in the offline stores and mobile applications. The smart mirrors have supported various functions, such as not just simulating the users' make-up styles or recommending suitable cosmetic items, also sharing through SNS or E-mail and even controlling the LED lights.

These systems show the recent trends of smart mirrors to help customers to try on the various make-up styles and recommend the appropriate cosmetic products. Most of the existing beauty mirrors are utilized in the store to provide customers who are visiting their cosmetic stores and selling their products based on the result of the displayed simulation. The other mirrors have the purpose to sell their physical devices (HiMirror) or using their apps (Modiface) supporting the function of beauty simulation. These mirrors have been developed with cutting-edge technologies, such as face tracking, AR, and matching algorithms. Therefore, our research team investigated what users and beauty professionals want through the SBM as 'Beauty Expert', and the development of the beauty mirror industry today has not been popularized. Many merchants use new technology to sell their makeup products, so the existing mirrors are more of a linkage sales model. The products that improve the user's beauty and makeup experience are few, which is one of the starting points of our research team. However, as far as the application of technology is concerned, many hardware aspects, such as touchable electronic display, voice control system, etc. have mature applications, which are aspects that we can learn from and use. At the same time, how to improve the user's beauty and makeup experience is the focus of our attention.

3.3 Interview with Beauty Industry Experts

The purpose of this section is to examine the current cosmetics market situation and process of change in the smart beauty industry through in-depth interviews with a smart beauty-related expert.

Research Method. First of all, based on the insight obtained from the preliminary study, we looked for a suitable expert for the interview. We found that we needed an interview with an experienced cosmetics industry expert who has experience in in planning smart mirror products. We got a connection with the executive in charge of cosmetic marketing planning at 'E' company, who has been working for more than 20 yrs in a global cosmetic group. We conducted an in-depth interview for three hours and recorded the dialogue

Table 1. Summary of case study about smart mirror for beauty/cosmetics.

No	Name	Company	Platform	Interface	Functions
1	MemoMi (MemoryMirror)	MemoMiLabs	Public (Store)	Touch screen mirror	Digital image recording during the make-up Virtual wearing eyewear & clothes Smartphone & SNS sharing, etc
2	MagicMirror	Charlotte Tilbury	Public (Store)	Touch screen mirror	Show the result of cosmetics style Import images through email, etc
3	Digital counseling Mirror	Shiseido	Public (Store)	Touch screen mirror	Support the product information with 3D images Skin check & results
4	New Magic Mirror	Panasonic	Public (Store)	Touch screen mirror	Take a photo with skin condition care Apps that allow you to digitally "try on" make-up
5	Hi Mirror	Hi Mirror	Personal (Home)	Touch screen mirror, Voice control, LED lights	Adjustable LED lighting Skin analysis Recommend cosmetic products Makeup tutorial SNS sharing
6	Modiface	Modiface	Personal (Home)	Mobile touch screen	Simulating the various cosmetic effects and hairstyles Recommend cosmetic products
7	Lumini Kiosk V2	Lulu-Lab	Personal (Home)	Touch screen mirror kiosk	Skin analysis based on the algorithm Recommend skincare and cosmetic products Compares skin conditions with people through big data
8	Z Mirror	Icon AI	Personal (Home)	AI speaker, Touch screen mirror, LED ring	Adjustable LED lighting Skin analysis Recommend cosmetic products Show makeup on YouTube Virtual makeup based on AR

(*continued*)

Table 1. (*continued*)

No	Name	Company	Platform	Interface	Functions
9	Morror	The Morror team	Personal (Home)	LED ring, Touch screen mirror	Adjustable brightness Skincare and makeup tutorial Show weather information

contents. Table 2 is the phases of the interview including the questions extracted from the preliminary studies. The questions consist of analysis by industry market experts, which is difficult to obtain out of the industry, and about smart mirrors placed in offline stores.

Table 2. Preliminary questionnaire for expert interview.

No	Interview phases	Explanation/Questions
1	Introduction of the research purpose	Concept of the smart mirror Technical methodology for a smart mirror Product Service System (PSS) design
2	Inquiry about the expert role	Cosmetic manager's role Past experiences in cosmetic companies Cosmetic company's expectations for the smart mirror
3	Need of customer	Categorization of the cosmetic products Product recommendation (sales) process for consumer Features of the customers Industry market analysis tools of the cosmetic company
4	Smart mirror for offline cosmetic stores	The beginning of the offline smart mirror Trends of the smart beauty market The value of the personalized beauty service for marketing

Interview Result and Discussion

Smart Mirror for Offline Cosmetic Stores: The interview with an expert in the cosmetic company showed the purpose and effect of the company's installation of the smart mirror in cosmetic stores. The main purpose of smart mirrors installed in beauty stores is to make the customer look more beautiful. The initial models of the smart mirror have changed since they originated in the backstage mirrors of fashion shows that the shape with the light attached to the mirror (Table 3).

Opportunities for the Smart Mirror in the Cosmetic Market: The expert predicted that the department store which was the main channel of selling brand cosmetics will be changed as a showroom. Their sales report shows the main shop of cosmetics will be a

Table 3. History of smart mirror for cosmetic stores.

Backstage mirror with lighting (15–20 years ago)	LED lighting panel	Color/Brightness changing	Camera for selfie (5 years ago)
Initial Appearance of the smart mirror in a cosmetic store	Make the mirror flat and it can be added angle for side mirror to look the side face of the customer	Complement the difference between natural light and interior lighting in a department store	To recognize the face of the user To apply virtual make-up to user To save the image

multi-brand store. The Multi-brand store is represented as SMC which means Specialty Multi-Channel. (e.g., Olive Young, Boots, Sephora, CiCHOR, LOHBs) The cosmetic companies including high-end brands try to expand their selling channel to SMC. In that channel, the user's experiences with brand products are more important because products from various brands are sold in one space. The expert said that the smart mirror could be used as an efficient 'Untact' marketing material. The interview with the expert has determined that providing technologies that consumers can use on their own will be an important factor in smart mirrors. As the technology penetrates the industry, new features and sales objectives have been added, and more recently, it has evolved into a smart mirror with facial recognition, finally applying virtual makeup to what they sell.

4 User-Centered Interface for Customized Service

4.1 Survey of Users' Needs

The beauty industry is integrating technology to provide efficient services along with pleasurable user experiences. While there are varying beauty technology services that have been invented, not many people have had the chance to use them. Therefore, designing a new smart service integrated system that meets customers' expectations in a user-friendly way is important. Therefore, we have conducted an online survey to specify user needs for exploring design applications of 'SBM', a mirror that provides users adaptive recommendation services based on users' preferences, styling application contexts, and sociocultural trends. Our research contribution is two folds: First, user needs have been explored based on their daily beauty-related lifestyle activities and patterns. Second, design criteria in terms of both product and service components for a beauty mirror are suggested.

Method. People in their 20–30's are the technology 'Savy' generation. This generation has already applied technology within various aspects of their daily lives, and they are more likely to accept and adapt to new technology. To understand how people in their 20–30's apply makeup and discover their needs and expectations for an "SBM", we have conducted a semi-structured online survey. Participants: Our main target group is both Korean males and females in their 20–30's because they are the population that has a high interest in beauty-related activities. A total of 24 participants (Male = 9, Fe-male = 15) have answered the survey, and the average age of the participants was 27.29 years old (SD = 2.79, Min = 23, and Max = 34). Survey Contents: The user needs survey has been conducted according to a predesigned set of questions. The survey is composed of three main sections that are composed of subsections First, the demographic of the participants were asked to understand the general backgrounds of the participants. Second, questions regarding beauty activities and behaviors were asked to understand participants' beauty lifestyles and needs. Third, users' expectations and needs for the "SBM" in terms of both service and product aspects have been inquired.

General Beauty Related Activities: To understand how participants gather information or tips about the latest trends or beauty-related activities, "Q3. How do you gather information about health and beauty-related activities/issues, tips and trends?" was asked. Most participants answered that they use the internet to find such information. Unlike magazines or commercials, SNSs or personal blogs show step-by-step guidance of beauty product applications along with the user experiences of the real customers. It can be inferred that participants are seeking more user-oriented products and application methods. To understand users' experiences or familiarity with using digital devices or technology, "Q5. Have you used digital applications to enhance or aid health and beauty-related activities?" was asked. 37.5% of the participants answered "Yes" to this question. Some of the examples the participants have listed were massage chairs, weight-watching applications, workout tutorial applications, or make-up store online applications. The core functions of these apps were recording daily activities, watching pre-recorded tutorials, or product sales information. However, these functions do not provide real-time personalized information or guidelines.

Specific Beauty Related Activities: To understand the general makeup application process, the participants were asked to list all the beauty-related products that they use daily (Q2). 22 participants answered that they use basic products (e.g., toner, lotion, serum, cream). Foundation and color cosmetics (e.g., eyeliner, lipstick, blusher) were listed as daily applied cosmetics. Q3. asked how long a participant spends applying daily makeup. This question was intended to predict the usage time of the 'SBM'. Most participants answered that they spend 10–15 min, and on average participants spend 16 min applying makeup or conducting styling activities. Because some people especially take a long time to put on makeup. To determine design space in terms of user experience, Q4. was asked to determine the goal or reasons for applying makeup or styling products. The participants' reasons to look neat or attractive could be under-stood from two different perspectives. First, they apply cosmetics for self-satisfaction. This indicates that providing pleasurable experiences is important. Second, the act of taking care of appearance is part of a social act. One participant answered that "Because it is a manner to do so (Female, 25 yrs)." This indicates that the recommendation service should also consider social norms. To understand further considerations when determining design rules for the recommendation system. Q7. was asked. 20 people (83.3%) answered that they apply different styles on different occasions. One of the participants answered "...some trends, time of the year, occasions. For example, I like bright colors for spring/summer and dark colors for winter. I only wear eyeshadow for a special event or if I am going to a club (Female, 23 yrs)." This indicates that different recommendation rules should be pre-defined depending on the makeup application context as well as the season. To understand the evaluation criteria of the final results of the make-up application, Q8, 'How do you determine whether the style suits you or not?' was asked. Following are the excerpts from the participant's answers; when I am satisfied, friend compliments, personal evaluation, reactions from friends or family, how I look in photographs. The answers indicated the lack of objective evaluations but relied most on subjective opinions of the self or acquaintances. This highlights the potential need for an expert system for the evaluation of the results. Q9. directly asked what difficulties people had when putting on makeup. Following are examples of answers: 'I have trouble selecting the right product as there are too many brands', 'I cannot find the right color for me', and 'It is difficult to try new styles'. The answers yet again proved the need for a personalized recommendation service to select the right product as well as guidance for selecting appropriate styles for the user.

SBM Ideation: Following are the functions that participants have listed: 1) Virtual application of different styles, 2) Style recommendations, 3) Product recommendations and 4) Make-up tutorials. A question regarding the expected size of the mirror was asked to discover the product family of smart mirrors to define its design features. Most participants imagined a face-sized mirror for the smart mirror. It can be inferred that the participants are looking for a mirror that is similar to the ones they are familiar with. Another question was asked for the preferred method for using the mirror to determine the appropriate user interface when the 'SBM' will be implemented. Voice control was most preferred followed by gesture and touch interfaces. Almost half of the participants answered that they wanted to interact with the mirror through voice control because they wanted to use the mirror while they were applying make-up. The reasons for touch-based interfaces were that the participants are familiar with the method and it prevents errors. Both advantages and disadvantages of adopting different interfaces were explored.

4.2   Interview with Makeup Artist

On top of the market trend, it is important to understand how people do makeup. However, putting on makeup that looks good is a kind of expert knowledge, which might require talents or years of training. It is common to see people searching for video tutorials, or even hiring the actual expert, to do their styling and makeup for special occasions such as parties and weddings. It is reasonable to assume that users of SBM would like to receive expert recommendations to aid them in getting ready. For this reason, we had an in-depth semi-structured interview and a makeup demo session with an experienced makeup artist. We aimed to understand the decision-making process and the know-how of the professionals when they serve customers with different facial features and preferences, from that we can extract the general rules and design them into the PSS.

Study Method.
Participant: The interviewee Kim has been a specialist in wedding makeup and styling for more than eight years by the time of the interview. The interviewee was recruited

through an acquaintance. Her participation was voluntary. Kim reported that her customers included both males and females in their 20 s to their 50 s, while female customers in their 20 s or 30 s were the majority. As our research targeted the Korean market, Kim was a qualified interviewee who frequently communicated and understood the needs of our potential consumers and users.

Setting: The interview and the makeup demo were conducted at the interviewee's workplace, a wedding shop in the city of Daejeon, South Korea. The advantages of choosing the workplace are threefold. For the first thing, the interviewee is familiar with the environment so that she can be more comfortable and willing to speak out. For another thing, the space is equipped with a variety of makeup tools and products for the demo. Lastly, this enabled the researchers to observe how the makeup artist interacts with the client in a natural setting, as well as the makeup room configuration.

Study Design: The execution overview of the expert interview and makeup demo are given below in Table 4. The interview and the makeup demo session were designed according to the think-aloud protocol, which aims at encouraging the interviewee to explain herself.

Table 4. Overview of expert interview and makeup demo.

Briefing (About 5 min)	In-Depth interview (About 1 h)	Male makeup demo (About 11 min)	Female makeup demo (About 24 min)
To explain the goal and the procedure of the study To have the participant consent form signed	To understand how experts analyze clients' features and apply makeup	To observe and understand how experts apply daily makeup application for men or women	

For the interview, we designed a question set which covers the interviewee's experience as a makeup artist, trends in makeup, and the general principles and skills of doing makeup. Table 5 accounts for the details of the question set. The flow of the interview did not strictly follow the question set. It allowed room for flexibility to skip questions on the part which the interviewee has already mentioned, or to ask additional follow-up questions to make clear the details.

Followed by the interview, we invited the interviewee to perform a daily makeup on our researchers, both male and female, in the usual way she interacted with her clients. The researchers not only observed the interviewee but also asked questions regarding her decision-making process for every procedure she performed, every tool and product she used. Both the interview and makeup demos were taped for later analysis.

Environment Setting: The makeup demo session was conducted in the makeup studio which has a desk with a large wall mirror. All the makeup tools and products are organized by their usage on the desk. The lighting is right on top of the seat. Figure 2 shows the environment and setting of the makeup studio where the demos took place.

Table 5. The question set of interview with makeup expert.

Category	Questions
Background and field knowledge	How long have you been working as a makeup artist?
	Is there a trend? If so, how do you get to know the makeup trend?
Consultation with clients	Who are your main clients? Their demographic features?
	How do the clients ask for the style they want? Do they describe a style or a celebrity?
	How do you make plans to meet the client's goals or needs?
	How do you decide the suitable style for each occasion and each client?
	Do you encounter any difficulty or problems? If so, what is it?
Knowledge and techniques	How do you analyze the features of the clients?
	How do you complement face shape or maximize certain facial features of the clients?
	(E.g., clients of different skin tones, face shape, eye shape, lip shape)
	How do you determine what products or colors to use?

Fig. 2. The makeup studio environment and setting

There are reasons for the big mirror and the lighting to be installed. The interviewee explained that the size of the mirror should be large enough to show the whole upper body so that the user can check if the makeup matches one's outfits and styling. It should be placed vertically in front of the user, at about 30 to 50 cm from the seat. In such a position, the user can observe better if the makeup is put on symmetrically. Talking about it is common for people to get closer and closer to the mirror to work on the details of the makeup, the interviewee said "that's why the lighting is important, people have to do so usually because the room is not bright enough." White light is more preferred than yellow light when observing how the makeup looks on one's face. These apply not only to the makeup studio but also to the home environment. Not all customers have enough space for a big smart mirror with a bunch of light bulbs in their house, therefore the physical SBM should be designed with the flexibility to fit in a different room environment. For instance, considering users might put the mirror in the bedroom with dim, yellow lighting, attaching a white light bulb to the mirror will provide additional light for the user to aid their makeup process.

Decision-Making and Procedures of Makeup: As observed in the makeup demo sessions, doing makeup usually follows a set of common procedures. It includes but is not limited to skin condition check, preparatory care such as putting on moisturizer or eyebrow trimming, face, eyebrow, eye, lip makeup, and a final fix and set. Some of the steps might be omitted depending on the client. For instance, people who have shaped, sparse or thin eyebrows might not need additional trimming. Meanwhile, male makeup is much simpler than female makeup because some of the steps are omitted. The observed time needed for each step is summarized in Table 6.

The preparatory stage of makeup application included observation and consultation with clients. The knowledge that the makeup artist learns from the client would be the fundamentals of her later decision-making during the makeup application stage. In other words, observing and consulting with the clients help the interviewee to know what to do next, and how to choose suitable products for them. The things the makeup artist observed included the skin condition, skin tone, hair color, and the shape of the face and facial features of the client.

Table 6. The observed time needed in daily makeup.

Step	Procedure	Observed time needed (in second)	
		Male daily makeup	Female daily makeup
1	Check skin condition and skincare	120	240
2	Eyebrow trimming	180	N/A
3	Face makeup	360	300
4	Eyebrow makeup	10	300
5	Eye makeup	N/A	180
6	Lip makeup	N/A	180
7	Final fix and set	N/A	240

Based on the skin condition, such as the extent of dryness, the interviewee would wipe the client's face with toner to calm the skin, then apply moisturizing cream or essence to prepare the skin. For clients with dry lips, she would put a lip mask with a thick layer of Vaseline which the excessive grease would be wiped off right before applying lip makeup. The goal was to exfoliate, soften and lubricate the client's lips. The interviewee also suggested that sunscreen would be needed to protect the skin. At the makeup stage, the interviewee used different products for different skin conditions and tones. Specifically, she chose the base product, foundation, and concealer of suitable shade, as well as decided the overall color tone, all based on the skin tone. The hair color was the reference to choose the eyebrow pencils, powders, or mascara of matching color. By observing the face shape and the facial features, she could later decide which parts to emphasize or not. On top of observation, the interviewee had to consult with the client for the things that are not immediately observable. For example, she would confirm with the client to see if he or she was allergic to any cosmetic products. She would also discuss with the client about the makeup style he or she preferred, his or her skin type, and skincare habits. In particular, she would choose makeup products of different textures according to the skin type so that the makeup could last longer, such as powder type for oily skin, cream type for dry skin.

Makeup Knowledge. When asked if there are trends in makeup, the interviewee agreed. She observed that mass media and celebrities influenced the trend, which has changed over time. Arched eyebrows became popular a few years later. Commonly, clients would bring the celebrities' photos with them, to show and discuss with her the makeup style they admired. She also found these helpful in understanding the clients' preferences and expectations. The trend is always changing, but the interviewee suggested three strategies to choose colors and products to put on. First, pick the matching colors for the season. For instance, colors of pastel tone, pink, and coral are used a lot in the spring, more vivid tones such as sky blue and khaki are used in the summer, burgundy for the fall, and white for the winter. Second, make use of the trending colors of the year selected by the experts. Third, look up the brand stories and the models as these give hints on whether the products would suit oneself. All this information can help one to judge whether a product would fit him or her. Nevertheless, the interviewee put the client's preference as the priority. From the design perspective, the PSS should be able not only to retrieve data on the latest trend but also to learn from the user.

Makeup Strategies and Techniques. When the interviewee was asked if there is any goal of doing makeup, she suggested that there are two common concerns that apply to most kinds of makeup except for prosthetic makeup. The first concern is about how to make the skin look clear and flawless, and the second is about how to symmetrize, balance the facial features. Following that, doing makeup is mainly about correcting the skin tone, balancing the asymmetry, and covering the blemish or the imperfection of which the client is concerned. Table 7 summarizes the strategies she adopted to achieve these goals.

Even though there are millions of makeup tutorials available online, many people still recruit professional artists to do their makeup for important occasions, such as a wedding. Indeed, the skills and experiences are parts of the expertise of the beauty practitioners with which need time to be trained and hard to be replaced.

Table 7. Summary of strategies and techniques used by makeup experts.

Goal	Strategy	Technique
Even up skin tone	1. Less is more 2. Use of complementary color 3. Avoid using a particular color 4. Change of hair color	1. Use minimal products to present a clear base with the natural contour 2. Use reddish products to vitalize and brighten the dull, yellowish, or bluish tone 3. Avoid red for people with skin redness; avoid yellow and hot pink for people with yellowish skin tone 4. For people with darker skin tone, dye dark hair lighter to brighten up the face
Balance out the face shape	1. Shift of focus 2. Highlight and contour 3. Change of hairstyle	1. For people with long face shapes, extend the eyebrows and eyes horizontally by drawing them thicker and longer 2. Highlight the part one wants to emphasize and shade the part to make a part less noticeable 3. For people with a square chin, put up the hair to makes the edges less obvious; for people with asymmetric faces, sweep the hair aside to cover it; cut a fringe to cover the forehead
Symmetrize the face	1. Symmetry check 2. Symmetry creation 3. Different extent of emphasis	1. Maintain a distance from the mirror, blink, and keep a poker face which the muscles are at a natural, relaxed state 2. For eyebrows at slightly different levels, reshape the eyebrows by trimming or drawing them 3. For eyes and eyebrows at different levels, apply lighter makeup to make the asymmetry less noticeable
Enhance the beauty	1. Repeated use of the same color 2. Use of tools	1. Tint the lips, cheeks, eyelids, and eyebrows with the same color to create a harmonious effect 2. Apply products with hand helps absorption, with a brush creates the glows, with sponge or puff to supply moisture

5 Discussion

The online survey and expert interview have provided the research team with insights and ideations which can be implemented into the PSS design. Through the online survey, we could notice most participants preferred a face-sized mirror, voice control, touch interface for a smart beauty mirror. Also, they emphasize 1) Virtual application of different styles, 2) Style recommendations, 3) Product recommendations and 4) Make-up tutorials. for assisting makeup function. Experts said a smart mirror might have the function to detect and adjust the environmental lighting to what is proper for putting on makeup. The system can also learn users' preferences and knowledge from beauty professionals at the same time to offer personalized recommendations. When the interaction between the user and the system is as natural, smooth, and satisfying as having a personal makeup artist, the marketability of smart mirrors is very likely to improve.

5.1   User Persona

Personas are fictional characters that can represent a potential user of a specific service. This section describes the main user of this service who can represent the main target group. Also, it explains how the persona uses the service proposed by this paper. The woman is selected for persona because they had a relatively higher frequency of looking in the mirror and doing makeup than men. First, we wrote the personal information (sex, age, work, family, and nationality). Second, we focused on specific attributes such as attitude, behavior, and pain points. Third, we described her biography, career, and technology comfort level. Lastly, we set up her beauty and style goals (Fig. 3).

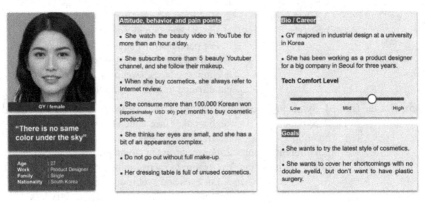

Fig. 3. An evaluation persona extrapolated from research

5.2   Service Blueprint

This Smart Beauty Mirror service blueprint (Fig. 4) is divided into four sections (User Actions, User Interface, Backstage Actions, and Supporting Processes). The time is divided into two parts, from 5 to 30 s, which refers to the overall smart mirror process from the start of mirror operation to before makeup. From 5 to 120 min are the time from the start to the end of makeup and the time to finish the smart mirror operation. User action proceeds in the following order. The user operates the smart mirror through a button and voice control interface. 1. When the user says Hello to the mirror, the mirror is turned on and informs weather and time, and shows the account options (public/private). 2. User selects an account, the purpose of make-up (Usual, Special, Recommended), and select the process (tutorial, virtual makeup, product recommendation) 3. The user starts the makeup by playing the video, listing up the recommended products, showing the virtual makeup. 4. When the user wants to end up the makeup, just leave the seat and the smart mirror is turned off.

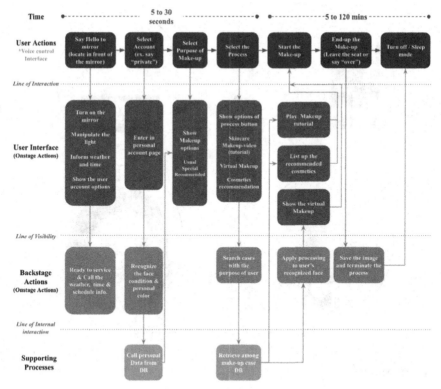

Fig. 4. Smart beauty mirror service blueprint

5.3 Wireframe

For the wireframe (Fig. 5), we made a concept image based on a Smart Beauty Mirror user interface. The first image shows when the user turns on the mirror by voice or touch, the mirror informs today's weather and time. When the user clicks the personal account, the schedule and the user's past makeup data come out. The second image indicates showing makeup options such as usual, special, and recommended depending on weather or the users' past makeup data through AI recommendation algorithms. The third image shows the situation where the user plays a skincare and makeup tutorial. When the user follows the makeup through video, the cosmetics information and price used in makeup are shown. Therefore, users can use the same products or choose similar products from the tutorial. The fourth image shows when the user chooses the virtual makeup. The user can see various options (Eyeshadow, eyeliner, lipstick, blusher, shading) to choose or a full makeup style. If the user's face is recognized, the virtual makeup goes on the face, so it helps the user to find which makeup is suitable.

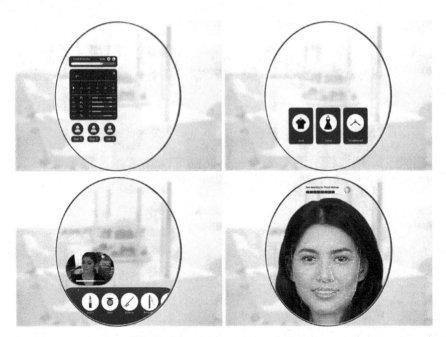

Fig. 5. Smart beauty mirror wireframe

6 Conclusion

The online survey and expert interview have provided the research team with insights and ideations which can be implemented into the PSS design. Through the online survey, we could notice most participants preferred a face-sized mirror, voice control, touch interface for a smart beauty mirror. Also, they emphasize 1) Virtual application of different styles, 2) Style recommendations, 3) Product recommendations and 4) Make-up tutorials. for assisting make up function. Experts said a smart mirror might have the function to detect and adjust the environmental lighting to what is proper for putting on makeup. The system can also learn users' preferences and knowledge from beauty professionals at the same time to offer personalized recommendations. When the interaction between the user and the system is as natural, smooth, and satisfying as having a personal makeup artist, the marketability of smart mirrors is very likely to improve.

Currently, the smart beauty mirror presented in this study is only presented up to the wireframe, and the prototype has not been proposed. In addition, the user feedback on smart beauty mirrors for the makeup process presented in this study was not reflected. In order to compensate for the shortcomings, reviewing the Smart Beauty Mirror process and function with beauty industry experts and makeup artists remains a future task for researchers. Also, it is necessary to verify and supplement the Smart Beauty Mirror by conducting many user tests in order to identify the satisfaction of our SBM function. If the prototype is developed through future works, we strongly believe that our SBM as product service system design can be commercialized and effective for people's make up.

References

1. Allied Market Research. https://www.alliedmarketresearch.com/cosmetics-market. Accessed 2 Feb 2021
2. Athira, S., Francis, F., Raphel, R., Sachin, N.S., Porinchu, S., Francis, S.: Smart mirror: a novel framework for interactive display. In: 2016 International Conference on Circuit, Power and Computing Technologies (ICCPCT) (2016). https://doi.org/10.1109/iccpct.2016.7530197
3. Gold, D., Sollinger, D.: Indratmo: SmartReflect: a modular smart mirror application platform. In: 2016 IEEE 7th Annual Information Technology, Electronics and Mobile Communication Conference (IEMCON) (2016). https://doi.org/10.1109/iemcon.2016.7746277
4. Nguyen, T.V., Liu, L.: Smart mirror: intelligent makeup recommendation and synthesis. In: Proceedings of the 25th ACM international conference on Multimedia (2017). https://doi.org/10.1145/3123266.3127926
5. Morelli, N.: Developing new Product Service Systems (PSS): methodologies and operational tools. J. Clean. Prod. **14**, 1495–1501 (2006). https://doi.org/10.1016/j.jclepro.2006.01.023
6. Parida, V., Sjödin, D.R., Wincent, J., Kohtamäki, M.: Mastering the transition to product-service provision: Insights into business models, learning activities, and capabilities. Res. Technol. Manag. **57**(3), 44–52 (2014). https://doi.org/10.5437/08956308X5703227
7. Tukker, A., Tischner, U.: Product-services as a research field: past, present and future. Reflections from a decade of research. J. Clean. Product. **14**(17), 1552–1556 (2006). https://doi.org/10.1016/J.JCLEPRO.2006.01.022
8. Marilungo, E., Papetti, A., Germani, M., Peruzzini, M.: From PSS to CPS design: a real industrial use case toward industry 4.0. Procedia CIRP **64**, 357–362 (2017). https://doi.org/10.1016/J.PROCIR.2017.03.007
9. Mele, C., Pels, J., Polese, F.: A brief review of systems theories and their managerial applications. Serv. Sci. **2**, 126–135 (2010). https://doi.org/10.1287/serv.2.1_2.126
10. Beverungen, D., Müller, O., Matzner, M., Mendling, J., vom Brocke, J.: Conceptualizing smart service systems. Electron. Mark. **29**(1), 7–18 (2017). https://doi.org/10.1007/s12525-017-0270-5
11. The design of Smart Product-Service Systems (PSSS): an exploration of design characteristics, http://www.ijdesign.org/index.php/IJDesign/article/view/1740. Accessed 11 Nov 2022
12. Lee, C.-H., Chen, C.-H., Trappey, A.J.C.: A structural service innovation approach for designing smart product service systems: case study of smart beauty service. Adv. Eng. Inform. **40**, 154–167 (2019). https://doi.org/10.1016/J.AEI.2019.04.006
13. Kuo, T.C.: Mass customization and personalization software development: a case study eco-design product service system. J. Intell. Manuf. **24**(5), 1019–1031 (2012). https://doi.org/10.1007/s10845-012-0643-8
14. Kato, Y.: A study on application of Artificial Intelligence (AI) for cosmetics: quantum Computer is necessary for beauty-field analysis. In: 2018 International Conference on Electronics Packaging and iMAPS All Asia Conference (ICEP-IAAC) (2018). https://doi.org/10.23919/icep.2018.8374693
15. Cosmetics and Your Health – FAQs. Womenshealth.gov. November 2004. Archived from the original on 12 March 2013
16. Kumar, S.: Exploratory analysis of global cosmetic industry: major Players, technology and market trends. Technovation **25**, 1263–1272 (2005). https://doi.org/10.1016/j.technovation.2004.07.003
17. Lau, K.: Uncovering Chinese stereotypes and their influence on adolescent male makeup purchasing behavior. J. Soc. Sci. Stud. **5**, 248 (2017). https://doi.org/10.5296/jsss.v5i1.12329

18. Weber, J.M., Capitant de Villebonne, J.: Differences in purchase behavior between France and the USA: the Cosmetic Industry. J. Fash. Mark. Manage. Int. J. **6**, 396–407 (2002). https://doi.org/10.1108/13612020210448673
19. Choi, J.-Y., Kim, K.-H., Kim, M.-S.: Cosmetics buying patterns and satisfaction among female university students in China, Japan and Korea. J. Korean Soc. Cloth. Text. **31**, 1772–1783 (2007). https://doi.org/10.5850/jksct.2007.31.12.1772
20. Interaction Design Foundation. https://www.interaction-design.org/literature/topics/service-design. Accessed 2 Nov 2022

Opportunities and Challenges
for the Near Future Smart Environments

Dynamic Environmental Plugins: Programmable Architectural Elements Reactive to Socio-environmental Conditions

Mostafa Alani[1]($\boxtimes$), Michael C. Kleiss[2], Muwafaq Shyaa Alwan[1], and Sida Dai[2]

[1] Aliraqia University, Baghdad, Iraq
mostafa.waleed@aliraqia.edu.iq
[2] Clemson University, Clemson, SC, USA

Abstract. This paper employs Research through Design (RtD) approach to customizing building components to address Socio-Environmental issues within the built environment and utilizes shapeshifting artifacts that can be integrated into existing spaces to extend those spaces' functionality, consequently improving occupants' social and physical experience. The paper focuses on the steps and processes necessary to design, program, and fabricate such components and present two types of Dynamic Environmental Plugins that are inspired by Islamic tessellated structures.

Keywords: Reconfigurable structures · Form transformation · Tessellations · Built environment · Embedded computation · Interaction design · Algorithmic thinking · Architectural robotics

1 Introduction

Tessellated structures are one of the most prominent features of Islamic architecture that has been employed for decorative, cultural, and environmental purposes. A wide variety of geometric patterns exist geographically in the region that expands from central Asia in the east to Morocco in the west. Such structures weren't arbitrary; rather, it was based on extensive knowledge of geometry designed to fill spaces perfectly while leaving no gaps [1, 2]. Figure 1 shows the tessellated structures and other, historically exist, types of patterns in Islamic architecture—floral, and calligraphic patterns.

Ancient artisans and mathematicians mastered the production of such geometric patterns and generated morphologically related designs. It has been found that the most segmented design in Islamic tessellations is morphologically related to the least segmented design; that is, the components of each design can be reconfigured to display the other design [3]. Figure 2 shows such morphological transformation between three designs. Inspired by such morphologies, this study employs tessellations to subdivide and morph surfaces to address socio-environmental issues.

© The Author(s), under exclusive license to Springer Nature Switzerland AG 2022
N. A. Streitz and S. Konomi (Eds.): HCII 2022, LNCS 13325, pp. 363–371, 2022.
https://doi.org/10.1007/978-3-031-05463-1_25

Fig. 1. Geometric, floral, and calligraphic patterns cover various surfaces inside the Qalawun complex in Cairo, Egypt.

Dynamic building components are common elements within the built environments. The idea of reconfiguring a building component to extend or alter the function of the built environment has been an essential part of architecture since its early days. For instance, doors and windows are some of the earliest examples of dynamic building components. Moreover, more complex examples are well established within architecture, such as escalators and elevators, to mention a few.

Nowadays, digital technologies can be embedded within dynamic building components to sense the surrounding environment and respond accordingly. The *Institut du Monde Arabe* in Paris, designed by the award-winning architect Jean Nouvel and built between 1981 to 1987, can be considered one of the earliest examples of a responsive dynamic building component (see Fig. 3) [4]. The geometric tessellations in the exterior building façade of the Institut du Monde Arabe are inspired by al mashrabiya (shanshūl)—a perforated, crafted pieces of wood that provides a view to the outdoor, natural lighting, and ventilation while preserving the occupants' privacy. The Institut du 'Monde Arabe was followed later by a series of projects that aimed to use reconfigurable building structures to extend or enhance the performance of the building. One prominent recent example is Al Bahar Towers where the façade of the towers is covered with traditionally inspired, environmentally sensitive dynamic shading devices that shapeshift in response to the surrounding environmental conditions [5].

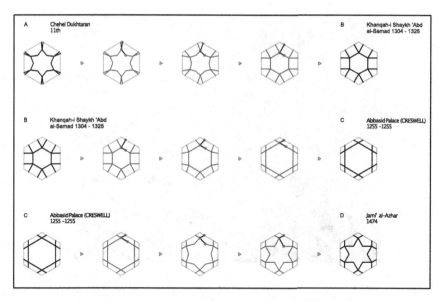

Fig. 2. The morphological transformation of Islamic tessellations for three different historical designs. Designs shown on the left and right are authentic Islamic tessellations. Designs shown in the middle are the gradual transformation of those designs.

2 Research Method

The presented design-research work started as an experiment in a design studio as a response to socio-environmental conditions in public spaces. It aims to answer the question of how to develop an adaptable environment that responds to human needs. Thus, the research utilizes Research through Design (RtD) research approach. The RtD approach allows exploring various facets of a problem in a creative way while creating "conceptually rich artifacts" [6] while documenting the processes taken to create such artifacts. Thus, this research conducts developmental work to "customize a piece of technology" to do something new and then "communicate the results," focusing on the design goals and iterative design and fabrication processes [7–9].

3 Dynamic Environmental Plugins

This paper builds on the historical and contemporary applications of dynamic building components and develops Dynamic Environmental Plugins (DEPs). The developed Dynamic Environmental Plugins (DEPs) are shapeshifting artifacts that can be added to an already established space to provide extra features that enhance that space's functions and improving occupants' social and physical experience [7].

Fig. 3. Top the façade of the *Institut du Monde Arabe. Bottom:* Interior shot explaining the dynamic shading devices (images credit: Wikimedia).

The paper presents two types of Dynamic Environmental Plugins (DEP): pre-fabricated and pre-structured. The following sections discuss the hardware and software development of each system.

3.1 Pre-fabricated DEP

The pre-fabricated DEPs are shapeshifting building components that can be installed in various spaces by mounting them on existing building components, such as floors, walls, columns, and ceilings, to extend the functionality of those spaces to respond to various physical and social issues. The pre-fabricated DEPs are designed for rapid deployment and are beneficial for quick upgrades of the built environment.

The Audio Columns is an exemplar case of a pre-fabricated DEP that can be deployed in public spaces to respond to the issue of hearing impairment. The project builds on the "DeafSpace" concept [10]. This project aims to extend existing public spaces' features to be deaf-friendly by integrating dynamically morphing skin to communicate messages with deaf individuals. The presented prototype was developed to be mounted on columns within public spaces. System hardware consists of a hexagonal grid covered by stretchable material that can be actuated through rotating rods attached to a motor. Figure 4 shows the designed digital model and the physical prototype, and its actuation mechanism.

The software was developed to measure the surrounding audio intensity through sensors. The data collected through sensors is then fed to the algorithm and remapped into a rotation value. The rotation values speed and intervals are then associated with meanings to signal messages to deaf individuals—for instance, rapid movement signaling an emergency (see Fig. 5). In addition to the above input method, the algorithm can be hardcoded and fed the data directly through a human operator.

3.2 Pre-structured DEP

Pre-structured DEPs are modular shapeshifting components that can be installed on a repetitive structure. The repetitive structure is to be part of the existing space. Thus, it requires the prior installation of the repetitive structure. Pre-structured DEP offers many advantages such as structural flexibility, customization, ease of maintenance, and long-term cost-effectiveness.

The reTessellate system is an exemplar case of Pre-structured DEP. It consists of two main components: a repetitive structure and a repetitive unit. The repetitive structure was designed to be reconfigurable; that is, the same units can be put together to assemble the three types of regular tessellations: triangular-, hexagonal, and rectangular-structures which add another level of flexibility to the system [11]. Then, the repetitive units can be inserted within that structure. We designed the repetitive units to be modular and can host various modules to perform different functions to meet occupants' continuously changing needs [12]. In the case of the reTessellate, both linear and rotary actuator modules were designed. The linear allows actuating surfaces through a push-pull function, ultimately achieving something similar to the actuated surfaces used in the Audio Columns. The rotary actuator modules were used to build morphable star-like elements using the origami techniques to shapeshift and allow or prevent light to pass through (see Fig. 6).

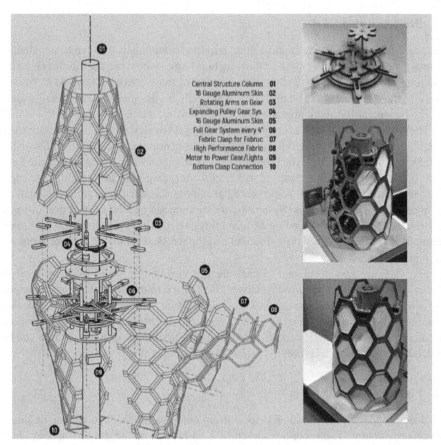

Fig. 4. Audio Columns project. Left: exploded view of the unit. Right: a prototype that can communicate various messages (this project was developed in a design studio setting by Brandon Arroyo and Farhaan Samnani)

4   Tessellations and Dynamic Built Environments

The understanding of tessellations significantly advanced the design and research of the two presented dynamic environment plugins both in software and hardware development.

In the case of the Audio Columns project, the visual communication mechanism with deaf individuals is conducted through a morphable skin that is based on hexagonal tessellations. The use of hexagonal tessellations makes it possible to link the response generated by the algorithm to the physical model in an organized manner. The data was sent to each cell accordingly to actuate the whole design (see Fig. 7).

In the case of the reTessellate, tessellations informed the design of both the repetitive structure and the repetitive unit. The repetitive structure can be reconfigured to assemble the three possible regular tessellations. Additionally, the tessellations system can be transformed in a gradient fashion from one regular tessellation to another. This gave the system greater flexibility to meet various functions and makes it suitable for configuration

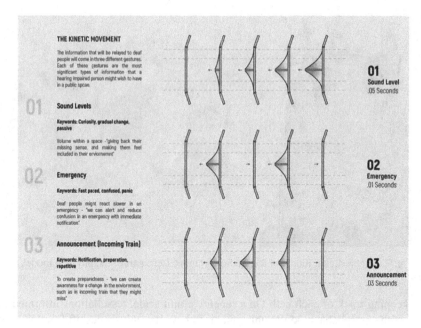

Fig. 5. Various actuation modes of the audio column.

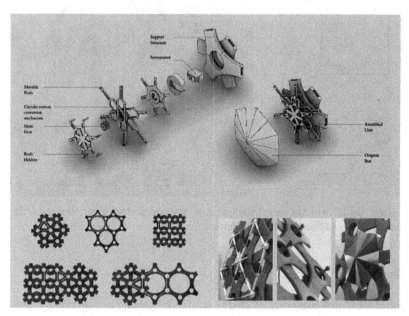

Fig. 6. The reTessellate system. Top: exploded view of the repetitive unit. Bottom left: stacking possibilities of the repetitive unit ("minimum inventory maximum diversity"). Bottom right: the system with various modules installed.

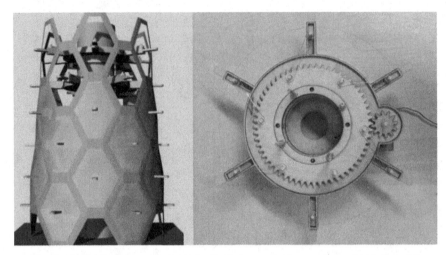

Fig. 7. Right: digital model of the Audio Columns. Left: part of the physical model.

while keeping track of each cell. On a repetitive unit scale, tessellations informed the design of the morphable modular units; that is to have the unit shapeshift from one state to another to respond to a social or physical condition (see Fig. 8).

Fig. 8. Right: digital model of the reTessellate. Left: assembled physical model using a triangular repetitive structure and linear actuator modules.

5 Discussion

This paper presented two types of DEPs: pre-fabricated and pre-structured. Both systems utilize tessellated structures that Islamic Geometric Patterns inspire as a base for the morphing skin. The Audio Columns utilizes a basic hexagonal cell covered with stretchable fabric, which allows it to initiate the communication process with deaf individuals. We argued that such system is better suited for an already established environment and can another level of functionality to inhabitable spaces. The presented pre-structured DEPs, on the other hand, are based on the "minimum inventory maximum diversity" design strategy [12]. It utilizes a more complex tessellated structure capable of forming the all-possible regular tessellated structures hexagonal-, triangular-, and square-based structures, which gives it greater flexibility to cope with a wide range of scenarios. In addition, the repetitive unit can hold various modules with a variety of cores that can be customized as needed. The software design of both systems utilizes skeletal mapping data fed to Rhinoceros computer software and its Grasshopper plugin as inputs [13]. The data processed, and the system produces an output in the form of physical transformation. However, considering the modular nature of the Pre-structured DEP, additional sensing devices were also tested. Such system needs a pre-planning to be integrated into the space fabric, yet it promises versatility.

The next step for the presented prototypes is to set up on-site usability tests, conduct associated hardware improvements for the tessellated structure and actuation mechanism, and conduct additional software improvements.

References

1. Gülru, N.: The Topkapi Scroll: Geometry and Ornament in Islamic architecture. Getty Publications (1996)
2. Jan, A.S., Salman, A.S.: Symmetries of Islamic Geometrical Patterns. World Scientific (1994)
3. Alani, M.W.: Algorithmic investigation of the actual and virtual design space of historic hexagonal-based Islamic patterns. Int. J. Archit. Comput. 16(1), 34–57 (2018)
4. Branko, K., Parlac, V.: Building Dynamics: Exploring Architecture of Change. Routledge (2015)
5. Peter, O.: Al Bahr Towers: The Abu Dhabi Investment Council Headquarters (2014)
6. William, G.: What should we expect from research through design? In: Proceedings of the SIGCHI Conference on Human Factors in Computing Systems (2012)
7. Evan, G.K.: Architectural Robotics: Ecosystems of Bits, Bytes, and Biology. MIT Press (2016)
8. Christopher, F.: Research in art and design. Royal College of Art Research Papers, vol. 1, no 1, 1993/4 (1994)
9. John, Z., Forlizzi, J., Evenson, S.: Research through design as a method for interaction design research in HCI. In: Proceedings of the SIGCHI Conference on Human Factors in Computing Systems (2007)
10. "DeafSpace." – Gallaudet University. www.gallaudet.edu/campus-design-and-planning/dea fspace
11. Mostafa, A., Soleimani, A.: reTessellate: Modular dynamic surfaces reactive to socio-environmental conditions. In: Streitz, N., Konomi, S. (ed.) HCII 2019. LNCS, vol. 11587, pp. 113–123. Springer, Cham (2019). https://doi.org/10.1007/978-3-030-21935-2_10
12. Peter, P.: Structure in Nature is a Strategy for Design. MIT Press (1990)
13. Andrew, O.P., Johnson, J.K.: Firefly: interactive prototypes for architectural design. Arch. Des. 83.2, 144–147 (2013)

Interpreting the Development of Information Security Industry from Standards

Jie Liu, Yongxin Kong, and Guochao Peng[✉]

Sun Yat-sen University, Guangzhou 510006, China
penggch@mail.sysu.edu.cn

Abstract. Information security has been a significant concern in personal life, enterprise development, city construction, and national competitiveness. Information security standards, as an important regulatory and guiding tool, reflects the consensus reached by the industry and therefore are important references to understand an industry. This study explores a new angle to understand the development of the information security industry by analyzing the external and content features of related standards. Based on the available metadata and the possible dimensions, a standards' features index system and a roadmap of analysis are constructed. The Chinese and ISO information security standards are selected to verify the method. The result shows the evolution of the industry, the status quo, and the future trend of the information security industry.

Keywords: Information security · Standards · Bibliometrics · Thematic analysis · Standards' features · Index system

1 Introduction

In the era of big data, information and data are indispensable for personal life, enterprise development, and national development. However, information security problems such as information leakage, information pollution, information infringement, and information destruction have become increasingly prominent [1], causing huge losses and laying great impacts on individuals, enterprises, and the country. The most common security issues include ransomware attack, code injection, XSS attack, data breach, malware, DDoS attack, credential stuffing attack, brute force attack, weak passwords, and authentication issues, social engineering, SPAM and phishing, insider threat, sensitive data leak, etc. [2].

Personal information is becoming more valuable for business operators and therefore is a new target for criminals [3] (Xianghua Deng 2021). Emerging technologies and services like voice assistants [4, 5], mobile app, cloud computing [6] and so on, bring new concerns of privacy protection. According to the Information Leakage report of ENISA (the European Union agency for Cybersecurity), in the first half of 2019 only, an astonishing number of 41 billion data records were exposed globally, and E-mail and passwords were the top of the list [7].

For enterprises, information is not only the raw material of production, but also an intangible asset [8]. Solms [9] pointed out that protecting enterprise information security is to protect enterprise information assets, and that information security should be called business security. According to the Data Breach Investigation Report (DBIR) released by Verizon, the data leakage events covered almost all types of enterprises around the world [10]. In merely 2 years from 2019 to 2021, the number of confirmed data leakage events increased sharply from 2,013 to 5,258 [10, 11], up by more than 160%.

On the level of countries, the production and control capacity of data has become a new embodiment of national influence and dominance [12]. The Global Cybersecurity Index [13] and the National Cyber Security Index [14] are constructed to evaluate the security level of countries across the world. Moreover, smart city construction has a growing demand for information security. In this reformation of city construction, information security is one of the biggest challenges [15, 16]. However, it is also noted that this problem cannot be fixed by a single vendor or manufacturer, but by applying appropriate standards in the entire industry or city [17].

Information security standards play an important regulatory and guiding role in information security [16]. Although, researchers are keen to study topics like information security technologies, management, behaviors, and performance of organizations, only in recent years, information standards attract more and more attention as many researchers become more interested in the information security management system and ISO/IEC 27000. Nevertheless, most of the studies are about a single standard. There is no study found about information security standards as a whole.

This study explores a new angle to study the development of information security technologies, management, and applications by analyzing all the related standards. The related standards of ISO and China are selected to verify the method. The standards are divided into 3 groups according to their current status. By analyzing the data of all the issued standards, the evolution of information security development is presented. By interpreting the data of all currently applicable standards, the status quo of the information security industry is demonstrated. And the data of standard plans, which are expected to be completed within 5 years, draw a clear developing path in the near future of information security.

2   Literature Review

It is nonnegligible that the standards issued by a country contain technical content agreed by the experts and industry, and even approved by the country. To somehow, they are the imprint of the development of the country. Researchers have explored many ways to study the standards. The researches on information security standards are mainly about the standards system construction, content comparison between different standards or standards systems, and the problems in implementing the standards. Many Chinese researchers have studied information security standard systems of different industries, such as smart cities, intelligent networked automobiles, industrial Internet, nuclear power plant, industrial control system, digital archives, railways, etc. Zhao Wen et al. [17] combed China's information security standard system and introduced the relationship between main standards. Chen Xuehong [18] studied the industrial information security standard system. Guan Hongpeng [19] analyzed the hidden dangers of information security in China's industrial Internet and put forward suggestions on the information security standard architecture of industrial Internet.

Some researchers are keen to compare standards and standards systems to look for enlightenment, especially in China. Prameet P. Roy [20] compared the advantages and disadvantages of the NIST network security framework and ISO 27001 Information Security Standard. Xie zongxiao [21] introduced ISO/IEC 27036 and ISO IEC 27036-3, analyzed ICT supply chain information security risks, and put forward suggestions for the implementation of ICT supply chain information security management in China. Chen Tian et al. [22] combed the information security standard systems of ISO/IEC, ITU-T, NIST, and China, and analyzed the problems that existed in the standard system framework from the aspects of practicability, applicability, and cohesion. Sun hang [23] compared ISO, ITU-T, the United Nations World Forum for harmonization of vehicle regulations and SAE information security standards in the United States, and put forward suggestions on the construction of China's automobile information security standard system.

The implementation of standards, especially the implementation of ISO 27000 family standards of information security management system, is also a keen concern of researchers. Susanto et al. [24] developed a set of integrated solution modeling software for testing the organization's implementation of ISO 27001 readiness in six categories: organization, interested parties, tools & technology, policy, culture, and knowledge. Through empirical research, Shuchih Ernest Chang et al. [25] found that managers' ability, environmental uncertainty, industry type, and organization scale are all factors affecting the implementation of BS7799. Stefan Fenz [26] created the formal expression of the ISO 27002 standard and showed how to use security ontology to improve the efficiency of the compliance inspection.

It can be seen that the mainstream of existing researches on information security standards focuses on the content comparison of standards in specific industries and the implementation of a specific standard. Despite the many different ways to interpret standards of information security standards, there is no index system found and applied to the information security standards.

3   Construction of the Index System

This research seeks a solution to understanding the information security industry by analyzing the external and content features of related standards using bibliometric and thematic analysis.

Bibliometrics is a discipline that studies literature or literature-related media using econometric methods such as mathematics and statistics to master the dynamic characteristics of science and technology [29]. Since the beginning of the 21st century, bibliometrics has been applied to the research of agricultural standards, traditional Chinese medicine standards, scientific and technological archives standards, publishing standards and other industries' standards [30–33]. Although some researchers have applied the bibliometric method in studying standards in various industries, most of them focus on external features like quantity, time, and number [32, 34]. As for the content features, ICS (International Classification of Standards) is used to classify the industry, and the high-frequency keywords are used to know the focus of standards [34, 35].

Based on the existing researches, the index system of standards literature is constructed as shown in Fig. 1.

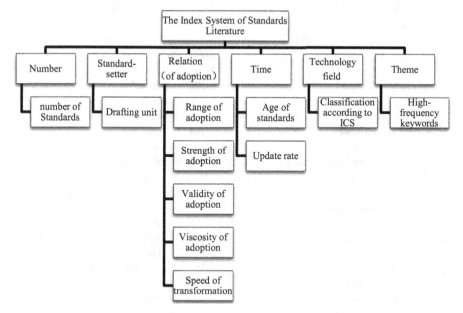

Fig. 1. The index system of standards literature based on [30–33]

Nevertheless, the index system only considers the available metadata of Chinese standards. In order to construct an index system that could be applied to both Chinese standards and international standards, it is necessary to analyze the metadata of both Chinese and foreign standards and understand the features they represent.

According to the Chinese national standard of "Metadata of Standard Literature" (GB/T 22373—2021), the metadata of both Chinese and foreign standards are compared. The availability of the metadata of information security standards is marked as shown in the following table. The possible analytic dimensions of available metadata of both Chinese and foreign standards are also marked (Table 1).

Considering the availability of metadata of both Chinese and ISO standards, the dimensions of number, relation, time, technology field and theme could be used to analyze the information security standards. Although ICS classification can show the industrial distribution of the standards, a fine-grained thematic evolution and distribution are left unsolved. Therefore, a co-occurrence analysis and thematic analysis are favored in this study. As a result, a new index system of standards features is constructed (see Fig. 2).

Based on the available metadata of standards, the external and content features can be analyzed. The scale, timeliness, and advancement reflect the external features of standards, and can be measured through the number, release time, and age of standards. The source of content and thematic distribution reflects the content features of standards. The source content can be identified through whether the standards adopt foreign standards.

Table 1. Metadata of standard literature.

No.	Foreign standard metadata				Chinese national standard metadata			
	Identifier	Name	Analytic Dimensions	Availability	Identifier	Name	Analytic Dimensions	Availability
1	000	Record status	/	✗	000	Record status	/	✗
2	001	Record ID	/	✗	001	Record ID	/	✗
3	100	Standard number	N	✓	100	Standard number	N	✓
4	101	Release date	T	✓	101	Release date	T	✓
5	102	Issuing agency	R	✓	102	Issuing agency	R	✓
6	200	Standard status	N, T	✓	200	Standard status	N, T	✓
7	205	Implementation or trial date	T	✓	205	Implementation or trial date	T	✓
8	206	Abolition Date	T	✓	206	Abolition Date	T	✓
9	207	Confirmation date	T	✓	207	Confirmation date	T	✓
10	208	Original classification Number	/	✓	209	Drafting unit	/	✓
11	298	Chinese standard name	D	✓	298	Chinese standard name	D	✓
12	301	Original standard name	D	✓	302	English standard name	D	✓
13	302	English standard name	D	✓	305	Audit items	/	✗
14	305	Audit items	/	✗	390	English subject words	/	✗
15	390	English subject words	/	✗	461	Substitute standard	/	✓
16	462	Replaced standard	/	✓	462	Replaced standard	/	✓
17	461	Substitute standard	/	✓	800	Degree of consistency	R	✓
18	800	Degree of consistency	R	✓	820	Amendment	/	✓

(*continued*)

Table 1. (*continued*)

19	820	Amendment	/	✓	823	Supplement	/	✗
20	823	Supplement	/	✗	825	China Classification of Standards	/	✓
21	825	China Classification of Standards	/	✗	826	International Classification of Standards	F	✓
22	826	International Classification of Standards	F	✓	835	Chinese subject words	/	✗
23	835	Chinese subject words	/	✗	840	Chinese free words	/	✗
24	846	Collection mark	/	✗	846	Collection mark	/	✗
25	871	Technical Committees	/	✓	871	Technical Committees	/	✓

Note: in analytic dimensions, "N" is short for "number", "R" for "relation", "T" for "Time", "F" for "technology field" and "D" for "thematic distribution".

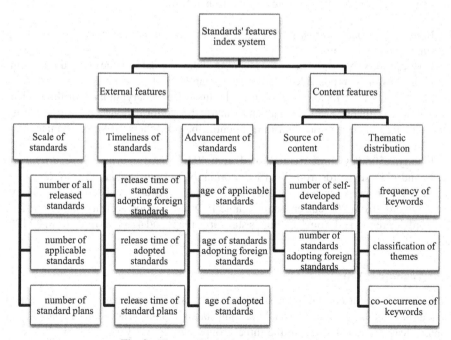

Fig. 2. The standards' features index system

And the frequency of keywords and co-occurrence can help to identify hot issues in the industry and generate a knowledge map. The classification of themes can help to look into the evolution of themes during industrial development and compare standards of different countries, regions, or organizations.

4   Data Procession

4.1   Collecting Data

The National Public Service Platform for Standards Information (NPSPSI) in China provides the most complete and up-to-date data of standards. Therefore, NPSPSI is selected as the database for the Chinese standards. As for ISO standards, the data of the ISO official website are collected. In order to ensure the authority and comparability of the data, only the standards developed by ISO/IEC JTC1/SC27 and SAC/TC260 were collected. And the standards issued by Mar. 5th, 2021 are collected. The collected data include the standards' title, current status, release time, implementation time and the title, relation of adoption, consistency of adoption. In total, 402 standards and 71 standard plans developed by SAC/TC260, and 378 standards and 82 standard plans by ISO/IEC JTC1/SC27 were collected.

4.2   Marking the Keywords

As the standard titles are the most accurate concision of the content, we mark keywords from the title. The specific marking method is as follows:

1. Remove auxiliary words, punctuation marks, and numerical numbers, and keep substantive nouns only;
2. On the premise of not changing the meaning of the original text, the title is divided into phrases as small as possible according to semantics. For example, the keyword of the title "Information Technology, Security Technologies, Encryption Algorithms, Identity Based Ciphers, SM9 Mechanism" is marked as "information technology, security technologies, encryption algorithms, identity-based ciphers, SM9, mechanism".

Finally, 1506 keywords were marked from 402 China's information security standards, and 1715 keywords from 378 ISO information security standards; 1167 keywords were marked from 312 currently applicable information security standards in China, and 905 keywords from 207 currently applicable ISO information security standards; 374 keywords were marked from 71 China's standards plans and 428 keywords from 82 ISO standards.

4.3   Analysis of Data

According to the current status, the standards are divided into three groups: all the issued standards, currently applicable standards, and standard plans. The external features and content features of standards in the three groups will be analyzed respectively. Coordinating with the research questions, the roadmap of analyzing the development of the information security industry based on standards is constructed as shown in Fig. 3.

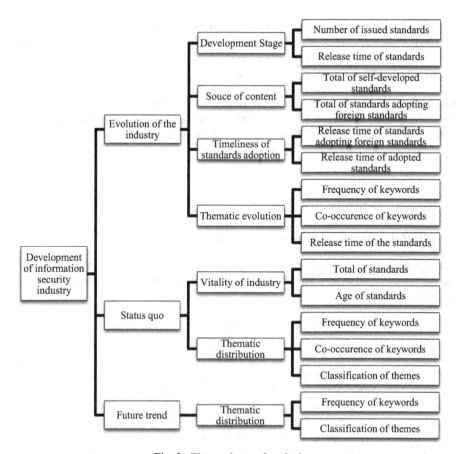

Fig. 3. The roadmap of analysis

Frequency Analysis. The number of information security standards released over the years is counted, and the evolution trend of the number of standards released over time is analyzed. The release time of Chinese standards and that of their adopted international standards is recorded, and the time difference is calculated to know the timeliness of adopting international standards in China. The age of the standards and their changes reflects the aging of the standards.

Co-occurrence Analysis. Instead of a rough classification by ICS or pure high-frequency keywords, this study uses co-occurrence analysis to study the characteristics and changes of standards' themes. Co-occurrence analysis is a content analysis method that uses subject/keywords to analyze the subject composition of the research field [36]. This study conducts a co-occurrence analysis of the keywords marked based on the standards' titles.

Knowledge Map. Knowledge map aims to visually describe the development process and relationship of scientific knowledge. It features with intuition, quantification and knowledge discovery. This study uses VOSviewer to process and generate knowledge maps. Set 3 as the minimum co-occurrence frequency to generate the thematic evolution map and the thematic distribution map based on keywords of all the issued standards and current applicable standards respectively. Set 1 as the minimum co-occurrence frequency to generate the density map of standard plans.

Thematic Analysis. Thematic analysis is a qualitative description method for identifying, analyzing and reporting patterns (themes) in data, including "bottom-up" coding and "top-down" coding [37]. This study use "button-up" coding of keywords marked from the standards titles to classify the themes.

5 Empirical Study

5.1 The Information Security Standards of China

According to the roadmap as shown in Fig. 3, the development of information security industry is analyzed from 3 aspects: the evolution of the industry, the status quo and the future trend.

Evolution of Information Security Industry. According to the total number, release time, and adoption relation of the information security standards, the information security industry has experienced 3 stages: the initial stage (1994–2004), the growing stage (2005–2014) and the leap stage (2015-present). China's information security standardization has been launched since 1987. Nevertheless, after 2004, China's information security standards have developed rapidly. Especially after 2014, it has developed dramatically. At present, the total number of China's information security standards exceeds ISO. The development mode of China's information security standards has also changed from the passive mode dominated by adopting international standards to the active mode dominated by self-development.

In the initial stage, Chinese national standards lag 3 years on average behind the adopted international standards. From 2005 to 2014, the average lag time increase to 6.1 years. After 2015, this number decreases to 5.8 years. This shows that self-developed standards are the main content of China's information security standardization, and the standards adoption efficiency needs to be improved further.

Table 2. Development stages of information security industry in China

Stage	Period	Number of issued standards	Number of self-developed standards	Number of adopted standards	Proportion of adopted standard	Average lag time (years)
Initial stage	1994–2004	21	3	18	86%	3
Growing stage	2005–2014	141	107	34	24%	6.1
Leap stage	2015–2021	240	200	40	17%	5.8

The Fig. 4 demonstrate how the themes of standards change overtime. It can be seen that the themes of China's information security standards have generally experienced changes from safety technology, information security technology, public key, network security, information security management, to application security, IoT and personal information.

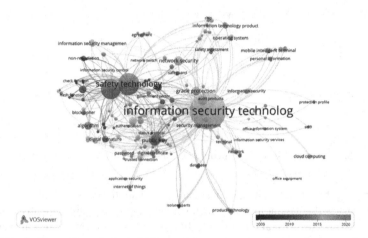

Fig. 4. Thematic evolution of Chinese information security standards overtime

Status Quo of Information Security Industry. Currently, there are 312 applicable standards in China. The data shows that the standard age of China's applicable information security standards is between 1 and 21 years, and the average standard age is 5 years. And standards under 5 years constitute 62.8% of the total number. 24.7% of the standards are between 6–10 years old, and 12.5% are between 10–21.

In view of the timeliness of standard adoption, the national standards issued by China lag an average of 6 years behind the international standards, including 40.7% of 5 years and below, 55.6% of 5–10 years and 3.7% of 10 years and above. It can be seen that China still needs to improve the timeliness of the standards adoption. Otherwise, it may cause inconsistency of domestic and foreign technical requirements, and therefore damage the export of Chinese products and services.

The main themes of China's applicable information security standards are information security technology, safety technology, information system, public key, network security, algorithm, information technology product, cloud computing, application security and information technology product. This shows that the current focus of the industry is on the technology and application issues (Fig. 5).

Future Trend of Information Security Industry. As Fig. 6 shows, information security technology is the hottest topic in the near future, followed by information technology, safety technology, evaluate, and infrastructure.

Conduct a thematic analysis of the high-frequent keywords (no less than 3 times) and classify the keywords. It is found that Chinese information security standards can be divided into 3 categories: technology issues, management issues and application issues (see Table 3).

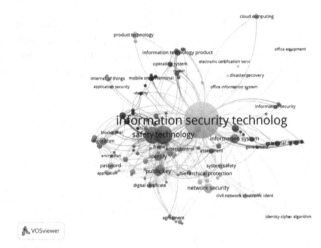

Fig. 5. Thematic distribution of current Chinese information security standards

Comparing the thematic changes between current applicable standards and standard plans, we can see that technology, management and application are basically balance in weights. The data security and the application of emerging technologies attract attentions. In terms of application, more scenarios have emerged, such as the information security of products and services that closely related to people's lives and the system security that related to enterprises. In management, although the protection of personal information, information security management system, evaluation and hierarchical protection have been upgraded, improvement is relatively limited compared with the other two categories.

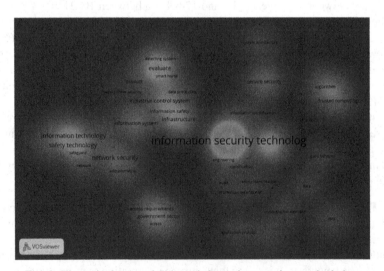

Fig. 6. Thematic density of Chinese information security standard plans

Table 3. Thematic analysis of Chinese information security standards

Category	Applicable standards		Standard plans	
	Sub-category	Main keywords	Sub-category	Main keywords
Technology	Network	Network, network security, Internet	Network	Network, Internet, inter network communication, mobile Internet, virtual private network
	Algorithm	Algorithm, trusted computing, elliptic curve, cloud computing, hash function	Algorithm	Confidentiality algorithm, integrity algorithm, cloud computing, cryptographic algorithm, trusted computing
	Password	Public key, password, key, block cipher	Password	Key, block cipher, public key infrastructure
	Autograph	Digital signature	Data security	Data security, data recovery, data backup, data processing, big data security, network data
	/	/	Emerging technologies	Face recognition, gene recognition, voiceprint recognition, gait recognition
Management	Information security management	Information security management system and information security risk	Information security management	Capability requirements, risk management and use specifications
	Evaluation	Controllable evaluation, evaluation, index system and evaluation method	Evaluation	Index system, safety assessment and risk assessment
	Personal information	Personal information, citizen network electronic identity	Personal information	Personal information security and personally identifiable information
	Hierarchical protection	Grade protection	Hierarchical protection	Grade protection

(*continued*)

Table 3. (*continued*)

Category	Applicable standards		Standard plans	
	Sub-category	Main keywords	Sub-category	Main keywords
Application	System	Information system, system security, operating system, industrial control system, office information system	System	Information system, industrial control system, important industrial control system
	Product	Information technology products	Product	App, scan products
	Application scenario	Internet of things, mobile intelligent terminal, e-government, website, smart card, mobile terminal	Application scenario	Smart home, Internet of things, mobile Internet, supply chain, mobile intelligent terminal, social network platform, government website
	/	/	Service	Electronic credentials, automobile, telecommunications, cloud computing, Internet information services, instant messaging, logistics, social online shopping, express logistics, online payment, online audio and video

5.2 The Information Security Standards of ISO

Similarly, ISO standards are also analyzed from 3 aspects: the evolution of the standards, the status quo and the future trend.

Evolution of ISO Information Security Standards. Since 1987, ISO has issued 378 information security standards and abolished 171. The specific chronological distribution is shown in Fig. 3. The first ISO information security standard was published in 1987. From 1987 to 1995, the number of ISO information security standards issued was small, a total of 12. From 1996 to 2003, the release of ISO information security standards increased. After 2004, the annual release of ISO information security standards remained relatively stable and reached its peak in 2015.

Figure 7 show that the theme of ISO information security standards changes from cryptographic technology, IT security, information technology, security techniques, information security management, information security, cybersecurity, to privacy protection.

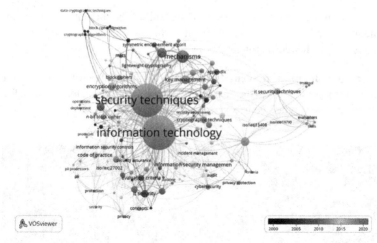

Fig. 7. Thematic evolution of ISO information security standards overtime

Status Quo of ISO Information Security Standards. Currently, there are 207 applicable ISO information security standards. The standard age of them is between 0–23 years, and the average standard age is 6 years. 51.7% of the standards are below 5 years old, 33.8% are between 6–10, and 14.5% are between 10–23.

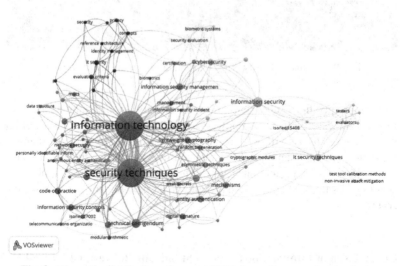

Fig. 8. Thematic distribution of current ISO information security standards

The themes of current applicable standards as shown in Fig. 8 are information technology, security techniques, information security, entity authentication, digital signature, information security management and IT security. More weights are on technology issues and management issues. This is consistent with result of the thematic analysis of applicable standards (see Table 4), which shows that the most concern of ISO standards is technology issues, followed by management.

Future Trend of Information Security Industry. Figure 9 shows that the focus of ISO information security standards in the near future will be information technology, followed by security techniques, cybersecurity, information security, and privacy.

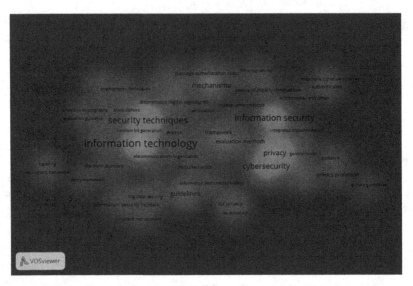

Fig. 9. Thematic density of ISO information security standard plans

To be more specific, ISO weighs more on technology and management security than application security. In technology issues, ISO focuses on algorithms, encryption technology. Data security will be a new focus in the future. In terms of management, the information security management system continues maturing, the evaluation is more concrete, and the privacy protection is more comprehensive. In terms of application, ISO moves from generality to detail, and has deployment in application scenarios, products and services.

5.3   Comparison of Information Security Standards Between China and ISO

Comparing the total number and age of standards of China and ISO could help to evaluate the development status of the information security industry of China. The annual increment of issued standards represent the activity of standardization, or in other words, the vitality of the information security industry. Figure 10 shows that the information security industry keeps a growing vitality since 2005 and surpass the international level since 2017.

Table 4. Thematic analysis of ISO information security standards

Category	Applicable standards		Standard plans	
	Sub-category	Main keywords	Sub-category	Main keywords
Technology	Network	Cybersecurity, network security	Network	Network security, cybersecurity, network security framework development, internet security, network visualization security, network virtualization security, communication
	Algorithm	Hash function, encryption algorithm	Algorithm	Encryption algorithm, elliptic curve generation, elliptic curve, hash function
	Password	Key management, block public key, encryption technology, lightweight cryptography, asymmetric technology, weak secret, symmetric technology	Password	Key management, cryptography, multiple public keys, cross domain cryptography, password based key derivation, public key infrastructure, authentication encryption
	Autograph	Electronic signature, anonymous electronic signature	Autograph	Anonymous digital signature, rewritable signature scheme, blind signature
	/	/	Data security	Big data privacy, big data security and storage security
Management	Information security management	Information security management system, information security control, event management, audit, certification, iso 27002	Information security management	Risk management, implementation, event management, capability requirements, risk management, technology maturity

(*continued*)

Table 4. (*continued*)

Category	Applicable standards		Standard plans	
	Sub-category	Main keywords	Sub-category	Main keywords
	Evaluation	Evaluation criteria, evaluators and safety assessment	Evaluation	Evaluation criteria, evaluation methods, evaluation laboratories, evaluation activities, it security evaluation, evaluation guidelines
	Personal information	Identity management	Personal information	Personally identifiable information, deletion of personally identifiable information
	Privacy protection	Privacy protection	Privacy protection	Privacy criteria, privacy protection, privacy preference, privacy impact assessment, privacy enhancement data
Application	Application security	Biometric system Application security	Application scenario	Telecommunication organization, mobile equipment, industrial internet platform, communication, internet of things, smart city
	/	/	Product	App
	/	/	Service	Timestamp service

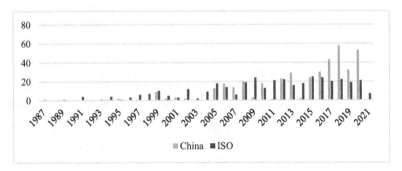

Fig. 10. Annual increment of issued standards

The age of applicable standards reflects the updating speed of the industry. The faster the standards are renewed, the faster the industry updates. The statistic shows that China is 11% more than that of ISO, and the average age of China's standards is 1 year less than that of ISO. China has more and younger standards than ISO. This means that Chinas' information security industry is growing faster than the average international level (Fig. 11).

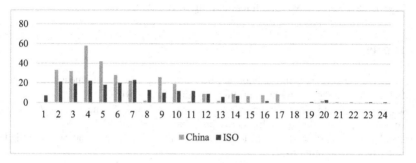

Fig. 11. Age of applicable standards

Compare Table 3 and 4. The differences of themes of information security standards can help us to find the problems and advantages in the development of China's information security industry. Both the China and ISO have deployments in all three issues of technology, management and application, and keep almost the same concerns on technology issues. Differently, China lacks enough attention to information security management and privacy protection. Nevertheless, China outperforms ISO on new technology and application scenarios, and this advantage will still be kept in the near future.

6 Conclusion

This study explores a new angle to understand the development of information security industry by analyzing the development path of information security standards, their status quo and development trend. A bibliometric analysis and a thematic analysis are used to understand the external features and content features of standards, and a standards' features index system and the roadmap of analysis are constructed accordingly.

Based on the bibliometric analysis of external features of standards, the development status, vitality and updating speed of standards are evaluated. The thematic analysis supplements with the thematic evolution and distribution of standards. In this way, a relatively comprehend understanding of the development of information security industry is achieved.

The information security standards of China and ISO are selected to verify the standards' features index system and the roadmap constructed in this study. The result proves that this method can help to interpret the development of information industry of a country and compare it with the international standardization organization to know the problems and advantages in its development. Moreover, the standards' features index system and the roadmap of analysis can also be used to analyze standards of other industries if the metadata required are available.

The limitation of this study may lie in the keywords' generation process. In this study, the keywords are marked from the titles of the standards. Although the standard title is the most accurate concision of the content, it is still too limited. In the future, NER and machine learning can be applied to process the texts of standards to generate more keywords and improve the understanding of the standards.

References

1. Zhang, H.: Research on information security problems and countermeasures in modern information technology environment. Inf. Syst. Eng. **8**, 81 (2018)
2. Escobedo, J.: Top 15 most common security issues and how to fix them. https://www.liquid web.com/blog/five-common-web-security-problems/. Accessed 2 Jan 2022
3. Deng, X., Yan, M.: Research on the Legal Protection of Personal Information in the Big Data Era. CIBDA 2021, IOP (2021)
4. Hoy, M.B., Cortana, A.S., et al.: An introduction to voice assistants. Med. Ref. Serv. Quar. **37**(1), 81–88 (2018)
5. Pal, D., Arpnikanondt, C., Razzaque, M.A.: Personal information disclosure via voice assistants: the personalization–privacy paradox. SN Comput. Sci. **1**(5) (2020)
6. Nikkhah, H.R., Sabherwal, R., Sarabadani, J.: Mobile cloud computing apps and information disclosure: the moderating roles of dispositional and behaviour-based traits. Beh. Inf. Technol. 1–17 (2021)
7. ENISA, ENISA Threat Landscape. https://d-russia.ru/wp-content/uploads/2020/10/etl2020-a_year_in_review_ebook_en.pdf. Accessed 2 Jan 2022
8. Zuo, J., Yang, J.M.: On information assets. Reform. Strat. **05**, 27–30 (2000)
9. Von Solms, B., von Solms, R.: From information security to…business security? Comput. Secur. **24**(4), 271–273 (2005)
10. VERIZON: 2021 data breach investigations report. https://www.verizon.com/business/resour ces/reports/dbir/2021/masters-guide/introduction/. Accessed 2 Jan 2022
11. VERIZON: 2019 data breach investigation report. https://enterprise.verizon.com/resources/reports/dbir/2019/introduction/. Accessed 2 Jan 2022
12. Leng, X.Y: Research on information security strategy in big data era. Inf. Sci. **37**(12), 105–109 (2019)
13. ITU. Global Cybersecurity Index. https://www.itu.int/en/ITU-D/Cybersecurity/Pages/global-cybersecurity-index.aspx. Accessed 2 Jan 2022
14. e-Estonia. The National Cyber Security Index ranks 160 countries' cyber security status. https://e-estonia.com/the-national-cyber-security-index-ranks-160-countries-cyber-sec urity-status/. Accessed 2 Jan 2022
15. Abdi, H., Shahbazitabar, M.: Smart city: a review on concepts, definitions, standards, experiments, and challenges. J. Energy Manage. Technol. **4**(3), 1–6 (2020)
16. Lai, C.S., Jia, Y., Dong, Z., Wang, D., et al.: A review of technical standards for smart cities. Clean Technol. **2**(3), 290–310 (2020)
17. Pishva, D.: Internet of things: security and privacy issues and possible solution. In: Proceedings of the 19th International Conference on Advanced Communication Technology (ICACT). IEEE (2017)
18. Wu, Z.: Preliminary study on information security standard system. Inf. Network Secur. **03**, 37 (2005)
19. Zhao, W., Su, H., Hu, Y.: Analysis of the relationship between information security standards. Inf. Network Secur. **11**, 48–50 (2009)

20. Chen, X.H., Liu, C.Y., Yang, S.F.: Research on industrial information security standard system. Conf. Sci. Technol. **07**, 25–28 (2019)
21. Guan, H.P., Li, L., Li, X., et al.: Research on information security standard system of industrial. Internet Autom. Expo. **03**, 50–53 (2018)
22. Roy, P.P.: A high-level comparison between the NIST cyber security framework and the ISO 27001 information security standard, NCETSTEA, IEEE: Durgapur, India (2020)
23. Xie, Z., Kunxiang, D.: ICT supply chain information security standard ISO/IEC 27036–3 and system analysis. China Stand. Rev. **03**, 16–21 (2016)
24. Chen, T., Zhang, Y., Zhao, S.: Research on the status quo of international information security standards and thoughts on the construction of standard system in china. Inf. Secur. Commun. Confident. **11**, 41–47 (2016)
25. Sun, H., Hanguang, X., Zhao, W.: Construction of information security standard system of intelligent networked vehicle and research on industrial policies. Chin. Autom. **12**, 38–43 (2018)
26. Susanto, H., Almunawar, M.N., Tuan, Y.C.: Information security challenge and breaches: novelty approach on measuring ISO 27001 readiness level. Int. J. Eng. Technol. **1**(1) (2012)
27. Chang, S.E., Ho, C.B.: Organizational factors to the effectiveness of implementing information security management. Indust. Manage. Data Syst. **106**(3), 345–361 (2006)
28. Fenz, S., Plieschnegger, S., Hobel, H.: Mapping information security standard ISO 27002 to an ontological structure. Inf. Comput. Secur. **24**(5), 452–473 (2016)
29. Qiu, J.: Definition of bibliometrics and its research object. Lib. Sci. Commun. **02** 71 (1986)
30. Wang, Y., Dan, X., Shusong, M.: A bibliometrics analysis of standardization for traditional Chinese medicine from 2010 to 2014. Introd. Trad. Chin. Med. **22**(13), 60–63 (2016)
31. Wu, K.: Bibliometric analysis of standard documents of scientific and technological archives in china. Electromech. Warship Arch. **01**, 66–70 (2018)
32. Wang, P., Wei, X.: Research on standardization of publishing industry based on standard literatures' bibliometrics. Technol. Publish. **10**, 116–124 (2019)
33. Liu, T., Yang, L., Qiuhong, Z.: Analysis of the application of occupational health standards based on bibliometrics. Chin. J. Labor Health Occup. Dis. **01**, 49–52 (2019)
34. Liu, H.: Comparisons of information and documentation standards between china and developed countries based on bibliometrics. Lib. Inf. Serv. **55**(12), 51–55 (2011)
35. Li, J., Liu, Y.: Literature metrology analysis on domain distribution and hotspots of Chinese agricultural standard--taking national library of standards' holdings from 2006 to 2008 for examples. Lib. Inf. Serv. **53**(18), 44–47+78 (2009)
36. Li, X., Qiu, J.: An informetric analysis on public culture service standards. J. Chongqing Univ. (Soc. Sci. Ed.). **21**(06), 132–139 (2015)
37. Braun, V., Clarke, V.: Using thematic analysis in psychology. Qual. Res. Psychol. **3**(2), 77–101 (2006)
38. GB/T 20000.2.: Guidelines for Standardization—Part 2: Adoption of International Standards (2010)

Immersive Entertainment Environments - From Theme Parks to Metaverse

Xueying Niu[1][(✉)] and Wei Feng[2]

[1] Beijing Normal University, Beijing 100875, People's Republic of China
15318809121@163.com
[2] Shandong College of Tourism and Hospitality, Jinan, Shandong, China

Abstract. This paper explores the interaction between the virtual world and the real world through the integration of the analysis of the metaverse and the theme park. At the same time, case studies of the application of the concept of metaverse in games and movies are conducted to explore the current manifestations of metaverse and critically explore the ethical issues it raises. The theme park here represents not only an IP, but also a broader cultural symbol. Under the development trend of metaverse, how real world theme parks should convey their cultural symbols, and in what form we can bring real world theme parks into the world of metaverse will become urgent issues to be solved. This paper will illustrate the process of a real theme park elements by transforming them into digital artworks through a design concept. This transformation not only enables virtualization of the real world, but also enables cultural dissemination to the world while virtualizing.

Keywords: Metaverse · Theme park · NFT · Case studies

1 Metaverse and Theme Park Background Elaboration

1.1 Metaverse Background Statement

The concept of metaverse originated from Neal Stephenson's book Snow Crash in 1992, which constructed a virtual world parallel to the real world, and this virtual world is the metaverse. The metaverse is a deep integration of the virtual world and the real world, where people in the virtual world can find projection in the real world. One of the Four Great Masterpieces of Chinese ancient times, A Dream of Red Mansions, once described a Taixu fantasy world, in which a couplet reads, "Truth becomes fiction when the fiction's true; Real becomes not-real where the unreal's real." The imagination of virtual worlds has emerged from the Chinese Qing Dynasty or even earlier. It has gradually become possible to construct a virtual world in people's imagination by using evolving science and technology.

The metaverse concept was born as a conceptual expansion of the game world, the construction and operation of a larger and richer game scene; It is now gradually being given a new meaning. The metaverse is managed and run as a parallel world to the real world, or even an augmented world that merges with the real world. Characters and scenes from the real world will be projected and constructed in the metaverse. The essence of the metaverse is deep interaction with the real world, and at its core is big data. The metaverse can both project the real world and break the pattern of the existing world in a virtual scenario, reconstructing and creating the real world in the virtual world, which makes the metaverse full of infinite possibilities. However, it is certain that the metaverse cannot completely replace the experience and value of the physical environment at the physical level. Thus, the metaverse as a virtual digital world will have a higher level of multifaceted immersion and personalization, a world where the real and the virtual coexist and the virtual and the real intermingle. It is a beautiful vision, and of course full of challenges.

1.2 Properties of Theme Parks

Theme park usually refers to the entertainment activity space shaped by virtual environment, garden environment as the carrier, while the theme plot throughout the amusement facilities, such as Universal Studios, Disneyland, etc. As society further expands the definition of theme parks, any park with a theme can be considered a theme park, such as Zhuhai Chimelong International Ocean Resort. The original intent of the theme park is more entertaining and clearly directed to entertainment, generally supported by popular IP. During the entertainment process, the realistic IP in the theme park and the environment that goes with them bring the audience and entertainers into an ideal, completely different world from reality, allowing people to experience a different life. The expanded theme park incorporates diverse themes such as plants, animals and even famous sites and traditional culture into the park design, and the broader theme park has the same goal orientation and positioning as the original theme park.

The theme park, as a typical product of the realization of the virtual world, is the expansion of the human spiritual world. If the meta-universe is to bring reality into the virtual, the theme park is to go from the virtual to the real. If the metaverse is the reality in the virtual, the theme park is the virtual in the real. The theme park in this paper is relatively broader in scope and has the following basic attributes in a narrow sense:

Entertainment and Game-play. Theme parks are first and foremost entertaining, which is the fundamental factor of its existence. There are many theme parks around the world, large and small, from Universal Studios in the United States, Disneyland, Changlong Resort in China, etc., to small museums and amusement parks in various places. Although all have different themes and business concepts in order to generate their own appeal, they all have typical entertainment and gaming attributes.

Virtuality and Immersion. Theme park facilities and environments are, on the one hand, virtual worlds built on scenes that never existed or have disappeared from the real world. These places are inaccessible to visitors in their daily lives, so they can be constructed using unlimited imagination to satisfy visitors' rich and diverse desire to explore and immerse themselves in them. For example, science fiction movie theme, cartoon theme, dinosaur theme, alien life theme, etc. On the other hand, the construction of theme parks is based on a collection of real things in the real world, thus meeting the historical traces left by people in the process of historical development, such as various types of rivers, lake parks, sites of human civilization, etc. Disney applied for a patent in July 2020 called "virtual-world simulator", the purpose is to allow visitors to travel freely between the real world and the virtual world, thereby increasing the immersion of play. Whether immersed in imagining the future or tracing history, the virtual nature and immersion of a theme park are crucial.

Reality and Interactivity. Theme park facilities and environments are real in real life, a product of moving from virtual to reality, where visitors can personally experience and interact with stories, scenes and characters from the virtual world. For example, the recently very popular LinaBell (shown in Fig. 1), an IP image released by Shanghai Disney on September 29, 2021, is a character that has not appeared in any previous animated film. But it was released immediately caused people's pursuit, many tourists specifically to Disney long lines with LinaBell photo, LinaBell dolls around is a short period of time in short supply. Reality and interactivity not only reflect the interaction between visitors and the theme park, while the theme park relies on IP to obtain offline economic benefits, thus realizing the real interactive behavior of the two.

Fig. 1. A figure of Lina Belle (Photo credit: Baidu Encyclopedia)

Thematic and Commercial. Theme parks generally have a clear theme and popular IP support, with the ultimate goal of profitability and obvious commercial attributes. A clear theme and IP are created to attract a specific group of customers for the purpose of sustainable business.

These attributes coincide with the concept of metaverse. The theme park's audience tends to be the IP that supports it, attracting a segment of the population interested in such IP, while the metaverse's audience tends to be "everyone". In the virtual digital environment of the future world, every person, every scene, every city, even every country, expects to find its own place, both reconfigured and maintained (as shown in Fig. 2).Theme parks can be seen as pieces of the meta-universe scattered around the world, and the meta-universe is the carnival of the whole world.

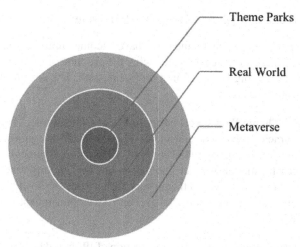

Fig. 2. Diagram of the relationship between the theme park and the meta-universe (Photo credit: Author)

The "ego", "self" and "superego" were introduced by psychoanalyst Freud's structural theory in 1923. It profoundly reveals the human characteristics of both contradiction and unity in the structure of the human spiritual world. In the context of this new era of the meta-universe, we have a new understanding of it and give it a different meaning. In the context of this paper, we can see the theme park as the "ego", which is the desire, the potential need of human nature based on relaxation and entertainment. The real self in the real world is the "ego", which lives according to a set track. The meta-universe is the "superego", the ultimate goal of the virtual world idealized by human beings (as shown in Fig. 3). And the three natures of the world can be explained as the ego expressing the entertainment of the world, the ego expressing the reality of the world, and the superego expressing the future of the world.

Fig. 3. A figure of the extension of the three divisions (Photo credit: Author)

1.3 Limitations and Prospects of Theme Park Development

As the epidemic continues, many theme parks have become unprofitable, or even closed at a loss. Many of China's theme parks are facing the problem of transformation. In this large social context, the big IP is still in a profitable state. The reasons for this can be broadly divided into four areas:

Design and Build Theme Parks According to Local Conditions. Theme parks need to rely on local characteristics for design and development, and designing an IP cannot be separated from the local environment. The blind choice of government and developers to copy the successful model of other parks does not suit the different needs of each place. At the same time, the size of a theme park varies from city to city, and the size of a theme park should take into account the level and development capacity of the city in which it is located.

Focus on Innovation and Creativity. The creation of IP should be based on solid market research, determine the regional audience, and reasonably develop a multi-level, multi-element and multi-form innovation park. With the continuous development of the social and economic level, people's aesthetic and experiential needs have gradually improved, and the single form of paradise has been difficult to meet people's needs. Continuous innovation, construction can make visitors, players refreshing play experience in order to obtain the theme park to maximize the benefits.

Gamification Design. Yu-Kai Chou has given a definition of gamification design that" I originally created the term 'Human-Focused Design' to contrast with 'Function-Focused Design' in 2012, but it should not be confused with 'Human Centered Design,' or 'User Centric Design' by IDEO [1]." Human-Focused Design focuses on the core drivers, so when we apply gamification design to theme parks it is based on the human experience. Unique route planning and product design for different groups of people will break through the original meaningless handling and piling up, and give tour participants a new experience and sensory enjoyment.

Diversified Profit Model. Creating a theme park not only needs to give a novel experience offline, but also should have the ability to transform cultural products into economic benefits. For example, when entering Disney, a street at the entrance is entirely devoted to selling Disney's peripheral products. At the same time should also "offline + online", that is, the combination of offline and online, the theme park IP projected online, using a variety of forms of exposure and publicity to increase the penetration of the brand. Based on the general background of the meta-universe, projecting the real world to the virtual world may also be a new attempt.

1.4 Metaverse and Theme Parks

Metaverse and theme parks are analyzed from their attributes, they have both commonalities and significant differences. What they have in common is that: Firstly, they are virtual and beyond reality; Secondly, they are based on and have sources and are not entirely empty; Thirdly, they are idealized and cannot be fully realized at present. Theme parks are easier to regulate and manage. The metaverse is currently in the conceptual and embryonic stage, involving ethics, safety and other aspects that are still being explored, and there are no effective means and measures for regulation and management.

The metaverse concept was initially very game-like and entertaining, and could be seen as a theme park in a virtual world. As it has been studied and theories have evolved, its entertaining nature has gradually diminished, getting closer and closer to the idealized state of the real world, moving from entertainment to reality. Theme parks, whether in the past, present or future, will always uphold its entertainment properties, existing in the real world or nested in a meta-universe, building virtual spaces that do not belong to the real world at all. In comparison, the theme park can be seen as the prototype of the meta-universe, which will evolve into a symbiotic meta-universe with the real world in the future after the integration and mapping with the real world.

In our life, they are both contradictory and unified, an organic whole. Theme parks built based on metaverse can be both real and virtual. According to our own needs, we can build a virtual theme park unique to ourselves in the world of metaverse, or visit other open theme spaces with individuality, in order to achieve the purpose of releasing self-awareness and thus reduce the mental pressure of self in life.

2 Metaverse with Game and Movie Retrospective

2.1 Metaverse and Games

The year 2021 is called the meta-universe year. The improvement of many technologies such as content production, 5G technology, data processing technology technology, and interface has laid a good foundation for the development of metaverse. At the same time, the epidemic also accelerated the development of the social "house economy", which stimulated the formation of the metaverse. The metaverse is not a purely virtual world, but a fusion of the real world and the virtual world. The game, on the other hand, is an artificially constructed virtual space, and the metaverse is an extension of the game.

The meta-universe has been shown in several games and film productions as early as. Under the influence of the epidemic, more and more people choose to get a sense of excitement and satisfaction in the virtual world of games, and to communicate with real human relationships in the game. Because of the strong interactive nature of the game, players are able to communicate on multiple levels and with strong feedback in it. From ancient times to the present, whether it is literature, paintings, or movies and games, people have been pursuing the sense of compensation of the virtual world to the real world. And also try to feed the real world through the construction of the virtual world, so as to make up for what people cannot achieve or are missing in the real world, so the sense of participation and immersion become important indicators of measurement.

For example, in the era of Web 2.0, "Second Life" developed by Linden Lab was launched in 2003, which reproduces people's real life in the game in the form of online games combined with social networks. Players will not only be able to socialize in the game, but will also be able to spend or start businesses through its proprietary currency, the Linden Dollar, selling the fruits of their labor to other players. Nintendo of Japan's 2020 release of "Animal Crossing: New Horizons" also constructed a space in the virtual world exclusively for players. The time setting of the island is consistent with the player's geographical location, enabling the interaction between reality and virtual space. Players in the game through the construction of the island to get their ideal living environment, in the island using "bell money" as currency, players need to work (shell collection, fruit, fishing, etc.) to get paid for their labor, and then convert the goods into "bell money" and repay the loan, so as to enhance their living experience on the island. At the same time, friends can also visit each other in the game by virtual plane and give gifts, thus realizing the strong social attributes of the game. But in contrast, "Animal Crossing: New Horizons" is still a relatively closed world, and only those who participate in it can exchange news.

Thus, in terms of the degree of openness of the game environment, it can be roughly divided into three levels. The first level is similar to "Minecraft", "Animal Crossing: New Horizons" and other games with a low degree of openness, in which players are able to interact on a small scale. During the epidemic, there were also schools conducting graduation ceremonies in both games to meet the social needs of people who could not meet offline. The second level is a moderately open gaming platform similar to the early Roblox. Roblox is dedicated to connecting the world through games, and it builds community content that is all about the developers. Players juggle the roles of player and developer in the community, making games in the community with Roblox' authoring tools. At the same time, there is undoubtedly economic behavior in the Roblox community as well, with players acquiring Robux through real-world currency and then paying Robux to developers and platforms by playing games and buying game skins. The third level is the meta-universe - a highly open world, at which point the game will be just one part of it.

From the current point of view, the construction of metaverse will gradually weaken or even break the social barriers and rebuild a borderless world in the future. In the process of game category design, players also began to pay more attention to the independent choice and the play of personal subjectivity. In addition to massively multiplayer online games, many other categories of games are also starting to focus on player choice to a certain extent. So in addition to multi-category games, interactive video games have emerged. For example, New One Studio's adaptation of the creation of "The Invisible Guardian", wartime spy design allows players to have full scope for choice. The different choices players make in the game correspond to very different game endings. In addition, there are "The Shapeshifting Detective", "Late Shift", etc. all belong to the category of interactive video games.

To varying degrees, these games have introduced a digital social component. On the one hand, digital socialization in the game brings people closer to each other, and on the other hand empowers players while strengthening the control for them. "The connections allowed by these systems are always double-edged: they liberate exploration, expression and are thus potentially empowering; on the other hand, the constant contact with social networking services also enables new technologies of uninterrupted control. (Crawford, G, 2013) [2]" By taking a critical look at these open links, players are enjoying a more open and free gaming experience, but are also being "watched" and controlled.

2.2 Metaverse and Movies

Film also plays an important role in the conceptual imagination of the "metaverse". For example, 1999's "The Thirteenth Floor" depicts the interchange between the virtual and real worlds. "Avatar" in 2009 showed the idea of the human neuronal system being "split" by a machine. The 2010 film "Tron: Legacy" is based on an immersive video game that constructs a virtual space." Inception" depicts the vision of multiple spaces. In the movie "The Congress" in 2013, the heroine sells her image to a company, which can then process "unmanned" movie works by computer. The movie became a product of the re-creation of one public figure's image possession after another. After that, Spielberg's "Ready Player One" in 2018 and "Free Guy" in 2021 show a "bounded" virtual space that can be accessed through VR devices. In addition, there are "The Truman Show", "Hardcore Henry", "Jumanji", "Westworld" and many other similar film and productions.

The role of film in the construction of metaverse is relatively single, similar to that of games, and the role of audience is gradually changing from "watching" to "participating", and the boundary between film and game is gradually blurred. For example, the first interactive films were shown at the Montreal World's Fair in 1967. The movie "Kinoautomat: One Man and his house" allows the audience to vote on the ending of the movie by using the red and green buttons while watching the movie. In addition, there are "Detroit: Become Human", "Black Mirror: Bandersnatch" and other interactive film and game works that combine film and game.

While most films present the metaverse from the perspective of decentralization and new human-machine relationships, we should also consider the ethical issues of the metaverse itself. As shown in "The Congress", in the real world, people establish their self-subjectivity through the other, but in the utopian world depicted by movies, people use hallucinogens to turn themselves into symbols themselves, losing the subject of self-care. People are like works of art in the era of mechanical reproduction, losing not only the "aura" as Benjamin said but also Freud's "ego, self, and superego". The metaverse constructs a huge landscape society, every virtual user will be a digital laborer in the metaverse, all operations performed by the user in the metaverse are labor, while the user's means of production are controlled in the hands of a larger capital, and behind the more open virtual environment is a more repressive, exploitative and precise algorithm. At the same time, this virtual world does not have a second life as in the game Second Life, so it is real domination of the politics of life.

Dave Baszucki, CEO of Roblox, has summarized the metaverse into eight core characteristics: Identity, Friends, Immersive, Low Friction, Variety, Anywhere, Economy and Civility. Professor YU Guoming has mentioned in his article that from the perspective of product form, games are the prototype of metaverse. And the metaverse adds the features of low latency, unlimited devices (anytime, anywhere) and diversity to satisfy the basic characteristics of games, and the metaverse thus achieves perpetual development [3]. The authors also suggest that the development of the metacosmos will gradually internalize the construction of the mental world from the external "five senses" (hearing, seeing, smelling, tasting, and touching). At present, both games and movies, which are regarded as the "prototypes" of the meta-universe, still have certain boundaries, and the re-creation of the meta-universe itself and the value of human subjects in the meta-universe is still in development.

3 A Vision of Linking Metaverse and Reality Theme Park

3.1 Design Objectives: NFT Digital Artwork Design as an Example

NFT covers a variety of categories, such as digital artwork, digital music, digital real estate and game props. Take digital artwork as an example, in the construction of metaverse, the theme park in reality is transformed into digital artwork through NFT so as to realize tokenization. Not only is it possible to virtualize the real world, but it is also possible to spread culture to the world while virtualizing.

The uniqueness of NFT makes it a symbol of rights in the virtual world, rights that belong not only to the purchaser, but also to the creator. Artists will no longer need to worry about plagiarism and copyright disputes, and this uniqueness provides protection to both buyers and sellers. As we increasingly feed culture into NFT products, NFT becomes the small link between the virtual world and the real world.

This paper locates the NFT practice in the landscape design within a theme park, and the design subject is selected from Shandong Province, China. The design plan transforms a traditional Chinese theme park into a digital artwork through design, thus projecting the real world into the virtual world. The author and the team used a combination of software, such as Aseprite, Photoshop, After effects, and Magicavoxel. Later on, a series of modeling and lighting setups were carried out for the digital artwork based on an attempt to diversify the means of promotion.

3.2 Production Process Description

In the early stage of design, we conducted a thorough data review process, compared different software, and finally selected Aseprite software for the pixelated landscape design. For the performance content part, the first focus on the regional culture and architectural style in the theme park of China's Shandong Province, selected images with regional characteristics and representative landscapes such as the willow tree, Daming Lake cruise ship, Qingdao Beer Museum, etc., a series of cultural tourism elements are planned to be drawn. The group adopted a production strategy of drawing elements first and then combining and adjusting them, starting with a static single element drawing of the plant class (as shown in Fig. 4).

After the unified drawing of the plant elements, the group reviewed the original materials for the drawing of the building, prepared many reference pictures and selected the most suitable ones. Physical color extraction and post beautification were carried out based on cultural element extraction, and the objects were summarized with impactful colors, and the painting of Daming Lake painted boats, Chaoran Building, Dacheng Hall of Confucius Temple, and Qingdao Beer Museum were carried out respectively (as shown in Fig. 5).

In the static single element drawing, the group finally performed the drawing of the character element (shown in Fig. 6). The first two pictures (left 1 and left 2) show the design extracted from traditional Chinese elements, while the third picture (right 2) shows the design extracted from woodblock prints from Weifang City, Shandong Province. The last picture (right 1) shows the design with the element of running dry boat.

Fig. 4. A figure of plant elements drawn (Photo credit: Author)

Fig. 5. Design of some architectural elements (Photo credit: Author)

Fig. 6. Part of the folklore character elements drawing (Photo credit: Author)

After completing the static single element drawing, proceed to the dynamic element design using Aseprite. The process of creating dynamic elements is basically the same as that of animation, which is accomplished by changing the shape of the screen in different key frames. The figure below shows the dynamic performance of the lion dance in the costume folk culture (as shown in Fig. 7). Such dynamic elements can be synthesized and then disseminated independently on mobile using gif format as WeChat emoji packs, etc. They are also able to enter the blockchain as unique small animations.

Fig. 7. A figure of the dynamic process of "lion dance" (Photo credit: Author)

Afterwards, we performed a picture composition to make a complete motion picture (as shown in Fig. 8).第The first line on the left shows the scene around Daming Lake. We try to make the lake dynamic to achieve the effect of shimmering, and at the same time use the combination of scenery such as willow trees, painting boats and Chaoran Building to form the mood beauty of reflecting thousands of scenery on the shore of Daming Lake. The picture on the right shows a signal hill and a lighthouse on the seaside of Qingdao, Shandong Province, as representative elements with a certain degree of interest and expressiveness. The second row, shown on the left, is a scene of Nanshan Mountain in Yantai. The picture on the right shows a scene of Mount Tai in Tai'an, Shandong Province, with clouds in the mountain and a view of the mountains from a high place.

Fig. 8. Part of the illustration screen synthesis (Photo credit: Author)

3.3 Conclusion

Take China's theme parks as an example, except for big IP such as Disney and Universal Studios, which have landed in China and gained good economic benefits, many local Chinese theme parks are facing some degree of hardship. Especially under the impact of the epidemic, many theme parks that are already struggling to make ends meet are even worse. In understanding the above issues, in addition to focusing on the representation and external connections of the metaverse, a critical understanding of the various ethical and social issues it raises is indispensable. When the theme park is facing the status quo of virtualization, the gradual penetration of small aspects may not be a bad way to go. Extracting the representative elements of theme parks and turn them into innovative pictures and videos through design to enter the Non-Fungible Tokens market. This blockchain-based crypto asset not only protects the creativity, but more importantly, attracts more attention by taking up space in the market to promote these unique landscape designs. By transforming the real world landscape into digital artwork and thus tokenizing it, this transformation not only enables the virtualization of the real world, but also enables cultural dissemination to the world at the same time.

References

1. Chou, Y.: Actionable Gamification: Beyond Points, Badges, and Leaderboards, pp. 8–9. Packt Publishing Ltd., Birmingham (2019)
2. Crawford, G., Gosling, V.K., Light, B.: Gamers: The Social and Cultural Significance of Online Games. Taylor & Francis., Abingdon-on-Thames (2013)
3. Yu, G.: The evolution logic of future media: the iteration, reorganization and sublimation of human connection–from the age of context to the metaverse to the future of the mental world. Journal. Mass Commun. (10), 54–60 (2021)

Enabling Real-Time and Big Data-Driven Analysis to Detect Innovation City Patterns and Emerging Innovation Ecosystems at the Local Level

Eleni Oikonomaki[1,2(✉)] 🆔

[1] Aristotle University of Thessaloniki, 541 24 Thessaloniki, Greece
[2] Northeastern Boston University, Boston, USA
oikonomaki.e@northeastern.edu

Abstract. Innovation indicators have been the main subject of many prior studies, most having focused on the structural patterns of innovation ecosystems and the complementary relationships between a pair of actors rather than the dynamic aspects of their hybrid identity, both physical and digital settings. There is also extensive bibliography on the definition and the different forms of innovation ecosystems. For this, the current paper aims at contributing to innovation ecosystems research from a different view. The first section introduces the topic by addressing the research question: In an era of digitalization and teleworking, how can digital data and recent technologies serve in providing the most up-to-date information about innovation performance measurement of innovation ecosystems? The second section summarizes current bibliographies on the framework of the use of big data for detecting city patterns and some constraints identified. The third section provides an overview of metrics-based management toolkits and frameworks, scoreboards, and indicators from several sources for measuring innovation at different scales. The findings are presented to shed light on the gaps and opportunities of the current toolkits used for measuring a growing divergence of national, regional, and local innovation success, but also provide new insights for innovation policymakers and governments seeking to identify dynamic interactions within innovation ecosystems at the local level. This study emphasizes these toolkits' capabilities to use big data to detect real-time innovation patterns while it explores how these new technologies are enabling innovation in ways other studies have not considered. The paper concludes with a reflection on this study's limitations and advancing recommendations for future research on success factors associated with physical, geographical settings and digital patterns with the innovation performance of an ecosystem. The proposed approach aims at providing useful insights and meaningful recommendations for stakeholders and policy makers to orchestrate the emerging ecosystems of the next generation of innovators and entrepreneurs.

Keywords: Innovation ecosystems · Innovation success factors · Innovation indicators · Big-data · Innovation governance · Innovation patterns · Metrics-based management toolkits · Innovation performance measurement · Data analytics · Optimization · Intelligence · Open data

© The Author(s), under exclusive license to Springer Nature Switzerland AG 2022
N. A. Streitz and S. Konomi (Eds.): HCII 2022, LNCS 13325, pp. 404–418, 2022.
https://doi.org/10.1007/978-3-031-05463-1_28

1   Introduction and Context

1.1   Background and Research Questions

The main aim of the paper is to identify existing frameworks and scoreboards of innovation, gather some of the current indicators used to measure innovation in multiple scales (from national to regional and local), and understand the main success factors that drive innovation. Its secondary purpose is to highlight some of the challenges of the current toolkits to measure innovation and explore new ways that big data analytics can be used as an additional method to the existing ones, to identify innovation patterns. In addition to that, the paper works in the direction of previous studies, which identified the need for more efficient tools to measure innovation at the local level, since most of the existing measurement toolkits have focused on innovation indexes from a top-down perspective and hardly measure innovation in a smaller than the regional scale, almost neglecting the fact that innovation is mainly built from bottom-up processes.

This article also builds upon two previous studies. The first one discusses the transformations of city business ecosystems and the ways cities worked to restore their vibrancy since the start of the pandemic [22]. The second study [23] uses data from the platforms and repositories of international organizations (such as OECD library) to analyze local policy responses to COVID-19 from different cities all over the world. Both studies concluded on the need for monitoring the cities' transformation through the lens of local efforts. Local focus is needed to expand the different types of innovation opportunities even after the pandemic needs are met. The spread of the virus has led governments to adopt unprecedented measures to support city business ecosystems and enhance entrepreneurship and innovation at the local scale.

The current study examines the lessons we can learn from the current crisis and explores new ways to use big data analytics and other technologies to apply new policies to support local communities' innovation and provide insights on the ways they can profit off their own data for the good of many people instead of a select few large companies. The economic, social, and environmental benefits of the use of big data cannot be ignored. Internet and World Wide Web platforms, big data analytics, software, social media, and civic technologies contribute to the "creation of smart ecosystems in which connected intelligence emerges and disruptive social and eco-innovation flourishes" [28]. Localities that will take advantage of the current technological advances shown, will achieve a faster recovery and get better prepared for future crises. Connecting physically and digitally heterogeneous entities [human intelligence, unrelated areas of science and technology, and methods from different disciplines; artificial intelligence, mining large datasets, supervised learning, and analytics; and collective intelligence, knowledge and resources distributed in communities, organizations, and places] is crucial to deal with the challenges of 21st [28].

The paper sets out the findings of the study as follows:

Section 1 introduces the topic of big data as a tool for enabling successful real-time, data-driven identification of city patterns and leads to the question: How can digital technologies and big data analytics serve in providing the most up-to-date information about innovation performance measurement. (Sect. 1.1); The answer to the question will provide support to innovation policy makers to improve the current tools that they use to identify bottom-up initiatives at the local city scale. This section also describes some parts of the current discussion and an overview of those studies that provide critique at big data (Sect. 1.2).

Section 2 provides significant considerations in the discourse of real-time & big data-driven processes (Sect. 2.1) and analyzes significant constraints for detecting patterns (Sect. 2.2). It also attempts at exploring new opportunities for using big data in innovation assessments at the local level (Sect. 2.3).

Section 3 contains an evaluation framework which can provide insights into how a metrics-based management toolkit for innovation is structured (Sect. 2.3); This section also provides a summary of the range of innovation indicators identified across all the scales of ecosystems (national, regional, local) as well as an overview of the key issues and constraints of these studies (Sect. 2.4).

Section 3 provides recommendations for further study based on the overview of innovation toolkits and indicators presented in Sect. 2.3.

1.2 Methods, Scope, and Data Collection

To address these questions, the study has been informed through a literature review which mainly focuses on publications on the way cities can use real-time data to detect city patterns. This section firstly provides a bibliographic analysis of other studies and initiatives using real time, big data analysis as a tool for improving city governance. It also aims at revealing the gaps in research in regards with the use of big data to identify current and emerging innovation patterns of different city ecosystems and localities. The study continues with the identification of existing innovation scoreboards and metrics-based management toolkits that measure the national, regional, and local innovation. However, the search approach cannot be considered fully systematic or exhaustive; since there may be examples and literature which have not been included. This paper attempts to provide a useful and informative summary of the main directions of the literature and an overview of the indicator dimensions for innovation assessment that can potentially incorporate big data analytics. The study considers big data a crucial method to understand innovation at the local level and explores new ways that these indicators may afford more opportunities than was previously examined in the innovation assessment. It aims to set as a basis for future work in developing an innovation scoreboard for local ecosystems which incorporates an ecometrics approach. Although the trend while measuring innovation shows that most of the innovation assessment toolkits and emerging practices are supporting a national or regional scaled analysis, it is important to further evaluate whether these indicators can be applicable for an innovation assessment at the local level or new indicators and tools are needed to support this process.

The paper introduces big data adoption and their opportunities as other tools to measure local innovation and provide efficiency, optimization, and intelligence. To address the question posed at the beginning, the collection and classification of 289 innovation indicators is used as a main method to facilitate the discussion around existing metrics-based management innovation toolkits used across different locations and scales [Fig. 3]. The 298 different innovation indicators that are examined for this study (adopted from 2006 until 2022) from 6 main scoreboards/sources which are listed in the next chapter [Fig. 1], are categorized based on their dimensions/pillars [Fig. 2].

The study provides a short catalog of different innovation scoreboards adopted during the last decade, without exhaustively examining all existing indicators used. It mainly focuses on the identification of the indicators, which could be measured through big-data analytics. This method will facilitate local communities to identify recent innovation initiatives that have been initiated either by the local authorities (top-down) or by the community (bottom-up approaches).

2   Theoretical Framework of Detecting City Patterns Through Big Data

There is extensive bibliography on the capabilities of big data analytics to reveal "hidden patterns and secret correlations named" [39]. In contrast to traditional data collected from surveys, observations, and experiments, which are often limited in size, collected only once annually, "seeing the city through big data" can provide information by tracking events and conditions in real time across the city and give us an insight into how constituents engage with government service [35, 36].

The distinctiveness of "big data" with "3 Vs": volume, or "big"-ness; velocity, or the fact that many of these data update often, sometimes in real time; and variety, or breadth of content, have been examined by many urban scholars [25, 26]. Robert Kitchin and Gavin McArdle analyzed the factors that distinguish big data from other types of data and recognized volume as one of them [26]. In his book "The Urban Commons: How Data and Technology Can Rebuild Our Communities", O'Brien discusses analytically about the possibilities of tracking neighborhood characteristics in the digital age and emphasizes on the fact that the opportunity that modern digital data offer urban science is an enhanced ability to track events and conditions across the urban landscape. This is reflected in the colloquial understanding of 311 systems as the "eyes and ears of the city". Moreover, O'Brien claims that an ecometric approach in the use of naturally occurring data is necessary to measure social & physical conditions, due to the nature (volume) of the big data. This ecometric approach provides a quantitative assessment of the physical and social settings of an area and appears to be a rigorous method for data analysis, which involves combining statistical and mathematical data modeling with techniques that help understand the urban dynamics.

Ecometrics as a method was first developed in the 1990s by Sampson and Raudenbush. The researchers applied tools of psychometrics to gather quantitative, first-hand information about behavior and space through surveys and audits and advanced these tools to measure physical and social disorder. Since then, using naturally occurring big data has made collecting data richer in variety and much more effective. Even though the 'data deluge' can become overwhelming due to their unlimited volume, variety, and constant updates, they allow the ecometrics approach to get more breadth, be complemented with low-cost options to understand human behavior and therefore, improve public policy [36].

In the same direction, in the article "Is the Cost of 311 Systems Worth the Price of Knowing?" Tod Newcombe discusses the ways cities can receive data from these systems regarding complaints and requests for service and proactively tackle urban problems before they get serious [34]. We are informed that some cities are using 311 to push out information to citizens. Cities with the most sophisticated 311 systems can capture all these data and use them to track work, measure performance, and make strategic decisions that affect services, policies, and budgets, but mostly they can enhance community engagement. These systems are great tools to make accurate projections on where scarce resources should be used and detect patterns that might otherwise have not been noticed. Moreover, the 311 system manages to detect reliable patterns, but they also provide insights when the normal patterns are disrupted, as callers help provide real-time insight into what's really happening.

In the article "What a Hundred Million Calls to 311 Reveal About New York", Steven Johnson talks about the most intriguing thing about NYC Data Analytics, which is the fact that "all the information it supplies back to the city" [21]. The complaints get logged, tagged, and mapped in big datasets and then analyzed. In some cases, 311 data help New York City authorities respond more intelligently to needs that were obvious to begin with. It is considered that cities which can manage to be smart by leveraging the detailed available information from systems such as 311 and NYC Analytics, will be able to better understand local challenges and opportunities but also inform improvements in policies and programs. These systems have become a helpful technological tool for mayors and city managers to make smart decisions for policy making, while they are ensuring transparency in budget allocation.

Several governments have embraced open & big data, in support of their effort to enhance data-sharing among agencies, sharing with external partners and catalyzing new insights and tools. During the last years, Boston and many other cities in the world have provided their residents with mobile apps through which they can submit geotagged photos of potholes and broken lights and then track the status of the problem. In this way, citizens are being transformed to "sensors", who report real-time data [18]. Similar lessons have been learnt through the study "Towards a comparative science of cities: Using mobile traffic records in New York, London, and Hong Kong.", conducted by Senseable Cities lab. Grauwin et al. discuss the similarities & differences between cities and more specifically, the cultural, technological, and economic factors that shape human dynamic behaviors. They used clustering analysis of cell phone data as a method to detect similar patterns at both city and local level of 3 metropolitan cities (London, Hong Kong, New York). The study revealed that these three cities display a broadly comparable rhythm, common to all components of activity. However, what was interesting was that even if New York and Hong Kong are located almost at opposite sides of the globe and have so many cultural differences, they appear to have more similar signatures than other cities with more cultural and linguistic similarities such as New York and London.

This fact reveals that the way these signatures happen is affected by many factors. Technology, economy, culture, but also the physical settings can play a significant role in the way people behave. Senseable Cities Lab's study can set as a basis for further studies which will explore the way that this type of big-data analysis can be used additionally to the land use maps as another way to identify current changes of land uses, emerging central business districts and current commuting transit patterns.

2.1 Constraints and Limitations in the Use of Big Data

Despite all the benefits of the use of big data systems, there are significant pitfalls and challenges that this type of systems appears to have. To start with, the technology behind the collection of data, which keeps evolving, consists of one of the main challenges. The software that undergirds the systems needs continuous refinements and updates to keep up with the latest in mobile technology, social media, and self-service tools. Cities need to stay on the cutting edge. However, smaller cities find it hard to adapt at the same pace. As Tod Newcombe explains in his article, big data systems require high costs which make it a target for budget cutters, while issues with staff training and retention make it hard for managers to use the systems to their fullest capability [34].

On the other side, Daniel O'Brien provides critique on 311 systems and points out the fact that they do not fully describe community issues. Although the vast majority of 311 data refer to real problems, their distribution might not reflect the relative needs of a city's neighborhoods [36]. Firstly, O'Brien supports that when people report street light outages or graffiti, this is a proof of care and basic sense of territoriality for that space. Based on his study, 80% of reports come from reporters living within two blocks of the problems they report, which might be considered limiting.

Moreover, there are other significant drawbacks when dealing with such large data sets. It results in "noisy" content, which makes it more confusing to understand what questions it might answer. A data collection process can create bias and consequently it gets hard to discern the scale, scope, or context from reading the data. O'Brien suggests three main ways when using ecometrics to deal with the drawbacks of the big data sets. Firstly, it is important to extract constructs - isolate the importance of the research information and get rid of the "noise". He also suggests validating the data to address the bias by identifying their source. Finally, establishing reliability criteria is an important part of this process to understand what kind of data are reliable for repeated use.

At the same time, the disparities between community members and between different neighborhoods or different cities increase [35]. In other words, community members who are supposed to benefit from this new data have little influence on the processes by which they will be used, as they are lacking the analytic skills needed to use new data resources. On a larger scale, cities like Boston, New York, and Chicago are leaders in terms of urban informatics, however the gap between well-resourced and poorer cities is widening.

In addition to this, Kontokosta & Hongin report bias and inequality in the nature and distribution of data received through 311 systems [29]. As they explain, this bias stems from the representativeness of self-reported condition assessments, which differ based on socio-cultural characteristics and neighborhood context. Therefore, data used for city service delivery models can lead to over-allocation of resources to households and neighborhoods that tend to report more, regardless of the actual conditions.

On the other hand, Senseable Cities Lab's work used communication data points from citizens to inform decision-making and anticipate events based on the emerging patterns. The clustering analysis of mobile data studied by the Senseable Cities lab, can be used as a way for cities to better understand human behaviors even in the landscape of local innovation, since this type of analysis of mobile data can provide useful insights to the city authorities on the way people interact with their cities, where they live, commute, work etc. As discussed in the previous section, the maps of mobile phone activities or pedestrian activity can be a complementary urban analysis tool to urban designers and planners to tackle urban problems. Despite this fact, we see that the conclusions from the mobile data analysis have the risk to be subjective as they can easily be interpreted in a biased way. In the case of the 311 systems, there might be over-reporting and under-reporting cases, while in the case of Seansible's work, there might be people that do not have the option to use mobile data. For this, data analysts should consider the socioeconomic, racial, gender differences, when making recommendations based on mobile data. If younger, older, or marginalized communities do not have access to raise their own issues, the city resources will not get equitably distributed.

In addition, interpretations from mobility data analyses may change depending on whether citizens regularly use their cell phone and can be biased to who has the access. Not all people have access to a stable internet connection. Also, the cost of mobile data plans might not be affordable to them. Such is the example of London, where Grauwin et al. realized that the London request signature presents a daily cycle with higher variations than the New York and Hong Kong ones, and a relative drop of activity in the weekend compared to workdays [18]. This revealed that the cost of mobile data plans being higher in London than in other parts of the world might make Londoners use (cheaper) wifi whenever available to connect their mobile devices. These transitions from mobile network to wifi network are not recorded in the dataset. This is only one example of how patterns of mobile data can easily lead to biased ways to interpret the city. In that case, finding ways to make smart mobiles and mobile data affordable to all the citizens might be key as more cities will look to rely on mobile data for policy making or detecting mobility changes. The same study elaborates on the fact that two individuals facing similar conditions may provide different data based on their expectations for how their neighborhood should be, but also based on their levels of trust in government or as stated "differing expectations about whether the government will actually respond [1, 2] that make them more or less likely to report a problem".

In his article" The real-time city? Big data and smart urbanism", Kitchin describes the politics of big urban data, technocratic governance and city development, corporatization of city governance and technological lock-ins, buggy, brittle and hackable cities, and the panoptic city as the main five emerging concerns of big data [25].

Also, websites such as "LinkNYC" [30] and "Sidewalk labs" [41] show some of the downsides of urban big data use, such as concerns over data mining and data privacy. Without a doubt, this kind of city technologies need to address important questions regarding privacy and the way data can be used. Based on "Sidewalk Labs" Urbanist approach in Toronto, smart cities vision is quite new, and it is missing substantial regulations on data collection. Governments should lead this effort. Otherwise, big corporations will decide their policies.

Boston Smart City Playbook provides some critique at the technology companies, scientists, researchers, journalists, and activists that make up the "Smart City" community and asks them to "stop sending salespeople and start solving real problems, for real people" [42]. The playbook points out the need for cities to "fight for better decisions - not just better data". Most smart city pilot projects have ended with PowerPoint presentations of data; however, cities need first to gain a better understanding into how to affect that sort of behavior change within city government.

All the above factors influence individual levels of civic engagement or participation which can lead to inconsistent patterns of reporting. For this reason, it is essential that city leaders carefully use data collected for decision-making, to avoid provoking biased outcomes and therefore unfair or inequitable city interpretations.

2.2 A Big Data-Driven Approach for the Identification of Innovation Patterns at the Local Scale

There is an extensive bibliography on the definition and the different forms and components of innovation ecosystems [10, 17, 20, 32] and innovation indicators [9], most having focused on the structural patterns of innovation ecosystems and the complementary relationships between a pair of actors rather than the dynamic aspects of their hybrid identity, both physical and digital settings. For this, the current paper aims at contributing to innovation ecosystems research from a different view.

More specifically, the paper introduces to the capabilities of innovation performance measurement toolkits at the sub-regional (local) level to incorporate big & real-time data analytics. Several studies concluded with the consideration that local innovation indexes might be useful sources of information for policymakers, given the fact that microregions appear to have specific strengths and weaknesses in terms of innovation and therefore they face specific problems and require differentiated policies even within a given region [2, 5]. Autant-Bernard & LeSage identified that innovation performances change dramatically between different localities within a region [4]. Even though the sub-regional measurement of innovation performance has attracted relatively weak attention, primarily due to the problems of data availability, it is identified by several authors as an area for future research, mainly because innovation activities have inherently a local aspect. This local focus is also identified by Mytelca who examines more closely the way in which local clusters can be transformed into innovation systems [33]. Breschi & Lissoni also provide a critical assessment of the recent fortunes met by the concept of "localized knowledge spillovers" [8], while Isaksen focuses on the local character of innovation, by identifying the unique competence of firms, which is strengthened by the fact that locally sited, state-owned higher education and research institutions have adapted activity to the needs of key local industries [19]. Cooke, P. also points out that whilst 'information is relatively globally mobile (…) knowledge is remarkably spatially rooted' [12, 13]. Similar issues about the local aspect of innovation are discussed by Porter, who discusses local companies' ability to gain competitive strength in regional clusters, primarily due to the better access to specialized and experienced employees, suppliers, specialized information, and public goods, and by the motivating force of local rivalry and demanding customers [37].

A range of additional commentary on the subject will be used for this section to better understand how these aspirations for empowering innovative localities can find their tangible manifestation in the use of cutting-edge technologies and big data analytics into the innovation assessment process.

In Technopoles of the World, Castells and Hall attribute the technopole phenomenon to three 'revolutions'; the information technology revolution, the consolidation of the global economy and lastly the Knowledge Economy [11]. They focus on the importance of cities and regions in this new economy and recognize that "local powers, even not having the power of national governments, have the flexibility to harness continuously changing global trends"; the locality is "responsible for fostering the growth of small and medium endogenous firms".

On the other side, Westley discusses the capability of complex ecosystems to build resilience by strengthening cultures of innovation and encouraging the communication between disparate elements. Culture that supports social innovation, will take in turn resilience [45]. In other words, cities that support their existing components of the knowledge economy and create dense communication networks can enhance high rates of technological innovation and strengthen their global and regional competitiveness [40].

In addition, the paper "Smarter More Competitive Cities" provides insights into how cities can develop economically by achieving a balanced growth of business, talent, and technology. City leaders need to understand that technology plays an important role in value creation and innovation and that cities can cultivate the three core attributes - charisma, resiliency, and vitality - by implementing integrated solutions in the areas of planning and management, infrastructure, and people [43]. More specifically, IBM suggests that the 'smart cities' approach should incorporate three important goals. The first of them is about cities' intention to lead with vision and deep insight, by leveraging the right technologies to make informed decisions and right prioritization, increased efficiency, enhanced collaboration and improved and quicker responses.

Having explored some of the broader issues associated with local innovation assessment and being greatly influenced by the potentials of new technology systems and services, big data analytics and cloud solutions have become complementary tools to the existing metrics-based management toolkits that detect city patterns, the study explores the potentials of the use of big data to detect innovation patterns. We see that in periods of crises, the transformations of cities' business ecosystems and central business districts happen at such a fast pace due to the change of mobility patterns. New centers of innovation emerge, while traditional innovation ecosystems respond with amendments and other up-to-date policies to restore their vibrancy and business activity [23]. In this context, big data analytics are assessed as a new method to capture dynamic interactions and real-time information regarding the transformations of business and innovation city districts.

2.3 Overview and Analysis of the Current Metrics-Based Management Toolkits for Innovation Assessment

Big data analytics can support the innovation performance measurement at the sub-regional (local) level. To better understand where the opportunities for incorporation of these technologies might be, this section analyzes the existing metrics-based management toolkits at the sub-regional (local) level, as well as their indicators, which are aimed at identifying outcomes related to national and regional innovation growth and development.

- Entrepreneurship and Business Statistics Global Entrepreneurship Index (GEI) by GEDI Institute has gathered and provided entrepreneurship and business statistics on a country's entrepreneurial ecosystem through Global Entrepreneurship Index (GEI). The GEI is an annual index that measures the health of entrepreneurship ecosystems in 137 countries. This process creates 14 'pillars' which GEDI uses to measure the health of the regional ecosystem [14].

- The European Innovation Scoreboard 2021 provides a comparative analysis of innovation performance in EU countries, other European countries, and regional neighbors. It assesses the relative strengths and weaknesses of national innovation systems and helps countries identify areas they need to address. The 2021's EIS report is also accompanied by the 2021 edition of the regional innovation scoreboard which provides comparable results for 240 regions in 22 EU countries [15].
- The Regional Ecosystem Scoreboard for Clusters and Industrial Change. This Scoreboard encompasses different levels of individual indicators that are assigned to sub-dimensions and dimensions. On this base, the overall composite indicator is calculated. Composite indicators are calculated for all sub-dimensions, as well as for the eight dimensions of industrial change, and the six dimensions of entrepreneurship and innovation. In total, the Regional Ecosystem Scoreboard of the European Observatory for Clusters and Industrial Change covers 15 dimensions and 36 sub-dimensions [16].
- Knowledge Assessment Methodology and Knowledge Economy Index developed by the World Bank, provides a way to build a national knowledge economy to understand national strengths and weaknesses, as well as the strengths and weaknesses of actual and potential competitors. Countries must then articulate their goals and develop policies and investments to achieve them. The most recent version of the KAM 2008 makes comparisons based on 83 structural and qualitative variables that serve as proxies for the four knowledge-economy pillars. Some 140 countries can be compared, among them most of the developed economies of the Organization for Economic Co-operation and Development (OECD) and about 100 developing countries [27].
- Kauffman Foundation Research Series on City, Metro, and Regional Entrepreneurship consists of reports from 2015 that explore the entrepreneurial ecosystems of medium-tier cities, as well as ways to measure and support entrepreneurial ecosystems [24].
- The World Economic Forum, the Global Competitiveness Report series has since its first edition in 2006 aimed to prompt policymakers beyond short term growth and to aim for long-run prosperity. The 2020 special edition is dedicated to elaborating on the priorities for recovery and revival and considering the building blocks of a transformation towards new economic systems that combine "productivity", "people" and "planet" targets [44].

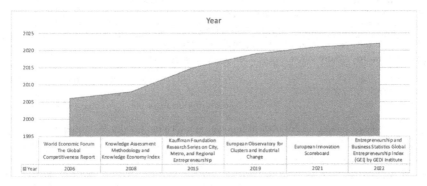

Fig. 1. Graph 1.1 Name & year of published innovation scoreboard/toolkit

Dimensions/Pillars of Indicators

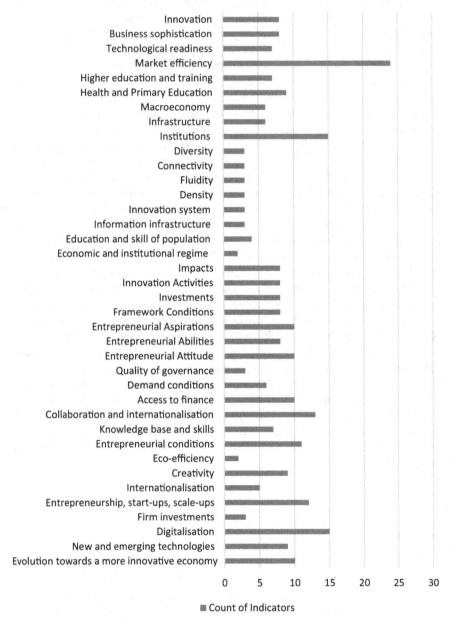

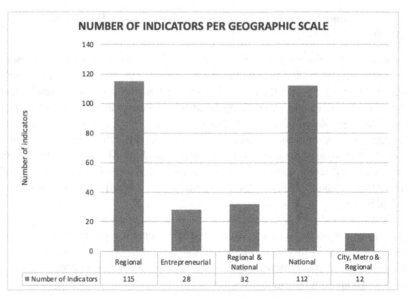

Fig. 3. Graph 1.3 Innovation indicators describing nation, region, local ecosystems Source: own elaboration

The current study analyzed 289 different innovation indicators provided by institutions from all over the world. The findings suggest that the existing toolkits focus mainly on national and regional innovation assessment. This leads to the need for introducing new scoreboards at the local level. In terms of the indicator dimensions, the most popular types of dimensions are market efficiency, institutions, digitalization, collaboration, and internationalization, with entrepreneurship, start-ups, scale-ups, and entrepreneurial conditions following (Fig. 4).

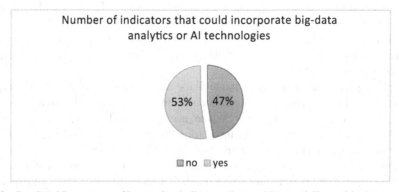

Fig. 4. Graph 1.4 Percentage of Innovation indicators that could potentially use big data analytics as a complementary method of assessment Source: own elaboration.

2.4 Summary and Capabilities of Current Innovation Toolkits to Incorporate Big Data Analytics

The overview of the current frameworks used for innovation evaluation has shown that there is much effort to identify innovation on a larger scale (national to regional) and revealed that there is a gap in the research regarding smaller scale ecosystems. In other words, this study reflects the current need towards new metric based management toolkits that can detect innovation of the city localities.

In addition, looking at the different indicators, it is difficult to identify which ones are evaluated based on high-quality statistic analysis and robust analyses, but also which ones are measured using open and real-time data. Moreover, from a quick examination, more than the half of the indicators examined could incorporate big-data analytics technologies.

In the same direction, the creators of the different toolkits need to consider the incorporation of open big datasets which will complement more traditional statistical studies and sources. In this way, the innovation assessment process can be optimized, and city authorities can be more effective in their effort to help initiatives coming both from top-down and bottom-up approaches.

3 Conclusions

Even before the pandemic, many urban centers needed to change their innovation approaches to meet their innovation goals. The Covid-19 pandemic crisis revealed inefficiencies and highlighted new challenges, but also created opportunities for the adoption of technologies in the process to re-evaluate urban strategies for innovation, resilience, and sustainability. This study concludes that most scoreboards (with some notable exceptions) measure indexes to identify the dynamics in terms of regional or national innovation. This happens mainly due the fact that statistical data are mostly produced by the regional entities. To bridge this gap, the paper explored the capabilities of innovation assessment tools to incorporate new technologies that will lead to the identification of innovation patterns at the local level. This method of analysis aims at encouraging researchers, policymakers, practitioners, and civic leaders to analyze real-time records, digital data relevant to local innovation that will allow them to respond to the emerging reality and cities' weaknesses.

It was helpful to find that most of the toolkits' methods follow a similar path, mainly using traditional data sources to measure innovation performance. Although innovation indicators have been studied by policymakers across the world for several years, more research in this area with a focus on the unexploited big data analytics and AI technologies could create expectations for a new approach into the innovation landscape. The two questions that remain unanswered concern the privacy and the capabilities of these data to provide meaningful correlations when overlaid with traditional social, geographical data. A further study could explore how these new data technologies can effectively provide city transparency but also clear insights on the success factors of the local innovation ecosystems. In this context, it gets clearer that as the big data analytics and AI evolve and the challenges of measuring the innovation initiatives in a smarter way need to happen.

Funding. This research received funding from the European Union's Horizon 2020 Marie Skłodowska- Curie (MSCA-RISE-2018) project TREND—"Transition with Resilience for Evolutionary Development". Grant agreement 823952.

References

1. Analytics, N.M. (n.d.). https://www1.nyc.gov/site/analytics/index.page
2. Anselin, L.V.: Local geographical spillovers between university research and high technology innovations. J. Urban Econ. **42**(3), 422–448 (1997)
3. Audretsch, D.B., Feldman, M.: Knowledge spillovers and the geography of innovation. Handb. Reg. Urban Econ. **4**, 2713–2739. Elsevier (2004)
4. Autant-Bernard, C., LeSage, J.: Quantifying knowledge spillovers using spatial econometric models. J. Reg. Sci. **51**(3), 471–496 (2011)
5. Bajmocy, Z.: Constructing a local innovation index: methodological challenges versus statistical data availability. Appl. Spat. Anal. Policy (6) (2012). https://doi.org/10.1007/s12061-012-9080-5
6. Baudenbush, S.W., Sampson, R.J.: Ecometrics: toward a science of assessing ecological settings, with application to the systematic social observation of neighborhoods. Sociol. Methodol. 1–41 (1999)
7. Boston Smart City Playbook. (the Mayor's Office of Urban Mechanics in Boston). https://monum.github.io/playbook/
8. Breschi, S., Lissoni, F.: Knowledge spillovers and local innovation systems: a critical survey. Ind. Corp. Chang. **10**(4), 975–1005 (2001)
9. Cai, Y.: What contextual factors shape innovation in innovation? Integration of insights from the Triple Helix and the institutional logics perspective. Soc. Sci. Inf. **54**, 299–326 (2015). [Google Scholar] [CrossRef]
10. Carayannis, E.G.: Mode 3 and quadruple helix: toward a 21st century fractal innovation ecosystem. Int. J. Technol. Manag. **46**(3/4), 201–234 (2012)
11. Castells, M., Hall, P.: Technopoles of the World: The Making of Twenty-First-Century Industrial Complexes. Routledge, London (1994)
12. Cooke, P.G.: Regional innovation systems: institutional and organizational dimensions. Res. Policy **26**(4–5), 475–491 (1997)
13. Cooke, P.H.: An Evolutionary Approach. In: Regional Innovation Systems: The Role of Governance in a Globalized World (2nd edn.). Routledge, London (2004)
14. Entrepreneurship and Business Statistics Global Entrepreneurship Index (GEI). (GEDI Institute). https://thegedi.org/tool/
15. European Innovation Scoreboard: Innovation performance keeps improving in EU Member States and regions. (European Commission). https://ec.europa.eu/commission/presscorner/detail/en/ip_21_3048
16. European Observatory for Clusters and Industrial Change. (EASME/COSME/2016/035). Accessed European Observatory for Clusters and Industrial Change (2019)
17. Granstrand, O.: Innovation ecosystems: a conceptual review and a new definition. Technovation **90**, 102098 (2020)
18. Grauwin, S., Soboleysky, S., Moritz, S., Godor, I., Ratti, C.: Towards a comparative science of cities: using mobile traffic records in New York, London and Hong Kong (2014). ArXiv, abs/1406.4400
19. Isaksen, A.: Innovation dynamics of global competitive regional clusters: the case of the Norwegian centers of expertise. (2009)
20. Jackson, D.J.: What is an innovation ecosystem? (2011). http://www.erc-assoc.org/docs/innovation_ecosystem.pdf

21. Johnson, S.: (n.d.). What a Hundred Million Calls to 311 Reveal About New York. Wired Magazine
22. Kakderi, C., Komninos, N., Panori, A., Oikonomaki, E.: Next city: learning from cities during COVID-19 to tackle climate change. Sustainability **13**, 3158 (2021)
23. Kakderi, C., Oikonomaki, E., Papadaki, I.: Smart and resilient Urban futures for sustainability in the post COVID-19 era: a review of policy responses on urban mobility. Sustainability **13**, 6486 (2021)
24. Kauffman Foundation Research Series on City, M. a. (n.d.)
25. Kitchin, R.: The real-time city? Big data and smart urbanism. **79**, 1–14 (2014).https://doi.org/10.1007/s10708-013-9516-8
26. Kitchin, R., McArdle, G.: What makes big data, big data? Exploring the ontological characteristics of 26 datasets. Big Data Soc. (2016)
27. Knowledge Assessment Methodology and Knowledge Economy Index. (n.d.). (World Bank). https://web.worldbank.org/archive/website01030/WEB/IMAGES/KAM_V4.PDF
28. Komninos, N.: Smart Cities and Connected Intelligence: Platforms, Ecosystems and Network Effects (1st ed.). Routledge, Abingdon-on-Thames
29. Kontokosta, C., Hong, B.: Bias in smart city governance: how socio-spatial disparities in 311 complaint behavior impact the fairness of data-driven decisions. Sustain. Cities Soc. **64**, 102503 (2021). ISSN 2210-6707
30. LinkNYC. (n.d.). https://www.link.nyc
31. Measuring an entrepreneurial ecosystem: (Kauffman Foundation Research Series on City, Metro, and Regional Entrepreneurship). https://www.kauffman.org/wp-content/uploads/2019/12/measuring_an_entrepreneurial_ecosystem.pdf
32. Mercan, B.: Components of innovation ecosystems: a cross-country study. Int. Res. J. Financ. Econ. (76), 13 (2011)
33. Mytelka, L.K.: Local systems of innovation in a globalized world economy. Taylor Francis J. Ind. Innov. **7**(1), 15–32 (2000)
34. Newcombe, T.: The cost of 311 systems worth the price of knowing? Governing
35. O'Brien, D.T.: The Urban Commons: How Data and Technology Can Rebuild Our Communities. Harvard University Press, Cambridge, MA and London, England (2018)
36. O'Brien, D.T.: How Public Data Can Improve Services and Empower Communities. Scholars Strategy Network, Harvard Book Press, Cambridge
37. Porter, M.E.: Clusters and the new economics of competition. Harv. Bus. Rev. Repr. **7**(6), 77–90 (1998)
38. Raudenbush, S.W., Sampson, R.J.: Ecometrics: toward a science of assessing ecological settings, with application to the systematic social observation of neighborhoods. Sociol. Methodol. **29**(1), 1–41 (1999)
39. Sagiroglu, S., Sinanc, D.: Big data: a review. In: 2013 International Conference on Collaboration Technologies and Systems (CTS), pp. 42–47 (2013)
40. Saxenian, A.: Regional Advantage: Culture and Competition in Silicon Valley and Route 128. Harvard University Press, Cambridge, MA (1994)
41. Sidewalk Labs–Sidewalk Toronto. https://www.sidewalklabs.com/toronto
42. Smart City Playbook: (the Mayor's Office of Urban Mechanics in Boston). https://monum.github.io/playbook/
43. Smarter: More Competitive Cities Forward-thinking cities are investing in insight today. (IBM Smarter Cities). https://s3-us-west-2.amazonaws.com/itworldcanada/archive/Documents/whitepaper/ITW248B_Smarter_Cities_overview.pdf
44. The Global Competitiveness Report Series: The World Economic Forum
45. Westley, F.: The evolution of social innovation building resilience through transitions (2017)
46. Zenker, A.: Methodology report for the regional ecosystem scoreboard for clusters and industrial change. (European Commission, Executive Agency for Small and Medium-sized Enterprises, Publications Office) (2020). https://data.europa.eu/doi/10.2826/623149/

Mapping the Research Space Shaped by EU-Funded Projects in Relation to Cyber-Physical Systems, Human-Machine Networks and Their Connection to Resilience

Anastasia Panori[1(✉)] and Artemis Psaltoglou[1,2]

[1] URENIO Research, Aristotle University of Thessaloniki, Thessaloniki, Greece
apanori@plandevel.auth.gr
[2] White Research SRL, Saint-Gilles, Belgium

Abstract. The relationship between humans and machines has been thoroughly investigated throughout existing literature focusing on various angles of everyday life. Research on cyber-physical systems and human-machine networks has tried to shed light on the connection between social and technological aspects, offering insights and helping on a better matching and exploitation of the revealed space amongst those elements. In several cases, the exploration of human-machine networks has offered new ways to engage with vulnerable and marginalized groups more effectively, as well as to foster the well-being of individuals and communities. This can be perceived as a hidden potential of cyber-physical systems and human-machine networks towards empowering resilience, which can be approached by various developmental dimensions, like community engagement, transport safety, energy production and consumption, as well as new techno-economic orientations. The study targets on mapping the links between elements being part of cyber-physical systems, human-machine networks and resilience, that have been created through research and innovation projects funded by the European Commission under the programme Horizon 2020, between 2014 and 2021. A total set of 7,859 projects are analyzed in relation to their title and abstract for revealing bridges that have been constructed between human-machine features and resilience. Our analysis further explores the main fields of application of projects on cyber-physical systems and human-machine networks and reveals the ways in which the relate to two resilience characteristics, connectivity and collaboration. It shows the increasing focus of European research projects on cyber-physical systems and human-machine networks and their rising potential for resilience.

Keywords: Cyber-physical systems · Human-machine networks · Resilience · Research projects · Knowledge space · Europe

1 Introduction

Resilience is a complex notion that can be perceived as a system's ability to react and confront unexpected changes [1]. Factors shaping the resistance, recovery and reorientation potential of systems during a crisis should be carefully considered when exploring resilience [2, 3]. Recently, the European Union (EU) has experienced a significant digital transition through which it tries to boost the resilience of various European regions towards making them more competitive, sustainable and inclusive towards external shocks. In this regard, investigating the interactions rising between the social and technical elements of regional systems is an essential point when considering the prospects of resilience at the regional level [4, 5].

Cyber-physical systems (CPSs) and human-machine networks (HMNs) are two key expressions encompassing both social and technical elements. In the first case, CPSs form complex networks characterized by interactions between individuals and machines, that can be used towards increasing their connectivity. These networks integrate computational and physical capabilities that enable interaction with humans through many modalities. In the latter case, HMNs can be used to conceptualise significant synergetic effects produced through socio-technical interactions, affecting in this way their collaboration ability. The synergistic effects of HMNs are expected to go beyond the joint effort of the individual actors involved [6]. Therefore, both CPSs and HMNs are essential expressions of socio-technical systems that trigger aspects closely connected to the ongoing debates on resilience, focusing on connectivity and collaboration.

The main research question rising within this framework is how applications developed under the topics of CPSs and HMNs can be used for empowering regional resilience. What are the main channels through which CPSs and HMNs can boost regional responses to external shocks? What is the current situation in relation to the knowledge space shaped by EU-funded research?

The present paper argues that elements deriving from CPSs and HMNs can be of high relevance to resilience, as they enable significant interactions in relation to collaboration, trust and sustainability aspects. We place our empirical application under the framework of Horizon 2020 (2014–2021), exploring a set of 7,859 research projects, towards revealing any ties that have been constructed among human-machine features and regional resilience. The analysis shows that there are variations regarding the space shaped around CPSs and HMNs, with the first one focusing mostly on cybersecurity and interoperability aspects, whilst the latter one on human-robot interaction and autonomous driving. Co-occurrence analysis also provides information on relevant areas of applications that have been explored throughout EU-funded research to which we try shed additional light.

The paper is structured as follows. Section 2 investigates existing literature related to HMNs and regional resilience, trying to shed light on the main theoretical frameworks underpinning these fields of research and the points of their interaction. Section 3 provides a detailed description on the data and the methodology being used in our analysis, whereas Sect. 4 presents the main findings of our empirical application regarding the knowledge space that has been created under the Horizon 2020 framework bringing together human-machine networks and regional resilience. Finally, a general discussion and the main conclusions deriving from this study are given in Sect. 5.

2 Literature

Various theories have tried to shed light on the processes and the norms underpinning CPSs and HMNs, assuming they are complex systems that can be understood from the interactions between their various parts. According to the theory of socio-technical systems, real-world systems are formed through the interactions rising between both human-centred and technical aspects aiming to achieve a common target [7]. In this context, HMNs are considered complex systems of humans and technology in which the formation processes of technology and its social context are intertwined [8]. At the same time, actor-network theory points out that technology is part of a broader social context, indicating the need to reconsider social systems by providing equal weight to human and non-human entities [9]. From another perspective, cyber-physical-social systems theory has introduced the social dimension in the interactions within human-machine networks using computational techniques to develop and observe them [10]. More recent studies have used a fourth angle, establishing the emerging theory on social machines that tries to unify both computational and social processes taking place within HMNs, under the key idea that computing means connecting [11].

There are different approaches on characterizing CPSs and HMNs based on their specific features and properties. On the one hand, CPSs can be described using a corresponding set of characteristics: *technical emphasis, cross-cutting aspects, level of automation, and life-cycle integration* [12]. Examples of CPSs are critical infrastructures, such as power grids, railways, air traffic control, industrial automation in manufacturing, water and sewage infrastructure, etc. On the other hand, HMNs can be differentiated based on possible variations of interaction between the actors. In this context, Tsvetkova et al. [6] identify eight types of HMNs: public-resource computing, crowdsourcing, web search engines, crowdsensing, online markets, social media, multiplayer online games and virtual worlds, and mass collaboration.

According to the abovementioned theories, there are some key elements that underpin the functionality of CPSs and HMNs introducing two significant dimensions in their system entities: *connectivity* and *collaboration*.

In the first case, CPSs and HMNs encompass infrastructural elements bridging the gap between the cyber (machine) and the physical (human) systems, creating interactions amongst them [13]. Connectivity is a key notion that penetrates the abovementioned aspects referring both to their physical and social perspectives, ensuring interoperability between the different elements of CPSs, as well as an effective human-machine interaction of HMNs. Connectivity in this sense is a crucial step for their operation, but at the same time it can be perceived as a significant outcome of these systems. Studies on resilience have also spotted connectivity as one key parameter underpinning the effectiveness of systems in various application fields, such as energy [14, 15], urban communities [16, 17] and environmental hazards [18–20]. Applications of resilience related to society and well-being highlight the importance of connectivity for community resilience [21], whereas connectivity referring to the built environment and infrastructure increases disaster resilience, being also closely connected to governance and institutional aspects [22]. Connectivity in all these cases refers to the ability of a system to create information flows between its actors or across different systems [23].

Second, CPSs and HMNs can be approached as organizational structures encompassing aspects related to collaboration which is closely connected to activities, value creation and risks during operation [24]. Collaboration in this case refers to the ability of systems to increase their productivity outcomes or create innovative ways for re-combining their existing assets towards creating new value, as well as their potential for ensuring safety while performing. Empirical studies establishing collaboration as a key parameter for increased resilience cover various fields of research, including productiv-ity and supply chains [25, 26], mobility [27–29] and environmental management [30, 31]. Collaboration in most of these cases relates to the ability of a system to build trust and sustainability between its actors and structural elements.

Hence, we can see that enhanced resilience is closely connected to increased connec-tivity and collaboration within systems. In this regard, we argue that research on building regional resilience could be further strengthened by exploring the effects of CPSs and HMNs on these two dimensions and the factors affecting them, such as interoperability, trust and sustainability. In the next sections, we will explore the links between CPSs, HMNs and resilience. To do so, our empirical analysis will first identify basic character-istics of CPSs and HMNs that have been boosted by EU-funded projects, for example security, interoperability and interaction. Second, it will connect those characteristics to specific application fields, including energy (smart grids), governance (digital services), mobility (autonomous vehicles) and productivity (robotics), for identifying the ways in which CPSs and HMNs empower resilience in those fields. Finally, we will discuss the ways in which this analysis can help to better understand how novel channels triggered by CPSs and HMNs through EU-funded research could be a useful tool towards boosting resilience.

3   Data and Methodology

Our empirical analysis focuses on mapping the links related to human-machine networks with the broader knowledge space that has been created via research and innovation projects funded by the European Commission (EC) under the programme Horizon 2020. A total set of 7,859 projects have been analyzed in relation to their main objectives for revealing knowledge bridges that have been constructed between human-machine networks and other fields of research. We will try to analyse the results of this mapping exercise under the prism of resilience.

Data used in this mapping exercise cover Research and Innovation Actions (RIA), Innovation Actions (IA) and Coordination and Support Actions (CSA) that have received funding by the H2020 programme between 2014 and 2021. We were able to derive word co-occurrence s for a set of selected terms that are relevant for our paper by applying text mining algorithms on the abstracts for the selected projects. The abstracts included the main objectives of each project. The list of terms that have been used as key search terms for the empirical analysis is given in Table 1, alongside a short definition for each one of them. We used R as our main programming language and we applied the '*tm*' and the "*openNLP*" packages to build the corresponding corpus for each term and perform the text mining analysis.

Table 1. List of key search terms that have been used as main references for calculating word co-occurrence in the knowledge space shaped by EU-funded research.

Term	Short definition
Cyber-physical	Cyber-physical systems refer to the integration of computational and physical processes [32]
Human-machine	Human-machine networks refer to networks where humans and machines work together to provide collaborative effects for their goals [33]
Smart grid(s)	Smart grids change conventional grids by integrating advanced communication and computing methods to improve the control, efficiency, reliability and safety of the system [34]
Digital service(s)	Digital services are based on applications adopted by the market and offered on a regular basis as a service via viable business models [35]
Autonomous vehicle(s)	Autonomous vehicles refer to technologically equipped cars and light vehicles for reducing accidents, energy consumption, pollution and costs of congestion [36]
Robot(s)/Robotics	Robotics refer to processes extending human motor capabilities with machines [37]

It is important to highlight at this point that the terms included in Table 1 can be divided into two groups. The first group captures the main theoretical terms that we want to investigate in our analysis, "cyber-physical" systems and "human-machine" networks. The outcomes of co-occurrence analysis in relation to these terms will help us to better understand their positioning within the research-space developed in the Horizon 2020 programme, as well as identify potential differences rising between them. The second group of terms focuses on a set of applications closely related to the terms of the first group that have been identified based on the results of the co-occurrence analysis applied on our dataset. These include smart grid(s), digital service(s), autonomous vehicle(s) and robot(s)/robotics. A detailed analysis for links between the abovementioned terms will be provided in Sect. 4.

Figure 1 presents the evolution of the number of projects related to these terms throughout the period under investigation. As we can see, research projects related to cyber-physical systems and robotics are the ones attracting increased attention in relation to the other terms under investigation. Projects referring to smart grids also indicate increased values between 2015 and 2017. However, projects exploring human-machine networks seem to be very sparse in the sample we are analysing.

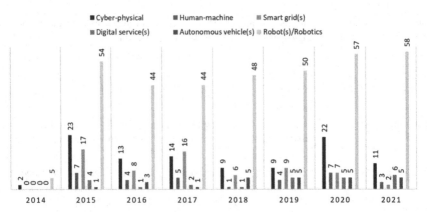

Fig. 1. Number of funded Horizon 2020 projects by year that relate to our key search terms.

4 Results

Figure 2 shows the results of the co-occurrence analysis using the term "cyber-physical" as our key search term. We can see that the CPS term is highly related to terms such as "security", "privacy" and "interoperability". In the first two cases, security and privacy are significantly connected with terms referring to cybersecurity indicating a strong orientation of CPS towards developing dependable systems for protecting against cyber-attacks. Trust is a critical issue in this case, as the extended use of CPS has brought threats related to users' privacy and data protection [38, 39]. At the same time, another orientation of CPS in EU-funded projects seems to be present towards distributed systems and cloud computing, aiming at improving the interoperability between digital services and smart systems. Interoperability Literature highlights interoperability as a key element for empowering the overall sustainability of CPS enabling them to achieve better performance and user engagement [40, 41].

Evidence suggests that some indicative applications that are closely related to research projects focusing on CPS include smart grids and digital services. To further investigate the knowledge-space created around these areas, we have also performed a co-occurrence analysis using these two as our main search terms (Fig. 3, Fig. 4). Below, we summarise the main findings for each one of them.

Smart Grids. Results deriving from co-occurrence analysis in relation to smart grids indicate that there is a strong orientation on applications related to energy (Fig. 3). More specifically, we can see that energy distribution, flexibility and storage lie in the heart of our co-occurrence network, surrounded by terms referring to renewable energy, microgrids and demand. Significant links arise between the terms "energy", "heat" and "building", verifying a close connection between research on smart grids and sustainable buildings. Existing literature also highlights the importance of these applications towards building resilient cities and regions from an energy perspective, as CPS can provide significant inputs for redesigning power grids towards increasing their safety and reliability [4, 42, 43].

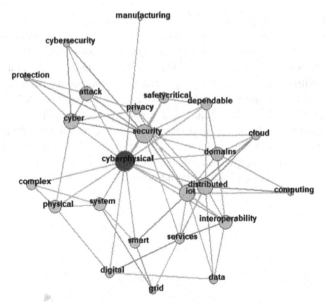

Fig. 2. Word co-occurrence network using "cyber-physical" as the main search term in the knowledge space shaped by EU-funded research projects. Note: Nodes with less than 2 edges have been removed. The search term has been highlighted with blue colour and the co-occurrent terms with orange. Edges with a significance of at least 50% of the maximum significance in the graph are drawn in orange. The size of the nodes follows their degree of networking.

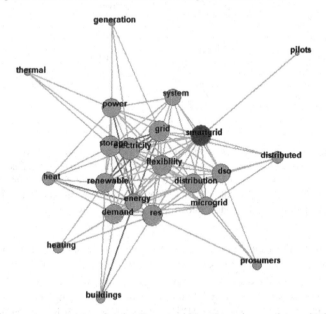

Fig. 3. Word co-occurrence network using "smart grid" as the main search term in the knowledge space shaped by EU-funded research projects. Note: Nodes with less than 2 edges have been removed. The search term has been highlighted with blue colour and the co-occurrent terms with orange. Edges with a significance of at least 50% of the maximum significance in the graph are drawn in orange. The size of the nodes follows their degree of networking.

Digital Services. The empirical research results shown in Fig. 4 in relation to digital services co-occurrence analysis indicate that projects emerging in this field are closely related to governance and security aspects. More specifically, there seems to be a close connection between the terms "e-government", "citizens" and "trust" –apart from "digital services'- with the latter one being significantly connected to "privacy". Following the significant links deriving from "privacy", we can see that the knowledge space being created around cyber-physical systems, with a specific focus on digital services, aims at improving trust through enhancing privacy, data, services' interoperability and openness. This is in line with existing literature suggesting that building trust on digital services requires a significant effort towards empowering privacy and openness, regarding interoperability of services and user data [44, 45].

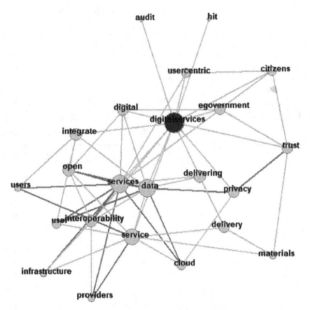

Fig. 4. Word co-occurrence network using "digital services" as the main search term in the knowledge space shaped by EU-funded research projects. Note: Nodes with less than 2 edges have been removed. The search term has been highlighted with blue colour and the co-occurrent terms with orange. Edges with a significance of at least 50% of the maximum significance in the graph are drawn in orange. The size of the nodes follows their degree of networking.

Moving on to the term "human-machine" as our key search term, the empirical findings from co-occurrent analysis seem to vary. In this case, EU-funded projects encompassing HMNs have been found to mostly relate with the terms "interaction" and "cognition", as well as "safety", "autonomous" and "driving" (Fig. 5). In the first case, we see that there is a focus of HMN-related projects on investigating the interactions rising between humans and robots and the ways in which more cognitive links arise. Both cognitive and interactive aspects of HMNs are closely related to increased collaboration outputs, that are key elements for achieving more resilient environments

[46, 47]. Second, there seems to be a mobility-related area where HMN-based projects expand their knowledge space, exploring the ways in which HMNs affect road safety, traffic and autonomous driving. This relates to existing studies investigating ways to enhance resilience in autonomous driving systems-of-systems [48, 49].

Key field applications that are closely related to research projects focusing on HMNs include robotics and autonomous vehicles. To further investigate the knowledge-space created around these areas, we have also performed a co-occurrence analysis using them as our main search terms (Fig. 7, Fig. 6). A summary of the main findings for each case is presented below.

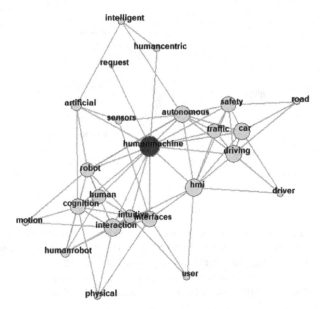

Fig. 5. Word co-occurrence network using "human-machine" as the main search term in the knowledge space shaped by EU-funded research projects. Note: Nodes with less than 2 edges have been removed. The search term has been highlighted with blue colour and the co-occurrent terms with orange. Edges with a significance of at least 50% of the maximum significance in the graph are drawn in orange. The size of the nodes follows their degree of networking.

Robotics. Regarding the first application related to HMNs, Fig. 6 shows the co-occurrence network calculated for the term "robot", encompassing the terms "robots" and "robotics". As we can see, the analysis points out a close connection with terms such as "abilities", "motion" and "tasks", indicating a strong orientation of EU-funded research towards HMN applications that investigate the ways in which robots can improve their interaction with physical environment and humans. It interesting to notice that there is an additional branch -not fully independent from the previous- focusing on aspects more connected to autonomous robots and including the terms "control", "sensors" and "navigation". Both perspectives capture a trend of EU-funded projects to further improve robots' capabilities in relation to their interactions with human and physical environment, which has been stressed as an essential aspect for boosting their role in building resilient spaces [47, 50].

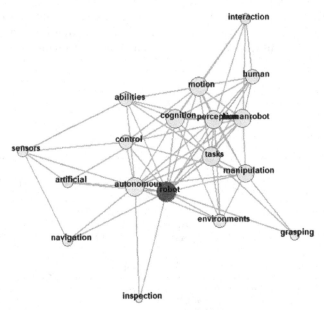

Fig. 6. Word co-occurrence network using "robot" as the main search term in the knowledge space shaped by EU-funded research projects. Note: Nodes with less than 2 edges have been removed. The search term has been highlighted with blue colour and the co-occurrent terms with orange. Edges with a significance of at least 50% of the maximum significance in the graph are drawn in orange. The size of the nodes follows their degree of networking.

Autonomous Vehicles. When exploring the results from the co-occurrence analysis regarding the term "autonomous vehicle" we can see that most terms, as expected, are related to transport issues. A core is formed in Fig. 7, including the terms "road", "vehicle", "traffic" and "transport", that indicate links with high significance. Even though these terms genetically relate to our research term, there is a second level of connected words that provide additional information of this research. This includes aspects referring to "urban", "air", "safety" and "navigation systems", highlighting a close connection between research on autonomous vehicles and urban resilience in terms of environmental and safety aspects. This connection is in line with existing literature, as empirical studies suggest that urban mobility can be used as a significant driver for boosting resilience in cities [51, 52].

In the next section, we try to provide a more systematic connection of all this information with existing literature on resilience to better understand the way in which knowledge space related to CPS and HMNs that has been created through EU-funded research empowers aspects of resilience.

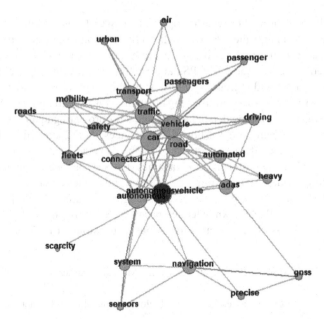

Fig. 7. Word co-occurrence network using "autonomous" as the main search term in the knowledge space shaped by EU-funded research projects. Note: Nodes with less than 2 edges have been removed. The search term has been highlighted with blue colour and the co-occurrent terms with orange. Edges with a significance of at least 50% of the maximum significance in the graph are drawn in orange. The size of the nodes follows their degree of networking.

5   Potential Impact of EU-Funded Research Related to CPS and HMNs on Resilience

This section provides a discussion on the ways in which the findings of our empirical analysis relate to ongoing debates on resilience. Table 2 provides an overview of our main findings. We can see that the key related terms to CPSs and HMNs-related EU projects include interoperability, security/privacy, cognition/interaction and safety. At the same time, the main fields of application, as they have been identified from our topic analysis, include digital services, smart grids, autonomous vehicles and robotics. By combining the key related terms with the application areas, we can see that EU-funded research related to CPSs and HMNs can be highly linked to urban and regional resilience, as all the identified aspects cover relevant areas of interest pointed our by previous studies on resilience [15, 17, 19].

First, we have shown that CPSs and HMNs-related EU projects can effectively promote connectivity as a key element of resilience. The focus of these projects on distributed systems and cloud computing aiming at achieving better performance can reinforce their interoperability. Moreover, aspects related to exploring the ways in which they can improve road safety, traffic and energy distribution, can also provide significant inputs in relation to connectivity between different urban and regional systems. This is an essential element for resilience, as it improves the overall sustainability of urban and regional systems and helps them to more efficiently respond to external shocks [4, 53].

Second, based on the findings of our research terms' topic analysis, we can argue that EU-funded projects related to CPSs and HMNs can also affect to a large extent collaboration in urban and regional systems, as they both promote the development of features that can impact trust and user engagement. More specifically, CPSs projects' orientation towards developing dependable systems for protecting against cyber-attacks can play a key role in increasing trust on digital services. At the same time, the focus on improving cognitive and interactive aspects of HMNs can lead to increased collaboration outputs, not only between humans and machines, but also between humans. This is in line with existing evidence suggesting that digital technologies can become an inherent aspect of collaboration by empowering it and changing its nature [54, 55].

Overall, we argue that the knowledge space created through EU-funded research on CPSs and HMNs is closely related to various dimensions of resilience -urban and

Table 2. Links between CPS, HMNs and resilience.

	Key related terms	Fields of application	Impact on resilience
Cyber-physical systems (CPSs)	**Interoperability** – focus on distributed systems and cloud computing, aiming at achieving better performance **Security/Privacy** – strong orientation towards developing dependable systems for protecting against cyber-attacks	**Digital services** projects aim at improving trust through enhancing privacy, data, services' interoperability and openness. EU-funded projects relate to governance and security aspects **Smart grids** projects are essential for building resilience from an energy perspective. EU-funded projects relate to energy distribution, flexibility and storage lie in the core of their applications, surrounded by terms referring to renewable energy, microgrids and demand	CPSs can provide significant inputs for redesigning power grids and increasing their *safety* and *reliability* CPSs can build *trust* on digital services by empowering privacy, openness and interoperability of services and user data CPSs can increase interoperability and achieve higher *user engagement*

(*continued*)

Table 2. (*continued*)

	Key related terms	Fields of application	Impact on resilience
Human-machine networks (HMNs)	**Cognition/Interaction** – focus on investigating the interactions rising between humans and robots and the ways in which more cognitive links arise **Safety** – interest in exploring the ways in which HMNs affect road safety, traffic and autonomous driving	**Autonomous vehicles** projects closely relate to urban resilience in terms of improving environmental and safety conditions, through air quality, navigations systems and traffic management **Robotics** projects investigate the ways in which robots can improve their interaction with physical environment and humans, indicating a specific focus on autonomous robots	HMNs offer cognitive and interactive aspects that are closely related to increased *collaboration* outputs HMNs can improve urban mobility resilience by increasing *safety* of autonomous vehicles and their *environmental* impacts HMNs can improve robots' *capabilities* in relation to their interactions with human and physical environment

regional- and thus, it can be considered as a significant asset for improving it. However, our analysis has been mostly an exploratory exercise that provides an initial mapping of potential connections that might arise between CPSs, HMNs and resilience. Additional efforts should be made towards including statistical analysis on the significance of these factors on resilience. To this end, future research can focus on integrating those findings together with variables capturing urban and regional characteristics and levels of resilience. In this way, we will be able to get an evidence-based assessment on the actual impact of these projects on resilience.

References

1. Martin, R.: Regional economic resilience, hysteresis and recessionary shocks. J. Econ. Geogr. **12**, 1–32 (2012). https://doi.org/10.1093/jeg/lbr019
2. Bristow, G., Healy, A.: Introduction to the handbook on regional economic resilience. In: Handbook on Regional Economic Resilience, pp. 1–8. Edward Elgar Publishing (2020). https://doi.org/10.4337/9781785360862.00005
3. Psycharis, Y., Panori, A., Athanasopoulos, D.: Public investment and regional resilience: empirical evidence from the Greek regions. Tijdschr. voor Econ. en Soc. Geogr. (2021). https://doi.org/10.1111/tesg.12499
4. Komninos, N., Kakderi, C., Mora, L., Panori, A., Sefertzi, E.: Towards high impact smart cities: a universal architecture based on connected intelligence spaces. J. Knowl. Econ. 1–29 (2021). https://doi.org/10.1007/s13132-021-00767-0

5. Panori, A., Kakderi, C., Komninos, N., Fellnhofer, K., Reid, A., Mora, L.: Smart systems of innovation for smart places: challenges in deploying digital platforms for co-creation and data-intelligence. Land Use Policy **111**, 104631 (2021). https://doi.org/10.1016/j.landusepol. 2020.104631

6. Tsvetkova, M., et al.: Understanding human-machine networks: a cross-disciplinary survey (2017). https://doi.org/10.1145/3039868

7. Sony, M., Naik, S.: Industry 4.0 integration with socio-technical systems theory: a systematic review and proposed theoretical model. Technol. Soc. **61**, 101248 (2020). https://doi.org/10. 1016/j.techsoc.2020.101248

8. Eide, A.W., et al.: Human-machine networks: towards a typology and profiling framework. In: Kurosu, M. (ed.) HCI 2016. LNCS, vol. 9731, pp. 11–22. Springer, Cham (2016). https:// doi.org/10.1007/978-3-319-39510-4_2

9. Latour, B.: Reassembling the Social: An Introduction to Actor-Network-Theory, p. 301. Oxford Univ. Press. Oxford, UK (2006)

10. Sheth, A., Anantharam, P., Henson, C.: Physical-cyber-social computing: an early 21st century approach. IEEE Intell. Syst. **28**, 78–82 (2013). https://doi.org/10.1109/MIS.2013.20

11. Burégio, V., Meira, S., Rosa, N.: Social machines: a unified paradigm to describe social web-oriented systems. In: WWW 2013 Companion–Proceedings of the 22nd International Conference on World Wide Web, pp. 885–889. ACM Press, New York, New York, USA (2013). https://doi.org/10.1145/2487788

12. Törngren, M., et al.: Characterization, analysis, and recommendations for exploiting the opportunities of cyber-physical systems. Cyber-Phys. Syst. Found. Princ. Appl. 3–14 (2017). https:// doi.org/10.1016/B978-0-12-803801-7.00001-8

13. Mishra, A., Jha, A.V., Appasani, B., Ray, A.K., Gupta, D.K., Ghazali, A.N.: Emerging technologies and design aspects of next generation cyber physical system with a smart city application perspective. Int. J. Syst. Assur. Eng. Manag. 1–23 (2022). https://doi.org/10.1007/s13 198-021-01523-y

14. Andrei, H., Gaiceanu, M., Stanculescu, M., Arama, I.N., Andrei, P.C.: Power systems connectivity and resiliency. In: Mahdavi Tabatabaei, N., Najafi Ravadanegh, S., Bizon, N. (eds.) Power Systems Resilience. PS, pp. 45–79. Springer, Cham (2019). https://doi.org/10.1007/ 978-3-319-94442-5_2

15. Jesse, B.-J., Heinrichs, H.U., Kuckshinrichs, W.: Adapting the theory of resilience to energy systems: a review and outlook. Energy Sustain. Soc. **9**(1), 1–19 (2019). https://doi.org/10. 1186/s13705-019-0210-7

16. Zuniga-Teran, A.A., Gerlak, A.K., Mayer, B., Evans, T.P., Lansey, K.E.: Urban resilience and green infrastructure systems: towards a multidimensional evaluation (2020). https://doi.org/ 10.1016/j.cosust.2020.05.001

17. Mouratidis, K., Yiannakou, A.: COVID-19 and urban planning: built environment, health, and well-being in Greek cities before and during the pandemic. Cities **121**, 103491 (2022). https://doi.org/10.1016/j.cities.2021.103491

18. Cariolet, J.M., Vuillet, M., Diab, Y.: Mapping urban resilience to disasters–a review. Sustain. Cities Soc. **51**, 101746 (2019). https://doi.org/10.1016/J.SCS.2019.101746

19. Lu, Y., Zhai, G., Zhou, S., Shi, Y.: Risk reduction through urban spatial resilience: a theoretical framework. 1–17 (2020). https://doi.org/10.1080/10807039.2020.1788918

20. Carvalhaes, T.M., Chester, M.V., Reddy, A.T., Allenby, B.R.: An overview & synthesis of disaster resilience indices from a complexity perspective. Int. J. Disaster Risk Reduct. **57**, 102165 (2021). https://doi.org/10.1016/J.IJDRR.2021.102165

21. Bohn, J., Hogue, S.: Changing the game: college dance training for well-being and resilience amidst the COVID-19 crisis. Health Promot. Pract. **22**, 163–166 (2021). https://doi.org/10. 1177/1524839920963703

22. MacAskill, K., Guthrie, P.: Disaster risk reduction and empowering local government–a case comparison between Sri Lanka and New Zealand. Int. J. Disaster Resil. Built Environ. **7**, 318–329 (2016). https://doi.org/10.1108/IJDRBE-05-2015-0030/FULL/XML
23. Ahern, J.: From fail-safe to safe-to-fail: sustainability and resilience in the new urban world. Landsc. Urban Plan. **100**, 341–343 (2011). https://doi.org/10.1016/j.landurbplan.2011.02.021
24. Mikkola, M., Jähi, M.: Inter-organizational perspective to cyber-physical system modelling in industrial production. In: Balint, G., Antala, B., Carty, C., Mabieme, J.-M.A., Amar, I.B., Kaplanova, A. (eds.) Modelling and Simulation 2020–The European Simulation and Modelling Conference, ESM 2020. pp. 216–220. Eurosis-ETI (2020)
25. Dubey, R., Gunasekaran, A., Bryde, D.J., Dwivedi, Y.K., Papadopoulos, T.: Blockchain technology for enhancing swift-trust, collaboration and resilience within a humanitarian supply chain setting. Int. J. Prod. Res. **58**, 3381–3398 (2020). https://doi.org/10.1080/00207543.2020.1722860
26. Nikolakis, N., Maratos, V., Makris, S.: A cyber physical system (CPS) approach for safe human-robot collaboration in a shared workplace. Robot. Comput. Integr. Manuf. **56**, 233–243 (2019). https://doi.org/10.1016/j.rcim.2018.10.003
27. Singh, R., Miller, T., Reid, D.: Collaborative Human-Agent Planning for Resilience (2021)
28. Floetgen, R.J., et al.: Introducing platform ecosystem resilience: leveraging mobility platforms and their ecosystems for the new normal during COVID-19. Eur. J. Inf. Syst. **30**, 304–321 (2021). https://doi.org/10.1080/0960085X.2021.1884009
29. Benko, J., et al.: Security and resiliency of coordinated autonomous vehicles. In: 2019 Systems and Information Engineering Design Symposium, SIEDS 2019. Institute of Electrical and Electronics Engineers Inc. (2019). https://doi.org/10.1109/SIEDS.2019.8735632
30. Morris, J.C., McNamara, M.W., Belcher, A.: Building resilience through collaboration between grassroots citizen groups and governments: two case studies. Public Work. Manag. Policy. **24**, 50–62 (2019). https://doi.org/10.1177/1087724X18803116
31. Hartley, K.: Environmental resilience and intergovernmental collaboration in the Pearl River delta. Int. J. Water Resour. Dev. **34**, 525–546 (2018). https://doi.org/10.1080/07900627.2017.1382334
32. Gushev, M.: Dew computing architecture for cyber-physical systems and IoT. Internet Things (Netherlands). **11**, 100186 (2020). https://doi.org/10.1016/j.iot.2020.100186
33. Liang, X., Yan, Z.: A survey on game theoretical methods in human-machine networks. Futur. Gener. Comput. Syst. **92**, 674–693 (2019). https://doi.org/10.1016/j.future.2017.10.051
34. Ghofrani, M., Steeble, A., Barrett, C., Daneshnia, I.: Survey of big data role in smart grids: definitions, applications, challenges, and solutions. Open Electr. Electron. Eng. J. **12**, 86–97 (2018). https://doi.org/10.2174/1874129001812010086
35. Komninos, N., Kakderi, C., Panori, A., Tsarchopoulos, P.: Smart city planning from an evolutionary perspective. J. Urban Technol. **26**, 3–20 (2019). https://doi.org/10.1080/10630732.2018.1485368
36. Anderson, J., Kalra, N., Stanley, K., Sorensen, P., Samaras, C., Oluwatola, O.: Autonomous vehicle technology: a guide for policymakers (2016). https://doi.org/10.7249/rr443-2
37. Trevelyan, J.: Redefining robotics for the new millennium. Int. J. Rob. Res. **18**, 1211–1223 (1999). https://doi.org/10.1177/02783649922067816
38. Gol Mohammadi, N.: Trustworthy cyber-physical systems. Trust. Cyber-Phys. Syst. (2019). https://doi.org/10.1007/978-3-658-27488-7
39. Ashibani, Y., Mahmoud, Q.H.: Cyber physical systems security: analysis, challenges and solutions. Comput. Secur. **68**, 81–97 (2017). https://doi.org/10.1016/J.COSE.2017.04.005
40. Broo, D.G.: Transdisciplinarity and three mindsets for sustainability in the age of cyber-physical systems. J. Ind. Inf. Integr. 100290 (2021). https://doi.org/10.1016/j.jii.2021.100290
41. Gürdür, D., Asplund, F.: A systematic review to merge discourses: interoperability, integration and cyber-physical systems (2018). https://doi.org/10.1016/j.jii.2017.12.001

42. Mohammadpourfard, M., Khalili, A., Genc, I., Konstantinou, C.: Cyber-resilient smart cities: detection of malicious attacks in smart grids. Sustain. Cities Soc. **75**, 103116 (2021). https://doi.org/10.1016/j.scs.2021.103116

43. Allgöwer, F., et al.: Position paper on the challenges posed by modern applications to cyber-physical systems theory. Nonlinear Anal. Hybrid Syst. **34**, 147–165 (2019). https://doi.org/10.1016/j.nahs.2019.05.007

44. Tsampoulatidis, I., Kompatsiaris, I., Komninos, N.: From e-government to we-government: an analysis towards participatory public services in the context of the H2020 WeGovNow project. In: International Conference on Information Society and Smart Cities (ISC 2018), Cambridge, U.K., 27–28 June 2018 (2018)

45. Komninos, N., Panori, A., Kakderi, C.: Smart cities beyond algorithmic logic: digital platforms, user engagement and data science. In: Smart Cities in the Post-Algorithmic Era, pp. 1–15. Edward Elgar Publishing (2019). https://doi.org/10.4337/9781789907056.00007

46. de Visser, E.J., Pak, R., Shaw, T.H.: From automation to autonomy: the importance of trust repair in human–machine interaction. Ergonomics **61**, 1409–1427 (2018). https://doi.org/10.1080/00140139.2018.1457725

47. Tokody, D., Papp, J., Iantovics, L.B., Flammini, F.: Complex, resilient and smart systems. In: Flammini, F. (ed.) Resilience of Cyber-Physical Systems. ASTSA, pp. 3–24. Springer, Cham (2019). https://doi.org/10.1007/978-3-319-95597-1_1

48. Madni, A.M., Sievers, M.W., Humann, J., Ordoukhanian, E., D'Ambrosio, J., Sundaram, P.: Model-based approach for engineering resilient system-of-systems: application to autonomous vehicle networks. In: Madni, A.M., Boehm, B., Ghanem, R.G., Erwin, D., Wheaton, M.J. (eds.) Disciplinary Convergence in Systems Engineering Research, pp. 365–380. Springer, Cham (2018). https://doi.org/10.1007/978-3-319-62217-0_26

49. Fernandez, F., Sanchez, A., Velez, J.F., Moreno, B.: Associated reality: a cognitive human-machine layer for autonomous driving. Rob. Auton. Syst. **133**, 103624 (2020). https://doi.org/10.1016/j.robot.2020.103624

50. Andriella, A., Torras, C., Alenyà, G.: Short-term human-robot interaction adaptability in real-world environments. Int. J. Soc. Robot. **12**, 639–657 (2020). https://doi.org/10.1007/S12369-019-00606-Y/FIGURES/11

51. Thombre, A., Agarwal, A.: A paradigm shift in urban mobility: policy insights from travel before and after COVID-19 to seize the opportunity. Transp. Policy **110**, 335–353 (2021). https://doi.org/10.1016/j.tranpol.2021.06.010

52. Johnson, E., Nica, E.: Connected vehicle technologies, autonomous driving perception algorithms, and smart sustainable urban mobility behaviors in networked transport systems. Contemp. Read. Law Soc. Justice **13**, 37 (2021). https://doi.org/10.22381/crlsj13220213

53. Mora, L., Wu, X., Panori, A.: Mind the gap: developments in autonomous driving research and the sustainability challenge (2020). https://linkinghub.elsevier.com/retrieve/pii/S09596 52620341329, https://doi.org/10.1016/j.jclepro.2020.124087

54. Kattel, R., Lember, V., Tõnurist, P.: Collaborative innovation and human-machine networks. Public Manag. Rev. **22**, 1652–1673 (2020). https://doi.org/10.1080/14719037.2019.1645873

55. Komninos, N., Panori, A.: The creation of city smartness: architectures of intelligence in smart cities and smart ecosystems. In: Smart Cities in the Post-Algorithmic Era, pp. 101–127. Edward Elgar Publishing (2019). https://doi.org/10.4337/9781789907056.00012

From Interactive Experience to Behavioral Participation–A Probe into the Expression of Public-Interest in the Era of Digital Intelligence

Jian Zhou and Jieru Zhou[✉]

Nanjing University of the Arts, Nanjing, China
870713727@qq.com

Abstract. The expression of public-interest directly influences societal engagement, and in the era of digital intelligence it not only involves publicizing to and calling on the general public but also allows the general public to directly perform participatory public-interest behaviors through interactive experience. The original intention of the interactive expression of public-interest is to transmit the philosophy of public-interest, more specifically, to allow the audience to open up and receive public-interest information. When an audience experiences interactive public-interest works, it is imperative to allow them to gain a sense of participation in public-interest activities, as the behavior at this moment represents both experience with the works and participation in public interest. This possibility requires the expression of public-interest to make breakthroughs at the levels of content design, interactive behavior, and interactive emotion.

Keywords: Expression of public-interest · Interactive experience · Behavioral participation · Interactive emotion

1 Introduction

Public interest is an abbreviation of public-interest undertakings and refers to the well-being and interests that are related to the general public. Public interest is about doing meaningful things for societies, while at the same time it can help disadvantaged groups develop faster. Public interest requires societal engagement in order to improve in scale and quality and to make societies become more harmonious. The question of how to motivate more people to engage is a determining factor in public interest, thus the expression of public-interest becomes especially important. At a certain level the expression of public-interest represents a kind of publicity and appeal, but in the era of digital intelligence, interactively experiential expression is shifting more than ever before towards the form of behavioral participation. Of course, this also requires the design of specific expression.

© The Author(s), under exclusive license to Springer Nature Switzerland AG 2022
N. A. Streitz and S. Konomi (Eds.): HCII 2022, LNCS 13325, pp. 435–443, 2022.
https://doi.org/10.1007/978-3-031-05463-1_30

2 Content Design in Public-Interest Expression

2.1 Refining Content with Public-Interest Themes

The refining of content with public-interest themes involves highly generalizing the concepts of public-interest and implying them within the contents of works to allow the audience to acquire the spirit of public interest through interaction. Interactive design for the expression of public-interest should closely encompass public-interest themes and conduct content design that is always surrounded by public interest.

First, let us define a public-interest theme. An accurate theme is a precondition for design to occur, and the theme directly affects the nature of expression while also pointing out the direction for interactive design. Defining a public-interest theme includes the screening and planning of the subject, type, conception, emotion, values, and other elements of public interest, while the scope and subjects covered by the theme should be effectively controlled to avoid empty and superficial experience brought on by excessively broad scopes.

Second, let us outline the refining of public-interest content. The determination of a public-interest theme lays a foundation for content presentation, while at the same time the quality of expression largely depends on the content of the interaction, and refined and ingenious content design is the cornerstone of wonderful presentations. In some sense, the expression of public interest is a kind of publicity, where excessively informative content would overwhelm the audience and be counterproductive to conveying public-interest themes and emotional experience, thus making the refining of public-interest content even more important. Such refining is not a simple shortening and paring-down, but rather involves generalizing and extracting under the guidance of the theme, to highlight important information with specific directivity.

2.2 Behavior-Oriented Content Swapping

Behavior-oriented content swapping involves the design of similar content conversion in public-interest expression with public-interest behavior as the reference. According to content design, the behavioral participation of the general public is both an important step for ensuring the integrity of expression and is also kind of public-interest behavior. Therefore, such transformation needs to be guided by content in order to achieve conversion between these two.

First, content swapping and expression need to be logical. The transformation of content expression into public-interest behavior would be impossible without logical support inherent in the interactive content. The process of planning behavior is behavioral logic. The essence of interactive content is based on the casual association between the different linking modes and different outcomes of behavioral logic. The reasonableness of content and plot settings in public-interest expression is particularly important in the design of interactive content, as smooth and clear logic can provide an assurance for high-quality interactive content, and such logic manifests in expression as connection before and after the content, guidance of audience's behavioral participation, and the audience's behavioral reaction to the content. The swapping between the content of expression and the audience's behavior cannot proceed without securing the intrinsic connections. In the interactive expression of public-interest, the participatory behavior of the audience is a natural product of the content elaboration process, in which the content guiding the behavioral participation needs to be both specific and gradual in the setup process. A critical part is to perform this in a way that not only ensures the smoothness of the interaction process and orderly connection between behavior generation and subsequent content, but also enlightens the audience ideologically and allows them to receive a deeper spiritual impact.

Second, interactive content needs to spark audience engagement. The presentation of the expression content should be appealing, which will allow the the audience to develop a strong curiosity or inquisitiveness after exposure to effectively arouse their interest in participation. If rigorously logical, the content of interactive design still won't appear richer unless more novel and interesting elements are added. Moreover, the narratives in interactive content expression need to be concise and specific, which will fully motivate the audience to subjectively engage and drive the immersive experience to further complete the interaction.

3 Construction of Interactive Behavior for the Purposes of Public-Interest Participation

3.1 Content-Led Interactive Model

A content-led interactive model describes a model in which public-interest content determines the behavior of interactive participation, where the interaction process unfolds around the content, and the form and specific behavioral interaction in a specific design need to be determined based on the theme or content expressed.

First, the connection between interactive behavior and design content must be analyzed. Behavioral transformation means the audience behavior shows a series of changes due to the influence of the externally communicated information, and it is the interactive content in public-interest expression that leads to the behavioral transformation of the audience. Interactive behavior is formed under the guidance of content, and the design of content stimulates the audience to generate certain kinds of behaviors or thinking, thereby immediately unfolding the interactive experience. At this moment, the content should be purposeful or directly or implicitly remind the audience, which will allow them to generate behavioral consciousness and perform interactive actions that will ensure a connection with the subsequent content. Both positive experience and positive feedback are based on the setting of public-interest content, which has an important influence on interactive behavior.

Second, an interactive model based on design content must be established. From the human perspective, content should result in changes to the audience's behavioral model. Interactive design should consider the behavioral variable and behavioral model of human beings, as the attitude and response to the same stimulus will inevitably be biased due to differences between people in terms of educational level and aesthetic experience. This phenomenon suggests the need to constantly envision and simulate when constructing the behavior, to summarize the responses of different populations to advertising content in actual communication, classify possible scenarios, and further sort out the characteristics of the model. This process mainly relies on information acquired from theoretical research and practical investigation, and is immediately followed by extending and summarizing in conjunction with guidance from the content. From the perspective of scenario, content will result in changes to the interactive scenario model. The participatory behavior in interactive design has to be present in a particular scenario in order for the audience experience to be real, and a scenario exists to allow the audience further associate with the advertising content. It occurs to narrate the background and describe the methods of interaction between the audience and advertisement, as well as influencing the generation of the audience behavior. Therefore, the establishment of the scenario should serve to trigger the audience's interactive behavior, and the design should not only simulate ideal interactive behavior based on the scenario narrated by public-interest content, but also elaborate and analyze the many possibilities presented in the behavior process, pinpoint the targets of the interactive content, construct the ultimate model for the scenario, and repeatedly verify it.

3.2 Interaction Between Virtual and Real Behaviors

Interaction between virtual and real behaviors means the audience's real behavior interacts with the virtually expressed content, and that the virtual content triggers participatory behavior. This participatory behavior in turn affects the virtual content in a mutually connected manner.

First, suitable digital technologies must be selected based on the characteristics of the content. In the process of the expression of public-interest, interactive behavior plays a decisive role in that the audience's behavioral participation affects the integrity of the content and determines whether the public-interest content can be effectively presented. The man-machine interaction between virtual and real behaviors is a striking characteristic of interactive expression, and man-machine interaction is supported by digital technologies. With the developments in the era of digital intelligence, sensing control and other technologies have endlessly emerged as technologies available for choice. These technologies bring unlimited possibilities to the development of the interactive expression of public-interest, but the suitability of the expression of public-interest content is the ultimate yardstick for choosing a technology, and the natural connection and mutual integration between technology and content is the ultimate purpose.

Second, we follow the concept of putting people first in creating the interactive expression of public-interest. In the interactive process for the expression of public-interest, interactive interfaces serve as the bridge between man and machine and between the virtual and real, or in other words, the audience realizes interactive experience through direct contact with interactive interfaces. Upholding the concept of putting people first, human beings are the recipients of expressed information, meaning the interactive design requires humanizing the behavioral construction. In terms of the design of interactive interfaces, virtual interfaces are generally comprised of images, texts, colors, voice, and other elements, which should be implemented with reference to psychology-related studies and integrated with theoretical knowledge to not only express the true intention of the expression of public-interest but also meet the atheistic needs of the majority of people, thereby allowing the audience to read and understand and letting people of all age brackets and educational attainments to participate in it. In terms of the design of interactive behavior, realistic interactive behavior should be presented to the general public in a concise and convenient form, and behavioral design is one that leads the audience's behavior or awareness to achieve the ideal interaction by design, which is required to both achieve the content-led behavioral objectives and proximity to life, by adding daily behavior into the interaction which can be easily accepted by the general public.

Third, physical elements must be added to bring the audience back to real-world public interest. Adding physical elements to behavioral participation involves connecting the virtual environments with the real world at the level of human perception as an effective way to help the audience develop a sense of reality. The behavior of touching and perceiving physical objects is also a process of leaving behind the traces of public-interest in a way that enhances the authenticity of expression and the experiential feeling of the audience, as well as reminding people to pay attention to the public-interest content behind the expression from a realistic perspective. The determination of the form of such an element is inseparable from the content expressed. In design, the expressed content should be dealt with in a fragmented manner to find the representative elements for physical presentation, before integrating them into the expression based on the characteristics and attributes of the physical elements.

3.3 Participation of Interactive Experience in Public Interest

The participation of interactive experience in public interest means that the setting of behavior in the interactive design of the expression of public-interest should meet the needs of the audience for experience and allow them to gain a sense of participation and experience in public-interest activities. The behavior of interactive experience needs to combine interaction and public interest. When an audience experiences interactive public-interest works, it is imperative to allow them to gain a sense of participation in public-interest activities, as the behavior at this moment represents both experience with the works and participation in public interest. In a specific work, interactive behavior is inseparable from the expression of public-interest, as these two mutually serve and accomplish each other. In the design of behavior, public-interest behaviors should be gathered and classified and screened in light of their conditions, such as the theme and content of public interest and the difficulty of implementation, thereby simulating the interactive process, in which the inherent connections between interaction and public interest are considered, and the best possible solution is chosen. "With You, We Are Not Alone" is an interactive work created for the platform of Nanjing Charity Foundation for autistic children. It takes the image of brain nerve fiber as the basic visual expression element. With Every donation has been done on the platform, "the image of brain nerve fiber" will gradually become clear from a vague state. The interactive process also allows the audience to experience the help that donations will bring to autistic patients (See Fig. 1).

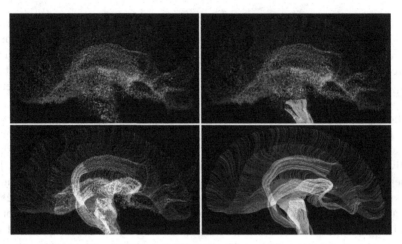

Fig. 1. The work *"With You, We Are Not Alone"*

4   Interactive Emotion in the Expression of Public-Interest

4.1   Triggering of Multidimensional Perception

The triggering of multidimensional perception means that the interactive design of the expression of public-interest arouses emotions from multiple dimensions, including content, form, and concept, as content provides the intrinsic framework for expression and acts as the foundation for the triggering of perception. The selection of topics, construction of the framework and perfection of the narrative set the emotional tone for the expression of public-interest, with subsequent designs all building on the content. In the interactive expression of public-interest, content that can mobilize perception should have powerful informational support. It should also incorporate the role of audience, highlight the priorities for preparing the content, emphasize the triggering of perception, and arouse empathy.

From the perspective of form, form provides the extrinsic state for expression and serves as a direct contributory factor to triggering perception. The construction of scenario, choice of technology, and setting for the behavior determine the behavioral participation of the audience and affect the generation of emotions. In the interactive expression of public-interest, the forms that effectively arouse perception should follow the characteristics of human senses and combine with novel means to attract participation. The success or failure of an interactive mode determines the degree of smoothness of the content experience and the authenticity of public-interest environments. Interaction in the expression of public-interest needs to create public-interest spatial environments for the audience, provide spatial information, and arouse spatial feelings, which arguably has a great effect on the triggering of perception. When designing, efforts should be made to find the point of entry into communication with the audience based on the stimulus to be released from the expression of public-interest, and appropriate interactive behavior and triggering of audience perception should be formally constructed. "The Sky Under Your Feet" is an interactive work that promotes the spirit of the Red Army's Long March.

When the audience is entering in a narrow passage, the video of The Red Army walking with straw sandals will be project on the top of the passage. The combination of the video and the form makes the audience feel that The Red Army walk past on frosted glasses on the top of the passage. The time-travel-style presence immediately gives the audience a strong emotional resonance (See Fig. 2).

From the perspective of concept, concepts provide spiritual support for expression and are the inner soul of triggering perception. The public-interest theme, means of conveying, and ideological stamp all determine the theme of expression. Concept refers to the reality in human impressions and is a subjective reflection of objective things, which is deeply rooted in mind and is formed under the influence of growth process and social environments. In interactive design, the concept that arouses perception should carry a particular symbolic element, which needs to be both popular and representative, and the occurrence of which can arouse the audience's memory and unconsciously lead the direction of emotions such that self-identification more easily occurs, as expression is easier to understand when the interactive design comes closer to concepts that the audience is familiar with. The acquisition of symbols requires screening and consideration of the common memories of the times, thereby endowing them with new meanings and scenarios to meet the emotional needs of the audience.

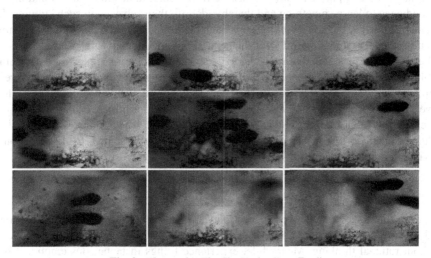

Fig. 2. The work *"The Sky Under Your Feet"*

4.2 Driving and Resonance of Emotions

The driving and resonance of emotions starts with cultural identity. Emotions are generated subjectively and vary from one individual to another due to different personal experiences. In order for an audience's emotions to converge and achieve the effect envisioned by the expression of public-interest, using cultural identity can effectively guide and promote themes in completing the audience's train of thought and arousing resonance. Cultural identity means a particular individual or group believes in a certain cultural system (values and lifestyles, etc.) that is inherent in their mental and personality structure, which they consciously follow in order to evaluate things and normalize behaviors. The characteristics of the cultures that are identified with are also elements that should be presented in the interactive design of the expression of public-interest. First of all, the ideology and culture implied in the expression of public-interest should please the majority of the people in the society, i.e., the popular culture. The "popular language" under such a culture is easily accepted and spread and is more capable of producing an empathy effect. Second, the ideology and culture implied in the expression of public-interest should conform to the social trends in thinking, i.e., the mainstream cultures. Mainstream cultures generally have a positive significance and can bring positive effects. Under the influence of the positive energy advocated in modern societies, the people can feel warmth, inspiration, health, and happiness. Accordingly, whether it is to advocate notions and thoughts, or to trigger the attention of special populations, the interactive expression of public-interest should be based on group interests, should be positive, and should increase the audience's ideological consciousness before emotions can be generated accordingly. Last, the ideology and culture implied in the expression of public-interest should demonstrate national style and features, i.e., traditional cultures. Such cultures have deep implications, withstand scrutiny, and merit lingering consideration, which can play an educational role in the communication process and allow the audience to learn something and thereby identify themselves with such cultures. In interactive design, the conveying of public-interest thinking represents a manifestation of cultural connotations. In order for the general public to identify themselves with the cultures implied in works, it is necessary to understand the cultural appeals of the general public, ensure that the audiences identify with the original intention of cultural expression, and determine the direction of the interaction before distinguishing the parts that have been advocated and not yet valued. One should set priorities, examine their significance and value from the public perspective, and judge whether they conform to the values of the majority of the people, thereby gaining the cultural identity of populations, driving emotions, and arousing resonance through spiritual indoctrination.

4.3 Rational Thinking on Interactive Experience

Rational thinking on interactive experience means that public-interest works utilize logical thinking to trigger an emotional experience and that emotions cannot be induced without rational thinking. Meanwhile, experience brings instantaneous emotions, but what merits further consideration is the profound meaning behind the interaction, which requires the audience to reflect. Emotions are a product of a logical setting. The original intention of the interactive expression of public-interest is to transmit the philosophy of public-interest, more specifically, to allow the audience to open up and receive public-interest information, which can be summarized as moving the general public using emotions. In order to spark the audience's emotions and arouse resonance, it is necessary to apply logical thinking, rationally examine the objectives of the expression (what kind of emotions are to be conveyed), consider the process of information transmission (what kind of methods are to be adopted), and analyze the results of the expression (whether the transmission was successful or not). By focusing on the setting of the process, the gap between the objective and reality as well as the influencing factors can be identified, and solutions can be enumerate and adapted to situations, choosing the best possible one.

Rational thinking reveals the connotations of public interest. In the process of experience the audience should generate instantaneous emotions, including feeling moved, shocked, proud, and happy. However, as the interactive process is transient, such emotions will fade away over time, whereas the expression of public-interest is meant to cause the information conveyed by the interaction to permanently remain in people's minds. To achieve the ultimate objective of publicity requires sublimating emotions, arousing the rational thinking of the audience and revealing the connotations of works and the essence of public interest. When designing, one should accurately grasp the rhythm of the interaction, arrange the content and steps according to the speed at which people receive information, and ensure that emotions are aroused to the maximum extent. Meanwhile, the process should be brief and efficient, and the content should be refined. The questions raised after the end of the interaction should lead the audience to think as much as possible, and deepen the audience's memories using the thinking process, while will allow them to understand the deep meaning of the content and endow their experience with meaning, instead of merely remaining a surface-level interaction.

5 Conclusion

The creation of public-interest is a long-term process and is also a behavior that brings art closer to social relations and reflects the social value of art. Social civilizations are continuously evolving and increasing numbers of people are very willing to understand and participate in public-interest undertakings, but the rapid pace of work and life makes the broader public so overwhelmed that they can only mentally participate in an image or video advertisement for public interest even if they saw one. With the advent of the era of digital intelligence, interactive public-interest works allow the general public to experience public-interest behavior and truly participate in public-interest undertakings in a way that combines interaction, experience, and participation, which is the future trend for public-interest works and is also our mission and responsibility as members of the media.

References

1. Xu, S., Zhang, H., Zhang, J., Dai, Z., Yuan, M.: Research on the significance and communication path of enterprise public welfare activities. China Mark. (17) (2020)
2. Shihu, X., Liu, Y.: Interaction design of a new design platform based on behavioral logic. Ind. Des. (3) (2020)
3. Feng, X., Jiang, L.: Research on united front work from the perspective of cultural identity. J. Shenzhen Univ. (Humanit. Soc. Sci.) (6) (2010)

Author Index

Printed in the United States
by Baker & Taylor Publisher Services